Buddhism Between Religion and Philosophy

Buddhism Between Religion and Philosophy

Nāgārjuna and the Ethics of Emptiness

RAFAL K. STEPIEN

OXFORD
UNIVERSITY PRESS

OXFORD
UNIVERSITY PRESS

Oxford University Press is a department of the University of Oxford. It furthers the University's objective of excellence in research, scholarship, and education by publishing worldwide. Oxford is a registered trade mark of Oxford University Press in the UK and certain other countries.

Published in the United States of America by Oxford University Press
198 Madison Avenue, New York, NY 10016, United States of America.

Library of Congress Cataloging-in-Publication Data
Names: Stepien, Rafal K., author.
Title: Buddhism between religion and philosophy : Nāgārjuna and the ethics of emptiness / Rafal K. Stepien.
Description: 1. | New York : Oxford University Press, 2024. |
Includes bibliographical references and index.
Identifiers: LCCN 2023043015 | ISBN 9780197771303 (hardback) |
ISBN 9780197771327 (epub)
Subjects: LCSH: Nāgārjuna, active 2nd century. | Mādhyamika (Buddhism) |
Buddhist philosophy—History.
Classification: LCC BQ7479.8.N347 S84 2024 | DDC 181/.043—dc23/eng/20231025
LC record available at https://lccn.loc.gov/2023043015

DOI: 10.1093/oso/9780197771303.001.0001

Printed by Integrated Books International, United States of America

MIX
Paper
FSC FSC® C183721

For my teachers

Contents

Acknowledgments ix

Introduction
Emptiness Between the Lines: Reading Buddhist Philosophy of/and/as Religion 1
0.0. The Dream Is Over 1
0.1. Nāgārjuna and the Ethics of Emptiness 4
0.2. Believing Between the Lines 9
0.3. Buddhism Between Religion and Philosophy 22
0.4. Contexts and Texts 35

1. Orienting Reason: A Religious Critique of Philosophizing Nāgārjuna 48
1.1. The Unimaginative Question 48
1.2. Unveiling the East 49
1.3. Orientalizing Reasons 56
1.4. Reimagining Religion and Philosophy 69

2. Logical, Buddhological, Buddhist: A Critical Study of the Tetralemma 87
2.1. Matters and Methods 87
2.2. The Logical Tetralemma 93
2.3. The Buddhological Tetralemma 111
2.4. The Buddhist Tetralemma 115

3. Nāgārjuna's Tetralemma: Tetrāletheia and Tathāgata, Utterance and Anontology 126
3.1. The Dilemma of the Tetralemma 126
3.2. The Exhaustive Tetralemma 130
3.3. Tetralemma as Tetrāletheia 133
3.4. Tetrāletheia as Tathāgata 135
3.5. Utterance and Anontology 137
3.6. Tetralemma and No-Teaching 141
3.7. Silencing Nothing 151

4. Abandoning All Views: A Buddhist Critique of Belief 156
4.1. Views on Abandoning Views 156
4.2. Nāgārjuna's Abandoning Views 158
4.3. Abandoning Nāgārjuna's Views 174

5. All-Embracing Emptiness: Nāgārjuna and the Ethics of Emptiness 201
5.1. The Abandonment of Ethics? 201
5.2. The Ethics of Abandonment 210
5.3. From Ethics to Eirenics 231
5.4. Abandoning All, Embracing All 248

Notes 257
Bibliography 357
Index 387

Acknowledgments

So it turns out that writing book acknowledgments is impossible. After all, where does one begin? Do ideas even have a beginning anyway?

At a loss, then, I have decided to attempt a start with thanking the one person most responsible for thwarting this work in every way I could imagine and many others I could not: my son. Eliot was born just as I was starting to write the doctoral dissertation, one chapter of which would eventually find final and much modified form as this book. Now that it's complete, I can thank him for forcing me, despite all my efforts, to wait for it to grow into what it has turned out to be—and for giving me new and infinitely better reasons to write it.

My doctorate was undertaken at Columbia University, and there my first thanks go to my advisors Chün-fang Yü, who remains a model of engaged mentorship, and Bernard Faure, who agreed to step in upon Prof Yü's retirement and who remains an inspiration in his erudition and encouragement. Both Souleymane Bachir Diagne and Robert Thurman agreed to be members of my committee without knowing me overmuch; I thank them both in turn for their unstinting support, great learning, and frank friendliness. In all, I was blessed with an advisory committee of exceptional breadth, erudition, and warmth, and express my heartfelt gratitude for the occasion to learn from and befriend such teachers.

My doctorate likewise proved to be an opportunity to forge working relationships with all manner of folk over three continents. At Columbia, I thank all my teachers, as well as the excellent administrative support of the Department of East Asian Languages and Cultures, at which I benefitted particularly from the assistance of Robert Hymes, Haruo Shirane, Tamara Kachanov, Joshua Gottesman, and Tracy Howard. At Harvard, where I spent my final year as an Exchange Scholar in the Committee on the Study of Religion, my thanks go in particular to Michael Puett and Barbara Boles for supporting my stay, to Parimal Patil and James Robson for constructive conversations and questions, and to all the wonderful staff at what was then still called the Andover-Harvard Theological Library. At Oxford, where I was an Academic Visitor at Wadham College during the 2012–2013 academic year, my thanks go to Edmund Herzig, who supported my stay; Ian Thompson and Tim Kirtley, who provided generous financial and library support at Wadham; and Janet Williams, who generously read over and discussed my inkling ideas.

Numerous shorter stints at various institutions also proved invaluable during the research phase of my doctoral work. Particular thanks go to the then Venerable Huifeng, now Matthew Orsborn, at the College of Buddhist Studies of Fo Guang University, the then Venerable Yifa at Fo Guang Shan, and all the faculty and staff at the Chung-Hwa Institute of Buddhist Studies and Dharma Drum Buddhist College in Taiwan as well as at the Centre of Buddhist Studies at the University of Hong Kong.

None of this could have happened without the generous support of numerous munificent organizations. Among these, most especial thanks must go to the Cihui Foundation for endowing the Faculty Fellowship in Chinese Buddhist Studies at Columbia, of which I am honored to have been the inaugural recipient. Other fellowships granted while still a student were a Mellon Fellowship in the Humanities for Dissertation Research in Original Sources awarded by the Andrew W. Mellon Foundation and Council on Library and Information Resources (CLIR), at which latter I particularly thank Amy Lucko; a Graduate Research Fellowship from the Chung-Hwa Institute of Buddhist Studies (CHIBS); an International Travel Fellowship from the Graduate School of Arts and Sciences at Columbia University; and a Chiang Ching-kuo Foundation Dissertation Fellowship from the Chiang Ching-kuo Foundation for International Scholarly Exchange. My profound thanks go to all these funding bodies. In addition, I likewise thank the Weatherhead East Asian Institute at Columbia University for a Weatherhead Fellowship; the Institute for Religion, Culture, and Public Life also at Columbia for a Graduate Research Fellowship; the South Central Modern Language Association for a Graduate Student Grant; and the New York Conference on Asian Studies for the Marleigh Grayer Ryan Graduate Writing Prize.

Unlike so many others, I was very lucky to find fulfilling employment following graduation. My first thanks in that regard thus go to Alan Hodder and Sue Darlington at Hampshire College, where I had the wonderful fortune to also meet fellow scholars from the Five College Buddhist Studies Program and other nearby institutions. Among these, especial thanks go to Jay Garfield, Maria Heim, and Andy Rotman within the Pioneer Valley and to William Edelglass and the late C. W. "Sandy" Huntington Jr. in the region for their friendship, mentorship, and all-round greatness.

I am also grateful to the powers that be at Hampshire for granting me leave to take up the inaugural Berggruen Research Fellowship in Indian Philosophy at the University of Oxford. In that regard, my profound thanks go, first of all, to Nicolas Berggruen and the Berggruen Institute for funding the fellowship. At Oxford, I would like to thank most especially Ulrike Roesler and Richard Sorabji at Wolfson College; Jan Westerhoff at the Faculty of Theology and Religion; Sarah Shaw at the then Faculty of Oriental Studies (now Faculty of Asian and Middle Eastern Studies); Richard Gombrich at the Oxford Centre for Buddhist Studies; Jessica Frazier at the Oxford Centre for Hindu Studies; and Edward Harcourt, Anil Gomes, and Paul Lodge at the Faculty of Philosophy. Meeting such people—among many others at Oxford—and conversing with them about all manner of matters philosophical and otherwise was and remains a profound privilege and pleasure.

I would next like to express my gratitude to the Alexander von Humboldt Foundation for the award of a Humboldt Research Fellowship for Postdoctoral Researchers. This was held at the then Heidelberg Centre for Transcultural Studies (now Centre for Asian and Transcultural Studies) at Heidelberg University, where I thank Oliver Lamers and Ina Buchholz for working administrative magicry; Chia-Wei Lin for her assistance in tracking down some Chinese-language sources; Christiane Brosius, Joachim Kurz, Axel Michaels, and Barbara Mittler for their unfailing *Freundlichkeit*; and above all Michael Radich for agreeing to act as my host and mentor at Heidelberg even before he had himself arrived there.

Leaving Heidelberg, I was lured into accepting a position as Assistant Professor in Comparative Religion within the Studies in Interreligious Relations in Plural Societies Programme at the S. Rajaratnam School of International Studies of Nanyang Technological University, Singapore. I have lived in almost a dozen countries, studied and worked at universities across four continents, but I have never encountered such an intellectually sterile, professionally corrupt, and morally destitute place. Although some of this book was drafted during this period, I have no one to thank there.

Happily, I was able to win a Starting Grant from the European Research Council (ERC) enabling me take up a Research Associate position at the Institute for the Cultural and Intellectual History of Asia (IKGA) within the Austrian Academy of Sciences, where as Principal Investigator I have now established and lead a team of researchers studying Sanlun 三論 Buddhist philosophy: the Chinese development of Nāgārjuna's Madhyamaka school. Words fail me in attempting to express the thanks I feel to the ERC for selecting me and the IKGA Director Birgit Kellner for agreeing to host me. This book was published after my arrival at the IKGA in Vienna, and I simply cannot imagine a more congenial professional and personal environment within which to have it at long last see the light of day.

During the course of the work eventuating in this book, I have also benefitted enormously from presenting papers at numerous professional conferences, invited lectures, and workshops. At these I had occasion to thrash out inchoate ideas that would eventually find formulation here, and speak on closely related topics with a view to forging connections between authors and ideas not immediately apparent. I thank the organizers, discussants, and participants at all these forums for their time, energy, and questions, and also to the following fellow scholars for all the conversations and correspondences that helped me in multifarious ways: Peter Adamson, Michihiro Ama, Naomi Appleton, Dan Arnold, Ankur Barua, Stefan Baums, Karl-Stéphan Bouthillette, Mikel Burley, Ethan Bushelle, Amber Carpenter, Francisca Cho, Alan Cole, Kate Crosby, Charles DiSimone, Jonathan Duquette, Malcolm David Eckel, Rafal Felbur, Marco Ferrante, Paul Fuller, Jonathan Gold, Marie-Hélène Gorisse, Natalie Gummer, Paul Harrison, Huanhuan He, Steven Heine, Chien-hsing Ho, Chris Jones, Sonam Kachru, Hans-Rudolf Kantor, Constance Kassor, Birgit Kellner, John Kieschnick, Yaroslav Komarovski, Gereon Kopf, Jowita Kramer, Michael Levine, Qiancheng Li, Dan Lusthaus, Anne MacDonald, Karin Meyers, Peggy Morgan, A. Charles Muller, Richard Nance, Karen O'Brien-Kop, John Powers, Wayne Proudfoot, Chakravarthi Ram-Prasad, Massimo Rondolino, Akira Saito, Jonathan Samuels, Rahul Santhanam, Michael Sells, Robert Sharf, Eviatar Shulman, Davey Tomlinson, Ben Van Overmeire, Lina Verchery, Joseph Walser, Nicholas Witkowski, Robert Yelle, and Brook Ziporyn. As for my students at various institutions, I thank them all for their intelligence and doubts, and for compelling me to clarify my thinking in so very many ways.

Of course, there are many more people—dead and living—whom I would like to thank for writing down their thoughts and thereby letting me talk with them in my mind. May this book, dedicated as it is to my teachers, be taken as a long letter of thanks to all who have contributed to my learning. That does not mean I agree with everything I've been taught, however, and indeed this book is witness to some serious disagreements I have with numerous scholars in the field. Chief among those whose genuinely beneficent influence I credit above but some of whose published positions I critique in the pages that follow are Jay Garfield and Jan Westerhoff. Given just how highly

I hold them in regard and just how much I have learned from them as people and as scholars (somehow they each manage to combine scholarly sagacity, warm wit, and conscientious kindness in a single human being), I sincerely hope that they (like the others whose views I contest) take my objections as signs of profound respect both for their work and for the material we study in common. Naturally, there will be challenges to my own proposals; these I welcome as efforts, like my own, aimed at moving a shared conversation forward.

Chapters 1 and 4 of this book are significantly revised and much expanded versions of my articles "Orienting Reason: A Religious Critique of Philosophizing Nāgārjuna" first published in the *Journal of the American Academy of Religion* 86, no. 4: 1072–1106 (Oxford: Oxford University Press, doi: 10/1093/jaarel/lfy021) and "Abandoning All Views: A Buddhist Critique of Belief" first published in *The Journal of Religion* 99, no. 4: 529–566 (Chicago: University of Chicago Press, doi: 10/1086/704844) respectively. I thank the publishers for permission to reproduce these materials, and to the editors and peer reviewers for their respective contributions. I also thank the peer reviewers for their comments and Piotr Balcerowicz and Brendan Gillon for their work in coediting an issue of the *Journal of Indian Philosophy* in which an earlier version of the material that now comprises Chapter 3 was accepted for publication, but which I ultimately decided to withdraw to use here.

Especially effusive thanks for publishing this book go to Theodore Calderara at Oxford University Press. Along with fellow editors Brent Matheny, Mary Pelosi, Leslie Anglin, and the Newgen team headed by Gigi Clement, Theo saw this book through from proposal to publication. Not only that, he somehow found reviewers who were both extraordinarily expert in the field and generous enough to read through the entire manuscript with consummate care (even twice!). The reviewers' detailed and nuanced comments improved the draft immeasurably, and the final book bears the imprint of their insights throughout. I thank them deeply. Indeed, to tweak somewhat Śaṅkarasvāmin's hymn the *Devatāvimarśastuti* (Nance 2020: 92), "They who have no faults at all, and in whom all virtues are present . . . they are my editors and peer-reviewers."

Profound thanks go likewise to Yachi Tseng 曾亞琪 for agreeing to let her beautiful artwork grace the cover of this book.

It is also a delight to give thanks to friends, without whom I could hardly complete a day, let alone a book. I am so very happy to consider a number of the scholars listed above as friends, but in addition to those, I would like to send my deep gratitude for the long-lasting and life-giving friendships I have been so gifted to enjoy while researching and writing this book with Mark Baynes and Monika Rutecka, Christophe Bachhuber and Elizabeth Frood, Jasmine Baetz and Joseph Frigualt, Frances Flanagan and David Ritter, Patrick and Majida Hamilton, Alana Harris, Marianne Hicks, Chris Hinds, Reto Hofmann, Faryal Iqbal, Erla Magnusdottir, Lorraine Sim, Hannah Skoda, Andrina Svindland, Yiannis Tsapras and Katrin Schulze, Katrina Whittred, Chris Wortham, and Savina Zanardo.

There are many others. But last, first, and in all ways between, I thank Nanor, who has been my confidante and critic, medium and meditation, love and life partner throughout this long adventure, and without whom none of this could have come to fruition. May our further travels take us further still.

Introduction

Emptiness Between the Lines: Reading Buddhist Philosophy of/and/as Religion

0.0. The Dream Is Over

> Fettered by the fetter of beliefs, the ignorant ordinary person is not freed from birth, ageing, and death, from sorrow, lamentation, pain, grief, and despair; he is not freed from suffering, I say.
>
> —The Buddha, *Sabbāsava Sutta* (*All the Taints*)[1]

Imagine, for a moment, that you're wrong. Speaking for myself, I can call to mind all-too-many instances of being wrong, occasions when some 'truth' I believed in turned out not to be true at all. Surely you have been there too, so presumably it shouldn't be too hard for us to reconstruct what it means for belief to morph into disbelief. Usually (at least for those of us not biased beyond redress or living in a 'post-truth' world), we take this transformation to be a good thing: in being shown that a given belief is false, we exchange it for another, which we now take to be true. That's called *learning*, and without it we would be lost, right? But what if being in the wrong is a question not of any particular beliefs, but of belief as such? What if *believing* is itself the problem, and the solution is to break free from its bonds? This book is an extended meditation on this idea, with the Buddhist philosopher Nāgārjuna (c. 150–250 CE) as our guide.

Before we get to Nāgārjuna, though, let's pause for a moment to consider the nature of 'the problem' itself. The First Noble Truth uttered in the very first discourse delivered by the Buddha upon his enlightenment is the truth of suffering, *duḥkha*.

> Now this, monks, is the noble truth of suffering: birth is suffering, ageing is suffering, illness is suffering, death is suffering; union with what is displeasing is suffering; separation from what is pleasing is suffering; not

Buddhism Between Religion and Philosophy. Rafal K. Stepien, Oxford University Press. © Oxford University Press 2024.
DOI: 10.1093/oso/9780197771303.001.0001

> to get what one wants is suffering; in brief, the five aggregates subject to clinging are suffering. (Bodhi 2000: 1844, slightly altered)[2]

By the 'five aggregates' (*skandhas*), the Buddha is referring to body/form (*rūpa*), feeling (*vedanā*), perception/cognition (*saṃjñā*), mental formations (*saṃskāra*), and discerning consciousness (*vijñāna*).[3] It is a foundational tenet of Buddhist philosophy that these five comprise the totality of the person, who is thus absent of substantial selfhood. This is the gist of the *anātman* doctrine. The long and short of this first and founding truth of Buddhism, then, is that suffering is an unavoidable feature of life. Its sheer ubiquity is underlined by the fact that, for Buddhists, *duḥkha*

> encapsulates many subtleties of meaning, but its application spans pain, suffering, disappointment, frustration, things going badly, hassle, unease, anxiety, stress, dis-ease, unsatisfactoriness, non-reliability of people and things, limitation, imperfection. It sums up the problematic aspects of life: its mental and physical pains, obvious or subtle, and also the painful, stressful, unsatisfactory aspects of life that engender these. (Harvey 2013a: 26)

Fortunately, the Buddha does not stop there, but goes on, in the remaining three Noble Truths, to describe the cause of suffering (its *samudaya*; i.e., *tṛṣṇā* / 貪愛 or thirst/craving), the cessation of suffering (its *nirodha*; i.e., *nirvāṇa* / 涅槃), and the way to attain such liberation (its *mārga*; i.e., *āryāṣṭāṅgamārga* / 八正道 or the Noble Eightfold Path).

Importantly for our purposes, this eightfold path—the very heart of Buddhist ethics—begins with 'right view' (*samyag-dṛṣṭi*). To hold right view is to see reality aright, and reality, according to the Buddha, is characterized by the operation of causality: "the central feature of Buddhist ontology" (P. Williams 2000: 64). Causality (*idaṃpratyayatā*) states that "When this exists, that comes to be; with the arising of this, that arises. When this does not exist, that does not come to be; with the cessation of this, that ceases to be" (e.g., Bodhi 2000: 579). This in fact underpins the impermanence (*anitya*) and selflessness (*anātman*) which, along with *duḥkha*, comprise the three marks (*trilakṣaṇa*) of *saṃsāric* existence in the Buddhist worldview. For the fact of things being causally dependent entails the phenomenal working of causally conditioned origination and cessation (hence impermanence), the absence of a causally (or otherwise) *in*-dependent selfbeing (*svabhāva*) (hence no-self), and the unavoidability of dissatisfaction so long as one continues to grasp for what are thus seen to be evanescent and essenceless phenomena (hence suffering).[4] The causal conditioning characterizing *saṃsāric* existence leads sentient beings such as us to cycle again and again around the wheel of dependent co-origination (*pratītya-samutpāda*).[5] Crucially for the entire Buddhist endeavor, causality not only engendered this mêlée but allows a way out of it, for causality occasions cessation just as it does origination. This is evident already in the formulation of the Second, Third, and Fourth Noble Truths, which, as we have seen, identify the cause of the problem, its causally brought about cessation, and the manner of causally bringing about that cessation.

To see causality at work is therefore the first step toward seeing reality aright, attaining 'right view'. Ignorance (*avidyā*) is the opposite of this vision, the first link in the wheel of blind enchainment. Since it is principally by means of ignorance that *saṃsāric* suffering arises, it makes perfect sense that the attainment of right view should prove the prime factor in leading one toward the ultimate liberation from suffering known as *nirvāṇa*. It is the extirpation of ignorance that drives the soteries and the soteriology of Buddhism.[6] Ignorance itself naturally admits of many sorts and shades. Nāgārjuna's Madhyamaka school accepts that what we hold to be mundane conventional truths may be right or wrong, or admit degrees of rightness and wrongness. At this level (the level of conventional truth: *saṃvṛti-satya* or *vyavahāra-satya*), to be shown wrong is to be shown ignorant of what are merely contingent facts. Having our conventional beliefs shown up as wrong may shake our self-assurance, but immediately we reassert ourselves: I may have been wrong before, but *now* I'm right. The deeper ignorance, ignorance at the level of ultimate truth (*paramārtha-satya*), is not touched by such superficial rightings.[7] For to eradicate ignorance—and with it suffering—completely, one must attain to the Buddha's insight, and thus to an altogether other "order of seeing, completely different from the attitude of holding to any view, wrong or right" (Fuller 2005: 1).

This book will attempt to unpack just what such abandonment of all views could possibly mean (spoiler: it means you stop searching for what it—or anything else—could possibly mean . . .). As a first step, recall that arising, abiding, and ceasing as a whole denote the very reach of *saṃsāra*, the realm of causally conditioned existence characterized as sufferful by the Buddha in the formulation of the very foundations of Buddhist philosophy, the Four Noble Truths. Now look at what Nāgārjuna says:

Like an illusion, like a dream
Like a castle in the sky
So has arising, so has abiding
So has ceasing been explained[8]

How can he say this? Doesn't this dreamy dismissal directly contradict the Buddha? Well, in the title to this section I referred to the song "God," in which John Lennon (that much later guru and pandit), having identified God as "a concept / By which we measure our pain," sings:

And so, dear friends
You'll just have to carry on
The dream is over

In the context of universal suffering caused by desireful grasping borne of ignorant belief-holding, the only way to really carry on, for Nāgārjuna, is by letting go of all ideals and authorities as illusory: 'killing the Buddha', as a much later Buddhist thinker would put it.[9] Believing being tantamount to dreaming, it turns out that we only awaken in *nirvāṇa* when all our dreaming is over, and we are finally freed from the fetter of beliefs.

0.1. Nāgārjuna and the Ethics of Emptiness

Following the Buddha himself, Nāgārjuna is the most important and influential of all Buddhist philosophers. The Madhyamaka or Middle Way school of Buddhist philosophy he founded became central to the history of Mahāyāna Buddhist thought in India, Tibet, China, Japan, and other Asian countries over some two millennia.[10] Given the sheer foundational importance of Nāgārjuna to the myriad trajectories of Mahāyāna Buddhist intellectual history in subsequent centuries throughout South, North, and East Asia, it is completely understandable that his thought should have been the subject of intense interest in recent years among scholars seeking to bring Buddhist texts and ideas to the forefront of attention in cross-cultural philosophy.

Unfortunately, however, much of this work has been beset by two interrelated problems. First, pronounced emphasis has been placed on rendering Nāgārjuna (along with his Buddhist philosophical heirs and brethren) as palatable as possible to contemporary, and particularly analytic, philosophers.[11]

Thus, rather than attempting to understand and explicate Nāgārjuna in his own terms, as an avowedly *Buddhist* philosopher and monk, manifold efforts have been made to 'naturalize' his thought; to shear it, in other words, of any overtly 'religious' elements. In consequence of this approach (and here we arrive at the second problem), inordinate attention has been paid to what are deemed his more 'philosophical' works, by which is meant those concerned with metaphysics and epistemology, as opposed to 'religious' ethics and soteriology.

I outline these and related developments in the study of Madhyamaka, Buddhist, and more broadly non-Western philosophy, and expose the Eurocentrism insidiously at work within them, in §0.3.[12] This leads directly to discussion of the very paradigms used to structure and to demarcate scholarship on 'philosophy', 'religion', and thus also 'philosophy of religion'. Using Nāgārjuna as a theoretical counterbalance, I critique the (largely unacknowledged) perpetuation of identifiably Christian/Western terms of reference as normative in the study of Buddhism. Instead, I see this book in its entirety as making a series of revisionary proposals by means of which non-Western traditions of thought and practice may be more adequately conceived and studied as fully sovereign epistemologies. Rather than continuing to attempt to accommodate Buddhist religio-philosophical modes and methods to Christian religious and Western philosophical ones (and thereby continuing to peripheralize the East and center the West), I propose that scholars of religion and philosophy adopt an approach at last capable of admitting full agency to globally resonant voices hitherto diminished, distorted, or silenced. In so doing, I hope to make a direct theoretical and methodological contribution to the study of religiously situated philosophically insightful primary sources across diverse traditions and cultures.

Having thus laid down the theoretical and methodological bases of my work in this Introduction, in Chapter 1, *Orienting Reason: A Religious Critique of Philosophizing Nāgārjuna*, I apply my approach in sustained fashion to the study of Nāgārjuna. In this chapter, I focus on the vexed question of the rationality—or irrationality—of Nāgārjuna's thought, and thereby bring to light the theoretical underpinnings of the hermeneutical project predominant among present-day scholars, which is to actively overlook or downright depreciate the religious motivation of Nāgārjuna's arguments. While this project has typically been pursued in an apologetic effort to justify Nāgārjuna, as truly worthy of the title 'philosopher', to mainstream (Western) philosophers, it has also had the effect among some scholars of dismissing him as insufficiently philosophical. Regardless of the glowing or dim light in which he is thereby cast, however, Nāgārjuna is appraised according to exclusively philosophical criteria such as cogency, consistency, and coherency. My "religious critique of philosophizing Nāgārjuna," then, is aimed at elucidating and problematizing this approach, however philosophically fruitful it may be, as at best tangential to and at worst seriously distortive of Nāgārjuna's thought as a whole.

Chapter 2, *Logical, Buddhological, Buddhist: A Critical Study of the Tetralemma*, advances my argument with specific focus on one of Nāgārjuna's most distinctive forms of discourse: the *catuṣkoṭi* or tetralemma. This fourfold form typically negates a given position, its contrary, both, and neither, as when Nāgārjuna states at the very outset of his masterwork, the *Fundamental Verses on the Middle Way* or *Mūlamadhyamaka-kārikā*, for example, that "Not from itself nor from another / Not from both nor without cause // Does any entity whatsoever / Anywhere arise" (MK:1:1).[13] The logicalizing approach predominant in contemporary scholarship on the tetralemma is motivated by a desire to demonstrate that, contrary to appearances, Nāgārjuna cannot possibly be serious in denying all four positions. I articulate and dismantle three major iterations of this approach, which I call the Mereological, Modal, and Qualitative Interpretations. I then propose an alternative reading; one which, I argue, is not only just as methodologically legitimate but also better adequated to the hermeneutical endeavor of describing Nāgārjuna's philosophy taken in its entirety. I thus outline an understanding of the *catuṣkoṭi* that takes it not as an abstract object of rational inquiry dissected from its philosophico-religious context, or as a datum adapted to the disciplinary conventions of contemporary academe, but as an organic part of Nāgārjuna's overall soterially motivated Buddhist project.

Chapter 3, *Nāgārjuna's Tetralemma: Tetrāletheia and Tathāgata, Utterance and Anontology*, turns from the critique of currently prevalent interpretive strategies to the construction of an alternative method. Having outlined the four positions of the tetralemma as instantiated in Nāgārjuna's text, I argue that the *catuṣkoṭi* must be taken exhaustively; that is, as embracing all logically possible propositional alternatives. In contradistinction to analyses—typical in the scholarly literature—aimed at demonstrating the classical logicality of the tetralemma via parameterization of one form or another, I propose an interpretation along what I call para-logical lines. In so doing, however, I argue for the inadequacy of the dialetheic reading currently in vogue, and therefore propose a new term, 'tetrāletheia', designed to more adequately represent the four-folded nature of the tetralemma. Subsequent sections of the chapter are devoted to its explication together with a reading of the tetralemma as embodied in the figure of the Tathāgata. In the final section, I propose another new usage, 'utterance', as an alternative descriptor for the totality of the tetralemma; one that I argue is better adequated to the para-logical and 'anontological' tetralemma than are terms in standard use insofar as it dispenses with their positive logical and substantialist ontological value(s).

Chapter 4, *Abandoning All Views: A Buddhist Critique of Belief*, ties my preceding discussions of the *catuṣkoṭi* to my original appreciation of the central role abandoning all views plays within Nāgārjuna's thought as a whole. For Nāgārjuna's masterwork opens and closes with salutations to the Buddha as one who taught the 'cessation of conceptualization' (*prapañcopaśamaṃ*) and the 'abandonment of all views' (*sarvadṛṣṭiprahāṇāya*) respectively. In addition, this and Nāgārjuna's other texts contain numerous analogous calls for the complete abandonment of views, which I survey and explain. Despite these copious, clear, and comprehensive disavowals of views, contemporary scholars almost unanimously interpret such statements as referring only to 'false' views (however these may be understood). In this chapter, I argue instead that Nāgārjuna's insistence on the abandonment of *all* views—including ultimately his own—constitutes his distinctive means to the metaphysical 'exhaustion' characteristic of *nirvāṇa*, wherein all views, theses, propositions (*dṛṣṭi, pakṣa, pratijñā*) are and must be abandoned as so many subtle affirmations of an only ever empty self. Finally, I argue that Nāgārjuna's reiterated use of the tetralemma to reject all four of the logical positions open to classical Indian philosophers is designed precisely to aid just such a 'no-view' position.

Chapter 5, *All-Embracing Emptiness: Nāgārjuna and the Ethics of Emptiness*, ties the preceding discussions in metaphysics and epistemology to the ethical and soterial mission undergirding Nāgārjuna's Buddhist project. Here, I address the perplexing question of how a teaching understood as espousing universal emptiness and the abandonment of all views can nevertheless entail a distinctively Mahāyāna Buddhist ethics. After all, how can Nāgārjuna justify an ethic of selfless care for all living beings based on the bodhisattva ideal of limitless compassion if he has denied any and all forms of foundationalism, including those standardly taken as grounding ethics? The answer, I argue, lies precisely in the emptying of all selfhood, for in a world emptied of self, self-interest is necessarily exhausted, and one is liberated from karmically harmful action by engaging with others in unhindered care. This, for Nāgārjuna, is 'the good life'; "Thus does this entire mass of suffering / completely cease."[14] Indeed, in this concluding chapter I propose that the socio-ethical import of Nāgārjuna's denial of autonomous selfhood in favor of a self only ever relational lies precisely in his corollary abjuration of doxastic positionality in favor of critical detachment from any op-positional grasping. Taken seriously, my interpretation of Nāgārjuna's 'position of no-position' thus undermines the very basis for prejudice, partisanship and, more broadly, rigid adherence to any of the sectarian positions implicated in conflict on the individual, communal, or geopolitical levels.

The foregoing summary should make clear that this book sets itself a simultaneously critical and constructive mandate. On the one hand, I am concerned to contribute to revising the way scholarship on Nāgārjuna, and more broadly Buddhist philosophy, and still more broadly non-Western philosophy, is undertaken (the critical project). On the other, I hope to contribute to charting that alternative path by presenting Nāgārjuna's vision in a manner that—to the extent possible within my own readerly horizons—does not do him 'hermeneutical injustice' (the constructive project).[15] Indeed, having formulated the distinction between 'textual hermeneutics' and 'philosophical construction' in Chapter 1, the following four chapters constituting the remainder of the book may be taken—*grosso modo*—as alternating between these approaches, with Chapters 2 and 4 geared toward ascertaining what Nāgārjuna's texts say and Chapters 3 and 5 more oriented toward elaborations based thereon. Each of these programmatic approaches reinforces the other, for I see the repeated (if unadmitted) refusal on the part of a significant segment of scholars working on Nāgārjuna to take him at his word—as evinced by the myriad attempts to qualify (i.e., twist) those among his statements not readily assimilable to their own (etic, historically contingent, and conventionally relative) fore-concluded frames of thought—as perpetuating a series of mis-construals in turn inevitably issuing in inadvertent ill-applications of Nāgārjuna's philosophy. I make this point in bold terms deliberately so as to provoke further reflection on the methods appropriate to the exegesis of Buddhist (and for that matter all manner of other non-Western) philosophical texts, as also for conceptual elaborations based thereon.

The clearest example of the tendency I am describing, and the one I see as most far-reachingly consequential for the textual hermeneutic task of interpreting Nāgārjuna's philosophy adequately, lies in the manner of approaching his reiterated dispousal of all views; his refusal to espouse any.

As the earlier summary has made clear, Nāgārjuna's call to abandon all views is the central thread running throughout this book, for I see it as playing an indispensable role in fully emptying the world of the holdfasts we are wont to seek out and suffer from. As C. W. Huntington has averred,

> the unqualified rejection of any sort of "definitely stated doctrine" [citation from Hayes 1994: 363]—whether in the form of a philosophical view (*dṛṣṭi*), thesis (*pakṣa*), or proposition (*pratijñā*)—is not only a leitmotif of Nāgārjuna's writing, it is arguably the defining feature of his work, its single most troubling aspect, one with which any serious attempt at interpretation must come to grips. (Huntington 2007: 109)

That the idea of not holding to *any* position is so 'troubling' in large part explains why it remains under- (or downright un-) appreciated in relevant scholarship despite its literal conspicuousness in Nāgārjuna's texts. It is a notion with which one cannot, by definition, 'come to grips', but which one must allow to slip, as it were, between the lines of interpretation and conceptualization. Although we will be exploring Nāgārjuna's (non-)position or 'abelief' throughout this book, its place as an ineliminably important element in his *śūnyavāda* obliges me, I feel, to introduce its sense and formal presence in Nāgārjuna's compositions in at least a little more detail here.

0.2. Believing Between the Lines

Philosophers are, by and large, awful readers of literature. Notwithstanding certain noteworthy exceptions, on the whole they are all too wont to ignore the literary dimensions of a text in an avowed effort to get at its philosophical substance; indeed, even to perceive such wanton disregard of what are taken to be 'merely' aesthetic features as a positive methodological principle.[16] It is thus unsurprising—yet simultaneously astonishing—that to my knowledge there exists not a single extended study of the formal literary properties of the *Mūlamadhyamaka-kārikā* (MK), despite the obvious fact that the text is composed in verses (*kārikās*). Given that there was no lack of prose treatises, Buddhist or not, on which Nāgārjuna could have modeled his own work, surely the fact that he composed the MK (and *all* his definitely attributed works) in verse is a noteworthy feature of his writing? Huntington is almost unique among all modern scholars in even referring to the literary qualities of the MK, as when he writes:

> It seems to me that the most serious shortcoming of this insistence on reducing the *Madhyamakakārikā*-s to a series of logical formulas is that such a reading lacks any sensitivity for the very features of textuality—symbol, metaphor, polysemy, multivalence—that might lead us (*à la* Candrakīrti) out of the compulsive desire to deal in certainties. In other words, this way of reading denies to the text its existence as a *literary* work, and in so doing it allows us to forget—or never to see—that "truth is in the act, not the content, of reading." (Huntington 2007: 126, emphasis original, citing Humphries 1999: 41)

Unfortunately, this is the sum total of Huntington's comments on the matter, but what he does say, and moreover the lacks I have noted, do lend credence to Alan Cole's claim that "Buddhist studies, though rather well developed philologically, has been less willing to engage Buddhist literature as literature" (Cole 2005: 9). This is certainly true of the textual corpus ascribed to Nāgārjuna.

0.2.1. Poetry as Philosophy

As such, the philosophical literature on Nāgārjuna is replete with argumentative positions derived from specific chapters, passages, or verses selected in support of a given commentator's take.[17] The structure of the MK as a whole, and the relation of this formal structure to the substantial content of Nāgārjuna's thought, have been matters given next to no attention in the scholarly literature. Even apparent exceptions, such as efforts to explicate why "Nāgārjuna starts with causation" (Arnold 2010: 367; see also Garfield 2002: 24–45) fail to appreciate, or even note, that Nāgārjuna does not start with causation at all, but with what the Chinese commentarial tradition succinctly refers to as an 'eightfold negation' (八不) informing Nāgārjuna's encomium to "the Fully Enlightened Buddha . . . the best of speakers" as the one who "taught" "Dependent co-origination / As the felicitous cessation of conceptualization" (MK:0:2):

Not ceasing, not arising
Not annihilated, not eternal

Not identical, not different
Not coming, not going[18]

In fact, such *maṅgala* verses of praise open not only Nāgārjuna's MK but many other Indian Buddhist philosophical texts, yet they and their fuller-fleshed brethren, "Buddhist praise poems or hymns (*stotra, stava, stuti*) . . . are texts to which contemporary philosophers have paid scant attention, perhaps assuming that little of philosophical interest can be gained from their study" (Nance 2020: 86).[19] The point to note here is twofold: first, that almost no effort has been made by philosophical exegetes to treat the MK (or any other relevant work) as a literary whole; and second, that even when some attention has been paid to its structuring, this has been carried out in a manner that overlooks textual elements deemed unbefitting of or irrelevant to philosophical exposition.

Yet Cole's statement as to the literary qualities of Mahāyāna *sūtras* may surely be applied to Nāgārjuna's works: these too are "carefully wrought literary constructions that assume their specific forms precisely because they were designed to inhabit and function in the literary space where one encounters them" (Cole 2005: 1). Now, I am not claiming that Nāgārjuna's style does not differ substantially from the highly wrought artifices of contemporary and later strophic poets such as Aśvaghoṣa, Kālidāsa, and Bhāravi. Nor am I quite going so far as to propose treating *kārikā* as *kāvya*, as it were; to apply poetic paradigms, be they from Nāgārjuna's own literary context or elsewhere, to what remains indisputably a philosophical treatise—even if one composed in verse of rare refinement in world literature. After all, as Huntington forthrightly asserts, "Nāgārjuna was not writing poetry" (Huntington 1995: 292), at least not of the epic, lyric, narrative, satirical, or prose kind. Nevertheless, it would be remiss of me not to underline certain features of Nāgārjuna's texts relating first and foremost to their poeticity rather than their philosophicality, to tarry on the underappreciated fact that "Nāgārjuna composed his magnum opus on the nature of reality in verse" (MacDonald 2015b: 375), for I hope to demonstrate that these features, far from being irrelevant to philosophical concerns, in fact play meaningful roles in the articulation of Nāgārjuna's philosophy.[20] My comments will be relatively brief on this score, for the mandate I have set for myself in this book is the explication and elaboration of what I will go on to call Nāgārjuna's 'religiosophy', and not his 'litero-philosophy'.[21] That said, studying in depth and detail the specifically literary qualities of Nāgārjuna's work, be it independently or in tandem with its philosophical content, is a scholarly enterprise to be distinctly encouraged. For given the wholescale scholarly neglect of the former in favor of the latter, and the unjustifiability of such neglect given the rhetorical subtlety with which Nāgārjuna wrote as well as the textual memorization such literary form facilitated, such an approach would doubtless be apt to open perspectives and initiate avenues of research on his work hitherto un- or under-appreciated.

As it happens, the notion that "there is, with respect to any text carefully written and fully imagined, an organic connection between its form and its content" (Nussbaum 1990: 4, also cited in Stepien 2020b: 12) is in fact not only unappreciated but downright denegated with respect to Nāgārjuna. Thus, for example, in the Introduction to their translation of the MK, Siderits and Katsura reduce Nāgārjuna's *kārikā* form to a "mnemonic aid": "Texts of this sort were originally used because it is easier to memorize information when it is put in verse form" (Siderits and Katsura 2013: 2). The first point to note about this characterization (designed as it is, as we will see presently, to minimize the role the text's poetic form plays in the explication of its philosophical content) is that it wholly ignores the well-attested corollaries to the mnemonic functions of verse. Perhaps the most visible external effect of the memorization of sacred scriptures and relatedly esteemed texts in religious communities (such as that within which the Buddhist monk Nāgārjuna lived and composed) is a socio-political one: the accumulation of social capital in the form of enhanced prestige. As with equivalent *virtuosi* in other religious contexts (such as the Qu'rānic *ḥāfiẓ* in Islam) Buddhist *dharmabhāṇaka*s or '*dharma* reciters', having memorized vast canons of scripture, were endowed with elevated intellectual, spiritual, and devotional *cachet*. More importantly for the history of religions, they played a crucial role in retaining and thereby maintaining the very teachings of the Buddha in the oral culture of pre-Mahāyāna Buddhist India, and did so with apparent—though inevitably disputed—success for several centuries until the Pāli canon was eventually written down around the turn of the millennium.[22]

In so memorizing the Buddha's teachings, moreover, *dharma* reciters actively enhanced their *community's* status. As David McMahan reminds us,

> The orality of early Buddhism was not only an instance of historical happenstance but also an important means by which the early Saṅgha made its claim to authority. Pre-Mahāyāna Buddhism was, in fact, quite self-consciously an oral tradition, relying on the oral recitation and hearing of the Buddha's

> discourses—talks that were maintained in the memories and mouths of monks who were, according to tradition, repeating, generation after generation, the very words that the Buddha himself spoke. This tradition of recitation, then, was the way by which the Saṅgha established its claim to the *Buddha-vacana*—the words of the Buddha—which conferred authority and legitimacy to the early Buddhist community. (McMahan 1998: 251)

Nor did the importance of mnemonics, and more generally of an oral function to Buddhist texts, dissipate with the adoption of the technology of writing in the composition of Mahāyāna *sūtra*s and *śāstra*s (Lopez 1995; Drewes 2015). And so, to return to Nāgārjuna, that "synecdoche for all things Mahāyāna" (Young 2015: 128), I cannot but speculatively propose that the *kārikā* form, far more than mere 'mnemonic aid', was consciously adopted by its author to play an effective and important social function as one among the various 'Strategies of Legitimation' (Lopez 1995: 23; McMahan 1998: 264) the Mahāyāna movement drew upon in the perpetuation and propagation of its texts, and thus in the eventual epochally significant diffusion of its teachings, philosophical and otherwise.[23]

This point concerns the text in the context of the histories of religion and philosophy, but the mnemonic function of the MK's verses may be seen to play a systematic as well as a historic role. The memorization of a religious text requires the devotion of immense amounts of time and energy on the part of the adept, and thereby itself already constitutes a 'spiritual exercise' in Hadot's sense. Indeed, Hadot speaks, in the contexts of Greco-Roman philosophy and Christian "monastic spirituality," of "*Prosoche* or attention to oneself, the philosopher's fundamental attitude" in terms of the "remembrance of God" enabled by textual forms of "Both the evangelical commandments and the words of the ancients . . . [that] could be easily memorized and meditated upon" (Hadot 1995: 131–133). The contexts Hadot writes of obviously differ greatly from that in which Nāgārjuna wrote, and unfortunately we know practically nothing of the devotional, ritual, soterial, or other uses to which Mahāyāna and other Buddhist scriptures were put by adherents in Nāgārjuna's time, let alone the uses to which Nāgārjuna's own texts were put. My comments here are therefore speculative, but based on relevant scholarship regarding the role of memorization of sacred and saintly texts both from Buddhist contexts and from others applicable to the Buddhist, surely I am justified if I suggest that Nāgārjuna's use of verse—specifically here as regards the memorization it invited and enabled—played a role in the spiritual development of those disciples who devoted themselves to thus internalizing it. Such phenomenological transformation of the embodied adept may be far removed from the aims of academic philosophy today, but it cannot be excised from Nāgārjuna without robbing his work of its entire *raison d'être*.

To elaborate on this point a little further, I propose that the poetic text necessarily renders the readerly experience more embodied than in a prose equivalent, in the sense that the reading of poetry calls into play not only the eye but also the ear in scansion and the tongue in voiceless rendition or, all the more so, in voiced recitation.[24] As mentioned, we know practically nothing of the recitative or ritualistic practices to which Nāgārjuna's texts may have been put in the India of his and succeeding times, but we can aver in general of religious contexts that

> Even the very sound of the words, as spoken or chanted, [is] judged to have spiritual power. . . . By chanting or listening to the rhythmic words of a sacred text, the teaching and inspiration in the words becomes renewed and reinforced. In this sense the oral recitation of a text is a sacramental act. (Coward 2000: 146)[25]

More than this, poetry involves touch too, in the sense that to read it, *as poetry*, is perforce to feel the rhythmic flow (and often the rhymic patterning) of its measured onward motion in the beat of one's own body.[26] Philosophers may well want to strip Nāgārjuna down to some mere skeleton of bloodless signification, but his MK and other works irreducibly represent a form of *Philosophy in the Flesh* (Lakoff and Johnson 1999).[27] In fact, this is so for any avowedly Buddhist text, for insofar as Buddhist, such a text must needs effect an alleviation of suffering (or at the very least constitute an effort toward that end). And suffering pertains to the sentient, the feeling, the embodied.[28] As such, the embodiment of the text in a form that foregrounds the embodiedness of both itself and its reader-reciters performs valuable work in conveying the philosophical message the text sets out. To adopt the formulation of Ryūichi Abé, "It is at this depth of *poiesis* where words demonstrate their affinity most vividly with the Buddhist theory of emptiness" (Abé 2005: 309).

Furthermore, there is an organicity to the poetic text that is not as pronounced in prose equivalents. I am referring here to the inextricability on the micro-level of a given syllable from a given verse, and on a larger level of a given verse from a given passage, without compromising the whole of which that syllable or verse forms an ineliminable part. Now, Nāgārjuna's *kārikā* is no Dantean *catena* of lines the removal of any one of which would send an entire *Canto*'s tower of *terza rima* crashing. Nevertheless, however, there is an imbrication of verses in tightly woven sequence that mirrors, and formally reinforces, the relationality of what are nominally conceived to be independent entities in Nāgārjuna's metaphysics. Without wanting to push the point too far, I am proposing that part of the philosophical work being done by a text such as the MK lies in the very construction of its textual fabric, the which exhibits to an enhanced degree the mutually dependent *co*-origination (*pratītya-samutpādaḥ*) and/as *correlative* designation (*prajñaptir upādāya*) of parts (things, words, people . . .) within the overarching system of *saṃsāra* that Nāgārjuna goes so far as to outright equate with his signature teaching of emptiness (*śūnyatāṃ*) and the middle way itself (*pratipat* . . . *madhyamā*).[29] To put this another way, if Nāgārjuna's philosophy argues for an understanding of the things of the world as irreducibly relational phenomena rather than the metaphysically self-standing, independent entities they are typically taken to be, then what more fitting form could he have used to convey it than one incorporating such relational intertwining within its very verbal web?

The indivisibility of literary form and philosophical content—of medium and message—in the construction of textual meaning is a well-worn given in literary studies,[30] and yet it still seems not to have penetrated the realm of (non-continental) philosophy. This is evident in what Siderits and Katsura go on to say about the MK's *kārikā* form. Since, they claim, "it would be difficult to clearly formulate and fully defend a sophisticated philosophical thesis within the form's constraints. . . . It is text plus commentary that together are meant to do the work of formulating and defending the philosophical thesis in question" (Siderits and Katsura 2013: 2). Now, without wishing to deny the explicative functions of commentary (in the Indian philosophical sphere and well beyond), I cannot but point out, on the one hand, that the sheer influence of Nāgārjuna's verses on the history of philosophical thought across almost two millennia, unto today, is surely evidence enough of the fact that they have succeeded very well indeed in 'formulating and defending sophisticated philosophical theses'. On the other hand, it is not as if prose philosophical treatises, of wheresoever a provenance, have proven free of needing commentaries! There is clearly a double standard at work here, and one clearly biased against poetic form in favor of the prose treatise format privileged within the modern Western philosophical canon. After all, I know of no student or scholar of Kant's *Critiques*, say, who does not read them in consultation with commentarial secondary works, yet no one appears to declare therefore that "it would be difficult to clearly formulate and fully defend a sophisticated philosophical thesis within the [*Critique*] form's constraints." On the whole, then, I see efforts such as this to downplay to the point of denial any "organic connection" (as per Nussbaum) between Nāgārjuna's verse medium and philosophical message as another straightforward instantiation of the apologist effort to render Nāgārjuna as palatable as possible to the prosaic tastes of contemporary Western philosophy.[31]

0.2.2. Circle as Soteries

Over and above calling attention to the distinctly poetic means of conveying the philosophical content of the MK (and thereby also serving to undermine the in any case conventional dualism between content and form altogether), I am concerned here to bring to the fore another formal feature of the text. This regards the structure of the text as a whole, and in particular its circularity, in line with my broader argument as to the centrality of the motif of the abandonment of all view-holding to Nāgārjuna's philosophy as a whole. For as stated earlier in my summary of Chapter 4, there can be no doubt that the MK opens and closes on this very topic. Given that the MK is the *magnum opus* of Nāgārjuna, the single most important philosopher of "The Golden Age of Indian Buddhist Philosophy" (Westerhoff 2018a), surely this is not without significance, be it for understanding the thought of Nāgārjuna or that of any of the later traditions influenced by him—in other words, practically all subsequent schools of Buddhist thought?

Most commentaries and exegeses of the MK simply neglect to include any discussion at all of the text's formal structuring.[32] This is all the more a pity because, like Jakubczak, I too "am convinced that in the case of Madhyamaka philosophy in particular, many problems related to the logical side of Nāgārjuna's thought can be solved precisely by taking into account the narrative structure of his texts" (Jakubczak 2010: 53).[33] Those that do take structural elements into account typically assert at best some loose arrangement of chapters into 'sections' (Garfield 1995: 91)[34] or 'clusters' (Lindtner 1997: 354 n. 63).[35] Thus, Pandeya and Manju initially state that:

> In the arrangement of his chapters apparently there does not seem to be any design or structure involved. All the known commentators of Nāgārjuna have paid no attention to the arrangement of chapters, implying that each

> chapter is devoted to one or the other concept taken either arbitrarily or for its prominence in a particular system. (Pandeya and Manju 1991: xxiii)

They go on in the following pages "to suggest, however, that there is *some* method involved" (Pandeya and Manju 1991: xxiii, emphasis added), without for all that specifying what it might be.

Kalupahana is an exception in that he details what he calls "a carefully executed plan or structure in the *Kārikā*" (Kalupahana 1986: 27). Notably, his division of the MK into four major sections reserves the final section—on freedom from views—to chapter 27 alone.[36] Regarding this, Kalupahana writes: "One could hardly expect a better conclusion to a text intended to bring about freedom from all obsessions (*prapañcopaśama*) than this last chapter. It represents an explanation of the highest form of freedom, that is, freedom from ideological constraints" (Kalupahana 1986: 31). It appears that, in this case at least, attention to the formal qualities of the text leads Kalupahana too to take Nāgārjuna's text as a whole to instantiate a coherent literary structure mediating a coherent philosophical message.

While it is not my intention to provide an alternative classification of the MK's chapters under one or other rubric, I wish to call attention to the acknowledged fact that Nāgārjuna's text is structured such that it surveys and deconstructs a broad range of competing views proposed by adherents of both Buddhist and non-Buddhist philosophical systems.[37] Indeed, much as the tetralemma is designed to exhaust all possible positions, so too the MK is intended to survey and reject all possible viewpoints.[38] This appears evident from the numerous instances in which Nāgārjuna argues from a particular example, only to state that his argument is designed to cover, *mutatis mutandis*, all other related positions. In this light, see, for example, the use of the phrase "and the rest" (*ādīni* or *ādayaḥ*) at MK:9:11 and MK:27:29.[39] Or see MK:5:7 where, having mounted an argument specifically with regard to space, Nāgārjuna extrapolates from his conclusion to include all other elements (*dhātus*).[40] Or for that matter see the vehemently worded statement at the conclusion of the argument in MK:10 where, having critically analyzed the fire/fuel analogy typically used by his (Pudgalavāda, Vaibhāṣika, or Sautrāntika) interlocutors to argue for the independent existence of a dependently co-originated subject, Nāgārjuna declares:

> From the analysis in terms of fire and fuel
> All ways without exceptions follow

Of analyzing self and attachment
In terms of pot, cloth, and the others[41]

These and other examples demonstrate that the arguments Nāgārjuna mobilizes are meant to refute not just one or another position, but to renege on positionality altogether. Indeed, as I argue extensively in Chapter 2, the tetralemma itself is the prime rhetorical means by which Nāgārjuna exhausts all thetical possibilities. Or, to expatiate a little, the *catuṣkoṭi* is to be read as the preeminent means whereby Nāgārjuna utters a tetrāletheic teaching not meant to be taken as itself posited in any of the four possible ways (of affirming, denying, both, or neither).[42]

Now, the details of which particular interlocutor Nāgārjuna is addressing at any particular point in any of his texts is the subject of much debate, and it is well beyond my purview to gauge the classical and modern commentarial literature on this point. The point I do wish to emphasize is that Nāgārjuna's distinctive argumentative strategy responds to and rejects whatever position any given interlocutor happens to advance, and that it is precisely by means of this serial *prasaṅgic* deconstruction that Nāgārjuna ultimately arrives at the abjuration of any and all positions. This means that Nāgārjuna's arguments are invariably *counter*-arguments; they serve to identify and eliminate positions or, in other words, truth claims. This is the purport of Westerhoff's observation that in Madhyamaka philosophy "there is no master argument for emptiness"; rather, arguments for emptiness are "opponent-relative" (Westerhoff 2016a: 372).[43] Indeed, more than being *invariably* so, this is *necessarily* so for consistency's sake, for any context-transcendent argument would entail that whoever makes it "believe[s] in context-transcendent truth-conditions" (Siderits 2019: 658). Nāgārjuna is no such believer, and so "There can, in short, be no master argument for emptiness. This is a consequence of the emptiness of emptiness" (Siderits 2019: 658).[44]

Of course, the proposing of truth claims (i.e., views) as to reality is the definitively philosophical endeavor, at least as it has been practiced in the West since the pre-Socratics, but also for the most part as it has been practiced in India and the rest of the world. After all, a philosopher (be s/he a *philosophos*, *fīlsūf*, *dārśanika*, *zhexuejia* 哲學家, or known by any other name) is one who proposes a (certain) view of (some aspect of) reality, and one's success as a philosopher is typically determined (at least theoretically) by the extent to which one's view of reality is determined to be true, or useful, or coherent . . . (by others, or at least by other philosophers). I said that this is 'for the most part' how philosophy has been practiced for, of course, there have been many dissenters over the many centuries of this enterprise; ones who criticized this approach and attempted to find ways out of it, often through recourse to non- or anti-logical discursive techniques and/or experiential as opposed to (what they would class as 'merely') intellectual insights. Unsurprisingly, in consequence of having thus attempted to expand the horizons within which philosophy, as the 'love of wisdom', may be enacted so as to include so much more of significance to human life, these radical innovators have been for the most part ridiculed, or simply ignored, to greater or lesser extents by mainstream philosophers, their approaches dubbed 'mystical' or misunderstood for understood from within the confines of a species of thinking they themselves claimed to have superseded.

I will devote substantial discussion in subsequent chapters to the multiple manners in which scholars of Nāgārjuna have explicitly or implicitly endorsed such a narrowly 'philosophical' interpretive lens by which to gauge his work. For the present, I want to argue for the ineliminably contextual nature of Nāgārjuna's *prasaṅgic* method, for I see him as employing this as an effective means of undermining all-comers' philosophies without affirming any of his own. Ethan Mills has identified this as a "parasitic method of defining the target of skepticism about philosophy," where the 'host' or "target of Nāgārjuna's skepticism is defined by his opponents" (Mills 2018a: xxvi, xxvii). His distinction between 'skepticism about philosophy versus epistemological skepticism' (Mills 2018a: xxii ff.) is useful here, for whereas Nāgārjuna is certainly no epistemological skeptic in the sense of proposing (skeptical) "truth-claims about knowledge" (Mills 2018a: xxiii), I agree that his method is, to adopt Mills's fivefold family resemblance schema of skepticism about philosophy,

> *dialectical* in that it is usually directed toward specific theories of other philosophers . . . [is] not attempting to adduce support for a truth-claim . . . is usually a wholesale refusal of the project of forming conclusions . . . constitutes a form of intellectual therapy with the goal of creating a mental coolness wherein one's impulse to form beliefs (at least about philosophical matters) is dissipated . . . [and] is—whether paradoxically or not—primarily cultivated through the use of philosophical arguments, although these arguments do not have as their conclusions truth-claims about philosophical matters. (Mills 2018a: xxvii, emphasis original)[45]

It makes perfect sense, of course, that Nāgārjuna should use—*need* to use—philosophical arguments to gainsay others' philosophical arguments, for otherwise his arguments would not hold any sway against them. If he had been a classical composer, he may have beaten Bach to counterpoint; if he had been a modern lyricist, he may have riffed on Lennon, since each of his works (and each of the individual chapters of the MK) amounts to Nāgārjuna countering, saying 'I don't believe' to whatever that work (or chapter) discusses, all the way on to *nirvāṇa* itself. But Nāgārjuna was a philosopher, and so he drove philosophical vehicles to arrive at philosophy's end.[46]

This method of silencing view after view after view forms a trajectory toward the silencing of all views, and this (as I will go on to argue in detail in Chapter 5) constitutes Nāgārjuna's distinctive contribution to the eirenic pacification of all conceptualization, and with it all *karma*—action—and thus all suffering. As already averred, I take the 'cessation of conceptualization' (*prapañcopaśamaṃ*) with which Nāgārjuna's major work begins and the 'abandonment of all views' (*sarvadṛṣṭiprahāṇāya*) with which it ends to function together as a—perhaps even *the*—hermeneutic key to the entire text falling within their bracketing. But as the preceding paragraphs have shown, the 'intellectual therapy' Nāgārjuna administers to those of us "afflicted with conceptualizations"[47] (and who is not?) features throughout his corpus.

Much of this book will be devoted to elaborating this Nāgārjunian 'anti-view', so for the moment I will restrict myself to a brief discussion of perhaps the clearest abjuration of all positionality to be found in any of Nāgārjuna's works, the justly celebrated verse 29 of his *Vigrahavyāvartanī* or *Dispeller of Disputes*. Having reviewed and repudiated his interlocutor's thesis as to the untenability of emptiness, Nāgārjuna rebuts the charge that his own view is prey to his own refutation by countering:

> If I held any thesis
> This fault would apply to me
> But I do not hold any thesis
> So I have no such fault[48]

Now, Burton has helpfully pointed out that when Nāgārjuna denies holding any thesis (*pratijñā*) at VV:29,

> he says this in the context of his critique of the Nyāya epistemology, according to which the *pratijñā* is the first of the five members of a valid

> inference, followed by the cause or reason (*hetu*) for the thesis, the statement of the example (*udāharaṇa*) [more widely known as *dṛṣṭanta*] supporting the thesis, the application (*upanaya*) of that example to the thesis and, finally, the conclusion (*nigamana*). (Burton 2004: 117)

The upshot of this is that *pratijñā* is the first, foundational, member of inferential knowledge. By refusing to hold a *pratijñā*, Nāgārjuna effectively denies the validity of the entire epistemological system of logical inference elaborated by his Naiyāyika interlocutors, the logicians foremost responsible for constructing the edifice of classical Indian epistemology and, with it, the canons of rational argumentation.[49] Indeed, on my reading he is doing even more than this, for not only is he refusing to grant validity to inferential knowledge, as symbolized in a given *pratijñā* on the Naiyāyika model, but he is also refusing to hold any view (*dṛṣṭi*) at all.[50]

Murti for one considers this 'view of no view' to be fundamentally constitutive of Nāgārjuna's Madhyamaka. He makes the point in several ways:

> The Mādhyamika *disproves* the opponent's thesis, and does *not* prove any thesis of his own; Negative judgment is the *negation of judgment*, and not one more judgment; Judgment *qua* judgment must always be affirmative, ascriptive . . . Negative judgment is the *negation of judgment*; *Śūnyatā* is negation of negations . . . Negation of positions is not one more position; Criticism of theories is not another theory; *śūnyatā* of *dṛṣṭis* is not one more *dṛṣṭi*, but is *prajñā*—their reflective awareness. (Murti 1955: 131, 155, 160, 161, 209, emphases original)[51]

It is on this basis that he is able to declare the Madhyamaka to be "the one system that is completely free from every trace of dogmatism" (Murti 1955: 334). Without subscribing to Murti's Kantianism, I can only agree with this analysis, and see it as being not only thoroughly consistent with the abandonment of all views espoused by Nāgārjuna throughout his opus but constituting a truly radical break with the warring of words constitutive of philosophical practice in Nāgārjuna's day as in our own, on the understanding that wars of any kind inevitably issue in the suffering of their conscripted troops.

Of course, the sheer radicality of Nāgārjuna's endeavor to rid us entirely of our dogmas—the very beliefs we live by—has perplexed those committed to its comprehension (myself very much included). But it is surely not for nothing that Nāgārjuna's works, like the Prajñāpāramitā *sūtras* from which he so evidently drew inspiration,[52] are strewn with deeply perplexing statements. Indeed, the evident, and often avowed, incomprehension with which commentators both ancient and modern, Eastern and Western, have been beset in confronting Nāgārjuna's views is surely itself something of a testimony to the success of his enterprise. After all, were his statements easily comprehensible to and explicable by commentators, either they would be readily assimilable to ordinary (read: unenlightened, dualistic) notions of reality (and thus fail to rouse us from these), or we commentators would be enlightened beings (for whom such statements would thus present no challenge at all). As it is, we being bound—alas—by our ignorance and desire to reiterate our unenlightened either/ors, we find Nāgārjuna's steadfast refusal to conform to them, be it as expressed in the fourfold negation of the *catuṣkoṭi* or the outright disavowal of views, baffling. This is necessarily so, for the unenlightened mind is inevitably attached to, and consequently involved in, oppositionality. The entire soterial thrust of Nāgārjuna's enterprise is, precisely, to free us from these bounds, these bonds, such that we are able to realize the "neither identity nor difference" (*anekārtham anānārtham*) with which he begins the first chapter of the MK (1:1). If this book can aid in the appreciation of that endeavor, then it has served a worthy purpose.

0.3. Buddhism Between Religion and Philosophy

The middle way is the way between, and this holds not only for the doctrinal extremes the Buddhist tradition abjures but also for the disciplinary identities the scholarly profession upholds. This book argues that Buddhism—or rather at least Nāgārjuna's brand of it—does lie *between* religion and philosophy as these disciplines have been traditionally understood and as they have been deployed to study their respective objects. For these disciplines arose and remain practiced within Western Christianate cultures and cultures of knowledge, from whence they have spread, like much else, to attain normative status around the globe. I will have more to say later about the relationships between Christianity, on the one hand, and philosophy and religious studies as academic disciplines historically situated in Western models of scholarship, on the other. More pointedly, I will argue for the relevance of those relationships to the study of Buddhism and, by analogy, to other non-Western philosophies, other non-Christian religions. But for the moment I want to explain the point I am making in terms of the coinage that I have just used and that will prove useful here and at various other junctures throughout this book.[53]

0.3.1. Islamicate, Christianate, Buddhate

In his awe-inspiring classic *The Venture of Islam*, Marshall Hodgson proposed a distinction between 'Islamic' and 'Islamicate'. These are respectively to stand "for what we may call religion and for the overall society and culture associated historically with the religion" (Hodgson 1974: 57). Hodgson goes on to specify that he restricts the adjective 'Islamic' to " 'of or pertaining to' Islam *in the proper, the religious, sense*" and uses his coinage 'Islamicate' to "refer not directly to the religion, Islam, itself, but to the social and cultural complex historically associated with Islam and the Muslims, both among Muslims themselves and even when found among non-Muslims" (Hodgson 1974: 59, emphases original). Unfortunately, despite their evident conceptual utility, Hodgson's terms have not found general acceptance within scholarship concerned with Islam, and equivalent terms have found practically no application to other religious spheres.

In what follows, then, I propose distinctions between 'Christian' and 'Christianate', 'Buddhist' and 'Buddhate', 'religious' and 'religionate' that are to function analogously to that first applied by Hodgson to Islam. Of these, as far as I am aware only the Christian/Christianate dichotomy has been put to any prior scholarly use. It has not been widely accepted by scholars of Christianity, however, and has therefore hitherto been predominant in relevant contexts only among a few scholars concerned primarily with Islam (see, e.g., Krstić 2015: 689). As for 'Buddhate', this is my coinage—preferable, I think, to 'Buddhistic', or for that matter 'Buddhistate' or 'Buddhisticate'—on the model of Hodgson's Islamic/Islamicate distinction. Subsequently to coining it I came across Charles Hallisey's comment that "It may be simultaneously fortunate and unfortunate that the academic community of Buddhist studies has not invented a term analogous to Hodgson's ungainly, but extremely useful one" (Hallisey 2020: 180–181). I can only hope my invention is taken as fortunate rather than unfortunate, though I freely admit it may appear ungainly at first![54] Finally, 'religious' and 'religionate', like 'Christian' and 'Christianate' or 'Buddhist' and 'Buddhate', refers to "what we may call religion" and "the overall society and culture associated historically with the religion" (Hodgson 1974: 57).[55]

The distinctions I propose are, of course, not unlimited in their appropriate ranges of applicability. Thus, most relevantly, I have seen no need throughout this book to make a distinction between the specifically 'Buddhist' elements of Nāgārjuna's religiosophy and those to be considered 'Buddhate'. This is so for the simple reason that Nāgārjuna (like the other Buddhist philosophers I mention) is unproblematically, avowedly *Buddhist*, his philosophy (their philosophies) conceptually assimilable to (and in fact historically assimilated by) the Buddhist religious tradition. What I am dealing with in this book, therefore, is clearly *Buddhist* philosophy (a religious one), not a merely *Buddhate* (religionate) product of Buddhist society and culture.[56] But how Nāgārjuna and his peers have been categorized, interpreted, and evaluated most certainly does have to do with religionate, and particularly Christianate, starting points.

To explain this, allow me first of all to aver in highly general (and therefore, admittedly, controversial) terms that the history of Western philosophy, at least from the time of Augustine and right unto today, has been embedded within self-identifiedly Christian societies and cultures, and is therefore wholly Christianate. For one thing, overtly proclaimed Christianity constitutes the intellectual bedrock of the vast majority of thinkers comprising the Western philosophical canon. But more broadly, I see the overall presuppositions and parameters of philosophical thought even as carried out among the minority of Western philosophers *not* self-identifying as Christian as being so steeped in the ambient Christianate intellectual culture they called (and call) home that even the critiques made by some of them of the Christianate (not to say Christian) terms governing Western philosophical discourse remain necessarily couched in, and thus informed by, those very same Christianate, if not downright Christian, terms. Over and above the incontestably Christianate (insofar as in fact Christian) philosophico-theology of Hegel, say (to say nothing of Descartes, Locke, Kant . . .),[57] the critiques made by Heidegger, say (to say nothing of Hume, Nietzsche, Derrida . . .), of the governing terms, the very questions guiding the venture of Western philosophy, I am thus here interpreting as religionate even if and when not explicitly religious, as Christianate even if and when not overtly Christian.

Naturally, and as my reference to Augustine should have made clear, my comments refer to the history of Western philosophy in the 'common era'; that is, *anno Domini nostri Jesu Christi.* That said, to the extent that Whitehead's quip to the effect that "The safest general characterization of the European philosophical tradition is that it consists of a series of footnotes to Plato" (Whitehead 1978: 39) is valid, my point may be restated as claiming that not only are the bulk of those footnotes Christian but all of them (after Constantine) are effectively Christianate. This is not to deny, of course, the enduringly definitive role pre-Christian Greek philosophers such as the very same Plato have played in shaping Western philosophy. Much has now, and particularly in the wake of Heidegger, been written on the determinative effects of what have thereby been shown to be idiosyncratically Greek modes and models of thinking upon what have until recently been widely assumed to be universal and unimpeachable principles of all thought. But while the Greeks have indubitably exerted pervasive influence, I am suggesting that to claim, *à la* Émile Benveniste, that "The whole diversity of Western metaphysics stems from particularities of the Greek language" (Faure 2004: 37) is to overstate the case. For it is to ignore, in the name of philosophy, that other guiding spirit of the Western mind, the Christianate nature of its culture I am emphasizing.[58]

My adoption of the coinage *Christianate* as a moniker applicable to Western philosophy conveniently sidesteps the question of whether, or the extent to which, such philosophy is *Christian.* That is convenient indeed, for the latter question has exercised just about every thinker accepted as a philosopher or a theologian (or a philosopher-theologian) since the time of Paul the Apostle, and resulted in anything but unanimity.[59] What is of most relevance to my discussion here, however, is the fact (or what I take to be a fact) that, certain 'philosophical theologians' aside, the vast majority of professional philosophers active today, and even of philosophers of religion among them, will doubtless rail vociferously against my claim, especially as it has been put in admittedly provocative terms. For quite apart from the professed atheism of many current-day philosophers, or the fact that many may well regard "theological language as either meaningless, or, at best, subject to scrutiny only insofar as that language had a bearing on religious practice" (Murray and Rea 2000: §1), philosophers have throughout the history of their enterprise made a point of grounding their avowed mandate—howsoever this may be conceived—in reason. For reason has been taken to be (ideally or definitionally) the light allowing access to truth unstained by bias or mere contingency, its use the defining characteristic of the *animal rationale, homo sapiens* itself.[60] Philosophers have conceived of their own method, moreover, as one of (not experimentation, say, as in the case of scientific method, but) argumentation premised upon contention and critique.[61] Crucially for the argument I am making here, however, none of this invalidates the idea that the history of Western philosophy has been overwhelmingly informed by Christianate paradigms.[62]

And yet, despite the convenience of sidestepping the issue, I do want to press for a further point. To make it, I take my bearings from Heidegger, and particularly from his acute understanding of the significance of what appear to be the mere abstract and abstruse arcana of philosophy to the socially situated practice of meaning-making. "Heidegger's claim is that by giving shape to our historical understanding of 'what *is*', metaphysics determines the most basic presuppositions of what *anything* is, including ourselves" (Thomson 2000: 298, emphases original). After all,

> The practices containing an understanding of what it is to be a human being, those containing an interpretation of what it is to be a thing, and those defining society fit together. Social practices thus transmit not only an implicit understanding of what it is to be a human being, an animal, an object, but, finally, what it is for anything to be at all. (Dreyfus 1993: 295, cited in Thomson 2000: 323 n. 3)

Applied to the context at hand, I propose that the circumambient Christianate culture within which so much of Western philosophy has been carried out has, to a significant extent, seeped into that philosophy, commensurately informing it with identifiably Christian forms of thought. The very understandings of 'what it is to be', be it *inter alia* in metaphysical, epistemological, or ethical constructions of self and world, truth and wisdom, or good and glory—and of how such things 'fit together'—have been fore-fashioned for us (all of us) by our culture, and thereby been rendered invisible to us. As Heidegger puts it in a justifiably famous passage,

> When tradition thus becomes master, it does so in such a way that what it 'transmits' is made so inaccessible, proximally and for the most part, that it rather becomes concealed. Tradition takes what has come down to us and delivers it over to self-evidence; it blocks our access to those primordial 'sources' from which the categories and concepts handed down to us have been in part quite genuinely drawn. Indeed it makes us forget that they have had such an origin, and makes us suppose that the necessity of going

back to these sources is something which we need not even understand. (Heidegger 1962: 43)

To the extent that this has been and remains so, the history of Western philosophy is seen to be not only *Christianate* but *Christian*. To substantiate this claim and thus comprehend in detail the exact extent of Christianity's influence on Christianate philosophy would take me far beyond my remit here and would in any case constitute an interminable task. But suffice it for now, before turning to the study of religion, to underline that howsoever great or small one may take such influence to be, its very existence problematizes the philosophical study of other religions—and here most pertinently Buddhism—in Western and Westernized contexts. For (to anticipate an argument fleshed out in Chapter 1) there can be no doubt that the study of Buddhist *philosophy* has in fact been carried out on the basis of paradigms and presuppositions alien to *Buddhist* philosophy. If we are committed to judging the value and validity of philosophers such as Nāgārjuna fairly, then, I suggest that we must first to the extent possible disillude ourselves of our *pre*-judgments, and the implicitly colonialist assumption of universality we effectively ascribe to them whenever we uncritically apply them to foreign worlds of thought.

0.3.2. Religionate Religious Studies

The case of religious studies will involve less discussion, not because it is any less complex or its history any less controversial than philosophy (far from it), but simply because, unlike philosophers, scholars of religion have on the whole readily and rightfully, if at times grudgingly, acknowledged the determining influence of Christianity upon the historical makeup of their field, and even on the very definition of their objects of study.[63] The nineteenth-century philological and then anthropological antecedents of today's 'religious studies' or *Religionswissenschaft* were themselves forged as intellectual and then professional disciplines in the study of textual data and human behaviors of immediate relevance and practical use to European—that is, Christianate, and most often outright Christian—interests and agendas. This was all the more so when the objects thus discovered and studied proved 'other' to regnant paradigms.[64] The predominance of Christianate cultures of study in the study of religion, and embedded within them of implicitly or explicitly Christian features of thought in thinking about religions, continues to this day. As one of the premier theorists of the field asserts, "The history of the history of religions is not best conceived as a liberation from the hegemony of theology . . . because such a claimed liberation has been, in so many moments of our history, an illusion" (Smith 2004: 362–363).[65] And another such theorist even points out that "*the* formative role in creating the discipline known as 'religious studies'" was played by none other than the "conservative and confessional" National Association of Biblical Instructors, "devoted to promote study of the Bible in higher education," renamed as the American Academy of Religion (Lincoln 2012: 133, emphasis added).[66]

This is not to deny, of course, that religious studies as an academic discipline has forged its very identity on a counter-positioning *vis-à-vis* (Christian) theology. But it is to deny that such an attempt has in fact succeeded in shedding religious studies of its Christianate (indeed, largely Christian) historical roots as an academic discipline. Eric Sharpe has traced those roots with acuity, demonstrating the extent to which Christian ideas, and perhaps most pointedly the idea that "Christianity is *die Religion*—the absolute religion, in which all others find their fulfilment" (Sharpe 1986: 127), played a determinative role in the discipline's historical "Quest for Academic Recognition." But he has also argued that the involvement of "liberal Christian (and other) theology" in shaping the discipline "has been fairly constant" even "in our own day," not least in its "bewildering ability to melt into its background and social setting" (Sharpe 1986: 294–295). This last observation in fact precisely describes the move from Christian to Christianate. But furthermore, as Tomoko Masuzawa has noted in a more recent context, and "as some adamantly secularist scholars—who constitute a sizable and vocal minority in the field—have observed with some displeasure, there is a higher concentration of unreconstituted religious essentialists in this department of knowledge than anywhere else in the academy" (Masuzawa 2005: 7). Indeed, given the overtly religious origins of the American Academy of Religion, what Masuzawa describes as the "religious (as opposed to scientific) and essentialist tenor of the AAR membership" (Masuzawa 2005: 7 fn. 10) today should come as little surprise.[67] Over and above religious affiliation or attitude (and there is, of course, no need to specify just *which* of the 'world religions' is being upheld here), and despite reiterated claims to being "a multitraditional and polymethodic discipline" (Sharma 2005: ix), the field of religious studies betrays, still, a preponderant privileging of its Christian heritage in myriad ways, be they structural-institutional (e.g., in the number of positions advertised and held, courses taught, books and journals published) or conceptual-hermeneutic (e.g., in the topics, templates, theories, taxonomies, and terminologies prioritized and prestigified).[68] Not only is the scholarly study of religion overwhelmingly Christianate, then, but it remains rooted in identifiably, if often implicitly, Christian terms of engagement.

Indeed, as one recent attempt at "Rethinking Concepts and Methods in the Sociological Study of Religion" puts it, "Christian templates profoundly shape religious and secular organization and practice, the role of religion in public life, *and research about it*" (Cadge, Levitt, and Smilde 2011: 439, emphases added). The authors go on to devote extended further discussion substantiating this claim, and do so precisely because "Christocentrism . . . is so omnipresent" (Cadge, Levitt, and Smilde 2011: 440) in the field. This is evinced by the data they cite, which demonstrates—shockingly—that *more scholarly attention is devoted to Christianity than to all other religious forms and traditions combined.* While Cadge, Levitt, and Smilde's analysis is limited to sociology,[69] their admonition as to "just how analytically dangerous and ultimately dishonest it is to try to fit all religious expressions into Christian boxes" (Cadge, Levitt, and Smilde 2011: 441) could certainly be extrapolated to the study of religion in general.

This explains why I refer to *religionate* religious studies in the title to this subsection. The term is only attested in a single verbal usage, meaning 'to be made religious', by Andrew Marvell in 1676, where the poet and essayist states that "There have been Martyrs for Reason, . . . but how much more would men be so for reason Religionated and Christianized!" (OED: religionate).[70] Of sometime 'martyrs for reason' this book will have much to say, but here I want to draw on the synonymity of 'Religionated' and 'Christianized' assumed by Marvell to propose an adjectival form signaling the religionate character of religious studies. As the foregoing discussion has shown, the scholarly study of religion remains a highly Christianate enterprise. One facet of this fact relates to the overtly religious—that is, Christian—identity of so many of its members. But in characterizing the field of religious studies as *religionate* (in addition to highly religious), I am adapting Hodgson's definition of 'Islamicate' to refer not directly to religion itself, but to the social and cultural complex historically associated with religion and religionists, both among religionists themselves and even when found among non-religionists.[71] The religion—*die Religion*—referred to is, of course, preeminently Christianity. But in speaking of the religionate character of religious studies, I want to both acknowledge the near-total overlap between the spheres of the religionate and the Christianate in the study of religion hitherto, and to open a space for alternative viewpoints. Religious studies, after all, could certainly benefit from more Islamicate, Buddhate, and other perspectives.[72] And as this book will demonstrate in detail, even scholars of such alternative perspectives may sometimes fall prey to Christianate premises.

Now, I freely acknowledge that my use of a single brush to paint the many departmental and disciplinary walls housed under the broad moniker of 'religious studies' obscures the varied hues of individual subfields (to say nothing of individual scholars). As one would expect in a field so large, there already is an immense variety of approaches and attitudes, though this detracts neither from the observation that some subfields are obviously more Christianocentric than others nor from my global characterization of religious studies as religionate. For example, I have previously argued that the subfield of philosophy of religion is a particularly egregious example of Christianocentrism, having been "solely based on the use of philosophy in the Christian religion, to the extent that it is often practically impossible to tell the divide between philosophy of religion and theology" (Stepien 2020b: 7).[73] The study by Cadge, Levitt, and Smilde I cited earlier shows like criticisms applicable to the sociology of religion, and further studies would doubtless uncover analogous silences (or silencings) in other subfields. It is this ubiquity of the disparity across the study of religion as a whole which, I feel, justifies the broad strokes of my critique. For my point relates not to any individual orientation, be it an exemplar or an outlier, but to the very geography of the field at large, wherein a single religion remains foregrounded, its particularities raised to become prerogatives. After all, if the place of 'other' religions in the ground plan of religious studies is prescribed by one among them (*the* 'one': "the only real religion in the proper sense of the term"—Masuzawa 2005: 144), which itself arrogates to itself exclusive centrality to the point of invisibility, then it is incumbent upon the scholarly community—mandated as it is, at least avowedly, to critically examine 'religion' as well as 'religions'—to redraw that map, to 'provincialize Europe' (Chakrabarty 2000) so as to excavate and expel as emphatically and entirely as possible the notion that "the unity of the world, or the world as totality . . . [is] a direct expression of European Christianity, or Europe as (erstwhile) Christendom" (Masuzawa 2005: 13). If this book can be of service in that endeavor, so much the better.

0.3.3. Buddhism as Religiosophy

This brings my discussion back to the relevance all this holds for the subject under study here. Has the study of Buddhism been affected by Christianate or Christian paradigms and presuppositions? Unfortunately, although Buddhism has not been viewed with the same "mixture of pity and disgust" as Judaism or the same "mixture of fear and hatred" (Sharpe 1986: 12) as Islam in the history of Christian confrontations with and exclusions of other religions,[74] it has nonetheless been subjected to all manner of misconceptions no less spurious or specious. This includes by writers ostensibly "jealous of their own scientific integrity as dispassionate investigators and empiricists" (Sharpe 1986: 295). Given the fact that religion has effectively—if, of course, not explicitly—been defined as "anything that sufficiently resembles modern Protestant Christianity" (Nongbri 2013: 18),[75] it should come as no surprise that Buddhism, this tradition "at once alien and familiar" (Masuzawa 2005: 121), should have been "embraced by the West as both an alternative religion and an alternative to religion" (Lopez 2005: 2)—and much else besides. But if "the European outlook on Buddhism [*as a religion*] was anything but consistent" (Masuzawa 2005: 121), then, contrariwise, modern Western philosophers have not been beset by any such inconsistencies or doubts. Indeed, ever since the recourse to *Racism in the Formation of the Philosophical Canon* in the wake of Kant (Park 2013), philosophy unto today has dismissed Buddhism as merely a religious 'Wisdom Tradition', of no relevance to any philosopher worthy of the name.[76] Perhaps still worse, and as Roger-Pol Droit has shown in exquisite detail, there is a long history of philosophers projecting their own fears and anxieties onto Buddhism, seen in this light "as a paradoxical and horrible religion of nothingness" (Droit 2003: 4).[77] Although Droit claims that this "old mistake . . . has vanished" (Droit 2003: 5), however, not only is the specter of Buddhism-as-nihilism not banished (see my discussion in §3.7), but the broader point as to Western philosophers' self-certain dismissal of Buddhism from the bounds of philosophy proper on the basis of ignorance and bias remains all too current. Indeed, for as long as Buddhist philosophy remains relegated to the margins of 'mainstream' philosophy, I see little more at work in its contemporary exclusion than the euphemized kin of the openly racist Christianate, and Christian, preclusions of yore.

Now, I have formulated the foregoing arguments as to the Christianate nature of philosophy as also of religious studies in provocative terms, and I have done so in a deliberate effort to press home what I see to be the inestimable yet largely unappreciated force and pervasiveness of frames of thought derived from Christianity in these fields of scholarship.[78] But I need not have done so for the purpose at hand, for this is simply to delineate the problems that such a Christianate theoretical pre-history produces in the study of a Buddhist religiosopher such as Nāgārjuna. The problems, as I see it, are two. One is that the identities of philosophy and religious studies as professional scholarly disciplines have been premised on an avowed disjunction between themselves and religion/theology that is not only problematic (if not downright deceptive) but does not apply, is alien to, the Buddhist context (among others, needless to add). No Buddhist school of thought or practice ever identified itself in opposition to, or even in contradistinction from, 'theology'. This is so even if, being generous, we interpret the term in so broad a manner as to dispense with the 'theo' element (obviously non-Buddhist) in favor of something like 'religiously informed reasoning'. The distinction is simply not operative in any Buddhist sphere. But the second problem is that, despite the rhetoric of distancing and differentiation, the fact is that philosophy and religious studies have both historically been and to this day remain utterly saturated with Christian frames of discourse, and in this sense remain clearly Christianate. So not only is the theoretical distinction inapplicable to Buddhist objects of study, but the overall failure to enact it, and thereby the fact of remaining in practice ensconced within terms of reference again inapplicable to Buddhism, entails that studying Buddhism from the vantage point of philosophy *or* of religious studies is prone to debilitating objections. Indeed, in one sense this book in its entirety is an effort to make these objections in as forceful a manner as possible, and concomitantly to proffer alternative terms and methods (or methodological grounds at least) more amenable to, recognizable to, the Buddhist religiosophical tradition itself as exemplified in the paradigmatic case of Nāgārjuna.

Thankfully, there is no need (anymore) to study Nāgārjuna from the vantage point of philosophy *or* of religious studies: these are not approaches necessarily to be conceived in terms of an either/or distinction. On the contrary, despite the stubbornness of departmental walls within the university, inter-, multi-, pluri-, and trans-disciplinarity have attained to normative-ideal status for original research (though not yet to the state of being normal-typical) across the humanities and well beyond. This is a good thing in general given the evident and amply attested advantages of inter-disciplinary and related approaches. And it is a good thing in particular for objects of study such as

Buddhism not assimilable (without more or less violent explanatory and/or descriptive reductionism) to the disciplinary boundaries standardly accepted and unquestioned in the academy heretofore.[79]

For as I will go on to discuss in some detail in the pages that follow (see, in particular, §1.4), Buddhism cannot adequately be understood as *either* a religion *or* a philosophy. Buddhism is thus what I am proposing to call a 'religiosophy'. I am not the first to coin the term,[80] but I use it here in a sense both new and hopefully useful for the study of systems such as Buddhism. The 'sophy' part of the coinage is straightforward insofar as it is meant to mean just the same 'wisdom' or 'knowledge' referred to in the word 'philosophy' (standardly rendered as 'love of wisdom', from the Greek etymons *phílo* and *sophía*). As for 'religio', I have in mind both of the Latin etymologies standardly given as candidates for 'religion', though each with an important modification. *Relegere* is the etymon proposed by Cicero, meaning 'to read over again' and thus leading to 'religion' being understood as 'painstaking observance of rites'. *Religāre*, meanwhile, is the etymon preferred by early Christian writers, stemming from a verb meaning 'to tie up or back, to restrain, bind fast, to make fast, secure' (OED: religate), and thus meaning 'that which ties believers to God' (OED: religion). In both cases, I propose removing the specifications extraneous to the original senses, thereby leaving us with 'painstaking observance' and 'that which ties' respectively. Religiosophy may thus be construed as both 'the painstaking observance of wisdom' and 'that which ties to wisdom'. Each of these senses has its own connotations, and one or other is to be foregrounded (though not to the outright exclusion of the other) in accordance with varying contexts. Thus, 'the painstaking observance of wisdom' emphasizes the practical orientation of religiosophy, according to which it serves to orient its adept toward a particular, virtuous, 'way of life' (to use Hadot's celebrated reconceptualization of philosophy: Hadot 1995). Religiosophy as 'that which ties to wisdom', meanwhile, emphasizes the intellectual bond tying an adept to wisdom, knowledge, insight into the nature of reality.

Now, in proposing 'religiosophy' and in defining it in contradistinction to either of its constituents, it is certainly not my intention here to offer definitions of terms so polysemic as 'philosophy' and 'religion,' not least since I would consider any attempt to do so hopelessly reductionist. Nor is it my intention to suggest that religiosophy somehow manages to override the etymological and conceptual incongruencies its two components bear with non-English near (but far from perfect) equivalents. Nevertheless, it should be clear that for present purposes I am foregrounding conceptions of philosophy that take it to be characterized by the rational search for abstract truth, and conversely of religion that take it to be characterized by the practical search for soterial end. Taking these as rough but useful heuristics, I am proposing to treat Nāgārjuna as an exemplary Buddhist, and an exemplary Buddhist religiosopher, in that he conceives his *philosophical* enterprise to be valuable, or even intelligible, only insofar as it serves the *religious*.[81]

This book thus argues for a religiosophical construction of Nāgārjuna's work, and it does so in a manner that, whatever its merits as textual hermeneutics, bases itself on identifiably Nāgārjunian grounds. As I demonstrate and criticize, many (I would not hesitate to say most) contemporary philosophically minded interpreters writing in English prefer to ground Nāgārjuna in analytical soil far removed from his native intellectual territory. They typically do so in an apologist effort to see Nāgārjuna approved as a true philosopher by professional philosopher peers. I propose that students and scholars of Buddhist philosophy (along with those engaged in the study of other non-Western philosophies) need to make a qualitatively different, and stronger, case for the objects of their studies being accepted as philosophy. Instead of apologizing for a Buddhist philosopher such as Nāgārjuna by attempting to square him with the presuppositions, parameters, and priorities animating contemporary Western philosophy (primarily as elaborated by the Analytic Church Fathers), we should not be reluctant or afraid to read Nāgārjuna on his terms, according to his words and worlds of thought. Given the divergent agendas at work (i.e., the divergent attitudes toward what philosophy is doing) as well as the divergent religious and religionate bases from which they start out, the frameworks within which Nāgārjuna's Buddhist philosophy holds together, within which it makes sense, differ in considerable and irreconcilable ways both from those of contemporary Analytics and (in other ways) from those animating the entire historical trajectory of Western philosophical thought in all its internal variegation. The overall upshot is that there is no such thing as 'philosophy' in the singular; there are philosophies. Since original thought thrives most fruitfully where it is placed in soils rich with multifarious nutrients, this should be cause for celebration, not for attempts to prune, merely transplant, or even uproot it as mere weed.

This point also serves to explain why, though this book be many things, one thing it is not is a work of analytic philosophy—even if the current philosophical establishment were to accept as valid such a rubric as 'Analytic Buddhist Philosophy'. Although as a student of philosophy trained in the late twentieth and early twenty-first-century West I have been led—not to say *forced*—to read a great deal of analytic philosophy, I do not consider analytic procedures and presuppositions to be particularly helpful in enabling comprehension of the vastly differing thought-worlds of Nāgārjuna's late second to early third-century India.

That said, I should not be taken as suggesting that we should desist from placing Nāgārjuna into conversation with the philosophers of twentieth and twenty-first-century Europe and North America. Apart from anything else, that would go directly contrary to the extolling of discursive multiplicity I have just avowed. But I do suggest that we should refrain from judging the East by the standards of the West, and attempting to approve it based on how well it satisfies those standards. I suspect academic philosophers would be up in arms if one were to evaluate Aristotle, Kant, or Wittgenstein in terms of how well *they* conform to the ideas and ideals of Vasubandu, Dharmakīrti, or Śāntideva, say, yet the occidento-centric converse approach is so prevalent even today—even among scholars of non-Western philosophies—that it effectively remains definitive of the field. Rather than forever defending our subjects and ourselves, the time has surely come go on the offensive on behalf of the un- or under-appreciated Nāgārjunas of the world. Whatever the individual approach, let us no longer disguise or distort those elements of whatsoever among the multifarious philosophies of the world we find fascinating which do not happen to accord with the prescriptions contingently distinctive of the Western canon in an apologetic effort to legitimate them. Instead, I propose that we decenter Europe and the philosophical traditions it gave rise to as but one of manifold roads toward truths just as manifold. This means adjudicating the merits and demerits of 'Buddhist philosophy' not as per 'philosophy' (still tantamount to nothing other than 'Western philosophy') but as per 'Buddhist philosophy' itself.[82] It also means getting on with the work of reading and working with it, and leaving those narrow-minded enough to fore-condemn it on the basis of nothing other than ignorance and prejudice to till their narrow rows.

0.4. Contexts and Texts

As this book proceeds, readers will notice that I propose numerous coinages designed to convey the particular Buddhist and Buddhist-derived ideas I entertain. I explain these neologisms *ad locum*, but a word may be in order here to explain *why* I have felt the need to coin such terms in the first place, not least since at least some of them will doubtless be deemed unfortunately exemplary of that philologist's bastard child, "Buddhist Hybrid English" (Griffiths 1981).[83] After all, are the prodigious resources of English vocabulary, benefitting as it does from several centuries of intellectually sophisticated discourse in its own idiom and many more centuries before that of inherited discourse in Greek and Latin, not adequate to the task of conveying Buddhist concepts? Put simply, the answer to this is "No, they are not." Indeed, it is not so much that the English language *has* a problem in this task, for it has certainly been used to convey philosophical ideas of immense sophistication, but that the English language *is* a problem. For it is precisely the inheritance of English, the entire Greco-Latino-Christian philosophico-theological religio-cultural complex so deeply sedimented into the language itself that it is blindingly invisible to all us worms toiling within it, that renders it at times—at philosophically important times—infelicitous soil. What Heidegger identified as the onto-theological bases of a particular understanding of Being (that born in Greece, wedded to Christianity, and propagated throughout all the modern European languages) permeates not only the very vocabulary we use to discuss all manner of philosophical and religious topics, but the underlying structures informing that vocabulary and thereby governing the ideological frameworks within which such topics can even be mooted.[84]

Without going too further afield into what can, in this context, amount to no more than an inchoate foray into the methodological hazards of comparative work in the humanities, I want simply to make the point that at least some of the misinterpretations of Nāgārjuna's texts I identify in this book stem from the inadequacy of the very terminology the scholars I cite employ. To speak, in English, of 'philosophy', for example, is already to accept a host of presuppositions missing from more or less, but never exactly, equivalent Sanskrit terms such as *darśana*, *vāda*, or *siddhānta*.[85] Like problems only multiply when dealing with overtly conceptual terms *within* a philosophical system such as Nāgārjuna's. Comparative work must remain acutely aware of the specific linguistic, intellectual, cultural, historical, and myriad other contours and contexts of the texts (in the broadest possible sense) it studies.[86] This naturally includes the present book, which is 'comparative' at least to the extent that it reads materials from one culture—Nāgārjuna's—from the interpretive horizon of another—my own. Unfortunately, despite broad awareness of the fact that translation is always a "matter of intercultural hermeneutics" (Ruegg 1992: 374), the study of Buddhism has hitherto been and continues to be riddled with the application of familiar conceptual schemas onto the unfamiliar other. Now, this would not necessarily be problematic on a theoretical level, were it not for the empirical fact that the paradigms and presuppositions determining the fields of philosophy and religious studies—and more pointedly their practitioners—as subjects differ so significantly from those of their objects of study. For as I have argued earlier, it is a historical fact that in their differing ways and across their disparate trajectories philosophy and religious studies as practiced unto today have deliberately and explicitly distanced themselves from their near relative theology.[87] This distinction, like that between religion and philosophy themselves and countless other conceptual parsings, is simply not operative in the Buddhist sphere. I have thus perceived it to be necessary at many points throughout this book to attempt an English rendering of a given Nāgārjunian term that, whatever one may think of its eloquence or lack thereof, tries to convey as best it may *Nāgārjuna's* message, rather than the religious or philosophical understructures of inevitably Christianate English.[88]

As for the works within which that message is found, I have concentrated throughout this book on the accepted works of Nāgārjuna, and most specifically on his magnum opus, the *Mūlamadhyamaka-kārikā* or *Fundamental Verses on the Middle Way* (MK). This delimitation has two reasons behind it, methodological and practical. First, I am methodologically concerned to explicate the philosophical positions Nāgārjuna espoused as these are to be found in his own words. This means that I have adopted a model of interpretation most often associated with literary exegesis; that is, close reading of a primary source text (or cluster of texts) with the aim of elucidating its contents and elaborating its implications. One significant consequence of this approach is that I do not read Nāgārjuna's texts so much as responses to "the specific demands of the social and institutional contexts in which he wrote" (Walser 2005: 2) but as exemplars of "a broad metaphysical account of reality, a diagnosis of the fundamental human condition that rests on that account, and a soteriological and ethical framework resting on that diagnosis" (Garfield 2015: 14). In other words, I am primarily interested here in "Madhyamaka's Promise as Philosophy" (Tillemans 2016: 17), though as should be amply clear already (and as will be clarified further as we move along), I see this philosophy as inextricably religious—Buddhist. I emphatically do not see it as the least bit less philosophically promising on that account.

Second, I am practically limited in the amount of time and space that can reasonably be devoted to the elucidation of Nāgārjuna's texts through the study of their metatexts. For Nāgārjuna, as the founder of Madhyamaka and one of the most far-reachingly influential of all Buddhist philosophers, has not only spawned entire schools of successors but generated a monumental corpus of commentaries, analyses, critiques, translations, and further elaborations. Although I occasionally make reference to later Indian and Tibetan Mādhyamikas such as Āryadeva and Candrakīrti, Tsongkhapa and Gorampa, as also to Chinese Mādhyamikas and other Buddhists indebted to Nāgārjuna such as Sengzhao 僧肇 and Jizang 吉藏, Zhiyi 智顗 and Linji 臨濟, these mentions are passing, and meant more as pointers toward entire galaxies of thought than as solid groundings of my given point. My primary interlocutors are my peers (isn't this the case for all works?), which is why the preponderant bulk of non-Nāgārjunian citations in the pages that follow derive from the writings of fellow scholars of Buddhism, and principally among them those writing in English (and to a lesser extent in Chinese, occasionally Polish or French). While some readers may baulk at the length and number of these, as it were, side-references, I feel they are needful to demonstrate that the arguments I am making about Nāgārjuna and how we read him relate to much more than merely Nāgārjuna and how we read him: to his Buddhist heirs across the premodern cultures of Asia, and to his scholarly exegetes across the contemporary disciplines of the global humanities.

This relative inattention to the lines of interpretation taken by the tradition self-identifiedly heir to Nāgārjuna is a lack, and one for which I may well be taken to task. I fully accept that a work able to explicate Nāgārjuna's words in the light of the full subsequent history of Madhyamaka thought is highly desirable. However, as with many desires, it is the stuff of fantasy, for in the present case such a work remains utterly impracticable given the sheer scale of the sources. Moreover, given precisely this volume of materials, a work that by practical necessity selected some small set of classical scholarship for discussion could not only be justifiably accused of cherry-picking but would despite its best efforts include but an infinitesimal fraction of the available material, and therefore be partial in the sense of both partisan and part. Do not get me wrong: there is ample space, and need, for scholarship on the later generations of Mādhyamikas and their Buddhist as well as non-Buddhist interlocutors throughout the centuries (up to and including the present day) during which Nāgārjuna's words were (and are) read and reflected upon in India, China, Tibet, and all the other cultural worlds of classical and contemporary Buddhism, as well as for scholarship on their lives and works and thoughts and influences. Indeed, I look forward to the day, distant though it doubtless lies, in which our historical and philosophical knowledge of the Buddhist and Buddhate worlds of Asia at least approaches our knowledge of their Christian and Christianate analogues to the West.[89] But given the present state of learning, and given the need for limits in a finite project's scope, my own is a rather narrower, though I hope no less valuable, agenda; viz., to explicate and elaborate the philosophy of Nāgārjuna as expressed in his own texts. If this may then serve to weave one thread of the infinitely intricate carpet of Madhyamaka—and more broadly Buddhist—intellectual history, so much the better.

Before moving on, however, I feel that one vitally important yet all-too-often unremarked fact bears underlining in regard to this history. In the ancient Indian context formative *for* and partly formed *by* Nāgārjuna, the very nature and scope of philosophical reasoning—including the formal and informal criteria according to which argumentative validity and soundness are to be determined, as well as the relationships obtaining among philosophical principles such as logicality, rationality, and consistency, and also among philosophical domains such as metaphysics, epistemology, and ethics—differ in significant ways from our own.[90] On the basis that rationality itself "is not a given universal norm, but is embedded within its own *Lebensform* and *Lebenswelt*" (McGrath 2018: 22)—that, in other words, human cultures exhibit "multiple situated rationalities" (McGrath 2018: 1)[91]—this means that the canons of reasoning we find in Nāgārjuna's philosophy, and the philosophies circumambient to it, simply do not conform to those so many scholars insist on imposing upon them.[92] This entails that the *history of* philosophical reasoning too took routes divergent from those trialed and trailed by Indian philosophers' Western brethren. Quite apart from the professionalization of Madhyamaka in Indian universities such as Nālandā, Valabhī, Vikramaśīla, and so on (a process which occurred, be it noted in passing, centuries before the first European universities were even founded),[93] the mutating meanings of key terms, the changing authorities and concomitantly shifting roles of authority in the construction of arguments and maintenance of tenets,[94] the evolving styles of and rules for inter- and intra-mural debates, the far-reaching yet ever-mercurial political dynamics determining, in no small part, the historically varying roles of diverse individuals and associations within their wider social spheres, all played their parts—among multifarious other factors—in the creation, and continual re-creation, of

Indian, and Indian Buddhist, modes and models of thought. And this is to say nothing of how and to what extent those were then transmitted to and transformed in China, Tibet, and much of the rest of Asia. While the thrust of much of my argument concerns modern Western interpretations of ancient Indian materials, what I am getting at here is that the history of Indian (and Chinese, and Tibetan . . .) interpretations of these same materials, Buddhist and non-Buddhist, as well as the history of the models and methods deemed principial by these historically and culturally diverse "epistemic territories and communities" (McGrath 2018: 3) for the successful performance of such exegeses, independent of any Western analogues or influences, presents a canvas both vast and varied in itself, and contrastingly colored to that charted within the margins of this book. Again, although my occasional references in the pages that follow to the Candrakīrtis and the Bhāvavivekas of later Buddhist philosophical developments hopefully go some small way toward tracing this picture, I can only hope that future work can fill in the expanses I must leave bare.

But what about intellectual *pre*-history? At various junctures in the book, I point out significant parallels between the thought of Nāgārjuna and that of earlier Buddhist traditions, most especially that collected in the *Discourses* of the Buddha himself. Like the aforementioned nods to Nāgārjuna's intellectual heirs, these references to his fores have significance for the history of religions and for the history of philosophy within the Buddhist religion. This is all the more so since the Madhyamaka school Nāgārjuna founded is typically considered highly innovative, and thus to greater or lesser extents at odds with, or at least in tension with, the Buddha's originary teachings.[95] Yet, as the points of overlap and influence I note attest, Nāgārjuna is as much one of those who "re-light the lamp of the True Dharma" (Young 2015: 114) as he is a "radical innovator" (Lindtner 1997: xxii). That is certainly how the diverse Buddhist traditions themselves see him. And though I merely advert to it in passing, it is surely no small matter to note, and to note with regard to a figure of such enduring importance within and without the Buddhist fold, that much of the most ostensibly radical of Nāgārjuna's teachings is to be found, *in nucleo* at least, in the Buddha's own.

Now, analogously to many other religious, philosophical, and intellectual traditions, the Buddhist tradition at large values fidelity to its foundational tenets far more than deviation from them. Ideological permutations, howsoever novel, are therefore invariably framed as perpetuations of prior truths at most, and at best, consummated within them. As such, it is only natural to find that Nāgārjuna is at pains throughout his works to portray his own ideas as not his own, as it were, but as reformulations of the Buddha's. This is evident in his multiple references to the Buddha's core teachings, and his explicit efforts to demonstrate the complete compatibility of what he articulates and 'what the Buddha taught'. That the then incipient Mahāyāna movement within which Nāgārjuna—as one of the "paragons of Indian Buddhist authority" (Young 2015: 115)—was to play such a historically prominent part and which was to become in the centuries succeeding him the dominant form of Buddhism throughout all but the South-Eastern portion of Asia was deeply committed to the task of proving itself an upholder of the Buddha's teachings—indeed, *the* upholder thereof—is well known. This feature is evinced perhaps most eloquently by Mahāyāna's procedure of naming what historians recognize to be its own new compositions '*sūtras*'. For in doing so the movement effectively claimed that its own works and words were discourses of the Buddha himself, hidden to a world not ready for them at the time, and not only rediscovered by but preeminently embodied in the Mahāyāna.[96]

The figure of 'Nāgārjuna' was itself to become a trope in this centuries-long concern to prove the Mahāyāna *bona fides*. Hagiographies portray him as nothing less than "the first propounder of Mahāyāna Buddhism itself" (Ray 1997: 129), a figure of mythic proportions, possessed of centuries-long life (Ray 1997) and author of over a hundred works (Westerhoff 2018a: 97). In such accounts,

> Nāgārjuna was depicted as a textual scholar and exegetical author, a master of debate and converter of kings. He revived the Dharma when it was dying and perpetuated it through master-disciple transmission. He also was a solitary wanderer admitted to the famed undersea dragon palace, and he was a master of "spiritual penetrations" who learned the art of invisibility through alchemy, observed the workings of heavenly beings, and conjured magical creatures through the use of Buddhist spells. (Young 2015: 153)[97]

Whatever we may make of such claims, the historical force of the perception (or conception) of Nāgārjuna as a Buddhist 'patriarch', an exemplary lineage-holder in a genealogy of 'sainthood' or arhatship stretching back to the Buddha himself, I see buttressed by the very real correspondences I note between relevant ideas within the authoritative works of Nāgārjuna and those ascribed to Śākyamuni Buddha himself.

Naturally, situating Nāgārjuna's works within its intellectual context (to the extent that we are able to do so) enables us to make sense of what I will go on (in §5.3) to describe as the apophatic (non-)position—the abandonment of all views—he espoused. In necessarily simplified terms, I take this historical intellectual context to be one in which the Abhidharmic mission to systematize the varied teachings of the Buddha and categorically classify the sum total of purportedly real entities had been thrown into turmoil by the twin Prajñāpāramitā claims to give voice to the Buddha himself and to deny any privileged status to any voice, be it even the Buddha's own, in the realization of the emptiness of all phenomena (including, of course, just such claims voiced in the Prajñāpāramitā corpus itself). Indeed, I take Nāgārjuna as being able to make the (revolutionary as/or conservative) step of systematically undermining all systematizations only on the basis of the Abhidharmic edifice and the Prajñāpāramitā critique thereof he inherited. In this context (though assuredly not in our own quite differently logically girded one), Nāgārjuna's repudiation of all views makes perfect sense . . . even if that sense is most assuredly not *logical*. At the very least, this book explores some of the ways in which it makes sense from Nāgārjuna's religiosophical perspective. While I consider the pursuit of Nāgārjuna's ideas to be a worthwhile endeavor (on pain of having simply wasted the all years I've spent writing this book!), it does mean that readers interested in more socio-historically inclined disciplinary orientations may be disappointed to find, for example, that among much else I do not "discuss any political repercussions of Mahāyāna [Nāgārjunian or otherwise] nor mention the specific, pragmatic interest that emperors, magistrates and gentry might have had in it" (Walser 2018: 12).[98] One book can only do so much, and so I hope to be forgiven for delimiting my disciplinary focus to a specific set of issues and approaches, while welcoming others as valuable, if differently accented, conversation partners.

These last comments notwithstanding, there is a further well-attested disciplinary problematic—that between 'Buddhology' and 'Buddhist studies'—which this book straddles and seeks to bridge. Buddhology as traditionally understood foregrounds linguistic training in relevant classical sources. It is, of course, justified in doing so to the extent that *any* engagement with primary written texts—be it oriented toward philological, philosophical, or any other disciplinary ends—requires thorough acquaintance with the language(s) of their composition and/or transmission. Buddhist studies, meanwhile, is usually characterized by a 'religious studies' approach. Though it may take multifarious forms, Buddhist studies (like religious studies) is united overall by a broadening of focal attention from narrowly philological to social and/or conceptual concerns. In summary then, the study of Buddhism as a whole has historically been marked (and continues to be marked) by something of a bifurcation of scholars into those engaged in text-historical research (Buddhology) and those more interested in conceptualizing the historical, philosophical, literary, and related manifestations of the Buddhist religion (Buddhist studies).

Naturally, this distinction is somewhat ill-defined given the overlap among both the materials under study and the aims and methods adopted toward those materials in these approaches, which therefore emerge as differing emphases rather than distinct disciplines. It has also sometimes shown itself to be downright counterproductive to scholarly collaboration and the production of knowledge insofar as it has led to the propagation and perpetuation of stereotypes such as those memorably parodied by José Ignacio Cabezón. According to these,

> North Americans are poor philologists; when they rely on primary textual material at all, they do so in an uninformed, extravagant and frivolous way as a means of substantiating overly broad hypotheses that are, in any case, of dubious scientific interest . . . [Contrariwise,] German and earlier French scholarship is so obsessed with the minutiae of textual criticism that it is incapable of achieving any kind of broad overview of the meaning of individual texts, much less an understanding of Buddhist doctrine / praxis in broad terms. (Cabezón 1995: 243–244)

Such silliness aside, one positive feature of the field partly attributable to the existence of such competing methodological approaches among scholars (all-too-often mutually antagonistic in real life as well as in stereotyped parodies!) is that the study of Buddhism has been and continues to be distinguished by sustained and sophisticated attention to the theories and methods undergirding it.[99] The relevant point for present purposes is that, given these dynamics besetting the field, I have tried to work across this disciplinary divide. This is not to say that the specifically philological corrections or suggestions I make in this book are anything more than passing or punctual. On the contrary, as should be apparent both from the list of textual sources I provide and from the overall conceptual thrust of the book, my project here would far more readily be classed within Buddhist studies than within Buddhology by any doxographer of sufficiently sectarian a cast as to undertake it. But over and above the adventitious fact that I have studied, researched, and taught Buddhisty matters in North America, Europe, and Asia (and am therefore professionally certified to be both 'extravagant and frivolous' with my interpretations and 'obsessed with the minutiae of textual criticism'), I trust that it should be clear to anyone reading this book that throughout it I meld philological and philosophical methods by attempting to deliver what I hope are forceful conceptual insights based on rigorous linguistic analyses.

Turning to the works of Nāgārjuna himself, though the man himself may well be dead, both literally and *à la* Barthes, his texts remain very much alive, and the laconic and complex nature of the textual evidence he has left at our disposal allows a multitude of varying, and even competing, interpretations. I hope it is clear that the interpretations I propose in this book should in no way be taken as final or exclusive. Apart from betokening a level of intellectual hubris on my own part surely itself an incontrovertible sign of feeble-mindedness, this would rob Nāgārjuna of a philosophical richness surely itself an indubitable sign of greatness. Of course, there are portions of the book in which I propose certain interpretations of Nāgārjuna's thought as I read them expressed in his extant writings; interpretations that I support in critical contradistinction to certain others I argue are less justifiably ascribable as being Nāgārjuna's positions. As I mention *ad locum*, however, this is not to conclude that such rival interpretations are lacking in philosophical value; on the contrary, many readers may well derive more plentiful ideas from them, especially as more often than not they reside more squarely than my own in the domain of contemporary analytic philosophy; a domain in which many readers will feel right at home. Likewise, there are portions of the book in which I consciously go beyond Nāgārjuna's own textual formulations to propose positions I take to be derived from and consonant with them, but nevertheless not immediately recognizable as strictly speaking Nāgārjuna's. This is because I see the scholarly tasks of both 'textual hermeneutics' and 'philosophical construction' as merited, but distinct (see §1.3). As distinct enterprises, we need to ensure we are clear which we are engaged in, especially as the slippage between them not infrequently leads to confusion and misattribution. Given all this, I hope it is clear that not everything I say in the pages that follow is to be found in Nāgārjuna's primary sources, but where I develop what I see to be Nāgārjuna's ideas along avenues he did not explicitly take, I hope to demonstrate that those destinations are at least implied by the directions he mapped out.

But just what are Nāgārjuna's primary sources? As adverted to earlier, my discussion throughout this book centers upon Nāgārjuna's major work, the *Mūlamadhyamaka-kārikā*. I refer to this text as MK, or as MK:X:Y, where the X:Y stands for the particular chapter and verse cited. The Sanskrit text is sourced from Siderits and Katsura (2013), which itself follows the edition by de La Vallée Poussin (1970 [1913]) as modified by Ye (2011), though I have also referred to the classic Chinese translation by Kumārajīva 鳩摩羅什 (344–413)—that is, 中論: T 1564—and the commentary therein ascribed to a certain 'Blue Eyes' or Qingmu 青目 (fourth century).[100] Along the same model, like formulations are used for references to Nāgārjuna's other texts: the *Vigrahavyāvartanī* (VV), *Yuktiṣaṣṭikā-kārikā* (YṢ), *Śūnyatāsaptati* (ŚS), *Vaidalyaprakaraṇa* (VP), *Ratnāvalī* (RĀ), and *Suhṛllekha* (SL).

The *Vigrahavyāvartanī* is extant in the original Sanskrit as well as Tibetan and Chinese translations. I have primarily relied on the Sanskrit edition by Johnston and Kunst reprinted in Bhattacharya (1978) and Bhattacharya (1986) and the transliterated Sanskrit version prepared by Yonezawa (2008), though I have also referred to the transliterated verses in Lindtner (1997) and classical Chinese translation (迴諍論: T 1631) by Gautama Prajñāruci 瞿曇般若流支 (active c. 538–543) in *Taishō* 32:1631, 13b–23a. Westerhoff (2010: 4–9) provides a history of the text and its translations, as well as (to my mind) convincing rebuttals of Tola and Dragonetti's (1998) arguments against the attribution of the VV to Nāgārjuna.

The original Sanskrit text of the *Yuktiṣaṣṭikā-kārikā* is largely lost, though Lindtner (1982: 102–119/1997: 174–175) provides the twelve Sanskrit verses he has identified from various sources, and Li and Ye (2014) have more recently recovered 37 Sanskrit verses (including five half-verses) "on the basis of quotations found in newly identified manuscripts from Tibet" (Li and Ye 2014: 154; cf. 17–18). As such, I have provided the verses where these are found in Li and Ye 2014, though I have omitted those which are mere reconstructions (for which, see Uryūzu 1985; Kumar 1993). Otherwise, I have relied on the English translations from Tibetan of Lindtner (1982: 102–119/1997: 72–93), the modern Chinese translation of Li and Ye (2014: 1–123), and referred also to Loizzo (2007), Tola and Dragonetti (1995a), and the French version of Scherrer-Schaub (1991). Loizzo and Scherrer-Schaub include critical editions and translations of Candrakīrti's commentary from extant Tibetan sources. Although a Chinese translation attributed to Dānapāla 施護 (d. c. 1000) exists (六十頌如理論， *Taishō* 30:1575, 254b–256a—Loizzo (2007: 26 fn. 8) mistakenly places the text's end at 265a), reliance on translations from the Tibetan has been necessitated by Lindtner's observation to the effect that "the Chinese version is usually too inaccurate to be of any philological value. . . . Few are the verses which say what Nāgārjuna actually had in mind!" (Lindtner 1982: 100 fn. 138). The truth of this statement is unfortunately borne out by comparison of the English and French translations from the Tibetan with the Chinese text, as these indeed often appear quite disparate.

No Sanskrit original of the *Śūnyatāsaptati* has been preserved; nor is there a classical Chinese translation of it. As such, I have relied on the translations from Tibetan found in Lindtner (1982: 34–69/1997: 94–119), Tola and Dragonetti (1995a: 72–81), Pandeya and Manju (1991: 140–148), and Komito (1987: 79–95). I am indebted to Anne MacDonald for referring me to the German-language scholarship on and translation of the ŚS by Erb (1990 and 1997).

Likewise, the original Sanskrit of the *Vaidalyaprakaraṇa* has been lost, and the text is only available in Tibetan. Fortunately, we now have the eloquent translation replete with philosophical commentary of Westerhoff (2018b), on which I have relied in due deference to doubts as to the authenticity of the text voiced by Tola and Dragonetti (1995b) and Pind (2001) and discussed in Westerhoff (2018b: 7–10, 233–234).

"The *Ratnāvalī* is only partially extant in Sanskrit" (Lindtner 1997: 292). The best one-stop textual shop for this work remains Hahn (1982a), as this includes the extant portions of the original Sanskrit as well as the canonical Tibetan translation and the Taishō edition of the Chinese version of the text translated by Paramārtha 真諦 (499–569); that is, the 寶行王正論 (T 1656). Hahn's Introduction includes discussions of the source texts, previous editions, and translations of these (Hahn 1982a: 1–34). Where the Sanskrit original is absent, I have relied on the translations in Dunne and McClintock (1997), Hopkins (1998), and Jampa Tegchok (2017), in consultation with the Chinese. The arguments for attributing the text to Nāgārjuna are usefully reviewed in Walser (2005: 271ff).

The original Sanskrit of the *Suhṛllekha* is lost, but there are three classical Chinese translations: the 龍樹菩薩為禪陀迦王說法要偈 (T 1672) by *Guṇavarman 求那跋摩 (367–431); the 勸發諸王要偈 (T 1673) by *Saṃghavarman 僧伽跋摩 (fl. c. fifth century); and the 龍樹菩薩勸誡王頌 (T 1674) by Yijing 義淨 (635–713) as well as one Tibetan version. Where I have dealt with this text in the book, I have relied on the classical Chinese versions and the modern translations in Della Santina (2002) and

Padmakara Translation Group (2013). It is perhaps worth noting that doubts have been cast on the traditional attribution of the *Suhṛllekha* to Nāgārjuna. Dietz, for example, concludes that "no clearly convincing evidence . . . can be found" in the text for the attribution on the basis that the *Suhṛllekha* "has few stylistic and philosophical characteristics in common with those of the indisputably authentic works of the philosopher of Madhyamaka" (Dietz 1983: 71, 60). I find this argumentation faulty, for along like lines we would be forced to conclude that the *Convivio* and the *Commedia* could not both be by Dante. Authors, after all, may over the course of a lifetime compose works differing significantly in style and content, so since there is nothing in the *Suhṛllekha* that contradicts Nāgārjuna's other works, I see no problem in accepting the work to be his.

Finally, it is to be noted that, as I am myself unfamiliar with Tibetan, I have refrained from including the Tibetan text in citations from the ŚS and VP and of the relevant portions of the YṢ and RĀ as I would consider this somewhat disingenuous as scholarly practice. Sources of other classical Buddhist texts mentioned are provided *ad locum*.

1

Orienting Reason

A Religious Critique of Philosophizing Nāgārjuna

1.1. The Unimaginative Question

> If I return to the unimaginative question "Is Buddhism a philosophy or a religion?" it is not in order to plunge through a door that is already ajar, but to underline the implications of such a question that are usually ignored.
>
> —Bernard Faure, *Double Exposure*, xii

Nāgārjuna is generally accepted by Buddhists and Buddhologists alike as one of the most important of all Buddhist thinkers. Indeed, his thought has been central to the historical shaping and reshaping of Buddhism throughout South, Central, and East Asia. It continues to fascinate, moreover, as evinced by the plethora of recently published inspirational and intellectual works devoted to him by adherents and academics. Recent scholarly interest in Nāgārjuna has been intense, with especial focus on the vexed question of the rationality, or irrationality, of his thought. For understandable reasons, debates in this regard have gravitated toward two points of friction between the arguments Nāgārjuna laid out in India almost two millennia ago and those considered acceptable by his philosophically minded interpreters today, trained as these latter have typically been in twentieth-century Western analytical philosophy. Briefly stated, the issues at question relate, first, to Nāgārjuna's use of the *catuṣkoṭi* or tetralemma,[1] according to which a proposition may be true, false, both true and false, or neither true nor false; and second, to Nāgārjuna's espousal of the "abandonment of all views" (*sarvadṛṣṭiprahāṇāya*). I will be treating these two topics extensively in later chapters. Here, however, I am concerned to bring to light the theoretical underpinnings of the hermeneutical project predominant among present-day scholars, which is to actively overlook or downright depreciate the religious motivation of Nāgārjuna's arguments. While this project has typically

Buddhism Between Religion and Philosophy. Rafal K. Stepien, Oxford University Press. © Oxford University Press 2024.
DOI: 10.1093/oso/9780197771303.003.0001

been pursued in an apologetic effort to justify Nāgārjuna as truly worthy of the title 'philosopher' to mainstream (Western) philosophers, it has also had the effect among some scholars of dismissing him as insufficiently philosophical. Regardless of the glowing or dim light in which he is thereby cast, however, Nāgārjuna is appraised according to exclusively philosophical criteria such as cogency, consistency, and coherency. My "religious critique of philosophizing Nāgārjuna," then, is aimed at elucidating and problematizing this approach, however philosophically fruitful it may be, as at best tangential to and at worst seriously distortive of Nāgārjuna's thought as a whole.[2]

1.2. Unveiling the East

In the case of numerous exegetes, there is little or no attempt made to understand Nāgārjuna within the framework of his own religio-philosophical enterprise. This is so on the implied or explicitly stated assumption that any position questioning or contradicting the canons of Western philosophical logic is irredeemable from irrationality and consequently not even worth serious consideration.[3] Thus it is that we find authors otherwise widely divergent in their interpretations of Nāgārjuna agreeing to indict Nāgārjuna's use or understanding of logic—without once questioning their own logical paradigms. Guy Bugault is especially frank in this respect. In his article, "Logic and Dialectics in the *Madhyamakakārikās*," Bugault proceeds "to outline the prolegomena to any reading of the *MK* by a Western trained in the school of Aristotle, *or, more generally, common sense*" (Bugault 1983: 8, emphasis added here and throughout subsequent citations), and refers repeatedly to "*our* instinctive logic" (Bugault 1983: 29) in his affirmations of the validity of applying "methods of contemporary [that is, contemporary Western] learning to *unveil* old Indian texts" (Bugault 1983: 53). That these latter, suggestively feminine and passive, are evidently in need of such active masculine methods to be "unveiled" is, of course, taken for granted. As such, the bulk of the article is in fact devoted to studying "*if* and *how* the principles to which we are accustomed function" (Bugault 1983: 19, emphases original) in the MK—note the "we"—with sections on the principles of contradiction, excluded middle, sufficient reason, and identity and haecceity (respectively, 19–26, 26–41, 41–46, and 46–61). These make reference to canonical Western philosophers from Heraclitus, Cratylus, Anaxagoras, Protagoras, Democritus, Empedocles, Parmenides, Diogenes, and Plato, to Descartes,

Spinoza, Leibniz, Kant, Hegel, Schopenhauer, Heidegger, and Russell, in addition to the ubiquitous Aristotle—though only Dignāga and Candrakīrti get any mention, albeit scarce, among Indian (or Tibetan, Chinese, Japanese . . .) Buddhist philosophers.

Having shown that "Nāgārjuna's way of thinking is diametrically opposed to *our* habitual way, *our own* being one which obliges us to choose at least, and at most, one of two contradictory assertions" (Bugault 1983: 33–34), and furthermore that "for a Buddhist, in particular a Mādhyamika, the principle of reason—or in this case, *pratītya-samutpāda*—is directly opposed to the principle of identity" (Bugault 1983: 46) (the which principle, being Aristotelian in origin, he is unable to question), Bugault tries to adopt "a fall-back position to *save common sense*" (Bugault 1983: 53). In so doing, he ends up claiming that Nāgārjuna's "Buddhism is a type (a rather special one) of positivism" (Bugault 1983: 57) and that Nāgārjuna's "doctrine, if it can be said to be one, is therefore completely practical" (Bugault 1983: 65). In arguing for this conclusion, Bugault declares that Nāgārjuna's "fundamental intention" is "not religious"—it cannot be, "for there is no God" (Bugault 1983: 58) in it. In other words, only theism counts as religion.

Quite apart from the deeply confused interpretation Bugault proffers, such unreconstructed orientalist foisting of Western logical categories and intellectual presuppositions onto Eastern thought is shocking in a late twentieth-century scholar.[4] Bugault, however, is far from being alone in appraising Nāgārjuna's thought according to criteria never themselves queried; criteria whose historical origins in a specifically Greek context render them (for Nāgārjuna certainly) as dependently co-originated, as conventional, and therefore as dubitable, as any other worldly phenomena, but which are unhesitatingly identified by the exegetes in question here as simply "the laws of thought" (Gunaratne 1986: 214). It is within the unquestioned limits of these "laws" that the scholars I critique here expound their critiques of Nāgārjuna: they attempt to fit Nāgārjuna into their own imported parameters and criticize him for his perceived inability to fully embody them.

Thus, among all too many examples, I cite one of the founders of the field, Richard Robinson, for whom "it is possible to transcribe the *Kārikās* entirely, chapter by chapter, into logical notation," but who nevertheless adjudicates that Nāgārjuna "makes mistakes in logic" (Robinson 1957: 307). K. N. Jayatilleke, meanwhile, writes, "there is little evidence that Nāgārjuna understood the logic of the four alternatives as formulated and utilized in early Buddhism" (Jayatilleke 1967: 82). Claus Oetke goes further, claiming to demonstrate "the fallacious character" of Nāgārjuna's argument regarding production and destruction at MK:21:1–6, and pondering, "perhaps Nāgārjuna and his contemporaries might because of historical reasons not yet have been able to give a correct diagnosis of the mechanisms involved in such a fallacy" (Oetke 1990: 94). Presumably, the "historical reasons" for the supposed lack of logical acumen among Indian philosophers such as Nāgārjuna and his contemporaries, their "pre-logical" primitivity, basically amounts to their being unschooled in what Oetke does not hesitate to call "common sense" (Oetke 1990: 91).[5]

This certainly appears to be how Richard Hayes sees the matter. His attempt "to ascertain Nāgārjuna's command of logical principles" (Hayes 1994: 323) concludes that "since Nāgārjuna employed faulty reasoning, he was able to arrive at conclusions that seem contrary to both reason and common sense experience" (Hayes 1994: 324).[6] Perhaps most tellingly, Hayes admits historicity to logic—as when he declares "the tetralemma was a fairly primitive framework" (Hayes 1994: 322)—but he nevertheless sees no problem in assessing "Nāgārjuna's logic . . . *by modern canons of validity*" (Hayes 1994: 323, emphases added).[7] It is as if his own modern canons of reasoning were somehow ahistorically unimpeachable. Indeed, this impression is driven home by Hayes's stunning assertion that the works of logically oriented scholars he approves such as "Schayer, Robinson, Bhattacharya, Ruegg and Williams . . . bear few characteristics that would identify them as works of the twentieth century" (Hayes 1994: 362). Apparently, the work of modern logicians such as these is timeless, their logic eternally valid. Incredibly, this is so despite the fact that in the very same article Hayes adduces a distinction between "exegesis" and "hermeneutics" more or less equivalent to that I will go on to propose between "textual hermeneutics" and "philosophical construction";[8] that he cautions "scholars [to be] clear in their own minds about which of these approaches they are taking" (Hayes 1994: 362); and that he characterizes his own approach as "a close look at Nāgārjuna's work *in the context in which it was written*" (Hayes 1994: 363, emphases added). One could wonder long and hard at how Hayes could possibly claim to be explicating Nāgārjuna's writings in *their own* terms given the manifestly anachronistic matrix of rationality he applies to them. The only explanation is that his own logic remains unseen: it is the eye of reason itself.[9]

Like criticisms apply to other exemplars of the tendency I am describing. Speaking generally of Nāgārjuna's philosophy as a whole, David Burton, for example, declares: "It is my contention—to which surely anyone who tries to read Nāgārjuna's texts will assent—that, far from being 'perfect', Nāgārjuna's thought, as expressed in his texts, is inchoate and obscure" (Burton 1999: 7). Burton soon specifies that what he calls "Nāgārjuna's blatantly fallacious reasoning" is such on the basis of the "obvious nihilistic consequences" (Burton 1999: 10) of his ideas, and most particularly of the "obscure" (Burton 1999: 53) doctrine of two truths. This doctrine, a key feature of Nāgārjuna's system, similarly defeats Mervyn Sprung, who ultimately gives up trying to understand it, stating, "in the end, it is not possible, I believe, to make the relation of *saṁvṛti* and *paramārtha* intelligible in any theoretical terms available to us" (Sprung 1973: 50).[10] Last, Frits Staal seems initially to be defending Nāgārjuna when he contends, "if Nāgārjuna got caught in paradoxes and contradictions, he is not worse off than most philosophers. What would make him an irrationalist is the desire to be illogical" (Staal 1975: 45). This, however, is something no right-minded philosopher would do, on the basis that "any violation of the principle of non-contradiction is irrational" (Staal 1976: 125).

Bugault and the other scholars I have cited all adhere to a form of epistemological foundationalism founded upon a combination of doxastic and epistemic basicality.[11] That is, they believe that their belief in the logical laws they take to be universally criterial to rationality is not itself dependent on other doxastic or epistemic principles. This is not necessarily problematic in itself as a philosophical position, but it is hardly appropriate when applied to the task of understanding a philosopher whose principles of reasoning differ from those of the exegete, let alone one whose entire *oeuvre* is devoted to demonstrating the absurdity of any and all forms of foundationalism. This goes as much for those scholars who are critical of Nāgārjuna's purported misuse or misunderstanding of such laws as it does for those eager to prove his correct use and understanding of them and thereby to habilitate him in the eyes of peers not *a priori* amenable to considering non-Western systems of thought as philosophy proper.

The apologist tradition *vis-à-vis* Nāgārjuna and the Madhyamaka school he founded goes back at least as far as David Seyfort Ruegg, who is adamant in maintaining "Madhyamaka reasoning (*yukti*) is based on the twin pillars of the principles of non-contradiction and excluded middle" (Ruegg 1977: 54, where he is summarizing Ruegg 1969), these being requisites for rationality, as we have seen.[12] Ruegg states this position even more forcefully when countering the claims of those who would see Nāgārjuna and his subsequent Mādhyamikas as irrational or mystical: "Although it has been alleged that Buddhist philosophers—and, indeed, other Indian thinkers as well—ignore or reject the principles of non-contradiction and excluded middle, this contention certainly cannot be sustained as concerns Nāgārjuna and his school, whose entire reasoning is in fact founded on them" (Ruegg 1977: 5). For his part, Tom Tillemans admits that "within Buddhist thought, the structure of argumentation that seems the most resistant to our attempts at formalization is undoubtedly the tetralemma or *catuṣkoṭi*," but concludes that "the structures of argumentation most frequently employed by Buddhists—including the Madhyamakas—do not present any violation of our classical logical laws" (Tillemans 1999: 189, 193).[13] Still more recently, Richard H. Jones has argued that Nāgārjuna's merely "apparent inconsistency . . . apparent paradoxicality" can in fact be "easily defused" and "restated without paradox" so as to demonstrate that Nāgārjuna was "entirely consistent and logical": his "arguments presume the basic laws of logic and are free of genuine paradoxes" (Jones 2018: 50, 51, 66, 42, 65). These and other like-minded scholars are clear that theirs is a self-conscious attempt to prove, in the words of Jay Garfield and Graham Priest, that "Nāgārjuna is not an irrationalist. He is committed to the canons of rational argument and criticism. He is not a mystic" (Garfield and Priest 2002: 96).

The latest book-length study of Nāgārjuna's philosophy, Jan Westerhoff's *Nāgārjuna's Madhyamaka: A Philosophical Introduction* (2009), is a further case in point. In similar fashion to Robinson, Katsura, and all the other scholars who try to explain away the "riddle" of the tetralemma through various logical stratagems,[14] Westerhoff at first admits that "it seems hard to make sense of it [MK:18:10], at least if we want to stay within the domain of classical logic" (Westerhoff 2009: 71)—which he evidently does.[15] Indeed, by "applying the familiar laws of logic" (Westerhoff 2009: 71),[16] Westerhoff is ineluctably led to conclude that the verse in question "is a contradiction" (Westerhoff 2006: 371/2009: 71). Characteristically, he immediately responds by asking, "How can this interpretation be avoided?" (Westerhoff 2006: 371 / 2009: 71)—without, of course, explaining *why* it should be avoided at all.[17]

This unquestioning attitude toward "classical logic" is typical of Westerhoff's work as a whole. In the course of presenting what he is content to describe as a "logically very conservative" (Westerhoff 2009: 90) interpretation of Nāgārjuna's *catuṣkoṭi*, Westerhoff expends his greatest efforts in tackling, as expected, the "important problem" (Westerhoff 2009: 80) of the stubbornly contradictory third lemma ("both P and not-P") to demonstrate that it is in fact logically explicable. The tenor of Westerhoff's approach may be summed up in his initial question as to this third lemma: "Why, we might well ask, does Nāgārjuna think we have to consider this contradictory option as well, *as if it constituted a real possibility*?" (Westerhoff 2009: 80–81, emphasis added here and throughout subsequent citations). For just as Raimundo Panikkar, for example, states that "internal contradiction is of its very nature nonsignifying" (Panikkar 1989: 63), so Westerhoff declares that a "contradictory alternative should . . . not constitute a genuine possibility" (Westerhoff 2009: 81 n. 55).[18] This is so despite the fact that Nāgārjuna obviously thought it did. Predictably enough, Westerhoff goes on to propose a version of the overtly contradictory third lemma that obviates its contradictoriness and neatly maintains logical cogency.[19]

Further to the particular arguments used with respect to one or other instance of the tetralemma, Westerhoff characterizes his project as a whole in this discussion as having "the specific objective of giving an interpretation of Nāgārjuna's employment of the tetralemma which makes both logical sense and *is in accordance with his general philosophical position*" (Westerhoff 2006: 368).[20] I have criticized his stance, and done so in such provocative terms, largely because Westerhoff and the other scholars I have cited implicitly or explicitly *do* claim to be providing an "accurate" or "honest" account of Nāgārjuna's philosophical enterprise—without for all that paying any heed to the overarchingly soterial aim of Nāgārjuna's endeavor. Indeed, given this last phrase about accordance with *Nāgārjuna's* philosophy (and let us not forget that Westerhoff's book is titularly concerned with *Nāgārjuna's* Madhyamaka), I find it remarkable that Westerhoff should then characterize his overall project as explaining "the methodological foundations of Nāgārjuna's arguments in the *catuṣkoṭi . . . entirely within the framework of classical logic*" (Westerhoff 2006: 393/2009: 90). In fact, such attempts to simultaneously do justice to Indian and Western philosophical traditions are commonplace in the literature. Thus, for example, the Cowherds—"an international collective of scholars in Buddhist Studies" (Cowherds 2016a: back cover)—"set themselves the task of working out [the ethical consequences of Madhyamaka metaphysics] in a way that does justice to the Madhyamaka tradition in the contemporary philosophical context" (Cowherds 2016a: 1). And the editors of *The Moon Points Back* (Tanaka et al. 2015) identify with its predecessor volume *Pointing at the Moon* (D'Amato et al. 2009) as being located "at the interface of contemporary logic and analytic philosophy and Buddhist philosophy . . . deploying a common analytic methodology" (Tanaka et al. 2015: xi).

Rather than citing further instances (which could easily be undertaken *in extenso*), I would like to end this section by pointing out that the common thread linking all the scholars I have mentioned is their unquestioning adherence to "*our* instinctive logic" (Bugault 1983: 29, emphasis added); this "classical logical reasoning" (Jones 2018: 65) imbued with all the onto-theo-logical presuppositions endemic to Western thought. By attempting to provide a "logically very conservative" (Westerhoff 2006: 392/2009: 90) and cogent account of the *catuṣkoṭi*, and of Nāgārjuna's thought as a whole, Westerhoff and his peers not only misrepresent Nāgārjuna but unwittingly do a cardinal disservice to the very reason for his repeated use of the *catuṣkoṭi*, for his espousal of "the abandonment of all views," and indeed for his entire philosophical edifice; that is, to enable the practitioner to pass beyond the oppositional confines of logical thought as classically defined.[21] In short, these scholars have succeeded only in fortifying the fixtures of the mind Nāgārjuna took such pains to undermine.

Indeed, I am tempted to ask: Is their unquestioning belief in reason not itself a species of mysticism? Or of theology? For mystics, theologians, and philosophers of many stripes have over the course of many centuries alleged that their proofs are vouchsafed by ultimate recourse to some self-proving power. Historically, the power in question endowed most augustly with superlatives has, of course, been "God." But if we attend specifically to the ascribed right of self-authentication, then there is little relevant difference between Him and any other such supposed Authority, including most pertinently Reason. Reason and its sharpest-bluntest instrument logic prove to be the refuge of not only avowed Rationalists such as Leibniz and Descartes, but of later commentators-cum-critics such as Kant and Frege (not to mention their heirs today). For these, despite their differences, "logic . . . provides constitutive norms for thought *as such*, regardless of its subject matter" (MacFarlane 2002: 35, emphasis original).[22] While Garfield may characterize attempts to render Nāgārjuna's philosophy logically consistent as "boring" (Smith College 2010), it should be clear by now that I see many contemporary exegetes as prey to just such a tendency.[23] Apart from any other misgivings, I am left tempted to ask why, if the aim really is to make Nāgārjuna philosophically interesting, there is so evidently felt a need to go to such great lengths to prove that he embraces logical laws when so many other philosophers so unproblematically do so, and when Nāgārjuna so lucidly exposes their limits. Surely, in addition to being unwarranted, it is also uncharitable to dismiss so central, so seminal, and so endlessly fascinating a feature of Nāgārjuna's thought as its paralogicality?[24]

1.3. Orientalizing Reasons

At the very outset of this section (a little playfully, a little provocatively) titled "Orientalizing Reasons," I would like to make it as clear as I can that I am *not* accusing the scholars I cite at work today of unfamiliarity with or approval of that particular brand of intellectual obtuseness known as orientalism. On the contrary, they are often explicit in railing against what they do not hesitate to call the "postcolonial racism" (Garfield 2002: 253) endemic to the exclusion of non-Western philosophy from the rubric "philosophy." When they are not actively arguing that "the entire conduct of philosophy as a discipline . . . celebrating European intellectual hegemony and excluding the 'natives'" is "intellectually and morally indefensible" (Garfield 2015: ix-x, ix), this is because "critique of the narrowness, arbitrariness, and ethnocentrism of this characterization is too easy and too boring to undertake" (D'Amato et al. 2009: xvii). And, of course, the entire project of philosophizing with Buddhist as well as Western sources is partially directed toward demonstrating that "it is appropriate to call them both 'philosophy'" (Siderits 2007: 5).

I would also like to express my deep affinity for "rational reconstruction" as opposed or in addition to "textual history" (Garfield and Priest 2002: 88),[25] for "doing Buddhist philosophy" as opposed or in addition to "developing an account of the history of Buddhist philosophy" (Garfield 2015: 320). Before going on, however, I believe it may be useful to remove some of the slippage between the two approaches characterized by Garfield and Priest as "rational reconstruction" and "textual history." This can be accomplished, first, by reducing the term "reconstruction" (with its implications of textual fidelity, and hence of hermeneutics) to "construction," since the point of this approach, as opposed to the historico-hermeneutical one, is precisely to build new ideas with the old textual material. Given the controversial nature of the role of rationality in Nāgārjuna's, and more broadly Buddhist, philosophy, moreover, I think it also prudent to expunge the "rational," since this unnecessarily and unfairly forecloses the constructions open to us, and replace it with the broader term "philosophical." This gives us "philosophical construction." As for the alternative approach, I will prefer "textual hermeneutics" to "textual history," and this for two reasons. One, I see the prime impetus for this methodology to lie in the properly hermeneutical endeavor of textual interpretation, which may be based on and/or be the basis of historical information, but which nonetheless stands (however slightly) removed from the aims and means of the historian. And two, because a potential confusion is thereby obviated between the study of a text in its historical context and the study of a text's history (or, to put it another way, between what a text said and says *vis-à-vis* its historical interlocutors and what a text historically underwent and undergoes). On this basis, then, I propose, and in the pages that follow will use, a distinction between "textual hermeneutics," on the one hand, engaged in the exegesis of a given text, and "philosophical construction," on the other, engaged in the elaboration of ideas and arguments based on but not necessarily found in a given text.

Returning to the point at hand, then, in terms Garfield proposes I consider "*engaging with*" (Garfield 2015: xiii, emphases original) Buddhist philosophy, by which I mean the theoretical project of adopting and adapting it in conversation with non-Buddhist philosophical partners, as much a valid and valuable intellectual enterprise as "*engaging in*" (Garfield 2015: xiii, emphases original) Buddhist philosophy, by which I mean "the exegetical project of figuring out what Buddhist philosophers said" (Garfield 2015: 320) and *a fortiori* what they *meant*. In other words, I consider a philosophically strict approach to Madhyamaka—and more broadly to Buddhist and even more broadly to non-Western religiously situated and philosophically rich texts, by which they are "purged of their religious elements" so as to ascertain whether "they present an overall attractive philosophical picture, or would they only be adopted by one who has a prior commitment to the religious tradition they form a part of" (Westerhoff 2017a: 1, 2)—to be methodologically sound. Indeed, such efforts in "comparative philosophy," "fusion philosophy," or "cross-cultural philosophy"[26] are highly sophisticated philosophical works in their own right and, as such, have been and will doubtless continue to be highly successful at increasing interest in Buddhist philosophy among Western philosophers. What is more, through the theoretical and hermeneutical reflections they occasion, coupled with the higher degree of generalization available to them than to counterparts restricted to a single tradition, these comparative works may lead, and have led, to manifold insights on important questions regarding concept and category formation, terminology, method, motive, and so on in the diverse academic fields with which they are identified (most readily religious studies and philosophy but also comparative literature, history, and area studies). Whatever its merits or demerits, the present chapter, based as it is on this body of scholarship, is a case in point of just such reflection.

Furthermore, I am not in entire agreement with Andrew Tuck when he discerns an ideological commitment to providing "interpretations and translations of ancient texts that are intended to be as 'accurate', 'objective', and 'close to the original' as possible" (Tuck 1990: 8) on the part of many of today's South Asianist scholars (and beyond). Such a commitment, rooted in traditional, nineteenth-century, hermeneutic attempts "concerned with the recovery of the original textual meaning" (Tuck 1990: 8)—a meaning which is taken, moreover, to be single and identical with the author's intention—are evidently what Tuck has in mind when he goes on to state that "it is extraordinary that readers of Indian texts still continue to be naïvely concerned with discovering the 'real meaning' of texts" (Tuck 1990: 14). Although Bugault, concerned as he is with "learning to unveil old Indian texts" (Bugault 1983: 53), may well be guilty of such hermeneutic essentialism, I do not perceive any such hermeneutic *naïveté* in the bulk of scholars active today. On the contrary, Garfield for one declares his awareness of such pitfalls pellucidly:

> We are not trying to recover authorial intent, if that is supposed to be something beyond textual meaning; we are not committing the historicist/objectivist fallacy. . . . We are instead trying to construct a reading of those texts that makes sense of them in the dual contexts provided by the textual milieu in which they figure historically—the context of their composition—and our own interpretive horizon, which is the only context in which we can read and understand. (Garfield 2008: 514)

Indeed, it should not need stating that I do not find problematic *per se* an approach to a text that endeavors to discern what it is saying, even if I freely admit that no particular reading is privileged with some singular access to its source (on which point more presently). I therefore have no problem at all with a philosophically constructive reading not "real" in the sense of "originally intended," provided that it is interesting—philosophically or otherwise—and provided that the exegete in question is not himself claiming to be getting at "what Nāgārjuna meant," and thereby, willy or nilly, shoring up credibility for his philosophical construction by presenting it under the guise of textual hermeneutics.[27]

Relatedly, the paucity of reliable information as to the socio-cultural context of the presumed producers of the texts under study is such that any attempt to provide what Nāgārjuna or any of his premodern peers "intended" is doomed to failure for historical reasons even before the theoretical project gets off the ground. Paul Harrison has written extensively regarding the socio-cultural context in which early Mahāyāna texts (such as Nāgārjuna's) were composed and in which their teachings were practiced. As he states of *sūtras*, but in a manner that is clearly extrapolatable to the Madhyamaka literature we are concerned with here, "The first objective is . . . to understand them not just as texts—although the usual philological operations are an essential preliminary—but to see past them to the lives of who produced them, to ask what impact those lives had on the texts, and *vice versa*" (Harrison 2003: 116).

Now, the difficulties concomitant with following through on this objective are formidable, as Harrison himself acknowledges on the same page. Perhaps foremost among them is the lack of reliable information as to the very lives of the presumed producers of the texts we study. This is so for Nāgārjuna just as much as for the authors of the early Mahāyāna *sūtra* canon. Despite Joseph Walser's attempts to "demythologize Nāgārjuna" (Walser 2005: 264) by "locating Nāgārjuna historically, socially, and institutionally" (Walser 2005: 2), we know nothing at all with certainty as to our writer's life.[28] I say "with certainty," for Walser does, in the course of his exposition, argue for specific monastic affiliations and geographic locations within which to place Nāgārjuna. But while it is no doubt true that, as per Walser, "many of the peculiarities of Nāgārjuna's writings can be more adequately understood if read as strategies devised to respond to the specific demands of the social and institutional context in which he wrote" (Walser 2005: 2), this boils down to little more than a truism based on a desideratum: We would more adequately understand Nāgārjuna's philosophy if we more adequately understood the circumstances in which Nāgārjuna's philosophy was composed. Although Walser does a fine job of mustering historical and institutional evidence in avowed support of his theses, ultimately he admits to being able to suggest only "a plausible (if, at times, diaphanous) picture of [Nāgārjuna's] career" (Walser 2005: 3). The tentative nature of this picture belies Walser's bold pronouncement in his Conclusion that "until someone can provide an alternative explanation of Nāgārjuna's institutional context, the reading of Nāgārjuna as refuting 'the *abhidharma*' (or even refuting all theses) is unlikely" (Walser 2005: 265). For even were we to grant Walser's hypotheses as to Nāgārjuna's context, surely Dan Arnold is right in pointing out that the relations among Nāgārjuna's claims "are not exhaustively explicable as a function of socio-historical pressures" (Arnold 2007: 688)—a point pertinent to thinkers well beyond Nāgārjuna, of course.

All of this goes to buttress my point here that a reading of Nāgārjuna's texts that purports to "unveil" him or them in some unreconstructed orientalizing fashion is a nonstarter. Quite besides which, Walser's avowed intention "to rescue Nāgārjuna from an overemphasis on his universality" (Walser 2005: 264) ignores the fact that Nāgārjuna's arguments are avowedly universal in scope. Since the relevance and significance of Nāgārjuna's arguments are not confined to the particular monastery or royal court in which he may or may not have composed them, their validity as philosophical arguments too should not be confined to, or by, the merely socio-historical contexts of their composition.[29]

Nevertheless, I feel that more than merely an inveterate historical philologist's urge toward deciphering the ur-truth of a text is at work when today's interpreters insist upon the logicality of Nāgārjuna's tetralemma, or more broadly of his philosophy as a whole. It will be expedient to frame my suggestions as to the reasons for this phenomenon in terms of a response to what I suspect are the two readiest potential objections to my foregoing critique. The first objection would accuse me, despite my denunciation of hermeneutic attempts to recover the authorially intended meaning of the MK and the use of the *catuṣkoṭi* therein, for example, of subscribing to just such an agenda in my insistence upon sticking to Nāgārjuna's own philosophical mission. In claiming that the exegetes I have criticized do a grave disservice to Nāgārjuna by ignoring, or at best marginalizing, the soterial intent of the tetralemma, am I not subscribing to exactly those monolithic notions of authorial intent, interpretive objectivity, and textual primacy as I have just now condemned?

My response is as follows: I am happy to go so far as to admit that any reading of a text is as valid as any other, and this on the grounds of the ineluctably grounded nature of hermeneutics as per Vico, the disavowal of textual finality as per Schleiermacher, the proclamation of authorial death as per Barthes, the deconstructive disavowal of logocentrism as per Derrida, or the dismissal of interpretive objectivity as per Gadamer, among the multifarious other factors that constitute me as a twenty-first-century heir to the continental philosophical and hermeneutical currents evoked by these few exemplary figures. But the crucial point to make here is that the scholars I criticize, despite their vocal admission of polysemicity, do not in fact hold such open-ended intellectual commitments as I have acceded to myself. Rather, these scholars remain closed to all but a single "right" way of thinking, which they typically refer to as "common sense" or "classical logic," but which is just as much in force when they apply deviant logics such as paraconsistency to the texts under study. For regardless of the details of their diverging approaches, they are united in accepting the universal sovereignty of "logic," "reason," or "rationality" as a neutral, objective criterion by which to gauge the validity of a given claim or the cogency of a given intellectual system regardless of its historical locus. Garfield states this with utmost clarity in declaring: "Logic transcends metaphysics: It is a canon of reason, not a theory of reality, and a canon of reason ought to be equally valid no matter how the world is" (Garfield 2015: 249), or "reason is . . . a transcendental condition of interpretation both in the sense that we can only vindicate an interpretation to the extent that we read the texts as rational, and we can only justify a reading rationally" (Garfield 2015: 332).[30]

When these scholars exclusively use such a closed interpretive lens to assess the validity and worth of Nāgārjuna's thought, I am forced to conclude that, far from acquiescing to a potentially infinite plethora of only-ever-relatively or conventionally true readings, they would—and doubtless will—denounce my own approach as "bereft of reason" (Garfield 2008: 526) and therefore misguided.[31] This is doubly ironic given that, as I have mentioned earlier and will go on to argue in detail, Nāgārjuna's entire enterprise is aimed at undermining belief in or reliance on any "transcendental conditions"—explicitly including those that structure our thinking. As T. R. V. Murti states in characteristically forthright terms, for Nāgārjuna "there is no such thing as a neutral logic which every philosopher accepts or has to accept. . . . Logic is metaphysical to the core" (Murti 1955: 152). To adopt the wording of the title to the present chapter, Nāgārjuna takes reason to be not some objective, neutral feature of "how the world is," but as *oriented*, as karmically driven, as causally constructed, as any other phenomenon. Thus, to posit logic/reason/rationality as some Archimedean point categorically removed from the ambit of conditionality is tantamount to affirming not only the existence of a metaphysical absolute but a position exactly antithetical to Nāgārjuna.[32]

To generalize, what I am attempting to argue here is that the preponderant bulk of scholarly activity on Buddhist philosophy, as it has been and continues to be undertaken, suffers from an unacknowledged prioritization of identifiably Western philosophical modes and models, which are, moreover, distinctly ill-suited to the material. While I can readily consider these efforts as so many exercises in twentieth- and twenty-first-century Western philosophy and hermeneutics—and of potentially great worth within this ambit—I am unable to consider them as exercises in *Buddhist* philosophy or hermeneutics. I am thus in stark disagreement with the Cowherds when they ask: "Are we doing real Buddhist studies when we deploy ideas and techniques from contemporary analytic philosophy to address questions arising from seventh-century Indian debates as adumbrated in fifteenth-century Tibet?" and reply: "We think so" (Cowherds 2011: vii). I am also thereby led to consider the claim made by Garfield that "the texts we and others publish are not *about*, but are moments *within* [the Buddhist philosophical] tradition" (Garfield 2015: 333, emphases original) to be deeply misguided in that they insist on interpreting Buddhist philosophy from *without*, from hermeneutical horizons *outside* it. In saying so, I realize I may be accused of falling into the danger of treating "the Buddhist tradition as a complete, mummified object of primarily curatorial interest" (Garfield 2015: 332–333), of suggesting that "the only way for scholars to show respect for the Madhyamaka tradition [is] to circumambulate the museum display containing their relics" (Cowherds 2016b: 620)—as if modern or Western interpreters are or should be barred from engaging with or in Buddhist thought simply by dint of being modern or Western. Here again we come across an acute irony, for it is precisely in evaluating Nāgārjuna in strict accordance with "the canons of rational argument and criticism" (Garfield and Priest 2002: 96) that these scholars do "set [them] selves up as privileged subjects writing hermeneutically closed texts that illuminate the Buddhist philosophical tradition with the cool light of scholarly objectivity" (Garfield 2015: 332). Indeed, in words that should pique the "curatorial interest" of Garfield and his peers, Bernard Faure rightly discerns the denaturing effect of such an enterprise:

> The apology for "philosophical" Buddhism is perfectly justifiable when it is a matter of winning recognition for Buddhism as a movement of thought in its own right. However, it becomes problematic when it insists on limiting itself to a narrowly rationalist, demythologizing and antiritualistic approach, thereby misrepresenting what Buddhism is and always has been.... Reconstructed (or rather distorted) in that fashion, Buddhism has become no more than a museum piece. (Faure 2004: 65)

Now, "what Buddhism is and always has been" is many things to many people, and the last thing I would want is to be taken as espousing a certain philosophical construction of Nāgārjuna as the one and only valid candidate. This is not to say that I do not have a favored reading, of course. Indeed, it should be clear by now that I consider an interpretation of Nāgārjuna that takes him to be "philosophico-religious"—indeed, "religiosophical"—to be preferable to one that takes him to be "philosophical-not-religious" insofar as this latter ignores or negates what I take to be central features of his thought.[33] The very fact that I consider an exclusively rationalist approach antithetical to Nāgārjuna, ill-suited to the textual material, is and should be taken as evidence of that. But that is beside the point. For the point I am making here (and as I go on to argue with reference to Wayne Proudfoot's distinction between descriptive and explanatory reduction later) is that the philosophical constructions based on a given text allow many perspectives, including, notably, those not rational, or even those not concerned with rationality.

Though efforts to present Nāgārjuna's MK (or any other Buddhist work) as "a philosophical text to philosophers" (Garfield 1995: viii)[34] may well bear multifarious fruit for "contemporary analytic philosophy," they are not at all "doing real *Buddhist* studies"; not at all "*within* that tradition." For in eschewing interpretive strategies that take seriously (or even consider at all) the Buddhist philosophico-religious premises within which Nāgārjuna's thought as a whole must be situated in order to understand *it* (i.e., on *its* terms), the readings proposed by these scholars effectively function only within the intellectual confines of Western academic debates. Within this context, they serve to proliferate the publication of views and counterviews; in so doing, however, they do not actually engage with the Buddhist philosophy of Nāgārjuna at all. In contrast, I am proposing that, as self-identifying interpreters (as scholars engaged, that is, in textual hermeneutics), we need to provide an interpretation of Nāgārjuna's thought that *he*, not "we," would recognize.[35]

Of course, Nāgārjuna may well have found much to disagree with, or even not recognize, in the exegesis of his own thought by later avowed Buddhists such as Jizang, Bhāvaviveka, or Tsongkhapa, say, let alone in twentieth-century ones such as Yinshun, Thích Nhất Hạnh, or the Dalai Lama. But whereas diversity of interpretation within an intellectual tradition is accepted, what distinguishes these exegetes from those I am discussing is, precisely, their taking seriously Nāgārjuna's text as (not "a philosophical text" but) a Buddhist text, regardless of their intended audience. They are, as it were, speaking Nāgārjuna's language, and are thus recognizably in conversation with him, rather than translating him into an alien idiom and either faulting him for his perceived lack of fluency in it, his remaining recalcitrantly "inchoate and obscure" (Burton 1999: 7), or congratulating him on at least grasping the grammar, "not deny[ing] any principles of logic" (Robinson 1957: 307). To be clear, and to reiterate a point made earlier, I am certainly not proposing some essential distinction between Buddhists and non-Buddhist scholars of Buddhism, whereby the former's interpretations of Buddhist texts are to be taken *a priori* as authentic and the latter's as invalid.[36] The point hinges not on some identity marker of a given exegete as "insider" or "outsider" but on whether or not the exegesis presented assumes principles of evaluation alien to those of the text it purports to interpret.[37] If a given interpreter insists that the text under interpretation conform to conditions of interpretability deemed imperative by *him* (and not the text), then he thereby reneges on positioning his interpretation within the text's own interpretive ambit.

As for where my own approach fits in, although it is an undeniable empirical fact that I write from and in a lingo far removed from Nāgārjuna's, and although (again) I claim no privileged ahistoricity (let alone Buddhisticity) for my own account, what I am attempting to do is insist, like the Buddhist authorities I have alluded to, on taking Nāgārjuna's words on their own terms. On one level, of course, I readily admit that this effort is and must be a failure, for no amount of anglifying will convey Nāgārjuna's Sanskrit, no channeling of his thought into my own ideas and idioms will deliver it, somehow, virginally inviolate.[38] But if that were the aim, then no translation (in the broadest sense of that term) would be possible.[39] Instead, I will be content if I succeed in presenting a reading that takes its place among others making sense of Nāgārjuna, and that does so in a manner as consonant as I can make it with his Buddhist religiosophy.[40]

The second potential criticism of my position (and one that stems from my immediately preceding comments as much as from my earlier critiques) is that the same interpretive techniques used by modern Western scholars were in fact used by classical Buddhist commentators, be they writing in Sanskrit or any other canonical Buddhist language. Being deeply versed in the various literatures constituting the history of Buddhist philosophy, the scholars I criticize regularly draw on sources considered unimpeachable authorities by the traditions themselves in support of their interpretations. More generally, the principles of rational argumentation recognizable to Western philosophers developed and were effectively deployed in Indian sources too.[41] Thus, Nāgārjuna and his Indian philosophical peers were well aware of and took as axiomatic the laws of non-contradiction, excluded middle, and double negation on whose bases classical Western logic is founded.[42] Indeed, Nāgārjuna's own texts, not to mention the vast commentarial literature surrounding them in premodern Indian as well as Tibetan and Chinese contexts, abound in arguments to the effect of proving or disproving theses on eminently logical grounds. Further, Nāgārjuna's primary argumentative strategy, *prasaṅga*, is explicitly designed to reduce his opponent's position to absurdity, an end oft achieved by means of demonstrating its violation of just such logical laws.

To this I would respond with the following observations. Although logical principles such as those mentioned do hold argumentative force in Madhyamaka texts, including the MK, the texts themselves make clear that the *function* of these principles differs markedly from that found in their modern Western utilization. Buddhist writers such as Nāgārjuna were engaged in a very different activity from that of the Western and Westernized scholars I have considered. This activity was informed not by the purportedly detached description of metaphysical truth espoused by academic philosophers but by, first, the avowedly Buddhist acknowledgment of the impossibility of such detachment within the realm of *saṃsāric* attachment and, concomitantly, the desire to rid oneself and others of the suffering necessarily entailed in such attachment. For the Buddhist *philosophical* project is irreducibly soteriological in its orientation; to marginalize or ignore the teleological end of texts such as the MK (i.e., ultimately, the attainment of *nirvāṇa*) is to engage in (presumably inadvertent) eisegetic catachresis (or, more briefly put, in critical abuse).[43]

The Buddhist *hermeneutical* project, furthermore, is informed by the same end. Therefore, in formulating a reading of Nāgārjuna's thought, be it in *catuṣkoṭi* form or not, the first and foremost aim of Buddhist exegetes was, and is, to aid in the liberation of sentient beings, the which goal is approached in the *śāstra* literature under study here through the apprehension of reality as it is; shorn, that is, of inevitably false conceptual reification. That this, the attainment of *nirvāṇic* liberation by means of the cessation of desire-driven ignorance, is the aim of the entire endeavor is either explicitly stated or simply taken for granted in *every* Buddhist text, including treatises such as the MK and its paratexts. (As a corollary point, I thus see no reason to propose a qualitative distinction, on this score at least, among scriptures, treatises, and commentaries—i.e., *sūtra*, *śāstra*, and *vṛtti* literatures—as has often been taken for granted in the scholarship.)[44] Let us not forget that the MK itself begins with dedicatory verses announcing that the purpose of Nāgārjuna's text is consonant with the teachings of "the Fully Enlightened Buddha, best of speakers, who taught dependent co-origination for the purpose of the cessation of conceptualization."[45] Although a study of this topos in Nāgārjuna's texts—and their relation to the broader contexts of Madhyamaka and other Buddhist literatures—will occupy us in subsequent chapters, I would hope that Nāgārjuna's espousal of the merely conventional nature of supposedly apodeictic logical laws, entailing as it does that his soterially motivated utilization of them is not implicative of any avowal of their ultimate (i.e., conceptually unconstructed, metaphysically independent) validity, should be sufficiently clear from his texts as to be beyond disputation.

As such (and to reiterate a point made earlier), if we are interested in discerning what interpretations of Nāgārjuna's texts proffered by classical exegetes such as Candrakīrti, Tsongkhapa, or Qingmu 青目, say, are up to, then we must understand them within the context of the avowedly Buddhist intentions of these authors (their *abhiprāya*). This is not to fall into some "historicist/objectivist fallacy" or deny our inextricability from our own "interpretive horizon" (see Garfield 2008: 514 quoted earlier). Rather, it is to maintain that if we are engaged in textual hermeneutics then we must take our texts' own formulations of their purpose and purport seriously; otherwise, we become engaged in the methodologically valid but different activity of philosophical construction.

Relatedly, it is not to allege some intuitive and inexplicable process of direct transmission whereby a given reader may divine the inner motivation or intent of a given author. Rather, in interpreting a text (or for that matter in interpreting a text's textual interpretation), we must confine ourselves, to the extent possible, to what the text in question actually says. Indeed, much of my disagreement with currently authoritative readings of Nāgārjuna's texts (and particularly of the *catuṣkoṭi* and the disavowal of all views) stems from my reliance upon this hermeneutical principle, in contradistinction to the manifold additions and parameterizations (proposed by the interpreters I criticize) that I systematically abjure.[46] The fact that we know next to nothing of the historical circumstances under which these texts were composed, nor of the practical aspects of their author's presumably monastic life, only renders circumstantially necessary what I take to be a valid and viable hermeneutic principle basically reducible to the old dictum "to the texts themselves."

While the objects of my critique may rail against any such precept, rejoining that it reduces the range of "permitted" readings and may even forestall the exploration of cross-cultural confluences (it does not, for that is a project of philosophical construction, not textual hermeneutics), it is in fact their accounts that prove reductive insofar as they enclose the horizons of interpretability in advance under the penumbra of reason. For if the texts themselves exceed the bounds within which their interpretations, it is claimed, must fall—recall Garfield's insistence that "a commitment to reason is a transcendental condition of interpretability" (Garfield 2008: 515)—then it is not the texts but the ostensible interpretations thereof that need enlargement.[47]

In the present case, Nāgārjuna's texts, I am claiming, while certainly availing themselves of the rationalist's toolkit, cannot legitimately be read by means of those tools alone. For they are explicit, and repeatedly so, in their repudiation of *any* foundation to the claims and counterclaims, the theses and antitheses, they denounce, and *all* of which, therefore, they renounce. To force Nāgārjuna into the very bonds he so entirely unlocks, unmasking them as more and mere metaphysical mysticism, is thus not only misinterpretation but contr-interpretation: it imports a "condition of interpretability" that is both alien and outright opposed to the stated purport of Nāgārjuna's philosophy.

All this will hopefully also put paid to the idea that I simply "see the application of logic and rationality as inimical to spiritual pursuits" (Siderits 2003a: 14–15). As Siderits alleges, this would indeed be "guilty of a bit of ethnocentrism," since it would be to apply a dichotomy between "philosophical rationality" and "soteriological value" foreign to the Indian Buddhist case (Siderits 2003a: 15).[48] On the contrary, as will become more apparent later, following Nāgārjuna I maintain that reasoned argumentation is an efficacious means toward the soteriological end of liberation. I am thus in full agreement with Siderits and Katsura's characterization of the MK as a work "designed to help foster liberation by enlisting the tool of philosophical rationality" (Siderits and Katsura 2013: 15). Importantly, however, I do not thereby aver (and definitely do not see Nāgārjuna averring) that reason stands removed from the net of conditionality as some kind of "substantive ultimate truth" (Siderits 2003a: 17) or structuring principle. The tool should be recognized as itself a product of tools, and not mistaken as some self-validating power transcendent to the tasks to which it is put. Indeed, while Siderits on the one hand defends a "semantic interpretation of emptiness, [according to which] the truth that liberates is the insight that there can be no truth apart from the contingent institutions and practices of social existence" (Siderits 2003a: 18), or in other words, that "there is no such thing as how the world is independently of the concepts we happen to employ" (Siderits 2003a: 21), on the other hand he never questions the "grand narrative" (Siderits 2003a: 20) of "discursive reason" (Siderits 2003a: 10) itself.[49] As such, although Siderits is more circumspect than Garfield when it comes to proclaiming the universal and transcendental authority of reason, he too could well be accused of turning out to be metaphysically realist about rationality itself.

This becomes all the more apparent in Siderits's discussions of what he calls Madhyamaka anti-realism. For Siderits, "The doctrine of metaphysical realism has three key theses: (1) truth is correspondence between proposition and reality; (2) reality is mind independent; (3) there is one true theory that correctly describes reality" (Siderits 1988: 311). Nāgārjuna, he rightly shows, undermines all three of these theses, and on Siderits's reading Nāgārjuna is thus to be accounted an anti-realist. Now, whatever we make of the anti-realist interpretation, what I want to emphasize is that Siderits fails to see the metaphysical character of the very "Canons of Rationality" his argumentation relies upon.[50] For in discussing Nāgārjuna's claim to have no thesis at VV:29, Siderits states that

> By this he appears to mean that the claim that all things are empty is not a substantive claim concerning the ultimate nature of reality. Nāgārjuna admits that were he to make such a claim he would be inconsistent, but he feels he need not. All he need do is show the impossibility of constructing a coherent metaphysical theory, *one which satisfies the demands of philosophical rationality*. (Siderits 1989: 235, emphases added)

More than this, Siderits alleges that "the content of ultimate truth is just those statements that are deemed acceptable *according to the standards of philosophical rationality*" (Siderits 1989: 233, emphases added). In so saying, Siderits effectively shows himself to be unaware that, for Nāgārjuna, "philosophical rationality" *is* a "metaphysical theory."[51] To posit it as anything more than a convenient and conventional means (an *upāya*); to rely on it as some transcendent tool used for the construction—or the deconstruction—of theories, is already to embrace rationality itself as a metaphysical absolute.[52] If for Nāgārjuna "There can be no such thing as the one true theory that corresponds to the nature of reality" (Siderits 1989: 235), if "the notion of the 'one right fit' between beliefs and world is empty" (Siderits 1989: 317), then Nāgārjuna cannot commit himself to philosophical rationality as the one true means of demonstrating that. To do so would indeed be inconsistent, for it would in effect be to espouse philosophical rationality (a belief) as uniquely rightly fitted to analyzing metaphysical reality (the world).

For a Buddhist philosopher such as Nāgārjuna, then, even if the soteriological mission at the heart of his project may (in part) be satisfied through the deployment of rational means designed to facilitate insight into reality as it really is (*yathābhūtadarśana*), this in no way implies that these or any other such efficacious means should be taken as transcendentally valid. Indeed, for Nāgārjuna, any such adherence to foundationalist bases would be taken as evidence of, precisely, ad-herence; that is, of one's still being affixed to, stuck with, afflicted by—not freed from—the infrastructure of suffering.

1.4. Reimagining Religion and Philosophy

My catalogue of the attempts to "rescue" Nāgārjuna, and in particular his *catuṣkoṭi*, from illogicality in §1.2 on "Unveiling the East" is, I trust, adequate testimony to an ongoing and often avowedly apologetic effort on the part of the exegetes involved to do Nāgārjuna a favor by ridding his philosophy of irrational oriental leftovers. In §1.3 on "Orientalizing Reasons," I argued that this has typically involved an imposition of logical models that fail to do justice both to the texts they purport to study and, more broadly, to the religio-philosophical paradigms within which authors such as Nāgārjuna lived, wrote, and practiced. The reasons for this inveterate demand for "reason" in Nāgārjuna's work are not hard to divine, and are certainly worth delving into.

We approach here one of the many places at which differing conceptual schemas at work in the Buddhist and Western philosophico-religious worldviews render meaningful critical analysis particularly fraught with the pitfalls of misunderstanding. Since Plato's instauration of the opposition between *doxa* and *epistêmê*,[53] Western philosophy has perceived itself as the preeminent realm of knowledge, as distinct from mere belief. Garfield puts this position into the mouths of philosophers in the following succinct terms: "There is a world of difference between philosophy and religion, and what passes for 'Eastern philosophy' is in fact religion misnamed. Western philosophy is independent of religion, and is a rational, religiously disinterested inquiry into fundamental questions about the nature of reality, human life, and so on" (Garfield 2002: 252).

The origins of such a partitioning of philosophical and religious endeavors have, of course, as much to do with the overtly paradoxical (and in this strict sense irrational) beliefs central to the Christian religion as they do with the rationalistic approach of the ancient Greeks. Such a net distinction is simply not operative in the Buddhist sphere, whose origins avowedly lie not in a call to belief but in a call to insight.[54] Of course, what I suggest here should not be misconstrued as a reductionist claim to the effect that Christianity and Buddhism can be characterized adequately, distinctively, and respectively as belief-centered and insight-centered. Rather, I am calling attention, first, to the understanding, of immense historical importance to the development of both "religion" and "philosophy" in Western (i.e., Christianate) culture, that these are distinct, if not mutually opposed, spheres of action, and second, to the fact that such an understanding is not operative within the classical Buddhist worldview of Nāgārjuna.

Indeed, despite the ostensible division between (Greek) philosophy and (Christian) religion in the West, each has in practice been saturated with the other over the many centuries intervening since their historical confrontation (a fact one surely need not read Augustine to observe). Thus, Garfield deflates the philosophers' claim to "religiously disinterested inquiry" with the objection that this would be to do away with the bulk of Western philosophy, on the basis that

> this distinction is supposed to deliver the result that St Thomas Aquinas's *Summa Theologica*, Descartes's *Meditations*, including the proofs of the existence of God, and Leibniz's discussion of theodicy are philosophical, while Dharmakīrti's investigations of the structure of induction and of the ontological status of universals, Tsong khapa's account of reference and meaning, and Nāgārjuna's critique of essence and analysis of the causal relation are religious. Anyone who has a passing familiarity with all of the relevant texts will agree that something has gone seriously wrong if this distinction is taken seriously. (Garfield 2002: 252)[55]

The adoption of etic methodological principles is to some extent a necessary feature of comparative work (including my own), and I am certainly not arguing that such a procedure is inherently erroneous and consequently that comparative work is indelibly flawed. In the scholarship on the *catuṣkoṭi* and other matters I have criticized earlier, however, the tendency to apply anachronistic and/or anachoristic[56] categories has been carried too far; to such an extent that these interpreters have, I have argued, effectively reneged on the emic project of understanding Nāgārjuna in his own terms (or at least in terms recognizable to him) altogether. In so doing, they have engaged in what Wayne Proudfoot has called "descriptive reduction": "the failure to identify an emotion, practice, or experience under the description by which the subject identifies it" (Proudfoot 1985: 196). As a methodological approach in the study of religion (or analogous fields), Proudfoot states forthrightly, "this is indeed unacceptable" (Proudfoot 1985: 196). His reasoning, with which I am entirely in accord, is that

> An experience must be specified under a description that can be ascribed to the subject, and it is the task of the historian of religions to identify the particular concepts and descriptions available to people in particular contexts and to disentangle them from our anachronistic [and anachoristic] tendency to ascribe our concepts to those people. This is what much of the study of religion is about. (Proudfoot 1985: 185)

Proudfoot goes on to contrast "descriptive reduction" with what he proposes to call "explanatory reduction"; this "consists in offering an explanation of an experience [or other religious phenomenon] in terms that *are not those of the subject and that might not meet with his approval*" (Proudfoot 1985: 197, emphasis added). Proudfoot immediately adds, "this is perfectly justifiable and is, in fact, normal procedure," but whether or not such an approach is normal, we must surely be wary of ascribing positions to a given subject with which s/he would disagree. Indeed, I admit to finding the stated distinction between descriptive and explanatory reduction ill-defined on the basis that, in both cases, the analyst reduces the subject's position to one intelligible to the analyst but not to the subject. I fail to see how such an explanatory approach avoids the inveterate tendency toward the ascription of "*our* concepts to *those* people." Such an approach, moreover, appears to lie at odds with Proudfoot's claim much later in the same book that "the distinguishing mark of a religious experience is not the subject matter but *the kind of explanation the subject believes is appropriate*" (Proudfoot 1985: 231, emphasis added). How, after all, can an analyst's explanation be taken as appropriate by the subject when it does not meet with his or her approval or even understanding?

It is important to note, however, that my suspicion as to Proudfoot's dichotomy and his defense of explanatory reduction in spite of a given subject's disapproval only stands if we, as analysts, are in fact avowedly engaged in the endeavor of understanding a given subject's experience, text, or position *as understood by that subject*. If this is not the case; if, that is, we are engaged in what I earlier referred to as philosophical construction and are thus unconcerned as to whether the given subject would or would not recognize our interpretation-cum-elaboration, then the reductionism espoused by Proudfoot is an effective practice. It is, moreover, one that may lead to great insights as to the subject at hand, as evinced by, for example, Freudian, Marxist, Feminist, or Existentialist explanatory approaches to subjects obviously unfamiliar with, indeed even predating, these intellectual currents. But a psychoanalytical reading of *Oedipus Rex*, say, takes as given the fact that Sophocles was unaware of Freudian theory and would not recognize its application to his text. An analogous case, however, cannot be made in the context of logically oriented Western scholarly interpretations of Nāgārjuna for, as I have shown, these analyses are avowedly exercises in textual hermeneutics; they are ones, moreover, that effectively posit a reading that is presupposed to be univocally valid. In other words, the scholars criticized earlier do *not* accept as given that Nāgārjuna would not recognize his words in their readings; rather, to cite once again the revealing mission propounded by Westerhoff, they aim to remain completely "in accordance with his general philosophical position" (Westerhoff 2006: 368). Despite the common claims to be "doing philosophy" by extrapolating from Nāgārjuna's stated positions to what these *would be* in the context of debates in Western philosophy, it is evident that these scholars are in fact "doing hermeneutics" by constantly making claims as to what Nāgārjuna's stated positions *are*. That is, they are not concerned solely with extracting philosophical metal from the ore of Buddhist texts and using this to construct philosophical edifices on foreign territory, as it were, but in determining how this material fit, or fits, within the surrounding strata of autochthonous ground. Or, to dispense with the metaphor, they are not (or not only) elaborating philosophical ideas drawn from Nāgārjuna but (also) elaborating what they claim are *Nāgārjuna's* philosophical ideas. This confusion, or melding, of what are in fact two methodologically distinct scholarly activities is evident in the very manner in which Garfield glosses what it means to "Engage *with* Buddhism" (Garfield 2015: xiii, emphasis added). If this, as Garfield proposes, means "to take up thinking through the point of view of this tradition" (Garfield 2015: xiii), then I am at a loss to understand how it might differ from engaging *in* Buddhism.

The slippage I have identified here between philosophical construction and textual hermeneutics stands in contrast to certain other prominent forays into Buddhist philosophy; ones, that is, which make clear that their attempts to think "with" Buddhist philosophy "might not really be Buddhist" (Flanagan 2013: 4–5) at all. Thus, for example, Flanagan's exploration of the question "whether Buddhism can be naturalized, tamed, and made compatible with a philosophy that is empirically responsible" (Flanagan 2013: xiii) states forthrightly that "Even if there is a minority movement that fits the bill of naturalized Buddhism . . . it does not follow that it really deserves to call itself Buddhism" (Flanagan 2013: 4). Indeed, Flanagan goes on immediately to aver that

> Actually it doesn't really matter to me whether the philosophical theory I am interested in talking about here is called "Buddhism," "buddhism," or just the philosophical theory—the metaphysics, epistemology, and ethics—that remains after you subtract the unwarranted nonnatural beliefs in Buddhism from Buddhism. (Flanagan 2013: 4)

Just so, Priest acknowledges that his construction of an ethics on the basis of Buddhist ideas and texts may well "not be accepted as Buddhist by some who regard themselves as Buddhist" (Priest 2014: 210),[57] but declares that "whether or not the ethics I describe should properly be called 'Buddhist' is, in fact, of little interest to me. All that concerns me is its truth" (Priest 2014: 210). Whatever we may make of the actual content of the philosophical constructions proposed by Flanagan or Priest, the point I am underlining here is that they clearly and unambiguously differentiate their mandate from that of textual hermeneutics. In so doing, they obviate the charge I have levelled at some of their peers earlier, and in the process advance the study of Buddhist philosophy "in the contemporary philosophical climate" (Priest 2014: xxiv) in a manner that does not, implicitly or explicitly, appear to do injustice to the Buddhist tradition itself. How could it, after all, since they do not claim to be advancing *Buddhist* ideas and arguments at all?

And yet, this is not to say that their positions are without problems. For one thing, a statement such as Priest's to the effect that "For what it is worth, I find disputes about whether something is *really* Buddhist unenlightening" (Priest 2014: 210 n. 2, emphasis original) misses the point. For although all manner of positions may be identified as "*really* Buddhist" (where this is to be taken in the sense of being attested in a given text identified by the tradition as within the tradition), my point is that there is a significant methodological difference between unearthing that material and building with it, between claiming it is indeed "Buddhist" and not so claiming. Relatedly, Flanagan's mission to "tame" Buddhism by naturalizing it effectively renders any version of Buddhism not so naturalized as *un*-tamed; that is, presumably, wild. It may even be straight-out labelled "bullshit" or, in a coinage Flanagan is apparently proud of, "Buddshit" (Flanagan 2013: 210 n. 6). Leaving aside for a moment the gross injustice of such a perspective, this characterization self-evidently rests on an all-too-smug assumption of superior epistemic status for naturalism in relation to what Flanagan does not hesitate to dub "the low epistemic standards that permit all manner of superstition and nonsense" (Flanagan 2013: xiii), the "epistemically speaking . . . incredible superstition and magical thinking" (Flanagan 2013: 3) of non-naturalized Buddhism.[58] Now, for one thing this kind of talk strikes me as woefully outdated, for in it we find Flanagan, the twenty-first-century self-avowed atheist analytic philosopher and philosophical naturalist (see Flanagan 2013: 209–210), echoing in alarmingly kindred terms the nineteenth-century Protestant pastor and theologian Cornelius Petrus Tiele, who dismissed Buddhism as "infected by the most fantastic mythology and the most childish superstitions" (Tiele 1884, cited in Smith 2004: 191). What that says about the claims to unbiased pure reason of naturalist analytic philosophy I leave to the reader's judgment.

But one additional, and important, relevant entailment of such a perspective is that it openly enacts a form of "*deep epistemic injustice*" (Kidd 2017: 393, emphases original) against Buddhists who hold beliefs not subsumable under a naturalistic umbrella. This is so because, for a naturalist such as Flanagan, "belief in them must be evidence of epistemic fault" (Kidd 2017: 393). On this model, Buddhism must demonstrate itself to be "compatible with the rest of knowledge as it now exists" (Flanagan 2013: xiii), not the other way round (or any other way in which differing epistemic systems may be related).[59] The onus is placed on Buddhism because it is assumed that "knowledge as it now exists" is naturalistic, meaning that "the very possibility of credibility or intelligibility is removed" (Kidd 2017: 393) from traditional Buddhism.[60] This procedure, however, self-evidently relies on but an alternative form of epistemic basicality that remains, as always, premised on the epistemic guarantors paradigmatic, and hence unquestionable, in a given era: those contingently conforming to "naturalism." That this particular disciplinary matrix or "metaphysical paradigm" should prove methodologically and semantically incommensurable with non-naturalist commitments such as those espoused within Buddhism is to be expected; that it should nevertheless be applied to it as a theory-independent rule is inadmissible.

My terminology here is obviously indebted to Thomas Kuhn, and in particular to his discussions of disciplinary matrices, incommensurability, and there being "no theory-independent way to reconstruct phrases like 'really there'" (Kuhn 1970: 181–187, 198–207, 206).[61] But my point may also be phrased in terms of Quine's insight that "for all its a priori reasonableness, a boundary between analytic and synthetic statements simply has not been drawn. That there is such a distinction to be drawn at all is an unempirical dogma of empiricists, *a metaphysical article of faith*" (Quine 1963: 37, emphases added). In relation to Nāgārjuna, such faith is amply evident in Flanagan's analytic *a priori* reliance on synthetic *a posteriori* facts. But it also plays an important role in Siderits's conventionalist reading of Madhyamaka.[62] This initially entails a consequence Flanagan would surely have done well to take note of; viz., that "if we find a culture that accepts beliefs that are irrational by our lights, and it turns out that those beliefs are warranted by that culture's standards of rational acceptance, we cannot criticize the members of the culture for holding those beliefs" (Siderits 1989: 239). Siderits immediately counters, however, that "This apparent consequence of anti-realism strikes many as clearly unacceptable. . . . [Indeed, it] is absurd, for what makes a proposition true or false is the facts, which do not vary across cultures" (Siderits 1989: 239–240).[63] Now, that facts do not vary across cultures is not only an "unempirical dogma of empiricists" but one that cultural psychologists the world over have documented to be empirically untrue. More relevantly, however, applying such a position to Nāgārjuna's philosophy is highly problematic, and this is so whatever we go on to make of Siderits's proposals to treat Prāsaṅgika Madhyamaka as relativism and Svātantrika Madhyamaka as non-relativistic pluralism. For there can be no doubting that Nāgārjunian "*Śūnyatā*, in breaking up the notion of absolute elements of experience, also breaks up the notion of an absolute analytic synthetic distinction between truths of fact and logic. Our ways of ordering affect what we are willing to call fact" (Waldo 1978: 297).[64] As such, although Siderits's account avoids the blatant ethnocentrism of Flanagan's, and although Siderits is keenly sensitive to "our imperialistic tendencies concerning our own styles of reasoning" (Siderits 1989: 246), nevertheless his presupposition of unvarying facts distinct from theoretical orders shows him to be holding Nāgārjuna to epistemic standards identifiably "independent of the particular practices of [his] culture" (Siderits 1989: 247).

In fact, there is a broader point to be made here regarding the dynamic of "hermeneutical injustice" at work. As coined by Miranda Fricker, this term designates "*the injustice of having some significant area of one's social experience obscured from collective understanding owing to a structural identity prejudice in the collective hermeneutical resource*" (Fricker 2007: 155, emphases original). I think a cogent case can be made for considering non-Western philosophers such as Nāgārjuna as indeed victims of "a kind of structural discrimination" (Fricker 2007: 161) along these lines, whereby they are "*hermeneutically marginalized* . . . a moral-political [notion] indicating subordination and exclusion from some practice that would have value for the participant" (Fricker 2007: 153, emphases original). In their case, the valuable practice from which they have been excluded is the professional practice of philosophy. Obviously, my claim here is to be understood with the important caveat that philosophers such as Nāgārjuna are dead and therefore do not themselves experience any first-person social subordination or marginalization. Rather, it is their *philosophies* which are done injustice, in the sense that these are excluded from instruction in philosophy curricula, their explications are excluded from publication in philosophy journals, and those researching them are excluded from employment in philosophy departments. All told, this appears quite straightforwardly to constitute the kind of "prejudicial exclusion from participation in the spread of knowledge" (Fricker 2007: 162) Fricker identifies as the specifically epistemic significance of hermeneutical injustice. Moreover, the prevalent endeavor to recast the intellectual paradigms of non-Western philosophers into the parameters deemed acceptable to those in contemporary positions of institutional power (i.e., Western academic philosophers) appears to fit Fricker's notion of "*situated hermeneutical inequality*." This designates a concrete situation in which the subject (in my application a non-Western philosopher) "is rendered unable to make communicatively intelligible something which it is particularly in his or her interests to be able to render intelligible" (Fricker 2007: 162); that is, the very content of his or her philosophy.[65] A Western philosopher such as Flanagan who appears committed to opening up professional philosophy to non-Western philosophical ideas may be aghast at this conclusion, but it would certainly seem to follow that by deracinating non-Western ideas in a manner he openly admits dismisses their "low epistemic standards" from the privileged vantage point of the Western episteme, he effectively perpetuates, albeit in more nuanced fashion than during the colonial era itself, the subjugation of the oriental other. After all, if "Modern

European philosophy emerged from a context of epistemic injustice toward non-European societies, and this injustice is perpetuated by legitimating ideas about intellectual superiority of European-American philosophy" (Alcoff 2017: 400), then it would be hard to see how *faux* inclusion *à la* Flanagan—whereby whatever is not recognizably modern/Western/scientific/naturalistic is excluded as "nonsense"—does not embody just such legitimation, and therefore just such injustice.

My point about "*faux* inclusion" maps well onto what Bret Davis terms "a *violence of inclusion* that is only relatively less pernicious than the more obvious *violence of exclusion*" (Davis 2019: 593, emphases original). Drawing on the work of Robert Bernasconi (2003) and Sarah Mattice (2014), Davis argues that non-Western philosophical traditions (and those studying them) find themselves in a double-bind, according to which they are

> either *excluded and ignored* or *admitted and misunderstood*. Either what they (and, full disclosure, much of what I) do is not counted as philosophy and they are sent off to be quarantined in an area studies or religious studies department, or they are invited in on the condition of conformity to pre-existing Western concepts and conceptions of what it means to do philosophy. (Davis 2019: 593, emphases original)

Given the internal dynamics of the field, it is no surprise to find that this is a common complaint among critically minded scholars. Having introduced it via discussion of ethnocentrism, injustice, and inequality, it behooves me to add that Davis's double-bind also ties in with distinctly colonial legacies. For it is, of course, precisely within

> colonial contexts, in which European and American military and economic power has led to conquest, domination and homogenization of other cultural traditions across the globe . . . [that] Western philosophies, despite their historically provincial frameworks and categories, were erected as the standards for universal thought and truth, while the philosophical traditions they confronted were often either measured against Western standards or dismissed as "unphilosophical." (Berger 2017a: 121–122)

In a still more forthright formulation, Jonardon Ganeri asserts that "Colonial rationalists' false claim to neutrality catches the excluded outsider in a vicious dilemma: make your use of reason like ours (in which case what extra value does your philosophy bring to the table?), or admit that you are outside reason and not actually engaged in philosophy at all" (Ganeri 2016a: 136).

Furthermore, on the basis that "some comparative methods perpetuate colonial legacies," Amy Donahue has in fact argued that the Cowherds', for example, is in certain important respects a "colonially problematic methodology" (Donahue 2016a: 597). Indeed, on the Cowherd's own telling, "Donahue contends that some Cowherds exhibit neo-imperialist bias by presupposing a monolithic common sense, presumably that of some oppressor class to which we either belong or owe ideological allegiance" (Cowherds 2016b: 618). For my part, I would hope that my explicit and unambiguous disavowals, earlier and again later, of any orientalist or racist tenor among contemporary scholars should render apparent that there is much in Donahue's critique with which I cannot agree.[66] That said, however, the Cowherds' retort that "this is simply wrong: we made no assumptions whatsoever as to what constitutes common sense" (Cowherds 2016b: 618) is disingenuous—certainly as it applies to the Cowherds themselves but, even more importantly, as it relates to the field at large. For there can be no gainsaying the fact that, as Donahue asserts,

> modern common sense philosophies tend to reinforce two asymmetries between "the West" and "the non-West" when they are extended cross-culturally, and tend to do so even when applied by scholars whose intentions seem to themselves to be sincere, benevolent, and "serious." They tend either to reflexively dismiss certain elements of non-Western philosophies as nonsense (e.g., "dismal"), or to subsume certain elements of non-Western philosophies beneath Western categories that are assumed to be intrinsically sensible. The particularities of these appropriated but still marginal others become irrelevant, while the particularities of Western categories are reinforced and preserved as ahistorical standards of philosophical value. (Donahue 2016b: 624)[67]

In preceding pages, we have in fact seen just such dismissals of those aspects of Buddhist philosophy deemed in advance to be "nonsense," be it insofar as "irrationalist" (Garfield and Priest 2002: 96), "illogical" (Staal 1975: 45), or simply "superstitious nonsense . . . Buddshit" (Flanagan 2013: xi, 210 n. 6). And we have seen more or less overt or covert claims to neutrality and universality along with repeated references to supposedly "intrinsically sensible" "laws of thought" (Gunaratne 1986: 214), "laws of logic" (Westerhoff

2009: 71), inherently unimpeachable "common-sense" (Bugault 1983; Oetke 1990; Hayes 1994), and other suchlike phantasms made by some modern and contemporary scholars. Donahue therefore has a point, and an important one given that "cross-cultural philosophical methodologies that superimpose the subject of modern common sense onto their readings of Madhyamaka philosophical texts will tend to reinforce exclusions of 'others' and asymmetries between 'the West' and 'the non-West' that are historically inextricable from modernity and coloniality" (Donahue 2016b: 623). While my approach in this book differs from Donahue's, not least in that I do not engage in detail with postcolonial or decolonial theory, I perceive that we are united in an effort to ensure that, when scholars do "engage philologically and philosophically with the Madhyamaka tradition not as curators or as acolytes but as interlocutors" (Cowherds 2016b: 617), they—and, of course, we—do so by locating these interlocutors truly as equals: able, as real philosophers are apt, to upturn even our most cherished creeds.

Now, all of this I state by way of an extended methodological caution against uncritically subjecting "others" to "our" modes, methods, and standards of thought.[68] An especially salient issue in this respect concerns answering "the unimaginative question" of the relationship between "religion" and "philosophy" in terms derived from the Greco-Christian/ate complex and therefore definitionally unsuited to the task of describing Indo-Buddhist/-Buddhate thought. For, to cite the characteristically insightful analysis of Ruegg:

> In the Western tradition, philosophy has indeed very often defined itself in opposition to religion, and the fact that scholars of Buddhism may regard the subject of their studies as both a religion and a philosophy has then led to the most extraordinary misunderstanding and confusion. (Ruegg 2010: 219)[69]

Such confusion is the result, not of willful obfuscation, but of the fact that the object under study—Buddhist thought—does not readily conform to the classificatory schemas imposed by the typical subject—the Western thinker—in unquestioning acquiescence to their purported universality. In saying this, my point is not to join what Tillemans calls "a long debate on the question of whether the tetralemma . . . stands as an example of a radical divergence between Asian logics and the classical logic of the West" (Tillemans 1999: 191). For the debate among commentators such as those I cite has not been conducted with regard to the greater or lesser degree of convergence or divergence between two logical systems taken on their respective terms. Rather, it has been concerned to demonstrate the greater or lesser degree of adherence of one (the Asian) to the other (the Western), where this latter has been taken as the principial yardstick to which the material other is to conform. In other words, the debate (if one may still call it that) has been rigged in advance in such a way that the only question remaining—surely as "unimaginative" as any—concerns the extent to which a certain phenomenological analysandum (viz., the religion-philosophy of Buddhism) can be reduced to one of its analytically predetermined categories (viz., philosophy).

In elaborating this point, I can do no better than to cite Ruegg again, who states unequivocally that in Buddhism:

> the philosophical side cannot usually be divorced and treated entirely separately from the religious without a certain more or less arbitrary compartmentalization, for no hard and fast dividing line can normally be drawn between the philosophical and the religious. . . . [Buddhism is] a comprehensive soteriological teaching necessarily involving a philosophical foundation. . . . In short, Buddhism is what is commonly referred to [in Western terms] as a philosophy and a religion. (Ruegg 1967: 5)[70]

Despite this, one need not look hard to still see in effective application the very pernicious distinction Ruegg identified decades ago.[71] Having already detailed at some length the efforts among modern and contemporary scholars of Nāgārjuna to demonstrate that, contrary to appearances, he is after all "logical," I want to shift in this section to a more explicit discussion of the binary opposition at work in such a characterization. For Garfield and Priest, "Nāgārjuna is simply too committed to rigorous analytical argument to be dismissed as a mystic" (Garfield and Priest 2002: 87). This and similar statements,[72] although doubtless intended to do some service to Nāgārjuna (on which more presently), evince that even readers such as Garfield and Priest who propose a dialetheic interpretation of the tetralemma (and thus one at odds with more classically oriented logical approaches) have been led astray by what Panikkar refers to in his essay "Aporias in the Comparative Philosophy of Religion" as "presuppositions."[73] There, Panikkar proposes "a fundamental distinction between 'assumption' and 'presupposition' " according to which an assumption is defined as "the conscious axioms that I set in order to study further," while a presupposition "is unconscious . . . underneath my constructions at their basis (supposition—*subponere*); they are also sent 'before' my examination, as it were, and before my eyes, so that they allow me to examine and see where I am standing (*prae-suppositio*)" (Panikkar 1980: 374). Though this final phrase appears to confer a positive role upon presuppositions, it is important to note that, on Panikkar's own formulation, "I am not aware of my presuppositions and take them so much for granted that I neither see them nor detect their possible problemacity" (Panikkar 1980: 374). Indeed, it is only through interaction with an "other who, although unaware of his own presuppositions, causes me to see mine by questioning a presupposition he cannot accept, and vice-versa" (Panikkar 1980: 374), that presuppositions are accepted (and thus turned into assumptions) or rejected (thereby modifying one's standpoint).

Now, in applying Panikkar's distinction here, I would like to nuance it by problematizing his characterization of assumptions as conscious and presuppositions as unconscious. Presuppositions in Panikkar's sense can, I propose, be as much conscious as unconscious, for I take the important point about them to be that they are unquestioned, or rather, from the perspective of those who hold them, unquestionable. (Besides which, it would be rather foolhardy for me to be claiming insight as to what is or is not conscious in a given scholar's mind!) One way in which presuppositions, in this sense, are evidently at work in the scholarly literature on Nāgārjuna is in the maintenance of the logical/rational/philosophical versus illogical/irrational/mystical dichotomy. Surely, whether Nāgārjuna is or is not a "mystic," like the related question of whether or not (or the extent to which) he is or is not a "Buddhist" philosopher as opposed to a philosopher *tout court*, is not only alien to the Indian and Buddhist traditions in which he lived and wrote but also utterly uninformative as to the worth of his work.[74] Thus, Garfield and Priest's comment that "none of the important commentarial traditions in Asia, however much they disagree in other respects, regard him in this light"; that is, "as simply a mystic or an irrationalist of some kind" (Garfield and Priest 2002: 87), says very little, if anything at all, for, of course no one of the classical thought traditions of Asia regarded Nāgārjuna as a mystic: they did not even know the term. Nor do the extant debates among those thought traditions regarding the in/adequacy of conceptual thought, of language, or of meditative absorption, for example, to arrive at truth/reality (*satya*) map unproblematically onto such a "philosopher vs. mystic" paradigm. What renders this paradigm not just another assumption but a presupposition in this case is not its unconscious avowal—the fact that Garfield et al. discuss the binary explicitly puts paid to that idea. Rather, it is that they presuppose it to be a binary opposition not as a "conscious axiom" but as the very function according to which to judge Nāgārjuna's thought. It is as if they were constructing a two-dimensional graph on a standard Cartesian coordinate system, taking "philosopher" and "mystic" unquestionedly and unquestionably as real variables, and trying to bring Nāgārjuna as close as possible to the "philosopher" axis.

The acknowledgment of one's own historicity (including one's own prejudices) is, of course, a necessary feature of critically aware scholarship. Yet, as the multifarious examples of occidento-centric perspectives I cite should show, too often "we" position "ourselves" at such a remove from the author at hand that we effectively lose all or most of his/her perspective altogether. In the debate between Garfield and Huntington as to "the Mādhyamika trick,"[75] for example, Garfield takes Huntington to task for Huntington's own use of argument in arguing that Nāgārjuna eschews all argumentation. Garfield presents an alternative approach, one that Huntington could have taken but did not take, according to which Huntington, like the Nāgārjuna he claims to speak for, presents no arguments for the conclusions he nevertheless hopes will be endorsed by his interlocutors. For, as Garfield points out, "Huntington is speaking to *us*": "21st Century interpreters of Nāgārjuna and Candrakīrti" (Garfield 2008: 514, emphasis original).[76] Garfield shows that such non-argumentation would inevitably lead to "an analytical dead-end" wherein we would simply "give up" the practice of reading and reasoning. Why? Because, of course, we would

> have no *reason* to believe [our anti-rationalist reading] ourselves, and no *reason* to believe that the fact that reason is self-subverting, or even that the fact, were it so, that reason is *always* self-subverting would be a good reason to reject reason. All we could say is that an argument we now regard as pointless has caused us to reject arguments.

Garfield rejects this approach because "As interpreters, we are obligated at least to the cogency of our own interpretive arguments. But we are also obligated to maximize the cogency of the texts we read." Huntington's reading of Nāgārjuna possesses no such cogency, for "cogency is hard to make sense of without a background assumption of rationality."

Throughout this passage, and the rest of his paper, Garfield unequivocally situates himself and his audience as "interpreters": twenty-first century scholarly, and primarily Western, ones at that.[77] His first response to the approach he sees Huntington to be taking is to ask "what should be *our* response *as interpreters* to this position?"[78] His argument that "to the extent that *we are interpreters*, and are comparing readings of texts, this [approach of Huntington's] leads us to give up" is buttressed, as already cited, by his understanding that, "as interpreters," we are obliged to the search for cogency in our own interpretations of texts as well as in these texts themselves. In the following paragraph, Garfield again situates us "as interpreters" who "read texts for *reasons*" (emphasis original), and precises that "in particular, *as philosophers*, we expect to learn from the texts we address." This we would be unable to do from Nāgārjuna and his *oeuvre* were we to grant Huntington's reading of the text, for it could not "be meaningful *to us* . . . be persuasive *to us*" as "this demand [for meaning, for persuasion] imposes a presumption of rationality." Garfield thus concludes his critique of Huntington's hermeneutical approach to the effect that "there are no good grounds for us *as readers and interpreters* to check reason or logic at the door when reading Madhyamaka, even if we conceive of ourselves *as good mādhyamika readers*."

Now, it may seem obvious, but I believe it to be of the utmost importance in this context to point out that Nāgārjuna was not speaking to *us* at all. Nāgārjuna was not addressing us twenty-first-century "interpreters, philosophers, readers" (to use Garfield's designations), but rather primarily the fellow Buddhists, and secondarily the fellow Indian religious thinkers, of his time. Though we may know nothing with any certainty as to their biographies, we are safe at least in asserting (based on the textual data we do have) that these contemporaries were no academic scholars interested merely in articulating the most cogent interpretation of a given text, but first and foremost religionists devoted to the one task incumbent upon them regardless of their sectarian affiliation: liberation. It is to these interlocutors—doubtless intellectually astute ones given the subtlety with which Nāgārjuna wrote, but primarily intellectually astute *Buddhists* nevertheless—that Nāgārjuna's text is addressed.

I stated that this is of the utmost importance to recall because I believe it drastically alters our understanding of what Nāgārjuna's text is doing, or at least is trying to do. From this perspective, the fact that Nāgārjuna does not make sense to "us," as logically minded analysts, in no way detracts from the coherence of his position within the context of his overall philosophico-religious (read: Buddhist) project.[79] If we take the alternative, and predominant, approach, according to which Nāgārjuna must "be meaningful *to us* . . . be persuasive *to us*" (Garfield 2008: 515, emphases added), we may as well go the whole hog and denounce Nāgārjuna as making no sense to us as English readers on the basis that he wrote in Sanskrit.

Of course, the inclination to demonstrate the logicality of Nāgārjuna to us, "as interpreters," on the part of a Garfield is motivated less by any racist security in the superiority of Western systems of thought[80] than by the felt need to have Nāgārjuna taken seriously by *us*—as Western philosophers—as a philosopher. Similar sentiments are felt by other scholars in the field, as when Christian Coseru, for example, states, "I am always happy to see mainstream philosophers take an interest in what is being said in the name of Buddhist philosophy" (Coseru 2014).[81] He goes on, however, to take Priest's dialetheic characterization of Nāgārjuna's *catuṣkoṭi* to task, and this not for any perceived invalidity of Priest's account but simply because it leads to "the notion that Buddhist philosophy is full of contradictions." Given this characterization, Coseru laments: "And so here we go again: Eastern thought is intuitive and mystical and Western philosophy is rational and argumentative, and the twain shall never meet." In the stead of Priest's contradictory and ineffably minded Nāgārjuna, Coseru urges us to turn to Westerhoff's account of Nāgārjuna's critique of Nyāya epistemology. "This," he announces, "is not a Madhyamaka wrapped up in paradox, but one *we* can make sense of" (emphasis added). There is no need, of course, for Coseru to explain just who his "we" is referring to.

In such apologetic attempts to render Nāgārjuna comprehensible to fellow contemporary Western scholars and philosophers, what I find most noteworthy is the aforementioned failure to appreciate and acknowledge the obvious fact that Nāgārjuna's intended audience was not comprised of "us" but of his fellow ancient Buddhist and non-Buddhist Indians. Surely it would be absurd for *us* to write treatises attempting to conform to the religious assumptions, philosophical criteria, and literary canons operative in some far distant future land we had not ever heard of. Yet that seems to be the prevailing demand made upon Nāgārjuna: that he, a Buddhist philosopher living and writing in India some two thousand years ago, make sense according to the intellectual frameworks we twenty-first-century Westerners take to be normative.[82] That this characteristic of contemporary scholarship, even in the twenty-first century, is not a neutral practice but one grounded in more-or-less unacknowledged presuppositions as to the superiority of "our" intellectual models is further evinced by the fact that the impetus toward logical justification as based on explicitly Western logical frameworks coupled with (effective, if not avowed) disregard for indigenous religiosophical paradigms such as those within which Nāgārjuna himself lived, wrote, and practiced, is only a one-way street. Nāgārjuna needs to abide by our road-rules, as it were, while the converse is distinctly not the case: the thought of present or past philosophers in the Western canon is not subjected to interpretation and evaluation in accordance with criteria operative in the Buddhist context, say, or for that matter according to any other criterial frames foreign to their world. Why so? Are we really, still, so assured of our own access to truth that we remain content to assess "others" by their ability to see what we see, but see no need to subject our own worldview to their perspective? And are we really so blinded by the invisibility of our own presuppositions that we even go so far as to "conceive of ourselves *as good mādhyamika readers*" when we do so? Besides which, if practically no Western philosopher satisfies the "secularity condition," according to which philosophy must be "religiously disinterested," then why should Nāgārjuna?

This last point leads me to observe that, despite their evident acute awareness of the fallacy of the position that religiosity does not characterize Western philosophy,[83] scholars such as Garfield, Coseru, and many others concerned with Buddhist philosophy nevertheless apply this fallacy to Nāgārjuna insofar as they insist upon reading Nāgārjuna in exclusivist fashion as "philosophical-*not*-religious." But while a demonstration of Nāgārjuna's philosophicality may serve to undermine some orientalist stereotypes among some Western philosophers convinced (unreasonably) of the areligiosity of their own tradition, this strategy must surely count as a rather disingenuous expedient means given that it is being deployed by scholars who also forcefully argue *against* the conviction that "Western philosophy is independent of religion" (Garfield 2002: 252). This strategy is mistaken substantively in that it does not serve to understand Nāgārjuna, whose philosophical arguments are inextricably interwoven with his religious aims. Consequently, efforts to remove the "religious" elements from his "philosophical" works either leave him unintelligent to others or unintelligible to himself. It is also mistaken methodologically in that it applies a norm (of religious disinterestedness) developed in twentieth-century Western analytical philosophy to a second-century Indian Buddhist thinker. Moreover, given that this norm in fact is fallacious insofar as it paints a picture of ancient, medieval, premodern, modern, and contemporary European and Euro-derived Christian and Christianate philosophers and philosophies whitewashed of their religious elements, surely the better, if admittedly more difficult, long-term approach for scholars (such as myself) committed to studying Buddhist philosophy as philosophy (and to having it recognized as such) would be to demonstrate, first, the historically determinative place of religion in the Western philosophical canon; acknowledge, second, the historically determinative place of religion in the Buddhist philosophical canon; and on this twin basis attempt, third, to understand the Buddhist philosophical canon's contributions to philosophy, be it Buddhist, Western, or of whatsoever provenance.[84] Only thus, I propose, can a full understanding and honest appraisal of the philosophical contribution of Buddhist philosophy be achieved; and only thus can its fruits be meaningfully then applied (if that is the project) to problems in Western philosophy.

Closely related to the failure to accept Nāgārjuna on his own terms is the twin failure to acknowledge that our terms, even our logical terms, are historically and culturally specific, and thereupon to adapt our use of these terms to his so as to enable meaningful dialogue and learning. After all, Nāgārjuna is unable to make the step across, as it were, the intellectual divide separating us from him. One, he never knew us; and two, he is now dead and so can never come to know us. But we, endowed with both our own intellectual apparatus (including the meta-hermeneutical facility to locate ourselves within our given milieu) as well as the linguistic and other scholarly tools required for entry into the Nāgārjunian *Weltanshauung*, are not so disabled. It is thus incumbent upon us, as interpreters, as philosophers, as scholars of religion, to read *Nāgārjuna* (in all his polyvalence), not what our ideologically predetermined disciplinary divisions would make of him.

To make sense of texts such as the MK in the dual contexts of their writerly and our readerly compositions, a shift needs to take place in our understanding of Philosophy *vis-à-vis* Religion. I capitalize these terms to draw attention to their accepted status as discrete fields of human life, susceptible to discrete *modi operandi* and, as such, studied in discrete departments of academic institutions. So long as philosophers perceive their endeavor as constitutively distinct from that of religionists, and of religious studies scholars, we will remain ill equipped to shoulder our share, the reader's share, of the compositional burden. And, to elaborate on a point I touched upon in the preceding paragraph, we will remain unable to actually *learn* from the texts we study and write about, even if—or rather especially when—they necessitate a rethinking of our intellectual structures. Given the richness of the material with which we are concerned, that would be "bereft of reason" indeed.

2

Logical, Buddhological, Buddhist

A Critical Study of the Tetralemma

Being, non-being, both being and non-being, and neither
Have been mentioned
Are not all named medicines
In accordance with illnesses?

—Āryadeva (third century CE), *Catuḥśataka* 8:20[1]

2.1. Matters and Methods

This chapter is both a study of the philosophy of the Buddhist philosopher Nāgārjuna and a study of the philosophical study of the philosophy of the Buddhist philosopher Nāgārjuna. Already, then, there seems to be a lot of philosophy involved . . . and this is precisely the issue at hand. For as will become clear in the course of this exposition, I am concerned with what I perceive to be an important stipulative circumscription on the part of certain philosophically minded, and more specifically analytically trained, contemporary scholars as to how to read Nāgārjuna's use of the *catuṣkoṭi* or tetralemma in his major work, the *Fundamental Verses on the Middle Way* (*Mūlamadhyamaka-kārikā*), and more broadly how to interpret Nāgārjuna's (religio-)philosophy as a whole. As already argued in Chapter 1, and as further exemplified here in the following, this methodological approach is circumscriptive in that it delimits what it deems to be a valid reading of Nāgārjuna to a single hermeneutical lens, which it stipulates, furthermore, as that of logic/reason/rationality.

While ample instances of this approach in general have been given in Chapter 1, and numerous more specifically related to the tetralemma will be provided in what follows, it is perhaps worthwhile here at the outset to delineate the overall thrust of and rationale for it. In doing so, I can do no better than to recapitulate from Chapter 1 certain particularly apposite and

Buddhism Between Religion and Philosophy. Rafal K. Stepien, Oxford University Press. © Oxford University Press 2024.
DOI: 10.1093/oso/9780197771303.003.0002

lucid formulations by Jay Garfield, who is not only one of the most prolific exponents of the methodology I am describing, but one unusually sensitive to and forthright about what its application involves. Thus, Garfield states unambiguously that "reason is . . . a transcendental condition of interpretation both in the sense that we can only vindicate an interpretation to the extent that we read the texts as rational, and we can only justify a reading rationally" (Garfield 2015: 332). This rationality model of interpretation, according to which rationality is to be used to sustain a rational reading of what thereby turns out to be a rational text, is then applied to Nāgārjuna in order to conclude that "Nāgārjuna is not an irrationalist. He is committed to the canons of rational argument and criticism. He is not a mystic" (Garfield and Priest 2002: 96). In general terms, this methodology is a clear instantiation of self-fulfillingly circular argumentation, for it explicitly selects its objects on the basis of its own predetermined criteria, and proceeds to interpret them as (unsurprisingly) in accordance with these very criteria. Those objects (such as the *catuṣkoṭi*) not *prima facie* conformant with the criteria are either dismissed as outside the purview of its operation (e.g., as "irrationalist . . . mystic") or forcibly reinterpreted so as to fit within the criteria after all ("committed to the canons of rational argument and criticism"). So much we have seen earlier.

In the specific case of Nāgārjuna's tetralemma, although there have been some scholars who have dismissed it as illogical,[2] the predominant tendency has been to "rescue" Nāgārjuna by forcing him, and it, through the predetermined parameters of Western logic.[3] Typically, this has taken the form of the Greek-derived classical logic constitutive of the first-order propositional and predicate calculus.[4] Lately, however, deviant logics such as paraconsistency have also been applied to Nāgārjuna's tetralemma, most conspicuously by Garfield and Priest (2002, 2009).[5] As I have previously stated with reference to these scholars, however (see §1.3), regardless of the details of their diverging approaches, they are united in accepting the universal sovereignty of "logic," "reason," or "rationality" as a neutral, objective criterion by which to gauge the validity of a given claim or the cogency of a given intellectual system regardless of its historical locus.

In contradistinction to this approach, I argue here that to interpret Nāgārjuna's *catuṣkoṭi* as instantiating the working out of rational solutions to rational problems through the exclusive, or at very least definitive, operation of rationality is deeply misguided. To put this another way, I am not proposing a way of reading Nāgārjuna that does not make *any* sense. But

I am proposing that reading Nāgārjuna so as to make him make *rational* sense is not the only way of reading him, on the understanding that rationality is but one of numerous faculties with which we are endowed. Contra, it seems, the predominant bulk of scholars in the field, I do not hierarchize these faculties on some implicitly or explicitly Platonic model according to which (as per the allegory of the *Phaedrus*) reason characteristically seeks to impose itself as the charioteer controlling and arbitrating over its unruly others, and is right to do so.

In this sense, the present chapter may be considered a development of the preceding one, wherein I launched an overt critique of the overall project I call "philosophizing Nāgārjuna." In the present case, I am concerned to apply this methodological intervention specifically to Nāgārjuna's tetralemma, arguing in the process for the untenability of interpretations of the tetralemma designed to philosophize Nāgārjuna into logicality—these being, as I demonstrate at length, the predominant approaches in the field. This will ultimately lead me to adumbrate and justify an alternative approach; one that I argue is just as methodologically legitimate, and in fact better adequated to the hermeneutical endeavor of describing Nāgārjuna's thought taken in its entirety. That is, I aim to outline an understanding of the *catuṣkoṭi* that takes it not as an abstract object of rational inquiry dissected from its philosophico-religious context, and/or as adapted to the disciplinary conventions of contemporary academic philosophy, but as an organic part of Nāgārjuna's overall Buddhist project. Herein lies what I referred to earlier as the *importance* of the rationalist stipulative circumscription: While an ethically indifferent, intellectually hermetic disengagement from the pressing problems of worldly suffering may make sense to an armchair philosopher, the attribution of such an abstracted attitude to the Buddhist Nāgārjuna, avowedly and actively involved as he demonstrably is in the soterially motivated project of alleviating and ultimately eradicating suffering, is not only textually unjustified but tantamount to a radical misreading of his entire religiosophical mission.

The further question of whether one takes such a (mis)reading to be charitable or uncharitable depends on whether one takes philosophy to be principally of theoretical or practical import. In the former case, one will presumably esteem the excision of what is taken to be adventitious religious content from the philosophy of Nāgārjuna to be beneficial insofar as it (purportedly) renders his arguments more cogent. In the latter case, one will presumably deem such abstraction of the "ineradicably" religious teachings of

Nāgārjuna to be deleterious insofar as it (purportedly) evacuates his tenets of their instrumental force. As will become all the more apparent in the final section, on "The Buddhist Tetralemma," my sympathies lie with the latter position, for I consider religiosity to be an ineliminable, integral part of Nāgārjuna's philosophy. That this should be so, moreover, I see as no reason to consider him any lesser a philosopher . . . but that brings up general issues as to the relation between religion and philosophy already adumbrated earlier and beyond the scope of my specific mandate in the present chapter.

That said, I feel it incumbent upon me to add that, to the extent that I am able to disassociate myself from my substantive views, I am in fact willing to navigate an ecumenical middle path through these methodological straits. For while my criticisms of the rationalist reading are apt to be taken as confirming my preference for the latter, religiously inclusive, reading, I want to emphasize here that it is not principally the rationalism of the rationalist reading to which I object but rather its exclusivism. For I do maintain that Nāgārjuna maintains that reasoned argumentation is an efficacious means toward the soteriological end of liberation. Corollary to this, I do not maintain that Nāgārjuna maintains that rationality is inherently inimical to attainment of this goal. Both of these twin positions are supported by the evident existence of reasoned argumentation throughout Nāgārjuna's corpus. To put this squarely in the context of my present concerns, I am not saying that the logical tetralemma propounded by the preponderant body of Buddhologists is not, or is not assimilable to, what I am calling the Buddhist tetralemma.[6] Rather, what I am concerned to argue here is that rationality is not the only (or the most efficacious) such means for Nāgārjuna, and that (therefore) rationality is not the only (or the most insightful) hermeneutical tool for comprehending Nāgārjuna. It is to these arguments—of matter and of method respectively—that the present section title refers.

To contextualize my position within the existing body of scholarship on Nāgārjuna's thought, and on the *catuṣkoṭi* in particular, it should be apparent already that I will have to criticize, and hence summarize, some of the more important contributions in the field.[7] This I have endeavored to do during the course of elaborating my own account in a bid both to avoid presenting a discrete "literature review" most readers would (be well-advised to) skip, and to critically engage with fellow exegetes even as I present them. In introducing my critique, I can do no better than to quote the cautionary words of David Seyfort Ruegg formulated precisely in the context of a discussion of studies of logical aspects of the *catuṣkoṭi*:

> A problematic has thus tended to be imposed on Buddhist thought in a form that does not in fact seem to be essential to the questions with which the Buddhist thinkers were actually concerned. It would seem obvious that such prejudgment in terms of another problematic imported from elsewhere is a rather ethnocentric procedure inasmuch as it is determined, not by the system of thought being studied, but by the modern analyst's culture and presuppositions. Hermeneutically it may be that such a tendency is difficult to avoid, but the difficulties require to be noted and taken careful account of. (Ruegg 1977: 52)

I will initially tarry (§2.2: "The Logical Tetralemma") upon three such hermeneutic techniques commonly encountered in the secondary literature. These are what I call the Mereological Interpretation (§2.2.1), according to which Nāgārjuna's tetralemma affirms a given quality of one part and negates it of another part of a given mereologically divisible subject; the Modal Interpretation (§2.2.2), according to which the tetralemma affirms a given quality of a subject in one respect or mode and negates it in another respect or mode; and, finally, the Qualitative Interpretation (§2.2.3), according to which it affirms a given quality of a subject and negates another quality altogether. In the course of my exposition, I will argue that these three (inter-related) readings are neither textually justified nor consonant with Nāgārjuna's explicitly stated soteriological aims. Following this, in §2.3 ("The Buddhological Tetralemma") I will provide further demonstration of the near ubiquity of the rationalizing mission, if I may so call it, within recent and contemporary European- and Chinese-language scholarship on the *catuṣkoṭi*.

The use of Chinese-language scholarship on Nāgārjuna is perhaps itself worth pausing upon given the near complete absence of it in European-language scholarship at large. In fact, apart from a desire to convey some of the substantive worth of the Chinese-language interpretations I do detail, I am also motivated to engage with this material for programmatic reasons. For it is clear that Western scholarship on the *catuṣkoṭi*, and more broadly on Nāgārjuna, Madhyamaka, and Buddhist philosophy as a whole, has been inordinately dominated by Indo-Tibetan perspectives. As a particularly conspicuous instance of this, I call as witness the symposium on "Madhyamaka and Methodology" that was held at Smith College (2010) in response to two articles by Huntington (2007) and Garfield (2008) on Nāgārjuna's stated abandonment of all views. At this three-day event, twenty Madhyamaka scholars (almost all based in North America) were invited to thrash out their understandings of how to go about reading Nāgārjuna's statements in this regard, and more broadly to clarify the methods by which the scholarly study of Madhyamaka philosophy should optimally proceed. Despite this turnout, not a single scholar dealt in any depth with Chinese interpretations of Nāgārjuna, be they classical, modern, or contemporary. Classical Indian and Tibetan commentators were called upon repeatedly, to the exclusion of all other Buddhist voices—a fact I take to be lamentable but unsurprising given the typical segregation of Buddhist scholars into either one of what are called the "Indo-Tibetan" and the "Sino-Japanese" worlds. One of the speakers, Peter Gregory, actually called attention to this fact during the symposium, stating that he would have liked to see some Chinese perspectives on Nāgārjuna included, but admitted that people who cross the disciplinary divide between Indo-Tibetan and Sino-Japanese are hard to find. Although the survey of Chinese scholarly perspectives I provide herein is far indeed from comprehensive, I hope that it may constitute an initial foray in this direction.[8] Apart from satisfying the methodological desideratum of including perspectives not hitherto adequately incorporated into the canon of Western Madhyamaka scholarship, I hope that my demonstration of the prevalence of the logicalizing tendency I have identified among East Asian exegetes too will prevent any orientalizing notions positing some kind of absolute disjunction between supposedly "insider" Eastern perspectives and "outsider" Western ones.[9]

Finally, §2.4 ("The Buddhist Tetralemma") is devoted to the formulation of an alternative conception of the *catuṣkoṭi*—one that is in accord with the soterial mission espoused by Nāgārjuna. To this end, I will survey some of the relevant passages from the Nāgārjunian philosophical corpus that state this aim with especial clarity, and I will conclude by proposing to read the tetralemma as functioning within what thereby turns out to be, on my understanding, a coherent religiosophical system. The critical stance I detail in the chapter as a whole will in turn inform my positive reading of the tetralemma in the chapter that follows.

Of course, the fraught yet fruitful relationships between argumentatively demonstrated conclusions and soteriologically beneficent truths within philosophico-religious primary sources, between philologically accurate and philosophically insightful textual reconstruction as methodological-cum-disciplinary approaches to their study, and among the former and the latter, go well beyond the disciplinary confines of (the study of) Nāgārjuna's *catuṣkoṭi*, of Madhyamaka philosophy, or even of Buddhism. It is hoped, therefore, that the arguments mobilized here may prove of benefit well beyond these fields.

2.2. The Logical Tetralemma

Prior to embarking on the properly hermeneutical project of proposing a particular understanding of the *catuṣkoṭi*, it would be well to describe it as neutrally as possible. This is not as easy as it would seem, and not only because all avowedly neutral descriptions are irrevocably already interpretations.[10] In the case of the tetralemma, my difficulties to (simply) describe it are compounded by its paradoxical nature . . . though, paradoxically enough, perhaps my task is made the easier after all by this very feature. After all, etymologically speaking, a "neutral" stance is one that adopts "neither one nor other" (*ne-utrum*) position of a given op-position—and we will eventually see that this is a uniquely adequate approach to describing the tetralemma.

In any case, briefly stated, the *catuṣkoṭi* utters all four of the logical positions available to classical Indian logicians.[11] Thus, for example, Nāgārjuna opens the first chapter of the MK with:

> Not from itself nor from another
> Not from both nor without cause
> Does any entity whatsoever
> Anywhere arise[12]

This constitutes a negative version of the tetralemma that can be formalized as:

> (-a) not 'x is A'
> (-b) not 'x is non-A'
> (-c) not 'x is both A and non-A'
> (-d) not 'x is neither A nor non-A'

Such negative versions of the tetralemma preponderate in the MK, also occurring, for example, at 12:1, 22:11–12, 27:13, and 27:15–18.[13] My formulation is designed to convey the understanding that the negation function involved in the negative tetralemma is external (negating the proposition as a whole), as opposed to internal (negating some component/s of the proposition).

The positive analogue of the *catuṣkoṭi* would run:

> (a) x is A
> (b) x is non-A
> (c) x is both A and non-A
> (d) x is neither A nor non-A.[14]

There is only one occurrence of this positive version of the tetralemma in the MK, at 18:8:

> All is real and is not real
> Is both real and not real
> Is neither real nor not real
> This is the teaching of the Buddha[15]

An inordinate amount of academic effort has been expended on "rescuing" Nāgārjuna through various means from the evident violation of the law of non-contradiction (and that of the excluded middle) that the tetralemma entails—or, on such analyses, at least appears to entail. Although such a logicalist stance enjoyed something of a heyday in the mid to late twentieth century among analytically minded scholars such as R. D. Gunaratne, K. N. Jayatilleke, P. T. Raju, and Richard Robinson,[16] it remains very much alive today. It is thus typical to read interpreters proposing a certain solution to the "riddle" of the tetralemma or, when faced with a clear contradiction in Nāgārjuna's text, immediately asking, "How can this interpretation be avoided?" (Westerhoff 2006: 371/2009: 71), without, of course, explaining *why* it should be a riddle or to be avoided at all. Thus, for example, Robinson states that a certain earlier "solution of the riddle doesn't make sense" (Robinson 1957: 305),[17] while Shōryū Katsura states that he "would like to propose another solution to the riddle [of the third lemma at e.g., MK:25:17] by applying the theory of two types of negation" (Katsura 2000: 203).[18] To call the tetralemma a riddle straightforwardly implies not only that there is a (single) correct "solution" to it, but also presumably that it amounts to nothing more than an intellectual diversion akin to a crossword puzzle or other word game. That this would hardly be consonant with the profoundly philosophical tenor of, let alone the earnestly religious motivation for, Nāgārjuna's text barely merits mentioning. For, in turning now to the three means I have identified by which the "riddle" of the tetralemma has been logically "solved," I want to state what I take to be an incontrovertible fact: The overarching aim of Nāgārjuna's religiosophy—indeed, of Buddhist thought as whole—is not to solve a riddle but to dissolve suffering. Any interpretation that discounts this can be considered incomplete at best, and at worst not relevant to its purported object at all.

2.2.1. The Mereological Interpretation

Jayatilleke provides perhaps the classic example of an interpretation of the *catuṣkoṭi* that argues for its logical validity on the basis that its lemmata refer to varying mereological parts of a given subject. Jayatilleke understandably concentrates his reading on the third lemma, since this constitutes an apparently obvious violation of the law of non-contradiction he is concerned to maintain. For him, (c) is not contradictory because he interprets it to state "S is partly P and partly non-P" (Jayatilleke 1967: 79). This interpretation is seconded by Alex Wayman (1977), who uses it in the context of MK:27:17–18, which says of a person:

> If one part were divine
> And another part human
> It would be both permanent and impermanent
>
> But that is not acceptable
> 'Both permanent and impermanent':
> If this were established
> Then 'neither permanent nor impermanent'
> Would likewise be established[19]

We need not concern ourselves with the latter verse here, but what is of relevance is to note that Wayman can only sustain his (and by extension Jayatilleke's) interpretation by reading "*ekadeśaḥ*" (one part) as "the same place" so as to then claim "Nāgārjuna does not here deny an alternative of 'both the permanent and the impermanent' per se; he denies this for one and the same place" (Wayman 1977: 7).[20] That is, Nāgārjuna is apparently denying that permanence and impermanence are to be found in the same place or part of a given object, which would mean that they could both, though binary opposites, be logically denied of that object. Robinson draws on Kumārajīva's Chinese translation of the MK (中論: T 1564) and the commentary therein by Qingmu in support of the same reading, according to which "one part is divine and one part is human" (Robinson 1978: 57).[21] While such an interpretation of Nāgārjuna's position clearly avoids logical self-contradiction, it runs into the inconvenient objection that Nāgārjuna himself rejects it outright in the final *pāda* here ("But that is not acceptable"). He even reiterates this rejection a few verses later in a structurally analogous passage:

> If one part were finite
> And another part infinite
> The world would be both finite and infinite
> But that is not acceptable[22]

It is "not acceptable" (*na yujyate*) or "not so" (不然) in both MK:27:17 and MK:27:25 because Nāgārjuna's purpose in these verses is explicitly to demonstrate the absurdity of holding that one part of a subject could be A and another non-A. As he goes on to declare explicitly, "this is non-sensical."[23]

The Mereological Interpretation is no mere historical curio, as it has recently been advocated by Jan Westerhoff. Given that "it is straightforward to assert that a chess board is black and not black if we mean by this that some parts of it are black and others are not black," Westerhoff proposes that "on this reading the contradiction [in the third lemma] is avoided by relativizing of the two properties involved to different mereological parts" (Westerhoff 2009: 82). Westerhoff goes on to graft this reading onto "the case of the tetralemma applied to causation" (Westerhoff 2009: 83) (apparently a textually unattested positive analogue to MK:1:1), such that "the third alternative constitutes a compromise between the first and the second: it says that things are partly self-caused and partly caused by other objects." The mereological purport of the crucial term "partly" here is immediately brought out: "But this possibility obviously does not imply the first alternative ["that things are caused exclusively by themselves"], any more than saying that a chess board is partly black and partly white implies that it is black all over" (Westerhoff 2009: 83–84).

In general terms, this would all be unproblematic, as it is self-evidently true that it is a mistake to take a statement relating to a part of an object as relating to the whole of it. What is strange about Westerhoff's discussion here is that in the preceding pages he considers and clearly rejects its applicability to Nāgārjuna's tetralemma. Specifically, he states that an interpretation of the third lemma according to which it "is to mean that some [objects] are white and some are not white . . . does not fit well with the employment of the tetralemma by Nāgārjuna" (Westerhoff 2009: 81). The crucial admission is that "given that Nāgārjuna wants to inquire into the applicability of particular concepts to objects *tout court*, we should also consider the four alternatives as giving alternative ways of the application of particular concepts to objects *tout court*, rather than as implying their application to some objects but not to others" (Westerhoff 2009: 82). Now, if Nāgārjuna meant the tetralemma to apply to "objects *tout court*"—if, that is, he did not mean it to apply to separate objects—then *a fortiori* he could not mean it to apply to the same object *taken as* separate objects. For to take the third lemma as applying alternately to the black and the white squares of a chess board is precisely not to take the chess board as an object *tout court*, but rather to take it as a juxtaposition of separate objects (black squares and white squares).[24]

In initially admitting that the Mereological Interpretation of Nāgārjuna's tetralemma is not textually justified, yet then going on to effectively use it anyway, Westerhoff presents a conspicuously clear case of ideologically motivated misreading; a reading motivated, that is, by the overwhelming imperative to banish all apparent illogicality from Nāgārjuna.[25] In fact, in the course of his chapter on the tetralemma, Westerhoff actually utilizes all three of the techniques I have identified in his effort to render it logical. Immediately following the passage I have just discussed, he proposes a version of the Modal Interpretation, stating that "the same result can be achieved by relativizing to different respects or perspectives under which the object is considered" (Westerhoff 2009: 82). And he frequently subscribes to the distinction between *prasajya* and *paryudāsa* negations invoked by Katsura (2000: 203–205) in support of a Qualitative Interpretation, as when he states that "*we have to assume* that the two occurrences of 'not'. . . [in MK:18:10] do not in fact refer to the same concept of negation" (Westerhoff 2006: 371/2009: 71, emphases added). That these interpretations are not merely considered but actively espoused by Westerhoff is made clear too, as where he declares that "these kinds of relativizing interpretations *are* present in Nāgārjuna" (Westerhoff 2009: 82, emphasis added). In the absence of textual support, these varied attempts to explain the *catuṣkoṭi* "entirely within the framework of classical logic" (Westerhoff 2006: 393/2009: 90) must be dismissed as efforts to comprehend Nāgārjuna in his own terms, and taken rather as apologetic attempts to justify him to inimically minded, analytically trained academic philosophers.

2.2.2. The Modal Interpretation

Jayatilleke states that "instead of *partly* we may substitute . . . synonymous expressions such as 'in some respects'" (Jayatilleke 1967: 79), and it is to this related interpretation that I now turn. As Frits Staal has correctly observed, "the principle of noncontradiction . . . applies only when both the affirmative and the negative clause are held to be valid *in the same respect*" (Staal 1975: 43, emphases original). It is for this reason that a host of scholars has sought to interpret the various lemmata of the tetralemma as referring to a given quality in various respects or modes.

Perhaps the most common technique along this line of interpretation has been to read the tetralemma, and particularly the positive version found at MK:18:8, as expounding a progressive or graded teaching. The notion here is more or less that the four lemmata are graded such that the first is true for an uninitiate, the second so for a neophyte, the third for an expert, and the final one for an enlightened (or near-enlightened) being. This reading finds classical support in the *Akutobhayā*, the earliest of all known Madhyamaka commentaries to the MK—and one traditionally (though dubiously) ascribed to Nāgārjuna himself—which "describes the four positions in the Buddha's teaching mentioned in [MK:18:8] as successive graded stages (*rim pa* = *krama*)" (Ruegg 1977: 37).[26] Candrakīrti (c. 600–650) too appears to adopt such an interpretation, for in his authoritative commentary to the MK, the *Prasannapadā Madhyamakavṛttiḥ*, he takes Nāgārjuna's use of *anuśāsana* at MK:18:8, and particularly of the prefix *anu-* ("progressive," "fitted"), "either as a teaching that proceeds progressively (*anupūrvyā śāsanam*) in introducing its recipients to reality (*tattvāmṛtāvatāradeśanānupūrvī*), or as a teaching fitted to those who are to be instructed (*vineyajanānurūpyeṇa vā śāsanam*)" (Ruegg 1977: 6). Although Tom Tillemans and Westerhoff both accept such a "graded teaching" interpretation,[27] Ruegg—whose summary of Candrakīrti's position I have just cited, admits that "the word *anuśāsana* is regularly used in Sanskrit, including the Buddhist literature, to mean teaching, instruction, without any specific reference to progressivity or fitness" (Ruegg 1977, 60 n. 19). Ruegg furthermore notes that neither of two slightly earlier and equally authoritative Mādhyamika commentators, Buddhapālita (c. 470–540, author of the *Madhyamakavṛttiḥ*) and Bhāvaviveka (c. 500–578, author of the *Prajñāpradīpa*), lays any special emphasis on the prefix *anu-* (see Ruegg 1977: 37–38). This, I might add, is so even though Bhāvaviveka's Svātantrika interpretation of Madhyamaka thought could only be reinforced by such qualification of Nāgārjuna's *prasaṅga* critique.

Apart from the commentarial disparity between Bhāvaviveka and Buddhapālita, on the one hand, and Candrakīrti, on the other, the first point to note about this interpretation is that it has been applied solely to the single occurrence of the positive *catuṣkoṭi* in the MK, at 18:8. As such, even if it were to hold here, this would leave unexplained the numerous uses of the negative *catuṣkoṭi* throughout the rest of the text. Secondly, and more seriously, to introduce a classificatory model of graded teachings into Nāgārjuna's thought on the basis of a single instance of a prefix—whose value, moreover, is disputed—strikes me as something of a stretch.

In fact, this would effectively make of Nāgārjuna's position in MK:18:8 a forerunner of the system of doctrinal classification (*panjiao* 判教) elaborated centuries later in China. According to the *panjiao* method, competing schools took their adversaries' core text or teaching as but a partial exposition of the fully flowered version found in their own. This doxographical practice of hierarchical classification—so well-attested in the history of Chinese Buddhist scholastic thought—sought to arrange the heterogeneous corpora of Buddhist literature inherited from Indian sources into some kind of meaningful order; an order that would allow adherents of one or another school to make sense of what appeared at times to be stubbornly contradictory teachings.[28] It would thus seem far removed from Nāgārjuna's *catuṣkoṭi*. And yet attempts to englobe the four lemmata of MK:18:8 within a single overarching meta-doxy, as a series of competing positions applicable to diversely endowed individual pupils, are amply evident among Chinese-language interpreters.

Thus, for example, Li Runsheng 李潤生has a discussion of the positive tetralemma at MK:18:8 in which he interprets the four lemmata as being formulated for the benefit of the three levels (superior, middle, and inferior: 上中下) of aspirant.[29] Li considers the first and second lemmata as being suited for the middle kind of aspirant. It is the third lemma, which encapsulates the both/and violation of the law of non-contradiction, which he takes to be for the inferior aspirant, while the fourth is reserved for the superior kind.[30] Li is following Qingmu's commentary to MK:18:8 here, with its like division of living beings into superior, middle/average, and inferior. Preempting Candrakīrti's "progressive" reading by some three centuries, Qingmu states:

> The superior see the characteristic of phenomena to be neither real nor not real [i.e., lemma (d)]. The average see the characteristic of phenomena to be completely real or completely unreal [i.e., lemmata (a) and (b)]. The inferior, whose powers of perception are meagre, see the characteristic of phenomena to be partly real and partly unreal [i.e., lemma (c)]. (T 1564: 25a23)[31]

For his part, Wan Jinchuan 萬金川 likewise frames his own attempt to overcome the logical problems inherent in the *catuṣkoṭi* through reference to the differing capacities of audience members ("受教者根器的不同," Wan 1998a: 122). Since the Buddha cannot be conceived as uttering a falsehood ("佛陀的說法不能為假," Wan 1998a: 122), any semblance thereof (as would be exemplified in an illogical statement) is explicable, on this reading, by means of a distinction Wan proposes between the incorrigible Buddhadharma (法) and mere doctrinal teaching (教法) (Wan 1998a: 123). It is as this latter that the tetralemma is to be interpreted, functioning in this capacity as a ladder (梯) along which practitioners may ascend (Wan 1998a: 124).

The motif of ascension likewise motivates Wu Rujun's 吳汝鈞 interpretation. Wu initially adopts a Hegelian-style dialectic in his commentary to the positive *catuṣkoṭi* at MK:18:8, whereby the first three lemmata represent the thesis, antithesis, and synthesis (正,反,合) of Nāgārjuna's position. He writes: "The first lemma is an affirmative statement: thesis. The second lemma is a negative statement: antithesis. The third lemma is a synthesizing statement: synthesis" (Wu 1997: 329).[32] In a twist to Hegel, however, Wu states that "the fourth lemma transcends the third lemma: transcendence" (超越) (Wu 1997: 329).[33] This therefore constitutes the moment of sublation, as it were, of the third lemma, which is itself the synthesis of the first and second (and therefore constitutive of their own sublation). Such a dialectical approach introduces an element of what could be called epektatic motion into Nāgārjuna's philosophy, but it is evidently still motivated by an ambition to fix the tetralemma within the static parameters of supposedly apodeictic logical laws—where I use "fix" in the sense of both "repair" and "anchor."

The overriding problem with the graded teaching interpretation, whatever the details of its specific elaboration, is that not only does it find no corroboration in Nāgārjuna's base text, but the contrary view (denying such progressive levels of teaching) is amply attested. Indeed, this is so both specifically in the passage cited and more generally throughout the MK. Thus, when Nāgārjuna continues his presentation of "the teaching of the Buddha" following 18:8, he uses the term "*śāsana*" without the *anu-* prefix but three verses later (18:11). Now, surely a reading not motivated by a deliberate hermeneutical agenda (in this case, to qualify Nāgārjuna's positive tetralemma) would take Nāgārjuna's parallel use of *anuśāsana* and *śāsana* in this continuous passage to betoken an equivalence in meaning between the two terms. To explain my point by way of an example (admittedly imperfect but hopefully adequate), suppose I were to use "view" and "viewpoint" interchangeably in a given passage, and one were to then construct a theory based on my usage of the suffix "-point" in the latter term according to which I there meant to specify a small, discrete unit of an idea rather than an ideology as a whole. I propose that the interpretation of Nāgārjuna's use of *anuśāsana* and *śāsana* in MK:18 as founding a theory of progressive teachings is as textually unjustified as this would be, especially given the complete absence of any other textual evidence in support of it. This is so also more generally because Nāgārjuna's well-known identification of emptiness (surely an ultimate teaching if Nāgārjuna has any) as itself empty, or his characterization of his own view as that of no view, precludes a hierarchization of views.[34] Such a gradation would necessarily entail that certain views could legitimately be held in preference to others; that they were, in other words, closer to the truth. This, however, would directly contradict Nāgārjuna's espousal of the "abandonment of all views" (*sarvadṛṣṭiprahāṇāya*) in the very final verse of the MK (27:30).[35]

Another way in which the various lemmata of Nāgārjuna's positive tetralemma have been qualified as stating something to be the case "in some respects" and not the case in others has been proposed by Garfield and Priest. To demonstrate that "the contradictions are mainly prima facie" and therefore that in fact "things are perfectly consistent," Garfield and Priest propose a "disambiguated" version of Nāgārjuna's text (Garfield and Priest 2009: 72). On their telling, MK:18:8 would state "something may be true (conventionally), false (ultimately), true and false (conventionally and ultimately, respectively), and neither true nor false (ultimately and conventionally, respectively)" (Garfield and Priest 2009: 72).[36] Westerhoff proposes an exactly equivalent strategy. His is likewise designed "to make sense of the seemingly contradictory statements we find in Nāgārjuna's writings," and more particularly "to dispel the appearance of paradox in instances of the tetralemma . . . by arguing that not all its negations relate to the same truth" (Westerhoff 2018a: 119). Westerhoff's treatment is thus of the negative rather than the positive tetralemma (he explicitly cites MK:22:11), but his "interpolation procedure" inserts the same qualifiers of "conventionally" and "ultimately" in much the same way as Garfield and Priest. Regardless of just which tetralemma is being dealt with, then, it is clear that the strategy here is to interpolate some parameters by means of which the contradictory quality of the tetralemma can be offset.

The first point to note about this strategy of parameterization is that it directly contradicts Garfield's and Priest's individual disavowals elsewhere of just such parameterization. Priest first describes this "stratagem for disposing of contradictions" in general terms:

> The stratagem is to the effect that when one meets an (at least *prima facie*) contradiction of the form P(a)!, one tries to find some ambiguity in P, or some different respects, r1 and r2, in which something may be P, and then to argue that a is P in one respect, P(r1,a), but not in the other P(r2,a). (Priest 1995: 166/2002: 151)[37]

He then goes on to list several reasons for its inadequacy:

> First, there is, in general, no reason to suppose that the property φ is parameterised. . . . Next, and even assuming that it is correct to parameterise φ, it is normally difficult to find independent reasons as to why the parameter must change from c to c' to give consistency. . . . Thirdly, and crucially, the parameterisation does not avoid the paradox, but merely relocates it. (Priest 2002: 153–154)

All this leads Priest to conclude that "parameterisation is less of a solution to the contradictions at the limit of thought than a manifestation of them" (Priest 2002: 155). As for Garfield, he is avowedly intent "to take very seriously Nāgārjuna's insistence on exactly what he says" (Smith College 2010). Indeed, in the same oral discussion from which this quote is taken, Garfield criticizes as unjustified the practice (common among not only Tibetan exegetes, as he mentions, but Western ones) of inserting a parameter such as "false" into the "abandonment of all views" espoused by Nāgārjuna at MK:27:30. Yet he goes on just a few minutes later to claim that this verse refers to "all views about the fundamental nature of reality." He does not appear to be aware that the phrase "about the fundamental nature of reality" is just as much a parameterization/interpolation as the term "false," or for that matter the alternation and combination of "conventionally" and "ultimately" at MK:18:8, is. Given Priest's demonstration of the inadequacy of parameterization in the context of Western philosophical paradoxes, and given Garfield's explicitly avowed adherence to the letter of Nāgārjuna's text shorn of any parameterizing insertions, their combined effort to present a "disambiguated" version of Nāgārjuna's tetralemma by interpolating just such parameterizing "respects" (of conventionality and ultimacy) into it constitutes not only a case of unjustified textual modification but a self-contradicting one at that.[38]

The second point to note about this reading of the tetralemma—be it of the positive one at MK:18:8 or the negative version at, for example, MK:22:11—is that its "various possibilities need to be disambiguated with respect to the two notions of truth operative for Nāgārjuna and quite generally in Buddhism" (Garfield and Priest 2009: 72). Westerhoff again echoes Garfield and Priest here, likewise proposing "the theory of the two truths" as "another hermeneutic device to help us understand what is going on with these apparently contradictory statements" (Westerhoff 2018a: 118). Now, Nāgārjuna only goes on to first state his celebrated theory of the two truths (i.e., of conventional truth/*saṃvṛti-satya* and ultimate truth/*paramārtha-satya*) some six chapters after MK:18, at MK:24:8, and in quite a different context:

> The teaching of the dharma of the Buddhas
> Is based on two truths
> Conventional worldly truth
> And ultimate truth[39]

Reading the two truths back from chapter 24 into chapter 18 (or in Westerhoff's case into chapter 22) requires quite some hermeneutic acrobatics, and is quite simply textually unjustified.

Now, it may be objected regarding this particular point that my own reading of Nāgārjuna's MK rests on an analogous reading back into the text, in my case by using the abandonment of all views espoused in MK:27:30 as a hermeneutic key to the work as a whole. In response, I would point out that surely there is a qualitative difference between inserting modifiers into a text on the basis of a foreconcluded hermeneutic agenda and proposing a reading of a text that attempts to make sense of it according to its own formulations. For there is no disputing the facts that Nāgārjuna's text begins and ends with endorsements of viewlessness, that its several chapters each deconstruct a given view or set of views, that it overtly repudiates readers who take even its most central tenets as views, and that not only the MK but Nāgārjuna's other works evince manifold explicit abjurations of view-holding (as detailed in §4.2). Contrariwise, what we find here are repeated invocations to the effect that "we *need* to understand . . . we *have* to distinguish . . . we *have* to presuppose" (Westerhoff 2018a: 118–119, emphases added) in a certain manner established prior to the reading and alien to the text read. In forcing such parameters onto the text, this method effectively reneges on the primary responsibility of textual interpretation altogether.

Returning to the text, even were we to grant the applicability of the two truths to MK:18:8 or MK:22:11, the interpretation of these verses proposed by Garfield, Priest, and Westerhoff here rests on an understanding of these two truths specific to the Tibetan Geluk (dGe lugs pa) school of Madhyamaka founded by Tsongkhapa (Tsong kha pa bLo bzang Grags pa) (1357–1419) in the fourteenth/fifteenth century. Westerhoff cites Tsongkhapa in "justification for this view" (Westerhoff 2018a: 119) directly, and for his part Tom Tillemans likewise refers to Tsongkhapa explicitly in formulating his own version of the Modal Interpretation, on the understanding that

> Some commentators—such as Bhāvaviveka, but especially some Tibetans—have tried to add qualifications such as 'truly established' (Tib. *bden par grub pa*) or 'established from an absolute perspective' (Tib. *don dam par grub pa*) so as to indicate clearly the level of discourse implicit in the use of the negation operators. This technique was used with great mastery by Tsong kha pa blo bzang grags pa, the great Tibetan commentator of the fourteenth century; he managed to transform the tetralemma into a sort of modal logic where the laws of double negation, excluded middle, and contradiction function in a classical manner. (Tillemans 1999: 197)

Although historically victorious over its rivals (and home to the Dalai Lamas), this school "differs sharply from other forms of Buddhist thought not only in Tibet, but elsewhere in the Buddhist world" (Duckworth 2022: §0). Apart from anything else, this means that the interpretation proposed is far indeed from being operative "quite generally in Buddhism" (Garfield and Priest 2009: 72)—a fact that should make us wary at least of proposing this interpretation as one acceptable to Buddhists of other schools of thought. But still more to the point, the Geluk interpretation has it that the two truths are "extensionally identical but intensionally distinct. . . . That is, the two truths are not different entities, but are conceptually distinct aspects of all entities" (Duckworth 2022: §1).[40] That this is the understanding Garfield and Priest are mobilizing is made clear toward the very end of their paper where, in reference to the dialectical play of Nāgārjunian deconstruction they represent as a series of De Morgan Lattices, they conclude: "we have effectively returned to where we started. True, from the standpoint of conventional reality, the first and last representations may look different. . . . But for the standpoint of ultimate reality, there is no real difference; they are the same" (Garfield and Priest 2009: 79). This understanding of the two truths, however, originated with Tsongkhapa over one millennium after Nāgārjuna, and thus is obviously nowhere to be found in the writings of Nāgārjuna himself. Nowhere does Nāgārjuna speak of the two truths in terms of "extensional identity but intensional distinctness." Indeed, the main thrust of the critique of Tsongkhapa's interpretation launched by his rival Gorampa Sonam Senge (Go rams pa bSod nams Seng ge) (1429–1489) is precisely

> that, if a Mādhyamika commentator adds that kind of ultimate parameter [i.e., qualifies Nāgārjuna's negative statements with 'ultimately' or 'truly'] and thus gives a nonliteral interpretation of Nāgārjuna's negative statements, he has in effect denatured the whole Nāgārjunian dialectic to the degree that it will no longer be able to accomplish its (religious) purpose of quieting philosophical speculation and attachment—and irenic quietism, or complete "freedom from proliferations" (*spros bral*, Skt. *niṣprapañca*), is, for Go rams pa, the main point of the Mādhyamika's negative dialectic. (Tillemans 2009: 93–94/2016: 77–78)[41]

Given all this, even if we were to grant that Nāgārjuna is already referring to the two truths in chapters 18 or 22 of the MK, they would be quite different from what Tsongkhapa's reading requires them to be. So using Tsongkhapa to interpret Nāgārjuna in this instance, as Garfield and Priest as well as Westerhoff do, is somewhat fraught, to say the least. Not only because Tsongkhapa proposed a reading unanimously rejected by other Buddhist schools but also, perhaps most importantly, because his interpretation is based quite evidently on some rather hefty textual interpolation. Indeed, the most damning evidence against the textual interpolations proposed by Garfield and Priest is that they are in fact directly contradicted by verse 18:8 itself, which explicitly states that *all/everything* (*sarvaṃ*) is its ambit. The following verse likewise speaks of "the character of reality" (*tattvasya lakṣaṇaṃ*) without any restrictive qualifications.[42] Westerhoff's citation of MK:22:11 runs into similar problems, for this verse likewise makes no mention of any qualifiers, even though Nāgārjuna shows himself perfectly able to use them when he needs to; indeed, he even does precisely that in the very same chapter, as when he asks just two verses earlier, "How can what does not exist through selfbeing exist through otherbeing?"[43] If he is careful to specify "*svabhāvataś* . . . *parabhāvataḥ*" here, why would he be so careless as to not specify "conventionally . . . ultimately" two verses later, especially as failing to do so certainly gives his verse, as we have seen Westerhoff acknowledge, "the appearance of paradox"?

In fact, Westerhoff appears to be acutely aware of the hermeneutic bind that his interpolative method entails, for he candidly admits that "The drawback with this interpretation is that we have to *presuppose* that the *sūtra*s and commentaries in question are incomplete" (Westerhoff 2018a: 119, emphasis added). This goes even further than Tillemans, whose reference to parameters mysteriously left "implicit" despite their apparently crucial importance to reasonable sense-making effectively functions as an inadvertent admission that the basis of his interpretation is textually unattested.[44] For Westerhoff here pursues a reading he himself openly admits finds no literal support in the texts themselves; a reading of Buddhist *sūtra*s and commentaries, moreover, which positions him as able to complete their incompleteness, to convey "what they *really* mean" "when *properly* understood" (Westerhoff 2018a: 119, emphases added). I have previously referred to the logicalizing mission as itself a quasi-religious pursuit (see §1.2), and here we find it pursued with unquestioning zeal to hermeneutic ends whose violence to the texts it purports to interpret could not be clearer. For it is not that "A casual reading of Nāgārjuna's works is likely to give the reader the impression that contradictory statements form an essential part of his philosophy (Westerhoff 2018a: 117); it is a *literal* reading that inevitably leads to such a conclusion. If Nāgārjuna had meant the lemmata of his *catuṣkoṭi* to refer alternately to conventional and ultimate truth in the manner Westerhoff, or Garfield and Priest, propose, surely he would have said so.[45]

2.2.3. The Qualitative Interpretation

The final hermeneutic technique by means of which the tetralemma has typically been "rescued" from logical contradiction that I will consider is one whereby it is said to affirm a given quality and negate another altogether. This has often gone hand in hand with the well-known distinction between two types of negation in Sanskrit grammar (to wit, *paryudāsa-pratiṣedha* and *prasajya-pratiṣedha*), as employed in a bid to avoid the conclusion that (-c) and (-d) are contradictory. *Paryudāsa-pratiṣedha* is "negation which indirectly affirms the existence of something else," while *prasajya-pratiṣedha* is "negation which leaves nothing in its place" (Huntington 1989: 58).[46] In practice, that which *paryudāsa* does imply is the affirmation of the contradictory of that which has been negated, whereas *prasajya* does not imply this.[47] Thus, the statement "The number seven is not even" would imply *paryudāsa* negation, whereby it would implicitly affirm the contrary; that is, that the number seven is non-even; that is, odd. By contrast, and to adapt an example well-known to contemporary philosophers, the statement "The present King of France is not bald" would necessarily entail the use of *prasajya* negation for, given that there is no present King of France at all, it would be false, indeed absurd, to imply that he is non-bald; that is, hirsute.[48]

Katsura is one scholar who proposes to use a combination of *prasajya* and *paryudāsa* negations to interpret the *catuṣkoṭi*, which thus finds itself neatly *encadré* within a Venn diagram in which the four alternatives coexist in logical coherence (see Katsura 2000: 203–205).[49] This treatment of the tetralemma reduces it to what Katsura calls a "method of enumeration" in which the possible combinations of two propositions are exhaustively listed, as in the following example, wherein people may be divided into (a) those who have eyes but not ears; (b) those who have ears but not eyes; (c) those who have both eyes and ears; and (d) those who have neither eyes nor ears (see Katsura 2000: 205).[50]

A like analysis is presented by Raimundo Panikkar, who sets himself the task "to demonstrate that a rejection of a proposition of type I ["A *is* B"] does not necessarily imply a proposition of type II ["A *is not* B"]" (Panikkar 1989: 64).[51] He does not, of course, explain *why* he deems it necessary to perform such a task, but the perceived necessity becomes apparent in the light of further comments he makes according to which the principle of non-contradiction is "a condition considered indispensable for our intellection" (Panikkar 1989: 64). Panikkar then proceeds to demonstrate that the proposition "A is not B" does not constitute a negation of "A is B" (i.e., "A is non-B," which would inevitably entail logical contradiction). Rather, "A is not B" constitutes the proposition "A is-not B." This does not, on Panikkar's analysis, so contradict "A is B," and therefore avoids logical inconsistency. For the sake of clarity, I cite Panikkar's argumentation in full:

> "A *is* B" is logically incompatible with: "A is non-B," but not with: "A *is-not* B." Indeed, if the first proposition is true—if A actually is B—then I may substitute A for B, and easily see which of the propositions containing a negative holds and which does not. "A is non-A" is a contradiction; "A is-not A" merely indicates that A is not absolutely identical with itself—which, after all, must be the case, for otherwise it could not have equaled B in any respect whatever, and the proposition "A is B" would have been a sterile tautology. (Panikkar 1989: 65, emphases original)

Mysteriously, he states that "the profound reason for this [that is, for not taking the first two lemmata as contradictory] seems to me to reside not in some misapprehension of the laws of logic on the part of Buddhism, but in the denial of a one-to-one correspondence between thinking and being" (Panikkar 1989: 64). Whatever this may mean, I take his argument as boiling down to Katsura's, wherein the first two lemmata affirm one quality and negate another. Note, however, that he also states that "the propositions that are simultaneously affirmative and negative . . . do not signify simple internal contradiction; they cannot, for internal contradiction is of its very nature nonsignifying" (Panikkar 1989: 63). He then proposes to replace the simple formulation of the proposition "the world *is* and *is not* temporally finite" with "the world is partially (or 'in one respect') finite and partially (or 'in another respect') not finite temporally," and thereupon concludes that "now the proposition becomes intelligible" (Panikkar 1989: 63, emphases original). Panikkar thus seems to be melding, or confusing, the Mereological Interpretation espoused by Jayatilleke with the Qualitative Interpretation also found in Katsura.

The arguments of Katsura and Panikkar run into the following problem: rather than identifying "A" and "B" as the two sides of a binary opposition, they have understood them to simply denote two different but not mutually contradictory attributes. This directly contradicts the actual statements which they are purportedly interpreting (viz., in Panikkar's case, "the world is temporally finite" and "the world is not temporally finite"). We are here irrefutably confronted with two mutually contradictory statements; statements, moreover, which exhaust the two poles of a binary opposition. Contrary to Panikkar's implication that though propositions (a) and (b) would only "*seem* to [but not really] exhaust the logical possibilities in respect of any affirmation" (Panikkar 1989: 64, emphasis added), the world really is and must be either finite or infinite; it cannot be something *else*. Indeed, when we get to propositions (c) and (d), or (-c) and (-d), of the tetralemma, we see that these statements too do not posit something else, something other to the claims proposed in (-/a)[52] and (-/b), but rather posit the affirmation (-/c) or the negation (-/d) of both (-/a) and (-/b) taken as a whole.

These comments therefore apply just as much to the negative as the positive tetralemma. For while it is evident that the conjunction of positive statements such as "the world is temporally finite" and "the world is not temporally finite" constitutes a contradiction, the attempt to adopt a face-saving combination of *prasajya* and *paryudāsa* negation to such statements could only succeed in restoring classical logicality were the objects of the tetralemmic lemmata qualitatively different, which they are not. That said, the negative claims that it is not the case that the world is finite and that it is not the case that it is infinite need not be contradictories, even if the positive claims that the world is finite and that the world is infinite are contradictories.[53] Indeed, this is precisely the point of bringing in the *prasajya/paryudāsa* distinction. But Katsura makes what appears to be a decisive error insofar as he applies the *prasajya* negation first to the positive rather than the negative *catuṣkoṭi*, and then to one component of the lemma under consideration rather than to the lemma as a whole.[54] The first move would transform the positive version of the third lemma ("All . . . Is both real and not real") from an affirmation and a negation of the same quality (in this case, reality) to an affirmation of one and a non-implicative negation of some other. What this other could possibly be—"blue"? "c-minor"? "swimming"?—is left unstated by Katsura . . . necessarily so since Nāgārjuna certainly says nothing on this score. In any case, why would Nāgārjuna employ such an argumentative strategy, when asserting that a given subject (e.g., a chess square) is, say, "both real and not-blue" is hardly consequential? The second move (applying the *prasajya* negation to one component of the lemma under consideration rather than to the lemma as a whole) is just as mystifying, however, for it entails that the third lemma should be taken as equivalent to "The present King of France is both bald and not-bald," where it is accepted that there is no present King of France at all. While this may (depending on one's views on the ontological status of referents) technically rescue the third lemma of the positive tetralemma from non-contradiction, it does so at the price of making no sense at all.

Moreover, the way that Panikkar chooses to formalize the *catuṣkoṭi* is itself problematic, for it obfuscates the unavoidable logical contradiction enacted by its propositions (-/a) and (-/b). We may, after all, agree with Panikkar that "'A *is* B' is logically incompatible with 'A is non-B' but not with 'A *is-not* B'" (Panikkar 1989: 65) and then conclude with him that Nāgārjuna (or for that matter the Buddha) avoided contradiction by effectively saying "A *is-not* B" but not "A is non-B." This is based, however, upon an initial setting up of the first two lemmata as "A *is* B" and "A *is-not* B" respectively (see Panikkar 1989: 64). Calling the two "A" and "B" implies that these are two of a logically possible multiplicity of attributes: A is not B; neither is it C, or D . . . just as an apple is not a banana, nor a cherry, nor a date. But it is invalid to use such labels—and by extension such an argument—when dealing with the two poles of a binary opposition, which is manifestly the case with a pair of statements such as "the world is temporally finite" and "the world is not temporally finite."[55] After all, I can only reiterate that we are *not* dealing here with a potentially infinite series of mutually compatible propositions, all of which may be attributed to a class "A" without ensuing contradiction, in the way that all kinds of fruits make up the category of "fruit" without thereby forcing that category into logical contradiction. In the case at hand, there is no third alternative according to which the world could be something else, something unrelated to either finitude or infinitude. We are here dealing with an exhaustive enumeration of logical possibilities; one that must consequently be formulated not in terms of "A" and "B" but in terms of "A" and "non-A" or "-A."

The reading proposed by Katsura and Panikkar would, if successful, render the tetralemma logically innocuous. Unfortunately for them, however, it cannot be what Nāgārjuna has in mind when he rhetorically asks, for example, how permanence and impermanence, finity and infinity, and the rest of their respective tetralemmas, could possibly apply to the *Tathāgata*—that is, the Buddha.[56] In other words, it is not the case that we are dealing with two qualities, such as Katsura's "having eyes" and "having ears," but with the possession or lack (or both or neither) of one. This is consistently the case with the tetralemma. Indeed, I have been unable to identify a single instance in the MK where Nāgārjuna applies the *catuṣkoṭi* to two (or more) distinct qualities, and am thus led to conclude that the tetralemma, in its negative guise, is deliberately designed to reject both the affirmation and the negation of one given quality (permanence, finity, emptiness, etc.).

2.3. The Buddhological Tetralemma

As I hope to have shown, interpretations such as those proposed by—among others—Jayatilleke, Wayman, Tillemans, Westerhoff, Li, Wan, Wu, Garfield, Priest, Katsura, and Panikkar, designed as they are in various ways to demonstrate the logicality of the *catuṣkoṭi* (be it according to the canons of classical or paraconsistent logic), are textually unjustified. They do not, in other words, accurately represent the tetralemma as it is employed in Nāgārjuna's MK. As I see it, these various though related attempts to rescue Nāgārjuna from logical contradiction all impose some kind of parameters onto the tetralemma, be these mereological, modal, or qualitative. It is perhaps Wayman who embodies most evidently this effort to parameterize the *catuṣkoṭi*, however, for in a somewhat cavalier manner he proposes that the third lemma in MK:25:14

> can be resolved in various ways, for example, one may deny both a presence and an absence of *nirvāṇa*, adding "that is, in the same place"; or, with a different subject, adding perhaps, "that is, at the same time"; or, with still other subjects, perhaps drawing upon the two truths, "that is, with the same truth." (Wayman 1977: 17)[57]

It seems not to matter, in other words, just how one parameterizes the tetralemma, so long as one does do so.

Richard Robinson adopts a similar approach. Concerned as he avowedly is "to establish the logical form of the tetralemma" (Robinson 1978: 57), Robinson proposes two approaches: either "the four lemmas are modes of one proposition" or "The other likely possibility is that the four lemmas differ in the quantity of their constituent terms" (Robinson 1978: 57). The first of these is self-evidently a version of the Modal Interpretation. As for the latter strategy, we have already seen Robinson deploy it regarding MK:27:17 (see §2.2.1), where he utilizes it to support a straightforward version of the Mereological Interpretation. In any case, Robinson is clear that, "If we assume" in these or other such ways, "There do not seem to be any real paradoxes in the *Stanzas* [i.e., MK]. The seeming paradoxes are easily resolved" (Robinson 1978: 57–58).

A like approach characterizes Claus Oetke's efforts to provide a "satisfying interpretation" of the "apparent tensions and inconsistencies in Nāgārjuna's writings" (Oetke 1991: 315). Oetke effectively proposes another version of the Modal Interpretation,[58] according to which "a sentential operator 'on the level of highest truth (it is the case that)' and a negated existential proposition . . . must be kept in mind" when dealing with the tetralemma (Oetke 1991: 318). He then generalizes this procedure, however, such that any qualification whatsoever may be permitted if it serves "to dissolve apparent inconsistencies" (Oetke 1991: 316). This apparently shows Nāgārjuna to be "much less silly" (Oetke 1991: 321):

> For seen in this light, the fact that *bhāva* as well as *abhāva* are rejected and that there are statements to the effect that both 'it is' and 'it is not' are disapproved can be understood as logical consequences of the main tenet, if only we asume [sic] that what is at stake in all these cases is the possibility of saying *of* something that it exists or does not exist at certain times or certain places, or more generally, of ascribing predicates to things. (Oetke 1991: 318, emphasis original)

As expected, Oetke concludes that "seen in this way, the tension of [the tetralemma] turns out to be merely apparent" (Oetke 1991: 318).

That the techniques I have cited—of part, mode, or quality—consistently impose parameters where the MK states none should, I hope, by now be apparent. Before going on to attempt to provide an alternative to this tendency toward logicalization of the *catuṣkoṭi* on the part of latter-day scholars, I would like to evoke the near ubiquity of this approach. For in case any doubt remains in the reader's mind as to the prevalence of these attempts to prove the logicality of Nāgārjuna's tetralemma, I cite in passing a further handful of preeminent instances. Raju, for whom the *catuṣkoṭi* "can be explained with the help of the difference between contrary and contradictory opposition of western logic" (Raju 1954: 710); Gunaratne, for whom the "*catuṣkoṭi* has an isolable or a consistent logical structure" (Gunaratne 1980: 212); Tachikawa, who affirms that the *catuṣkoṭi* "does observe basic rules of logic" (Tachikawa 1997: 133); and Jones, who claims that "logic is at the center of Nāgārjuna's argument" in the *catuṣkoṭi*, such that the merely "apparent paradoxicality of Nāgārjuna's treatment of the four options can be explained away" (Jones 2018: 47, 51), all invoke Western philosophical models to explain away the violation of logical laws enacted so evidently in the *catuṣkoṭi*. Westerhoff

(2006: 367 nn. 1–7 and, in slightly expanded form, 2009: 67–68 nn. 1–7) mentions several other hermeneutic techniques used for the same purpose, including the utilization of intuitionist logic (Chi 1969: 162–163), the quantification (Robinson 1967: 57–58) and non-quantification (Schayer 1933: 93)[59] of the four lemmata, and the interpretation of any such quantification in substitutional or referential terms (Tillemans 1990: 75), among others. Likewise, Staal (1975: 39), whom Westerhoff also mentions, proposes a three-valued or many-valued logic, as developed to account for Brouwer's intuitionistic logic, to explain the "rationality" of the MK as found in the *catuṣkoṭi*.

A further example is provided by Tom Tillemans, whose stated remit "will essentially concern the adequacy of certain formal translations of the structures of Buddhist thought and the formal properties of the calculi employed in such translations" (Tillemans 1999: 192).[60] Given the evidently lamentable fact that "we must admit that the initial attempts at applying classical logic to the most recalcitrant structures of Mahāyāna Buddhist thought—most notably the tetralemma—have been failures" (Tillemans 1999: 191), Tillemans promptly goes on, of course, to ask: "How then are we to dissipate the seeming paradoxes of the tetralemma's four negations within an adequate translation of that structure into modern logic?" (Tillemans 1999: 196).[61] He then proceeds to "sketch out a solution by proposing two ways of understanding the quantification implicit in the Buddhist's statements" (Tillemans 1999: 197). It is noteworthy, here as in the numerous other examples already given, that the paradoxes/contradictions/inconsistencies directly expressed by the *catuṣkoṭi* are perforce taken to be "seeming" rather than serious[62]—and this despite the fact that Tillemans himself, as we have seen in our discussion of the Modal Interpretation earlier, explicitly recognizes that parameterization "denature[s] the whole Nāgārjunian dialectic" (Tillemans 2009: 93/2016: 78).[63] The reference here to a "solution," moreover, shows that the tetralemma is still being treated as a riddle. As for the acknowledgment that the quantification Tillemans perceives is "implicit," I take this as an effective admission on his part that it is not actually in the text itself. Predictably, Tillemans echoes the numerous fellow logicalizing scholars cited earlier in concluding that

> We are now in a position to give a translation of the tetralemma into formal logic: . . . When we translate the Madhyamaka's statements into a logic with two types of interpretations,[64] we will not encounter any violation of the laws of contradiction, excluded middle or double negation, or of any other

> fundamental theorems of classical logic. There thus will not be any significant deviation. (Tillemans 1999: 199–200)

Riddle solved.[65]

Finally, I turn to the latest book-length study of the tetralemma, Graham Priest's *The Fifth Corner of Four: An Essay on Buddhist Metaphysics and the Catuṣkoṭi* (Priest 2018). The first point to note in this regard is that "The main aim of the book is to show how some ideas [on the *catuṣkoṭi*] drawn from Buddhist texts and some ideas in contemporary non-classical logic can profitably inform each other" (Priest 2018: xix). This means that Priest's endeavor may best be conceived as an instance of the "fusion philosophy" associated most closely with Mark Siderits, a method that draws on multiple philosophical traditions "to try to solve a philosophical problem" (Siderits 2016a: 129), as opposed to (merely) interpreting or comparing them.[66] Priest is thus forthright about the fact that his "book is not a scholarly work" in the sense that it consciously leaves aside "the correct interpretation of these [Buddhist] texts" (Priest 2018: xix). This frees Priest from any potential charge of misconstrual or mangling: textual hermeneutics "is *not* what I am engaged in here" (Priest 2018: xix, emphasis original).

Nevertheless, it turns out that the philosophical uses to which Priest puts Nāgārjuna's *tetralemma* align rather closely with his aforestated efforts to interpret *Nāgārjuna's* tetralemma. For be it in his prior writings or in this latest book-length engagement with the *catuṣkoṭi*, Priest is concerned above all to show that "Nāgārjuna is not an irrationalist" (Garfield and Priest 2002: 96), as he put it earlier, or, as he says here, "Nāgārjuna is a systematic philosopher" (Priest 2018: 75). Priest's main discussion of the tetralemma in Nāgārjuna's work specifically lies in chapter 5, devoted to what he calls the 'Fifth Corner' of ineffability.[67] For on Priest's account "Nāgārjuna has put together the *catuṣkoṭi* of four corners with an apparently incommensurable fifth" (Priest 2018: 63). Note the crucial proviso that this is so only "apparently." Indeed, Priest's central proposal in the ensuing discussion turns out to be that

> for Nāgārjuna, the *catuṣkoṭi* has split into two: a four-valued semantic *catuṣkoṭi*, and a 5-valued ontological *catuṣkoṭi*—the fifth value in the ontological case being ineffability. . . . It might have seemed that Nāgārjuna being committed to both four values and five values in the *catuṣkoṭi* is a paradoxical feature of his thought. It is not; once the distinction between the two kinds of *catuṣkoṭi*s is made, there is no contradiction here. (Priest 2018: 73)

That Priest's effort here is completely in line with his and others' reiterated attempts to logicalize Nāgārjuna is abundantly evident. Indeed, Priest himself explicitly echoes earlier attempts we have already seen in avowing that his approach "resolve[s] a puzzle of interpretation" (Priest 2018: 75) concerning Nāgārjuna's tetralemma. As he states, following his "*reinterpretation* of the notions involved, the whole machinery now makes sense" (Priest 2018: 68, emphasis added).[68] Yet again we find the riddle solved, the puzzle resolved, the whole machinery making logical sense—even if in Priest's case the logic involved is non-classical. In the words of a prominent reviewer, "As fun (if simplistic) as this is, from a different perspective, it would have been better if Priest sought in this way to disprove the validity of the *catuṣkoṭi* based on the notion that indeed the whole machine does *not* make sense" (Green 2020: 228, emphasis original). It is to charting why the tetralemma is designed, precisely, to *not* make sense that we now turn.

2.4. The Buddhist Tetralemma

Having detailed the logicalizing tendencies predominant in European- and Chinese-language scholarship on Nāgārjuna's *catuṣkoṭi*, in this final section of the present chapter I am concerned to demonstrate three inter-related points. First, I take it unassailably to be the case that, short of decontextualizing and thereby denaturing his thought completely, Nāgārjuna is engaged in the overall Buddhist project of alleviating, and ultimately eradicating, suffering (*duḥkha*). To this end, I will cite various passages from Nāgārjuna's texts wherein this is made particularly explicit. Second, I take it that the *catuṣkoṭi*, as an argumentative strategy used to great effect throughout Nāgārjuna's *oeuvre*, functions within this, his overall religiosophical soterial aim. There is no argument I provide for this specific point other than to aver that this is surely the most hermeneutically obvious, as well as philosophically charitable, approach. For the alternative would be to declare that one of the prime features of this philosopher's arguments is to be understood as unrelated to the prime thrust of his philosophy. Apart from there being no textual evidence for taking the *catuṣkoṭi* form of argumentation as somehow divorced from the arguments it actually expresses (I fail to see what such textual evidence could even look like), I take it that the point I am making here makes Nāgārjuna look "much less silly" (Oetke 1991: 321—see §2.3) than the alternative. For according to such an alternative, he would be repeatedly using an argumentative form unrelated, or even contrary, to his argumentative content . . . which would nevertheless somehow get conveyed by it. Lastly, and in consequence of the conjunction of these two points, I argue that interpretations of the tetralemma such as those I have detailed earlier (i.e., the Mereological, Modal, and Qualitative), concerned as they explicitly are in their various ways to provide a logical "solution" to the "riddle" of the tetralemma divorced from its function within Nāgārjuna's arguments taken as a whole, are thereby inadequate.

Quite apart from the salutation at the very beginning of the MK in which Nāgārjuna salutes "the Fully Enlightened Buddha" as "the best of speakers,"[69] his major work makes clear its overridingly soterial aim at numerous points. Perhaps the most salient instance of all occurs, as one would expect, in the chapter most directly concerned to defend the core teaching of the Buddha as to the nature, cause, release, and path toward release of suffering. These, the Four Noble Truths, are dealt with directly in chapter 24 in response to the accusation that

> If all this is empty
> There is neither arising nor cessation
> For you the non-existence
> Of the four noble truths follows[70]

The interlocutor goes on to claim that Nāgārjuna's notion of emptiness entails the non-existence of the Buddhist community (*saṃgha*), the Buddhist teaching (*dharma*), and even of the Buddha himself—all "three jewels" or "three refuges" (*triratna*) at the very basis of the Buddhist religion.[71] Nāgārjuna counters that, on the contrary,

> If all this is non-empty
> There is neither arising nor cessation
> For you the non-existence
> Of the four noble truths follows[72]

In the remainder of the chapter, Nāgārjuna proceeds to argue that it is only on the basis of dependent co-origination (which he identifies with emptiness and the middle way in the justifiably famous verse 24:18) that the Four Noble Truths, the three jewels, and indeed all understanding, action, and fruit of action—"all worldly conventions"[73]—can function, for nothing can occur in an unchanging world such as that effectively posited by the proponent of selfbeing (*svabhāva*).[74] Given the constitutively soterial import of the Buddhist project toward liberation from suffering, there can be no doubt that Nāgārjuna's reiterated support throughout the MK for canonical Buddhist teachings, as prominently evinced in this chapter, places his own project squarely within this tradition. Indeed, Nāgārjuna goes on in the following chapter to apply his teaching explicitly to this ultimate goal of the cessation of suffering.

Such a position is not limited to the MK, however. The colophon to the *Vigrahavyāvartanī* (VV) ends the text with the statement that it was written "for the benefit of all sentient beings"—as befits a Mahāyāna treatise. Nāgārjuna's text properly speaking is confined to refuting the erroneous views of interlocutors, but this does not stop him from stating in the autocommentary (*svavṛtti*) to the very final verse that

> For whom there is emptiness there are all things, mundane and ultimate. Why? For whom there is emptiness there is dependent co-origination; for whom there is dependent co-origination there are the four noble truths; for whom there are the four noble truths there are the fruits of religious striving and there are all special attainments; for whom there are all special attainments there are the three refuges of the Buddha, Dharma, and Saṃgha.[75]

As for the *Yuktiṣaṣṭikā-kārikā* (YṢ), this text makes clear from its dedicatory verse that the attainment of, in Candrakīrti's words, "that city of *nirvāṇa* whose nature is the termination of cyclic life [i.e., *saṃsāra*]"[76] is its goal:

> Obeisance to the Lord of Sages
> Who proclaimed dependent co-origination
> The principle by which origination and cessation
> Are abandoned[77]

Nāgārjuna's text then proceeds through a rebuttal of arguments not dissimilar to that found in his other major works (i.e., the MK, VV, and ŚS). Having argued against the origination or destruction of any *svabhāvic* things along familiar lines, Nāgārjuna explains the rationale for teaching dependent co-origination in explicitly soteriological terms:

> Therefore nothing whatsoever originates
> Nor does anything whatsoever cease

The path of origination and cessation
Was taught for a useful purpose

By knowing origination, cessation is known
By knowing cessation, origination is known
By knowing impermanence
Ultimate truth is known[78]

Nāgārjuna then concludes the YṢ with the following characteristically Mahāyānist benediction invoking the transference of merit:

By virtue of this [text] may all beings
Gather stores of merit and wisdom
Attain the two supremes
Arisen from merit and wisdom[79]

Finally, the *Śūnyatāsaptati* (ŚS) likewise enumerates objections to and rebuttals by Nāgārjuna as per standard procedure in his texts. Perhaps the most conspicuous instance of Nāgārjuna's defense of Buddhist principles and identification of his own philosophy with that of the Buddha occurs at ŚS:23:

[Interlocutor:]
In teaching the way to liberation
The Buddha spoke of origination and cessation, not of emptiness
[Nāgārjuna:]
To take the two as mutually exclusive
Is error[80]

Nāgārjuna goes on immediately to argue that it is only by means of his own understanding of emptiness as dependent co-origination that *nirvāṇa*, the soterial end of all Buddhist striving, can in fact be attained:

[Interlocutor:]
If there is no origination or cessation
Through the cessation of what can *nirvāṇa* arise?
[Nāgārjuna:]

Is liberation not by nature
That nothing arises or ceases?[81]

The text as whole ends, moreover, with an even more explicit claim that one who comprehends Nāgārjuna's philosophy is, *in so doing*, able to attain liberation:

Who faithfully seeks truth
Who logically abides by this principle [of dependent co-origination]
Relies upon the teaching that is without support
Abandons both existence and non-existence, attains peace
Upon understanding dependent co-origination
The nets of bad views vanish
Pure, one attains *nirvāṇa*
By abandoning attachment, ignorance, and aversion[82]

Hopefully, this brief survey of soteriologically oriented passages in Nāgārjuna's works, which could be supplemented extensively, should suffice to demonstrate the importance of the attainment of liberation for him and his philosophy.[83] Such an orientation is not unique to Nāgārjuna, of course, but informs the projects of later Mādhyamikas, and indeed of all Buddhist philosophers, even when pursued in the rather abstract garb of *śāstric* treatises. For example, the verse I have placed to open this chapter, by Āryadeva (third century), who is taken by the tradition to have been Nāgārjuna's direct disciple, clearly takes the four lemmata of the tetralemma as cures for varying mental ailments ("named medicines / In accordance with illnesses"). Śāntideva (fl. eighth century), meanwhile, not only devotes the bulk of Book Three of his *Bodhicaryāvatāra* to a succession of prayers for the deliverance of all sentient beings but also begins the final section of his text (Book Ten) with a like dedication of the merit accrued from the work's composition:

By the good that is mine
From 'Undertaking the Way to Enlightenment' [*Bodhicaryāvatāra*]
May all people
Adorn the way to enlightenment[84]

And even an ostensibly Svātantrika Mādhyamika such as Śāntarakṣita (725–788) writes, in the opening comments of his *Madhyamakālaṃkāravṛtti*, that:

> When one realizes that in reality
> There is no selfbeing
> Then all defilements and stains of knowledge
> Will be abandoned[85]

In all these texts, detachment from conceptual reification emerges as a soterially oriented goal. This is so on the understanding that the holding of such mental objects invariably keeps one enmeshed in the *saṃsāric* cycle of suffering. Paul Williams makes this point in his study of language and linguistic-conceptual construction in the Madhyamaka, which he begins with the following observation:

> The purpose of writing the *Madhyamakakārikā* [i.e., MK], according to a now lost commentary by Devaśarman preserved in fragmentary quotes in Bhāvaviveka's *Prajñāpradīpa*, was twofold; to destroy adherence to language and secondly to the referents of language. By refuting origination the referents are destroyed, and with the patent impossibility of reference language also must cease as lacking any objective substrata. (Williams 1980: 1)

As for Bhāvaviveka himself, it is well known that his position, contra those of his predecessor Buddhapālita and successor Candrakīrti, is to consider Nāgārjuna's arguments as autonomous inferences (*svatantra-anumāna*), on the basis of which to construct metaphysical theses. Furthermore,

> It is well known that Candrakīrti vehemently objected to Bhāvaviveka's logical method, on the grounds that it was a fundamental perversion of Nāgārjuna's project. Specifically, Candrakīrti maintained that the purpose of the *Madhyamakaśāstra* [i.e., MK] has nothing to do with "commanding rational assent,"[86] with demonstrating, proving or disproving anything. Rather the goal is to uproot altogether the very desire, or need, for rational certainty, and so to provide an anecdote [sic: antidote] to the intellectual and spiritual disease of clinging. (Huntington 2007: 122–123)[87]

In other words, a large part of Candrakīrti's gripe with Bhāvaviveka—as I read it at least—lies in his refusal to adopt Bhāvaviveka's thorough-going rationalism, and this on the preeminently pragmatic grounds that the appeal to abstract logic, and the construction—as opposed to the destruction—of philosophical theses for which this logic is utilized, undermines the soterial goal of the entire Madhyamaka enterprise. Yet despite all this, Bhāvaviveka too identifies the attainment of *nirvāṇa* as the aim of his own philosophical endeavor. He begins his *Prajñāpradīpa*, for instance, with a homage explicitly dedicated to liberation from conceptual thought:

> I pay homage to that [Buddha] who taught the reality of dharmas (*dharma-tattva*). Which is quite free from conceptual constructions (*vikalpa*).
> It pacifies all conceptual proliferation (*prapañca*) and destroys all the defective vision (*timira*) of false opinions (*blo ngan, *dhurmati*).
> Though [reality] is not an object of speech, [the Buddha taught] reality by means of imputation (*samāropya*),
> So that [beings] might acquire all levels [of existence and spiritual attainment]. (Ames 1993: 213)[88]

The emphasis on the principally soteriological import of Madhyamaka teachings therefore applies to both sides of the Svātantrika-Prāsaṇgika divide.

It would be all too easy to multiply such citations *in extenso* with reference to still other texts and Mādhyamikas, particularly (given my identifiably Prāsaṇgika understanding of Nāgārjuna), from Candrakīrti.[89] However, I will be referring (indeed, already have referred) to Candrakīrti not infrequently in the arguments that follow, so prefer to cite him *ad locum* rather than risk repetition.

In any case, to avoid a potentially near-infinite list of examples given the sheer magnitude of the textual canon, I will not follow this thread into the myriad other schools and sub-schools of Buddhist thought any further here, except to observe that the soteriological end of Buddhist discourse finds its beginning in the *Discourses* of the founder himself. For the Buddha's silence in the face of metaphysical questions of no soteriological utility—the so-called "unexplicated points" (*avyākṛtavastu*)—is itself eloquent testimony to this orientation, this understanding of silence as "a critical response to a metaphysical tyranny" (Yadav 1977: 464). In the context of a discussion of the Madhyamaka thinker Āryadeva, Jonardon Ganeri has coined the term "protreptic hermeneutics" to describe the Buddha's stance. He elaborates that "the Buddha's words aim at a transformation. Their primary purpose is neither to *refute* alternative views, nor to *prove* the truth of the Buddha's own. Their principal function is protreptic and not dialectic" (Ganeri 2007: 103–104, emphases original).

In like manner, and on the basis of the passages I have cited earlier and many other such statements in the primary literature, Huntington has referred to the Prāsaṇgika Madhyamaka philosophy epitomized by Nāgārjuna as "edifying philosophy," "soteriological philosophy," and "philosophical propaganda," in contradistinction to avowedly disinterested intellectual enterprises he dubs "systematic philosophy." He writes:

> This has been done, first, in order to emphasize the all-important point that this philosophy cannot, even in theory, be dissociated from a concept of practical application; and second, so that it might be more clearly distinguished as a truly radical departure from the type of philosophical enterprise through which one endeavors to discover or define an objective, value-free view of truth or reality. (Huntington 1989: xiii)[90]

This approach may profitably be juxtaposed with that of Yinshun 印順, perhaps the most prolific and highly regarded of all twentieth-century Chinese-language scholars in the field.[91] Yinshun categorizes Nāgārjuna's avowedly contradictory statements as constituting various complementary means by which practitioners may gain access to enlightenment. On this model, then, the tetralemma is designed to aid the various kinds of aspirants in comprehending ultimate truth (真諦) in line with their respective abilities. While this interpretation may appear to evince similarities to that utilized in support of a Modal Interpretation (see §2.2.2), there is an important qualitative difference at work, namely that the aim here is not to defuse the charge of illogicality. For it will be recalled that Li Runsheng and fellow proponents of the Modal Interpretation relied on the *śāsana/anuśāsana* distinction to espouse a gradualist solution to perceived—but on their interpretation merely apparent—paradoxicality in the tetralemma. This they did in order to render the tetralemma a logically (though not necessarily soteriologically) "expedient means of discoursing" (方便為言) (Li 1999b: 910–911). Their approach stands in marked contrast to Yinshun's reading. For the latter explicitly sees the tetralemma as being instrumentalized in Nāgārjuna's work toward soterial ends. This entails that any perception of a differentiation of teachings effectively espoused by the various lemmata in accordance with audience/aspirant ability is not in any way designed to "solve" the lemmata's illogicality. On the contrary, on Yinshun's account neither the internally contradictory third nor fourth lemma is reinterpreted along logicalizing grounds, and the four lemmata function as a coherent whole to aid all members toward liberating insight.

In case any doubt as to his attitude to the logicalizing tendencies apparent in peers' work should persist, Yinshun makes abundantly clear how his approach differs from theirs in perhaps his most famous work, *Investigation of Emptiness* (空之探究: Yinshun 1985).[92] There, he dismisses scholars who adopt an exclusively secular, logico-rational methodology when dealing with explicitly religious texts such as the MK:

> Modern scholars researching the MK through Sanskrit and Tibetan sources have made some progress, but they still adopt a secular methodology in their work so as to explicate the dialectical functioning of logic and proof according to which, on this account, Nāgārjuna worked. (Yinshun 1985: 226)[93]

For Yinshun, the tetralemma is used to *dispense with*, not reaffirm, "theories based on the mutual opposition between language and thought and developed via various deductive arguments" (Yinshun 1985: 227).[94] He goes on to make a great deal of the abandonment of conceptualization (*prapañca*/戲論), espoused by Nāgārjuna at MK:22:15.[95] This verse comes at the culmination of a series of rejections of any kind of tetralemma as being adequate to the description of the Buddha, perhaps most notably in MK:22:12.[96] Yinshun uses the negative tetralemma there in concert with similar examples from throughout the MK to deny that any merely intellectual inquiry can comprehend the import of Nāgārjuna's *prāsaṅgika* or deconstructive method. He goes on to state that ignoring the soterial aim of the MK risks denaturing Nāgārjuna's teaching as a whole:

> Speaking in terms of skillful analysis and precise differentiation has many great qualities. However, if one ignores the intent of the teaching and focuses solely on theoretical approaches to abstract principles, there is a risk one will miss Nāgārjuna's entire purpose and purport. (Yinshun 1985: 253)[97]

And he concludes his discussion with a reference to MK:27:30 by calling Nāgārjuna's approach an "exceptionally skillful form of teaching indeed"

(Yinshun 1985: 259).[98] There can thus be no doubt as to the overwhelmingly soteriological import of Nāgārjuna's philosophy as a whole, and of the abandonment of all views enacted in the rejection of all four positions of the *catuṣkoṭi* in particular, in the interpretation of his thought by Yinshun.[99]

Along like lines, I am proposing here that the four positions of the *catuṣkoṭi* function as an expedient means (*upāya*/方便) designed to aid in the rejection of all possible logical positions, and thus in the "abandonment of all views" (*sarvadṛṣṭiprahāṇāya*) memorably espoused in the final verse of the entire MK.[100] This does not mean, however, that Nāgārjuna's work is reducible to some conjurer's *trompe l'oeil* trick,[101] but rather that throughout his work Nāgārjuna has sought to disillude us of our desirous grasping at views through the expedient means of the tetralemma.[102]

If textual hermeneutics is the aim (i.e., if the aim is to understand what Nāgārjuna's texts are saying and doing), then it is unfortunate that few scholars treating the *catuṣkoṭi* have considered the soterial dimension, since for a devout Buddhist such as Nāgārjuna this is primary. Even Gunaratne merely acknowledges it in the final lines of his paper when he ventures that "Nagarjuna also uses the *catuṣkoṭi* as a means by which the *Karika* verses would lead one from the *saṃvṛti* to the *paramārtha* truth through a process of dialectical progression in thought and through meditation on the nature of things as 'exposed' in the text" (Gunaratne 1986: 231).[103] Staal too seems to make a similar acknowledgment when he says: "A sensible interpretation would be to regard the tetralemma not as a statement, but as a pedagogical or therapeutic device" (Staal 1976: 127). Crucially, however, he makes this claim only in an effort to *avoid* admitting any violation of the law of noncontradiction on the part of Nāgārjuna .

As we have seen in ample detail, attempts to logicalize the tetralemma in disregard of the soterial purpose it is aimed at serving within Nāgārjuna's overall religiosophical project have been and continue to be the norm. In the last analysis, however, the *catuṣkoṭi*, as utilized by Nāgārjuna for the systematic rejection of all four possible logical positions, for the abandonment of all views, is meant not to make logical sense but to blow us away. And I mean that literally, or at least as a literally leaning pun. For I am playing here on the etymological root of the term "*nirvāṇa*," which refers to blowing out, extinguishing, as the flame of a candle.[104] To get us to blow ourselves away—or rather to realize that there really is no self, no ignorance, in the first place to even be blown away, extinguished, enlightened—is the overarching goal of Nāgārjuna's entire enterprise. Without realizing that views (*dṛṣṭi*), like all things (*sarvam dharmam*), are empty (*śūnya*), we fall into the ignorance (*avidyā*) of ascribing existence to them. Only through what is *nirvikalpa* (free from invariably dichotomizing, or perhaps more aptly quaternizing, conceptualization), however, can we reach *nirvāṇa*. On this analogy, then, Nāgārjuna's view on views—as embodied in the fourfold rejection of views of the tetralemma—is like the candle flame that burns and, by burning, extinguishes itself.[105] And, to use a well-known Buddhist metaphor, just as it makes no sense to ask in which direction a flame has extinguished, so it makes no sense to ask what Nāgārjuna's view of no view holds, for it precisely holds no view at all.

If the foregoing account has proven in the least convincing, then it has succeeded in demonstrating the continuity between the Buddha and Nāgārjuna on the primary matter of this soterial end, and thereby in situating Nāgārjuna's *catuṣkoṭi* as a discursive tool eminently suited to the Buddhist enterprise. As such, it has also shown that accounts of the *catuṣkoṭi* that do not take this into account fail to function as interpretations of Nāgārjuna's thought at all. This does not render them of no use, of course, for the insights gained from an exclusively or overly rationalist approach to the tetralemma, or indeed to any other aspect of Nāgārjuna's philosophy, may lead to the articulation of interesting and internally coherent philosophical notions. It is just that they will not be Nāgārjuna's notions, dedicated as *he* is with using the tetralemma for ends beyond the remit of reason.

3

Nāgārjuna's Tetralemma

Tetrāletheia and Tathāgata, Utterance and Anontology

3.1. The Dilemma of the Tetralemma

This chapter forms a pair with the previous one in that both are concerned with Nāgārjuna's use of the *catuṣkoṭi* or tetralemma. However, whereas the foregoing discussion was devoted to a critical appraisal of overtly rationalizing scholarly readings, my approach here is primarily constructive. Indeed, this chapter should be taken primarily as a work of philosophical construction, though one based directly on the preceding textual hermeneutics. Now, on the one hand, I freely admit that Nāgārjuna would not have recognized the terms I propose here, not least since they deliberately innovate on his textual pronouncements. On the other hand, however, I conceive these innovations as developments of Nāgārjuna's stated views; attempts, in other words, to formulate philosophical ideas recognizably Nāgārjunian in the linguistic medium of twenty-first-century English. Given that Nāgārjuna's philosophy overall differs in multiple significant ways from any enshrined in the Western canon,[1] it makes sense that the terminology at our disposal, developed as it has been in and by that canon, should prove insufficient to the task of conveying it. Ideas can be expressed in multifarious ways: through musical compositions, paintings, sculptures, dances, rituals, and countless other non-linguistic as well as linguistic media. Philosophical ideas, however, wheresoever they have been humanly elaborated, have typically taken the form of linguistic expression. (I say "typically" for where one draws a line on admissible form comes down to where one draws a line on admissible philosophy, and if one takes a relatively inclusive view of what counts as the latter, then one is obliged to include many non-linguistic forms as philosophical media.) The linguistic and literary forms of philosophizing have themselves been myriad, of course,[2] and the histories of philosophies the world over are replete with countless instances of individual thinkers or schools inventing new words, or innovating old ones with new senses, so as to get their ideas

Buddhism Between Religion and Philosophy. Rafal K. Stepien, Oxford University Press. © Oxford University Press 2024.
DOI: 10.1093/oso/9780197771303.003.0003

across. Hence, in attempting to give voice to the philosophy of Nāgārjuna, I propose that not only is it not frivolous to propose neologisms, but that, on the contrary, it is downright needful. If recent newcomers to English such as "*karma*," "*dharma*," or even "Buddha" can attain widespread use, then I see no reason why, in the course of Buddhism's ongoing gradual acculturation to English-language contexts, the terms and senses I propose in what follows cannot do so too.

In light of the critical awareness occasioned by the preceding pages, then, in those that follow I argue initially that the *catuṣkoṭi* must be taken exhaustively; that is, as embracing all logically possible propositional alternatives. I will attempt to demonstrate this not only on the basis of such a reading being textually justified but also because it leads, I hope, to more interesting philosophical results. In other words, the exhaustiveness of the *catuṣkoṭi* is to be preferred on the methodological bases of the principles of hermeneutical fidelity and philosophical charity. Working from the *catuṣkoṭi*'s exhaustiveness, and in contradistinction to analyses—typical, as we have seen, in the scholarly literature—aimed at demonstrating the classical logicality of the tetralemma via parameterization of one form or another, I go on to propose an interpretation along what I am calling "paralogical" lines. In so doing, however, I argue for the inadequacy of a dialetheic reading, and therefore propose a new term, "tetrāletheia," designed to represent more adequately the four-folded nature of the tetralemma. Subsequent sections of the chapter are devoted to explicating this notion, together with providing a reading of the tetralemma as embodied in the figure of the Tathāgata. In the final section, I propose another new usage, "utterance," as an alternative descriptor for the totality of the tetralemma; one that I argue is better adequated to the paralogical and "anontological" tetralemma than are terms in standard use insofar as it dispenses with their positive logical and substantialist ontological value(s).

I am convinced that such a reading represents a more faithful interpretation of Nāgārjuna's thought than the logicalist readings I have criticized at length, distant as they have been shown to be from Nāgārjuna's own stated aims. That said, as mentioned I conceive my project here as methodologically located not within the field of textual hermeneutics but just over the border between it and philosophical construction. On the one hand, I do consider the interpretation of Nāgārjuna's *catuṣkoṭi* here proposed, according to which it is to be read in paralogical terms as a tetrāletheic utterance, to be hermeneutically sounder than those I have shown to be based on an "interpolation procedure" (Westerhoff 2018a: 119) designed and deployed so as to render the *catuṣkoṭi* logically innocuous. Indeed, rather than rescuing Nāgārjuna, on my understanding such efforts miss his tetralemma's most important aim: to help enlighten the reader not through the attainment of any particular knowledge but rather through the realization of "the perfection of wisdom which cuts like the thunderbolt" through all conceptualizations.[3] Nevertheless, having cited manifold relevant sources to undergird my interpretation in the foregoing discussion, I will not be presenting here any further substantive supporting documentation culled from the corpus of one or other classical commentator or exegetical school to buttress my reading. For while my position may be textually warranted (as I propose it is), the other side of my intent here is to provide, and to provoke, a philosophically rewarding discussion of the *catuṣkoṭi*; one, that is, which will remain interesting whether or not one agrees that this is what Nāgārjuna himself meant. For as we will go on to see in the next chapter (and as I therefore hope to be forgiven for stating but proleptically, and hence somewhat cryptically, here), I see Nāgārjuna's "abandonment of all views" (*sarvadṛṣṭiprahāṇāya*) or "view of no view," with which he concludes the entire MK, as indissolubly linked to what I term "exhaustion" in the present discussion. This, I argue, represents the soterial thrust of the tetralemma, the tetrāletheic utterance by which we are to be "exhausted"; extinguished, that is, in *nirvāṇa*. This last, after all, is the teleological goal of Nāgārjuna's entire enterprise.

Now, given that part of the argument I make in this chapter rests on what I take to be the inadequacy of analyses of the tetralemma rooted in the dualities typically taken by Western scholars as concomitant with the parameters of the supposedly apodeictic logical laws laid down by the *maestro di color che sanno*, it would be well to briefly outline the relevant views of their progenitor, Aristotle. As lucidly summarized in Garfield and Priest's opening statement on the topic, "The standard view in Western philosophy, dating back to Aristotle, is that every proposition is either true or false—not neither, and not both. There are just two possibilities" (Garfield and Priest 2009: 71). Indeed, the formulation of the dilemma, as well as of the laws of non-contradiction and of the excluded middle, are already present in early works of the Aristotelian corpus, as, for example, the *Posterior Analytics*, where the Stagirite states "That everything is affirmed or denied truly is assumed by demonstration *per impossibile*" (Aristotle 1984: 125: I, 11, 77a 22). Likewise, in *On Interpretation* he states "Of contradictory statements about a universal taken universally it is necessary for one or the other to be true or false; similarly if they are about particulars" (Aristotle 1984: 28: 7, 17b 27). The classic discussion, however, is to be found in Book IV of the *Metaphysics*. There, Aristotle formulates what he claims is "the most certain of all principles . . . naturally the starting-point even for all the other axioms"; that is, the principle that "the same attribute cannot at the same time belong and not belong to the same subject in the same respect" (Aristotle 1984: 1587: IV 3 1005b 19–33). Aristotle rejects the tetralemma offhand a little later in the text as either a basic error or as equivalent to saying nothing:

> our opponent himself confesses himself to be in error. —And at the same time our discussion with him is evidently about nothing at all; for he says nothing. For he says neither 'yes' nor 'no', but both 'yes' and 'no'; and again he denies both of these and says 'neither yes nor no'. (Aristotle 1984: 1592: IV 4 1008a 29–1008b 2)

He then goes on to declare that "there cannot be an intermediate between contradictories, but of one subject we must either affirm or deny any one predicate" (Aristotle 1984: 1597: IV, 7, 1011b 23). Indeed, according to Guy Bugault, Aristotle saw the tetralemma as quite simply "a despicable way to dodge a debate. He demanded that his adversary accept the dilemma, without the possible escapes of a third or fourth solution" (Bugault 1983: 17).

This is obviously not so in the Buddhist case. On the contrary, to continue the characterization provided by Garfield and Priest, "A traditional view in Buddhism, of equally ancient ancestry, is that there are four [possibilities]. A proposition may be true (and true only), false (and false only), both true and false, or neither true nor false—*t, f, b, n*. This is the *catuṣkoṭi*" (Garfield and Priest 2009: 71). Although Nāgārjuna's use of the tetralemma was and remains the most celebrated elaboration—and the one which occupies us here—it is important to note that this form of argumentation is already present in the Buddha's own *Discourses* as also in pre-Buddhist Indian philosophy.[4] Following Nāgārjuna, the tetralemma was put to use by a wide range of Buddhist (and non-Buddhist) philosophers in India, Tibet, China, and Japan (among others). Thus, for example, following expositions of the *catuṣkoṭi* as found in the Buddha's *Discourses* and the Abhidharma and Prajñāpāramitā schools, Priest charts its use among such figures as Sengzhao 僧肇 (374–414) and Jizang 吉藏 (549–623) of the Chinese Sanlun 三論 or Three Treatise school directly heir to Nāgārjuna's Madhyamaka, Fazang 法藏 (643–712) and Chengguang 澄觀 (738–839) of the Huayan 華嚴 or Flower

Garland (*Avataṃsaka*) school, and Dōgen 道元 (1200–1253) of the Sōtō Zen school (Priest 2018).

Prior to presenting my own reading, then, and in order to grasp something of the dizzyingly paradoxical heights to which the tetralemma was taken by later Buddhists, I will take a brief detour into the Chinese context (one not mentioned by Priest). There we find Guanding 灌頂 (561–632), disciple of Zhiyi 智顗 (538–597), who founded the Tiantai 天台or Heavenly Platform school highly influenced by Madhyamaka. In his *Commentary to the Mahāparinirvāṇa Sūtra* (大般涅槃經疏, T 1767), Guanding utters a *catuṣkoṭi* crystallized into the successive affirmation of negation, negation of negation, affirmation and negation of negation, and neither affirmation nor negation of negation. He writes:

> [Affirmation of negation:]
> Negate negation. Negate non-negation. Negate both negation and non-negation. Negate neither negation nor non-negation.
> [Negation of negation:]
> Not negate negation. Not negate non-negation. Not negate both negation and non-negation. Not negate neither negation nor non-negation.
> [Affirmation and negation of negation:]
> Both negate and not negate negation. Both negate and not negate non-negation. Both negate and not negate both negation and non-negation. Both negate and not negate neither negation nor non-negation.
> [Neither affirmation nor negation of negation:]
> Neither negate nor non-negate negation. Neither negate nor non-negate non-negation. Neither negate nor non-negate both negation and non-negation. Neither negate nor non-negate neither negation nor non-negation.[5]

If this is "logical," then I am at a loss to conceive what could possibly count as "paralogical."

3.2. The Exhaustive Tetralemma

There has been quite some scholarship devoted to the question of whether the tetralemma is logically exhaustive; that is, as embracing all logical possibilities. The general consensus—that it is[6]—is borne out not only by

Nāgārjuna's use of the tetralemma in the MK but also by its appearances in the Buddha's *Discourses* and in the pre-Buddhist Indian philosophical canon.

The only counterargument to the exhaustive view is one that interprets the *catuṣkoṭi* in what may be called a historical manner; that is, as being directed toward a limited set of historically identifiable interlocutors, be these Buddhist or non-Buddhist. Thus, for example, Wayman identifies the four lemmata at MK:12:1, and 1:1, as rejections of four specific non-Buddhist positions: (1) The denial of arising from self is a rejection of the Sāṁkhya position, "which is the *satkāryavāda* (causation of the effect already existent)." (2) The denial of arising from another is the rejection of the generally non-Buddhist notion of a creator being (*īśvara*), and also possibly of the specifically Jaina list of sources for "caused by another"; viz., destiny (*niyati*), time (*kāla*), God (*īśvara*), nature (*svabhāva*), and action (*karma*). (3) The denial of both is a rejection of the Vaiśeṣika (and also Nyāya) notion of *asatkāryavāda* (the opposite of Sāṁkhya *satkāryavāda*). And (4), the denial of neither is a rejection of the Lokāyata, "the ancient materialistic school" (Wayman 1977: 11–12).[7] Although Wayman does not spell it out, the (or at least an) implication of such an interpretation of the tetralemma is that, rather than exhausting all logical possibilities, it is merely a historically contingent enumeration of certain positions (among other conceivable ones) current among the philosophical schools of Nāgārjuna's India. The distinction is important, for were the exhaustive interpretation shown false, the tetralemma would effectively be deprived, on my reading, of most of its soterial thrust, based as this is on the paralogical overcoming of *all* logically possible positions.

In accordance with the "parasitic" or "opponent-relative" manner of his method (see §0.2), it is true that Nāgārjuna often states the view of an interlocutor prior to arguing, in *prasaṅga* fashion, for the absurdity of its consequences. Thus, to give a prominent example, the first six verses of MK:24 clearly state the view of such an interlocutor (whether Buddhist or non-Buddhist is not made explicit); one whom Nāgārjuna proceeds to castigate in the following verses as "not understanding," "weak-minded," and "like one who, though mounted on a horse, forgets that horse."[8] The remainder of the chapter is designed to reduce the views of the interlocutor to absurdity, as is routinely the case with Nāgārjuna's *prasaṅga* method of criticism. In the course of his critique, Nāgārjuna identifies his interlocutor's position with essentialism (the affirmation of own-being, *svabhāva*, 24:16), which is then shown to be incompatible with such unquestioned phenomena as arising and ceasing (24:17, 24:20), suffering and its end (24:21–25), and action and actors (24:27–29, 33–35). In effect, Nāgārjuna charges, "you reject all worldly conventions."[9]

This argument is explicitly grounded on Nāgārjuna's analysis of own-being (*svabhāva*), to which MK:15 as a whole is dedicated.[10] There, having deconstructed the notion of own-being, and its contrary, other-being (*parabhāva*), via the familiar *prasaṅgic reductio ad absurdum*, Nāgārjuna employs a foreshortened version of the *catuṣkoṭi* (i.e., the *dvikoṭi* or dilemma) to conclude

> "It exists" is grasping for eternalism
> "It does not exist" is the viewpoint of nihilism
> Therefore the wise should not depend
> On either existence nor non-existence[11]

This is a contextually unqualified position. That is, even if the historical Nāgārjuna is here combatting a view propounded by a particular philosophical adversary, his conclusion cannot be taken as remaining valid only within the limited ambit of that adversary's view. Rather, Nāgārjuna's method consists in taking certain tenets, propositions, or theses (*abhyupagama, pratijñā, pakṣa*) espoused by particular philosophical viewpoints or systems (*darśana, vāda, siddhānta*) current in his day, and showing them to entail not only consequences that are absurd, but consequences whose absurdity is universalizable. To claim that the consequences his arguments entail apply only to the given interlocutor would be tantamount to saying, for example, that the rejection by Plato's Socrates of Crito's offer to free him from jail by means of bribery could not be taken to posit a universal ethical standard, but only one relevant to Socrates and Crito. It would also go against Nāgārjuna's own overtly universalistic language, as, for example, in MK:15:10 just cited.

Nāgārjuna's *catuṣkoṭi*, then, must be taken as exhaustive; it comprehends, and typically rejects, all logically possible alternatives: affirmation, negation, both, neither. This exhaustiveness would not be problematic from a logical standpoint were Nāgārjuna to affirm one lemma to the exclusion of the others. To affirm, in other words, "all is real," and deny on this basis that it is not real, or both real and not real, or neither real nor not real (cf. MK:18:8), poses no logical problems. The insoluble logical conundrum of Nāgārjuna's *catuṣkoṭi*, however—and the consequently interminable attempts at its solution by logicians—consists in the fact that Nāgārjuna negates (or in one case affirms) *all* the lemmata. In any case, the logico-linguistic *exhaustiveness*

I have detailed thus far is a necessary condition for the epistemo-ontological *exhaustion* I will now go on to argue is the soteriological aim of Nāgārjuna's philosophical enterprise, and thus of the tetralemma as his preferred dialectical technique.[12]

3.3. Tetralemma as Tetrāletheia

Graham Priest has over the course of recent years been at the forefront of elaborating a philosophically robust notion of true contradiction. He terms this "dialetheia," by which he means "any true statement of the form: α and it is not the case that α" (Priest 2006: 4).[13] Understandably, this claim, and the extensive argumentation he provides in support of it, have faced a great deal of criticism from the "entrenched orthodoxy" (Priest 2006: 284) of analytical philosophers.[14] In turning his attention to Buddhist topics, Priest has teamed up with Jay Garfield to apply the notion of dialetheia to Nāgārjuna.[15] Contrary to those "who see consistency as a necessary condition of rationality," Garfield and Priest declare that "to those who share with us a dialetheist's comfort with the possibility of true contradictions commanding rational assent, for Nāgārjuna to endorse such contradictions would not *undermine* but instead would *confirm*, the impression that he is indeed a highly rational thinker" (Garfield and Priest 2002: 87, emphases original). Now, readers of the previous chapter will be aware that I am highly critical of the parameterization of the tetralemma as carried out by Garfield and Priest (among all-too-many others) as textually unattested and philosophically unwarranted. Nonetheless, I consider Garfield and Priest's attempt to read the tetralemma as dialetheic laudable on the grounds that it presents a reading both more philologically justified and more philosophically astute than the all-too-common attempts to prove it accommodated within the canons of classical logic. This is so even if their insistence on Nāgārjuna's "rationality," albeit dialetheic, shows Garfield and Priest still to be at work within precisely the parameters Nāgārjuna's *catuṣkoṭi* is designed to abandon.

The dialetheic understanding of Nāgārjuna is helpful, but not quite adequate. The inadequacy stems from Garfield and Priest's insistence upon a binary schema (di-aletheia) to represent what is a quaternary structure (tetra-lemma), and this despite their clear avowal of the difference between Western binary and Indian quaternary logical models.[16] Dialetheia has, in Priest's formulation, a "Janus-headed nature . . . [in that it] 'faces' both truth and falsity" (Priest 2006: 4 n. 4). Dialetheia thus explicitly functions within the binary parameters initially set by Aristotle, even (indeed, precisely insofar) as it argues for a "both/and" conception of truth as opposed to the "either/or" of the classical tradition.[17] In its stead, I propose to use a new term, "tetrāletheia," so as to more adequately represent the four-folded nature of the tetralemma; one not so much Janus- as Brahmā-headed. The term draws on, and plays with, etymological roots from both Greek and Sanskrit, and consequently requires some explication.

The prefix "tetra-" is of clear Greek provenance, and I use it simply to refer to the four *koṭi*s of the *catuṣkoṭi*. As for "aletheia," I use this with Heidegger's philologico-philosophical critical analysis in mind. It is in his seminal essay "Plato's Doctrine of Truth" (originally published in 1932) that Heidegger first discusses in detail why truth, for the Greeks, "was distinguished by the alpha-privative" (Heidegger 1998: 171).[18] He writes:

> Truth originally means what has been wrested away from hiddenness. Truth is thus a wresting away in each case, in the form of a revealing. The hiddenness can be of various kinds: closing off, hiding away, disguising, covering over, masking, dissembling. (Heidegger 1998: 171)

This Greek notion of truth, aletheia, as "the unhiddenness that is related to the hidden" (Heidegger 1998: 172) is closely related to that found in the Sanskrit term for conventional truth (*saṃvṛti-satya*).[19] Nagao notes that

> the Sanskrit texts have two spellings for worldly convention, *saṃvṛti* and *saṃvṛtti*. *Saṃvṛti* derives from the root *vṛ*, "to cover, hide, obstruct," thus suggesting that *saṃvṛti-satya* is covered or hidden truth (*satya*). But *saṃvṛtti* derives from the root *vṛt*, "to exist, arise, come about, activate," thus suggesting that *saṃvṛtti-satya* is truth that comes about within the world. (Nagao 1989: 39)[20]

Saṃvṛti-/Saṃvṛtti-satya can thus be read as the truth which is hidden within the world.[21] In quite Heideggerian terms, it is the truth which is concealed in its very unconcealedness. Crucially, although Nāgārjuna posits a difference between conventional and ultimate truth (*paramārtha-satya*),[22] on the predominant interpretation this operates only from the conventional perspective; once one has attained ultimate truth, one understands the ultimate identity between conventional and ultimate truth.[23] This amounts to the famous notion of the "emptiness of emptiness" (*śūnyatāśūnyatā*), according to which emptiness (absence of own-being) is also stated to be empty (absent of own-being), for otherwise it would constitute an exception to the truth of emptiness; a non-empty truth contradicting the truth of emptiness. In other words, "the ultimate truth is that there is no ultimate truth" (Siderits 2007: 182), only conventional truth (that is, emptiness) . . . which is ultimate truth.[24]

3.4. Tetrāletheia as Tathāgata

I am now *almost* in a position to explain the long "ā" in tetrāletheia. Before being able to do so, however, one final piece must be placed in the puzzle.[25] This regards the "Tathāgata"—a Pāli/Sanskrit term typically used by the Buddha in referring to himself. It is surely the single greatest pun in all Buddhist literature, for it plays with a grammatical feature known as *sandhi* (analogous to French *liaison*) whereby phonological elements at the boundaries of words or morphemes elide so as to facilitate pronunciation. In this case, the play consists in the fact that the term "tathāgata" may be read as a compound of "tathā + gata" or "tathā + āgata." Given that "tathā" means "thus," "gata" "gone," and "āgata" "come," we are left with two equally viable, and mutually contradictory, meanings of the word as a whole: "the thus-come one" and "the thus-gone-one." The Buddha is thus represented paradoxically as one who has both gone and come to thusness—or perhaps, in so doing, even as one who has passed beyond all such coming and going.

The ineradicably paradoxical nature of the Tathāgata is no mere playful pun for Nāgārjuna, who devotes an entire chapter of the MK to it.[26] Nor should we assume the topic could have anything less than cardinal importance, for let us not forget that the archetypal figure of the Tathāgata is universally taken by Mahāyānists such as Nāgārjuna to embody what the fifteenth-century Tibetan Mādhyamika Khedrupjey (Mkhas grub Dge legs dpal bzang) called "the great medicinal tree . . . the one who heals all beings" (Cabezón 2009: 136). Nāgārjuna begins the relevant chapter (MK:22) with a series of negations designed to demonstrate the untenability of any positive description applied to the Tathāgata. This reaches its *denouement* in true tetralemmic fashion, where Nāgārjuna concludes that, with regard to the Tathāgata, one must neither affirm nor negate:

> "Empty" should not be said
> "Non-empty" too should not be said
> Likewise with "both" and "neither"
> These are said for the sake of instruction[27]

Nāgārjuna then proceeds to drive the point home that no statement can logically apply to the Tathāgata. In the very next verse, he deploys the negative *catuṣkoṭi* to rhetorically ask:

> "Permanent," "impermanent" and the rest
> How could the fourfold apply here to the Peaceful One?
> "Finite," "infinite" and the rest
> How could the fourfold apply here to the Peaceful One?[28]

Subsequent verses display refined poetic play in their rejections of grasping (*grāha*),[29] discriminatorily conceptualizing (*vikalpa*),[30] and conceptualizing (*prapañca*)[31] the Tathāgata, the combined effect of which is to maintain that "no thought can apply to the by nature empty Tathāgata."[32]

And yet one must not stop at a merely negative characterization of the Tathāgata, for this would be tantamount to precisely such an "extreme view" (*antagrahadṛṣṭi*) as the "middle way" (*madhyamā pratipad*) of the Madhyamaka is out to avoid. Thus, in the very final verse of the chapter, Nāgārjuna writes:

> What is the Tathāgata's own-being
> That is the own-being of this world
> The Tathāgata is without own-being
> Without own-being is this world[33]

Having already denied that the Tathāgata can in any way be conceptualized, Nāgārjuna here effects an identification of that very Tathāgata with "this world." In so doing, he shows that a full account of the Tathāgata must do full justice to him as both thus-gone from the world and thus-come to it; that is in effect, to both the identity of and the difference between *svabhāva* and *śūnyatā*, *saṃvṛti-satya* and *paramārtha-satya*, *saṃsāra* and *nirvāṇa*. And to accomplish this one must both affirm and negate; indeed, affirm, negate, both affirm and negate, neither affirm nor negate. The upshot of all this is that the Tathāgata thus appears here as the embodiment of the tetralemma. He is the "truth-body" (*dharma-kāya*): real, not real, both, and neither; not empty, not non-empty, not both, and not neither. All this on the basis of a pun!

In like manner to the Tathāgata (who is both "tathā + gata" and "tathā + āgata"), I intend the tetrāletheia of Nāgārjuna's tetralemma to be read, therefore, both as "tetra + letheia" and "tetra + aletheia"; both as the four-folded negation or concealing of truth, and its four-folded affirmation or revealing. In the tetrāletheia, these two senses converge in mutual implication. For as Nāgārjuna comes to utter:

> "Finite" and "infinite"
> If both were established
> Then neither "finite" nor "infinite"
> Would be established[34]

3.5. Utterance and Anontology

I said "utter," for I am now in a position to explain this notion. "Utterance" is the term I propose to be used as referring to the totality of the tetralemma (and, by extension, to any of its four *koṭis* in functional relation to one another). It is preferable to other English-language renderings such as "statement," "declaration," "position," "proposition," "affirmation," and so on in that it avoids the ontologically substantialist presuppositions incorporated in the etymological components of these latter. Thus, for example, "*state*ment" presupposes something that "stands," "de*clar*ation" something that is brought to light, while the positivity of "*pos*ition," "*pro-pos*ition," and "*affirm*ation" as excluding negativity is all too evident. All these and numerous other synonymous terms implicitly assert the presence of some*thing*, which speaks volumes for the prevalence, even on the linguistic level, of what Heidegger called the metaphysics of Being. Of course, it is precisely on the linguistic level (i.e., grounded in and grounding the very manner in which we may construct our thoughts) that we should expect to see presuppositions so engrained that to demarcate them is already to call our thought as a whole radically (i.e., from the root) into question. I have proposed "utterance" as a term which embodies this radicality, this uttermost degree, and one which does so in an explicitly linguistic manner, as denoting an instance of uttering. For the tetralemma is an *utter* mode of speech: exhaustive, total, utmost. The English term recalls the Sanskrit *uttara*, moreover, meaning "superior," "beyond"—as the tetralemma goes beyond ordinary speech. And, in a final correlation which poetically figures my proposal to see the Tathāgata as the embodiment of the tetralemma, *uttara* even designates the Buddha himself, and does so in a tale tradition ascribes to none other than Nāgārjuna.[35]

An alternative to "utterance" in this sense would be an altogether new coinage: "āssertion." This new term I would propose as highlighting the paradoxically positive and negative formulation it embodies: it is both an assertion and the negation of assertion, the "a" functioning as both an intensive and a privative prefix.[36] But apart from losing the connotations of "utterance" just noted, I fear that the crucial diacritical mark on the initial "ā" would prove too much for easy incorporation into English, and so leave it as a potential resource for future English-language Buddhist work.

The utterance is inherently paradoxical. *Pace* Aristotle, a paradox as here understood is not simply "a divergence from pre-existing *doxa.*"[37] I use it to designate an opinion or belief (doxy) that is beyond or past (para) the parameters of ordinary language and classical logic (where these latter are understood to be roughly coextensive in the light of the etymological inherence of both "word" and "reason" in the Greek noun "logos"). Para-doxy is thus to be distinguished from ortho-doxy (right belief), pseudo-doxy (false belief), hetero-doxy (other belief), and what may be called homo-doxy (same belief). I pause on this point because I understand Nāgārjuna to be using the para-doxical tetra-lemma so as to enable the reader-practitioner to pass beyond (para) the oppositional meters of language and logic to a level of truth/reality (*satya*) no longer susceptible to them but, as shown earlier, both/neither conventional (*saṃvṛti*) and/or ultimate (*paramārtha*). In so doing, Nāgārjuna shows himself to be a worthy inheritor of the Perfection of Wisdom (*Prajñāpāramitā*—with an emphasis on the *pāra*) corpus of *sūtras* on which so much of his thought is based.

Nāgārjuna's tetrāletheic utterance, then, is "paralogical" in that it is intended to facilitate the passing beyond the entire edifice of reificatory thought at the basis of our reason and language. "Paralogical" is not meant so much here to mean "paraconsistent" (though I take the latter as a subspecies of the more generally paralogical), but rather as beyond (para) the logical (rational/linguistic).[38] I thus disagree with Robinson (and indeed with the entire exegetical project of proving Nāgārjuna to be "logical") when he states that "there is no evidence that Nāgārjuna 'uses logic to destroy logic'" (Robinson 1957: 307). Robinson is arguing here against Murti (among others), and in particular against statements such as "The sole aim of the Mādhyamika system is to free the human mind of the net of concepts '*vikalpa-jāla*' and verbal elaboration (*prapañca*)" (Murti 1955: 146 n. 1).[39] Huntington captures the relevant debate pellucidly in the following passage, which I thus cite in full:

> The very questions which, under the spell of reified thought, seem so engaging are invariably founded upon a tacit, deep-rooted presupposition that truth and reality can be discussed only in the language of epistemological and ontological propositions, that they must in some manner be susceptible to interpretation through the application of a rationalistic or idealistic grid over the data of everyday experience. The Mādhyamika's deconstructive analysis tries to illuminate and dissolve this presupposition by turning epistemological and ontological language back on itself so that it devours itself whole without leaving a trace. (Huntington 1989: 106–107)

Indeed, it is along just such lines that Nāgārjuna clearly sees logic, in the twin sense of rationality/language, as ultimately to be abandoned if one is to attain *nirvāṇa*.[40]

Furthermore, I have refrained in this context from speaking of Nāgārjuna's "ontology" because I understand his understanding of "what is" to be "anontological." By this term (and its nominal correlate "anontology"), I mean to convey in synoptic fashion something of the intellectually confounding content and deliberately disquieting form Nāgārjuna inherited from his Prajñāpāramitā forebears and exhibited in his own works. For to characterize Nāgārjuna as affirming or negating the existence of a certain entity (*svabhāva*, *śūnyatā*, etc.), and thereby as holding a certain *ontological* position, is already to miss the radical nature of his *prāsaṅgika* critique. Nāgārjuna refrains from holding any ontological position (indeed, any position), because any (such) position would be tantamount to one of the extreme views he—and the Buddha before him—denounced.[41] To say, with Murti, that emptiness is "the Absolute" (see Murti 1955: 229ff), or alternatively with Narain that Nāgārjuna's "*Śūnya-vāda* . . . [is] absolute ontological nihilism" (Narain 1977: 178) is to side with one or other of the doctrinal extremes (*antadvaya*) Nāgārjuna explicitly rejects in uttering, for example, that *nirvāṇa* "neither exists nor does not exist."[42] His position (such as it is . . .) is thus not ontological in the sense that ontology, at least as classically defined, is inevitably involved in pronouncing on what is and what is not.[43] Nāgārjuna refuses to affirm or to deny an ontological status of *bhāvas*;

his *prāsaṅgika* method criticizes any such ontological positioning, without arrogating any such position to itself. For as Nāgārjuna makes amply clear, to call a given thing "empty" is not to predicate emptiness of that thing, but rather to deny that any "thing" exists, or does not exist, or both exists and does not exist, or neither exists nor does not exist, such that emptiness, or anything else, could be predicated, or denied, or both, or neither, of it. To speak of the emptiness of things, to characterize reality as empty, is thus not equivalent to making any predicative statement in regard to things or reality. Rather, it is to deny the applicability of any ontological status to a given thing, on the basis that the ascription of any ontological status requires the existence of some identifiable thing; that is, *that very thing* to which one would thereby be ascribing an ontological status. This applies even if the ontological status ascribed is a negative one; that is, even if one is denying that *that very thing* (really) exists.[44]

Nāgārjunian emptiness is thus anontological because it rejects the very object to which ontological status could be ascribed. As such, it is not ontological, but nor is it non-ontological, where this latter would entail a negative ontological status tantamount to nihilism. That which "exists, does not exist, both exists and does not exist, neither exists nor does not exist" is no *that* at all. This is why I have preferred to coin the term "anontology," on the basis of the negatory prefix "a-" ("an-" before a consonant), to denote "without ontology," "ontology-lessness." In addition, however, there is an enjoyable ambivalence in the term set up by the consequent presence of the letters forming the prefix "anon" as per the common abbreviation for "anonymous." Coupled with "ology" ("the science or discipline of")—via a linking "t" for phonological ease as per Sanskrit *sandhi* or French *liaison*—"anon" forms "anon-t-ology": the study of the nameless. Now, names and things are mutually constitutive for Nāgārjuna, as evinced by his adoption and repeated use of the term *nāmarūpa*, "name-and-form," as this was used already in the twelve *nidāna*s or links of dependent co-origination within the Buddha's *Discourses*.[45] On Nāgārjuna's account, then,

> With the cessation of the domain of thought
> Comes the cessation of the expressed in language[46]

Given this, "anontology" functions as an alternative to "ontology" (or "non-ontology," or even "de-ontology") in describing Nāgārjuna's understanding of the study or analysis of (not what is or is not but) what equates to emptiness.

Only the anonymous, the nameless, after all, can be the object of Nāgārjuna's *prasaṅga*. Only with

> The cessation of all cognizance
> The felicitous cessation of conceptualization[47]

can it be the case that

> Nowhere for anyone was any teaching
> Taught by the Buddha[48]

3.6. Tetralemma and No-Teaching

The notion of a "teaching of no-teaching" Nāgārjuna touches upon here brings into view, as it were, the "view of no-view" he will go on to espouse. I devote the following chapter specifically to explicating and substantiating this (non-)position, and in the final chapter I present a case for considering Nāgārjuna's abandonment of all views as the (or at least a) distinctive feature of his Mahāyāna ethics. To prepare the ground for those readings, in this section of the present chapter I will argue that it is in fact the *catuṣkoṭi* which instantiates, for Nāgārjuna, the exhaustive means whereby to abandon all views. As such, I want first to return briefly to the exhaustive character of the *catuṣkoṭi*, and in so doing to show that this enables Nāgārjuna to abjure the holding of views and the concomitant clinging to things constitutive, for him, of *saṃsāric* suffering. Non-attachment to things need not and should not issue in attachment to nothing, however, and so in the final section (§3.7) I will argue that Nāgārjuna's silencing of views is not tantamount to mere silence.

I formulate my comments here in response to the following paragraph by Gadjin Nagao:

> *Catuṣkoṭi* consists of any four alternative propositions such as, for example, "exists," "does not exist," "both exists and does not exist," and "neither exists nor does not exist." It is observed that the existence of all things is summed up and represented by these four propositions and that, dialectically speaking, there is no other possibility. Nāgārjuna's argument consists of probing into whether each proposition can stand on its own. Through

> this examination, he attempts to point out that if a proposition is stated with a belief in a "self-nature," that is if it is based on a substantive realistic view, it necessarily falls into a contradiction of antinomy and cannot stand on its own. Therefore he concludes that if a proposition is to be established, it must have no "self-nature," that is, it must be empty. (Nagao 1991: 179)[49]

The first thing to note here is that Nagao does not provide any textual support for his claim that "if a proposition is stated with a belief in a 'self-nature,' that is if it is based on a substantive realistic view, it necessarily falls into a contradiction." There is in fact no such textual basis, for Nāgārjuna does not say "I do not hold any thesis stated with a belief in a self-nature;" he simply says "I do not hold any thesis" (VV:29). But this I leave for discussion in Chapter 4.

It is also worthwhile to note that, contrary to Nagao's final sentence, for Nāgārjuna a proposition that has no self-nature (or, as I translate *svabhāva*, selfbeing), that is empty, simply cannot be established. To be established (*pratiṣṭhita*) would mean precisely to be fixed and hence not empty. Indeed, only a proposition that "has self-nature" (to use Nagao's phrase) could logically be established—were anything to be established, or establishable, at all, which, given reality is as it is, it is not. Logically speaking, a being or proposition that has no self-nature (that is, in other words, empty) cannot be established. And reality being characterized by dependent co-origination (aka emptiness aka the absence of *svabhāva*), no *bhāva* and no *prapañca*/*dṛṣṭi* are or can in reality be established. But this requires some explanation.

Perhaps it would be best to conceive of Nāgārjuna's argumentative strategy (in the tetralemma, and more broadly in the overall structures of the MK and his other works, wherein, as already noted, he systematically surveys and destructs all his interlocutors' views) as twofold. First, he agrees with his interlocutor that only a *svabhāvic* self could exist (were any "thing" to exist), and analogously that only a fixed proposition could hold. Second, however, in contradistinction to his interlocutor he argues that no such *svabhāvic* self actually does exist, no such fixed proposition actually does hold, for all that "exists" "is" empty.[50] So, (hopefully) to simplify: logically speaking, only a selfbeing (*svabhāva*) can be and only a proposition (*pratijñā*) or view (*dṛṣṭi*) can hold, for, in order to be or hold, it must exist *as* some certain thing or hold *to* some certain basis, and this certainty requires fixity of identity. Since no such fixity is found, however, no such *svabhāva* actually exists and no such *pratijñā* holds (as per VV:29).

Now, I placed "exists" and "is" in scare quotes in the foregoing paragraph because these are terms betraying implicitly conveyed ontological commitments that are precisely unfit for Nāgārjuna's purpose here. Instead of "exists" we should really say "dependently co-arises" or "inexists" and instead of "is" we should really say "equates to/equivales emptiness," or simply "empts." Inexistence is a notion I take from Paul Williams, who in relation to (what an early Chan text from Dunhuang calls) "the ceasing of notions" states:

> Since the Madhyamaka holds that actually nothing exists so it follows as clearly demonstrated that the referents of language are all *prajñaptisat* entities which 'exist' (perhpas [sic] 'inexist') only as referents and are therefore themselves caused by *saṃjñā* [perception/cognition]. *Saṃjñā* hypostasises, operates counter to impermanence, and therefore operates counter to *yathābhūtadarśana* and liberation. Liberation itself is either a result of, or much facilitated by, the suppression of *saṃjñā*. (Williams 1980: 25)[51]

As for "empt," the *Oxford English Dictionary* defines this term in both intransitive and transitive senses. Intransitively, it means "to become empty" as well as "to be or make oneself free for an activity." This accords beautifully with Nāgārjuna's retort to the anti-emptist that

> You reject
> All worldly conventions
> In rejecting
> Emptiness as dependent co-origination
>
> Nothing at all could be done
> No action begun
> No actor could act
> If emptiness were rejected[52]

As for the transitive sense, the *Oxford English Dictionary* gives "to empty out," "to make (a vessel, receptacle, etc.) empty . . . to cause to be rid of an attribute, characteristic, etc.." This again tallies well with Madhyamaka usage as applied to *svabhāva*-cum-*lakṣaṇa* (selfbeing as defining characteristic), and thus of *śūnyatā*-cum-*alakṣaṇa* (emptiness as absence of defining characteristic), treated in MK:5. Given the felicitousness of the verb in treating these topics, then, I propose to habilitate "empt" for use in English-language treatments of Buddhism, in the following three senses: (1) "to become empty" (intransitive); (2) "to empty" (transitive), and (3) "to equate to emptiness," "to equivale emptiness." It is this latter sense I had in mind earlier where I suggested that instead of "all that exists is empty" we should more correctly say "all that inexists empts" in a Nāgārjunian context. This sense of the term denotes not an intransitive or transitive verbal act but rather an alternative to the copula; one able to convey the (anontological) existential status of what may here be referred to as (not *svabhāvics* but) *śūnyatics* (not existents but) emptents.

Returning with this in mind to the argument at hand, we see that Nāgārjuna and his interlocutors agree that only a being can be; that is, that only a *svabhāvic* entity can validly be said to exist. This first move is strictly speaking definitive; it defines a self or thing (*atman* or *bhāva*) as that which is possessed of selfbeing (*svabhāva*). Whatever exists, in order to exist, must, by definition, be independent of causes and conditions, possess self-identity—in short, be, precisely, a *svabhāvic* entity (i.e., an entity *tout court*). As such, Nāgārjuna and his interlocutors are united in their assessment of what could possibly count as a *valid* characterization of the real in this context. A characterization that were to define a *svabhāva* as dependently co-originated, for example, would without hesitation be discarded by both Nāgārjuna and his interlocutors as invalid. Indeed, this would be rejected as definitionally absurd in that it would be to qualify the stipulatively independent as, precisely, dependent. For a *bhāva not* possessed of *svabhāva* is a philosophical absurdity, equivalent to an *anātmanic atman*, a selfless self. This is so for both Nāgarjuna and his interlocutor, who may be conveniently called a "selfist" or "Svābhāvika" if this application of the term be permitted—it is certainly apt. It is on the basis of this shared premise that in the second phase of his argument Nāgārjuna goes on to demonstrate, along Prāsaṅgika lines, the absurd consequences of a view holding that such a *svabhāvic bhāva* (strictly speaking a tautological phrase) actually exists, and thereby to conclude that no such *svabhāvic bhāva*, indeed no *bhāva* at all, actually exists.[53]

In analogous fashion, Nāgārjuna and his interlocutor agree that only a fixed proposition could hold. His critic's criticism at VV:1, for example, to the effect that "Your statement, lacking selfbeing, cannot refute selfbeing,"[54] implies just such a view of views: Only a non-empty, a fixed view could hold, for only such a view could be based/grounded/fixed, and some such base/ground/fixity must obtain for a view to function as a view. The difference, of course, is that the selfist (more fundamentally any viewer/believer/

proponent) does in fact maintain some such view or views (at least one, though typically many). Foremost among these is none other than the view that a (*svabhāvic*) *bhāva* exists. Nāgārjuna, however, does not strictly speaking hold a contrary view, according to which no such (*svabhāvic*) *bhāva* exists. Rather, Nāgārjuna applies the selfist's view to close *prāsaṅgika* scrutiny, and finds no such thing.

It is crucial in this context to note that this does not tie Nāgārjuna to a view, be it the contrary one to that of the selfist or any other. My comments here anticipate my argument in the following chapter, but in order to explain the relevant point as to the view of no view for the present discussion, I propose the following analogy. Say you were to believe in sky-flowers or horned rabbits or God, and upon subjecting such beliefs to *prāsaṅgika* scrutiny I were to not find them justified. This would not necessarily tie me to a contrary belief. To simplify the example in terms of Īśvara (God) alone, that I would not be a theist would not necessarily entail that I would be an atheist. For I would in fact be an atheist (only) were I then to affirm that there is no God—but I am not obliged to do so. Rather, along the lines of the tetralemma's second lemma, I may subject the atheist denial of a God to the same *prāsaṅgika* scrutiny and likewise find it to be baseless. As such, I would be, if anything, agnostic. If agnosticism (i.e., "abelief") can be called a belief, then only in that limited—I would argue invalid—sense would I be a believer: a believer in abelief. But it would be more correct, not to mention philosophically generous, to accept my abelief as abelief and refrain from ascribing to me any belief.

All of this goes to show that while Nāgārjuna shares what could be called a common meta-ontological framework with his peers (a framework, that is, concerning which entities count or logically should count as ontological), where he parts ways from his Abhidharmic co-religionists as much as his non-Buddhist interlocutors is in his understanding of the true state of affairs in the real world. Whereas his interlocutors, even the Ābhidhārmikas, go on to affirm the being of beings on the basis of the definition that "only a being can be," Nāgārjuna denies that any such being really exists.[55] Indeed, Nāgārjuna's entire philosophical enterprise may well be characterized as a related series of attempts to dismantle what he regards as the untrue belief in any selfbeing (*svabhāva*); in short, in any being (*bhāva*). For Nāgārjuna, no such thing is found in the realm of reality. It is but a delusion; one, moreover, which conduces, as per canonical Buddhist teachings, to constantly reiterated suffering on the part of the believer. Nāgārjuna attempts, by means of deconstructing every reificatory belief (and every belief reifies), to relieve the unenlightened of this hindering ignorance, to show them reality as it really is.

Only such an *anātmanic* understanding of reality, and the emptiness of views or what I call "abelief" necessarily concomitant with it, is *true* for Nāgārjuna. And (to reiterate, for the sake of clarity, a point made earlier) such emptiness of views is empty of negative as well as positive views. That is, both sides of the polarity of being and non-being, *bhāva* and *abhāva*, *svabhāva* and *niḥsvabhāva*,[56] are doctrinal binary extremes (*antadvaya*), and are therefore equally to be avoided. Nāgārjuna does indeed avoid both, and the *catuṣkoṭi* is the perfect discursive vehicle for such a wholescale avoidance, for it exhausts the whole scale of logical possibility: affirmation, denial, both affirmation and denial, and neither affirmation nor denial.[57]

So, to return more directly to Nagao's statement, I propose that this also makes a categorial error by confusing, or at least confounding, the logical and the an/ontological spheres of argument. For while it is indeed the case that "propositions with self-nature cannot be established because they have self-nature," this is so anontologically, but the contrary is true logically speaking. That is, Nagao's position is anontologically true but logically invalid. It is logically invalid because it runs counter to the framework (in Carnap's sense of the term) within which philosophical argument functioned for both Nāgārjuna and his interlocutors. This is so because this framework, like that of their Greek counterparts, avowed, indeed allowed, only propositions with self-nature/selfbeing to function as propositions, since only such propositions could meaningfully be said to propose anything at all. In this context, the phrase "proposition with self-nature" is, strictly speaking, as tautological as "being with self-nature." This is so because every proposition must be "with self-nature" in order to function as a proposition at all; that is, in order to even enter into the arena of possibly establishing some actual, an/ontological truth-position or other. It must be endowed with selfbeing in the sense that, in order to be valid, its very claim to establish its object as true (fixed, independent in the sense of "not *pratītya samutpanna*," "not *śūnya*") must itself explicitly or implicitly accept the claim that claims such as itself can and do make valid assertions as to the truth or untruth of actual things. In so doing, and in so doing alone, this proposition functions as a *pratijñā*, a "propositional thesis,"[58] a claim, in other words, as to reality . . . and therefore a claim which necessarily affirms the validity of a meta-onto-logical framework within which claims are themselves not empty.[59]

For to propose that a given proposition can affirm, or deny, some truth regarding reality is already to propose that propositions function within a realm of validity wherein, as valid or invalid, they are valid vehicles of such truths. This applies whether the reality truth-claims claim truth of is understood in a standard ontological way whereby things actually are or are not, or a Madhyamaka anontological way whereby things neither are nor are not but rather equivale emptiness, empt. To be valid vehicles in the manner described, propositions must actually carry some ontological load; they must themselves *be* in an ontological—and not an anontological—way, on pain of nonsense. Propositions are thus seen to be inherently apophantic; they cannot avoid at least implying an onto-logical background within which the contents of their predication *are*. In short, any proposition must pro-pose; it must put forward some*thing*, and in so doing it already pre-sup-poses its own status as some*thing*. To put it in play: a proposition must "pose it" (posit), where "it" is an ontologically defined something, and thereby "pose itself" (positself?) as something too. One cannot build on air; to establish something as true, the logical means used to do so must already be established as valid. What establishes must itself already be established. Therefore, every proposition/view/belief "has self-nature," to use Nagao's phrase, which however is why his statement that "propositions with self-nature cannot be established" is logically invalid.[60]

On the anontological level, however, Nagao's statement (viz. "propositions with self-nature cannot be established because they have self-nature") in fact (that is, in reality) turns out to be true. This is so not because those particular propositions which happen to have self-nature cannot be established whereas other propositions which happen not to have self-nature can be established, but rather because all propositions without exception cannot be established. Why? Because all propositions are propositions with self-nature, and, for Nāgārjuna, *there really exists nothing that has self-nature.*

This last notion—that there really exists nothing that has selfbeing—is the expression of an anontological view of reality. As stated, however, it is undoubtedly subject to misunderstanding and consequent miscriticism. Perhaps, then, I need to explain that, on my understanding of Nāgārjuna's anontology and the preeminent role played by the *catuṣkoṭi* in giving discursive expression to it, one should, for the sake of clarity, consistently adopt a fourfold description when speaking from an anontological viewpoint. To illustrate: My use of "viewpoint" in the last sentence is amenable to easy criticism according to which I have denied that Nāgārjuna adopts any viewpoint and yet, contradictorily, here foist just such a viewpoint upon him.[61] Given the tetralemmic form adopted by Nāgārjuna to guard against any and all viewpoints or theses, what I really should have said instead of "anontological viewpoint" was "anontological viewpoint / non-viewpoint / both-viewpoint-and-non-viewpoint / neither-viewpoint-nor-non-viewpoint." This, and this alone given that the *catuṣkoṭi* uniquely expresses in uttered (or āssertive) form all possible permutations of a given case, adequately expresses the Madhyamaka perspective (or better: "perspective / non-perspective / both-perspective-and-non-perspective / neither-perspective-nor-non-perspective"). My use of "viewpoint" earlier in this paragraph is thus to be taken as a shorthand way of referring to this tetralemmic utterance. Just so, from the anontological perspective (!) of a Mādhyamika, any expression regarding a thing, belief, truth, emptiness . . . anything at all, should strictly speaking be couched in such a fourfold format. This use of the tetralemmic utterance would obviate a great many misunderstandings, for there could be no question of contradicting anontological abelief through an apparent assertion (in the standard sense) of ontological belief via the simple use of conventional language. Thus, from the anontological perspective (which may be considered equivalent to that of ultimate truth/*paramārtha-satya*), any affirmation—where any use at all of a noun already constitutes an affirmation of the ontological status of its object—should be countenanced by a correlate negation, affirmation of both the affirmation and negation, and negation of both the affirmation and negation (see Guanding's formulation in §3.1). This, of course, would make for some strange and convoluted reading, which is why I, and Nāgārjuna, typically resort to a shorthand which uses the conventional (*saṃvṛti*) noun or related term for its ultimate (*paramārtha*) equivalent.

An analogy from Buddhist literature on ontology may be of use to explain my point. Adapting Nagao's formulation, it is not the case that a given *svabhāvic* self cannot be established because of the adventitious fact of that particular self having *svabhāva*, but that no self can be established at all because any self would, by definition, be *svabhāvic*. As already stated, logically speaking there is and can be no such thing as an *asvabhāvic svabhāva*, an *anātmanic atman*, for these would be self-contradictory. Just so, there is and can be no such thing as an empty proposition (or an empty belief, or an empty view . . .), for this would amount in like manner to a self-contradiction: a proposition which does not propose (a belief which does not believe, a view which holds no view). Therefore, to recapitulate, Nagao's characterization of

Nāgārjuna's conclusion as "if a proposition is to be established, it must have 'no self-nature'" is logically invalid but anontologically true—a claim which, I hope, is the clearer for having been explicated at length.

All that said, however, perhaps we can rehabilitate the logical validity of Nagao's statement after all. This we can accomplish on the basis that Nāgārjuna presumably must view his *prāsaṅgika* critique of views to be valid (on pain of absurdity, or at least of wanton sophistry). If we adapt Nagao's statement to say "if a critique (*prasaṅga*) is to be valid, it must have 'no self-nature', that is, it must be empty," this obviates the potential criticism, already foreseen and forerefuted by Nāgārjuna in his response to VV:1, to the effect that, for it to be valid, Nāgārjuna's critique must itself selfbe (i.e., be endowed with *svabhāva*), and therefore not empt. For *prasaṅga* is precisely the analytical means by which the absence of selfbeing is demonstrated by the Mādhyamika. Were the critique to function in a manner that affirmed its own selfbeing in contradistinction to the absence thereof in the object of its critique, this critique, insofar as it is meant to be universal, would itself fall into obvious self-contradiction. *Prasaṅga* avoids this trap, however, by steadfastly refusing to posit selfbeing even of itself. This is explicitly stated by Nāgārjuna at MK:13:8 and VV:29, for example. Indeed, for Nāgārjuna, any critique that attempts to deconstruct a given object only to construct in its place another falls into the same apophantic framework as its object, and is therefore just as invalid. Rather, *prasaṅga* deconstructs all propositions, including critical ones, demonstrating them all to be empty; it can only do so consistently by admitting to its own emptiness. It is thus incorrect to view *prasaṅga* within the standard philosophical terms of truth-bearing premises and conclusions, for all such propositions are necessarily involved in a species of Heideggerian "onto-theo-logy." This is so, and not just in the broadly speaking Western metaphysical tradition, in that all propositions pro-pose some*thing*, including most saliently them*selves* as positions.

In other words, *prāsaṅgika* critique is not propositional at all: It posits no-thing; it has no predicative force; nor is its conclusion clusive.[62] Rather, it is the maieutic means by which one may come to realize the universality of dependent co-origination as/or emptiness, and thereby allow the myriad phenomena of the conventionally perceived world to open into their flourishing—a process that is perennially in progress in spite of being ostensibly occluded by those perspectives confined to seeing but static thinghood.[63] I refer here to the idea, espoused by Nāgārjuna most sustainedly in MK:24, that, contrary to common-sensical—and mostly unspoken-for-unquestioned—assumptions as to being and meaning, to be or to mean something precludes the possibility of processual phenomenality; of anontological, ever-opening and open-ended, becoming (~~be~~coming), or what I will now propose to call "meandering" (me-ander-ing).

As Nāgārjuna puts it:

> Unoriginated and unceased
> Unchanging
> Without manifold appearances
> Would the world be if selfbeing[64]

By "becoming" I here aim to indicate the "comegoing" of the Tathāgata: a ~~being~~ in gerundial form, never fixed and ever ongoing/oncoming, or (what amounts to the same thing) one in participial form, ever come/gone, the Thus Comegone. It is such comegoing that really characterizes the way "things" "are"—where "things" are understood to be *dharma*s, dependently co-originating phenomena empty of selfbeing; and where "are" is understood to entail no ontological state, but rather an anontological fluidity equivalent to emptiness. Thus, more precisely, comegoing characterizes the way emptents empt. By "meandering," moreover, I aim to indicate the only-ever-relative nature of *prajñaptir upādāya* (correlative designation); a meaning innately ennetted (*jālata*) in mutual signification with other signs. The coinage (in this sense) is based on the English definite pronoun "me," referring to "myself," coupled with the German indefinite pronoun "*ander*," meaning "other," "another," to make the gerundial form of the verb "meander." To meander, in this sense, is to move in meaning at the confluence of oneself and one's other: something that all words do in that they can only ever be defined relatively through other words, and thus can never really attain to definition. I see MK 15:5, and especially 15:5cd, as making much this point in relation to things (*bhāva*s):

> If being is not established
> Then non-being is not established
> For an othered being is not
> A being, people say[65]

It is just such comegoing and meandering that *prasaṅga* aims to uncover; comegoing is how reality is and must be as it is, and meandering is how meaning works and must work to work at all. The alternative, as Nāgārjuna argues through apogogic demonstration, is a world of things fixed in being as selfbeings (*svabhāva*), unable to undergo or overcome any change; and of terms fixed in meaning as selfpositings (*svamata*), unable to communicate any signification for forever locked in self-referential solipsism. "Thus," states Lindtner, "Nāgārjuna is able to argue—or at least to *suggest*—that all theories etc. generated through the operations of *vikalpa* are, in the final analysis, untenable as they impose absurd implications (*prasaṅga*) on the proponent of any kind of *bhāva*" (Lindtner 1982: 274, emphasis original)—where I would only specify that all "theories" (under which blanket term I here include all those used to denote any kind of propositional stance or view, *dṛṣṭi*, whatsoever) implicitly or explicitly actually do entail their proponents in the affirmation of *bhāva*.

Reality, then, is anontological. To describe it ontologically (in terms of beings rather than comegoings) is to remain enmeshed in beliefs and meanings. It is to continue holding on to beliefs and meanings on the (mis) understanding that they and their purported objects are real. The alternative or antidote, for Nāgārjuna, is liberated abelieving and meandering. This, I believe, is what Murti is getting at in calling Nāgārjuna's method the "*śūnyatā* of *dṛṣṭis*," which he describes as "the negation of standpoints, which are the initial negation of the real that is essentially indeterminate (*nirvikalpa*, *niṣprapañca*). Correctly understood, *śūnyatā* is not annihilation, but the negation of negation" (Murti 1955: 271).[66]

3.7. Silencing Nothing

The final sentence just quoted is evidently aimed at a view quite prevalent in the critical literature surrounding Nāgārjuna during Murti's time (and beyond); one that considered Madhyamaka "annihilationist" or nihilist.[67] Unfortunately, such a one-sided derogation of the Mādhyamika's middle way persists to this day. For the most one-sided exemplars of this interpretation, see Narain, who declares that "the Mādhyamika philosophy, *Śūnyavāda*, is absolute nihilism" (Narain 1964: 311), and Wood, according to whom "For the Mādhyamikas, emptiness (*śūnyatā*) . . . [is] simply sheer, unqualified, absolute nothingness" (Wood 1994: 279–280). In a book already amply stocked with examples of ideologically motivated forced readings, it is worth underlining that Wood's nihilistic interpretation is supported first and foremost by his wholly unjustified gloss of *śūnya* as "unreal" (Wood 1994: 200)—literally the very opposite of Nāgārjuna's understanding that emptiness characterizes *reality*.

Perhaps the most recent witness to the fact that—borrowing Spackman's quip—"Rumors of the death of the nihilist interpretation of Nāgārjuna are, it appears, greatly exaggerated" (Spackman 2014: 151) is Shaoyong Ye's "Nihilistic Interpretation of Nāgārjuna's Refutations" (Ye 2019). This claims that

> Nāgārjuna finds all concepts to be self-contradictory, and rules out the possibility of any concept to refer to its referent/own-being. Hence, he establishes a nihilistic philosophy by asserting that the whole world perceived by us is merely concepts (*vikalpa-mātra*) without referents (*niḥsvabhāva*), namely, empty (*śūnya*). That is to say, nothing within our ken can possibly exist. (Ye 2019: 759).

The nihilistic conclusion here has multiple problems. For one thing, for it to hold, we need to accept Ye's understanding of the self-contradictoriness of concepts, according to which, "if the referent of any concept has to undergo change, the concept cannot be held true, i.e., it is self-contradictory" (Ye 2019: 752). This is already problematic on at least two grounds. First, it is not at all clear why a conceptual referent's undergoing change would render that concept untrue, let alone self-contradictory, unless we uncritically assume Ye's "confinement principle" (Ye 2019: 750–754). Second, and even irrespective of our stance on this principle, not being true is obviously not equivalent to being self-contradictory. On top of that, for Ye's reading to hold, we would also need to accept his ascription of the earlier understanding of the self-contradictoriness of concepts to Nāgārjuna, and this runs into textual difficulties too many and too tangential to my principal concerns to enumerate here. Besides which, even were all this granted, we would still be left with the fact that Ye's interpretation relies on both an equivocation between "self-contradictory" and "without referents," and an identification of the latter as "nihilism." Apart from anything else, the equivocation betrays a classical logicalist refusal to countenance self-contradictoriness, the which is obviously far from equivaling nihilism—just ask Hegel.[68] It is the conflation, however, that constitutes a more serious argument against Ye's reading. For by simply reinterpreting Nāgārjuna's repudiation of *svabhāvic* referents as being tantamount to nihilism (rather than emptiness), Ye effectively reneges on the task of interpreting *Nāgārjuna* altogether. Far from "show[ing] that epistemological nihilism is a straightforward interpretation of Nāgārjuna's position" (Ye 2019: 760), Ye's argument straightforwardly relies on a deliberate reinterpretation of nihilism to mean emptiness. He acknowledges this directly in admitting "I use the word 'nihilism' to convey the meaning of *śūnyatā* in Nāgārjuna's context" (Ye 2019: 760). If only taking one thing to mean something completely different were all that were needed to make it so.[69]

Nāgārjuna's works exhibit counter examples to the nihilistic reading too numerous to enumerate here; nor is it my intention to debunk at length what I consider to be an all too obvious misreading. For, as Nāgārjuna makes clear at MK:15:5:

> If being is not established
> Then non-being is not established[70]

While Wood, Narain, Ye, and others may attempt (*do* attempt) to argue such passages away in order to insist on their nihilistic interpretations, what such exegetes fail to realize is that, for Nāgārjuna, *bhāva* and *abhāva* are inextricably bound in relational co-dependency: One cannot posit the one extreme without implicitly positing the other. Nāgārjuna makes this point several times in his works (e.g., MK:15:10 cited in §3.2), and perhaps most explicitly in the RĀ where "In verses 43–62 Nāgārjuna argues for an ontological middle-way according to which the world truly does not exist or non-exist.... Existence and non-existence are terms that necessitate each other and therefore cancel each other out" (Shulman 2011: 317).[71] Indeed, on the basis of this extended passage Shulman concludes that "The rare ability to transcend both existence and non-existence is what, according to Nāgārjuna, defines the Buddhist truth. . . reality is truly beyond existence and non-existence" (Shulman 2011: 318–319).

To put the matter a little obliquely, just as Newton's Third Law of Motion states that for every action there is an equal and opposite reaction, and thus that forces cannot but come in relationally co-dependent pairs, so Nāgārjuna's "Law of Emptiness," if I may put it in such terms, states that for every *bhāva* there is an equal and opposite *abhāva*, and thus that things cannot but come in relationally co-dependent pairs. Binary opposites (and their quaternary elaborations into both/and and neither/nor forms as per the tetralemma) are bound to each other. And being bound to them is suffering (*duḥkha*).

This is so on the ontological level just as on the epistemological one, which is why Nāgārjuna's emptiness of views (*dṛṣṭiśūnyatā*) is indissolubly tied to his emptiness of things (*svabhāvaśūnyatā*). Believing entails being and being entails believing. To coin a Sanskrit term, I see the Buddhist "view of self" (*ātmadṛṣṭi*) as entailed by and entailing a "self of views" (*dṛṣṭyātma*).

The understanding I am here proposing of the Mādhyamika's intertwining of the ontological and the epistemological, of the concomitance of the rejection of *svabhāva* and of *dṛṣṭi*, will occupy us again in the next chapter when it comes time to develop just what Nāgārjuna's abandonment of all views means. What is salient to note in the present context is that Nāgārjuna's rejection of nihilism as I have explained it here differs from, and complements, his rejection of what Westerhoff refers to as the "five different conceptions of nihilistic positions that the Mādhyamika explicitly rejects" (Westerhoff 2016a: 362).[72] It rests not on any nominal repudiation of extreme positionality in favor of a doctrinal middle way, or demonstration of the contradictoriness of annihilationism in the face of permutating phenomena, or rejection of the identification of the insubstantial (i.e., the empty) with the non-existent, or dismissal of the reification of emptiness as nihility, or rebuttal of consequentialist worries as to moral anarchy, for example. While these are all valid as explications of Nāgārjuna's non-nihilism, the present context necessitates an interpretation that rests on a logical or, if one prefers, definitive point regarding the mutually entailing nature of opposites (be they binary or quaternary). For Nāgārjuna, being entails non-being and vice-versa, not in some causal sense but in the sense that each is the logical antithesis of the other, the other without which the one could not be.[73]

Importantly, this means that for Nāgārjuna the exhaustion of ontological positionality in anontological emptiness does not entail lapsing into mere silence. Now, there is a long tradition in Buddhism, dating back to the Buddha himself, of responding to metaphysical questions with silence.[74] Such an approach found ample, and paradoxically prolix, elaboration in the myriad Chan/Zen schools of East Asia, who universally claimed ancestry from the silence enacted by Vimalakīrti when asked to "elucidate the teaching of the entrance into the principle of nonduality."[75] A silence (of thought as much as of language) as opposed to views (*dṛṣṭi*), discriminatory conceptualization (*vikalpa*), conceptualization (*prapañca*), and in short the entire domain of logico-linguistic construction (*kalpanā*), would embody a dichotomization alien to the ultimate utterance of each, both, and neither.

Such an oppositional silence would therefore disable one from realizing the reality of things in their sheer thusness:

> With the cessation of the domain of thought
> Comes the cessation of the expressed in language
> Not arisen, not ceased
> Like *nirvāṇa* are things as they are[76]

In other words, although Nāgārjuna aims to pass beyond conventional truth into ultimate truth (and thereby affirms that the latter is, soteriologically speaking, beyond the former), this attainment cannot be achieved if one still conceives of ultimacy as opposed to conventionality.[77] Such a standpoint would still locate one within logic as opposed to paralogic, within affirmation/negation as opposed to utterance—where "paralogic" and "utterance" are meant to convey what may be called the "opposition to opposition."[78] Nāgārjuna's authoritative commentator Candrakīrti may admit that "ultimate truth is a matter of venerable silence" (*paramārtho hi āryas tūṣṇīmbhāvaḥ*), but he immediately goes on to affirm the use of conventional language "for the sake of enlightening others" (*parāvabodhārtham*) (de La Vallée Poussin 1970 [1913]: 57).[79] It is for the same reason, and by means of the *catuṣkoṭi*, that Nāgārjuna expresses ultimate truth (*paramārtha-satya*) in the conventional garb of language (*saṃvrti-satya* or, perhaps more appropriately here, *vyavahāra-satya*).[80] And it is thus that the very final words of the *Mūlamadhyamaka-kārikā*, wherein Nāgārjuna affirms a teaching which nonetheless leads to the abandonment of all teaching, apply to him as much as to the Buddha:

> For the abandonment of all views
> He taught the true teaching
> By means of compassion:
> I salute him, Gautama[81]

Which takes us directly to the topic of the following chapter.

4

Abandoning All Views

A Buddhist Critique of Belief

4.1. Views on Abandoning Views

Nāgārjuna opens and closes the MK with salutations to the Buddha as one who taught the "cessation of conceptualization" (*prapañcopaśamaṃ*) and the "abandonment of all views" (*sarvadṛṣṭiprahāṇāya*) respectively—terms I take to be largely equivalent.[1] Furthermore, the text contains numerous calls for the complete abandonment of views, and it repeatedly uses the tetralemma (*catuṣkoṭi*) to survey and reject all four of the logical positions open to classical Indian philosophers. Despite these copious, clear, and comprehensive disavowals of views, contemporary scholars typically interpret such statements as referring only to false views (however these may be understood). In this chapter, I argue instead that Nāgārjuna's insistence on the abandonment of *all* views—including ultimately his own—constitutes his distinctive means to the thoroughgoing metaphysical, epistemic, and doxastic exhaustion characteristic of *nirvāṇa*, wherein all views, theses, propositions, (*dṛṣṭi*, *pakṣa*, *pratijñā*)—all beliefs—are abandoned as so many subtle affirmations of an only ever empty self.

My arguments for this interpretation will rely on a close reading of Nāgārjuna's MK and other philosophical works, which I will initially survey for evidence in support of my reading. Of course, the corpus of texts attributed to Nāgārjuna is vast: he is "justly famed for his many works of undoing—works deconstructing, dismantling, unraveling, even pulverizing the 'net of views' to which beings in their predictable ignorance inexorably cling" (McClintock 2023: 2). I have restricted myself to the *Vigrahavyāvartanī* (VV), *Yuktiṣaṣṭikā-kārikā* (YṢ), and *Śūnyatāsaptati* (ŚS) for four reasons. First, I have preferred to confine myself as much as possible to the MK throughout this chapter since this is universally acknowledged as the locus of Nāgārjuna's most characteristic and developed philosophy; the references here to the other three works are meant to buttress my point as

Buddhism Between Religion and Philosophy. Rafal K. Stepien, Oxford University Press. © Oxford University Press 2024.
DOI: 10.1093/oso/9780197771303.003.0004

to the soterially motivated necessity of abandoning all views for Nāgārjuna. Second, the authenticity of the traditional ascription of these works to Nāgārjuna is largely unquestioned. Third, these are the most "philosophical" of Nāgārjuna's works, as evinced by their universal categorization by Tibetan doxographers among the "collection of six texts among reasoning" (*rigs pa'i tschogs drug*). By contrast, the other two texts in this "*yukti*-corpus" are either not always included in it (*Ratnāvalī*) or continue to face contested claims of authorial attribution (*Vaidalyaprakaraṇa*; see e.g., Tola and Dragonetti 1995b; Pind 2001). That these most "philosophical" of Nāgārjuna's works (if by that term is meant something like "metaphysical" or "intended to describe reality") should nevertheless prove irreducibly soteriological in orientation (as per the abandonment of all view-holding) supports my argument as to the ubiquity of such an orientation in Nāgārjuna's opus as a whole more forcefully than were such an orientation found (as indeed it is) in his less abstract, more overtly "religious" (in the sense of "devotional") works—I am thinking most directly of the hymns of the *Catuḥstava*, the lay ethical precepts of the *Suhṛllekha*, and the practical applications of Madhyamaka principles found in the *Ratnāvalī*. Lastly, it is necessary to draw a line somewhere, and the plethora of works attributed to Nāgārjuna renders the dangers of cherry-picking choice verses or passages more conspicuous than is the case with many another author.

In the course of my exposition in this chapter (as, of course, throughout this book), I will have occasion to engage with, and hopefully make contributions to, several debates very much alive in contemporary scholarship on Nāgārjuna specifically, and in the study of religion, philosophy of religion, and philosophy broadly speaking. Since it will soon become clear that my views on Nāgārjuna's espousal of abandoning views stand in contrast to those voiced by many fellow scholars in the field, I take this opportunity both to explain my approach in the pages that follow and to provide it with methodological justification so as to forestall (at least some of) their objections.

The first point to note is that this chapter is primarily a work of textual hermeneutics as opposed to philosophical construction; one, that is, concerned with "developing an account of the history of Buddhist philosophy" as opposed to "doing Buddhist philosophy."[2] In other words, I am primarily engaged here in the exegetical project of providing a reading of Nāgārjuna's texts, less in the (no less intellectually valid, but methodologically distinct) task of extrapolating philosophical arguments from those texts. This is not to say that I am wholly unconcerned with the philosophical implications of my reading of Nāgārjuna; on the contrary, I will argue at quite some length in §4.3 on "Abandoning Nāgārjuna's Views" that the interpretation I propose makes of him a far more radical and profound thinker than do the competing analyses I cite, which in my view rob his position of its very thrust. But it does explain why much of the present chapter (particularly §4.2 on "Nāgārjuna's Abandoning Views") grapples with the precise purport of Nāgārjuna's textual formulations.

Prior to detailing such textual evidence, however, it is incumbent upon me to explain the methodological justification for my approach. For it is self-evident that merely marshalling passages is of no probative force if the purport of those passages is precisely the point at issue among rival interpretations. Indeed, it would not only be hermeneutically naïve for me to take the meaning of a given passage as simply singular, self-evident, and/or authorially intended; it would also beg the question against interpreters proposing alternative readings of certain passages if I were to rely on simply quoting what those passages say. In response to this, I will naturally attempt to justify my use of the passages I adduce in support of my reading *ad locum*. Here, however, I want only to aver in general terms that the sheer number of these examples does add weight to my reading, at the very least by forcing the burden of proof onto any interpreter whose reading goes directly against the *prima facie* sense of these statements. While no passage anywhere *self-evidently* warrants any particular interpretation, in order to make sense at all it must *evidently* warrant some interpretation over others; otherwise its infinite polysemicity renders it merely meaningless. There may be many things under the sun, as the Ecclesiast reminds us, but some are more textually warranted than others. Given that both I and the exegetes I mention are avowedly engaged in the exegetical task of interpreting what Nāgārjuna said about views (and not just speculating about them ourselves), I see their interpretation(s) as falling on the sharp side of Ockham's razor by consistently relying on extra-textual additions and interpolations.

4.2. Nāgārjuna's Abandoning Views

The primary source for Nāgārjuna's views on views, and their ultimate abandonment, is his major work, the MK. This text contains manifold espousals of the abandonment of all forms of intellectual positionality, which I will now proceed to cite.[3] Having referred to the opening and closing lines of the text at the outset of this chapter, I can do no better than to cite the opening verses in full. The text begins:

> Not ceasing, not arising
> Not annihilated, not eternal
> Not identical, not different
> Not coming, not going
>
> Dependent co-origination
> As the felicitous cessation of conceptualization
> This is what the Fully Enlightened Buddha taught
> I salute him, the best of speakers[4]

The simple fact that Nāgārjuna begins his major work with an explicit call for the "cessation of conceptualization" is evidence in favor of the importance of this motif in his thought as a whole (that he ends the work on a like note can only strengthen this point). What he means by such a call will, I hope, become clearer as we go on.

The text of the MK then proceeds by critically reducing to absurdity a series of positions all in one way or another foundationalist. Thus, for example, having refuted the Abhidharmic classification of space and the other elements (*dhātus*) as possessed of defining characteristics (*lakṣaṇas*) and as such taken to be ultimately real, in the final verse of MK:5 Nāgārjuna bemoans:

> But those of unenlightened intelligence
> Accepting the existence or non-existence of things
> Do not see the felicitous cessation
> Of what is to be seen[5]

Siderits and Katsura note in relation to this verse that "the *Akutobhayā* [commentary] explains that by 'auspicious cessation' ['felicitous cessation' in my translation] is meant *nirvāṇa*, which is the cessation of hypostatization" (Siderits and Katsura 2013: 64).[6] This last phrase recalls directly the *prapañcopaśamaṃ* used at MK:0, and therefore creates a first direct link in the text between the cessation of *prapañca* and the attainment of *nirvāṇa*.

The final verses of MK:9 constitute another occasion where Nāgārjuna makes a radical claim as to the inapplicability of any kind of intellectual positionality to reality, in this case arguing against the non-existence—as well as the existence—of mental cognitions. Having refuted the claim (characteristic of the Pudgalavāda school of Buddhist thought) that a person must exist as an ontologically prior entity to the act of perception, Nāgārjuna expands his claim to include not only the perceiver but perception itself:

> Seeing, hearing, and the rest
> Feeling and the rest
> If that to which these belong is not found
> These also are not found[7]

The upshot of the repeated phrase "and the rest" (*ādīni*) is that no perceptual acts exist. Crucially, on the Buddhist account there are six faculties of sense perception, including consciousness as well as the five familiar ones (to "us") of seeing, hearing, smelling, tasting, and feeling. As such, Nāgārjuna's argument here explicitly includes mental perception or cognition. In the very next verse, he is careful to explain that this act, and the actor purportedly "prior" to it, are not non-existent (which position would render him susceptible to the "extremist" charge of nihilism), but rather that "the notions of existence and non-existence do not apply" to them:

> That which is prior to seeing and the rest
> Or simultaneous with them, or posterior to them—
> That is not found
> The conceptual constructions of existence and non-existence
> do not apply there[8]

Apart from obviating the charge of nihilism, in this verse Nāgārjuna identifies the very categories structurally primary to ontology ("existence and non-existence") as "conceptual constructions," and therefore without metaphysical foundation independent of any such conventionally constructive activity. This point will bear richest fruit at MK:24:18, where Nāgārjuna equates dependent co-origination (*pratītyasamutpādaḥ*) with emptiness (*śūnyatāṃ*), correlative designation (*prajñaptir upādāya*), and the middle way itself (*pratipat . . . madhyamā*).[9] The upshot of this for present purposes is that Nāgārjuna unambiguously categorizes even the core metaphysical tenets of his philosophical system (preeminently *śūnyatā*) as conventional designations.

It is in MK:13 that the necessity of abandoning any and all such constructions is elaborated. This chapter as whole is concerned with what is composite/compounded/constructed/conditioned (*saṃskṛta*), and there can be no denying that, for Nāgārjuna, all types of conceptual-linguistic construction (*prapañca*/conceptualization, *vikalpa*/dichotomizing conceptualization, *kalpanā*/conceptual construction, *saṃjñā*/notion, as well as *dṛṣṭi*/view, etc.) are *saṃskṛta*.[10] It begins with an unequivocal rejection of *all* such *saṃskāra*s:

> "Whatever is deceptive is false"
> Thus did the Blessed One say
> All conditioned phenomena are deceptive
> Therefore they are false[11]

Nāgārjuna goes on in the succeeding verses to argue for emptiness as the antidote to such deception, before concluding the chapter in a pellucid rejection of views:

> Emptiness as the relinquishing of all views
> Has been proclaimed by the Victorious Ones
> But those who have taken emptiness as a view
> They are the incurables[12]

In this verse, Nāgārjuna explicitly states that even his most central tenet, emptiness, must not be taken as a view, and that anyone who takes even this most refined of teachings as a view is not simply wrong but incurable. Yet perhaps unsurprisingly, the typical gloss on this verse holds that "the 'views' in question concern the ultimate nature of reality, or metaphysical theories" (Siderits and Katsura 2013: 145).[13] This interpretation is buttressed by an extra-textual and hermeneutically motivated insertion in Siderits and Katsura's translation, according to which not "those who have taken emptiness as a view" but "those for whom emptiness is a [metaphysical] view" are incurable. The insertion of "metaphysical" reduces Nāgārjuna's claim here from one pertaining to views *tout court* to just views contrary to Nāgārjuna's anti-foundationalist metaphysics.[14]

Now, much of the following section will deal in critical manner with interpretations of Nāgārjuna's point. To foreground that discussion, however, I want only to underline in the present context that such parameterization of

Nāgārjuna's statements as I have just cited robs them of much of their philosophical radicality. Thus, in the present instance, rather than making a bold claim to the effect that view-holding, of even the most refined kind, is necessarily implicated in the suffering (*duḥkha*) characteristic of cyclical *saṃsāra*, Nāgārjuna appears to merely be stating that metaphysical views (i.e., views contrary to his own) are so implicated. In other words, he would merely be saying here that those whom he takes to be wrong are wrong—hardly a point worth making at all, let alone as the culmination to an entire chapter. Not only is this philosophically uncharitable, but it goes against the grain of Nāgārjuna's argument as this develops. For on the basis of MK:13's rejection of conditioned phenomena as deceptive, it makes perfect sense that Nāgārjuna goes on to argue in MK:16 that no such conditioned can attain *nirvāṇa*:

> That conditioned phenomena could attain *nirvāṇa*
> This is utterly nonsensical[15]

Indeed, just as at MK:9:12 it is said that "existence and non-existence do not apply" to actors or acts, so at MK:16:5 it is said that:

> Conditioned phenomena, arising and ceasing
> Are neither bound nor liberated[16]

For to side with one extreme view would necessarily entail the very holding of a view which Nāgārjuna is at such pains to abjure. And just to bring the point home that conceptual phenomena of all kinds are to be included under this rubric, and consequently that the *holding* of a view or concept in mind is tantamount to the *grasping* at the core of suffersome attachment, Nāgārjuna ends this chapter with a rhetorical question withholding any soterial utility to dichotomizing conceptualization (*vikalpa*) itself:

> "Without holding on, I will attain *nirvāṇa*
> *Nirvāṇa* will be mine"
> For those who grasp thus
> There is great holding on to grasping
>
> Where there is no attainment of *nirvāṇa*
> Or cessation of *saṃsāra*
> What becomes of *saṃsāra*?
> How is *nirvāṇa* to be dichotomously conceptualized?[17]

Having already spoken of "emptiness as the relinquishing of all views" at MK:13:8, Nāgārjuna here applies a like analysis to even the conceptual formation of—and ineluctably consequent attachment to—the desire for soterial liberation. Indeed, we see here that Nāgārjuna considers even the ostensibly benign formation of a desire for an end to desire (the "so-called paradox of liberation"—Siderits and Katsura 2013: 169) to be actually malign—precisely insofar as it is the formation of a conceptualization.

Nāgārjuna brings out the necessity of abandoning conceptual-linguistic elaboration altogether in order to liberate oneself from *karma*-creating action and defilement in the course of his analysis of the self in MK:18. There, he states unequivocally:

> With the cessation of action and defilement there is liberation
> Action and defilement arise from dichotomizing conceptualization
> These from conceptualization
> But conceptualization is extinguished in emptiness[18]

As Siderits and Katsura comment slightly later in this chapter,

> while all [Buddhists] agree that hypostatization [conceptualization] lies at the root of the problem of suffering, only Madhyamaka appreciates that it is not just hypostatization [conceptualization] concerning "I" and "mine" that is problematic. The realization that all things are devoid of intrinsic nature is required in order to bring to a halt our tendency to see ultimately real entities behind what are merely useful concepts. (Siderits and Katsura 2013: 200)

I would only add that, on Nāgārjuna's analysis, *all* concepts (notions, positions, views, beliefs, etc.)—howsoever "useful" they may be—turn out to be impediments. This is so for the simple reason that reality, whose realization is the sum goal of the Buddhist endeavor—is devoid of them:

> Not dependent on another, peaceful
> Not conceptualized through conceptualization
> Without dichotomizing conceptualization, without distinction
> This is the nature of reality[19]

Contrary to the predominant scholarly interpretation, it would therefore be incoherent in the extreme for Nāgārjuna to allow the holding of any view. Reality, after all, is on his understanding wholly—not partly—"without dichotomizing conceptualization, without distinction"; the realization of it must therefore necessitate the complete abandonment of what is ultimately seen to be unreal, said only "for the sake of instruction":

> "Empty" should not be said
> "Non-empty" too should not be said
> Likewise with "both" and "neither"
> These are said for the sake of instruction[20]

This verse follows from the rhetorical question in the preceding one in which Nāgārjuna asks:

> How can the Tathāgata, empty
> Be conceptualized through what is empty?[21]

Paul Williams's summary of *prajñapti* is to the point here:

> the word '*prajñapti*' in the Madhyamaka designates the status of an entity which has no existence apart from that postulated to fulfil the requirements of verbal reference. The *prajñapti* is the referent of a term with no ultimate referent, and is created by language due to the requirement that all terms have referents in order to be meaningful. Such terms create their referents by generalisation and hypostasisation, and it is a doctrine peculiar to the Madhyamaka that all entities whatsoever simply enjoy *prajñaptisat*. The category of *prajñaptisat* is for the Madhyamaka the true way of seeing the empirical world, it both implies and is an implication of *śūnyatā*. (Williams 1980: 14)

In this passage from MK:22, then, Nāgārjuna yet again states, without qualification, that conceptualization of any kind is constitutively inadequate to the task of attaining liberation and should consequently be abandoned. As he goes on to declare a few verses later:

> Those who conceptualize the Buddha
> Who has passed beyond all conceptualizations and is unvarying
> They all, afflicted with conceptualizations
> Fail to the see the Tathāgata[22]

The state of Buddhahood/Tathāgatahood is therefore one which is "beyond *all* conceptualizations." Not only does Nāgārjuna not qualify this statement, but he explicitly uses the nominative plural *sarve* to designate any holder of any position; such a one, on this account, "*afflicted* with conceptualizations (*prapañcahatāḥ*)," is far from attaining enlightenment.

In MK:25, Nāgārjuna returns to the topic of *nirvāṇa*, to which the chapter as a whole is dedicated. MK:25:21 includes an uncharacteristically qualified statement as to views:

> Views as to what is beyond cessation
> Or what ends or what is eternal
> Depend on *nirvāṇa*
> The end, and the beginning[23]

At first sight, this verse seems to limit the kinds of views Nāgārjuna is dealing with, at least here. Indeed, this verse, like MK:25:17–18, refers to the "unexplicated points" (*avyākṛtavastu*) the Buddha refused to answer with anything but silence.[24] Yet in the verses that immediately follow, Nāgārjuna makes clear that he is denying that any and all views could pertain to *nirvāṇa*. He calls upon classic negative tetralemmata to do so, rhetorically asking:

> All things being empty
> What is infinite? What is finite?
> What is both infinite and finite?
> And what is neither infinite nor finite?
>
> What is identical? What is different?
> What is eternal? What is non-eternal?
> What is both eternal and non-eternal?
> And what is neither?[25]

The upshot of these reiterated questions is to negate the ostensive force of any purported description of *nirvāṇa*. In the very next verse (the final one of the chapter), Nāgārjuna expands his deconstructive critique still further, to embrace all views and teachings, all acts of cognizance, whatsoever:

> The cessation of all cognizance
> The felicitous cessation of conceptualization:
> Nowhere for anyone was any teaching
> Taught by the Buddha[26]

If this is not an unambiguous rejection of conceptual-linguistic construction of any kind, including even the very teachings of the Enlightened One, then I am at a loss to conceive what could be.

Were there any doubt as to the soteriological import of Nāgārjuna's critique, the fact that he devotes the entire next chapter to describing the origination and the cessation of the twelvefold causal chain of suffering should surely put paid to it. In MK:26, Nāgārjuna charts a parabola according to which he first explicates (in MK:26:1–9) the arising of the twelve causes (*nidānas*) constitutive of suffering (*duḥkha*) along the cycle of dependent co-origination (*pratītya samutpāda*), only to then descend (following the volta at verse 10) the other arc toward the cessation of ignorance and of all the other consequent factors of *saṃsāric* existence:

> Thus does this entire mass of suffering
> Completely cease[27]

It is with this conclusion to MK:26 that Nāgārjuna leads us to his final topic, the one to which the entire text thitherto has been leading: views (*dṛṣṭi*).

The bulk of MK:27, the final chapter, is devoted to surveying and rejecting views as to selfhood as per the standard Buddhist doctrine of no-self. It is only in the two very final verses of the MK as a whole that Nāgārjuna brings in his own notion of emptiness so as to deny that any view can really be held by anyone at all:

> So since all existents are empty
> Where? To whom? Based on what?
> Could there be views
> As to eternity and the rest?[28]

If one has understood universal emptiness aright, one cannot hold any view, for one has realized the emptiness of oneself. Indeed, in the very final verse of the MK, Nāgārjuna goes a step further to propose that the teaching of the Buddha, including notably the teaching of no-self itself with which he has foregrounded it, is itself to be abandoned, together with all views whatsoever:

> For the abandonment of all views
> He taught the true teaching

By means of compassion
I salute him, Gautama[29]

This is the culmination of the entire text; the verse Nāgārjuna composed and chose to place as the end-marker of his major work. In it, as I will argue more extensively in §4.3 on "Abandoning Nāgārjuna's Views," Nāgārjuna, having passed from analyzing the emptiness of purported selfbeings (*svabhāvaśūnyatā*), and on from even the holding of emptiness as a view (*śūnyatādṛṣṭi*), finally attains to what may be called the emptiness of views (*dṛṣṭiśūnyatā*), according to which "the abandonment of all views" (*sarvadṛṣṭiprahāṇāya*) follows.[30]

Moving on from the MK to Nāgārjuna's other works, that *all* things are empty, including Nāgārjuna's own views, is also apparent from the *Vigrahavyāvartanī*, a source for Nāgārjuna's philosophy second in importance only to that of the MK. It is surely noteworthy—though unremarked in the secondary literature—that this text both opens and closes, in its first and final verses, with explicit reference to "all things":

If the selfbeing of all things is not found anywhere
Your statement, lacking selfbeing, cannot refute selfbeing
. . .
For whom there is emptiness there are all things
For whom there is no emptiness there is nothing at all[31]

Nāgārjuna responds to his interlocutor's argument as voiced in VV:1 with the rejoinder that:

If my speech is neither in combination with
Nor distinct from causes and conditions
Then the emptiness of beings is established
Due to their lack of selfbeing[32]

In other words, Nāgārjuna here explicitly includes his own statements as within the ambit of emptiness, and thus as among the "all things" devoid of own-being. There is thus no reason to propose a distinction in this respect between the emptiness of things (in the domain of ontology) and the emptiness of statements or views (in the domain of epistemology) by means of which to allow the latter to be true/real (*satyam*) in a manner somehow superior to, or at least different from, the former. Indeed, this passage of the VV in reference to the interlocutor's first argument culminates in the famous disavowal of theses or propositions (*pratijñā*) announced in VV:29:

If I held any thesis
This fault would apply to me
But I do not hold any thesis
So I have no such fault[33]

This is doubtless the most celebrated, and commented, verse in the VV.[34] In his auto-commentary to this verse, Nāgārjuna reiterates "I have no thesis."[35] And as if that were not enough, he goes on to refer explicitly to "the emptiness of all things" as applying to linguistic elements such as names (*nāma*) and theses (*pratijñā*):

[Interlocutor:]
If things were without selfbeing
Then the name 'lack of selbeing'
Would be without being
For there is no name without an object

[Nāgārjuna:]
The emptiness of all things
Was established earlier
This criticism therefore
Is of a non-thesis[36]

As Westerhoff rightly observes in his commentary to VV:59, "as Nāgārjuna asserts a thesis of *universal* emptiness, it should be clear that the constituents of language are subsumed under this as well" (Westerhoff 2010: 107, emphasis original). Of course, theses, as themselves constituents of language, fall under the same rubric, which problematizes Westerhoff's characterization of Nāgārjuna's verse as asserting a thesis, particularly in the light of VV:63:

I do not negate anything
There is nothing to be negated
Therefore you malign in saying
"You negate"[37]

Nāgārjuna here again invokes the equivalence of things and statements in terms of universal emptiness; linguistic elements such as theses and propositions—be they affirmative or negative—must fall under the sway of emptiness on pain of positing an extra-empty (i.e., *svabhāvic*) entity. It should be clear from this that, were Nāgārjuna to hold on to a thesis, howsoever refined or "ultimate," he would thereby undermine the entire thrust of his insight into universal emptiness. It is all too easy to treat emptiness in Nāgārjuna's thought as a thesis, but this would be to treat it as another answer to the question "What is reality?" Nāgārjuna refuses to have his non-position be classed alongside other positions as just another position. He deals with this misunderstanding explicitly in the following verse:

> [My] statement renders the non-existent known
> It does not negate[38]

This is a matter to which we will return in the following section; for the moment, let us continue detailing the textual evidence.

The *Vaidalyaprakaraṇa* as a whole aims "to refute the sixteen Nyāya categories" (Westerhoff 2018b: 10) taken to govern rational debate. In the course of this overall deconstructive project, Nāgārjuna finds himself accused, naturally enough, of not only negating the propositions upheld by his interlocutor but of negating negation itself, and thereby annulling any validity that any refutation he himself might seek to effect may hold. To the claim that Nāgārjuna's "rejecting the establishment of the epistemic instruments and objects . . . would simultaneously reject the possibility of asserting any negations at all," including his own, however, Nāgārjuna responds that "all that is necessary for successful negations is the assertion of mere words (*brjod pa*) to which the negation can become attached. No ontological commitment to the object of negation having to exist in some form or other as the referent of these words is necessary" (Westerhoff 2018b: 89–90, 95). In other words, we are dealing here with a "mere" negation, a *prasajya-pratiṣedha* that negates without (logically, or ontologically) positing in place of the negated assertion a contrary or in any case other assertion. This accords with the passages of the VV just discussed in clearly repudiating the charge of implicitly if not explicitly making an assertion, in this case one in the form of a negation. Nāgārjuna again echoes the VV at VP:49, where his interlocutor accuses him of establishing a thesis (*pratijñā*) ("the thesis is asserted": Westerhoff 2018b: 183) with an analogous rebuttal to the effect that "the thesis does in fact not exist" (Westerhoff 2018b: 183).[39] VP:52 again finds the interlocutor attempting to pin a position on Nāgārjuna, insisting "there is a position and an opposing position for you" (Westerhoff 2018b: 197). But again Nāgārjuna replies that no, "The debate does not exist, since the expressing and expressed do not exist" (Westerhoff 2018b: 197).

I am not concerned here to delve into the specific arguments Nāgārjuna mobilizes at various points in the VP to support these and other such non-assertions. Rather, what I want to convey is the sheer literal unambiguity and textual recurrence of Nāgārjuna's repudiation of assertoric positionality. As befits a tightly structured text, this reaches a crescendo at the VP's conclusion, where the final two *sūtras* (VP:73–74) state:

> Objection:
> Negation does not exist either, like the object of negation, epistemic instruments, and so forth.
> [Reply:]
> If you say that, it is to be replied:
> Because both are not asserted. If that is not established, it amounts to no more than just not being established.
> . . .
> It is said to be thus; expressions do not exist. (Westerhoff 2018b: 280, 282)[40]

As Westerhoff observes, the argument in VP:73 is to the effect that "If some Nyāya category is not established, this does not entail any more than the absence of its establishment; it does not imply that its negation is now established" (Westerhoff 2018b: 282). As for VP:74, Nāgārjuna's auto-commentary declares that, since everything falls under the sway of emptiness, according to which "identity, difference, and both together do not exist, all things are said to be nonexistent. Therefore, while things do not exist, referents and expressions do not exist" (Westerhoff 2018b: 282). This brings into the open the equivalence between things and statements I noted earlier regarding the VV, and it presents a final pellucid rejection in the VP of taking Nāgārjuna's own *prasaṅgic* negations as holdable positions.

Despite being a relatively short text, the *Yuktiṣaṣṭikā-kārikā* likewise contains several references to the abandonment of all views. Following a dedicatory verse, Nāgārjuna's text begins with an encomium to detachment from all positions:

Those whose enlightened intelligence
Transcends being and non-being, is groundless
They know the profound and imponderable
Meaning of 'condition'[41]

In his concluding remarks against the claim that *svabhāvic* entities originate or cease, Nāgārjuna further states:

Those who know
Dependent co-origination
Abandon origination and cessation
Cross the ocean of existence of views[42]

A hermeneutically unmotivated reading of these verses clearly shows Nāgārjuna to be espousing a groundlessness beyond the ocean of views as characterizing those of "enlightened intelligence . . . those who know." Given this, Nāgārjuna goes on to provide his longest sustained verse passage against holding to views:

It is strange indeed
That those who rely on the path of the Buddha
Advocating universal impermanence
Should yet cling to things with arguments

When analysis reveals
That neither 'this' nor 'that' is found
What sage will argue
For the truth of 'this' or 'that'?

Woe to those who posit
An independent self or world
They are gripped by views
Such as 'permanence' and 'impermanence'

For those who posit selfbeing
Of dependently co-originated things
How can faults not arise
Such as attributing 'permanence' to those things?

> Those who accept dependently co-originated things
> As being like the moon in water
> Neither true nor false
> Are not gripped by views
>
> As soon as one affirms
> Views—painful and malignant—arise
> Which produce attachment and aversion
> And the arguments that spring from them
>
> That is the cause of all views
> Without it defilements do not arise
> Therefore when this is understood
> Views and defilements cease[43]

There is no ambiguity here as to Nāgārjuna's feelings regarding views: He sees them as obstructions regardless of the position they espouse. Whether one clings to permanence, impermanence, or any other "this" or "that," one is nevertheless gripped by, and thereby afflicted with, defilement. Indeed, views and defilements emerge in the final verse quoted as so mutually entwined as to arise and cease concomitantly. This is why, as Nāgārjuna goes on to write,

> Great ones hold no thesis
> Are beyond dispute
> For those who hold no thesis
> How could there be an opposing thesis?
>
> In holding any standpoint at all
> One is seized by the writhing snakes of defilement
> They alone are liberated
> Who hold no standpoint[44]

Surely a more unambiguous denunciation of view-holding would be difficult to write.

Moving on to the *Śūnyatāsaptati*, we find only one instance of the Sanskrit term *dṛṣṭi* in the reconstruction from Tibetan proposed by Lindtner. Tellingly, this occurs in the very final verse of the text:

Upon understanding dependent co-origination
The nets of bad views vanish
Pure, one attains *nirvāṇa*
By abandoning attachment, ignorance, and aversion[45]

The appearance of the term here translated as "bad views" (*kudṛṣṭi*) could well lead one to propose that Nāgārjuna, at least here if not elsewhere, is espousing the abandonment of false, as opposed to all, views. Yet the context makes clear that what Nāgārjuna means by *kudṛṣṭi* is nothing other than *sarvadṛṣṭi*—all views. The verse states that the nets of bad views vanish upon understanding dependent co-origination, at which point one becomes pure (*alipta*), the defilements (*kleśa*s) are abandoned, and *nirvāṇa* is attained. Now, dependent co-origination has been described in preceding verses as equivalent to emptiness,[46] which itself characterizes "all expressible things" as well as *nirvāṇa*.[47] As such, to understand dependent co-origination is to understand emptiness, which is to understand all reality—be it conventionally expressed (*vyavahāra*) or ultimate (*paramārtha*). Ignorance (*avidyā*) is consequently defined by Nāgārjuna as that which arises from any of the four (i.e., tetralemmic) positions; in other words, as that which stations one at any position at all as to reality:

In understanding reality
Ignorance, which arises from the four erroneous judgments, ceases[48]

It is on this basis that Nāgārjuna ends his text at ŚS:73 with reference to the "nets of bad views." The state of utter purity spoken of in this ultimate verse is introduced in the penultimate in terms of the peace (*śānta*) concomitant with the "teaching that is without support":

Who faithfully seeks truth
Who logically abides by this principle [of dependent co-origination]
Relies upon the teaching that is without support
Abandons both existence and non-existence, attains peace[49]

In context, this peace can only (or at least most straightforwardly) be understood as concomitant with the cessation of all views.

4.3. Abandoning Nāgārjuna's Views

In the preceding section, I have provided textual sources in support of the interpretation of Nāgārjuna's abandonment of all views I am propounding. Textual sources, however, are amenable to all manner of interpretations, such that even interpretations that appear to go directly counter to the letter may claim to go straight with the spirit of the text.[50] As such, in this section I will argue against the prevailing interpretive stance on the grounds that my own renders Nāgārjuna's philosophical project both more coherent and more interesting. That is, I propose a reading that takes Nāgārjuna at his word to be not only more philologically responsible but also more philosophically charitable. It is the sense I now propose to make of Nāgārjuna's philosophy that I take to clinch the philologically informed reading I have adumbrated heretofore.

4.3.1. Parameterizing Paradox

Before surveying the critical literature on this issue and elaborating my position in contradistinction to it, I want to reiterate what I take to be a supremely noteworthy fact. Among all the instances I have cited in which Nāgārjuna espouses the abandonment of views, in not a single one of them is this statement parameterized so as to confine its purview to "false" views or "views as to *svabhāva*" alone. As I have shown, even the one occurrence of the term *kudṛṣṭi* (bad or false views) at ŚS:73 is, in context, found to be equivalent to *sarvadṛṣṭi* (all views). And the one place wherein Nāgārjuna appears to qualify the purview of the views he is dealing with to "Views as to what is beyond cessation / Or what ends or what is eternal" (MK:25:21ab) has been shown, again in context, to entail "The cessation of all cognizance / The felicitous cessation of conceptualization" (MK:25:24ab).

Despite this, parameterization for the sake of "rescuing" Nāgārjuna from the evident philosophical absurdity of abjuring all views has been an extremely common hermeneutic strategy.[51] Since VV:29 is taken to be the *locus classicus* of Nāgārjuna's (non-)position, a great deal of this scholarly effort has gone into interpreting this verse. The stakes are the familiar ones of absurdity and/or paradoxicality, for, as Frits Staal puts it, "unless this statement itself is not a proposition, we have a paradox here" (Staal 1975: 45).[52] But it is Dan Arnold who sets out the dilemma facing the exegete most lucidly:

> the characteristically Mādhyamika claim not to have any thesis forces . . . [an] interpretive choice: One can take it at face value and convict the Mādhyamika either of self-referential incoherence or of making a vacuous statement, or one can work to understand "thesis" as specifically referring to some particular kind of thesis. (Arnold 2005: 133)[53]

It is no surprise that the latter strategy of modification or parameterization has been the almost ubiquitous strategy of contemporary exegetes, on the understanding that taking the Mādhyamikas at their word forces one to "convict" them of incoherence or vacuity.[54]

In relation to VV:29, Jan Westerhoff shows himself to adopt just such a strategy in claiming that "what Nāgārjuna wants to say here is that he does not have any thesis *of a particular kind*" (Westerhoff 2010: 64, emphases original). Having dismissed offhand the idea that the verse might "amount to the paradoxical claim of someone asserting that he is not asserting anything" (as if Nāgārjuna might actually mean what he says when he says "I do not hold *any* thesis"), Westerhoff specifies just what this "thesis *of a particular kind*" is as follows: "What Nāgārjuna wants to say is that he does not hold any *substantially existent* thesis, that is, any thesis *which is to be supplied with a realist semantics that spells out meaning and truth in terms of correspondence with a mind-independent reality*" (Westerhoff 2010: 12, emphases added). I have italicized the parameterization here to highlight just how extensive it is. Westerhoff explains that "the insertion of such modifiers is often necessary when interpreting Madhyamaka texts" (Westerhoff 2010: 64 fn. 30). Given that the text itself exhibits no such modifiers, one can only conclude that their insertion is "necessary" so as to maintain an antecedently concluded reading.

Tellingly, Westerhoff justifies his use of such modifiers here—just as he did with reference to dispelling the apparent contradictoriness of the *catuṣkoṭi* in §2.2.2—by referring to their extensive use in the Geluk school founded by Tsongkhapa. But Arnold acknowledges that premodern Geluk interpreters "had a particular stake in defending the canons of dialectics and debate," and "typically qualif[ied] Nāgārjuna's claim—for example, suggesting that the kind of 'thesis' Nāgārjuna thus disavows is only that *kind* of thesis that is thought to presuppose the sort of 'essence' (*svabhāva*) that it is Nāgārjuna's business to reject" (Arnold 2005: 261–262 n. 12, emphasis original) on the basis of that agenda. Garfield is even more forthright in stating that Geluk authors starting with Tsongkhapa "simply argue that when Nāgārjuna speaks of relinquishing 'all views', he means 'false views', or 'all views according to which things are inherently existent'" (Garfield 2002: 47—also quoted in Thakchoe 2007: 98). He rightly notes that, contra the Geluk insistence on the need for inserting qualifiers, for the Nyingma school and its prominent proponent Ngog blo ldan shes rab (Ngok Loden Sherab), "Nāgārjuna means just what he says. The central teaching of Madhyamaka is that one should relinquish all views, and that if Madhyamaka becomes a philosophical view, one has fundamentally missed its point" (Garfield 2002: 48).[55]

While not denying the creative element ineradicably part and parcel of any and all interpretation, it would appear obvious that deliberately *not* taking Nāgārjuna to mean "what he says," but rather repeatedly and extensively modifying his text—whose message is purportedly being determined—in order to discern what one feels he "wants to say," inevitably introduces an unacceptably significant degree of arbitrariness into the hermeneutic endeavor; a degree, that is, of being "decided by one's liking; dependent upon will or pleasure; at the discretion or option of any one" (OED: arbitrary). Such a tendency is in full evidence in Westerhoff's interpretation of VP:52 cited earlier. Indeed, Westerhoff is completely upfront about both the literal absence of his qualifiers in the original text and the reasons he finds it "tempting" to insert them:

> Even though Nāgārjuna says explicitly, and without any modifiers, that neither the expression, the expressed, nor debate exist, it is tempting to insert some suitable modifiers here, having him say that there is no substantial (*svabhāvatas*) relation between words and referents, i.e., no relation that is not wholly explicable in terms of conventions. To assert any more would be dangerously close to a performative contradiction, since Nāgārjuna presumably wants his own statements in the VP and elsewhere to be conventionally meaningful. (Westerhoff 2018b: 203)

Now, I take the interpretation Westerhoff proposes here to be coherent, in the sense that it makes sense according to its own sense of what constitutes making sense, which it moreover assumes to be universal and unquestionable.[56] Furthermore, anyone familiar with Nāgārjuna's texts will be in no doubt as to the acuity of his argumentative vision, so I see no problem in even going so far as to suppose that Nāgārjuna could reasonably have foreseen such a possible and internally coherent reading of his text. But it certainly does not exhaust the range of justifiable readings. I for one quite like the idea of Nāgārjuna's "performative contradiction" in VP:52, expressing as it does that neither expressing (*vācya*) nor expressed (*vācaka*) exist, acting as a kind of "proto-gongan," stunning the reader into non-discriminatory *prajñā* (see also VP:74: "identity, difference, and both together do not exist"; Westerhoff 2018b: 282).[57] Other readers proffer other readings, and while there are no limits to the readerly horizons from which a given text may be interpreted, I take it that inserting what a given exegete happens to consider "*suitable* modifiers" into a given author's text and thereby "*having* him say" what one supposes in advance he *should* say is detrimental to learning what the text actually means in saying what it says.

Like comments apply to VP:32, which deals with the Nyāya category of conclusion (*siddhānta*). Westerhoff here initially outlines an interpretation of the verse according to which "Nāgārjuna cannot . . . hold a conclusion" (Westerhoff 2018b: 141). He immediately rejects this, however, in favor of what for him "seems to be a more satisfactory conclusion . . . Rather than claiming that the Mādhyamika cannot hold any conclusion whatsoever, we would want to say that he cannot hold a conclusion that is established intrinsically" (Westerhoff 2018b: 141). A footnote here specifies that "this rejection of the *siddhānta* should be interpreted along the same lines as the rejection of the *pratijñā* in VV 29, as the rejection of a conclusion or thesis that is to be interpreted according to a realist semantics" (see discussion of Westerhoff 2010 earlier). In other words, "Nāgārjuna does not reject any conclusion or *siddhānta*, but only conclusions of a certain kind"; viz., conclusions that rely on "a semantics based on correspondence with a mind-independent world" (Westerhoff 2018b: 141). Quite apart from anything else, this proposal clearly ignores the concordance of an unqualified rejection of the conclusion here with the multiple and likewise textually unparameterized repudiations of affirmation and negation, theses and positions, to be found throughout the VP and VV (see §4.2). But even irrespective of the merits or demerits of the philosophical construction Westerhoff proposes here, I would hope that by now it should be clear that such efforts to have the text say what "we would want to say" amount to derogations of the task of textual hermeneutics.[58]

Westerhoff's reference to VV:29 acts as a convenient bridge to Garfield and Priest's reading of this important verse. Much like Westerhoff, Garfield and Priest state that "Nāgārjuna's reply [at VV:29] does not deny that he is asserting anything. How could he deny *that*? Rather, he *asserts* that his use of words does not commit him to the existence of any convention-independent phenomena (such as emptiness) to which those words refer" (Garfield and

Priest 2002: 98, emphases original). Despite Garfield's stated intention to take Nāgārjuna at his word,[59] and to do so on the understanding that he "means just what he says" and "says what he means" (Garfield 2002: 48),[60] (not to mention his, Priest's, Westerhoff's, and others' often highly sophisticated philosophical constructions based on Nāgārjuna), this is another clear instance of an evidential exegetical fallacy according to which the evidence presented by the text itself is deliberately skewed so as to support a foreclosed philosophical presupposition.[61]

Now, Garfield and Priest may well respond that they are channeling Garfield's own earlier article on "Emptiness and Positionlessness: Do the Mādhyamika Relinquish All Views?" There, Garfield presents a richly nuanced argument for what he calls a "nonassertorial understanding" (Garfield 2002: 52) of Nāgārjuna's abjurations of view-holding. Suffice it for present purposes to observe, however, that Garfield's position appears to be inconsistent insofar as, in the just-mentioned article originally published in 1996, Garfield maintains that "Madhyamaka philosophy must be understood as, in the end, positionless" (Garfield 2002: 51) unqualifiedly, and that "Nāgārjuna *does* sincerely claim to assert no proposition, not merely to assert no inherently existent proposition" (Garfield 2002: 56, emphasis original), while in the remainder of his published work on the topic he nonetheless insists upon adding just such qualifiers. Thus, in attempting to explicate Nāgārjuna's unqualified abjuration of conceptualization at the very outset of the MK, Garfield immediately calls upon Candrakīrti to buttress his own position, taking Candrakīrti to be taking Nāgārjuna to be saying (merely) that "the Mādhyamika philosopher will make no positive assertions *about the fundamental nature of things*" (Garfield 1995: 100, emphases added)—a qualifier absent from Nāgārjuna's root text. Garfield then proposes that this already qualified rendering of Nāgārjuna's "claim must be qualified in several ways" (Garfield 1995: 100), first and foremost on the basis that "we must take the phrase 'the nature of things' [which is, again, absent from Nāgārjuna] very seriously" (Garfield 1995: 100). In the 2002 article coauthored with Priest, moreover, Garfield specifies that "The views that one must relinquish are views *about the ultimate nature of reality*" (Garfield and Priest 2002: 96, emphases added). And although he subsequently acknowledges (in his highly influential response to Huntington 2007) that "As one who has argued strenuously for taking Nāgārjuna's avowals of rejecting all views, and of positionlessness seriously, I am sensitive to the charge of now saddling him with a view, a position" (Garfield 2008: 523), nevertheless Garfield goes on to argue that "Nāgārjuna in his insistence that Madhyamaka not be taken as one more *dṛṣṭi* is emphasizing that this really is the rejection of *any* view *regarding the fundamental nature of reality*" (Garfield 2008: 525, emphasis on "any" original, emphasis on final phrase added). But views "about the fundamental nature of things," "about the ultimate nature of reality," or "regarding the fundamental nature of reality" are not *all* views; and the point is that it is *all* views that Nāgārjuna rejects.[62]

For as demonstrated earlier, when Nāgārjuna states "I do not hold any thesis (*pratijñā*)" at VV:29, he does not qualify this absolute with some relative clause limiting its scope. He does not, for example, state "I do not hold any thesis that proposes a *svabhāva* (but I do hold a thesis that does not propose a *svabhāva*)." Similarly, when Nāgārjuna states that "those who have taken emptiness as a view / They are the incurables" at MK:13:8, he does not qualify this "view" in any way. And finally, the final verse of the entire MK (27:30) pays homage explicitly to Gautama as one who "For the abandonment of all views / . . . taught the true teaching." In attempting to propound a philosophically charitable interpretation of these and all of Nāgārjuna's kindred statements which does not denature them, I propose that, for Nāgārjuna, views—or positions, propositions, beliefs . . . indeed, all "discursive development (*prapañca*) and dichotomizing conceptualization (*vikalpa*)" (Ruegg 1977: 12)—are mental reifications metaphysically equivalent to and epistemically causally constitutive of the self. By "equivalent to" I mean that they are just as invalid, as empty, as are the *svabhāvic* substances normally taken to ground existence; and by "constitutive of" I mean that the process by which such views are constructed is itself at least partly responsible for the false belief in any such substance (including the self).

4.3.2. Holding and Clinging

Now, I have consistently used the term "hold" of a position or view. This I have done as a deliberate strategy intended to bring out the relation—for Nāgārjuna inevitable—between what may be called the holding *of* and the holding *onto* positions/views/beliefs. As evinced at MK:16:9–10 and MK:18:5, for example,[63] there is a direct and reflexive relationship between these. The holding of a view is never innocent, is always a commitment, and therefore necessarily involves one in attachment (*upādāna*), thereby reinforcing one's enmeshedness in the wheel of *saṃsāric* rebirth. Holding is always also clinging. There is no such thing as a completely objective position; one that would entail no subjective affirmation but would be affirmed, rather, with utterly detached neutrality. As such, the holding *of* a view is inextricably entwined in the holding *onto* views. This is why Jakubczak's claim that for Nāgārjuna "Not holding a view means not having an egotistical attitude toward it" (*Nie mieć poglądu to znaczy nie mieć do niego egotycznego stosunku*) (Jakubczak 2019: 341, echoing Jakubczak 2017c: 89) subtly misses the point: For Nāgārjuna, view-holding is necessarily, inevitably, egotistic, an act of attachment, so one could not possibly hold a view egolessly. In fact, as Charles Muller observes, "the concept of 'grasping' in Buddhism (Skt. *grāha*; Chi. *qu* 取, *zhi* 執) is often a virtual synonym for *dṛṣṭi*" (Muller 2018: 368). Even relatively unquestioned views (what are typically called "assumptions") such as logical or physical "laws" necessarily entail a hermeneutic framework within which to function; one that is typically ontologically substantialist, and consequently affirmative of what for Nāgārjuna is a metaphysically false, and soteriologically harmful, view of reality.[64]

It is in this relationship between holding and clinging that the realms of metaphysics and epistemology converge upon soteriological concerns. For, to put the matter another way, to affirm one's view is always also to affirm oneself. In affirming a view or belief—even a belief in no-self or emptiness—I affirm my affirming self, and my belief in turn affirms me in my belief. Such a reflexively affirmatory relation is reflexively reificatory; I affirm my belief as true, and am affirmed by my (holding of my) belief as real. For to affirm a belief is to affirm it as a given, while in being affirmed my belief affirms me to me as its giver. I am unable to believe without affirming my belief as some*thing*, and my belief is unable to be believed without its believer being affirmed as some*one*. All beliefs, in other words, are involved in (and involved in *constructing*) an ontological framework; one that, as ontological, is reificatorially populated with individual existents.[65]

This helps to explain why, despite averring that Nāgārjuna "is writing with specifically soteriological goals in mind" (Garfield 1995: 107), Garfield's efforts to restrict Nāgārjuna's multiply reiterated and utterly unqualified abandonment of views to a merely "technical sense of *proposition* in the sense of *pratijñā*" (Garfield 2002: 66, emphasis original), or to the relatively inconsequential domain of semantics,[66] do undermine (contra Garfield's own protestations) the soteriological thrust of Nāgārjuna's Madhyamaka, based as this is on the universal baselessness constitutive of emptiness. For while Garfield correctly notes that Nāgārjuna's understanding of emptiness as itself empty relies on its being treated "on a cognitive par with other nominal entities" since "All linguistic and conceptual activity is implicated simultaneously in ontic constitution and assertion" (Garfield 2002: 271 n. 27),[67] I would argue that he fails to follow this insight through to its conclusion, or at least appears to vacillate on just how far to go. In addition to the inconsistencies already mentioned, Garfield's apparent vacillation on the topic is evident from his forthright declaration that "for the arhat who directly realizes emptiness . . . there is no view to be expressed," only to specify "where a view is something that can be given assertoric voice" (Garfield 2002: 53). Or by his subsequent acknowledgment, on the one hand, that Nāgārjuna's statements "must be understood as pure denials" and his immediate undercutting of that very "purity," on the other hand, by their qualification as "denials that phenomena, including emptiness, have any nature—showing the way that things are when seen *per impossibile, sub specie aeternitatis*" (Garfield 2002: 66). But a locally qualified denial is no longer pure in the sense of universal. Besides which, to claim that Nāgārjuna's abandonment of all views is "*impossibile*" undermines the entire thrust of the *prasaṅgic* dialectic, which is to see reality (certainly not "*sub specie aeternitatis*"!) *sub specie veritatis*—as utterly, unqualifiedly empty. In other words, it is to see reality aright, "through direct, nonconceptual consciousness" (Garfield 2002: 269 n. 16). For while Garfield is perfectly right to say that once we have "transcend[ed] that [conventional] standpoint, no matter what we try to say, and no matter how carefully we hew to a *via negativa*, we can say nothing at all consistent with the *via media* Nāgārjuna is determined to limn" (Garfield 2002: 58), Nāgārjuna's point as to the universality of emptiness (or, to put it another way, as to the ultimate unity of the conventional and ultimate) is precisely that the transcendence of the conventional into the ultimate is simultaneously the pervasion by the ultimate of the conventional. Indeed, to dispense with hierarchy altogether (or *archē* altogether), it is their utter inter-penetration and/as inter-identification. The *via media* turns out to be the *via omnia*.

I mention *archē* because in the final words of his article Garfield equates "the relinquishing of all views" with "an *archē* beyond discourse" (Garfield 2002: 68, referencing Sellars 1997). This is dead wrong, on whatever sense of "*archē*" we choose to take: "origin, beginning" (the relinquishing of all views is the *end* of all discourse); "power, authority" (it is *exhaustion*); or "rule, order" (it is *deconstruction*). In short, the abandonment of all views—that is, the attainment of enlightenment—amounts to *anarchy* in the strict sense that, contrary to the fundamental posit of ancient Greek philosophy, there simply is no first principle. To understand Nāgārjuna to be positing "an *archē* beyond discourse" is therefore effectively to smuggle in old Theo by the (heavenly) back door—a consequence that Garfield may well not have intended (indeed, that may well horrify him) but that remains a consequence of his claim nonetheless. That the absence of ultimate metaphysical ground is what enables all conventional discourse—indeed, all conventions determining imputed "orders" of "things"—to function is the upshot of Nāgārjuna's further move (most perspicuously elaborated in MK:24) to the effect that only universal emptiness enables the intertwining of local functionalities constitutive of the world.

Now, Garfield's unwillingness to countenance the universal ambit of abandonment goes hand in hand with his insistence on maintaining a clear distinction between conventional and ultimate truth.[68] Yet in this context it is crucial to note that Nāgārjuna's ultimate abandonment of conceptualization *in toto* necessitates the abandonment of all distinctions, and with them the very distinction between ultimate and conventional.[69] The abandoning of all views and the collapsing of the two truths are two sides of the same coin. Nāgārjuna is clear about this, as it is precisely in the culminating verse of the book of the MK specifically devoted to *nirvāṇa* that he speaks of "The cessation of all cognizance / The felicitous cessation of conceptualization"[70]—a conclusion prefaced by the unreserved inter-identification of realms:

> Between *saṃsāra* and *nirvāṇa*
> There is no difference at all
> Between *nirvāṇa* and *saṃsāra*
> There is no difference at all
>
> What is *nirvāṇa*'s limit
> That is the limit of *saṃsāra*
> Between them is not found
> Even the slightest difference[71]

Given all this, every *dṛṣṭi*, *pakṣa*, *pratijñā*, and *prapañca* is to be abandoned not only on some putative ultimate reality transcendent to all views, propositions, theses, and conceptualizations, but on the only kind of ultimate Nāgārjuna recognizes: ultimate-cum-conventional, where the very distinction between ultimate and conventional has been done away with as yet another dichotomy constitutive of illusory conceptual proliferation.

In the conceptual construction of one's worldview (or perhaps I might more aptly say "of one's world"), therefore, the role of conceptualization (*prapañca*) and/as dichotomizing conceptualization (*vikalpa*) is crucial. As Paul Williams states, "the use of '*vikalpa*' [in the Madhyamaka]—as expressed by the divisive prefix '*vi-*'—is to place emphasis on the creation of a referent through the ability of language to partition and create opposition, to divide a domain into mutually exclusive and contradictory categories" (Williams 1980: 27).[72] It is thus precisely in the activity of dichotomizing conceptualization that referents—that is, the myriad things of the world—are constructed.[73] While Williams is right to locate this definitive function of *vikalpa* in the domain of language, for language (at least as ordinarily understood and used) is indeed consistently dichotomizing, I prefer to speak here of "belief" as an umbrella term for the various technically nuanced expressions present in the literature pertaining to the holding of a doxastic and/or epistemic propositional attitude. I speak of belief because I want to emphasize precisely that *holding*, rather than the linguistic *expressing*, of whatever is so held.[74] Without going into a fully fledged theory of mind and/or of language, and without insisting overmuch on any structural primacy to belief (as the intentional locus of a given propositional attitude) over language (as the verbal expression of that propositional attitude), I am thus arguing that, for Nāgārjuna, the practice of dichotomizing conceptualization (*vikalpa*), and indeed of conceptualization (*prapañca*)/conceptual construction (*kalpanā*) more broadly, is causally implicated in (false, deceptive) ego construction.[75]

This particular point does not seem to me to be revolutionary. Indeed, it is already prefigured in the twelve *nidāna*s or causal chains of the wheel of dependent co-origination espoused by the Buddha. In this classical formulation, composite mental formations (*saṃskāra*) are founded upon delusion (*moha*) or ignorance (*avidyā*), and lead to the arising of discerning consciousness (*vijñāna*). This last term, be it noted, is also formed with the divisive prefix "*vi-*," and standardly opposed in the primary Buddhist literature to *jñāna*—liberating (that is, non-divisive) knowledge or gnosis. So, without realizing that views (*dṛṣṭi*), like all things (*sarvam dharmam*), including the self (*ātman*), are empty (*śūnya*), we entangle ourselves in attachment (*rāga*) and aversion (*dveṣa*) with regard to them on the basis of that primal ignorance (*avidyā*) which ascribes substantial existence to them, and thereby fall prey to the three poisons (*triviṣa*) or afflictions (*kleśa*) constitutive of *saṃsāric* suffering (*duḥkha*).

So understood, the Mādhyamika's position of no-position is but the application to positions or views (*dṛṣṭi*) of the Buddha's liberatory insight into the impermanence (*anitya*), and (hence) selflessness (*anātman*), of what are conventionally referred to as "things." There is no permanent view; there can be none because fixed views cannot possibly describe unfixed phenomena, comegoings. To propose a fixed view is therefore both metaphysically mistaken and soterially harmful. It is mistaken because it attempts to meld incommensurables (ephemeral anontological comegoings onto/into a fixed ontological framework of thinghood).[76] And it is harmful because this conceiving of views as fixed is analogous to conceiving of selves as fixed, and is thus tantamount to espousing a *svabhāvic* conception of reality—one that, as per the Buddha's central insight, invariably brings about suffering (*duḥkha*). Indeed, as Murti eloquently summarizes, "the root cause of *duḥkha*, in the Mādhyamika system, is the indulging in views (*dṛṣṭi*) or imagination (*kalpanā*). *Kalpanā*, (*vikalpa*) is *avidyā par excellence*" (Murti 1955: 271).[77]

4.3.3. *Nirvikalpa* and *Nirvāṇa*, *Prasaṅga* and *Prajñā*

The necessary implication of this point is that only through what is *nirvikalpa* can we reach *nirvāṇa*.[78] Given that the attainment of *nirvāṇic* liberation is the teleological end of the entire Buddhist enterprise, and given that for Nāgārjuna "They alone are liberated / Who hold no standpoint,"[79] it is of the utmost relevance to note that descriptions throughout the Buddhist tradition of *nirvāṇa* and of the Tathāgata who has attained it invariably characterize them as "profound, immeasurable, unfathomable" (Ñāṇamoli and Bodhi 1995: 593), or with any number of like terms designed to convey their sheer inconceivability. Therefore, I do not consider the conceptual difficulty (even impossibility) of conceiving what such wholescale abandonment of views would consist of to constitute an argument against my reading Nāgārjuna as espousing it. On the contrary, our very inability to conceive this I see as yet further evidence in favor of my interpretation, for were we able to conceptualize *nirvāṇa* (taken here precisely as the non-conceptualizable), it would no longer lie beyond the very mental bonds its attainment is explicitly meant to sever.

In elaborating how such abandonment of all views is supposed to function, allow me a silly analogy. Let's say Nāgārjuna had written a work of culinary theory replete with claims that we must abandon all curries, admonitions to cease consuming any spicy saucy dishes, and dismissals of those who take even his own most distinctive recipe to itself be of a curry as incurables. Of course, we could work through every instance of such statements, interpreting him to only mean "vindaloo" here or only "rogan josh" there, but what the text would actually say in every case would just be "all curries" or some equivalent phrase. Now, my analogy falls down because we can easily conceive of living without curry (however bland that might be), but we find it extremely difficult (if not downright impossible) to conceive what living without views would be. Indeed, the refusal on the part of the preponderant bulk of exegetes to take Nāgārjuna's statements to this effect seriously, their dismissal of them as self-referentially incoherent or vacuous, is eloquent testimony to this difficulty. For as we have seen, the radicality of Nāgārjuna's claim to hold no claims leads many commentators to reject offhand the possibility that he denies asserting anything at all (recall Garfield and Priest rhetorically asking "How could he deny *that*?"). Admittedly, the abjuration of all positionality is a radical (non)position, and one that appears to fly in the face of the apparently indubitable existence of positions, propositions, and oppositions expounded by Nāgārjuna throughout his works. Yet Nāgārjuna's work is replete with claims that fly in the face of the (typically substantialist) presuppositions generally taken as "common sense," so it will hardly do to dismiss his abandonment of views (or indeed his rejection of any and all forms of foundationalism) on these grounds alone.[80] Moreover, Nāgārjuna is well aware of the difficulties concomitant with taking him at his word; as we have seen, he explicitly and repeatedly states that this teaching is extremely hard to swallow (like some curries after all!).[81]

The point I am making here is reminiscent of that made by Jonathan Gold in his reply to Dan Arnold:

> Granted, any tradition that claims that all of our conceptualizations are, in an important way, false, is asking that we change the rules of the language game in which we ordinarily understand how meaning and reference operate. We are asked to read such expressions as merely pragmatic, as not affirming any essential nature, as figurative, *sous rature*. This is not how words seem to work, including the words that express these ideas. But we are being asked to look at things in a new way. And it is not an appropriate response to a proposed rule change to say that to accept it would be against the rules. (Gold 2014b: 1067–1068)[82]

For his part, Arnold had charged that "altogether to abandon the commonsense view of the mental, as Lynne Rudder Baker puts the point, 'would be to relinquish the point of view from which the idea of making sense makes sense'" (Arnold 2014: 1064).[83] More generally, Arnold confesses that, if it involves the abandonment of all views, then "I do not see what sense the idea of Buddhahood makes; indeed, it seems that nobody *could* make sense of this apart from assent to the Buddhist tradition's testimony to its possibility" (Arnold 2014: 1065, emphasis original). But it is surely incumbent upon scholars of Buddhism to take seriously positions forcefully iterated and reiterated throughout the Buddhist traditions, even if (or especially when) they "make sense" not according to the interpreter's imported intellectual paradigms but to (what are thus seen to be) radically other "rules." And that the various classical Buddhist thought traditions of South, East, and North Asia *have* taken the abandonment of all views seriously has been convincingly shown. It is a position that *makes sense* within the parameters of the Buddhist path—or rather, as its end—even if it makes sense only, precisely, as the end of all such making sense. Thus, Paul Fuller (whose treatment remains the most comprehensive) states unambiguously that "The aim of the path is not the cultivation of right-view and the abandoning of wrong-views but the relinquishment of all views, wrong or right. . . . The early texts do not understand right-views as a correction of wrong-view, but as a detached order of seeing, completely different from the attitude of holding to any view, wrong or right (Fuller 2005: 1).[84] He goes on to refer to the facts that what he calls the "no-views understanding" he finds well attested in the Pāli canon "has been termed 'Proto-Mādhyamika' by Luis Gómez," and that "Richard Hayes has used the term 'doxastic minimalism' to describe this understanding within Buddhist thought" (Fuller 2005: 3).[85] My references earlier to Vasubandhu, Dharmakīrti, and Candrakīrti among Indian Buddhist philosophers, and to Sakya Paṇḍita and Gorampa among the Tibetans, is evidence of substantial and sophisticated philosophical elaborations there of this "transcendence of all views."[86] As for East Asia, Charles Muller's article argues that the Chan, Seon, and Zen schools of China, Korea, and Japan respectively became "almost completely absorbed in the non-abiding in views above all other practices" (Muller 2018: 373), and also provides numerous examples of the varied efforts to undermine view-holding of any kind in the East Asian strands of Yogācāra and Tathāgata-garbha thought, to which the Sanlun and Tiantai traditions explicitly heir to Nāgārjuna could well be added.[87]

Of course, I am not claiming that Nāgārjuna (or any other Buddhist thinker), asks us to dispense with any and all view-holding in our as-yet-unenlightened conventional worldly interactions. Arnold is right to aver that "it is only *as* conventionally experiencing subjects that we can understand any claims at all" (Arnold 2014: 1064, emphasis original). But this is to neglect what for Nāgārjuna is the very point of the path; that is, to reach its end, to go from *laukika* to *lokottara* and thence abandon the distinction itself, to turn us from "conventionally experiencing subjects" to transcendent come-gone Tathāgatas. This is so even if, as per Arnold, "what a Buddha knows is simply that ordinary experience does not require—indeed, that it is inconsistent with—the idea that there is something that we 'really' are" (Arnold 2014: 1065).[88] For Nāgārjuna, to understand this truth, to attain realization, is precisely to dispense with views propounding certain truths, certain conceptualizations of reality. What Arnold describes as "the commonsense view of the mental" is simply not adequate to the enlightened mental state, which (whatever else can or cannot be said about it) *cannot* hold or "understand any claims at all" in anything like the same sense that the rest of us hold or understand them.[89]

Views (all views, without exception) thus turn out for Nāgārjuna to be hindrances. His *prasaṅgic* deconstruction is designed to clear the ground, as it were, of all supposed supports (metaphysical, epistemic, and doxastic), and thereby to open the Mādhyamika's mind to *prajñā* (an etymological brother of *jñāna*), the enlightened awareness of emptiness.[90] As Lindtner says,

> *prajñā* performs its task in the systematic intellectual endeavour to demonstrate that the *jāla* [net] of *prapañca* [conceptualization] is empty, that it lacks 'objective' foundation (cf. YṢ, 25–27 etc.). This is achieved by bringing to light that *asti* and *nāsti* [being and non-being] hypostasized by the activity of *vikalpa* [dichotomizing conceptualization] do not appertain to reality (*tattva*). (Lindtner 1982: 271)[91]

In short, "there really is no *dharma* or *bhāva* to fix one's mind upon as support" (Lindtner 1982: 272), and thus upon which to construct a doctrine (*mata*) or view (*dṛṣṭi*). The adequate propositional attitude toward it, therefore, is one that is neither propositionally contentful nor attitudinally oriented at all.[92]

All of this goes some way, I hope, to rebutting Arnold's claim that

> Mādhyamika arguments are (apparent claims to the contrary notwithstanding) offered in defense of a particular truth-claim—that is, these arguments are not simply methodological or "therapeutic" exercises that are equally compatible with just any ontology or metaphysics; rather, they fundamentally aim to make a point about how things exist. (Arnold 2005: 137)[93]

The "apparent claims to the contrary" must be taken seriously. If Nāgārjuna (and Candrakīrti) had meant to say that he was eschewing only certain claims (rather than claims as a whole), surely that is what he would have said. Instead, he explicitly espouses the abandonment of *all* claims. It is not that his statements "are equally compatible with just any ontology or metaphysics"; rather, they constitute the abandonment of all ontologies and metaphysics, in short of all belief paradigms through which reality is viewed and hence distorted, not seen simply "as it is," in its "suchness" (*tattva*).

My point here is supported by Mills, who writes: "Of course, there is a longstanding debate about whether 'all views' (*sarvadṛṣṭi*) here [at MK:24:30] means all views whatsoever, or all *false* views, as is commonly interpreted by many Indian, Tibetan, and Western commentators. I think we should take Nāgārjuna at his word" (Mills 2018b: 97–98, emphasis original).[94] Mills eloquently elaborates on this in the context of Nāgārjuna's denegation of causality in MK:1 as follows:

> If Nāgārjuna meant for us to accept some theory about conventions, regularity, or conceptual construction, one wonders why he would not have said so. There would be no point in going the extra step to tell us that theories of emptiness undermine themselves. It might be the case that Nāgārjuna didn't really mean what he said or that he didn't mean for those statements to be taken straightforwardly (perhaps he meant "all *false* views" or "I have no *essentialist* thesis"). But this is not what he said, and my skeptical interpretation is based on the attempt to take him at his word. Supposing Nāgārjuna really did mean exactly what he said, there are no final theories about causes and conditions to be found—that is precisely the point. (Mills 2018a: 63–64, emphases original)

While I have reservations regarding the use of the moniker "skeptic" to describe Nāgārjuna, as a term with what I see to be inalienable features irrelevant and/or inapplicable to him, it should be clear that I am in substantial agreement with Mills's point here, as indeed with his understanding of Nāgārjuna's overall aim as "to offer a therapy for Buddhist intellectuals prone to grasping at philosophical theories" (Mills 2018a: 65). The only caveat I would make to this statement relates to the generality of its ambit, for I take Nāgārjuna's therapeutical work to apply not only to "Buddhist intellectuals" and "philosophical theories" but to everyone and all views.[95]

This last point brings more fully into focus Arnold's claim that "Mādhyamika arguments . . . are not simply methodological or 'therapeutic' exercises." It is unfortunate that Arnold does not spell out what exactly he means by, and what is or are the scope/s of, "methodological" and "therapeutic." Judging from the context, however, I understand him to imply that such exercises are opposed to properly metaphysical endeavors; that they, unlike the latter, are not interested in making truth claims *per se*, or indeed at all. But at the risk of making a rather sweeping claim, I aver that no Buddhist, *qua* Buddhist, "fundamentally aim[s] to make a point about how things exist"; that is, fundamentally aims to make a metaphysical truth claim. The over-riding—or, to use Arnold's term, *fundamental*—aim of Buddhist discourse, be it in the Buddha's own *sūtra*s, the philosophical *śastra*s, the poetic *kārikā*s, or any other genre, is avowedly *not* metaphysical but soteriological; that is, it is aimed at liberation. Buddhist philosophers such as Nāgārjuna "make a point about how things exist" not *fundamentally* but only insofar as that point is *effective*; otherwise, they would be engaged in precisely the kind of vacuous, sophistical "eel-wriggling" that the Buddha disparaged on the grounds that it only served, and serves, to bind its practitioner more tightly in the grip of (self-)affirmation.

In this sense, the authorial intent of Buddhist religiosophical texts such as the MK is not primarily zetetic but protreptic; indeed, zetetic only insofar as protreptic.[96] In other words, these texts seek to instruct the reader/practitioner as to the means toward detachment from irreality in the form of conceptual elaborations such as "self" and "truth." The deconstruction of such fictions and consequent description of reality as it truly is (i.e., devoid of them), *even where this deconstruction and description comprises the bulk of the text*, is subservient to this ultimate end.[97] It is telling that Arnold neglects to deal in this context with what is—certainly for Nāgārjuna and the Mādhyamikas—the centrally important concept of "expedient means" (*upāya*). As is abundantly clear from his multiple formulations to this effect, Nāgārjuna considers his philosophical enterprise as being wholeheartedly soteriological in intent.[98] Rather than constituting "a properly metaphysical claim . . . a universally obtaining truth claim" (Arnold 2005: 120), Nāgārjuna's central teaching (of dependent co-origination as emptiness) is meant to disabuse one of suffering by enabling one to proceed along the Buddhist path toward unadulterated vision of reality (unadulterated, that is, by any and all conceptual lenses). In other words, Nāgārjuna (together with his fellow Mādhyamikas) conceives of his own enterprise as valid only insofar as it proves soterially efficacious; not insofar as it merely "make[s] a point" (Arnold 2005: 137).

On a Mādhyamika's understanding, theism (as mentioned by Arnold—see the citation from Arnold 2005: 137 earlier) represents just one branch of the larger tree of substantialism. For whether one believes that there is one intrinsically/independently existing thing or many such things, the metaphysical basis for the belief in the existence of such a thing is equivalent, and consequently dealt with in the same way by Nāgārjuna. Thus it is that Nāgārjuna considers his argument against the existence of any selfbeing (*svabhāva*) as effectively refuting also the existence of any otherbeing (*parabhāva*) derived therefrom:

> Without selfbeing
> Where is otherbeing?
> For otherbeing is said to be
> The otherbeing of an other being[99]

So, although it is true that Nāgārjuna's central claim that

> Since no non-dependently co-originated thing
> At all is found
> Therefore no non-empty thing
> At all is found[100]

contradicts a—indeed, the definitive—truth claim of substantialists (and thus of theists), this is to ignore what is equally and concomitantly true; viz., that this Madhyamaka claim contradicts the definitive truth claim of nihilists (i.e., anti-substantialists) too. Arnold has, as it were, stated the truth but not the whole truth, but to state the whole truth is to transform the truth. He is right to point out that the Mādhyamikas contradict the substantialists, but in pointing out that they also contradict the opposing view of the nihilists, I am endeavoring to show that Arnold's conclusion (viz, that the Mādhyamika claim "is proposed as *true*") is no longer tenable, or at least no longer tenable in the same sense, for it rests upon a one-sided interpretation—perhaps what Nāgārjuna himself would call yet another example of an extreme view (*antagrahadṛṣṭi*).

For, to elaborate on an earlier point, to state not-P in opposition to some proponent of P is indeed to make a claim. Thus, for example, the atheist (in opposition to the theist) claims that there is no God, much as the nihilist (in opposition to the substantialist) claims that there is no thing. Were Nāgārjuna to be making such a negative claim, Arnold would be right in characterizing him as indeed making a claim; one that happens to be negative. However, to state neither-P-nor-not-P, and to propose no third alternative (say, T—for "thesis"),[101] is no longer to make an opposing claim, but rather to refuse to play at making claims altogether. This, on my reading, is the force of Nāgārjuna's *prasaṅga* critique. For Nāgārjuna (and Candrakīrti), both the theist and the atheist, the substantialist and the nihilist, are what I propose to call "thesists." They are engaged in the enterprise of making claims, or theses/propositions (*pakṣa*/*pratijñā*).

Arnold goes on to argue for his "reconstruction of Mādhyamika arguments as transcendental arguments" (Arnold 2005: 139) in terms of the debate in which Nāgārjuna and Candrakīrti engage with "a proponent of 'normative epistemology' (a *pramāṇavādin*)" as to the charge "that if Nāgārjuna's thesis (*pratijñā*) is correct, then he cannot possibly claim to know that fact by virtue of any reliable warrant (*pramāṇa*)" (Arnold 2005: 145).[102] Given that Arnold's (and Nāgārjuna's) discussion here centers on perception, I would like to reformulate the justly celebrated analogy for Nāgārjuna's view of no view proposed by Candrakīrti in the *Prasannapadā*.[103] According to this, a man who has nothing to sell is being asked to sell that very nothing. Now, let us imagine instead that the man is a blind, and therefore declares that he sees nothing. Unless we do some serious damage to the standard notion of "reliable warrant" (*pramāṇa*), his visual non-perception does *not* rely on any warranted object (*prameya*). According to Nāgārjuna's and Candrakīrti's supposed *pramāṇavādin* interlocutor, the blind man is thus in no position to claim any certainty (*niścaya*) as to his claim that he perceives no objects, for he possesses no *pramāṇa* through which to make any claim as to any *prameya*.[104] *Pratyakṣa* (perception) cannot be at work, for it is precisely visual *non*-perception that informs the man's claim to not perceive any visually perceptible object. Nor can *anumāṇa* (inference) be called upon, for although he may infer—or even, at a stretch, postulate (i.e., rely on *arthāpatti*: postulation, presumption, derivation from circumstance, circumstantial implication)—the existence of a visually perceptible object based on my prior knowledge that he is in fact blind (the which knowledge would itself presumably need to be derived from *śabda*: authority, word, testimony by reliable expert), any such inference (or postulation) is logically posterior to his present episode of non-perception. Besides which, if as per the Nyāya logicians "inferential knowledge requires knowledge of an invariable concomitance (*vyāpti*) between the perception of a sign and the presence of that which is to be inferred from the presence of that sign" (Perrett 2016: 70), then this condition is certainly not met here. Indeed, the only *pramāṇa* that might be legitimately called upon in such a case is *anupalabdhi* (non-cognition, non-perception, non-apprehension, negative proof), but apart from the fact that this is only accepted as a valid *pramāṇa* by Bhāṭṭa Mīmāṃsā and Advaita Vedānta, this is taken by Naiyāyikas to itself rely on inference, which we have already seen to be inadmissible in the present instance. Perhaps most importantly, however, *anupalabdhi* is used by relevant Mīmāṃsakas and Vedāntins to explain the non-existence of a given object (such as an elephant in the room: see Perrett 2016: 102), whereas what is at stake here is the non-perception of a perceptible (hence existent) object.

The upshot of all this is that it would be an error to take the man's statement "I see nothing" as working on the same level as grammatically like statements such as "I see something" made by sighted people. In this latter case, and to the extent that we accept his "normative epistemology" (cf. Arnold 2005: 144), the *pramāṇavādin* is justified in asking the perceiver for a warrant, and will presumably be satisfied upon receiving certification of the functional status of the perceiver's means of perception. In the former case, however, wherein the Mādhyamika non-perceiver non-perceives an object, how is he to provide satisfactory certification? To ask him for it is to force him into an epistemologically biased framework of perceptual certainty; biased, that is, toward positive (perhaps we can say kataphatic) assertions of successful perceptions. Our blind Mādhyamika fails this test, but not because he has failed his eye exam but because he has *attained* to blindness. In other words, it is not that he has failed to live up to the criteria governing the normative epistemological framework to which he would thereby still be bound, but rather that he has abandoned the entire edifice of epistemological certainty. Arnold, like Nāgārjuna's *pramāṇavādin* interlocutor, is therefore unjustified in claiming that "the object that Nāgārjuna 'might' (counterfactually) thus apprehend (*artham upalabheyam*) is a *svabhāva*, an 'essence' of existents" (Arnold 2005: 145). Nāgārjuna's gripe here is not, strictly speaking, with the apprehension of *svabhāvic* existents, but with the epistemological framework within which such perception could function. For, although Arnold is right in perceiving that Nāgārjuna denies the existence of any such *svabhāvic* entity, and consequently of any apprehension of any such *svabhāvic* entity, this is a secondary point; a corollary to the exhaustive abandonment of what I am here referring to as acts of perception, but which I have called elsewhere throughout this book "beliefs," "positions," or "theses."

To put this another way, Nāgārjuna would certainly agree with Arnold's characterization of his position as one that considers the positing of a *svabhāvic* essence "fundamentally incoherent." Indeed, much of the MK and VV in particular are devoted to reducing such a position to absurdity. However, on my reading Nāgārjuna considers views and theses (i.e., belief positions of any sort) as themselves *svabhāvic*. That is—and to again use Arnold's position as a foil—Nāgārjuna agrees that arguments (positions, views, theses . . .) "fundamentally aim to make a point about how things exist;" in so doing, arguments are indeed "proposed as *true*." It is just that, for something to be *true*, that something must *be*.[105] Being, however, is precisely what Nāgārjuna's critique refutes, since for Nāgārjuna there *is* no way that "things" exist, for no things really do "exist." Propositions of any kind satisfy, in other words, the ontological criterion: Like the *pramāṇas* or epistemological warrants on which they rely and which they validate, metaphysical positions (indeed, positions of all kinds, for all positions implicitly if not explicitly make metaphysically "absolute presuppositions"—Arnold 2005: 140) "must surely be counted among 'all existents' " (Arnold 2005: 145). As such, it is a mistake to claim that "the Mādhyamika claim contradicts a truth-claim" (Arnold 2005: 137) made by others: The Mādhyamika does not make a claim and consequently does not contradict any other such claim—Nāgārjuna deflects this criticism explicitly at VV:29. For the Mādhyamika's *prasaṅgic* critique does not propose or construct but only deposes or deconstructs. One cannot agree with it, for as soon as one has, one has reified it into a fixed position amenable to agreement and disagreement, and hence to the whole range of epistemic criteria according to which truth claims are judged.[106] As such, and to adapt the point made by Gold earlier, Nāgārjuna is seen to agree to the rules of the game, as it were, according to which theses posit things, but simply to reject playing it.

4.3.4. Abandonment and Athesism

The thread linking Arnold's, Westerhoff's, and many other modern and premodern critiques of the Madhyamaka claim to be not making any claims may be termed "thesism." Thesism, which includes Garfield's technique of smuggling appropriately qualified views in by the back door despite avowing their complete abandonment, amounts to the view that the Mādhyamikas are proposing a thesis after all, which each critic then criticizes on the basis of some alternative thetical paradigm.[107] Arnold, for instance, is forced to argue for Nāgārjuna's and Candrakīrti's propounding a thesis so that he may go on to distinguish this thesis from that of their "not sufficiently reductionist" (Arnold 2005: 166) Ābhidhārmika forebears. But although much of what Arnold and the other scholars I mention here say as to the content of the Mādhyamikas' (provisional) theses is, to my mind, highly insightful, I believe that they fail to grasp the truly radical nature of the Mādhyamikas' project, motivated as this latter is by a soterial push toward something beyond the bounds of reason.[108] For the enlightened state—to the extent I feel qualified to say anything about it at all—is surely a state radically different from that of the *saṃsāric* delusion in which we—alas—are all involved. This is why Nāgārjuna resorts, as he must, to explicitly paradoxical formulations when describing *nirvāṇa*, the Tathāgata, and other such unformulatables. To help us get there, to attain to such radical liberating insight, Nāgārjuna must use appropriately radical techniques; techniques that have traditionally been classed under the general term *prasaṅga* or deconstructive critique. To be completely successful, *prasaṅga* must deconstruct *all* theses; on this Nāgārjuna is repeatedly explicit, and to interpret him nevertheless as espousing the application of *prasaṅga* only to the limited scope of theses affirming *svabhāva* or the like is philologically disingenuous and philosophically uncharitable.

Of course, to arrive at such a thoroughgoing athesism, Nāgārjuna must systematically deconstruct particular theses through the application of specific *prasaṅgic* critiques. These function provisionally as theses but—as with the famous raft in the *Lotus Sūtra* which one should discard once having reached the farther shore—they should not be hauled along after having served their purpose. In other words, once the *upāyic* effect has been attained—the particular thesis deconstructed—one should abandon the *prasaṅgic* deconstruction in search of the next thesis to be deconstructed. Otherwise, one is liable to take the *prasaṅgic* deconstruction of theses itself as a thesis. This is a danger Nāgārjuna was acutely aware of; as we have seen, he describes it colorfully at MK:13:8 as characteristic of the "incurables." It is thus of the utmost importance to realize that *prasaṅga*, the deconstruction or discarding of theses, should not be construed as itself a thesis. The *prasaṅgic* method is that of meta-thetical critique: a critique of theses *qua* theses, including those it uses to critique theses. For any species of thesism necessarily impedes one from *nirvāṇic* liberation.

Given all this, Nāgārjuna's "point about how things exist" is only "true," as per Arnold, provisionally. The theses espoused by Nāgārjuna, though theses (or perhaps ~~theses~~), are only functional within the over-riding Prāsaṅgika project of the abandonment of theses/views. As such, they can legitimately only be called theses in a provisional sense, and preferably not at all if we are aiming to avoid the confusions concomitant with apparent self-contradiction. For by calling them theses (*pratijñā*) or views (*dṛṣṭi*) uncritically, interpreters both misconstrue the force of Nāgārjuna's *prasaṅgic* critique and facilitate the (unfair but unfortunately common) criticism of the Mādhyamikas as illogical and/or/because incoherent. If I have to use a given means so as to arrive at a given end, that does not mean that I take the means as an end. Theses, for Prāsaṅgikas, are nothing more than expedient means (*upāya*); they do not possess any validity in themselves (nothing does). In other words, they are not to be believed, for they are nothing (are functionally useless) if they are not means toward the abandonment of belief itself.

Seen in this light, Garfield's critique of Huntington's reading may be read as indicative of Garfield's not going far enough in his avowal "to take very seriously Nāgārjuna's insistence on exactly what he says" (Smith College 2010). According to Huntington, Nāgārjuna

> was interested in conjuring up a philosophical and religious world in which it appears possible completely to cease identifying with any doctrine, tenet, thesis, or point of view, a groundless world of "non-abiding" in which one might surrender attachment to the elaborate and convoluted project that grows out of the compulsion to know something for certain, to command, demonstrate, prove or disprove something once and for all—including the validity of rational argumentation itself . . . [and espoused] the admittedly perplexing belief that one may somehow come to relinquish all attachment to belief. (Huntington 2007: 129)

Garfield criticizes Huntington for going "too far in his reading, and hence not far enough philosophically. As a consequence, Huntington sees Nāgārjuna as rejecting philosophical analysis entirely, hence abandoning his own corpus" (Garfield 2008: 524). But of course, 'abandoning one's own corpus' is espoused by the Buddha himself, as in the famous analogy I referred to just now, of the *dharma*, the Buddha's own teaching, as a raft. Just as this is to be abandoned, so too the extensive textual evidence I have presented convincingly demonstrates that the "point" of Nāgārjuna corpus is precisely to abandon that corpus, and with it *all* corpora. This, I submit, is precisely the sense in which Nāgārjuna "is positionless in a sense of great moment to philosophy, thus giving point to that corpus" (Garfield 2008: 524).

In support of his position, Garfield claims that "a lot hangs on the ambiguity between *dṛṣṭi* and *darśana* in *Mūlamadhyamakakārikā*, . . . and on the sense of *pratijnā* [*pratijñā*] in *Vigrahavyāvartanī*. . . . Nāgārjuna argues that anyone for whom *śūnyatā* becomes a *dṛṣṭi* is hopeless, not that one should not achieve *śūnyatā-darśana*" (Garfield 2008: 524). Garfield makes a similar point regarding Candrakīrti later in the same paper: "Candrakīrti emphasizes that the Mādhyamika has no *pakṣa*. But it does not follow that the mādhyamika has no position of *any* kind, or endorses no arguments of *any* kind" (Garfield 2008: 526, emphases original). But this is surely to inadvertently reintroduce philosophical views even while claiming that "the deepest and most radical idea advanced by Nāgārjuna and Candrakīrti is the idea that Madhyamaka is the rejection of *all* views (Garfield 2008: 524, emphasis original). Nāgārjuna espouses the abandonment of all philosophical views (*dṛṣṭi*); just because he does not enumerate all the synonyms for view (such as *pakṣa* or *darśana*) surely does not mean that he nevertheless does *not* espouse *their* abandonment. Along like lines to my earlier point about "view" as opposed to "viewpoint" (see §2.2.2), it is as if I were to say "I hold no view" and were interpreted to thereby mean that I *do* hold positions and theses. Nor is Garfield acknowledging, as I have in §4.3.3, the inevitability of view-holding in the context of unenlightened conventional worldly interactions. In fact, Garfield makes the thrust of his hermeneutic endeavor clear on the preceding page, where he claims that "Nāgārjuna in his insistence that Madhyamaka not be taken as one more *dṛṣṭi* is emphasizing that this really is the rejection of *any* view regarding the fundamental nature of reality" (Garfield 2008: 525, emphasis original). Just as we have seen with other such parameterizations, however, views "regarding the fundamental nature of reality" are not *all* views, and it is *all* views that Nāgārjuna rejects. This book as a whole, and most particularly the present chapter, is an attempt to explicate this fact.

As for Garfield's response to Huntington, this ends in oracular terms:

> Being irrational is cheap, and takes one nowhere, or anywhere. To be truly radical is to be rationally radical. We follow Nāgārjuna and Candrakīrti as guides down the chariot path of rational inquiry to the city of liberation. Huntington we leave to wander, bereft of reason, aimless and alone in the trackless wilderness of saṃsara [*saṃsāra*]. (Garfield 2008: 526)

Now, the textual basis for such pronouncements as "To be truly radical is to be rationally radical" remains unclear. As for Huntington wandering aimlessly in the trackless wilderness, this, far from characterizing *saṃsāra*, actually reiterates quite accurately Nāgārjuna's description of *nirvāṇa*![109] For it is *saṃsāra*, not *nirvāṇa*, that is characterized by the kind of goal-oriented activity evoked by Garfield's image of the chariot path; a path leading not to the city of liberation but rather ineluctably further into the ignorance of delusion memorably evoked in Nāgārjuna's image of the "city of [mythical] Gandharvas."[110] After all, the canonical Buddhist analysis of ignorance (*avidyā*, *moha*), attachment (*rāga*), and aversion (*dveṣa*) as the three poisons (*triviṣa*) or afflictions (*kleśa*) constitutive of *saṃsāric* suffering (*duḥkha*), coupled with the understanding that among these it is ignorance which lies at the root of desire (*tṛṣṇā*) (positive, as in attachment; or negative, as in aversion), makes clear that activity (*karma*) directed by desire (i.e., activity directed toward any goal) is the characteristic condition of cyclic existence (*bhavacakra*).

In this context, Garfield's use of the chariot metaphor is particularly apt, for the chariot is a stock example in Buddhist discourse (used by the Buddha, Nāgārjuna, Candrakīrti, and many many others)[111] of the apparently existent independent entity which, upon insightful analysis, is seen to be nothing but a conventional conglomeration of parts. That Garfield should choose to ride the chariot rather than realizing its emptiness is unfortunate for him, for thereby he is left not to wander aimlessly, as befits the Tathāgata, but to ride in certain directions together with all other suffering beings; directed whithersoever he goes by the poisons (which he takes to be medicines) infused by what Nāgārjuna memorably called "the writhing snakes of defilement."[112] In contrast, Nāgārjuna himself, in what doubtless appears to unenlightened path-takers as wild wandering, is free to comego beyond attachment and detachment, ignorance and insight.[113] After all,

> Since there is no fruit
> No path to liberation or to heaven is established
> There follows the pointlessness
> Of all activities[114]

Given, then, that Nāgārjuna espouses the abandonment of all views (and all activity!), how are we to read him? After all, to interpret, to propose a certain understanding, is already to hold a view. Bhāvaviveka (or some like interlocutor)[115] asks this question of Candrakīrti in the latter's *Prasannapadā*: "Do those with deep insight really have no conclusive argument?" To which Candrakīrti provides eloquent answer:

> Who can say whether they do or they don't? For those with deep insight the truth of the highest meaning is a state of silence. This being so, how is there any possibility of discursive thinking out of which we might find either a conclusive argument or no real argument at all?[116]

Although "those with deep insight" may well be satisfied with "the truth of the highest meaning" in their "state of silence," we as yet uncured curables, stuck in the "dispositional disease called *prapañca*" (Yadav 1977: 467), are left to grapple with this important methodological issue. The question is of great import, for it concerns all hermeneutical and philosophical activity; indeed, all thought, and all practice based on it, whatsoever. For contrary to common sense (by which is meant ordinary false thinking),

> According to the Mādhyamika, genuine philosophical activity is possible for the philosopher and practiser of the Middle Way despite—or rather, perhaps, precisely because of—the suspension of all the . . . components of a proposition or thesis presupposing the self-existence of a hypostasized entity. (Ruegg 2000: 232)

To this statement by Ruegg I would only add that is indeed "precisely because of" the suspension—or rather, negation—of all propositions or theses whatsoever that allows the Mādhyamika to engage in philosophical thought. This is so for reasons analogous to those Nāgārjuna adduces as to the possibility of the existence of conventionally perceived, impermanent, reality. For Nāgārjuna states that, contrary to what may be called "conventional wisdom," which sees entities as really existing (i.e., as *svabhāvic*), such a view necessarily entails the absurd consequence that nothing at all could be subject to change.[117] Only the Madhyamaka understanding of universal emptiness allows reality on the conventional (*saṃvṛti*) level to function as it appears to do. Just so, and also contrary to the ordinary view, philosophical activity is effectively rendered impossible by the proposition, on the part of a philosopher, of a particular view/thesis. For as I have argued earlier, in making a proposition the philosopher disallows any progress toward the (or a) truth by foreclosing the argument within the confines of a particular definitive view (and all views are definitive). What is left is thus not philosophy (understood as a dialogic and mutually enlightening progress toward truth) but static dogma (and all dogmas are static).

In other words, any assertion of the type "reality is thus" ineluctably proposes, or presupposes, a fixed view of reality, such that the reality described is, precisely, "thus" and not otherwise. And since all philosophical propositions—if they are to count as philosophical propositions at all—can ultimately be reduced to the form "reality is thus," they are all without exception rejected by Nāgārjuna as invalid, *svabhāvic* reifications/hypostatizations of what can only be accurately described as indescribable/empty/dependently co-arisen/relative indication/the middle way.[118]

It is just such an understanding of the MK which informs Garfield's claim that "Nāgārjuna's text is aimed primarily against philosophy. But its soteriological goal is the extirpation of the very root of suffering" (Garfield 1995: 88 n. 2). Now, although I fundamentally agree with Garfield on both these points,[119] one way of elucidating my rejection of Garfield's avowal that Nāgārjuna is best understood as "a highly rational thinker" (Garfield 2002: 87) is to rebut his use of "But." For in placing this little "but" between the rejection of philosophy (as thesis-holding) and the extirpation of suffering (as self-grasping), Garfield implies a qualitative distinction separating the two.[120] But (!), as I hope to have shown, Nāgārjuna saw the extirpation of suffering as concomitant with the abandonment of all views; indeed, this latter he proposed as the preeminent means whereby to effect the former and thereby attain to liberation from all teaching.

This does not mean that Nāgārjuna himself abjured all rationality or held no views. Apart from anything else, such an unremittingly radical stance would have disabled him from performing the innumerable ordinary functions of everyday life, not to mention have doubtless barred him from inclusion in the Buddhist monastery in which he, as a historical Buddhist man, presumably resided and attained to some renown.[121] But the fact remains that we do not know anything with certainty about Nāgārjuna the man; all we have is Nāgārjuna the author; or rather, Nāgārjuna-the-author's authored works. It is these latter, and foremost among them the MK, that have sustained my reading, for it is only upon their basis that we can say anything about Nāgārjuna's views at all. That Nāgārjuna the man must have held views, and consequently held the view that some views are superior to others, I find unproblematic, but both irrelevant to my argument and uninteresting to the philosophical purport of his stated no-view, or for that matter to his use of reason in aid of its ultimate overcoming. What I derive as useful from such a reading as Wu Rujun's of Nāgārjuna's *catuṣkoṭi* in terms of transcendence is not a recourse, by the back door as it were, to some kind of hierarchy of views.[122] Rather, I see it as leading to the transcendence/abandonment of all views on the basis that any and all views enmesh their holders in suffering. It is to this final topic—suffering and the soteries of emptiness—that we now turn.

5

All-Embracing Emptiness

Nāgārjuna and the Ethics of Emptiness

5.1. The Abandonment of Ethics?

And so, we have abandoned all views: what of it? What consequences ensue? Specifically, how can Nāgārjuna espouse a particular ethics if he has reneged on holding any position?

In this final chapter, my aim is to tie the preceding discussions in metaphysics and epistemology to the ethical mission undergirding Nāgārjuna's Buddhist religiosophical project in its entirety. As mentioned in the Introduction, I here address the perplexing question of how a teaching understood as espousing universal emptiness and the abandonment of all views can nevertheless entail a distinctively Mahāyāna Buddhist ethics. After all, how can Nāgārjuna justify an ethic of selfless care for all living beings based on the bodhisattva ideal of limitless compassion if he has denied any and all forms of foundationalism, including those standardly taken as grounding ethics? The answer, I argue, lies precisely in the emptying of all selfhood, for in a world emptied of self, self-interest is necessarily exhausted, and one is liberated from karmically harmful action by engaging with others in unhindered care. This, for Nāgārjuna, is "the good life"; "Thus does this entire mass of suffering / completely cease."[1] Indeed, in this concluding chapter I propose that the socio-ethical import of Nāgārjuna's denial of autonomous selfhood in favor of a self only ever relational lies precisely in his corollary abjuration of doxastic positionality in favor of critical detachment from any oppositional grasping. This means that, rather than constituting an abandonment of ethics as might be assumed, Nāgārjuna's "position of no-position" turns out to be precisely what is needful for the enactment of an ethics truly committed to the Buddhist ideal of universally eradicating suffering.

Nāgārjuna was not the first, and hardly the last, philosopher—Buddhist or otherwise—to propose a way to do away with suffering. But I will argue in the following pages that Nāgārjuna's approach differs—and differs

Buddhism Between Religion and Philosophy. Rafal K. Stepien, Oxford University Press. © Oxford University Press 2024.
DOI: 10.1093/oso/9780197771303.003.0005

qualitatively—from those positing an ethical system based on the espousal or embodiment of certain views or positions. For of howsoever universal an application any such ethical system may be, or may have been conceived to function, on my understanding Nāgārjuna sees it as running aground on the wreckage of views which he has wrought. Or rather, given that Nāgārjuna's *prasaṅgic* project wrecks all views without replacing them with any alternatives, ethical systems will not run aground anywhere, but dissolve into the fathomless, horizonless ocean of emptiness. But this needs explaining.

There is a twofold sense in which Nāgārjuna's ethics differs from, and confounds, ethical systems as traditionally understood; that is, as being founded on certain views in the form of fixed positions, grounding principles, and the like. First, there is the *prasaṅgic reductio*, according to which Nāgārjuna reduces any and all views to absurdity. We have seen him do this to metaphysical and epistemological positions, dismantling in inexorable sequence over the course of his philosophical works (the *yukti* corpus) any and all of the manifold positions taken by fellow thinkers. We have also seen that the exhaustive *catuṣkoṭi* permits Nāgārjuna to survey and refute all possible positions on a given topic. Ever rigorous, we have even seen Nāgārjuna apply the *prasaṅgic* method to himself, arguing that even his signature teaching of emptiness must be taken as (not some alternative foundation but, like all teachings,) irredeemably, utterly empty. Ethical positions are no exception to the ambit of emptiness, so any ethical system that attempts to set itself up on the basis of some particular view will prove to be prey to just the same deconstructive critique as any other view. As such, whatever ethical views other, non-Prāsaṇgika philosophers may have put forward, Nāgārjuna's method of relentless repudiation may (indeed, must) be taken to function as an antidote to them. However successful or unsuccessful we may take Nāgārjuna's critique to be, the point here is that the aim of his enterprise is to deconstruct views, and thereby to obviate their holding.

Following from this, the second point to note is that whatever constructs Nāgārjuna may propose in light of the *prasaṅgic* ground-clearing, whatever actions or attitudes his ethics enjoins or denounces, are to be taken as following from, and thus coherent with, his wholescale abandonment of view-holding. For just as Nāgārjuna recognizes that he would clearly fall into self-contradiction were he to erect emptiness as a substantial pillar upon which to build a metaphysical edifice, so too he realizes that the establishment of an ethics founded upon some analogous basis—some transcendental ethical premise—would load the emptiness of emptiness with precisely the kind of philosophical bedrock emptiness itself has cleared away. This means that, just as we saw Nāgārjuna deny that emptiness is to be taken as yet another postulate of metaphysics or basis for epistemology, so too what I will go on to call his eirenics (explained later) cannot be taken as yet another standard system of ethics.

For the purposes of the present chapter, this also means that I will not be concerned to detail much of the *content* of Nāgārjuna's ethics. Apart from the allusions and suggestions we may adduce in the MK (and the still lesser ethical conclusions we may draw from texts such as the VV, YṢ, and ŚS), the ethical values Nāgārjuna espoused and the prescriptions and proscriptions flowing from them can most readily be gleaned from texts not studied in depth in this book. Among those texts whose ascription to Nāgārjuna is largely uncontested, I am referring primarily to the *Precious Garland* (*Ratnāvalī*: RĀ)[2] and *Letter to a Friend* (*Suhṛllekha*: SL), both often categorized as Nāgārjuna's "epistolary works" (see Westerhoff 2020: §1). Shulman eloquently summarizes the content of the RĀ as follows:

> The text treats topics as diverse as Buddhist meditation, Buddhist philosophies of different sorts, Buddhist practice, worship, and the path to Buddhahood, the nature of Buddhahood in its physical and spiritual manifestations, and Buddhist polemics and politics, while all these diverse Buddhist realms of inquiry are intertwined with a long lecture on recommended royal policy in the fields of construction, governance, economics, society and religion. (Shulman 2011: 302)[3]

Given the text's overt emphasis on social and political theory (insightfully studied in Scherrer-Schaub 2007), it is hardly surprising that, as Shulman also notes, "To date, the philosophical aspects of the RĀ have been neglected in the modern study of Madhyamaka" (Shulman 2011: 306). While I have on occasion referred to the RĀ (and Shulman's analysis of it) in my treatments of nihilism and the mutual correlativity of existence and non-existence in Nāgārjuna's philosophy (see §3.6), the RĀ's subject matter falls largely outside the scope of my present concerns. Indeed, the same may be said of the SL, which "is mainly concerned with an exposition of the ethics of a layman (Lindtner 1997: 298).[4]

I propose that the ethical precepts espoused in these works and sparsed throughout Nāgārjuna's corpus as a whole are broadly consonant with those of early Buddhism. More pointedly, they embody the bodhisattva ideal developed in the centuries immediately surrounding Nāgārjuna and constituting the preeminently distinctive feature of the major vehicle of Mahāyāna then emerging. Indeed, along lines not dissimilar to the much later Mādhyamika Śāntideva (c. 685–763), whose *Guide to the Bodhisattva Way of Life* (*Bodhicaryāvatāra*) is typically taken to be the definitive work of Madhyamaka ethics,[5] Nāgārjuna clearly attempts to synthesize the Mahāyānic innovations in his teachings with those of the preceding canon dating back to the Buddha. In so doing, it is evident that he is concerned to demonstrate the consonance of Madhyamaka ethics with those animating the broader Buddhist tradition. Thus, for example, Nāgārjuna begins the culminating chapter of the RĀ with a long passage detailing fifty-seven faults the aspirant to enlightenment should avoid—a list taken directly from an Abhidharmic treatise.[6] These range from such obvious obstacles to attainment as anger (*krodhaḥ*), hatred (*upanāhaḥ*), regret (*kaukṛtyam*), and doubt (*vicikitsā*) (the first and final two faults of the entire enumeration), to such minor transgressions as hinting (*naimittikatvam*), consideration of relatives (*jñātisambandho vitarkaḥ*), attachment to the life in the countryside (rural life) (*jānapadā tṛṭ*), and lack of delight in food (*bhaktāsaṃmadaḥ*).[7] But having thus delineated something of a code of conduct (*prātimokṣa*) incumbent upon the aspirant to *bodhi* recognizable to (indeed, adapted from) earlier forms of Buddhism, Nāgārjuna immediately supplements this list with the characteristically Mahāyānic features of the bodhisattva. These take the form of the six perfections (*pāramitā*s) and ten stages (*bhūmi*s) distinctive of the bodhisattva path.[8] Importantly, Nāgārjuna conceives the six perfections—of generosity (*dāna*), moral virtue (*śīla*), patience (*kṣānti*), vigor (*vīrya*), meditation (*dhyāna*), and wisdom (*prajñā*)—as being crowned with compassion or care (*karuṇā*). For, as he declares,

> From generosity there arises wealth, from moral virtue happiness,
> From patience there arises beauty, from vigor brilliance,
> From meditation peace, from wisdom liberation,
> From compassion all aims are accomplished.[9]

Working out just how all aims are to be accomplished for Nāgārjuna is a legitimate way of construing the purpose of this chapter. As we will see, this has everything to do with how all views are to be abandoned.[10]

In pursuit of that end, I will not be describing in much further detail the whats and hows by which the bodhisattva path is traversed on Nāgārjuna's account. For one thing, as we have seen, these contents of Nāgārjuna's ethics are conventional in the sense of according with the norms accepted by Mahāyāna and pre-Mahāyāna Buddhist systems alike. (It should go without saying that, for Nāgārjuna, they are conventional also in the sense of appertaining to conventional reality: there is no need for precepts and proscriptions among the perfected.) Although much work remains to be done unpacking the specifics, the overall agreement of Nāgārjuna's ethics with those of his compeers renders their content subsidiary to my present concerns. For above all, I have not seen need to engage with Nāgārjunian texts such as the RĀ and SL in detail here because my aim is not to reconstruct or interpret Nāgārjuna's ethics but to theorize its relation to his metaphysics and epistemology. To use Mark Siderits's formulation, I am interested in "the soteriological significance of emptiness" (Siderits 2003a). More precisely, I want to understand how the realization of the emptiness of all views and the consequent application to views too of the Nāgārjunian refusal to take refuge in, to hold on to, any construct at all relates to the soterial end of complete and universal liberation. Put another way, this means that the thread guiding my thinking in this chapter is not Nāgārjuna's "religiosity" *per se* (i.e., not his religious-cum-ethical-cum-soterial mission in itself) but the relationship between Nāgārjuna's philosophy and his religiosity—where these are to be understood heuristically as referring to the ostensibly abstract critiques of metaphysical and epistemological positions comprising his most celebrated and studied works, and the overtly soteriological orientation of works such as the RĀ and SL respectively.

Now, I speak of *ostensibly* abstract critiques of metaphysics and epistemology because I perceive the link between these and the ethics to which we are specifically attending here to be intimate. Naturally, I am hardly the first to draw a link between Buddhist metaphysics and ethics; on the contrary, their interconnection is well-established and only to be expected of a globally coherent system of thought.[11] But given that I have interpreted Nāgārjuna's thought as a whole through the lens of his espoused abandonment of all views, it is this distinctly Nāgārjunian (non-)position that will be my focus here. In other words, what this final chapter of the book explores is just how such wholescale abandonment relates to Nāgārjuna's ethics. How, in the avowed absence of *any* view, can Nāgārjuna endorse a particular ethical view?

We will return to this question presently, but before we do we need to clarify what it is we are really talking about. As we have already seen, throughout this book I have seen reason to modify the prevailing terms of philosophical and religious discourses, or indeed to propose neologisms in their stead, on multiple occasions where current usages were apt to mislead the exegete of Nāgārjuna's religiosophy into misinterpretation. This chapter will be no exception, and so before we proceed any further I would do well to critically analyze two of its central terms—"metaphysics" and "ethics"—to begin delineating Nāgārjuna's approach to the topics we are discussing.

"Metaphysics" in fact turns out to be not a particularly apt word in this context. This is so not only because it derives from specifically Aristotelian premises as to the relation between "physics" and "metaphysics" alien to the Buddhist sphere. More substantively, the term "metaphysics" in Western philosophy has historically been used to denote a sphere of reality (descriptively denoted as) transcendent of, (ascriptively denoted as) superior to, and (prescriptively denoted as) teleologically after the physical world.

It is worth noting that the latter two denotations, though they are often assumed as following directly and unavoidably from the first, are not strictly implied by it at all. Just because a certain sphere of reality is described as transcendent of another does not imply that it is necessarily to be ascribed a superior status to it. The implication only follows if we ascribe superiority to transcendence (however "superiority" is to be understood in such a context). In like manner, just because a certain sphere of reality is described as transcendent of another does not imply that it is necessarily to be prescribed as the telos of that other; its final end and consummation. The implication only follows if we not only ascribe superiority to transcendence but also prescribe said superiority as the teleological aim of the initial sphere of reality. (Or in any case if we prescribe said transcendence as the teleological end, whether or not we ascribe superiority to it: one may, after all, seek the not-superior). To put this another way, just because a certain state is taken to be superior to another does not necessarily imply that the superior state is to be taken as a goal. The ethically charged prescription of "ought" is not consequent upon the evaluatively charged ascription of "be," and neither of these is consequent upon the empirically charged description of "is." I use "ought" and "is" here in oft-used senses, but since my usage of "be" is neologistic, I precise that it here designates the stipulative function; that is, one according to which a given thing is stipulated to "be" superior to another. And to reiterate a point just made in this regard, "superiority" may be understood here in various senses, such as, for example, "more good," "more true," or "more beautiful." The point is that, irrespective of the specific criterion or criteria according to which the two things or states or spheres of reality are evaluated, to one is ascribed a criterially superior status.

Now, none of these denotations (descriptive, ascriptive, prescriptive) applies to the status of ultimate (as opposed to conventional) truth/reality in the Nāgārjunian Buddhist sphere. First, ultimate reality is not (descriptively denoted as) transcendent of conventional reality; rather, ultimate reality is realized (made real) precisely when ultimate reality is realized (ceived as real) to be (nothing other than, identical with) conventional reality.[12] The second and third implications follow directly from the collapse of the descriptive divide instantiated in the first. Ultimate reality is not (ascriptively denoted as) superior to conventional reality, and ultimate reality is not (prescriptively denoted as) teleologically after conventional reality, for that which is identified with another cannot be superior to or teleologically after it.

But apart from this simple logical deduction, we also arrive here at a source of considerable philosophical substance for Nāgārjuna and his intellectual heirs. For the relationship between ultimate and conventional reality is, of course, not one of mere identity, as this would effectively collapse any differentiation between them and thereby render the "two truths" one. Apart from anything else, this would go directly against the explicit statement in MK:24:9 that

> Those who do not understand
> The distinction between these two truths
> Do not understand the profound truth
> Of the Buddha's teaching[13]

But nor are the two truths wholly distinct, as this would undermine Nāgārjuna's explicit identification of them in MK:25:19–20:

> Between *saṃsāra* and *nirvāṇa*
> There is no difference at all
> Between *nirvāṇa* and *saṃsāra*
> There is no difference at all
>
> What is *nirvāṇa*'s limit
> That is the limit of *saṃsāra*
> Between them is not found
> Even the slightest difference[14]

Perhaps the best way to broach my interpretation here is via Garfield's statement in relation to MK:24:8 that "despite their ontic unity, the ultimate truth is epistemologically and soteriologically more significant than the conventional" (Garfield 1995: 297 fn. 108). Like myself, Garfield here proposes three senses in which to frame the relation between ultimate and conventional truth, but I believe his demarcation of ontic, epistemological, and soteriological senses maps a different, albeit complementary, constellation of relations. For Garfield, if I understand him aright, is making the following series of inter-related points. "Ultimate" and "conventional" describe, for Nāgārjuna, the same sphere of reality. However, the epistemological realization of the nature of the ultimate differs from the epistemological realization of the nature of the conventional insofar as—whereas the epistemological realization of the nature of the conventional is constituted by the epistemological realization that the nature of the conventional is, conventionally, different from the nature of the ultimate—the epistemological realization of the nature of the ultimate includes—may even be said to be constituted precisely by—the epistemological realization that the nature of the ultimate is, ultimately, nothing other than the nature of the conventional. This epistemological realization of the ultimate "ontic unity" of conventional and ultimate, moreover, has a distinctly soteriological dimension according to which said epistemological realization constitutes the ontological realization of the soteriological goal of insight as to the ultimate nature of reality as a whole.[15] Insofar as this explication (if such it is) of Garfield's analysis is accurate, I agree with it entirely. However, my own analysis here in terms of the descriptive "is," ascriptive "be," and prescriptive "ought" is geared toward a related but different set of points, and these have to do directly with how we conceive of "ethics."

Notwithstanding these considerations, and partly because in any case "there is no simple term in classical Sanskrit that translates perfectly 'metaphysics'" (Tillemans 2023: 278), I have decided to retain the term "metaphysics" here. Alternatives (such as "realology" or "realogy," "emptics" or "*śūnyatics*") do suggest themselves, and these might seem preferable insofar as they would imply or presuppose neither a purported transcendence of some merely physical realm to some metaphysical plane (as per, well, traditional *meta*-physics) nor a reduction of the metaphysical-cum-transcendental to the physical-cum-empirical (as per physicalist species of ontological reductionism). But if we understand "metaphysics" (relatively) uncontroversially as "the attempt to find the widest ranging and most fundamental description of what exists and how it exists" (Tillemans 2018: 87; cf Tillemans 2023: 278–279), then I see no problem in continuing to use it here as a marker simply denoting that aspect of Nāgārjuna's (and more broadly Buddhist) philosophy concerned with the comprehension of reality.

As for "ethics," it should already be evident that Nāgārjuna is not—cannot—be concerned with the identification, definition, or elaboration of "moral principles, or a system of these" (which is how the *Oxford English Dictionary* defines the term—in what perhaps betrays an overly deontological orientation on its part here). Indeed, Nāgārjuna's brand of Madhyamaka ethics (let us call it the "proto-typical Prāsaṅgika Madhyamaka" stance)[16] cannot be mapped—certainly cannot be mapped unproblematically—onto *any* of the notions of ethics or morality standardly accepted in Western philosophy, be they descriptive or normative (regarding which, see Gert and Gert 2020). It is certainly not my intention to substantiate this point by working through every such definition in *prāsaṅgic* fashion, so suffice it for now to state only that, though the *path* Nāgārjuna enjoins may hold manifold similarities with other such schemas of ethical progress, his *goal* differs, and differs qualitatively, insofar as it may legitimately be characterized only as uncharacterizable (a point to which we will have occasion to return later). Far from, say, the soul destined "to fill all the infinitude of time and space with stages of perfection in thought that grow on to infinity, and which has to approach as it were step by step the goal of the supreme excellence of the Deity, without, however, being ever able to reach it" (Kant 1900 [1755]: 167, cited in Ward 1971: 338), the telos toward which the Nāgārjunian seeker proceeds has, and can have, no identity as such. There is no "Deity" there—or here—and therefore as it were no approach by which to approach it. Given that *nirvāṇa*, on Nāgārjuna's understanding, is *nirvikalpic*, the ethical end of his religiosophical project cannot be dissociated from, and is in fact consequent upon, the metaphysical/epistemological abandonment of all views.

This hopefully serves to explain why I will speak here of Nāgārjuna's ethics as eirenics. For perhaps the most that we will ultimately be able to say of the attainment of *nirvāṇa* is that it is intrinsically conditioned by peace. And at this point I hope it should be clear that if I say "intrinsically conditioned," this is to be taken as not implying any intrinsicality or conditionality at all; and if I speak of "peace," this qualification is itself to be taken as the complete absence of qualifiers—the soterial equivalent, and concomitant, of Nāgārjuna's ultimate abjuration of positionality.[17]

Put another way, where what I am calling Nāgārjuna's eirenics parts ways with other systems of ethics is in its utter disavowal of any and all (metaphysical, epistemological, ethical) foundations, and in its understanding of peace (the soterial end of eirenics) as indissolubly concomitant with, inter-defined with, just such universal emptiness. For Nāgārjuna, then, *all* ethical theories, as ethical theories, are to be avoided, for they invariably and unavoidably, implicitly or explicitly, partake in one or other species of foundationalism, and *all* foundationalism is false. Now, some foundations are easier to spot than others, of course, as for example those grounding and in some sense guaranteeing theistic ethical systems. But less obvious examples of what nonetheless count as kinds of ethical foundationalism on the Madhyamaka analysis are not hard to find if one accepts Nāgārjuna's "irenic quietism" (Tillemans 2009: 94/2016: 78).[18] I am referring here not so much (or not only) to the various forms of what Westerhoff calls Nāgārjuna's "epistemological non-foundationalism," "linguistic non-foundationalism," and "non-foundationalism about truth" (Westerhoff 2017b) but also to what I have previously analyzed under the rubric of Nāgārjuna's "sortal essentialism" in the sense of the "negation of ontologically foundational status to what are epistemic phenomena" (Stepien 2021c: 887). These include, of course, views, ethical and otherwise.

Given that ethical theories (the meat of our matter here) rely upon certain foundational principles and presuppositions, and foundations of any sort are not to be found in Nāgārjunian emptiness, such theories are to be dispensed with along with all others. In fact, the issue goes far beyond ethical theories (or even metaphysical and epistemological ones). For Nāgārjuna's rejection is of all theorization; indeed, of all conceptualization. How this can possibly be squared with a given adept's ethical perfectionment (along the ethical path) or perfection (at the path's end) is at the nub of our concerns.

5.2. The Ethics of Abandonment

I stated at the outset of this chapter that my concern would be to explicate how Nāgārjuna could coherently espouse a particular ethics after having reneged on holding to any views. Charles Goodman begins his own foray into this topic with a clear statement of the question and its import:

> Is emptiness compatible with ethics? . . . The profound teaching of emptiness subtly undermines all our dogmatic convictions and beliefs, and points toward a compelling realization of the core Buddhist ideal of "freedom from view." But if we are to realize such an ideal, what will happen to our ethical commitments? (Goodman 2016: 141)

Goodman goes on to sketch a "road map" from Madhyamaka to consequentialism, and I will return to analyze the details of that reconstruction later. For the moment, however, I want to lay out the problem facing a non-foundationalist Mādhyamika such as Nāgārjuna in order eventually to argue that standard charges (of incoherence, inconsistency, and/or incomprehensibility) are ill-founded. The problem is that, if all views have been abandoned, then on what basis would the Mādhyamika act in accordance with Madhyamaka (or more broadly Mahāyāna, or more broadly Buddhist, or more broadly *good*) principles? The key to a Nāgārjunian response lies in the very structure of the question: "On what *basis*?"

The entirety of my foregoing analysis should make clear that the immediate response would naturally be "On the basis of no basis." That is, on the "basis," as it were, of emptiness, whose universality encompasses and undermines not only the basis of all posited substantial material entities but also that of all posited substantial abstract and immaterial entities, including logical laws, metaphysical grounds, epistemological axioms, and indeed ethical principles. But in response to this response, it is clearly open to the critic to interrogate in turn why such basis of no basis, such sheer absence of ethical principles, would give rise to *this* or *that* action or attitude as opposed to any other. More particularly, why would the abandonment of all views, including most relevantly in this context all ethical principles, issue in action on the part of the Mādhyamika practitioner that is nonetheless concordant with Madhyamaka ethical ideals such as care (*karuṇā*)?

The objection may be phrased in terms analogous to those of the contextualist-constructivist approach to mystical experience associated with the likes of Steven Katz and Wayne Proudfoot, as opposed to the universalist-perennialist approach of Robert Forman and Walter Stace.[19] There, an argument is made to the effect that the content of purportedly contentless mystical experience is nevertheless conditioned by a given mystic's doctrinal and practical training within a particular religious tradition, and that the experience is therefore contentful and contextual.[20] Claims to paradoxicality or ineffability make no sense, for "the terms 'paradox' and 'ineffable' do not function as terms that inform us about the context of experience, or any given ontological 'state of affairs'. Rather, they function to cloak experience from investigation and to hold mysterious whatever ontological commitments one has" (Katz 1978: 54).[21]

To bring this back to Nāgārjuna's avowed abandonment of all views, for Katz this would be tantamount to saying "I don't mean what I say and I don't say what I mean" (Katz 1978: 40)—a non-sensical non-stance entailing the impossibility of establishing "any view whatsoever" (Katz 1978: 40). Now, if no-view is in any way conditioned, then it is no longer no view, for it is thereby no longer viewless, contentless. Applying like reasoning to the sphere of ethics with which we are here concerned, if action taking place in the absence of any ethical principle is in any way guided by ethical principle, then that action is no longer absent of ethical principle.

As such, to deflect the charges of incoherence and inconsistency (and without lapsing into incomprehensibility), there must be something distinctive about Nāgārjuna's abandonment of all positionality which itself leads to certain ethical actions as opposed to others—leads *inevitably* on a strong version of the claim, *potentially* or *typically* on weaker versions. This distinctiveness cannot reside in any particular action or kind of action promoted on whatever grounds by the broader philosophical system (in this case, Madhyamaka) for, again, such contentfulness would undercut the very feature—all-embracing abandonment—distinctive of such a system. Rather, a fully fleshed version of this eirenic pacification lies (and *must* lie) in the overall relation between abandoning all and, as it were, embracing all. To abandon all must be to embrace all. *How* this is so is the crux of the matter.

This cannot be a matter of acting in accordance with certain universal principles. This means that it is not a version of deontology. Nor can it be a matter of acting in accordance with certain virtues the cultivation of which (in oneself or in others) is accepted as the aim of said action. It is thus not a version of virtue ethics either. And nor can it be a matter of acting in accordance with preformulated norms so as to maximize the normatively right or good consequences of said action. It is thus not a version of consequentialism either. Rather, it is and can only be a matter of acting without cognizance or conceptualization, in utter spontaneity, free-floating in emptiness. Whatever we may think, therefore, of the various models adapted from the history of Western philosophy to conceptualize Buddhist ethics in more or less general terms, it is evident that Nāgārjuna's eirenics differs, and differs qualitatively, from them.[22]

5.2.1. The Emptiness of Ethics

In seeking to comprehend Nāgārjuna's ideas in this ethico-soterial regard, it should surely come as no surprise by now to find our insights in his metaphysics. For Katz is surely right—and certainly right in regard to Nāgārjuna—that "for Indian systems metaphysics *is* soteriology" (Katz 1978: 58, emphasis original). Specifically, we need to look at the overall structure of an utterly empty universe. Our first clue comes in realizing that this is tantamount to looking at the overall structure of an utterly *unstructured* universe. For the universe ceived as empty is utterly an-archic, un-structured.[23] This is so in that such a world is bereft of the conceptualizations governing even the individuation of objects (or of subjects from objects), let alone their hierarchization into any constructed orders of being or value. We are looking here at a universe completely empty of entities, and thus empty of any constructs whatsoever according to which they could be ordered, empty of rules according to which they could be ruled. For be it noted (and the point will turn out to be crucial) that all rules imply rulers and ruled, all orders violate emptiness and are thereby violent. Indeed, the very identification of putative entities is already a violence enacted upon reality, empty as it really is of any such fixity, be it everlasting, temporary, or even momentary.

Having taken our starting point as emptiness, we naturally find that "when emptiness itself is subjected to analysis, we find not it, but its emptiness, and so on all the way down. This is the emptiness of emptiness" (Garfield 2002: 270 n. 60). Garfield does not make the point explicit (unless we interpret "all the way down" in the appropriate manner), but it will prove relevant to Nāgārjuna's eirenics to note that the consequence of this metaphysical analysis is that the emptiness of emptiness entails an infinite regress. For if the emptiness of emptiness is what we find upon analyzing emptiness, then what we find upon analyzing the emptiness of emptiness is the emptiness of the emptiness of emptiness, and so on *ad infinitum*. This is not a conclusion inimical to Nāgārjuna. On the contrary, a bottomless descent into ever-deeper, never-sounded emptiness is precisely the right result corollary to the clearing of *all* metaphysical grounds to which Nāgārjuna's multiple arguments lead. The regress is thus not vicious in that it does not undermine the conclusion Nāgārjuna is seeking; rather, it is virtuous in that it actively promotes the conclusion. Indeed, the conclusion that emptiness is inconclusive in this sense turns out to be just right given both that emptiness is what turns out to be the ultimate nature of reality and that the ultimate nature of reality turns out to be indeterminate. Reality is ultimately indeterminate—meandering—because on Nāgārjuna's analysis it turns out to be natureless. The conventional determination of reality into discrete entities along essentialist lines is precisely the process according to which reality is irrealized, denatured, moved away from its natural naturelessness into unnatural naturedness. (This is "unnatural" both because it denatures reality, is not in keeping with reality's nature, which is to be without nature, and because it is governed by conventions, which are constructions absent from ultimate reality.) As we will soon see in greater detail, this denaturing process does not merely occur in but is an ineluctable concomitant to the epistemological processes of mental cognition, consciousness, conceptualization.

The ethical implication of this is that the regress (according to which emptiness is analyzed to be empty, and this emptiness of emptiness is likewise analyzed to be empty, and so on . . .) turns out to be not a regress at all, but what could well be called a "virtuous progress." To understand what I mean by this it is necessary to accept, first, that it is no coincidence that the word "determination" simultaneously refers (among other things), on the one hand, to "a bringing to an end . . . ending; termination" and "the determining of bounds or fixing of limits; delimitation; definition; a fixing of the extent, position, or identity (of anything)," and, on the other hand, to "the definite direction of the mind or will toward an object or end" and "the mental action of coming to a decision; the fixing or settling of a purpose" (*Oxford English Dictionary*: "determination," senses 1, 5, 9, and 10). The former may be called the ontological senses of the term since they define a given object's ontological status and metaphysical identity; the latter are what I call the mental senses of the term since they define the orientation of the mind and/as will toward a given object. Let us take these definitions sequentially in their inter-relatedness.

That determination is termination means, in this context, that what the other definitions of the term refer to in sum amounts to the ending of the object of determination. To determine reality in the sense of fixing the limits of it is to put an end to reality, for reality is, on Nāgārjuna's analysis, indeterminate. To determine the indeterminate, to identify the unidentifiable, to self the selfless, to ent the empty, is no longer to deal with it at all. Reality so determined (i.e., determined in any way) simply is no longer reality. Rather (and this is where the collocation of ontological and epistemologico-mental senses begins to reveal some hefty philosophical presuppositions), determinate reality is a mental artifact, the construction resultant upon a given subject's mental orientation toward it. Crucially for the ethico-soterial purpose of Nāgārjuna's analysis as a whole, the mental orientation of a given subject toward a given object—indeed, the very construction by the subject of that object as *an*, and as *that*, object, and the concomitant construction of the subject's own subjectivity in relation to it—is volitive; that is, a function of the will. Hence my reference just now to the mind *and/as* will.

It is thus (to prefigure a little) that we arrive at *karma*. For not only *what* we take an object to be (i.e., how we determine it, be this in terms of avowedly "subjective" values or alternatively in terms of what are typically taken to be "objective" facts about its identity) but *that* we take it as an object at all is a function of the karmically conditioned deludedly desirous mind. I say "deludedly desirous" to bring out the key relevant feature here of the basic Buddhist understanding of sentient beings' *saṃsāric* entanglement; that is, the mutually entailing nature of delusion and desire. For the delusion according to which subjects ceive objects (in short, reification) gives rise to the desire on the part of those subjects for (or for the absence of) those objects, and this desire in turn (re)inforces the delusion. That these are mutually entailing is eloquently attested in the Buddhist tradition by positing a cyclical nature to the relation between beginningless ignorance and beginningless desire (and related links in the chain of dependent co-origination). That delusion/ignorance (*avidyā*) is foundational to *saṃsāric* suffering is in turn eloquently attested by its being placed as the very first link in the entire round of rebirth. And that *saṃskāra*s (constructions, fabrications, and more pointedly *volitional* formations) ensue directly from ignorance renders my point as to the inter-related nature of the ontological and epistemologico-mental aspects of determination all too clear: On the Buddhist account, to direct the mind (anywhere)—that is, to fix upon an identity (any identity)—is (not karmically neutral but) already to engage the will; it is therefore already deluded, and therefrom already karmically suffersome. As Chakravarthi Ram-Prasad declares concisely, "Suffering comes with conceptuality" (Ram-Prasad 2001: 153).

Nāgārjuna's alternative, his antidote to the three poisons of delusion (*moha*) as to reality and desire for (*rāga*) or against (*dveṣa*) it, is to undermine the entire onto-mental complex on which *saṃsāric* suffering rests, to take away the ground upon which any determination could be made. The "virtuous progress" of infinitely embedding emptiness "all the way down" (or up, or across, or in . . .) thus indicates not only an onto-epistemological map charting how to ceive reality aright but also an ethical path toward that map's ultimate destination (though we will soon see that the notion of pathhood here is itself not as simple as often assumed). For realizing reality as empty (and thus as empty of emptiness . . .) in an epistemological sense (as ceiving to be real) functions both as cause and effect of realizing reality as empty in an ontological sense (as making real). On the one hand, the process by which the onto-epistemological truth of emptiness is promoted (e.g., via the *prasaṅgic* arguments Nāgārjuna deploys) entails the cessation of ignorance as to reality, and thus the deconstruction of the grounds of desire, and thus of suffering.[24] Conversely, the silencing of suffering in the embodying of desirelessness itself enables the Buddhant ception of reality emptied of all determination.[25]

Let us recall at this point Goodman's concern that "if we are to realize such an ideal, what will happen to our ethical commitments?" (Goodman 2016: 141). To understand Nāgārjuna's conception in its full radicality, we must admit that all "our ethical commitments" will indeed dissolve: there simply is no way to maintain any such certainties or fixities in the face of emptiness. For Nāgārjuna, however, far from constituting a blow to his ethics, it is precisely this absence which will prove to be what allows moment-to-moment non-(pre)conceptualized ethical action to take place. For one who has abandoned all views there is no ethics (in the sense of ethical system or theory) to adhere to, but this absence of (fore)thought is exactly what enables such a one to act without intention (*cetanā*), and thus to act without accruing karmic consequences. This is *karman* without *karma*, for it is action enacted without the intentional directionality of *cetanā*: the lynchpin structurally causative of karmic consequence.

5.2.2. Intention and Action

To explain this, we need to delve a little more deeply into *cetanā*, and thereby into its relation to view-holding and action-taking. The importance of *cetanā* for the Buddhist account of action is difficult to overstate. Indeed, as remarked by Williams, "The Buddha is reported to have said of *karman* (*kamma*), action: 'I assert that action is volition (*cetanā*), since it is by willing that one performs an action with the body, speech or mind' (*Aṅguttara Nikāya* III: 415)" (P. Williams 2000: 68). This assertion is also cited (and alternately translated) by Meyers, who takes it to be "a kind of *mahāvākya* ['great saying'] around which scholars construct theories of Buddhist ethics" (Meyers 2010: 138).[26] My intention here is not to enter into debates as to the precise senses in which, or degrees to which, *cetanā* implies, or does not imply, such mainstays of argument within philosophical ethics as freedom or free will, moral responsibility or culpability, or cognitive as opposed to conative mental dimensions. Rather, I want to focus upon the ineliminable role intention (*cetanā*) plays for Nāgārjuna in conditioning action (*karma*)—well, this side of enlightenment anyway.

Nāgārjuna refers directly to the Buddha's statement just cited at the outset of his most extended treatment of action (*karma*) and its fruit (*phala*) in the MK. He writes:

> Action was said by the Supreme Sage to be
> Intention and what is brought about by intention
> Manifold distinct kinds of that action
> Have been proclaimed
>
> Among these, that action said to be 'intention'
> Is called mental
> And conversely that said to be 'brought about by intention'
> Is bodily and verbal[27]

We thus see that in MK:17:2 Nāgārjuna takes the Buddha "to have taught a twofold kind of action: intention-action (*cetanākarman*) and action following intention (*cetayitvā karman*, lit. 'action after having intended')" (Kragh 2006: 221). The threefold division into "bodily, verbal and mental action (*kāyikam*, *vācikam* and *mānasam*) . . . [in MK:17:3 is] correlated with the twofold division into intention and action following intention, because intention is said to correspond to mental action and action following intention is said to correspond to bodily and verbal action" (Kragh 2006: 226).[28] Indeed, in line with the Buddha's assertion that "action is *cetanā*,"[29] Nāgārjuna's text here shows him to understand action to be either intentional alone (mental action) or the bodily or verbal expression of intention. Whichever type of action we commit, then, it is evident that it is ineliminably characterized by intentionality.[30]

Now, whatever we may make of its conative aspect, there can be no doubt that intention is necessarily cognitive, and hence conceptual.[31] Given, moreover, the ineradicable role of intention in action (be it mental, bodily, or verbal), we are led to conclude that, for Nāgārjuna, conceptuality is part and parcel of action. It stands to reason, therefore, that the soterial end of abandoning all views-cum-conceptions (*dṛṣṭi*-cum-*prapañca*) entails—may even be said to be concomitant with—the abandoning of all actions-cum-intentions (*karma*-cum-*cetanā*). Nāgārjuna's abandonment of all views, of all conceptualization, is thus seen to have monumental consequences for Buddhist ethics. One way to approach this significance is through the rubric of sentience, for Buddhist ethics is premised on the existence of sentient beings. But what is sentience? In the context of the founding truths of Buddhism as a whole, sentience may be defined as the ability to suffer; indeed, sentience is defined by suffering. And suffering has a cause: it is caused by ignorance (*avidyā*), principally in the form of the mistaken view that the suffering self exists. The eradication of suffering is thus concomitant with—or in any case certainly necessitates—the eradication of any view affirming a self. And crucially, as Nāgārjuna perceived, all views affirm a self. Therefore, the avowed teleological end of Buddhism—enlightenment as the eradication of suffering—is attained concomitantly with the eradication of view-holding (i.e., conceptualization). The liberated one, unsuffering, holds no views. For precisely

> With the cessation of action and defilement there is liberation
> Action and defilement arise from dichotomizing conceptualization
> These from conceptualization
> But conceptualization is extinguished in emptiness[32]

That is, the Buddha does not conceptualize, for to do so would inevitably be to superimpose selfhood onto a reality empty of self, to divide subject from object where reality countenances no discretion. To see reality as it really is is indeed to see it as empty of self, but Nāgārjuna perceives that this is tantamount to seeing reality as empty of suffering too. As the critic accuses in MK:24, there really is no one to save if all are empty—a point I will return to presently.

The very nature of sentience is drastically changed here. For the typical Buddhist account, and most notably the typical Mahāyāna Buddhist account, has it that sentient beings are suffering. The defining innovation of Mahāyāna is precisely the avowal to eradicate the suffering of *all* sentient beings. But this presupposes a binary division between those beings that are sentient and those that are not. This division, like all divisions, is the work of conceptualization. Nāgārjuna's disavowal of any and all conceptualization thus entails that, for him, the distinction collapses such that all beings are as sentient, or insentient, as all others. One immediate (and potentially rather radical) consequence of this appears to be that it expands the remit of the Mahāyāna Buddhist ethical mandate to embrace all *beings* without qualification, for the division between sentient and insentient, suffering and unsuffering, has been abolished. From an alternative perspective, it declares the Buddhist path to have been already travelled by all, insofar as none are not already arrived at emptiness.

Another way to get at the same point is to (attempt to) explicate the role of (or the role of the absence of) intention in the actions of the Buddha—if we can still call them actions, that is. Given that *cetanā* is "*cognitive, conceptual*," it must be that "Morally positive action, however free from duality we might hope it can become, is hence *intentional*, hence *conceptualized*, hence implicated with subject-object duality, objectification, always conditioned by ignorance, and therefore, in the end, with *saṃsāra*" (Garfield 2016: 92, emphases original). As Garfield goes on almost immediately to observe, "Even appropriate conception is *conceptual*; even positive karma is *karma*, and a Buddha does not generate karma, does not objectify, does not engage conceptually. A Buddha, therefore, acts without *cetanā, non-intentionally*" (Garfield 2016: 92, emphases original). This is why Garfield is led to infer that "inasmuch as ethics is concerned with the *path* to perfection, we can say that a Buddha has accomplished all that ethics is intended to enable. She or he therefore does not continue to practice ethics, but transcends it. The para-ethical is the goal, not the continuation of the ethical" (Garfield 2016: 94 fn. 15, emphasis original).

The "para-ethical" is indeed the goal, but it is natural to note that we are here treating the *ultimate* attainment of the Mādhyamika's ethics. Given that we have seen the abandonment of all views to be crucial to Nāgārjuna's overall religiosophical project, I am attempting here to spell out the ethical consequences of this attainment-cum-abandonment; to work out how one liberated from the grip of views, no longer beholden to belief, could and would—or should—act. The necessary absence of ethical theory, and therefore of action principled on its basis, at this *end*, is not to be taken to entail that the *path* toward that end systematically laid out to greater or lesser extents by

Madhyamaka ethicists is to be altogether dispensed with.[33] Ultimate abrogation is not the same as wholescale dismissal. For while it is true that the path toward one's end must be left off once one has arrived, it must nevertheless have been traversed for that end to have come into view. This means that the elaboration of ethical and moral guidelines governing one's mundane actions and interactions (or what may perhaps most conveniently be termed conventional Madhyamaka ethics), as found most prosaically among Nāgārjuna's accepted works in the *Suhṛllekha*, remains both a valid enterprise for the Madhyamaka ethicist and a source of salutary guidance for the Madhyamaka practitioner.

This also ties in to earlier discussions regarding reason. Indeed, it helps to explain why Nāgārjuna is at such pains to make unparameterized statements overtly inimical to reason, such as espousing the abandonment of *all* views, while nonetheless utilizing reason as an indispensable tool in dismantling what he perceives to be *wrong* views.[34] For reason—for Nāgārjuna as for "us"—is the very bastion of distinctions and dualities; as such, it finds ample scope for prosecution in the procedure of progressing one along the path *toward* liberation, but it can have no place at all *in* the empty realm of liberation. This is why Dunne is justified in saying, of "Dharmakīrti and his fellow Buddhist thinkers, [that] reason is crucial to obtaining *nirvāṇa*" (Dunne 2004: 251). But to claim, as Dunne immediately goes on to do, that the "goal is thus obtained by judicious, rational persons. In short, *nirvāṇa* is not beyond reason—*it is perfectly in accord with reason*" (Dunne 2004: 251, emphases original) is to make a fundamental error of conflation between what pertains to the path toward *obtaining nirvāṇa* and what pertains once one has *obtained* it. I speak not for Dharmakīrti here, but if my account of Nāgārjuna is at all just, then it should be clear that he is certainly *not* to be accounted among any such "fellow Buddhist thinkers." On the contrary, irrespective of the indubitable role that reason plays in *prasaṅgic* critique of interlocutors, it can play no role once all positions and oppositions have been cleared away at liberation's end. There are no "judicious, rational persons" possessed of *bodhi*, for *bodhi* is and can only be beyond rationality.[35] Taken in a merely descriptive tenor, then, Dunne's statement is incorrect, at least as applied to Nāgārjuna, but certainly also to manifold other Buddhists, "thinkers" or not.[36] Indeed, as Ram-Prasad says in explication of a highly Nāgārjunian statement by Prajñākaragupta (c. 750–810), a commentator of none other than Dharmakīrti,

> Whatever is said is said from within the conceptual realm of the unliberated, and that applies equally to what is said of liberation. Every conception of liberation is, as it were, an unliberated conception, for there can be no other type of conception. So it is already misleading to have a conception of liberation when liberation is a transcendence of conceptuality. (Ram-Prasad 2001: 147)[37]

Given the ineliminability of rationality in the application of conceptuality, one may legitimately repurpose Ram-Prasad's final phrase to read "liberation is a transcendence of *rationality*," and thereby show that, whatever else we can or cannot say about it, the state of ultimate attainment, of Buddhahood, in *nirvāṇa* is non-dual and thus ir-rational.[38] Nāgārjuna makes this clear at numerous points in his corpus, as when in the *Paramārthastava* (*Hymn to the Ultimate*) he declares that "The Buddha is neither nonbeing nor being, neither annihilation nor permanence, not noneternal, not eternal. He falls into no category of duality" (Williams 2009: 178, citing the original text in Tucci 1932: 322). And yet there is no need to resort to Nāgārjuna's hymns, especially as exegetes such as Dunne would presumably argue that these "poetical" works should be discounted from the canon of truly "philosophical" works. For as we have seen repeatedly throughout this book, the tetralemmic repudiation of all logically possible alternatives, and with them all dualities and quaternities, may be found strewn throughout Nāgārjuna's *yukti* corpus of "logical" works.

In any case, as alluded to earlier, all this also means that the position voiced by the interlocutor in MK:24, who says that Nāgārjuna's claim that *ultimately* all are empty entails that the Buddhist path and the ethical action concomitant with it are dispensed with, is right—ultimately. For ultimately, there really is no one to save, no one saving, no saving. But none of this removes the conventional occurrence of all these phenomena. Indeed, one lesson to be derived from this is that Buddhist ethics functions only within the ambit of conventional reality; ultimately, there is no need, or place, for ethics.[39]

5.2.3. A Buddha's Ethics

My foregoing discussion of path and goal, and of the disjunct between them on Nāgārjuna's account, and indeed of the place (or placelessness) of ethics and even of action within their differing ambits, may fruitfully be further explicated through counterposing with Bronwyn Finnigan's conception of what she calls "a Buddhist account of ethical agency" (Finnigan 2011a). Finnigan begins by delineating her guiding assumption in general terms as follows:

> Significantly, for any ethical theory that is 'progressive' in the sense of positing a strategy or pathway toward a desired teleological end, there will be a symmetric relation of dependence between the teleological end and the strategy employed to achieve that end. That is, not only will the stages of the pathway posited for overcoming the trouble be justified in relation to their role in constituting or producing the teleological end, but the teleological end itself will be determined by this process. (Finnigan 2011a: 134)

She then applies this principle to the Buddhist case specifically, proposing that

> there is a relation of dependence between the teleological end of a Buddhist ethical theory that takes the Four Noble Truths as a framing assumption and the strategy employed to achieve that end. If the teleological end (i.e., that of buddhahood) is not coherent, this fact problematizes (or, more strongly, undermines the justificatory status of) the pathway posited to achieve this end. (Finnigan 2011a: 134)

The first problem with Finnigan's assumption is that it is unargued for; that is, it is simply taken as a given—and givens are always giveaways. In the present instance, we may break the assumption down into what are effectively two subclaims. The first posits a "symmetric relation of dependence" (or justificatory relation) between the "stages of the pathway" and "their role in constituting or producing the teleological end." The second, meanwhile, posits such a relation as (somehow) constitutive/determinative of that end ("the teleological end itself will be determined by this process"). Not only is neither of these assumptions argued for, but both are in fact problematic.

Indeed, this brings us to the second problem with Finnigan's account. This relates to the fact that it is unclear what exactly the relation actually is (in either subclaim), given that it is supposed to be a "symmetric relation of dependence." What exactly the "symmetry" posited amounts to here and how it relates to "dependence" are unexplained, even though there are countless readily conceivable instances wherein a dependence relation obtains between radically differing (and thus presumably "asymmetrical") phenomena.

The contextual discussion appears to render the "symmetrical" aspect of the relation in subclaim 1 reducible to a sort of causally efficacious sortal correspondence. Thus, we are effectively left with the positing of a causal dependence relation according to which acts of a certain sort "a" undertaken along the proposed path toward the proposed end lead to states of a certain sort "z" (recall that they are to be taken as "producing the teleological end"), where "a" and "z" are assumed to be "symmetrical" or, as I have glossed, sortally alike. On subclaim 2, "z" is said to be constituted or determined by "a." In either case, the relation in both claims may be understood as obvious; indeed, painfully so: On the one hand, it is self-evident that, if "a" is assumed to be an action that produces "z," and the performance of "a" is for the purpose of producing "z,"[40] then the performance of "a" will be justified precisely insofar as it will in fact produce "z." To give an example: if acts of compassion produce a state of bliss in me, and I perform acts of compassion to enter into such a state of bliss, then I will be justified in performing acts of compassion insofar as they do in fact lead me to that bliss. On the other hand, if "a" is assumed to produce "z," and no other supporting or countervailing factors obtrude,[41] then "z" will be constituted/determined by "a" precisely insofar as it is in fact produced by "a." Thus, if bliss is brought about in me by my acting compassionately, and acting compassionately does not bring about any other (potentially complicating) states, then my state of bliss will be constituted/determined precisely insofar as it is brought about by my acting compassionately. Both hands come out empty, as it were, for if understood in the manners I have proposed then both subclaims amount to little more than tautologies.[42]

Is there another way to interpret Finnigan's account to obviate this charge? Yes, there is, but it leads directly to what I see as the third problem with it. Teleologically oriented acts often—perhaps even typically or, on the strongest version of this criticism, invariably—lead to end-states of an obviously different sort. This entails that Finnigan's dual assumption is in fact inapplicable to any number of readily conceivable non-ethical and ethical contexts. Let us take the first subclaim first. In non *prima facie* ethical contexts, I can train to be an athlete and thereby become rich, clean the house and thereby make my wife leap for joy, fell a tree in a forest and thereby engender a millennia-long debate between idealists and realists, where it is understood that in each of these cases: (1) the "thereby" betokens a causally productive dependence relation; (2) the end-state was not the intended causal result of the action (it was not geared toward that teleological end); and (3) it is not at all clear what kind of non-trivial "symmetry" or sortal correspondence could be said to obtain between the end-state and the action. As for overtly ethical contexts, I can take hallucinogenic drugs and thereby enter meditative absorption (*samādhi*) (a consequentialist example), practice truth-telling (*satya-vacana*) and thereby get fired by my dishonest boss (virtue ethics), or (deontologically) follow the Noble Eightfold Path (*āryāṣṭāṅgamārga*) and thereby become a celebrity, where all the same conditions (1 through 3) apply. In these and countless other such conceivable cases, although the causal links between actions "a" and end-states "z" may well be as empirically discernible as any other causal chains are (if any can be said to function in an empty world), it is not in the least clear how *any* "progressive" ethical theory could make sense of them in terms of ethical progress when in fact the end-states are unintended consequences of, and (as such) ethically unrelated to, the actions by means of which they were technically (efficiently) occasioned. And it is even less clear how any such end-states could be said to have been constituted or determined by their efficient causes.

The most serious problem with Finnigan's account here, however, has to do not with its internal coherence or cogency but with its applicability (or not) to the Buddhist context. Now, in his response to Finnigan's paper, Garfield has already forcefully argued that, among other perceived faults, "Finnigan's own account of a buddha's action . . . is not, as she believes, acceptable *within a Buddhist framework*" (Garfield 2011: 175, emphases original).[43] My intention here is obviously not to rehearse those criticisms, which have to do with diverse aspects of how to "explain a buddha's awakened thought and action" (Garfield 2011: 175), but to focus specifically on Finnigan's central premise.

Put simply, the positing of a dependence relation in the terms proposed is unjustified in a context such as the Buddhist where the identified teleological end (*nirvāṇa*, Buddhahood) is overtly and repeatedly characterized by the tradition in terms that are not only radically other to those characterizing the identified path toward it (i.e., "not coherent" with it), but outright internally *incoherent*. In fact, the *internal* incoherence, according to which *nirvāṇa* or Buddhahood is characterized in explicitly *self*-contradictory terms, constitutes precisely the relevant distinction—the absence of coherence—between it, as beyond duality, and the duality-laden pathway leading toward it. Regarding Buddhahood, for example, Finnigan draws on Garfield to spell out the multiply self-contradictory characterization of Buddhahood, according to which, "For instance, a buddha is considered to be able . . . to be aware that there is no distinction between subject and object and that kinds are merely conventional, but where this awareness of nonduality is, itself, nondually cognized; and to see reality '*as* it is' but without the mediation of any concepts" (Finnigan 2011a: 154 n. 11, emphasis original).[44]

Unfortunately, Finnigan's response is simply to dismiss the nuttiness of the issue and pick the cherries she can work with. For she freely admits that "There are various accounts of the nature of buddhahood within the Buddhist tradition, many of which are transcendental and posit god-like qualities," but decides to simply "set aside these transcendental interpretations of buddhahood" (Finnigan 2011a: 155 n. 16). Much like the parameterization of the tetralemma or other efforts (addressed earlier) to render Buddhism respectable as a "philosophy," this is effectively an inadvertent admission that the (naturalized, analyticized) Buddha she is theorizing is not the Buddha of Buddhism.[45] In fact, things get even worse, for Finnigan actually appears to try to have it both ways—to keep both cherries and nuts—by stipulating that "the buddha I am concerned with is the historical, human Buddha (Siddhārtha Gautama), who chose to remain on earth to transmit the *dharma* to his disciples via teachings and as recorded in the early Buddhist canons" (Finnigan 2011a: 155 n. 16). But this is to willfully ignore the facts that, first, "the early Buddhist canons" are largely silent on the state of Buddhahood/ *nirvāṇa*, and that when they do address it they do so in terms directly inimical to the kind of rationalization Finnigan is engaged in, and second, that the subsequent tradition *in toto* only forcefully reinforces this twin tendency, which Panikkar calls "the double silence of the Buddha" (Panikkar 2006: 22), and which Finnigan herself encounters lucidly exposited by her object of study, Dharmakīrti. Finnigan's cherries, alas, are sour. Indeed, the historical Buddha himself is attested as refusing to address the issue or, insofar as addressing it, as addressing it in terms of its inaddressability. Thus, for example, in a discussion directly on the topic of path and goal, the Buddha answers a series of questions posed by the monk Rādha as to "the purpose" of the various stages along the path of perfection. Having arrived at dispassion and been told that "The purpose of dispassion is liberation," Rādha naturally asks: "And what, venerable sir, is the purpose of liberation?" The Buddha responds tautologically: "The purpose of liberation is Nibbāna." So Rādha pursues: "And what, venerable sir, is the purpose of Nibbāna?" But here the Buddha cannot but stop:

> You have gone beyond the range of questioning, Rādha. You weren't able to grasp the limit to questioning. For, Rādha, the holy life is lived with

Nibbāna as its ground, Nibbāna as its destination, Nibbāna as its final goal. (Bodhi 2000: 984–985)[46]

The overall upshot is that, irrespective of whatever one *makes of* the Buddha's characterization of the "final goal" as uncharacterizable as anything other than the endpoint, as it were, of characterizability, the fact remains that in the Buddhist case that end *is* ineliminably of a qualitatively radically different (asymmetrical) kind to the path leading toward it. There is a (constitutive and determinative) disjunct between the enlightened and the unenlightened states: the historical Buddha acts and knows, but how he does so is and necessarily remains, somehow, *asaṃskṛta*, *avyākṛta*.[47] This is precisely whence Nāgārjuna's radically aporetic collapsing of the very distinction between *saṃsāra* and *nirvāṇa* draws its force. After all, if this were not the case, if *nirvāṇa* (or its realization in Buddhahood) were assimilable to the norms and forms of *saṃsāra* (or suffersome immersion in its pre-Buddhic ignorance), then where would be the point of the path? For unlike the paths and chains familiar to us denizens of *duḥkha*, the final footfall of this path, the final link of this chain, is unlike any of those preceding it, leading as they were toward it whereas it leads nowhere and thereby unmakes them in their final realization.

This shows in the present context that any and all efforts such as Finnigan's to rationalize *nirvāṇa* or Buddhahood in order to render it compatible with *saṃsāra*, explicable in terms of the categories obtaining within *saṃsāra*, cannot but fail. They are, to use Panikkar's helpful neologism, katachronic, where "katachronism" is defined as "interpretation of a reality or doctrine with categories that are extraneous or posterior" (Panikkar 2006: 280).[48] The present case is but another form of the efforts we have seen time and again throughout this book to resolve into reason's terms what is (and must remain on pain of internal incoherence) an irresolvable aporia beyond reason's remit.[49]

This is not to say that other conceptions of Buddhahood and *nirvāṇa* have found no place in the Buddhist tradition. On the contrary, much as Steven Collins distinguishes between "nirvana in and out of time" (Collins 1998: 119ff),[50] so too Guang Xing distinguishes between "the human Buddha" and "the superhuman Buddha" (Xing 2005: 7–18). Indeed, Collins identifies several dynamically interacting "varieties of Buddhist salvation" along what he calls "a spectrum of felicities" (Collins 1998: 101, 109), while Xing distinguishes among no fewer than five historically successive conceptions of the Buddha (Xing 2005: 179–181) within the tradition.[51] There can thus be no doubting the capacity of Buddhism to hold within it a multiplicity of (more or less complementary, more or less competing) conceptual spaces for its identified structuring principle and end. A consequence of this plurivocality is that some room at least is in fact cleared in at least some conceptual regions for the kind of "symmetry" between path and end within Buddhism that Finnigan calls for, though there are, of course, clear limits beyond which any such account ceases to be recognizably Buddhist at all.[52] And this applies, I would argue, even when relatively "human," as opposed to "superhuman," conceptions of Buddhahood or *nirvāṇa* are at work given that these in fact function, within Mahāyāna as much as within Śrāvakayāna, as "the moment of ending that gives structure to the whole" (Collins 2010: 113).[53]

But regardless of what we make of any conceptualization of *nirvāṇa* as more or less continuous with the *saṃsāra*-laid path leading toward it, our concern is principally with Nāgārjuna, and it is clear that no such conception can be applied to him. Indeed, I have tarried on Finnigan's presentation precisely because it brings out, through counterpoint, a central feature of Nāgārjuna's notion of Buddhahood/*nirvāṇa*. Nāgārjuna like fellow "Mahāyānists concentrated exclusively on the abstract notion of the Buddha, not on the historical Buddha. This provides the foundation for the Mahāyānist doctrine of the concept of the Buddha" (Xing 2005: 180). We see this in evidence throughout Nāgārjuna's corpus (*yukti* and otherwise), but expressed perhaps most clearly in the culminating verse of his direct treatment of the Tathāgata in the MK, where he explicitly identifies the "altogether empty" (cf. MK:22:10) Buddha with the world in its entirety:

> What is the selfbeing of the Tathāgata
> Is the selfbeing of this world
> The Tathāgata is without selfbeing
> This world is without selfbeing[54]

This is the Buddha as no mere human teacher, but the very reality of reality. And given that view-holding denatures reality (disables the realization of reality), view-abandonment is, in Nāgārjuna's eyes, an ethical act—one needful for the realization of Buddhahood.

And yet, here as elsewhere, the Madhyamaka approach of Nāgārjuna shows itself to be "the knotty exception"[55] to any easy either/or . . . though hopefully this "knot" will prove to be of a kind with Siddhartha's top-knot: cut through in renunciation of conventional dualities. For although "the state of awakening . . . [is] para-ethical" (Garfield 2016: 81), if we take this to designate simply the consummation of the ethical prescriptions and proscriptions laid down along the path as conditions for the successful traversal of it, then we are left with a rather standard model of ethical progress and perfection. Much as Descartes, say, sees no need to delineate an ethics for those attained to the "supernatural bliss" (*béatitude surnaturelle*) of the next life (see Rutherford 2019: §1), so Nāgārjuna would take the Buddha to represent precisely the figure of the "Supreme Sage" who, standing atop the summit of ethical perfection, finds himself no longer in need of any path leading thereto. But although I have previously characterized the abandonment of all views as the telos of Nāgārjuna's Buddhist path, acknowledging in the process that Nāgārjuna asks us not to dispense with view-holding in our as-yet-unenlightened conventional worldly interactions, the time has come to problematize somewhat this suspiciously neat binary, and with it the very structural setting of Nāgārjuna's Buddhist ethics. For while a specified path as distinct from and leading toward a specified goal would make perfect sense were the goal identifiable with a specific nature, the very naturelessness of the goal in Nāgārjuna's system undermines the dichotomy of path and goal itself. This is so because the end of the path in this case is the realization of the emptiness of all things—including of the path itself. The goal is, as it were, the path's "end" in both the sense of telos and terminus, achievement and annulment. More exactly, one attains to *nirvāṇa* by realizing that it is nothing other than *saṃsāra*; that, as Nāgārjuna writes near the culmination of his most sustained treatment of the topic, "Between *saṃsāra* and *nirvāṇa* / There is no difference at all" (MK:25:19ab).[56] But this realization cannot but entail—indeed, equivale—the dissolution of the very distinction itself, and thus the distinction between the path of perfecting and perfection attained. And this necessarily transforms the entirety of the relation.

Recall that, as Nāgārjuna explains earlier in the very same book of the MK as the foregoing quotation,

> What comes or passes
> In dependence or relation
> That, in neither dependence nor relation
> Is taught to be *nirvāṇa*

And the Teacher taught the abandonment
Of becoming and passing
Thus it is acceptable to say that *nirvāṇa*
Neither exists nor does not exist[57]

Nirvāṇa is thus explained to be the very same as "What comes or passes / In dependence or relation," in other words the very same as what comprises and constitutes the suffersome round of *saṃsāra*, but seen "in neither dependence nor relation."[58] And in direct textual anticipation of the abandonment (*prahāṇāya*) of all views (MK:27:30), Nāgārjuna here (MK:25:10) immediately goes on to observe that the Buddha "taught the abandonment (*prahāṇaṃ*) / Of becoming and passing." Crucially, however, the argument is set up in such a way as to undermine what turns out to be a merely apparent kataphatic affirmation of '*nirvāṇa* as opposed to *saṃsāra*' in favor of an apophatic abandonment of both based on their inter-identification. For as Nāgārjuna will go on to utter of the very embodiment of *nirvāṇa*, the Buddha,

Beyond cessation, the Blessed One
Is not to be said 'to exist' nor 'to not exist'
Neither 'both' nor 'neither'
Is to be said[59]

That the Buddha should be characterized as uncharacterizable "beyond cessation" (i.e., after death, in *nirvāṇa*) is not at all unexpected given the reiterated refusals to qualify *nirvāṇa* with anything other than non-qualifications.[60] But that he should be likewise uncharacterizable "during abidance" (i.e., while alive, in *saṃsāra*) shows the dichotomy itself to be untenable:

During abidance, the Blessed One
Is not to be said 'to exist' nor 'to not exist'
Neither 'both' nor 'neither'
Is to be said[61]

The Buddha here emerges as the ineffable cipher of *nirvāṇa*, which itself is seen to be one side of a binary opposition with *saṃsāra*—a binary that itself is undone in the very attainment of (unattained, and indeed unattainable: MK:25:3a) *nirvāṇa*.[62]

The apophatic undermining of the differentiation between *nirvāṇa* and *saṃsāra* in *nirvāṇic* liberation from this and all other dualities need not detain us any further here except insofar as it affects our understanding of Nāgārjuna's ethics. For the upshot is that the differentiation between path and goal accepted along the conventional path is shown to be inapplicable upon attainment of the ultimate goal . . . and therefore in turn inapplicable to the entire conventional-cum-ultimate path-cum-goal. To put this another way, although some vehicles (*yāna*) may be more or less conducive than others along the paths (*mārga*) or ways (*pratipad*) and through the stages (*bhūmi*) constitutive of progress toward the various perfections (*pāramitā*) definitive of Buddhist, or certainly at least Mahāyānist, ethical achievement, final attainment of what the tradition as a whole calls "remainderless *nirvāṇa*" (*nirupadhiśeṣa nirvāṇa*) shows that "All things being empty" (MK:25:22a: *śūnyeṣu sarvadharmeṣu*) from the start and to the end,[63] what is "remainderless" turns out in the end and from the start to be nothing other than "all things" (*sarvam dharmam*), nothing other than that very *saṃsāra* between which and *nirvāṇa* "There is no difference at all" (MK:25:19). The paradoxicality of such formulations is in fact already prefigured in, and explains, the paradox implicit in stating that the Buddha "acts without *cetanā*" (Garfield 2016: 92). For as we have seen both the Buddha and Nāgārjuna avow, "action is *cetanā*."[64] So how can action, irreducibly intentional, conceptual, view-ridden, be rid of any such *cetanā*?

The question brings us back to the problem we began with, the problem at the heart of our entire discussion: that of what I call in the subtitle to this chapter, and this book, "the ethics of emptiness." The problem is put by Owen Flanagan in the following terms:

> I still do not see, despite trying for many years, why understanding the impermanence of everything including myself makes a life of maximal compassion more rational than a life of hedonism. And isn't that the problem that we keep coming back to, the problem or question that doesn't go away? I am not distraught over not seeing this connection, but then again I am not a Buddhist. If I were a Buddhist I would be troubled by not understanding how Buddhist ethics follows from Buddhist metaphysics and epistemology. (Flanagan 2013: 206–207)

Perhaps we are now in a place to allay any such disquiet. For on my analysis, so far from "destroying the bodhisattva path" (Williams 1998: 164),[65]

Nāgārjuna's avowal of universal emptiness and the abandonment of all views concomitant with it emerge not only as reconcilable with Madhyamaka ethics but as the *uniquely* adequate metaphysics and epistemology to an ethics of universal compassion (*karuṇā*).[66] For compassion is understood here precisely not merely as the absence of passion, but as the absence of any thought of self, and thus of any division between oneself and another. The realization of the metaphysical truth of the emptiness of self and other, and thus of the emptiness of any posited division between them, is concomitant with the realization of the ethical reality of all-embracing compassion.[67] One simply cannot think a selfish thought, let alone act a selfish action, once one has realized the emptiness of self and other. But that still needs some explaining.

5.3. From Ethics to Eirenics

What is the nature of the relation between the holding of views and the committing of actions?[68] This is a matter of some importance, for it is on the basis of what he perceives to be their interwovenness that Nāgārjuna is able to set forth what will turn out—if my analysis is valid—to be a tightly knit relationship between his Madhyamaka metaphysics of emptiness, epistemology of abandonment, and ethics of pacification.[69]

5.3.1. Conception, Perception, Ception

Now, I have had occasion in the foregoing discussion to put the coinage "ceive" to use, and the time has come to explain it along with correlates such as "ception." The aim here is to bring out the implications these notions hold for Nāgārjuna's religiosophy as a whole—comprising as this does not only ethics, metaphysics, and epistemology but also philosophy of mind and of language. Put simply, "ceive" and "ception" are designed to capture the sense of both "conceive" and "perceive," "conception" and "perception."[70] This is proposed on the basis of the fact that the standard Buddhist model of personhood includes the mind (*manas*) as one of the six sense organs, and correlatively the mental as one of the six sensory modes of experience. In so doing, the Buddhist conception effectively undermines the distinction between conception (as the ception of mental objects by the mind) and perception (as the ception of bodily objects by the eye, ear, nose, tongue, skin).

Not that the distinction is altogether abrogated, for collecting and analyzing the senses' data remains an important meta-function of the mind. But at the level of data-ception (as opposed to data-ception analysis), the point is that the mind is functionally on a par with the other sense organs. This means that the mind and its objects are not ontologically privileged *vis-à-vis* the other senses and their objects. All six are senses and sense objects: hence the undermining of a conception/perception distinction.

The *āyatana* model is addressed directly by Nāgārjuna in MK:3, which begins:

> Seeing, hearing, smelling,
> Tasting, touching, and mind
> Are the six sense faculties;
> What is seen and so on are their fields.[71]

In the remainder of this chapter, Nāgārjuna mounts a critique of standard accounts of seeing and its correlative fields of operation, and explicitly declares in the closing verse that his argument applies to the five other sense faculties and fields:

> It should be understood that
> Seeing, hearing, smelling, tasting, touching, and mind
> Are explained by means of seeing
> As are the hearer and the heard, etc.[72]

In passing, it is certainly worthwhile noting that this standard Buddhist *āyatana* model of six rather than five sense faculties and fields, explicitly subscribed to by Nāgārjuna, clearly gives the lie to Hayes's claim that in their philosophy of mind "the views available to Buddhists are mind-body dualism and mind-only monism" (Hayes 2013: 395). On the contrary, we find here a model differing in a philosophically important way from this "duality-or-unity" mode of thinking; one that proposes in its stead a six-fold mode of ception that collectively exhausts under a single rubric all epistemic processes—and indeed all ontology according to one of the Buddha's *Discourses*! Thus, in a section of the *Saḷāyatanavagga* titled "The All" the Buddha declares "The eye and forms, the ear and sounds, the nose and odours, the tongue and tastes, the body and tactile objects, the mind and mental phenomena. This is called the all" (Bodhi 2000: 1140 (IV.35.III.23

(1)).[73] The Buddha certainly seems to be making a ontological claim here, though in the context of everything else he says we would be grossly mistaken to take this as positing *svabhāvic* selfhood, not least since any and all of the "five aggregates" (*skandhas*) constitutive of selfhood are "nonself."[74]

Whatever we make of this specific issue, the more philosophically important point for present purposes regards the need for a single term to designate an epistemic process that may be undertaken by the mind (in what ordinary English parlance refers to as conception) or any of the other five sense organs (perception). I see this need buttressed by the fact that the term I have translated throughout as "conceptualization"—*prapañca*—"is actually not confined to conceptual mechanisms . . . [*prapañca*] refers both to ontic and to epistemic diffusion—both to the universe as the totality of the contents of perception and to language and conceptual thought" (Huntington 1989: 209 n. 101).[75] The need for a term such as "ception" I see as also evident in a statement such as the following, where I take the two to be legitimately conflated: "For Nāgārjuna . . . it is a mistake to distinguish conventional from ultimate reality—the dependently arisen from emptiness—at an ontological level . . . The difference—such as it is—between the conventional and the ultimate is a difference in the way phenomena are *conceived/perceived*" (Garfield 2002: 39, emphases added).[76] Note also, however, that elsewhere Garfield distinguishes between "*perception* and *reflection* or *conceptual thought*" (the latter amenable, I take it, to being alternatively rendered as "conception") based on the notion that "When we perceive, we engage directly with particulars, and hence with *reality*. When we reflect, we *conceive*, and apprehend unreal universals" (Garfield 2016: 92 fn. 12, emphases original). Regardless of whether we take Garfield's slash mark in the previous quote as undermining or supporting the distinction, I do not take Nāgārjuna in relevant passages to be subscribing to the particular/universal distinction along these lines.[77] On the contrary, apart from the fact that his teaching of universal emptiness undercuts even particulars' claims to "*reality*," Nāgārjuna, as we have seen earlier, is at pains to deflate *all* distinctions. This has implications for the distinction between the ontological status/es of the organs of what is standardly termed "perception" (i.e., eye, ear, nose, tongue, and body) as opposed to the organ of what is standardly termed "conception" (i.e., mind), as well as for the epistemic status/es of the processes at work in knowledge-episodes among them. These are worthy of brief further consideration, for not only do they still further reinforce the inter-wovenness of the various facets of Nāgārjuna's religiosophy (and thus both the internal coherence of it and the need to study it holistically in order to do it justice), but, in tightening the linkages between the realms of things, views, and actions, they are directly relevant to our purposes here.

The issue of ception, and the problem it presents for enlightened action, is acute for the Mādhyamika. For, as Ram-Prasad explains,

> The account must somehow square the freedom from conception of liberating cognition with the richly textured attitudes of the compassionate *bodhisattva* . . . There is, then, a double challenge for the philosopher of this school: the epistemic one of reconciling cognitive purity with unavoidably conceptual understanding, and the moral-soteriological one of reconciling that purity with compassionate attitudes and activity. (Ram-Prasad 2001: 160)[78]

We have already had occasion to touch upon the issues of action and compassion earlier, and we will return to them again, but for the moment let us focus on the epistemological question.[79] This revolves around the fact that, on a broad view of conceptuality such as that I have ascribed to Nāgārjuna, "Given that conceptuality is bound to (or identical with) ignorance, it would seem that perceiving *an object* (let alone responding to it correctly) is, itself, beyond the ken of a buddha" (Finnigan 2010: 291).[80] Note, first, that Finnigan's account of *con*ceptuality here explicitly involves *per*ceiving objects, and this is right given that the issue relates to any and all of the sixfold forms of ception. But the more substantive philosophical problem is that, if enlightenment ensues from the eradication of ignorance, and thus of concepts, and thus of speech, then there can be no escaping the conclusion forcefully made by Dunne:

> Not only does such a buddha not see the ordinary things of the world, he does not even know ultimate reality because nothing at all occurs in a buddha's mind. Indeed, it would seem that Candrakīrti's [and we may say Nāgārjuna's] buddhas do not know anything at all. If such is the case, we might feel compelled to conclude that buddhas are entirely outside our reality in some state of complete "isolation" (*kaivalya*) . . . It would certainly seem that such a buddha would be completely incapable of doing anything in the world, for s/he would not have any cognitive relation to the world whatsoever. One might even conclude that such a buddha is simply dead. (Dunne 1996: 548)[81]

Linji may have called for killing the Buddha (see §0.0), but surely this is not what Nāgārjuna meant?

5.3.2. The Aporia of Ethics

I propose that what we approach here is an acute and distinctively Buddhist form of "the *aporia*—the unresolvable dilemma—of transcendence" (Sells 1994: 2, emphasis original).[82] There is no reasonable way for Nāgārjuna (or Candrakīrti or Dharmakīrti for that matter, or any other Buddhist thinker) to explain away the paradox at the heart of Buddhahood and *nirvāṇa*.[83] Dunne is right to point out that the Buddha, the perfectly enlightened one (*samyaksaṃbuddha*), must speak and, in so doing, employ concepts, the which are defined, however, as ignorance, whereas the "Buddha is omniscient, possessed of *sarvajñatva*, *sarvajñāna*, or *sarvākārajñatā*" (Griffiths 1994: 69).[84] And we may add that the Buddha, the unsurpassed (*anuttara*) and perfected in knowledge and conduct (*vidyācaraṇasaṃpanna*), must also act and, in so doing, enact *karma*, the which is defined, however, as suffersome, whereas the "'Buddha's defining characteristic is the purification of the actuality of all things from the two obstacles: those of affliction and those which obstruct objects of awareness' (*kleśajñeyāvaraṇadvayāt sarvadharmatathatā viśuddhilakṣaṇaḥ*)" (Griffiths 1994: 76, citing the *Mahāyāna Sūtrālaṃkāra*). There is no way to conceive of speech or action otherwise without transforming their very notions into unrecognizably alien forms. This, of course, is precisely what the Buddhist tradition does in invoking notions such as "wisdom without dichotomizing conceptualization" (*nirvikalpajñāna*) (and thus speech without conceptualization (*niṣprapañca*))[85] or "acts without *cetanā*" (and thus *karman* without *karma*) as regards the Buddha, or indeed in proposing that while the "Buddha appears to act in the world physically (through its *kāya*), verbally (through its *vāc*), and mentally (through its *citta*) . . . Every act done in one of these three ways by Buddha . . . [is] itself classified as an instance of magical transformation (*nirmāṇa*)" (Griffiths 1994: 102). This echoes other attempts to explain (or explain away) the problem through the postulation of three bodies for the Buddha (viz., the "reality body"/"*dharma* body" or *dharmakāya*, "celestial body"/"enjoyment body" or *saṃbhogakāya*, and "emanation body"/"transformation body" or *nirmāṇakāya*).[86] But what are explanatory recourses to "magical transformations" or "emanation bodies" but effective admissions of the impossibility of explanation, discursive white flags signaling reason's defeat? Naturally, theistic religious traditions have faced analogous problems and have proposed analogous solutions in discussing how, for example, the Impassible and Immutable 'Ēl 'Elyōn could possibly live and die humanly incarnated as Jesus, or how the Incomparable (*badī'*) and Hidden (*bāṭin*) Allāh could possibly give voice to the divine discourse (*kalām*) of the *Qu'rān*.

Returning to the Buddhist case, we find that Nāgārjuna's insistence on the transcendence of the duality of transcendence and immanence, ultimate and conventional, *nirvāṇa* and *saṃsāra*, amounts to an aporia according to which the attainment of the path's end undermines the very distinction between that end and the path leading toward it. Let us look, then, a little more closely at Sells's account, according to which a statement of the sort "X is beyond names" "generates the aporia that the subject of the statement must be named (as X) in order for us to affirm that it is beyond names" (Sells 1994: 2).[87] The applicability of such a mode of discourse to the case of Nāgārjuna's Buddha should be evident, for as we have seen, Nāgārjuna conceives of the Buddha as beyond concepts/actions, but likewise needs him to employ concepts in speaking the *dharma* and to undertake action in alleviating *duḥkha*. Sells charts three responses to this dilemma of transcendence. "The first response is silence" (Sells 1994: 2)—a response we have seen embodied in Nāgārjuna's references to the "unexplicated points" (*avyākṛtavastu*) of the Buddha and Candrakīrti's "silence of the saint" (*ārya-tūṣṇīmbhāva*) (see §4.2 and §4.3 respectively). "The second response is to distinguish between ways in which the transcendent is beyond names and ways in which it is not" (Sells: 1994: 2). This is a form of what I have called parameterization of Nāgārjuna's overtly paralogical utterances, be they in tetralemmic form or otherwise, by today's Buddhist scholars. But it also applies to some of yesteryear's Buddhist philosophers insofar as they took refuge from (what Nāgārjuna saw to be the ultimate refuge of) viewlessness and its correlates in the postulation of metaphysical fantasies such as magical transformations and graded multitudes of Buddha-bodies.[88]

Finally, however,

> The third response begins with the refusal to solve the dilemma posed by the attempt to refer to the transcendent through a distinction between two kinds of name. The dilemma is accepted as a genuine *aporia*, that is, as unresolvable; but this acceptance, instead of leading to silence, leads to a new mode of discourse. (Sells 1994: 2, emphasis original)

I have already identified this "new mode of discourse" in prior chapters as the tetralemmic utterance and, more broadly, the avowed abandonment of all views such utterance serves. It is also apparent in what I have previously referred to, drawing on Muller and Mills, as the "two levels" or "two phases" of Nāgārjuna's *prasaṅgic* method, where (in general terms) one sets up a position or view only to overturn or undermine it in the subsequent discursive move.[89] In fact, there is a striking analogy here between Nāgārjuna's setting up of conceptual constructions and relentless deconstruction thereof, and Sells's understanding of apophatic language. The analogy will help us discern yet another aspect of the relationship between enlightenment and the wholescale abandonment of views in Nāgārjuna's thought.

5.3.3. Apophatic Ethics

Sells uses the term "apophasis" not so much in its usual sense of "denial" or "negation," but by referring back to its etymological components (*apo-phasis*) to signify "un-saying" or "speaking-away." This is in contrast to "kataphasis," which according to Sells signifies an "affirmation," "saying," or "speaking-with."[90] On Sells's analysis, a "mystical language of unsaying" (to adapt the title of his book) "is a discourse of double propositions, in which meaning is generated through the tension between the saying and the unsaying" (Sells 1994: 12).[91] That is, he argues that the mystic writer is one whose discourse continually shifts between the saying and the un-saying of a given position, and that meaning is constructed in such a discourse not through any one or other of these statements, but rather through their interplay or tension. As he puts it: "The writer must continually turn back to unsay the previous saying" (Sells 1994: 215) so as to create an aporia; the "unresolvable dilemma" (Sells 1994: 2) in which full meaning resides. Such an act of apophatic speech creates a "meaning event" wherein the duality initially posited or presupposed falls away into a semantic synthesis: "The meaning event is the semantic analogue to the experience of mystical union. It does not describe or refer to mystical union but effects a semantic union that re-creates or imitates the mystical union" (Sells 1994: 9). This leads on the epistemic front to a condition of 'agnosia': "an unknowing that goes beyond rather than falling short of kataphatic affirmations" (Sells 1994: 35).[92]

Applying Sells's terms and ideas to the arena of our own concerns, we find that time and again the Nāgārjunian textual corpus does indeed exhibit a "discourse of double propositions," whereby a given position is "said" (be it by an assumed interlocutor or in postulative mode) only to be "unsaid" in its subsequent *prasaṅgic* taking-down.[93] This is acknowledged even by an interpreter so concerned to maintain logical consistency as Westerhoff, who inadvertently echoes Sells directly in admitting that Nāgārjuna's MK resembles the Perfection of Wisdom *sūtras* in that in these texts "one sentence asserts something which the next one then goes on to deny" (Westerhoff 2018a: 118). This is a classic formulation of Sellsian apophasis.[94] Such apophasis is in evidence perhaps most clearly of all within the *catuṣkoṭi*, whether positive or negative, where the first lemma is directly contra-dicted (un-said) by the second and so forth, but it is in fact discernible in the *catuṣkoṭian* structure as a whole, where we find Nāgārjuna positing all four logically possible positions only to abjure them one and all.[95] In line with my overarching argument regarding the centrality of the abandonment of all views to Nāgārjuna's overall program, this last point reminds us that Nāgārjuna not only turns back to "unsay the previous saying" but to unsay *all* sayings. To push the metaphor a little further, if we can picture Nāgārjuna turning his back on one after another position, then we must try to imagine him ultimately turned away from all positionalities, oriented in no direction at all.

What "meaning event" comes of this? Well, as Mills eloquently states with regard to what he calls the "two phases" in Nāgārjuna's textual mode of argumentation (and which Sells would rightly identify as Buddhist instantiations of his two discursive moments of saying and unsaying), "Nāgārjuna transforms this uneasy dichotomy into a cohesive dialectical practice: he tries to show that the practice of analysis, when pursued all the way to the emptiness of emptiness, can be used as a means to the practice of making an assault on conceptualization itself" (Mills 2018b: 99). This means that, for Nāgārjuna, there is not so much a "semantic synthesis" as an "athesis"; the realization of what I have referred to earlier as "abelief" (see §3.6). This in turn entails that the "mystical union" Sells proposes as the experiential corollary of the mystic's discursive unsaying is in a sense inapplicable to the Buddhist Nāgārjuna, or rather applicable only with the crucial qualification that, in place of any God with which Sells's mystics may aspire to unity, the only locus of union for Nāgārjuna is *reality*.[96] Of course, this does not impinge on the attainment of a recognizably Sellsian form of agnosia on the part of the Buddhist, for not only is this precisely the epistemic state (or "state of no state") corollary to the doxastic abandonment of views (or "view of no view") encapsulated by the what I am calling abelief, but it also recalibrates and clarifies the discussion earlier of the Buddha's inherently paradoxical state of omniscience in the absence of conceptualization. More than this, however, Nāgārjuna's effective espousal of a form of "apophatic nonknowing" (Sells 1994: 213)[97] as the attainment of Buddhant *jñāna* in the realization of *nirvāṇa*, and indeed more generally his refusal to "solve" the "riddle" of transcendence, encompasses not merely a realm of discourse but no less than the entire ambit of view-holding and action-taking.

In fact, there is an important sense in which the postulation, in Nāgārjuna's texts, of what he or any other Mādhyamika would take to be a "wrong" view (such as, say, the espousal of *svabhāva*) differs qualitatively from the postulation of a "right" view (such as, say, the espousal of *śūnyatā*), and this has consequences for the sense in which, or extent to which, Sells's "languages of unsaying" model of discourse applies to Nāgārjuna. To bring out the relevant distinction, I will return momentarily to the analysis of views in early Buddhist texts undertaken by Paul Fuller to which I have already had recourse in the previous chapter. Here, however, I wish to tease out a slight slippage in Fuller's work between what it means to abandon *wrong* views and what it means to abandon them *all*.

Fuller stipulates that "It is not all views that should be abandoned, but all attachment to views," or (what is to say much the same thing) that "To abandon wrong-views, or all views, is to abandon attachment to doctrine, not doctrine itself" (Fuller 2005: 157, 159). Now, this is true (and true for Nāgārjuna's understanding as much as it is for the Pāli texts Fuller studies) insofar as views—all views—invariably and unavoidably enmesh one in attachment. In this sense, all views *are* wrong views: "Any position is an expression of attachment, an apperception (*saññā* [*saṃjñā*]), a mental object" (Fuller 2005: 146).[98] I have spent many pages of this book explicating Nāgārjuna's understanding on this, substantiating it with textual references and elaborating on its religiosophical implications.

But *śūnyatā* is not the same as *svabhāva*, and the relevant difference in this context is as follows. Whereas *svabhāva* is precisely a graspable object, its positing a position, *śūnyatā* is itself self-undermining, necessarily entailing the *śūnyatā* of *śūnyatā*, and thus (in this sense) *not* the positing of any position. Insofar as the Mādhyamika takes emptiness to be "right view" (*sammā-diṭṭhi*/*samyag-dṛṣṭi*), then, it "is 'right' because it *cannot* be grasped and it *cannot* be an object of attachment" (Fuller 2005: 156, emphases added).[99] Understood this way, emptiness is not only not a "thing" that can be grasped; in fact, it denotes the very absence of any such thing. It is precisely in this sense and for this reason that, taking *śūnyatā* as *samyag-dṛṣṭi*, emptiness as right view, "Attaining right-view *is* to relinquish all views" (Fuller 2005: 157, emphasis added).[100]

Crucially, on this understanding Nāgārjuna's call to abandon *all* views still holds. Not only that, but we come to see that to "hold" emptiness just is to hold no views. For understood in this way, the so-called view of emptiness simply "does not have the usual attributes of 'viewness', as the expression of some position" (Fuller 2005: 235 n. 15). It is the very *dharma*, and "The *dharma*, by definition, cannot be a view" (Fuller 2005: 143).[101] Emptiness (*śūnyatā*) is therefore not to be taken as a view (*dṛṣṭi*) at all: *śūnyatādṛṣṭi* here equivales *dṛṣṭiśūnyatā* and is thereby found to be beyond the purview of *sarvadṛṣṭi*. What cannot be held cannot be abandoned.

To understand Nāgārjuna's quintessential view/doctrine/position in this way is thus to understand it as utterly bereft of quintessentialization, as necessarily neither view nor doctrine nor position. The implication of this for Sells's discursive model is that the initial kataphatic moment of "saying" already *is* its own apophatic "unsaying." To "say" *śūnyatā* is already to "unsay" *śūnyatā*: emptiness empts itself.[102] It is inherently deinherentant, its averment is neither a positive statement nor a negative denial but itself already something of an *utterance*, though rather than being four-folded like the tetralemma it is as manifold as the world's phenomena. "*Sunyata* is not, therefore, Ultimate Reality; rather, it is an apophatic marker which denies the ultimate validity of all conceptual and discriminative views, whether they be affirmative or negative" (J. Williams 2000: 46).[103] As such, whereas Sells proposes a positive positing and its negating as both working together to forge an aporetic meaning event, if we understand Nāgārjuna's apparent affirmations of the doctrinal "position" of emptiness and its equivalents—what Muller or Mills would call his first discursive level or phase—as themselves signaling the denegation of positionality, then we find that this first ostensible affirmation already betokens negation. Perhaps still more radically, we must conclude that neither Nāgārjuna's ostensibly positive nor his ostensibly negative positings are to be taken as positings at all; that, therefore, his entire discursive endeavor is geared toward the dissolution of all putative "meaning events" as unfounded. For if, as Sells asserts, the "Meaning event indicates the moment when the meaning has become identical or fused with the act of predication" (Sells 1994: 9), and neither Nāgārjuna's so-called views (bereft as they are of viewness) nor obviously his unconditional abjurations of views can meaningfully count as "acts of predication," then Nāgārjuna is seen to have abandoned the search for "meaning" altogether. Having seen through it, as it were, he has seen the search for meaning as nothing more nor less than yet another manifestation of goal-oriented path-activity—indeed, perhaps the most stubbornly rooted of them all, yet ultimately eradicable nevertheless. Far from providing meaning, *nirvāṇa*, "the ultimate goal of Buddhist soteriology" (Collins 1998: 188), frees one from seeking to find it.

Concomitantly, this understanding modifies the sense in which *nirvāṇa* is "the moment of ending that gives structure to the whole" (Collins 2010: 113, cited in §5.2.3). For while *nirvāṇa* gives structure to the path in the sense that it fulfils the function of the path's teleological end, its actual attainment effects the undoing of structure, indeed of *archē* as a whole; the realization of its emptiness. Collins himself appears alive to this dual function of *nirvāṇa* as both structuring principle and principle of deconstruction. On the one hand, he "want[s] to see nirvana as having the syntactic value of a *closure-marker*, structurally and narratively" (Collins 1998: 189, emphasis added). On the other, however, in a passage highly evocative of Sells,[104] Collins states in the context of a discussion of *nirvāṇa* as *asaṃskṛta* ("the Unconditioned") that "This Unconditioned exists, semantically, in a relationship to what is said, as a silent, unsayable Unsaid, a moment in the dynamics of discourse. . . . Correspondingly, what is left when conditioned consciousness goes out of being is also Unsaid: Buddhist final salvation, one might say, is *open-ended*" (Collins 1998: 206, emphasis added). In this sense, then, *nirvāṇa* is not only "a silence in discourse that creates meaning as such" (Collins 1998: 283; see also Collins 2010: 186) but also (in the case of Nāgārjuna certainly) a silence that empts "meaning as such."[105]

This dual nature of Nāgārjuna's abelief, according to which his espousal of emptiness and his eschewal of views are seen as two paths along the same middle way,[106] also holds implications for how we understand the epistemic outcome of such wholescale abjuration of doxastic positionality. On this point, Mills states that he "part[s] ways with interpreters who claim that Nāgārjuna supports some sort of nonconceptual knowledge," for, he says, "While I agree with mystical interpreters that Nāgārjuna has no ultimate theories about philosophical matters, I disagree that there is some mystical insight intended to supplant such theories" (Mills 2018a: 64, 66 n. 1). However, if we combine my analysis earlier of the Buddha's "wisdom without dichotomizing conceptualization" (*nirvikalpajñāna*) with the interpretation of Nāgārjuna's "language of unsaying" I have just presented, we find that, much as Nāgārjuna's "views" are not to be taken as views, so the "knowledge" one attains in (not grasping but) realizing them, being non-conceptual, is not to be taken as knowledge—or certainly not in any ordinary sense. The "insight" such knowledge embodies does not "supplant" any theories by proffering its own; rather, as was made evident earlier, Buddhant *prajñā* is a form not of gnosis but of agnosia, where the former is taken to be necessarily contentful and the latter utterly contentless yet (or rather *therefore*) all-embracing. If *śūnyatādṛṣṭi* is equivalent to *dṛṣṭiśūnyatā*, the affirmation of emptiness the renunciation of view-holding, then what is attained in the epistemic attainment of emptiness is precisely that "knowledge" which is contained in "no theories." This, of course, is just another way of saying it is "silence," the very "nonconceptual knowledge" attained in *bodhi*.[107]

The upshot of this analysis is that, whether directly disavowing views or, as we may also put it, indirectly disavowing them in the avowal of their emptiness, Nāgārjuna makes abundantly clear that his words are not to be taken as objects of attachment. Of course, views—*all* views—inevitably *are* objects of attachment, which is why on Nāgārjuna's "view" what appears on the surface to be (and what standard ethical systems assume to be) a perfectly harmless activity—the holding of a view—turns out to lie at the very basis of suffering. One way to interpret the reason for this (alluded to in prior discussions) is that the holding of a view (and therefore the holding of an intention-cum-conceptualization) *orients* one. It is precisely what enables one to turn toward the world from a certain position, and in so doing it steers one toward a certain direction. It is thus not only that, for Nāgārjuna, "one's view of the nature of reality is a moral matter" (Garfield 2016: 90)[108]; it is that to *view* the nature of reality is already not to *realize* it as natureless.

More pertinently still in this context, to hold a view is to find oneself engaged in goal-oriented action: the very stuff of *karma*. Liberation, on the other hand, lies in leaving behind any and all such ineradicably suffersome intentional directedness. Let us recall to mind the discussion in the previous chapter of Nāgārjuna's renegation of goal-oriented charioteering (ineluctably desire-driven and so suffersome) in favor of "pointless" comegoing (as befitting the perfectly pacific Tathāgata). Given what I have referred to earlier as the ineliminable role intention (*cetanā*) plays in conditioning action (*karma*), we are arriving here at the realization that, for Nāgārjuna, "right action" (*samyak karmānta*) and "right view" (*samyag dṛṣṭi*) are mutually implicative. This is so in the sense that, on the one hand, all action is either "action-as-intention" (*cetanākarman*) or "action-consequent-upon-intention" (*cetayitvā karman*) (see MK:17:2–3 cited earlier), and on the other that all intention is already action.

What is more, on my understanding of Nāgārjuna, *karma* functions for him in an exactly analogous manner to views in that, just as in early Buddhism "The consequence of achieving right-view is that one does not hold *any* views. The aim of the path is the transcendence of all views" (Fuller 2005: 2, emphasis original), so too in Nāgārjuna the aim of the ethical path of perfection is the transcendence of all actions. Indeed, we find in what Fuller calls the "dilemma" (Fuller 2005: 1) at the heart of the study of *dṛṣṭi* a mirror-image of the kataphatic avowal and apophatic denial of difference between the *saṃsāric* and *nirvāṇic* realms I elaborated earlier. For as we saw in the previous chapter's discussion of views, there is what Fuller calls "the opposition understanding of views," according to which "The aim of the path is the cultivation of 'right-view' (*sammā-diṭṭhi* [Skt. *samyag-dṛṣṭi*]), and the abandoning of 'wrong-views' (*micchā-diṭṭhi* [*mithyā-dṛṣṭi*])," and there is contrariwise what he terms "the no-views understanding of views," according to which "The aim of the path is not the cultivation of right-view and the abandoning of wrong-views but the relinquishment of all views, wrong or right" (Fuller 2005: 1). We are now in place to see just how this relates to the eirenic pacification of action.

5.3.4. The Practice of Peace

Now, we have seen in quite some detail how the early Buddhist perspective Fuller details accords with, and doubtless informed, Nāgārjuna's views on views.[109] We find here, in the mirrored structure of *karma* and *dṛṣṭi*, action and view, an important linkage between Nāgārjuna's ethics (understood as that branch of his philosophy dealing with action and practice), epistemology (as dealing with belief and truth), and metaphysics (as dealing with conventional and ultimate reality). The nature of each of these, and thus the relationship among all of these, and thus (again) the nature of each of these, are, as we have seen and are seeing still, internally inextricably inter-related. They also differ significantly from their general manner of conception externally, be it individually or in their inter-relationality, in Western philosophy.

For what conventional Buddhist ethics calls "right action" thus turns out for Nāgārjuna to be no "action" at all. After all, right action is, in Nāgārjuna's thinking as in Buddhism generally, action that accords with reality, and if reality is seen to be empty of entities (as per Nāgārjuna's metaphysics), then right action will turn out to be action in accord with such emptiness. This means action undertaken not from the point of view of any subject, not directed toward any object, not governed by any belief, not aimed toward any end. Just as reality as such is suchness, so too such action as such must be "such-act." To act in this sense is not so much to "self-so" (action "self-so-ing"), as a strictly literal translation of the Chinese term *ziran* (自然) would have it, but simply to "so" ("so-ing").[110] Such action soes—and so sows no karmic seeds.

Indeed, just as we have previously seen that for Nāgārjuna logic, albeit useful to an extent, must ultimately be given up in the paralogical overcoming of *all* logically possible positions, and ontology be overcome in the anontological equation of emptiness with emptiness, so ethics—howsoever efficacious its formulations may be—must ultimately be sloughed off like any other conceptual attachment. In its place lies what I am calling eirenics: the practice of peace. Reserving now the term "practice" to designate just such soing, as opposed to *karma*-generating "action," I am led to conclude that Nāgārjuna's all-embracing emptiness entails just such practice of peace. "Peace" is to be understood here in a twin sense: as conditioning no violence, and as the (perfectly fluid) state of no-view. As we will soon see, these are not unrelated.

I have said that peace conditions no violence. By "condition" I mean both "to be the (precedent) condition of" and "to constitute or frame with conditions of being" (i.e., senses 4b and 5b of the verb "condition" in the *Oxford English Dictionary*). In one sense, then, I am effectively saying that peace cannot be the efficient cause of violence. In another, albeit related, sense I am claiming that peace is inimical to, irreconcilable with, violence. But what is violence? Most amply, violence is any action, and this includes any mental action. For action is that which generates *karma*, and as such is conditioned by ignorance, is not accordant with—violates—reality (*satya*). This may strike some readers as over-stating the ambit of violence, perhaps massively so; indeed, even to the point of meaninglessness. After all, if *all* action is violent, surely that renders "violence" meaningless? Yet such a criticism would be unmindful of the ambit of suffering announced by the Buddha in the very First Noble Truth, which is, precisely, universal: *saryaṃ duḥkhaṃ*.[111] All of *saṃsāra*, all conditioned existence, is unsatisfactory, sufferful, and it is so because it does not accord with the way reality really is. Conditioned existents posit *ātman* where there "is" *anātman*, *svabhāva* where there "is" *śūnyatā*.[112] Such fabrications (*saṃskāras*) of body, speech, and mind, born of ignorance (*moha*, *avidyā*) and the attachments (*rāga* and *dveṣa*) toward or away from putative objects it invariably entails, enact violence in that they violate truth/reality (*satya*). And all action, being prior to "the Peace which passeth understanding," enacts such violence; all action is karmically generative.[113]

I am therefore proposing a close—indeed, mutually defining—relationship between violence, suffering, and action. My justification for doing so rests on the analysis of non-*nirvāṇic* reality foundational to all Buddhist metaphysics as much as ethics: dependent co-origination/conditioned co-arising (*pratītya-samutpāda*), specifically with reference to the twelve links or *nidānas* causally constitutive of its maintenance. This analysis was, of course, instigated by the Buddha but, as should be becoming apparent, Nāgārjuna's ethics can be understood as a thoroughgoing thinking-through of the philosophical necessaries concomitant with such a vision given his own understanding of emptiness as the (natureless) nature of universal reality. The twelve links are, of course, well known, so there is no need to expound a particular vision of them here. What I wish to emphasize is the overall nature of this infrastructure of suffering codified in the wheel of conditioned co-arising. Its ambit is all conditioned existence, the entire realm of *saṃsāra*, and it shows just how this is characterized at all levels by suffering. At the first, instigative, link of the wheel lies ignorance. This is understood to be unknowing (*ajñāna*) of the nature of reality; that is, of reality seen as being conditionedly co-arisen. As Peter Harvey notes, "the first link can be seen, ironically, to be ignorance of this very principle" (Harvey 2013b: 51) of conditioned co-arising. This ignorance at the base of all suffering gives rise most immediately to *saṃskāras*: the constructing activities of body, speech, and mind. And as we have already noted, all such activities are karmically generative.

Now, since the ultimate aim of all Buddhist thought and action is to leave the realm of *saṃsāra* altogether, and since this is achieved through the unarising (*anutpāda*) and thence the cessation (*nirodha*) of karmically generative action (in a word, of *action*), *karma* is seen to have a dual nature. On the one hand, actions may be generative of positive or negative karmic consequences, to be auspicious (*punya*) and lovely (*kalyāṇa*) or inauspicious (*apunya*) and harmful (*pāpa*), or in other words to lead toward or away from liberation.[114] On the other hand, however, all *karma* is negative insofar as liberation is conceived as the cessation of all karmically generative activity, whether provisionally fruitful or harmful.[115] Although satiety may be achieved only through the consumption of sweet fruit, and not that of illness-inducing bitters, the ultimate aim is not fulness but emptiness. Or, to dispense with the metaphor, though karmically positive actions may bring one closer to the bliss of *nirvāṇa* while karmically negative actions lead one deeper into the mess of *saṃsāra*, the ultimate aim is the cessation of all karmically generative activity. Or, to put this yet another way, while "good" action furthers one along the path toward *nirvāṇa*, *nirvāṇa* itself is neither "good" nor "bad," but the transcendence of these and of all other categories and oppositions. *Karma* is thus seen to function at what may appropriately be called a conventional level and an ultimate meta-level. On the conventional level, we are enjoined to act in such a way as to merit "good" *karma* and to avoid acting in such a way as to deserve its "bad" analogue; ultimately, however, we are enjoined to dispense with (*karma*-generating) action altogether, on the understanding that the aim is the transcendence of the entire realm in which *karma* functions.

Karma itself thus turns out to be what the Mahāyānists would call an *upāya*; a skillful means that one should use to achieve an end concomitant with the abeyance of that means. The path of ethical progress is thus seen to be " 'the way leading to the stopping of karma', with the stopping of karma being 'that stopping of bodily action, verbal action and mental action by which one touches freedom' " (Harvey 2000: 44). In other words, action is to lead to the abandonment of action, its supplanting with what I have called "practice." This is so on the early Buddhist account of the wheel of dependent co-origination, and common to the analyses found in Nāgārjuna's texts. This is evinced, for example, by Nāgārjuna's reiterated (non-)qualifications of *nirvāṇa* and the Buddha as beyond any such dichotomies as karmic action requires,[116] or perhaps still more eloquently by his equating precisely "the cessation of action and defilement" with "liberation" and—importantly but unsurprisingly—his locating the cause by means of which action and defilement arise as "conceptualization." "But conceptualization is extinguished in emptiness."[117]

Practice is action that conditions no *karma*; as such, it embodies no violence and entails no suffering. And for Nāgārjuna, such peace as practiced by the inviolate Enlightened One goes hand in hand with peace as the (perfectly fluid) state of no-view, abelief.[118] For given that action conditions *karma*, and that *karma* is suffused with suffering, and that suffering is rooted in ignorance, and that ignorance informs views, and that views violate reality, and that reality is empty, and that the realization of emptiness brings about liberation, and that liberation releases from suffering . . . suffering—the fact founding Buddhism's First Noble Truth—is seen to cease with the abandonment of all views-cum-actions. We saw earlier that holding is tantamount to clinging; we see here that believing is tantamount to acting . . . and thus suffering. To put this another way, since Nāgārjuna's signature metaphysical insight—that emptiness embraces all—includes within its ambit the epistemic elements of views, beliefs, concepts . . . all those constructs with which we sentient beings structure our world, direct our propositional stance toward reality, imbue it with what we deem, in our misconceptions, to be its "logic," the metaphysico-epistemological realization of emptiness (both the realization that it *is* real and the realization of it *as* real) turns out to be an ineliminably ethical affair leading from action to practice, from suffering to peace, and culminating in the eirenic abandonment of ethics itself.

This also helps explain my fluid usage of "ethics" and "eirenics" throughout this chapter. At times I have spoken in quite conventionally unproblematic manner of the path toward *nirvāṇa* as an ethical one; a soterially motivated progress along definable stages toward an identifiable end. Analogously (but, I take it, more controversially), I have spoken of the eirenic abandonment of ethics itself (indeed, of action itself). It should be clear, I hope, that this and like phrases refer to the culminatory *nirvāṇic* post-state (post-non-state) characterized by (not characterized by) the practice of peace. But over and above these usages, which adhere to what is at bottom a binary model of path-ethics as distinguished from goal-eirenics, I have also spoken of Nāgārjuna's ethics *as* eirenics, or spoken not only of eirenics as the pacification of actions (the end as the ending of the path), but of eirenics as the *ethics* of the pacification of actions. This last way of phrasing the matter conceives the end *as* the path, the path *as* the end, and is therefore to be understood as referring to the ultimate undoing of the very distinction between ultimate and mundane, *nirvāṇic* and *saṃsāric*, in what may perhaps best be termed (though logicians will cavil) the attainment of non-attainment or the non-attainment of attainment.

The force of this understanding derives from the aporia I have identified earlier. According to this, the eu-topia of the path's end ending the path and the ou-topia of the entire path as its own endgoal turn out to be non-dual.[119] Here (nowhere, everywhere), the ultimate is nothing other than the perfectly ordinary, such that all telos-talk of the "farther" shore is silenced. Indeed, in the final analysis there is no shore at all, for we see here that to conceive of *saṃsāra* as a river to be crossed over to the shore of *nirvāṇa* is to engage in precisely the kind of dualistic thinking keeping one in (drowning one in) *saṃsāra* in the first place. Instead, *saṃsāra-nirvāṇa* is seen to be a single ocean, as boundless and bottomless as emptiness itself.

5.4. Abandoning All, Embracing All

I stated in the Introduction to this book that, if taken seriously, my interpretation of Nāgārjuna's ethics as eirenics undermines the very basis for prejudice, partisanship, and, more broadly, rigid adherence to any of the sectarian positions implicated in conflict on the individual, communal, or geopolitical levels. In these final pages of this final chapter, I will attempt to unpack just what that means in light of the foregoing analyses. In doing so, it behooves me to acknowledge that, whereas I have taken pains to remain within the bounds of Nāgārjuna's thoughts and formulations in the bulk of foregoing discussions (indeed, to reinstate these where I have seen them stretched or denatured), in what follows I self-consciously elaborate on his textual statements. In other words, in what follows I take Nāgārjuna in directions I understand to be not found within his verses themselves, even if I conceive them as concordant with him insofar as extrapolations from his work. Whereas I have often insisted on hewing strictly to Nāgārjuna's word, and whereas even the readings least directly tied to that word were proposed throughout this book as understandings of it, here I venture what is no longer so much an interpretation of Nāgārjuna at all as an amplification upon him.

The first point to reiterate is that the ultimate ethical aim, for Nāgārjuna as for all Mahāyāna Buddhists, is to eradicate all suffering of sentient beings. In what follows, I will propose that on Nāgārjuna's scheme the best means toward achieving this aim is to undertake what I will call *nonpathic caring practice* toward sentient beings. Such practice is best effected when based on empathic awareness and sympathic engagement with sentient beings. Such awareness and engagement are best attained in turn through realization of the emptiness of all beings, including sentient beings. Therefore, the ultimate ethical aim is best achieved through realization of the metaphysical truth of emptiness.

While my use of "practice" has been described earlier, "nonpathic" needs brief unpacking, in the course of which I trust that the rationale behind my use of "care," with its literal absence of "passion," to render *karuṇā* should also become clearer.[120] "Nonpathic" is to be understood as more or less equivalent to "apathetic" or "dispassionate," but the neologism is preferable on linguistic grounds—which, of course, are never far from philosophical entailments. The *Oxford English Dictionary* gives the primary definition of "apathy" to be "Freedom from, or insensibility to, suffering; hence, freedom from, or insensibility to, passion or feeling; passionless existence." Now, "freedom from suffering," and/as "freedom from passion," is surely as apt and succinct a definition of the overarching Buddhist ideal as can be. However, in an intriguing collocation of senses that says a great deal about Western philosophical conceptions stemming from the Stoics as to the (ideally absent) role of passion and emotion in virtuous action, this definition goes hand in hand with a series of inter-related connotations as far removed from at least Mahāyāna (if not altogether from pre-Mahāyāna) Buddhist ideals as can be. For "apathy" is also defined as "insensibility," which finds further elaboration in the term's secondary definition as "Indolence of mind, indifference to what is calculated to move the feelings, or to excite interest or action." The adjectival forms reinforce these latter senses, for "apathic" is defined as "Without sensation," and "apathetic" is initially defined somewhat uninformatively as 'Of, or pertaining to, apathy," but then further spelled out as "insensible to suffering or emotion generally; unemotional; indifferent to what is calculated to move the feelings or excite attention." Insensibility, indolence, indifference, inattentiveness: these are hardly the qualities of those (Buddhas and bodhisattvas) free from suffering and passion. Besides all this, the prefix "a" in "apathy" and related forms is privative, and surely the absence of suffering and passion should not be connoted as a privation.[121]

As for the other potential accepted alternative to "nonpathic," "dispassionate" is defined as "Free from the influence of passion or strong emotion; calm, composed, cool; impartial." Although the ideal Mahāyānist may well be characterized as free from the influence of passion, this does not mean that s/he lacks strong emotion, remains cool in the face of suffering, or impartial toward the plight of others. On the contrary, the development of the figure of the bodhisattva on the part of the early Mahāyāna movement may well be interpreted as a counter-reaction to what was perceived as an overly ataraxic conception of Buddhahood in terms of impassivity and indifference. The bodhisattva, one motivated to spurn final release from suffering for the sake of saving literally everyone else from it, is thus a deeply emotional figure; one, moreover, warm with care, ready for sacrifice, and constantly taking the part of, the side of, the suffering.[122] In this context, it merits mentioning that it is hardly historical accident that the most archetypal bodhisattva of them all was transfigured from being depicted in Indian pictorial and statuary form as a handsome male (whose name Avalokiteśvara, literally translatable as "lord looking down," may imply transcendent superiority) to being popularly depicted in East Asia in thousand-armed female form, ever at the ready to help the innumerable beings within her caring gaze (her name now being Guanyin 觀音 "hearer of cries," or more fully Guanshiyin 觀世音 "hearer of the world's cries"). East Asian stereotypes as to the attentive nurturance of the mother doubtless played a role in this transformation, which I note here only so as to press home my point that the bodhisattva is not impassive or indifferent, and therefore not best qualified by the term "dispassionate."[123] This is why I have preferred to coin "nonpathic" as a means of conveying the freedom from suffering in peace, action in practice, and passion in care, along with the simultaneous absence of impassivity and indifference characteristic of the bodhisattva.[124]

So what are we to make of such a bodhisattva, one who has consummated the ethical path in the eirenic pacification of action, nonpathically practicing care toward all, embracing them in full realization of their emptiness, aware of the multitude's infinite cries even as s/he ceives no subjects, holds no views? Well, without going into technical arguments as to whether or to what extent we can legitimately ascribe to this paragon of Nāgārjuna's Mahāyāna vision an "impartialist ethics" (Goodman 2017a), or whether Nāgārjuna's universalization of the Buddha's founding insight into *anātman* in the form of *śūnyatā* even rationally entails altruism (Williams 1998, Pettit 1999, Siderits 2000, Harris 2011),[125] I think it is safe to take the abandonment of all views Nāgārjuna sees as a necessary component of soterial fulfilment as a kind of "religious practice that contains neither beliefs nor propositional, nondoxastic faith" (Mills 2018b: 101). This means that the bodhisattva, so conceived, embodies what Mills calls "religiosity without belief" (Mills 2018b: 99–102; see also Mills 2018a: 39–41).

According to this account, Nāgārjuna "engages in philosophical destruction to bring about mental quietude, which is the absence of any faith or belief" (Mills 2018b: 99; see also Mills 2018a: 41). Crucially, this entails that Nāgārjuna—or Nāgārjuna's bodhisattva, the embodiment in this scheme of the successful accomplishment of this goal—holds no beliefs, including *Buddhist* beliefs.[126] Now, such a highly abstruse and religiosophically sophisticated—not to mention counterintuitive—notion, according to which the culmination of Nāgārjuna's Buddhist soterial path really lies in the abandonment of *all* views, even Buddhist ones, is, of course, liable to oversimplification and deformation, particularly in the hands of those inimical to Buddhism.[127] To explain these points further, I will draw here on Douglas Berger's study of what he calls "Nāgārjuna's Empty Ethics," in the course of which he proposes a thought-provoking conceptualization of *svabhāva* as "verbal and causal; it means to 'self-produce' or 'self-create', or to 'come about according to (one's) own principle' " (Berger 2007: 46). While Berger surely overshoots the mark in claiming that "There seem to be no good etymological or philosophical reasons" (Berger 2007: 45) for understanding *svabhāva* metaphysically in substantialist or essentialist terms, he is quite right to posit a sense of *svabhāva* with "palpable ethical relevance" (Berger 2007: 46). Indeed, taken in this sense we find that the metaphysical repudiation of *svabhāva* as "self-being" with which Nāgārjuna's philosophical project as a whole is most closely identified in fact has an ethical counterpart; a counterpart not any less important than the metaphysical but in fact constituting its soteriological end. For if we accept that "*Svabhāva* in both its metaphysical and ethical senses is much closer to 'autonomy', where that latter means 'to have one's own laws, principles, or norms', or to be a 'being from and unto oneself' " (Berger 2007: 46), then we see that Nāgārjuna's repudiation of views, as *svabhāvically* charged chains of *saṃsāra*, inaugurates precisely the freedom from enchainings of any sort characteristic of *nirvāṇa*.[128]

Where I would want to nuance Berger's discussion somewhat is in the explication of just what is meant by having 'one's own laws, principles, or norms', or "being from and unto oneself." For, of course, far from affirming some radically free "I" along Existentialist lines or in some or other forms of "First Person Realism" (Ganeri 2012: 312–317), there is no "oneself" here to which to refer or on which to ground "one's own" anything at all. Having abandoned all views, the single "law, principle, or norm" according to which one practices (not acts) is precisely the lack of any overarching "laws, principles, or norms" governing and orienting action. This is freedom: the Buddha's freedom to accord entirely with the law/principle/norm that is *dharma*, "the basis of things, the underlying nature of things, the way things are" (Gethin 1998: 35), where it is understood that on Nāgārjuna's *prāsaṅgic* analysis no "basis," "underlying nature," or "way" of things—indeed, no "things" at all—are to be found.

For his part, Berger proposes "a relational vision of interactional interdependence and mutual freedom" according to which "Nāgārjuna ends up . . . insisting in a very concrete way that injustice and justice, impurity and purity, unrighteousness and righteousness, exist only in co-productive relationship" (Berger 2007: 47, 52).[129] My earlier analysis of what I call the "relational co-dependency" of binary (or quaternary) opposite views (see §3.7) evinces my agreement with Berger's reading here, for there can be no doubt that ethical just as much as metaphysical positions entail and are entailed by their oppositions. But my own emphasis on the under-appreciated central role view-holding—and concomitantly view-abandonment—plays in Nāgārjuna's religiosophy leads me to take what I see to be a step further. This moves from the co-arising of "good" and "bad" to their overcoming/undermining in the abandonment of all and any such posits.

For the ethically meaningful distinction between "saying (no) evil" and "doing (no) evil" is, for one thing, a slippery slope. As Peter Harvey is unfortunately all-too-right to note, "Grasping at views can be seen to have led to religious and ideological wars (offensive or defensive), crusades, bloody revolutions, and gas chambers" (Harvey 2000: 240). Indeed, we find this understanding operative already in the earliest strata of Buddhist texts, as when, in the *Dīghanakha Sutta*, the Buddha works through all possible views as to "what is acceptable to me," and for each states that "If I obstinately adhere to my view . . . and declare 'Only this is true, anything else is wrong,' then I may clash with the two others . . . and when there is a clash, there are disputes; when there are disputes, there are quarrels; when there are quarrels, there is vexation" (Ñāṇamoli and Bodhi 1995: 604 (74.6)). Instead, in a passage directly anticipative of the kind of non-implicative negation (*prasajya-pratiṣedha*) Nāgārjuna will go on to employ to such devastating effect, the Buddha proposes that the sage "abandons that view and *does not take up some other view*" (Ñāṇamoli and Bodhi 1995: 604 (74.6), emphases added), concluding that "A bhikkhu [monk] whose mind is liberated thus . . . sides with none and disputes with none; he employs the speech currently used in the world without adhering to it" (Ñāṇamoli and Bodhi 1995: 606 (74.13)).[130]

But in a still deeper sense, and for Nāgārjuna certainly, views *are* acts, themselves already enactions of violence. Steven Collins proposes the equivalence in stating that "Just as the Buddha recommended non-violence (*ahiṃsā*) is the behavioural sphere, so too in the verbal," and citing in support a passage from the *Saṃyutta Nikāya* in which the Buddha advises:

> Those who take up a view and argue,
> saying 'only this is the truth!'
> to them say 'there is no-one here
> to oppose you in a war of words.'[131]

Nāgārjuna's point, as I see it, is to the effect that the holding of any view, any claim that "only this is the truth!," is not only mistaken, a de-realization of reality insofar as "there is no-one here to oppose you in a war of words" (both a reformulation of the *anātman* doctrine and a fore-formulation of VV:29—see §4.2) but, moreover, tantamount to engaging in conflict. Insofar as view-holding is ineliminably karmically charged, it is ethically significant; indeed, soteriologically deleterious.

The counter to this, as we have seen throughout this book, is not to hold (i.e., not to hold *onto*) any views, believe no beliefs. And as I am now proposing, just as emptiness itself does not lie beyond the ambit of emptiness, so Buddhist beliefs are themselves no exception to Nāgārjuna's call to complete abandonment. The ethical justification for this is first of all that since every belief embodies a position, and every position is an opposition, every belief involves its holder in an adversarial relation, and is therefore the cause of violence. This process we can all-too-easily see in the myriad ideological conflicts raging throughout our world, from full-scale wars and genocides, through the political playing-out of inter-communal prejudices and grudges, all the way down to the arguments and antagonisms besetting our individual lives.

Nāgārjuna's response, as we have seen, is to take recourse in what I have called abelief. This, as we have also seen, has two facets, since "believing" in emptiness is itself tantamount to reneging on doxastic positionality—belief—altogether, which is why emptiness can be understood as the kataphatic face of apophatic abandonment. As Robert McGuire rightly notes, "This is the crucial, and perhaps unforeseen, consequence of the universal truth of *śūnyatā* . . . For the Mādhyamika, there are no ultimately true propositions, and thus there is no core of ultimately true propositions at the heart of Buddhism. A Mādhyamika, therefore, cannot be seen to defend the ultimate truth of any Buddhist proposition" (McGuire 2017: 397, 398). Indeed, universally and for the same reasons, "a Mādhyamika cannot be seen to defend the truth, conventional or otherwise, of *any* proposition" (McGuire 2017: 398, emphasis added). The unavoidably adversarial nature of holding to certain views is evident already in the military metaphor of "defending the truth" here, as also more generally in our everyday talk of "offending others," or for that matter in philosophers' preoccupation with "winning" arguments (regarding which, see Stepien 2018b). In contradistinction to the causal role that belief plays in the enaction of not only such emotional or verbal but also physical violence, Nāgārjunian emptiness can be used to dissolve conflict at all levels. It can do so precisely because it is the ultimate "non-abrasive, or *frictionless*" truth (McGuire 2017: 393, emphasis original).[132] Itself empty, emptiness cannot be grasped; ungraspable, it cannot be held, or used to uphold a given view, let alone to enforce it.

This has far-reaching implications for Buddhist inter-religious relations. For whether the approach of a given religious adherent or proponent be exclusivist, inclusivist, or pluralist (as per the standard threefold typology), it is universally and naturally assumed that the adherent *adheres*; that is, that one is committed to one's own tradition, even if one is a self-confessed pluralist.[133] In fact, the point may be generalized further, for irrespective of one's own nominal religious identity (as a "Buddhist," say), the assumption is that one is committed to doxastic positionality *on one's own and others' parts*. Put another way, this means that the inter-religious encounter is always already oppositional. Even if s/he includes the other as a valid means toward attainment of what s/he believes to be the one true religion's end (the inclusivist approach), or accepts other religions as equally valid means toward equally valid ends (pluralism), the religious believer finds her or himself relating to other religious believers. Regardless of whether this relation be one of ecumenical dialogue, more or less respectful debate, or downright adversarial argument, Nāgārjuna shows us that it is rooted in a necessarily oppositional positionality; one utterly eradicated in abelief.

The radical reconceptualization of the very relation of oneself *vis-à-vis* one's other—religious or otherwise—that Nāgārjuna enjoins culminates in the wholescale deconstruction of "one" and "other." The metaphysical reality of *anātman*, universalized in *śūnyatā*, here finds its full ethical import. For far more than merely an "intellectual therapy leading to a peaceful state of mind" (Mills 2018b: 104), Nāgārjuna's "transcendence of views" in selfless emptiness is for him a necessary, albeit not sufficient, condition for the caring nonpathic practice toward all sentients that characterizes the core ethical aim of Mahāyāna doctrine. It is precisely in this sense that "The direct realization of emptiness . . . the 'actualization' of emptiness," understood in my own terms as the complete emptying of any thetic holding as/or karmic acting, "is the source of the bodhisattva's universal compassion [*karuṇā*: care]" (Huntington 1989: 59). Having emptied oneself of views, one no longer finds oneself positioned on any grounds to defend or from which to offend.

But more than just a *cause* of violence, view-holding itself *is* always already violent in that it inevitably violates the world by imposing its structures—its strictures—upon it. I have made this point earlier, but here, in viewing views *as* acts, we find perhaps the deepest reason behind Nāgārjuna's espousal of the abandonment of all views: to enact peace for all. Here we arrive at a sense of emptiness that not only functions as a source of care, but as its very enactment. One way in which Nāgārjunian emptiness has been interpreted along these lines is by understanding it as equivalent to dependent co-origination—a reading based above all on MK:24:18. Interpreted as "interbeing," the foundation for Engaged Buddhism (Hanh 1993), as "horizonless interrelatedness," enabling us to "let go of what should work to realize artlessly what does work" in ethical praxis (Hershock 2005: 68, 139),[134] or as "epectasic apophasis," permitting "participation in Buddha-nature itself as the activity of ceaseless practice" (J. Williams 2000: 188), emptiness enacted has understandably been the subject of much deliberation in efforts to unpack "The Connection Between Ontology and Ethics in Madhyamaka Thought" (Westerhoff 2016b). Now, Priest is right to assert that "the argument *simply* from interconnectedness fails. From the fact that a bunch of entities are interdependent, it in no way follows that each should look after the interests of the others" (Priest 2016: 229, emphasis original).[135] Nevertheless, as he goes on to observe, "the inter-being of people does indeed ground an important solidarity. In the end, my peace of mind cannot be divorced from that of those with whom I interact. Compassion is, indeed, the consequence of inter-being" (Priest 2016: 233). This is a vitally important ethical corollary of emptiness, but my own emphasis on the abandonment of views leads to a subtly different point.

Nāgārjuna accepts the pan-Buddhist account of action as karmically constitutive of suffering. For the Buddhist, action is our predicament, action enchains us. But right action unravels action, and action's undoing is our unchaining. What Nāgārjuna emphasizes is that this applies just as much to the mental sphere as it does to the verbal and bodily spheres, for all actions—including those of believing and conceiving as much as performing and perceiving—are intentional. In fact, Nāgārjuna's pronounced attentiveness to the crucial role the viewing, believing mind plays in grounding the attachment (*rāga*) and aversion (*dveṣa*) causative of all karmic action within beginningless ignorance (*avidyā*) testifies to his profound comprehension of the weight of this insight for the human condition. For the pride of place accorded to belief and related mental processes in Nāgārjuna's eirenics is only cemented by the singular role he sees them playing in keeping sentients such as us enmeshed in *saṃsāric* delusions and attachments. The ultimate import of viewing views as acts, then, lies not in any metaphysically situated universalization of *anātman* as *śūnyatā*, nor in an epistemologically oriented insistence on *karma* as *cetanā*. Rather, it lies in the ethical implications of belief-abandonment, in seeing abelief as eirenic.

For on my understanding of Nāgārjuna's overall program, the Buddha's *karma*-less action is precisely the bodhisattva's *karuṇā*-full action, where both embody what I have been calling practice: the enactment of emptiness as viewlessness. This I see as the final goal of Nāgārjuna's *prasaṅgic* clearing of views to the point of utter abandonment. Only one who has traversed the "infinite path of the bodhisattva" from beginning to end, a path "all 'middle' with no ends" (Hershock 2005: 162), is truly liberated from belief, and has thereby found eirenic freedom from the desire-driven directedness concomitant with it, the positionality of posits. Quite literally dis-oriented, attained to abelieving in the very realization of *bodhi*, such a practitioner is now Thus Comegone, one who meanders in nothing "other," nothing other than emptiness. As Nāgārjuna says in the concluding verse of his *Dispeller of Disputes*,

> For whom there is emptiness there are all things
> For whom there is no emptiness there is nothing at all[136]

In the final analysis, then, ultimate release from *saṃsāric* suffering, the aim of all Buddhist endeavor, is found in the *nirvāṇic* abandonment of all views, the grounds of all aims. Since for Nāgārjuna *dṛṣṭi* is *duḥkha*—belief suffering—*śūnyatā* is *śānta*, emptiness peace.[137]

Notes

Introduction

1. Ñāṇamoli and Bodhi 1995: 93. I have modified the translation slightly, most notably in rendering *diṭṭhi* (Skt. *dṛṣṭi*) as 'belief' rather than 'view' here so as to emphasize the broad ambit of doxastic positionality at large. For further discussion of *dṛṣṭi* as 'belief' or 'view', see Muller 2018: 364 cited in §4.3.2. While I am aware of the historically problematic nature of treating the *Discourses* of the Buddha—the *Sutta Piṭaka* of the Pāli canon—straightforwardly as the literal 'word of the Buddha' (*buddhavacana*), here and throughout I take it to be both historically the closest we are ever likely to get to that ideal of authenticity and literarily the functional equivalent thereof for the Buddhist traditions deriving therefrom.
2. This is from the *Dhammacakkappavattana Sutta / Dharmacakrapravartana Sūtra / Sūtra Setting in Motion the Wheel of the Dharma*.
3. Each of these terms admits of various English translations and has been the subject of much further exegesis and subcategorization by Buddhists and Buddhist scholars of various eras and areas, schools and sects. For an overview of the basic philosophical senses at work, see Harvey 2013a: 33.
4. Needless to say, over and above the Buddha's own multitudinous explications, this schema was elaborated in intricate detail and with differing emphases by various later Buddhist traditions of thought; I simplify here for ease of exposition.
5. For a thought-provoking but ultimately unconvincing argument to the effect that the original notion of dependent co-origination "is not an ontological teaching as such" relating to "the true nature of all phenomena" but rather "addresses the workings of the mind alone," see Shulman 2008: 299. For a reworking of this position, according to which "the category of dependent origination relates only to experience, not to the alleged external world" (473), see Jakubczak 2019: §1.5.
6. I coin 'soteries' here as the nominal form of the adjectival 'soterial', which I owe to Birgit Kellner as the term to be used "for cases where a notion is related to salvation (in Buddhist contexts: liberation) rather than to a theory or doctrine of salvation" (Kellner 2020: 39 fn. 2). Soteries is thus a notion pertaining to salvation/liberation.
7. My formulation here may appear to support a clear and qualitative binary opposition between conventional and ultimate, but though it may be inevitable at this introductory stage of exposition, such a reading would contradict Nāgārjuna's signature notion of the 'emptiness of emptiness' (*śūnyatāśūnyatā*), so I would ask the reader to withhold judgment until this topic is broached (in §3.3, and see also §3.4 and §3.5). For an excellent explanation of how "the Mādhyamika can have it both ways," denying "the intrinsic existence" of objects at the ultimate level and "giving up beliefs based on

perceptions that we earlier took to be veridical" at the conventional level, and doing so moreover without subscribing to an "appearance-reality distinction," see Westerhoff 2018b: 120.

8. MK:7:34. For further discussion and the original Sanskrit of this verse, see §4.3.4. Note that, here and throughout this book, I have dispensed with as much punctuation as possible in my translations of the MK in an effort to remain as close as possible to the original Sanskrit (which contains no punctuation). In particular, I have not end-stopped verses, preferring to use the line break itself as an effective semantic marker.
9. My reference is to Linji Yixuan 臨濟義玄 (d. 866), founder of one of the Five Houses (五家) of Chinese Chan 禪 Buddhism, and in particular to the following justly celebrated passage:

> On meeting a Buddha kill the Buddha, on meeting a patriarch kill the patriarch, on meeting an arhat kill the arhat, on meeting your parents kill your parents, on meeting your relatives kill your relatives, and you attain liberation. By not attaching to things, you freely pass through. 逢佛殺佛，逢祖殺組，逢羅漢殺羅漢，逢父母殺父母，逢親眷殺親眷，始得解脫，　不與物拘，透脫自在。(Sasaki and Kirchner 2009: 236, translation modified)

10. In introducing Nāgārjuna, I cannot but echo Westerhoff, whom I leave to expatiate in his own words:

> There is unanimous agreement that Nāgārjuna (ca 150–25 CE) is the most important Buddhist philosopher after the historical Buddha himself and one of the most original and influential thinkers in the history of Indian philosophy. His philosophy of the "middle way" (*madhyamaka*) based around the central notion of "emptiness" (*śūnyatā*) influenced the Indian philosophical debate for a thousand years after his death; with the spread of Buddhism to Tibet, China, Japan and other Asian countries the writings of Nāgārjuna became an indispensable point of reference for their own philosophical inquiries. A specific reading of Nāgārjuna's thought, called *Prāsaṅgika-Madhyamaka*, became the official philosophical position of Tibetan Buddhism which regards it as the pinnacle of philosophical sophistication up to the present day. (Westerhoff 2020: §0)

I would only note that the agreement is not quite unanimous (is any view?). Hayes, for example, claims that "Nāgārjuna's writings had relatively little effect on the course of subsequent Indian Buddhist philosophy. . . . Indian Buddhist intellectual life continued almost as if Nāgārjuna had never existed" (Hayes 1994: 299). Hayes may posit this to contrast more starkly with what he takes to be the inordinate attention paid to Nāgārjuna by modern scholars (or perhaps "he just wanted to make his paper more provocative at its outset"—Katsura 2023: 132), but he could not be more wrong.

11. If it is indeed true that "Buddhist studies was, for a long time, so cautious about the methods of analytic philosophy in general" (Tillemans 2016: 14), then it certainly proceeds with less caution now.
12. For a different but related critique—that of the racism I see at work in the continued exclusion of Buddhist and other non-Western philosophies from philosophical curricula—see Stepien 2022.

13. For further discussion and the original Sanskrit of this verse, see §2.2.
14. MK:26:12cd. For further discussion and the original Sanskrit of this verse, see §4.2.
15. The caveat regarding my own readerly horizons is to be stressed, as at no point do I wish the 'textual hermeneutic' element of my mandate to read Nāgārjuna to be misunderstood as implying I am somehow privy to any mysteriously privileged access—a point I elaborate further in §1.1 and §1.3. Without wishing to erase the significant methodological differences in our approaches, I propose that if Maria Heim may study one of the premier Pāli-language Buddhist philosophers "in the manner of an apprentice looking over Buddhaghosa's shoulder as he labors to create readers adequate to read him" (Heim 2018: 218), then perhaps I may be taken as adopting a like position regarding the Sanskrit-language Nāgārjuna. As for the term 'hermeneutical injustice', I use it here in a standard sense to more or less mean 'misinterpretation' or, more precisely, to designate a process whereby a reading proffered as textually justified or (more strongly) textually mandated in fact disaccords with the "principles for the retrieval of meaning" (Lopez 1988: 1) signaled by that text. In §1.4 I discuss how Miranda Fricker's notion of 'hermeneutical injustice' applies to the case of non-Western philosophy.
16. This is so despite Bernard Faure's cutting observation that "In its most academic aspects, philosophy is not so much a quest for truth as an esoteric literary genre" (Faure 2004: 26).
17. Thus, for example, Lindtner (1997: 354, n. 63) states that MK:18 is "the culmination" of the text; Garfield (among others: see Arnold 2005: 169) considers verse 24:18 to be "the climax of the entire text and [one that] can truly be said to contain the entire Mādhyamika system in embryo" (Garfield 1995: 304); while Dan Lusthaus considers verse 25:9 to be the climax of the text (Smith College 2010).
18. MK:0:1. For further discussion and the original Sanskrit of both verses 1 and 2, see §4.2.
19. Nance's article in fact itself opens with a discussion of Nāgārjuna's MK:0:1–2; see Nance 2020: 85.
20. Given their poeticity, I will, with a little license, occasionally refer in the following paragraphs to Nāgārjuna's work as 'poetry'.
21. The term 'litero-philosophy' I take from José Merquior, who uses it to denigrate "this tradition of philosophical glamour rather than rigour . . . Gallic philosophy in the twentieth century" (Merquior 1985:12, also cited in Stepien 2020c: 256 n. 31).
22. According to Collins, "there is universal scholarly consensus that the earliest phase of the Buddhist textual tradition was oral," and indeed, "despite the existence of written texts [from the first century BCE onward], the Buddhist tradition remained in various ways also an oral/aural one" (Collins 1992: 121).
23. My formulation is indebted to what Janet Gyatso refers to as "anthropological analyses of the embodiment of social memory in cultural processes, material media, and places, in which the emphasis is put upon the performative function of memory in the present, rather than on the mental storage or representation of past events" (Gyatso 1992b: 2). Gyatso's edited volume (1992a) remains the most sustained study

of Buddhist notions and practices of memory; for a more recent study of related Buddhist notions "in the light of some of the contemporary psychological and neuro-psychological theories and models of memory," see Ruseva 2015.

24. The enhanced oral/aural aspect of poetic texts *vis-à-vis* their prose cousins renders Steven Collins's perceptive observation of a "sensual dimension" to the lived experience of the Pāli scriptures among adepts all the more applicable to Mahāyāna verse texts such as the MK; see Collins 1992: 129.
25. Coward is drawing on Kitagawa 1979 and speaking in the first instance of the purposes and effects of the "remembered words" of the Buddha himself, though he goes on to suggest that ritual chanting in unison among Tibetan Buddhist monks "seems to evoke overtones of the interdependence of the universe—the point of the Buddha's enlightenment experience." Whatever one may make of this final phrase, any doubts as to the perceived sacrality of Nāgārjuna among later Buddhists should be dispelled by Young 2015 (see in particular his chapter 4 on "Nāgārjuna Divine and the Alchemy of Hagiography").
26. It should be mentioned that rhyme (or at least end-rhyme) is almost completely absent from Sanskrit poetry, including Nāgārjuna's, though metric rhythm is omnipresent.
27. In referring to Lakoff and Johnson's work on *The Embodied Mind and Its Challenge to Western Thought*, I am not claiming that Nāgārjuna's is "an empirically responsible philosophy" (Lakoff and Johnson 1999: 3) in the sense they intend. But insofar as it does in fact chime with their "Conception of an Embodied Person" (Lakoff and Johnson 1999: 555–557) in a manner and to an extent unmatched, broadly speaking, by "The Traditional Western Conception of the Person" (Lakoff and Johnson 1999: 553–555) as they describe it, I do perceive important and interesting—yet hitherto unstudied—means whereby Nāgārjuna's Buddhist philosophy could be applied to Lakoff and Johnson's project in a manner that for congruent reasons likewise "require[s] our [Western] culture to abandon some of its deepest philosophical assumptions" (Lakoff and Johnson 1999: 3). After all, in the words of Bibhuti Yadav, not only is it that "What the Buddha requests is to see that there is no such thing as disembodied thinking, and that the metaphysician, too, lives in the world as an embodied subject" but, in distinctly Nāgārjunian terms, "The metaphysician's claim that knowledge is objective insofar as it corresponds with reality is because of his forgetfulness that he has wishfully carved something and then posited it as an independent reality. This forgetfulness is called *dṛṣṭi*" (Yadav 1977: 465, 466).
28. I am not going to get into a discussion of the question of disembodied consciousness, be it (dubiously) in advanced meditative states in this world or (mythically) among other-worldly practitioners ensconced in the various realms of the 'form-world' (*rūpa-dhātu*) or 'formless world' (*arūpa-dhātu*) postulated by Buddhist cosmology. Suffice to say that I take Nāgārjuna's texts to have been directed toward human readers of the sensorial 'desire realm' (*kāma-dhātu*).
29. My reference here is to MK:24:18; for discussion, translation, and the original Sanskrit of this verse, see §4.2. It should be clear that I understand Nāgārjuna to be using the concept of *pratītya-samutpāda* in a manner that goes beyond its meaning in early

Buddhism (on which see Schmithausen 1997: 12-14, 52-59, echoed in Schmithausen 2000: 63-65; I owe the references to MacDonald 2015a II: 23 n. 61).

30. After all, Marshall McLuhan's celebrated phrase "the medium is the message" was coined all the way back in 1964 (see McLuhan 1964).
31. I critique such measures at length in Chapter 1. Perhaps a differentiation is called for here between 'Western' and 'Westernized', but for present purposes the former rubric should be taken to include forms of philosophizing not geographically originating in the West but whose contemporary norms evince deferential privileging of identifiably Western models.
32. This is not the case in the Chinese commentarial tradition. Following Jizang's lead, this makes "a distinction between the chapters 1–25 (considered as concerning Mahāyāna) from the chapters 26–27 (regarded as related to Hīnayāna)" (Travagnin 2009: 254; cf. Travagnin 2012: 256). I see this distinction as irrelevant to my concerns here, however, as it is based on a doxographical system historically subsequent to Nāgārjuna; one whose sectarian divisions, moreover, are but dubiously applicable to the conceptual content of the MK itself. Noteworthy in any case is the partition of the final portion of the text, including the concluding espousal of the abandonment of all views, into a distinct categorial space both here and in the alternative classificatory scheme proposed by Yinshun (see Yinshun 2000: 45–46 for the original Chinese-language table and Travagnin 2009: 259/2012: 270 for a translation thereof).
33. Pl. *Jestem przekonany, iż w szczególności w przypadku filozofii madhjamaki wiele problemów związanych z logiczną stroną myśli nagardżuny da się rozwiązać właśnie poprzez uwzględnienie. . . struktury narracyjnej jego tekstów*. Jakubczak's statement is made in the context of his lament on the same page that, in the study of Nāgārjuna, analysis of text-structural features "for a long time remained underestimated, or was perhaps grasped one-sidedly; that is, the importance of formal-logical research was emphasized, completely underestimating the importance of the analysis of the narrative structure" (*przez długi okres pozostawał niedoceniany, ewentualnie ujmowany był jednostronnie, to znaczy podkreślano doniosłość badań formalno-logicznych, całkowicie nie doceniając wagi analizy struktury narracyjnej*).
34. One page earlier Garfield makes clear that he sees his "own division, like these others [he mentions; i.e., Tsong Khapa's and Kaluphana's] simply as a useful heuristic device for parsing the argument" (Garfield 1995: 90 fn. 8).
35. It should be noted that the arrangement into chapters of the MK as a whole is due not to Nāgārjuna but to Candrakīrti.
36. For reference, Kalupahana 1986: 26–31 divides the MK into chapters 1–2 on causation and change, 3–15 on "the non-substantiality of phenomena (*dharma nairātmya*)," 16–26 on "the non-substantiality of the individual (*pudgala-nairātmya*)," and 27. While voicing several disagreements with Kalupahana, Salvini nonetheless likewise argues, based on Sanskritic sources, for a conceptually motivated structural division between the MK's conclusion (on Salvini's reading comprising chapters 26 and 27) and the entire preceding text; see Salvini 2011: 72 n. 19, and 77–80 for an analysis of the structure of MK:27.

37. Note also that I refrain from using the term 'opponent' to designate Nāgārjuna's supposed interlocutors, as this would be to class Nāgārjuna as a proponent of a position opposed to that of his opponent, and thus to place his *prasaṅgic* critique on a par with (other) metaphysical systems. More will be said in this regard in Chapter 4 especially.
38. For discussion of 'The Exhaustive Tetralemma', see §3.2.
39. For further discussion and the original Sanskrit of both these verses, see §4.2.
40. MK:5:7cd: "Like space / Are the other five elements." Skt. *ākāśasamā dhātavaḥ pañca ye pare.*
41. MK:10:15: *agnīndhanābhyāṃ vyākhyāta ātmopādānayoḥ kramaḥ / sarvo niravaśeṣeṇa sārdhaṃ ghaṭapaṭādibhiḥ*. The phrase translated as "All ways without exceptions" is *sarvo niravaśeṣeṇa*. As for the pot and cloth etc., these are "other stock examples . . . [of purported] asymmetrical dependence relations between inherently existent bases and the properties they support. Nāgārjuna is simply asserting the complete generality of his argument" (Garfield 1995: 195).
42. See, e.g., the discussion of MK:22:11 in §3.4 and §4.2. For 'tetrāletheia', see §3.3.
43. The absence of a "master argument" is also noted by Siderits and Katsura, who state that "Nāgārjuna's strategy is instead to examine a variety of claims made by those who take there to be ultimately real entities and seek to show of each such claim that it cannot be true" (Siderits and Katsura 2013: 7). That said, as I will go on to argue in §4.3, the only way that we can legitimately admit that the Madhyamaka method "relies essentially on specific theories that postulate or imply *svabhāva*" (Westerhoff 2016a: 372) or is "based on claims about the ultimate natures of things" (Siderits and Katsura 2013: 7) is by seeing that, for a Mādhyamika of Nāgārjuna's stripe, this constitutes no circumscription at all, for *all* theories/positions/views in fact 'postulate or imply *svabhāva*' and thus, in this sense, are 'about the ultimate natures of things'.
44. Another way of making the same point is to say that "Arguably, doing otherwise, that is, presenting baldly a master argument of his own, would be to engage in the same philosophical debate and thesis formulation he [Nāgārjuna] seeks to reject" (Tillemans 2017: 114). This explains why, though Oetke is right to emphasize that "A careful scrutiny of the [MK] reveals . . . that the different alternatives envisaged in pieces of reasoning cover or are presumably intended to cover all *conceivable* possibilities which can be implied by a tenet to be refuted" (Oetke 2015: 230, emphasis original; cf. Oetke 2015: 236), his criticism of Siderits and Katsura's underlining Nāgārjuna's interlocutor-specific method is misplaced.
45. To elucidate my own reading of Nāgārjuna as abandoning not only epistemological views but all, I have elided Mills's overt references to epistemology in the passage cited. I discuss Mills's theory in more detail in Chapters 4 and 5.
46. The 'vehicles', 'means', or 'tools' Nāgārjuna used (depending on one's pick of metaphor for *upāya*) are as heterogenous as those he used them *on*—and necessarily so if they are to prove apagogically effective (where the apagoge is taken to demonstrate the absurdity of a given position without for all that affirming its contrary). Thus, for example, Siderits and Katsura list 'Infinite Regress', 'Neither Identical Nor Distinct', 'The Three Times', 'Irreflexivity', and 'Nonreciprocity' among the "common patterns

of reasoning in his refutations" (Siderits and Katsura 2013: 7–9; cf. Oetke 2015: 236–239), while Mills notes that

> More fine-tuned instruments in Nāgārjuna's argumentative tool box include demonstrating that an opponent's thesis implies an infinite regress (*anavasthā*), circularity (*cakraka*), or mutual dependence (*anyonāśraya*), or—even worse—that it should be accepted with no cause (*ahetu*) or for no reason at all (*akasmāt*). All of these are often embedded within a larger *prasaṅga* structure and applied to specific options. (Mills 2018a: 53)

As Mills goes on immediately to underline, "it should be noted that these are problems for Nāgārjuna's opponent. They do not imply the acceptance of any particular theory on Nāgārjuna's part." In passing, it is worth noting that this explains why Betty's applying the same "criteria . . . that Nāgārjuna puts in the mouth of his imaginary opponent in the *Kārikās*" to assert "I see no way of salvaging the *Kārikās* from the scourge of their own conclusions" (Betty 1983: 124, 126) is misguided. As I will go on to argue at length, Nāgārjuna's use of a given argumentative tool in service of undermining a given position does not entail his asseveration of that tool, or for that matter his adherence to a given counter-position.

47. MK:22:15c; for discussion and the original Sanskrit of this verse, see §4.2.
48. VV:29; for further discussion and the original Sanskrit of this verse, see §4.2 and §4.3.
49. Given the centrality of the Naiyāyika schema to the practice of philosophy throughout classical India, it is only natural that this should not be the only occasion on which Nāgārjuna expends his energies in its refutation. As Westerhoff notes, "Nāgārjuna's aim in the VP [*Vaidalyaprakaraṇa*] seems very clear: it is to refute the sixteen Nyāya categories" (Westerhoff 2018b: 10) underlying epistemology, logic, and rational debate.
50. Kantor is thus perfectly right to deem that "the whole text of the *Vigrahavyāvartanī* (*Huizheng lun* 迴諍論) consists of Nāgārjuna's invalidating the objections and arguments of his opponents," but only right in stating that this "serves the purpose of strengthening and revealing his own view" (Kantor 2014: 344 fn. 10) if we stretch the interpretation of the latter to designate the abandonment of views *in toto*.
51. For further discussion of Murti's reading, see §4.3.
52. Westerhoff claims that "It was Nāgārjuna's aim to provide a set of arguments in support of the claims of the Perfection of Wisdom [i.e., Prajñāpāramitā] *sūtras*, to explicate their contents, and to demonstrate their philosophical feasibility" (Westerhoff 2018a: 93, and see also 105). This is a strong claim. Irrespective of whether the historical record justifies it or not, what I would emphasize is that, to the extent that Nāgārjuna's aim may indeed be accounted "to provide a set of arguments in support of" Prajñāpāramitā tenets, this is so only to the extent that those tenets are themselves, like Nāgārjunian emptiness, self-abrogating.
53. The following passage draws on and significantly expands on my brief explanation of 'Christianate' philosophy in Stepien 2021b: 2.
54. In any case, 'Buddhate' is to be distinguished from 'Buddhological', which I use here in a general sense to mean 'of or relating to scholarship of or relating to Buddhism'. It

is to be noted, however, that 'Buddhology' is also and indeed more typically used in a narrower sense to refer to a specifically philological scholarly approach to Buddhism, as opposed to 'Buddhist studies', which in this usage refers to a religious studies scholarly approach to Buddhism. I will touch again on this distinction later (see §0.4).

55. I will go on to discuss the religious/religionate dichotomy in greater detail when discussing religious studies in §0.3.2.

56. It is perhaps worth noting that the apologetic attempts to render Nāgārjuna's philosophy acceptable to contemporary Western philosophers I describe and criticize most directly in Chapter 1 are neither Buddhist nor Buddhate; on the contrary, they are typically attempts by non-Buddhists to assimilate Buddhist philosophy to Christianate paradigms. While I will go on to criticize the assimilation, I should note that there is, of course, nothing in the least wrong with the non-Buddhist identity of (some, many, even all) relevant scholars; indeed,

> the Buddhologist *qua* Buddhologist cannot be a religious enthusiast, proselytiser, or even, one might go so far as to say, Buddhist. The set of attitudes that a Buddhist usually has towards the texts of his tradition are quite different from, and to a large extent incompatible with, those that a Buddhologist should have towards the text he is studying. . . . This is not to say, of course, that no Buddhologist can also be a Buddhist, but only that any who claim to wear both hats—and many do—must be very careful to separate in their minds and their teachings the different functions of Buddhist and Buddhologist. To confuse the two is simply bad scholarly method. (Griffiths 1981: 21, 22)

The (distinctly messy, and rightly so) distinction between Buddhists and non-Buddhist scholars of Buddhism is one I come back to in §1.3.

57. Some readers may object to my inclusion of Kant in this list. Now, I am certainly not about to launch into a full-scale argument as to the central place of Christianity in Kant's thought, so suffice it for present purposes for me merely to echo Pasternack and Fugate in noting that throughout Kant's works we find "clearly affirmative" and "detailed treatments of biblical hermeneutics, miracles, revelation, as well as many distinctively Christian doctrines such as Original Sin, the Incarnation, Vicarious Atonement, and the Trinity"; that in addition "we find powerful defenses of religious belief in all three Critiques . . . [and] a considerable share of Kant's work in the 1790s is also devoted to the positive side of his philosophy of religion"; that, moreover, "the many positive elements of Kant's philosophy of religion have been eclipsed by its initial negative moments, moments not meant to oppose religion, but rather reflective of the Lutheranism (or more precisely, the anti-liturgical Lutheran Pietism) of his youth"; and in general that "One must, therefore, understand the negative elements in his philosophy of religion, such as his infamous objections to the traditional proofs for God's existence, in this context . . . [wherein] a central goal of the Critical project is to establish the limits to knowledge 'in order to make room for faith'" (Pasternack and Fugate 2020: §1).

58. My position here is not to be confounded with the famous statement by Levinas that "Europe is the Bible and the Greeks" (Levinas 2001: 137). While rhetorically powerful,

this is obviously a reductive view given that 'Europe' (whatever *that* is) is surely much else besides. What I am getting at is the dual influence on philosophy specifically.

59. See, for example, Nicholas Jolley's article on "The Relation Between Theology and Philosophy," which begins with a reference to Paul's warning against "philosophy and vain deceit" and goes on to discuss thinkers on the topic as disparate as Ambrosius Victor, Anselm, Aquinas, Arnauld, Augustine, Boyle, Clement of Alexandria, Des Bosses, Descartes, Desgabets, Gassendi, Glanvill, Hobbes, Huet, Jurieu, Leibniz, Locke, Malebranche, Mersenne, Mesland, More, Newton, Pascal, Rohault, Spinoza, and William of Ockham, among many others whose names could be added to this list. Unsurprisingly, Jolley sums up the entire discussion by stating—with remarkable understatement—that "The Christian tradition was thus marked by competing conceptions of the relation between philosophy and theology" (Jolley 2000: 364). Murray and Rea's more recent introduction to "Philosophy and Christian Theology" makes much the same point in livelier terms: "In the history of Christian theology, philosophy has sometimes been seen as a natural complement to theological reflection, whereas at other times practitioners of the two disciplines have regarded each other as mortal enemies" (Murray and Rea 2000: §1).
60. See, for example, Hastings Rashdall's claim from over a century ago, which acknowledges an overlap in subject matter between philosophy and theology (an overlap far larger than most contemporary philosophers would be content to admit), but which nevertheless seeks to carve out a distinctly philosophical approach to it:

    > Philosophy is largely occupied, indeed, with the same subject-matter as theology. It discusses the nature of the universe at large, the nature of God and His relation to the world, the nature of the human soul and its relation to God. All these things are also dealt with by theology. But philosophy investigates these things without presuppositions or assumptions . . . its methods are the methods of reason and not those of authority. (Rashdall 1920: 196)

    As if any human science can be "without presuppositions or assumptions"!

61. For relevant sources of this view and discussion of a Buddhist alternative, see Stepien 2018b.
62. Recall in this light Hodgson's definition of 'Islamicate' cited earlier, according to which it refers not to the religion itself, "but to the social and cultural complex historically associated with Islam . . . even when found among non-Muslims" (Hodgson 1974: 59).
63. As Brent Nongbri points out, "Many scholars have acknowledged that Christian assumptions have been a part of most definitions of religion" (Nongbri 2013: 154). He then goes on to characterize as "misguided" efforts to redefine 'religion' on the basis of "a widespread conviction that the history of religious studies has brought about a progressive purging of those Christian assumptions such that religion has become a more and more universally valid descriptive category" (Nongbri 2013: 154).
64. In tracing the foundational role of philology in *The Invention of World Religions* (and their study), Tomoko Masuzawa emphasizes that "the historical, empirical, and scientific study of languages—as philology was and has since been understood to

be—opened a new avenue to explore and to scrutinize *Europeans' own* past and future destiny" (Masuzawa 2005: 151, emphases added). Meanwhile, in tracing the role of anthropologically "Close Encounters of Diverse Kinds" in the eventual formation of the field (and beyond), Jonathan Z. Smith observes that

> Adopting the archaic Christian apologetic language for the relations of Christianity to classical culture, a notion of anthropologically significant survivals was developed in which the Christian scholar sought "seeds," "sparks," "traces," "footprints," "remains," or "shadows" of the original, essential unity of humankind amidst its palpable, contemporary diversity, and through which one could discern placement and reconstruct historical relations. (Smith 2004: 309)

As is to be expected, the scholarly literature on these topics is vast, so I hope to be forgiven for adducing these citations as exemplary without engaging in the endless and in any case peripheral task (to my agenda) of multiplying them.

65. The pursuit of transparency obliges me to note that, in the passage quoted, Smith is in fact *not* explaining 'such a claimed liberation' in terms of its illusory nature *per se* but in terms of what he calls "a more fundamental issue . . . between an understanding of religion based on *presence* and one based on *representation*" (Smith 2004: 363, emphases original). That argument is tangential to mine here, and in any case does not vitiate Smith's characterization of the discipline's liberation from theology as an illusion, so I hope my co-opting Smith in this manner does not ruffle too many methodological feathers.
66. Lincoln may overstate the role of the AAR in fashioning the field as a whole, not least in claiming somewhat simplistically that when "a discipline of religious studies took shape . . . it occurred not in Europe . . . but in the United States," and he surely indulges in some unwarranted essentialization in declaring that in the United States "attitudes toward religion consistently were—and remain—kinder, gentler, more cautious, and more reverent" (Lincoln 2012: 132), but none of this invalidates the genealogical point as to the avowedly Biblical agenda of the AAR at its outset.
67. Masuzawa notes that the AAR is "by far the largest association of religion scholars in the world," and so the religious stance of its membership is proportionately influential on the field globally, but I would not hesitate to apply her observation to other such professional organizations elsewhere.
68. Examples abound, but I will content myself with citing one each from the structural-institutional and conceptual-hermeneutic arenas. With regard to the former, a recent AAR Presidential Address notes that "The non-Christian portion of the AAR program"—that is, the portion concerned with the entirety of all religions save Christianity—still averages only "about 20 percent of the program" (Cabezón 2021: 808). To put this another way: at "the world's largest gathering of those interested in the study of religion" (American Academy of Religion 2021), there are, to this day, *four times* as many papers devoted to Christianity than to all other religions combined. As for the conceptual pervasiveness of Christianity, I cite Jonathan Z. Smith's "experience as general editor, on behalf of the American Academy of Religion, of the *HarperCollins Dictionary of Religion*" (Smith 2004: 163). Whereas

Smith finds that "other 'world religions' devote considerable space in their introductory essays to issues of definition and classification," this contrasts with "the persistence of an easy, unarticulated assumption of the universality of Christianity" (Smith 2004: 169). Smith elucidates that "As general editor I had to insert the adjective 'Christian' into the defining sentence fragment of the majority of the Christian entries. Articles in no other area presented that editorial problem" (Smith 2004: 169). Could any clearer mark of the continued centrality of Christianity in the mental world of scholars of religion be found than such singular unselfconscious *un*marking of this single tradition?

69. "In sociological studies, past and present, religion most often refers to Christianity, and, more specifically, to a narrow range of Christian forms practiced in the United States over the last few centuries" (Cadge, Levitt, and Smilde 2011: 440).
70. I owe the reference to Marcotte 2010: 27.
71. For Hodgson's original formulations, see §0.3.1.
72. That said, naturally I would caution against simply applying the paradigms regnant within the social and cultural complex historically associated with whichever 'other' religion a given scholar happens to (intellectually) reside within to whichever religious data they happen to study. Increasing diversity is well and good, but multiplying prejudices is hardly likely to enrich the field.
73. To my catalogue of exceptions (Stepien 2020b: 16–17, n. 6) should now be added Burley 2020 and Loewen and Rostalska 2023.
74. For a different but related point, see also Masuzawa's conclusion that "Islam was problematic in a way that the status of Buddhism, apparently, was not" insofar as the latter, unlike the former, was unproblematically classed as "a world religion alongside Christianity" (Masuzawa 2005: 120) during the formative period of the 'world religions' paradigm.
75. Nongbri points out that "Such a definition might be seen as crass, simplistic, ethnocentric, Christianocentric, and even a bit flippant; it is all these things, but it is also highly accurate in reflecting the uses of the term in modern languages" (Nongbri 2013: 18).
76. As Ganeri forcefully asserts, "The colonial power had philosophy, the rest of the world has only what was described as 'culture' or, more condescendingly still, 'wisdom tradition'" (Ganeri 2016a: 136). For a critique of the double standards involved in excluding Buddhism from the realm of philosophy on account of its religious nature, but willingness to forgive—or deny—the religious nature of the history of Western philosophy, see Stepien 2022, where I also discuss the 'wisdom tradition' claim on pp. 1072, 1075, 1082 n. 23, and 1083 n. 36. For related discussions, see especially Huntington 2019, Kantor 2019a, Stepien 2019b, and Ziporyn 2019a among the contributions to Stepien 2019a.
77. "Thinking they were talking about the Buddha, Westerners were talking about themselves" (Droit 2003: 21).
78. For an extended argument for the view that "religious belief is the most powerful and influential belief in the world . . . [one having] the single most decisive influence on everyone's understanding of the major issues of life ranging across the entire spectrum

of human experience . . . [and] exercise[ing] such influence upon all people independently of their conscious acceptance or rejection of the religious traditions with which they are acquainted," see Clouser 2005: 1. My own point here is not to be confused with this far more general and theoretical view. I make no claim concerning the power or influence of religious belief *per se*, but instead make what is a purely historical observation to the effect that Christianity has (contingently, but no less effectively for that) shaped the contours by which philosophy and the study of religion have been undertaken unto today in the West. Since these Western forms have exerted disproportionate influence upon the professional practice of philosophy and the study of religion in the rest of the world, my argument may be extrapolated to those other contexts too *mutatis mutandis*, but that is matter beyond my present remit.

79. For an extended discussion of the inadequacy of rigidly disciplinary approaches to the study of religion, see Stepien 2023c. For explanatory and descriptive reductionism, see my discussion of Proudfoot 1985 in §1.4.
80. An online search reveals a few (more or less dodgy) websites and blogs using it, one scholarly discussion of it "to reflect the apparent perennialist loadings [sic? leanings?] in Eliade's thought" (Ryba 1993: 18 n. 9), plus one use of it as an English translation of the Chinese collocation 宗教哲学 (Lü 2016).
81. I will return to and elaborate on this point in §1.4.
82. As Garfield laments, "European philosophy is just 'philosophy', the unmarked, privileged case, the 'core' as it is sometimes put" (Garfield 2015: ix). That 'philosophy' remains tantamount to 'Western philosophy' is also eloquently evinced by the recent launch of a "Buddhist Philosophy for Philosophers" series at Oxford University Press. To adapt what I said earlier about religion and Christianity, such singular unselfconscious *un*marking of this single tradition, whose practitioners are simply "Philosophers," reveals the sheer centrality of Western philosophy in the mental world of professional philosophers—in this case, strikingly, even among those committed to Buddhist philosophy.
83. Griffiths memorably dubs Buddhist Hybrid English "a bastardized form of the English language, so hag-ridden by Sanskrit syntax that almost every sentence is constructed in the passive, every technical term is translated by a series of hyphenated polysyllables, and the ideal of writing clear, precise, and elegant English hardly even comes to the conscious awareness of the translator" (Griffiths 1981: 24). He is referring directly to English-language translations of Sanskrit-language Buddhist texts, so, fortunately for me, I do not see his criticisms as applicable here insofar as this book is not a translation, and all the less so since I see my own task as consonant with Griffith's dictum to the effect that "philological expertise must be properly employed in the task of interpreting the sources and making them available for others; that is to say, philology must be properly related to hermeneutics" (Griffiths 1981: 30).
84. I thus echo Waldo in claiming that "Ordinary English terms like 'cause' and 'entity' have for us semiconscious connotations of empiricist logical geography that are far from parallel to those worked up by Buddhist philosophy from 'ordinary Sanskrit'" (Waldo 1975: 281).

85. For a related discussion of the traitorousness of translating "Nāgārjuna's Sanskritic Madhyamaka into terms current in contemporary English-language philosophical parlance . . . [given that] potential equivalents or analogues in fact possess quite different etymologies, intellectual histories, and hence senses," see Stepien 2021c: 878.
86. For a theoretically sophisticated and multi-disciplinary book-length argument "for the continued necessity—and relevance—of the comparative study of religion" (Patton and Ray 2020b: 1), see Patton and Ray 2020a.
87. Whether she is sister, mother, wife, daughter, or some mix of some or all of these, or for that matter an outcast pariah, is, as we have seen, up for never-ending debate.
88. I speak of inevitability, but this is naturally to be understood as a merely empirical, and hence defeasible, fact. Languages change as language communities change, and I suggest that the coinages proposed at various points in this book, or others like them likewise devised to convey Buddhist notions, may eventually prove needful if Buddhism is to seep into English vocabulary as it comes to permeate in centuries to come, as perhaps it will, English-language cultures. Chinese-language terms were invented or appropriated just as needfully in centuries long past as Chinese Buddhism emerged onto the world historical stage. Of course, the inveterate problem of conveying concepts across languages has led some scholars to "adopt a different strategy and reject both categories ['religion' and 'philosophy'] as inadequate. Instead of forcing Buddhism into foreign semantic structures, we can refer to the Buddhist self-awareness and simply acknowledge that Buddhism is dharma" (Jakubczak 2017b: 6). While this has the advantage of both "avoiding cultural domination" and "extending the analytical nomenclature" (Jakubczak 2017b: 6), and as stated I can certainly foresee indigenous Buddhist terms gradually fertilizing the soil of English-language discourse, nonetheless I feel that simply transplanting terms is an inadequate strategy. Indeed, this is effectively acknowledged by Jakubczak despite the proposed categorical rejection, for his discussion—like mine—remains couched in Buddhism as, precisely, "between religion and philosophy" (Jakubczak 2017a).
89. As per my aforementioned debt to Marshall Hodgson, in speaking of "Buddhist and Buddhate worlds," I am referring respectively to what are the naturally overlapping rubrics of, on the one hand, the specifically religious aspects of people and peoples identifying with Buddhism and, on the other, the broader social and cultural milieux wherein that religion has exerted influence; societies and cultures, that is, in greater or lesser part molded by Buddhism and Buddhists.
90. In emphasizing both the influence *of* the culture of reasoning shaping Nāgārjuna and the influence his own thought was to exert *on* the shapes that culture was subsequently to take, I am referring to the dynamic whereby "arguments are not only tradition-constituted (in a deterministic sense); they are also tradition-constituting in that they become foci for future debates within a tradition about itself" (Clayton 2006: 308).
91. See also Clayton's discussion of "localized rationalities" (Clayton 2006: 307) and his understanding that " 'Reasons' are always reasons for someone; they become persuasive when they are regarded as 'good reasons' by some audience" (Clayton 2006: 4).

92. See in this relation Eckel's discussion of the "canons of rationality and the formal requirements of a valid argument" (Eckel 2008: 6) in the Indian context. In that work, Eckel goes on to discuss a variety of what amount to significant disjuncts between 'our' philosophical praxes and those animating the sixth-century Mādhyamika Bhāvaviveka (Eckel's specific focus of interest) and ancient Indian philosophy more generally. These include "traditional Indian rules for debate" (Eckel 2008: 51), and indeed the very practice of "philosophy as a way to see" (38), of "philosophical analysis as a form of yoga" (83), and of "a philosophical argument not just as an 'idea,' a 'position,' a 'proposition', or any of the other conventional terms that can be used to name the currency of intellectual disputes . . . [but] as a trajectory of thought or an 'approach' that led eventually to a distinctive 'vision' of reality" (87). Meanwhile, on the topic of logic and validity, Balcerowicz markedly observes that

> The concept of formal validity was if perhaps not entirely absent, then certainly not thematised in it [Indian logic] at all, and the concept of tautology, a logical formula which remains true irrespective of the values of its variables, never consciously adopted. Consequently, the idea of logical truths as necessary truths was also absent in India. What remained was factual truths, but these were merely contingent truths. (Balcerowicz 2019: 937)

That Eckel's and Balcerowicz's analyses present us with Indian models of philosophy and argument, logic and logical truth significantly different from those developed on Greek models in the West should go without saying. What should *not* go without saying (and is in fact asserted and elaborated in Chapter 1 on "Orienting Reasons") is that unquestioningly acquiescing to occidental models and unhesitatingly applying them to oriental materials is problematic.

93. Nālandā—"the most famous of the Buddhist monastic universities of India" (Buswell and Lopez 2014: 565)—was founded around 427 and survived for a millennium or so thereafter, although its operation was vastly diminished following its sacking by Muslims in 1192.
94. On this, see Kevin Vose's study of "Authority in Early Prāsaṅgika Madhyamaka" (Vose 2010), which candidly admits that "Among the difficulties of evaluating Buddhism's rationality . . . is the breadth of concepts packed into the term 'reason'" (554), charts "a central tension between reason and authority in the Buddhist epistemological tradition, suggesting that the Buddha's authority may form for his followers a source of knowledge, on par with perception (*pratyakṣa*) and inference (*anumāna*)" (554), and studies a Madhyamaka view that "advocates the authority of Nāgārjuna as the sole means by which one can come to understand emptiness" (559).
95. The tension and even antagonism felt by adherents of the older Theravāda tradition toward the upstart Mahāyāna movement is memorably encapsulated in the quip, by a certain (unnamed) Theravādin monk, that "This so-called Mahāyāna was not spoken by the Buddha. It was fabricated by a clever man named Nāgārjuna" (Lopez 2005: 6).
96. Such "Parasitic Strategies of Mahāyāna" are studied in detail by Walser 2005: 153ff; other indispensable studies of the place of early Mahāyāna in Buddhist history (and

in Buddhist studies) are Schopen 1997, Silk 2002, Nattier 2005, Harrison 1987, 1995, 2003, the (other) essays collected in Williams 2005, and most recently and amply Walser 2018. Perhaps this is the aptest moment to acknowledge that my reliance on written texts may be criticized by some scholars as yet another embodiment of what Schopen (1997: 1ff) identifies as the 'Protestant Presuppositions' he sees as inordinately informing the study of Buddhism. In response, if "The implicit judgment, of course, is that real Buddhism is textual Buddhism" (Schopen 1997: 9), then I take the opportunity to explicitly deny, and decry, that judgment, for I readily admit as sources of philosophical thought all manner of 'texts' of a non-literary and/or non-formal nature not standardly accepted as such (see also §3.1). That said, in this book I do rely exclusively on Nāgārjuna's written texts. I do so because, on the one hand, this is all we have of his intellectual production and no historical evidence exists of his having furnished any other kind of work. On the other, I feel comfortable doing so because my point about admitting non-written texts into the ambit of philosophy obviously does not at all invalidate written texts as philosophical sources. And finally—if I am allowed a third hand—my sources are written ones because my own personal proclivities and predilections steer me toward the written word. I therefore see no theoretical or methodological obstacles to reading Nāgārjuna in this way.

97. Young 2015 is the authoritative study of Chinese hagiographies of Nāgārjuna and other Indian Buddhist 'patriarchs'. For summary lists of the principal sources for the 'life' of Nāgārjuna in Sanskrit, Chinese, and Tibetan, as well as a list of the premier scholarly treatments of his hagiography, see Ray 1997: 144–146 nn. 2–3.
98. Walser claims that his book "shows that what was at stake in the Mahāyāna championing of the doctrine of emptiness was the articulation and dissemination of court authority across the rural landscapes of Asia" (Walser 2018: blurb). This is an interesting and innovative claim, and one Walser buttresses with substantial historical data, but it is one that I neither feel qualified to evaluate nor am concerned with in this book.
99. The relevant literature in this subfield or meta-field (not a Buddhist Pure Land!) is vast and ever-growing, but two issues of the *Journal of the International Association of Buddhist Studies* dedicated to the topic may be taken as representative: that "On Method" containing the article by Cabezón just cited as well as Ruegg 1995, Gómez 1995, Tillemans 1995, Huntington 1995, and Hubbard 1995; and that on "Buddhist Studies in North America" containing Prebish 2007, Cabezón 2007, Freiberger 2007, and Gómez 2007. One particularly relevant attempt to explain "why there appears to be a basic difference in orientation toward Indian philosophy on the part of European and English-speaking scholars" (128), and moreover "to justify the philosophical approach to Indian philosophical texts by showing how it complements, in various ways, the historical-philological study of these materials" (125) is Taber 2013. For sustained further discussion of the relevance and importance of theoretical and methodological approaches for the study of Nāgārjuna specifically and the study of Buddhism—and religion—more generally, see Chapter 1 of the present book.
100. Qingmu has historically been identified as Piṅgala in part based on the Chinese transliteration 賓伽羅 given in the text, though there has been extended and still

unresolved (probably unresolvable) scholarly discussion concerning both this identification and more generally of the authorship of the commentary. See, for example, Bocking 1995: 395–405 for sustained argument in support of identifying Qingmu with "Kumārajīva's old Vinaya Master from Kashmir" (Bocking 1995: 98) Vimalākṣa 卑摩羅叉 (dates unknown). The whole debate as to the identity of this nebulous figure is in any case summarized in Goshima 2008, who concludes (333) that "in spite of a long history of research on the subject, almost nothing about Ch'ing-mu [Qingmu] has been clarified." Given this state of affairs, I take no stand on the authorship question and have thus referred to the commentator in neutral manner by the Chinese name Qingmu 青目 as this is what is given in the text's preface by Sengrui 僧叡 (dates unknown). Whatever we make of the commentary's original author, there can be no doubt in any case that Kumārajīva himself contributed significant authorial elements to the text as it has come down to us since Sengrui states that Kumārajīva "edited and amended all the errors, deficiencies and redundancies" in Qingmu's text. Would that we all had editors like that! (I cite the eloquent translation by Robinson 1978: 207 reproduced in full by Bocking 1995: 99. For the broader passage, see T 1564: 1a28: 其人雖信解深法而辭不雅中，其中乖闕煩重者法師皆裁而裨之，於經通之理盡矣，文或左右未盡善也).

Chapter 1

1. Here as throughout, I use the Sanskrit term "*catuṣkoṭi*" as equivalent to the Greek-derived "tetralemma."
2. It should thus be clear that I am not primarily concerned here to present a particular interpretation of Nāgārjuna, but rather, as the subtitle to the chapter denotes, to present a critique of the currently predominant mode of interpreting him. This is not because I have somehow managed to attain a Buddha's unperturbed reflective awareness (*ādarśajñāna*) and thereby passed beyond all hermeneutic horizons. On the contrary, as I go on to acknowledge, I do consider some interpretations of Nāgārjuna better (in the sense of textually justified) than others, but the sustained arguments and Nāgārjunian textual evidence in support of any such interpretive stance will have to await subsequent chapters. The "primary" objects of my critique at this stage are not the works of Nāgārjuna *per se* but the modern Western "secondary" literature surrounding them.
3. Although racist stereotypes are undoubtedly sometimes still at work in unquestioningly assuming the sole validity of Western logic as opposed to Indian/Buddhist varieties (such as those countenancing four as opposed to two truth values), Western analytical philosophers who refuse to toe the line are similarly ignored or disparaged. Graham Priest provides a textbook example of this. His groundbreaking book on dialetheism—a notion he rightly declares "*is* outrageous, at least to the spirit of contemporary philosophy" (Priest 2006: xv, emphasis original)—was initially rejected by ten major publishers before making it to print. In its second edition, Priest details how critical reviewers initially discouraged publication of the

book on the grounds that his position was "totally wrong-headed in the most radical way possible" (Priest 2006: xvii), not "serious" (Priest 2006: 284), or just plain "silly" (Priest 2006: xviii). Priest is left to conclude that "arguments against an entrenched orthodoxy have a hard time making any impact" since "people will disregard the arguments because they have already rejected the conclusion. What this says about rationality in operation, I leave the reader to ponder" (Priest 2006: xviii). While I do not presume to play in the same league as Graham Priest, I suspect that the present work will have similar trouble swimming against the current of "orthodoxy." After all, as Alister McGrath points out, "to hold patterns of thought that run counter to a deeply embedded cultural mindset or groupthink is potentially to be seen and judged as irrational" (McGrath 2018: 28, drawing on Taylor 2007). McGrath goes on to observe that "A similar point needs to be made in relation to the notion of 'common sense', which is often presented, especially in popular discussions of issues of rationality, as a straightforward and universal account of the way things are—or ought to be" (McGrath 2018: 28). We will in fact very soon find references to "common sense" abundant in the scholarly literature concerning Nāgārjuna.

4. Be it noted that Bugault, although relatively unknown among Anglo-American scholars (presumably on account of writing predominantly in French), was no academic lightweight. Until his death in 2002, he was Professor of Indian Philosophy and Comparative Philosophy at Paris-Sorbonne and member of both the Société Asiatique and the Association Française pour les Études Sanskrites. Bugault maintained his positions and methods to the end. In the "Methodological Precautions" to his article of 2000, for example, he announces his intention to again "seek and find quite unexpected help from Aristotle" in interpreting the MK (Bugault 2000: 386). In the introduction to his 2002 translation of the MK into French, furthermore, he reiterates in summary form his previously stated positions; see, for example, the statement that, though Aristotle "knows perfectly well the tetralemma" (*connaît parfaitement le tétralemme*), "he simply abhors it" (*simplement il l'abhorre*) (Bugault 2002: 20).
5. The relevant passage is worth citing in full, as it provides a perfect minor case study of the tendency I describe. Oetke states:

> This kind of argument [viz., that there can be no entities of a certain kind F that are G and that there can be no entities of the same kind F that are not-G] seems with regard to its formal structure intuitively sound and it can also be shown that its analogue in the classical predicate calculus is valid. Nevertheless the results of these proofs are implausible and the impression of implausibility is strengthened by the circumstance that in many cases the deduced propositions that there are no entities of the kind F serve as the basis for deducing in an apparently stringent manner the non-existence of further entities the existence of which is not questioned by common sense. (Oetke 1990: 91)

Oetke initially admits at least the seeming soundness of Nāgārjuna's argument, but, as is typical, he does not question the validity of applying the classical predicate calculus to Nāgārjuna; nor does he query the objectivity he ascribes to his own intuitions in assessing Nāgārjuna's argument as "intuitively sound." Even more problematically, Oetke does not explain why "implausibility" based on "common sense" should act as an argument against Nāgārjuna's positions, particularly as "the non-existence of . . . entities the existence of which is not questioned by [the substantialist presuppositions Oetke calls] common sense" is precisely the conclusion Nāgārjuna's well-known notion of emptiness entails. By adjudicating *a priori* as to what does and what does not count as "intuitively sound," "plausible," or "common sensical," and this on distinctly non-Madhyamaka *svabhāvic*/foundationalist grounds, Oetke shows himself to have missed the entire thrust of Nāgārjuna's *niḥsvabhāvic*/ antifoundationalist philosophy. On this, David Seyfort Ruegg's formulation of the matter is characteristically adroit: "Nāgārjuna was evidently convinced of the paradoxicality of many so-called common-sense views of the world and the real based on the assumption of entities or essences possessing own-being (*svabhāva*)" (Ruegg 1977: 5). Oetke in any case appears later to have conceded this point, for in 2007 he acknowledges that "compatibility with commonsense does not entail possession of objective justification" (Oetke 2007: 23), and furthermore avers that

> A tendency to present texts and their authors as propagating relatively unobjectionable views – even in defiance of philological standards and principles of exegesis – can be observed [within and] also outside Madhyamaka studies. Inasmuch as such endeavours are motivated by a desire to make Classical Indian Studies more attractive in the modern world they certainly deserve to be discarded. The value of a science is destroyed and not enhanced by substituting being pleasant for pursuit of truth(s). (Oetke 2007: 23)

As for my reference to pre-logicality, this should be taken not in the sense of an attempt to understand "the pre-logical underground of thought" (Graham 1992: 209) as itself conforming to an alternative but nevertheless coherent model of logicality (be it correlative, as per Angus Graham, or otherwise). Rather, I am pointing toward an orientalizing descendant of Lévy-Bruhl's (in)famous theory of "prelogical," "primitive," or "mystical" mentality, as developed most famously in his *Les fonctions mentales dans les sociétés inférieures* (Lévy-Bruhl 1910) and translated into English as *How Natives Think* (Lévy-Bruhl 1926).

6. See also Hayes 1994: 299–300: "Nāgārjuna's arguments, when examined closely, turn out to be fallacious and therefore not very convincing to a logically astute reader. By using faulty argumentation, Nāgārjuna was able to arrive at some spectacularly counterintuitive conclusions."
7. At least Hayes cannot be accused of subscribing to an essentialist vision of "eternal India"; indeed, he explicitly admits historical progression to Indian thought, as when he avers that "the conceptual tools at the disposal of intellectuals in India had improved considerably during the half-millennium that separated Nāgārjuna from the Buddha" (Hayes 1994: 322–323). He is even generous enough to claim that "Nāgārjuna's use of argumentation was in general at about the same level as Plato's" (Hayes 1994: 323). But, like some of the more adamant logical positivists, he is clearly unable to put into question the validity of his own era's *a priori*s.
8. "Roughly speaking, the former attempts to discover what a text meant in the time it was written, while the latter attempts to find the meaning of a text for the time in which the interpreter lives" (Hayes 1994: 362).

9. Such an "imaginary position of those who claim neutral objectivity for themselves—an unseen position that presumes to see all . . . [and can never] *itself* be subject to questioning or critique" is criticized by Gabriel Soldantenko (2015: 139–140). Within the context of an overall effort to decolonize philosophy, Soldatenko draws on analogous ideas, including Santiago Castro-Gómez's concept of the "zero-point" ("the imaginary through which an observer of the social world can occupy a neutral point of observation that is in turn not visible from any other point"—Castro-Gómez 2005: 18) and George Yancy's notion of the "oracle voice" (which "determines what counts as philosophy . . . is deemed *causi sui* . . . presumes to speak from nowhere"—Yancy 2007).
10. Note the "us." Sprung has already (Sprung 1973: 48) lamented that "*śūnyatā* is ambivalent in a frustrating way" in that it both expresses that things are "devoid" and is a synonym for reality ("*tattva*, *tathatā*, *paramārtha*, *dharmatā*, and *nirvāṇa*"). He appears to remain very much still caught up in the species of reifying thought according to which one or other—or both—of the two truths must be in some sense real/*svabhāvic*, without realizing the emptiness/dependent co-arising of both. In 1979, Sprung continues to bemoan "the mystifying Mādhyamika theory of two truths" (Sprung 1979: vii).
11. I follow Steup and Neta (2020: §4.1) in my usage of these terms, where "doxastic basicality" is glossed as "*S*'s justified belief that *p* is basic if and only if *S*'s belief that *p* is justified without owing its justification to any of *S*'s other beliefs"; and "epistemic basicality" is glossed as "*S*'s justified belief that *p* is basic if and only if *S*'s justification for believing that *p* does not depend on any justification *S* possesses for believing a further proposition, *q*."
12. For a historically informative and philosophically astute complication of what Indian Buddhists meant by the term *yukti*, see Nance 2007.
13. Note the "our" in both cases. Here and throughout this book, I adopt Tillemans's statement earlier in the same paper that "by the term 'classical logic,' we understand the first order propositional and predicate calculus that one generally finds in a work on elementary logic" (Tillemans 1999: 192).
14. For discussion of "solutions" to the "riddle" of the tetralemma, see §2.2.
15. Note that chapter 4 of Westerhoff's 2009 book is an almost verbatim reproduction of his 2006 article. In what follows, I cite one or the other (sometimes both). For reference, MK:18:10 states:

    Whatever comes into being dependent on something
    Is not the same as that thing
    Nor is it different from that thing
    Therefore it is neither annihilated nor eternal

    (*pratītya yad yad bhavati na hi tāvat tad eva tat / na cānyad api tat tasmān nocchinnaṃ nāpi śāśvatam*). Westerhoff translates the relevant portion of the verse (up to *na cānyad api*) as "whatever comes into being dependent on some object is not identical with that object, nor is it different from that object."
16. "Familiar," that is, to "us."

17. Westerhoff's approach is echoed by Jones, who tellingly insists that "Any paralogical theory that leads to the dialetheists' conclusion simply *must* be dismissed as misguided and only confusing our understanding of Nāgārjuna's thought" (Jones 2018: 61, emphasis added). Why *must* it be dismissed? Because this would be to contradict the "two basic laws of standard Aristotelean logic . . . [and] How can a self-contradictory statement be intelligible?" (Jones 2018: 45). For the dialetheic interpretation of the tetralemma, see §3.3.
18. After all, as Thomas Wood states in a similar vein, "from the logical point of view, truth is a univocal concept, for the claim of univocality is logically equivalent to the assertion that it cannot be the case that P and also the case that not-P at one and the same time. This assertion is fundamental to all logic. Any statement that violates this logical law of non-contradiction is meaningless or at least analytically false" (Wood 1994: 224). Wood is most closely associated with the "nihilistic" reading of Nāgārjuna, which we will have occasion to discuss in Chapter 4.
19. See in particular §2.2.1.
20. Westerhoff's language is slightly toned down in the 2009 version, wherein he claims to provide an interpretation "that both makes logical sense and sheds most light on Nāgārjuna's philosophical position" (Westerhoff 2009: 68).
21. I undertake detailed discussion of the soterial aim underpinning Nāgārjuna's enterprise as a whole and provide copious quotations from his *oeuvre* to this effect in the following chapters. In this context, it is especially ironic to find Jones, whose entire endeavor is explicitly designed to demonstrate that "Nāgārjuna does not violate any of the usual laws of logic and his use of logic is evident in all his texts," lamenting that "by focusing on possible logical matters within the four options, philosophers are missing the import of the arguments—in short, they miss Nāgārjuna's actual *reasoning* entirely" (Jones 2018: 45, 51, emphasis original). Of course, the logical confines Nāgārjuna was attempting to overcome were quaternary rather than binary in structure: see Chapter 3.
22. MacFarlane quotes Frege as stating that logical laws "prescribe universally the way in which one ought to think *if one is to think at all* (MacFarlane 2002: 37, emphasis MacFarlane's, citing Frege's *Basic Laws of Arithmetic*, xv), and Kant as stating that they are "the absolutely necessary rules of thinking, without which no use of the understanding takes place" (MacFarlane 2002: 43, citing Kant's *Critique of Pure Reason*, A52/B76). See also Zalta 2020: §2.7.1.
23. As we will soon see, this includes Garfield himself.
24. For discussion of Nāgārjuna's paralogic, see §3.5.
25. I take Garfield and Priest's "rational reconstruction" to be more or less equivalent to the "strong textualist" approach of Richard Rorty espoused by C. W. Huntington (1989: 8). Huntington cites Rorty 1982, but for further elaboration of a method of "rational and historical reconstruction," where past philosophical problems are related to contemporary philosophical ones, see Rorty 1984.
26. For "an alternative approach" to "fusion philosophy," which, "rather than asking what Asian philosophy can do for us, . . . set[s] out to investigate which theories, approaches and models from contemporary Western philosophy can [be] used to support,

analyze, refine and advance insights into the 'big questions' developed during the last three millennia of Asian thought," see Westerhoff 2015—and note the "us." For a stated preference for "cross-cultural philosophy" rather than "comparative philosophy," see Garfield 2002: viii. And for a suggestion to move away from "comparative philosophy"—which is not, on this account, "a branch of philosophy nor it is [sic: is it] a distinct philosophical method: it is an expedient heuristic introduced at a particular moment in world history as part of a global movement towards intellectual decolonization" (Ganeri 2016a: 134–135)—toward an "acolonial" age of "re:emergent philosophy"—which "consists in a retrieval and rearticulation of precolonial philosophical heritages in such a manner as to enable creative philosophical thinking in solidarity with others" (Ganeri 2016b: 164)—see Ganeri 2016a and the responses in Abu Sway 2016, Boghossian 2016, Stewart 2016, and Ganeri 2016b.

27. I use masculine pronouns here as almost all of the exegetes in question do so in reference to themselves. For an especially explicit acknowledgment that it is textual hermeneutics that is being practiced, see Dan Arnold's characterization of his own project in the following terms:

> I would here stipulate that by 'Madhyamaka,' I basically mean the thought of Nāgārjuna as expressed in the *Mūlamadhyamakakārikā* (particularly as interpreted by Cāndrakīrti), as well as in the *Vigrahavyāvartanī*. I mean by referring to these texts to say that I believe I can show my interpretation's adequacy to most if not all of what can be found therein; I would, indeed, propose my interpretation as representing a reading of these texts. (Arnold 2019: 698 fn. 1)

28. Luis Gómez already made this point in stating that among "problems arising from the data itself, one must count the absence of sociographic and biographic data. Specifically in the study of Nāgārjuna, reliable data on his life, to say nothing of valid data, is virtually non-existent" (Gómez 2000: 97).
29. See also in this connection my comments as to the exhaustiveness of the tetralemma in §3.3.
30. See also Garfield 2008: 515, where he states "cogency is hard to make sense of without a background assumption of rationality. In sum, a commitment to reason is a transcendental condition of interpretability." One can only wonder what Garfield would make of a claim such as that "In fact there is no equivalent to the concept of 'Reason' in the ancient Indian systems of knowledge" (Colas 2018: 87)! In any case, for a discussion of Garfield's characterization highly relevant to my argument here, see also Huntington 2020: 350–359, from which I echo the following passage:

> To assert, as [Garfield] does, that "we can only justify a reading rationally" is to make a methodological claim about how one ought to go about doing the history of Buddhist philosophy; a claim with which I happen to agree. . . . However, it in no way follows that in order to vindicate our interpretation of the original Buddhist texts as legitimately philosophical we must necessarily read them as instantiations of reasoned argumentation. (Huntington 2020: 354–355)

31. "Bereft of reason" is Garfield's characterization of Huntington in response to Huntington 2007. These two articles sparked a debate initially culminating in

Madhyamaka & Methodology: A Symposium on Buddhist Theory and Method (Smith College 2010). The present chapter is situated within and seeks to further this debate. Indeed, I hope to (re)ignite it, for I consider the Smith *Symposium* a disappointingly missed opportunity insofar as it was largely characterized by participants merely trotting out their pre-rehearsed positions rather than genuinely engaging in the kind of theoretical and methodological (self-)examination stated to be its aim. For the final related contributions by the debate's originator, see Huntington 2018 and 2020.

32. See again Garfield, who cautions that, "in commenting on Buddhist texts, or in using them for our own philosophical purposes, we must be careful of pretending to transcendence, of adopting a view, if not from *nowhere*, at least from some Archimedean point outside of the tradition we take ourselves to study" (Garfield 2015: 334, emphasis original). Garfield shows himself here, as elsewhere, to be highly sensitive to the problem, but seemingly unaware that his belief in reason as a "transcendental condition of interpretation" (Garfield 2015: 332) places him precisely in the u-topia—the *no-where*—he claims to eschew.
33. This issue has been broached in §0.3.3 and will be treated again in §1.4, but one way of conveying my point now is to reject the applicability of a net distinction between "philosophy" and "religion" to the Nāgārjunian, and more broadly the Buddhist, enterprise. For instead of dichotomizing the relation, I am arguing for the need to read Nāgārjuna according to a conception of the relation between "religion" and "philosophy" actually related to his Buddhist context. As we will see, this is in fact far removed from the exclusively analytical and hence (at least avowedly) non-religious conception taken to be definitive of the philosophical endeavor by the bulk of contemporary philosophers—and the bulk of contemporary philosophers of Nāgārjuna—and instead relies upon a non-exclusive and indeed mutually supportive relation between the two terms.
34. Note the unmarking of *Western* philosophers, and see also Garfield's much later comment on this issue (2015: ix) cited in §0.3.3.
35. For a deliberate effort "to avoid thinking of the West as 'us' and the non-West or the East or Asian as 'them,'" see Raghuramaraju 2017: 130, and for a survey of ways by which diverse thinkers have sought "to determine how we should position ourselves towards the other," see Moeller 2017: 127. See also Donahue's critique of Siderits's use (in Siderits 2011b) of 'we' in a related Indian Buddhist philosophical context. On Donahue's account, "Because it excludes the subaltern, the pronoun 'we' works in a royal sense, with a provincial group portraying itself, playfully, as global subjectivity" (Donahue 2016a: 604). I will address Donahue's broader criticisms as to the allegedly "colonially problematic methodology" (Donahue 2016a: 612) adopted by the Cowherds in §1.4.
36. The distinction in theory between these two groups is in any case impossible to implement in practice, for there is in fact substantial overlap between them. See, for example, the group of self-identified Buddhist Buddhism scholars assembled in Jackson and Makransky 2000, and Prebish's estimate that a full half of North American scholars of Buddhism are "scholar-practitioners" (Prebish 1999: 180). Both these are

discussed in Freiberger 2007, which explores with admirable lucidity the entire question of "Religious Commitment as Boundary-Marker" in the study of Buddhism.

37. "Purports to interpret" is an important qualifier here, for it precisely distinguishes what I am calling "textual hermeneutics" from "philosophical construction." I agree completely with Cabezón that "the presupposition that Eastern scholarly methods employed in the study of Buddhism must correspond to the world view in which Buddhism existed and evolved" would amount to "an almost theological stance" (Cabezón 1995: 247–248 n. 29, and see also Cabezón's discussion of "religious or theological, philosophical, and methodological" (256) normativity on pp. 256–260). This is not a stance I maintain! But if we are purporting to report what a text says, then we cannot presume to dismiss what it says if what it says is not what we say, or what we think it should or must say so that it may speak to us.

38. See again Cabezón, in particular his stereotype of the "philological positivist" who wants nothing so much as "to reconstruct the original text (there is *only one* best reconstruction): to restore it and to contextualize it historically to the point where the author's original intention can be gleaned . . . To reconstitute the texts in this way is to make it available in a neutral, untampered-with and pristine fashion" (Cabezón 1995: 245–246, emphases original). As for my own approach, I can only echo Berger:

    > I do not pretend to be making the case here that either I or any other cross-cultural philosophy scholar can completely transcend the conditions of being influenced palpably by the legacies of colonialism or the limits of historical and hermeneutic distanciation. We are after all doing our work within our historical contexts, writing, in the present case, in a Western language, and are motivated by concerns quite appropriately relevant to our own time and circumstances. (Berger 2017a: 124)

    Berger is, of course, drawing here on "what has come to be called the problem of 'prejudice' as it is connected to the 'hermeneutic circle' (Gadamer 1994)" (Berger 2017a: 122).

39. Gómez is one scholar of Buddhism who forthrightly asserts: "I believe translation is impossible" (Gómez 1995: 208). He, however, makes this claim because, as he rightly puts it, "The only perfect translation there can be is the original itself—which, of course is not a translation" (Gómez 1995: 208). What I am getting at is a different point: no translation may be perfect, but all translations convey, howsoever imperfectly, something of the original; otherwise, they would not be translations at all. This applies to translations generally; for some characteristically nuanced reflections specifically on translating Buddhist philosophical texts, see Ruegg 1992. Obviously, I am referring to "translation" here in a manner that slides—as translation inevitably *does* slide—into interpretation. On this point, Matthew Kapstein is characteristically adroit:

    > Interpretation is not translation, though no fixed boundary between these two arts can be defined. Interpretation invites us to occupy, so far as knowledge and imagination allow, the perspective within which a cultural object was born and nurtured, to understand it in its own world and then to articulate

> the understanding we have gained in the terms available to us in our world. (Kapstein 2017: 15)

This succinctly describes the unavoidable predicament of the textual hermeneut; it is to be contrasted with the task of the philosophical constructor, who seeks not (or not primarily) to understand the cultural object "in its own world," but to apply the understanding gained to his own. Kapstein is, of course, right to discern an inevitable element of construction within all interpretation, for since "we cannot in fact occupy other worlds, interpretation thus understood remains in some sense impossible. We can only aspire to construct, from the materials available to us, an imaginative simulacrum of the domain that gave meaning to the object of our concern" (Kapstein 2017: 15). In these terms, my methodological distinction between textual hermeneutics and philosophical construction resides precisely in the difference between imaginative simulacra and imaginative originals: simulacra, howsoever imaginative, aim to simulate and are therefore assessed as more or less accurate to the original; originals hold no mimetic aspirations at all and are therefore evaluated by entirely other criteria.

40. My insistence, within the realm of textual hermeneutics, on fidelity to the formulations found in a given text and simultaneous admission of textual polysemicity shares a great deal, as I see it, with Bronkhorst's statement that

> We can, and we actually do, refine our understanding of a text by confronting it again and again with the principal evidence we have, viz., its exact wording. In this way we can discard false interpretations, which are not simply outdated with reference to the latest philosophical theory in vogue in the West, but really false because in contradiction with the exact wording of the text. By eliminating one false interpretation after the other, we can be sure to get ever closer to the correct interpretation of the text, even if we are to believe that that correct interpretation can never be fully reached. (Bronkhorst 1993: 503)

I would only add that this in no way impedes the creative work of philosophical construction (see preceding note).

41. For recent book-length studies of Indian logic, see, for example, Vidyabhusana 1971, which includes an extended discussion (part II, section II) on "The Buddhist Logic"; Shen 1985, which refers to Buddhist logic throughout; Gokhale 1992, which discusses Buddhist as well as Nyāya logic; Matilal 1998, which deals with Buddhist logic most at length in chapters 4 and 5; and Ganeri 2001, which is *A Reader* not of classical sources but of classic twentieth-century essays on the topic. For an informed and illuminating inquiry into the question "Is There Anything Like Indian Logic?" that "will force one to seriously reconsider what so-called 'Indian logic' actually was and how its nature differed, if it at all did, from Western logic" (918), see Balcerowicz 2019. For studies of specifically Buddhist Indian logic, see, for example, Matilal and Evans 1986, which includes an initial foray into the question of "Does the Mādhyamika Have a Thesis and Philosophical Position?" by Ruegg fleshed out in much greater detail in Ruegg 2000; Wayman 1999, which treats of and translates Buddhist logical works from the millennium spanning from Asaṇga (c. 300–370) to Tsongkhapa (1357–1419); and Wang

and Zheng 2012, which focuses on scholastic history. The classic work is Stcherbatsky 1962 [1930]. Li 1986 is rare in crossing the Indo-Chinese divide in that it is a systematic and detailed comparative study of Indian and Chinese Buddhist thought.

42. See, for example, Ruegg 1977: 5 and 54 quoted in §1.2, and Siderits, who states that "Nāgārjuna's logical conservatism is attested to by his affirming all the standard principles of classical logic" (Siderits 2019: 646 fn. 2).
43. I can only hope that everything I say makes it abundantly clear that I am in full agreement with Kapstein when he writes "I do not believe that eisegesis ["the interpretation of the other through the projection upon it of one's own prior conceptions and judgments"] is inevitable, even if it can never be altogether eliminated" (Kapstein 2017: 26). I also take this opportunity to express regret at my wording on this point in a previously published version of this material (Stepien 2018a: 1088); to be clear now, I do *not* consider whatever eisegesis does characterize the interpretation of Nāgārjuna to be willful. For a related discussion of the pre-eminent place of soteriology in what may otherwise appear to be "pure" philosophy in the Buddhist sphere, and an acknowledgment that "Failure to appreciate the purport of a text can lead to a misreading, subordinating perhaps exactly those concerns that the tradition would foreground, or foregrounding those it would subordinate," see Garfield 2002: 243.
44. In oral comments made during the Q&A to his talk on September 29, 2014, at the Buddhist Studies Forum at the Mahindra Humanities Center at Harvard University, Jay Garfield stated that *sūtra* and *śāstra* texts are completely different genres. Sheldon Pollock, however, sees the *sūtra* as a "major sub-genre" of the *śāstra* (Pollock 1985: 500). R. C. Dwivedi's account of "the concept of the *śāstra*" appears to vacillate in calling the genre *śāstra* or *sutra*; see, for example, Dwivedi 1985–1986: 43.
45. I have paraphrased Nāgārjuna here; for a more literal translation of the relevant verse (MK:0:2) and the original Sanskrit, see §4.2.
46. This principle may thus be taken to explain why I "grant the possibility of multiple interpretations, while rejecting the notion that anything goes" (Cabezón 1995: 260) in textual hermeneutics.
47. See in this context Berger's proposal at "Cross-Cultural Philosophy and Hermeneutic Expansion" (Berger 2017a) and the responses of Moeller 2017, Raghuramaraju 2017, Roth 2017, and Berger 2017b.
48. To put the matter in more general terms derived from Oetke, I *agree* that "a prohibition to the effect that one should not search for ways of making the reasoning of the writer more intelligible cannot be tolerated", for I am certainly *not* "someone who advocates the maxim that it has to be presupposed that writers of texts of the Indian tradition *can* not conform in any respect to [*our*] familiar standards of rationality" (Oetke 2004: 97 n. 4, emphases original). That would be ludicrous, for it would debar Nāgārjuna (along with all those thinkers 'other' to 'us') from making *any* rational sense to us (or other Others). But since "it can occur that the author of a text did in fact not comply with 'standards of rationality' which the interpreter would *a priori* expect"; indeed, "it *might* occur that certain writers of texts belonging to remote times and cultures comply with standards of rationality which deviate from those which are (supposedly) common in the milieu of some interpreter" (Oetke 2004: 97

n. 4, emphases original), I maintain first, that we must be clear as to when we are attempting to interpret a given writer (the task of textual hermeneutics) and when we are attempting to embellish on or extrapolate from that writer (philosophical construction) and, second, that when pursuing the former task we refrain, to the extent possible, from importing to and imposing on a given writer our own "standards of rationality." This in any case aligns with the "presumptions of perfection" Oetke himself advocates on preceding pages (Oetke 2004: 95–96) as well as his recognition elsewhere that

> the imposition of concerns which were not operative for thinkers of the past is not merely suited to generate distorted pictures about the intentions of those persons and the authentic character of the works they created, but easily leads to unfairness by blocking the recognition of values pertaining to aspects that are not the interpreter's main concern. (Oetke 2011: 325)

49. Note that Siderits himself does not use these latter terms in the way I do here; I am using them merely to add rhetorical weight to my point as to Siderits's stance on rationality.
50. Evaluating Siderits's anti-realist interpretation is tangential to my concerns here, so suffice it for present purposes for me to agree, on the one hand, that

> In the context of Madhyamaka, anti-realism has the soteriological function of deflating the pretensions of philosophical rationality. It was Nāgārjuna's insight that, in order to become truly selfless, one must become profoundly skeptical about our ability to arrive at the ultimate truth about reality. The notions of ultimate truth and ideal rationality breed clinging and attachment, and thereby a sense of self. Skepticism about these notions undermines these last refuges of the self. (Siderits 1989: 247)

On the other hand, however, this soteriological function would very much remain operative on non-anti-realist readings of Nāgārjuna too, so it is hard to see how Siderits might argue for a distinctively anti-realist Madhyamaka soteriology. In any case, my own view on this aligns closely with that of Tillemans, who observes that "anti-realism would succumb to the same critique of intrinsic natures as realism," for it too relies on some kind of "*neutral* stuff . . . 'out there', real, and as it is intrinsically" (Tillemans 2017: 123–124, emphasis original). As such, I echo Garfield in asserting that "Nāgārjuna's Madhyamaka can . . . be seen as neither realism nor anti-realism, but a transcendence of the realism/anti-realism distinction through a critique of the very notion of reality it presupposes" (Garfield 2015: 65).
51. As Tillemans puts it, "There is thus, according to Madhyamaka, an all-pervasive type of metaphysical realism implicit in philosophical theses and debates, and it is somehow all wrong" (Tillemans 2017: 113).
52. *À propos* here is Bernard Faure's somewhat Heideggerian claim that "all Western logic . . . derives from a realist metaphysics" (Faure 2004: 34).
53. See, for example, *Republic* V 476D–477B on knowledge and opinion, 477B–478D on these two as faculties operating on distinct objects, and 478D–480A on the objects of opinion (Plato 2006: 183–189), which Plato states to lie "somewhere between pure

being and not being" (Plato 2006: 188). In relation to this passage, Szaif states Plato's argument to be one that:

> characterizes the doxastic state of mind as a state of deception and the objects a person in this state is acquainted with as being deceptive or 'untrue' insofar as they (like dream images) conceal their nature as mere copies. The only way to overcome this deception is philosophy . . . [which] make[s] us aware of the reality of the Forms. (Szaif 2007: 257)

For a far ampler account of Plato's theory of knowledge by the same author, see Szaif 1996. And for Nāgārjuna's uses of dream imagery as a simile for conventional reality, see MK:7:34, MK:17:33, and ŚS:66 discussed in §4.3.4. As for Plato's ontological characterization of conventional reality as "between pure being and not being," and more generally his notion of the "*metaxy*" (the "in-between" or "middle ground") in the *Symposium*, this has seemingly colored Bugault's reading of Nāgārjuna, for he declares that "Nāgārjuna . . . is the philosopher of the 'in-between'" (Bugault 1983: 27). Ruegg, however, cites the *Laṅkāvatārasūtra* in this regard, which "states that the wise person will not take his stand even in a middle position—a *metaxú*—located between the two extreme positions of existence and non-existence (i.e., Positions I and II of the *catuṣkoṭi*)—an important point that has sometimes been overlooked in discussions of the Madhyamaka as a Philosophy of the Middle" (Ruegg 2000: 114 n. 8). Nāgārjuna's "middle way" should thus not be taken as located *between* being and nonbeing, but rather as the rejection of both; indeed, of all four possible positions as per the *catuṣkoṭi*.

54. See, for example, Regington Rajapakse, who argues that the Buddha "is a religious teacher but also a philosopher" (Rajapakse 1986: 51). See also Mahinda Deegalle 2010, which includes a long section of papers delivered at the 2009 conference of the European Network of Buddhist Christian Studies on the topic of Authority in Buddhism and Christianity. These papers cover matters such as scriptural, spiritual, institutional, and political authority as well as "the crisis of authority" in the two religions.
55. Garfield reiterates and further contextualizes his point that "much of Western philosophy is religious, and derives its point from religious concerns" in Garfield 2002: 287 n. 1. Roy Perrett (2016: 4) makes the same claim in the context of his critique of what he calls the "secularity condition" on philosophy. See also my discussions of what I call, with direct reference to Garfield and Perrett, the "Religion Argument" (as also the "Historicist Argument," "Terminological Argument," and "Argument Argument," all variously used to dismiss Buddhist philosophy *as* philosophy) in Stepien 2019b: 13–14 and Stepien 2022: 1068.
56. The OED dubs "anachorism" a nonce word, which is unfortunate, since the need for a spatial equivalent for the temporal incongruity encapsulated in "anachronism" is evident.
57. Like Flanagan's argument that his "method makes sense *since* my target audience is not orthodox Buddhists or Buddhologists, but fellow analytic philosophical naturalists" (Flanagan 2013: 209–210 n. 3, emphasis added), Priest's resting the legitimacy of his

approach on the distinction between those who do or do not "regard themselves as Buddhist" is actually beside the point here. Whether a given exegete, philosopher, or reader identifies as Buddhist or not is independent of whether a given reading is or is not ascribable to a given Buddhist text (which is not to say, of course, that personal identification as Buddhist may not in fact sway one toward one or another set of readerly assumptions and underlying values).

58. See also p. xi, where Flanagan forthrightly declares that "some parts of Buddhism are superstitious nonsense." Presumably, the same goes for any and all systems of thought not grounded in a "commitment to scientific materialism," mere "untestable gobbledygook" (Flanagan 2013: 3, 219 n. 6). If Flanagan's aim is to demonstrate how "Buddhism naturalized can be achieved *without* a hostile takeover" (Flanagan 2013: 6, emphasis added), then I can only wonder what an outright hostile approach might look like.
59. Westerhoff clearly has Flanagan in mind when characterizing an approach which "assumes the superiority of the contemporary [naturalist] view [over the Buddhist view] but argues for a cherry-picking approach that accepts only those parts of Buddhist theory and practice that are consistent with naturalist assumptions or can at least be interpreted in such a way" (Westerhoff 2017c: 147–148).
60. For Flanagan's affirmation that "the burden is on the believers to give reasons for believing in their supernatural posits" or in "what I call hocus pocus," see Flanagan 2013: 210 n. 5.
61. I sometimes wonder whether the long-standing and pan-Indian commitment to *pramāṇa* theory or "theory of the instruments of knowledge" (Dunne 2004: 16), understood as "a particular mode of discourse in which subject matter, technical vocabulary, rhetorical style, and approach to reasoning are all shared by numerous philosophers from several traditions" (Dunne 2004: 15–16), could or should be interpreted as a variety of the Kuhnian paradigm . . . but that is matter for others to work through.
62. Siderits discusses Quine's rejection of the analytic/synthetic distinction with reference to Nāgārjuna at Siderits 1988: 321.
63. See also Siderits 1989: 231, where Siderits acknowledges that his reading of Nāgārjunian emptiness appears to be "committed to relativism about rationality: if what is rationally acceptable is partially dependent on human practice as shaped by human institutions, then given the cultural and historical variability of institutions, what is rationally acceptable cannot be canonized but must rather be relative to a concrete historical situation." The remainder of Siderits's article is in effect a response to this "charge of relativism" (231).
64. In discussing elsewhere Prāsaṅgika and Svātantrika Madhyamaka approaches, Waldo reiterates that their "line of reasoning has important consequences for our ideas about philosophy. It breaks down the empiricist's absolute distinction between science as the study of fact and philosophy as the study of logical relations" (Waldo 1975: 288).
65. This applies directly to contemporary non-Western philosophers; in the case of former ones such as Nāgārjuna, the aforementioned caveat applies. I am proposing that there is a legitimate sense in which we can understand the philosophies of the

past as having an "interest" in being communicated; if we speak of texts as "living" and ideas as "alive," it is surely because they continue to speak to us, to inform our own lives. Of course, I freely admit that much further constructive work would be needed to fully adapt Fricker's ideas, applying as they do in the first instance to the social experience of the living subject, to the distinct case of long-dead (non-Western) philosophers. May this brief treatment suffice for the moment as an initial Frickerian foray into the matter of "doing justice" to Nāgārjuna at the heart of this book as a whole.

66. This is only buttressed by the fact that a prominent Cowherd such as Garfield is found to give explicit and nuanced attention to issues of "temporality and alterity," to the lamentable fact that "We operate in the shadow of colonialism and its intellectual wing, orientalism," and to calling out "the odious character of this colonial approach to scholarship" (Garfield 2002: 231, 248).
67. In the course of her argumentation, Donahue draws on an important prior study—Lin et al. 1995—which "concluded that when modern Western categories and standards of evidence adjudicate the merits of 'an alternative philosophic tradition,' that tradition can appear only as 'an inferior variation on a Western theme'" (Donahue 2016a: 597).
68. As Davis notes, this is an endeavor demanding persistent attention at multiple levels, for

> Even if philosophy departments around the world were to become thoroughly pluralistic in content, they might still remain methodologically Eurocentric, meaning both Eurocentripetal and Eurocentrifugal: Eurocentripetal in the sense that texts and ideas from other traditions would be drawn into the circle of philosophizing in a modern Western academic mode, and Eurocentrifugal in the sense that this modern Western academic mode of philosophizing would continue to be exported to, and adopted by, Western-style universities in non-Western lands. (Davis 2019: 610)

69. This goes a long way toward explaining why "a major source of difficulty for reflection on Indian philosophy stems from conflicting intuitions in regard to the place of the study of religion within it" (Kapstein 2017: 17). The "extraordinary misunderstanding and confusion" and "major source of difficulty" Ruegg and Kapstein identify speaks to scholars' own "conflicting intuitions" as to "religion" and "philosophy"—certainly not those of Indian philosophers. In this context, the following passage is also worth citing in full:

> In deciding whether Buddhist doctrine—either as preceptive scriptural teaching (*deśanādharma*) or as a way of life to be practised (*adhigamadharma*)—is genuinely philosophical, much will of course depend on what we think philosophy is about. Were it to be considered to be unbridled speculative thought, or about the construction of a metaphysical system, Buddhist thought would no doubt not be pure philosophy. And a doctrine like Buddhism, which has represented itself as therapeutic and soteriological, would not be counted as essentially philosophical so long as philosophy is understood to be nothing but analysis of concepts, language, and meaning (though these matters do play an important part in the history of Buddhist thought, too). But the fact remains that, in

> Buddhism, soteriology, gnoseology, and epistemology have been closely bound up with each other. (Ruegg 2010: 223)

The soteriological import of Buddhist philosophy as expressed by Nāgārjuna has already been emphasized and will occupy our attention again later. To separate what for Nāgārjuna are two sides of the same coin (a coin only in circulation for the purpose of paying the ferrier to get one to the farther shore), I am proposing that Nāgārjuna is exemplary as a Buddhist philosopher in that he conceives the rational search for abstract truth typically taken (in Western currency) to characterize the philosophical enterprise to be intelligible, let alone valuable, only insofar as it settles the soteriological charge of the religious.

70. Huntington (1989: 14) cites the full passage I select from here. Alternatively, in terms I have used elsewhere,

> the relation between philosophy and religion in the Buddhist context is tighter still than mere overlap, for to the extent that Buddhism may be said to be a pursuit of liberation by any means useful (that is, a religion), the pursuit of truth by means of thinking (that is, philosophy) under its umbrella (that is, Buddhist philosophy) is religious, for the straightforward reason that thinking toward truth is one of the means useful toward liberation. (Stepien 2023b: 67)

71. Jin Park has recently formulated her critique of such "arbitrary compartmentalization" in much the same terms as my own. She writes:

> Mark Siderits, a scholar of Buddhist philosophy, began his book *Buddhism as Philosophy* (2007, 7) by analyzing the discipline of philosophy. Siderits distinguished Buddhist philosophy from religion, stating that Buddhist philosophy is not concerned about 'soteriology,' 'faith,' or 'theistic reality,' and instead focusing on attaining the ultimate goal of liberation through 'rational investigation of the nature of the world.' . . . Siderits' effort to present Buddhism as philosophy, ironically, indicates that Buddhism has yet to be fully accepted as a philosophy in the Western scene. In order to claim that Buddhism is a philosophy, Siderits had to impose on Buddhism the characteristics of the traditional Western philosophical categories. (Park 2017a: 186)

This also applies to my foregoing comments, most directly those regarding Flanagan and Priest.

72. See, for example, Garfield and Priest 2002: 96 cited in §1.2. In an article co-written by Garfield and Priest together with Deguchi, they elaborate, furthermore, that "Buddhism can be rational although inconsistent—indeed, ultra-rational, since the contradictions are the result of following a certain view of the world through to its logical conclusions" (Deguchi et al. 2008: 401). Note that Matthew Bagger is an exception in that he characterizes Nāgārjuna straightforwardly as a "mystic" (see Bagger 2007: 13), but it is telling that he is a specialist not of Nāgārjuna but of philosophy of religion. Steven Katz, another philosopher of religion, also classifies Nāgārjuna among the mystics based on his broadening of the traditional understanding of the term "mysticism" to include non-theistic religious traditions, as per his definition: "Mysticism is the quest for direct experience of God, Being, or Ultimate Reality,

however these are understood, that is, theistically or non-theistically" (Katz 2013: 3). The numerous problems with this formulation (e.g., the prioritization of "experience"; the onto-theological presuppositions at work in emphasizing "God," "Being," and "Reality"; and the simplistic dichotomization of these into "theistic" or "non-theistic") are beyond the scope of my concerns here. Besides which, I can only approve Denys Turner's declaration that "I do not know of any discussions which shed less light on the subject of 'mysticism' than those many which attempt *definitional* answers to the question 'what is mysticism?'" (Turner 1995: 2, emphasis original). This does not stop Krzysztof Jakubczak from drawing on William James's *Varieties of Religious Experience* (1902) to "specify the standard parameters of mystical experience (non-conceptuality, ineffability, paradoxicality, silence, oneness, fullness) and . . . conclude that they either cannot be applied to Madhyamaka or that the application is only illusory" (Jakubczak 2017c: 71, and see also Jakubczak 2019: 338, where he stipulates that mysticism, to be accounted such, must admit knowledge of "some form of absolute being, which has no place in either early Buddhism or Madhyamaka" [*jakaś forma absolutnego bytu, co zarówno we wczesnym buddyzmie, jak i w madhjamace nie ma miejsca*]). Moving on, Kamaleswar Bhattacharya states that "Nāgārjuna seems to be a mystic" but goes on to number him among those he calls "mystical philosophers" (Bhattacharya: 1978: 1). Finally, L. Stafford Betty's article (whose title, "Nāgārjuna's Masterpiece: Logical, Mystical, Both, or Neither?," is sufficient testimony to the unquestioned prevalence of the "logical vs. mystical" paradigm), concludes that it (that is, the MK) is "a mystical manifesto in philosophical guise. . . [a] unique hybrid of logic and mysticism" (Betty 1983: 133, 135), and that Nāgārjuna himself is "a mystic disguised as a philosopher" (Betty 1984: 449). To this I can only reiterate David Loy's critical retort that

> Yet, as Nāgārjuna would be quick to point out, it makes no sense to say that the *Kārikās* are *both* philosophical *and* a mystical tract, since, as these alternatives have developed in the West, they are indeed incompatible. For us, logic and intuition do not fit together very well; like mind and body, since they have been split it has become very difficult to rejoin them. So perhaps the best description of the *Kārikās* is that they fall into neither category as we have come to understand them in the West but are, rather, sui generis, requiring a new (to us!) view of how the philosophical enterprise relates to the path of liberation – as neither identical with it, nor divorced from it: a conclusion which I suspect Nāgārjuna would be pleased to agree with. (Loy 1984: 444, emphases original)

73. See also Panikkar 1988, where he proposes

> diatopical hermeneutics [as] the required method of interpretation when the distance to overcome, needed for any understanding, is not just a distance within one single culture (morphological hermeneutics), or a temporal one (diachronic hermeneutics), but rather the distance between two (or more) cultures, which have independently developed in different spaces (*topoi*) their own methods of philosophizing and ways of reaching intelligibility along with their proper categories. (Panikkar 1988: 130)

Perhaps "anatopical" could be used to supplement the term "anachoristic" suggested earlier. For a related discussion of this passage as it "concerns the very structure of the reader-text relationship when recognized boundaries of tradition are transgressed," see Garfield 2002: 243–244.

74. That "mysticism," no less than "religion," is a Western—and recent—invention has been convincingly shown in a plethora of scholarly monographs and articles (see, e.g., Proudfoot 1985: 184 and Masuzawa 2005, and see also Loy's (1984: 444) response to Betty (1983) cited earlier).
75. The phrase, played upon in the titles of both Huntington 2007 and Garfield 2008, is derived from Robinson 1972. There, Robinson sets himself the task of responding to the question "Does Nāgārjuna succeed in refuting all views without making any assumptions that are not conceded by the adherents of the particular view under attack?" His answer is a resounding "No," for on his analysis "The nature of the Mādhyamika trick is now quite clear. It consists in (a) reading into the opponent's views a few terms which one defines for him in a self-contradictory way, and (b) insisting on a small set of axioms which are at variance with common sense and not accepted in their entirety by any known philosophy" (Robinson 1972: 327, 331).
76. The citations in the remainder of this paragraph are all taken from the same article: Garfield 2008: 515, emphases original.
77. As Garfield himself avows (2008: 513, emphasis original), "Even if they [Nāgārjuna and Candrakīrti] do disavow reason, we would still have to ask whether, as contemporary Western interpreters, *we* should eschew logic and reasoning in interpreting their texts."
78. The citations in this paragraph are all taken from the same article (Garfield 2008: 515–516), though the emphases are added unless otherwise noted.
79. See also in this respect Gómez's effort to take "Madhyamaka *as a form of religious thought*" (Gómez 2000: 96, emphasis original).
80. Garfield's statements (2002: 252–253, quoted earlier) suffice to put paid to that idea.
81. The following citations in this paragraph are likewise from this (unpaginated) paper.
82. I speak of the twenty-first century, but unfortunately this is a problem already well attested over thirty years ago in the final decade of the twentieth, as when Ruegg denounces "as unfair and as untenable" attempts "to force [authors such as Nāgārjuna and Asaṅga] into the mould of modern philosophical thinking by making their works 'speak' to us as if their authors were the representatives of some modern philosophical movement" (Ruegg 1992: 371).
83. Again, see in particular Garfield's comments earlier (2002: 252) as to the arbitrariness of classifying the arguments of Aquinas, Descartes, and Leibniz, say, as "philosophical," but demarcating (and denigrating) those of Dharmakīrti, Tsongkhapa, and Nāgārjuna as "religious."
84. On this model, the present chapter would be conceived primarily as working toward the second desideratum.

Chapter 2

1. Skt. *sad asat sadasac ceti nobhayaṃ ceti kathyate / nanu vyādhivaśāt sarvam anuṣadhaṃ nāma jāyate*. Cited by Ruegg 2000: 128.
2. See, for example, Robinson 1957, Jayatilleke 1967, Sprung 1973, Staal 1975 and 1976, Oetke 1990, and Burton 1999.
3. My reference to "*Western* logic" is meant to designate asseverations such as that "Regarding the three basic laws of Western formal logic, these are in fact endorsed by Nāgārjuna" (西洋的形式論理的三原理，龍樹事實上亦是認許的; Kajiyama 1978: 81), and "the three 'Laws of Thought' of traditional Western logic are not denied" (Robinson 1978: 50). As will become clearer as my exposition unfolds, this is the truth but far from the whole truth, for it disguises the fact that Nāgārjuna uses such "laws of logic" as tools well suited for the *prasaṅgic* dismantling of his interlocutors' positions because such "laws" are subscribed to by *them* (not himself). Indeed, as I will go on to argue, Nāgārjuna does so in order ultimately to dismantle the very "laws" too.
4. Regarding which, see Tillemans 1999: 192 cited in §1.2.
5. See Westerhoff 2018a: 118: "Some modern interpreters have tried to address the puzzling occurrence of contradictions in Nāgārjuna's arguments by suggesting that he may have adopted a non-classical logic that tolerates contradictions." We will come to discussion of "puzzles" soon enough, but for the moment the point to make is that Westerhoff immediately dismisses such an approach in order to maintain logical non-contradictoriness: "we need to understand the contradictions proclaimed by the Perfection of Wisdom texts that the Mādhyamikas set out to explicate as merely apparent, but not as actual contradictions." Whether the logic be classical or non-classical, then, the thrust of these scholars' agenda is to prove that, one way or another, Nāgārjuna *must* be logical.
6. The distinction I am making between a "logical" and a "Buddhist" tetralemma, and the identification of my own interpretation with the latter, may open me to the charge of presumption insofar as I may be taken thereby as claiming that, in contradistinction to the scholars I criticize, I am somehow speaking straightforwardly "for Buddhism." This would be a misapplication of my distinction, which rather seeks to set interpretations that take logical/rational validity as the criterial yardstick by which to measure the success of Nāgārjuna's *catuṣkoṭi* apart from those that evaluate it instead according to its utility in moving one toward *nirvāṇa*. The implication is that this latter task is properly Buddhist. As should become clear in what follows, I support this implication and see it buttressed both by the specific textual evidence I present here (see §2.4) and more generally by the overwhelming body of Buddhist thought and practice.
7. For a book-length study of the Western interpretations of Nāgārjuna, see Tuck 1990. Ruegg provides an appendix of "Some Modern Interpretations of the *Catuṣkoṭi*" in Ruegg 1977: 39–55, and Gunaratne 1980: 235 n. 2 likewise provides a list of the major articles dealing with the *catuṣkoṭi* published unto his time. See also Huntington 1989: 25–32 for an alternative classification of the historical permutations of the Western study of Nāgārjuna.

8. For an extensive critical discussion of the prevalence of Indo-Tibetan perspectives in the study of Buddhist philosophy, see Stepien 2016. Note that space has constrained me to forego filling it with detailed discussions of the many other Chinese-language voices echoing throughout East Asian scholarship on Nāgārjuna. Indeed, the sheer plethora of material—even restricting oneself to that recently published—in the Chinese cultural sphere is such that any attempt to treat it in its variety and depth within the limits of a single chapter (one, moreover, not exactly bibliographical in intent!) would be hopelessly cursory. After all, if, as Jizang has an unidentified Hexi assert, some seventy authors had already written commentaries on the MK / 中論 by *his* time some millennium and a half ago ("河西云凡七十家": T 1824: 5a8; cf. Robinson 1978: 298 n. 27; Bocking 1995: 474 n. 468), then one can only imagine the sheer number of scholarly texts produced and available in our own (though Stefania Travagnin provides a comprehensive survey in 2009: 32–160). As such, the *modus operandi* I have settled upon is to focus on perspectives selected for their direct relevance to the discussion, though I have made a point of alluding also to other work by Chinese-language scholars on relevant topics in full acknowledgment that an adequate survey would require a monograph (or more) of its own. (As a side note, "Chinese cultural sphere" is my rather wretchedly wimpish circumlocution to designate the region without implicitly adjudicating on just how many administrations rightfully govern the Republic of China, People's Republic of China, and Hong Kong Administrative Region.)
9. It should be noted in passing that modern Chinese-language scholarship on Nāgārjuna is impressed with the influence of classical Chinese Madhyamaka thought as represented by thinkers such as Sengzhao 僧肇 (374–414) and Jizang 吉藏 (549–623). Since these latter are themselves primary sources for us (and ones of immense philosophical sophistication themselves), I have refrained from delving into them here, as this would take us too far afield of our prime concern: Nāgārjuna's *catuṣkoṭi*.
10. See Murti 1955: 152, cited in §1.3. The near-universally acknowledged fact of the inevitability of subjectivity, and hence of a motivationally constructed and pursued hermeneutic agenda, in ostensibly objective description, be it in the humanities or the sciences, is belied by its disavowal, in effect if not in name, by several of the scholars whose work currently shapes the study of Nāgārjuna—an issue already dealt with extensively in the foregoing chapter, and soon to occupy us once more. In case there should remain any uncertainty on the question, I am fully content to situate myself as a *subject* even in matters of logic, as opposed to those who affirm what they take to be the neutral objectivity of logic.
11. Regarding "utterance," see §3.5.
12. MK:1:1: *na svato nāpi parato na dvābhyāṃ nāpy ahetutaḥ / utpannā jātu vidyante bhāvāḥ kva cana ke cana.*
13. In addition, MK:25 as a whole (or at least 25:5–17) may be read as an extended negative tetralemma. Note that trilemmas (*trikoṭi*) and dilemmas (*dvikoṭi*), be they positive or negative, also occur throughout (see, e.g., 1:7, 2:24–25, 7:20, 12:9, and 21:13, 27:11).

14. See Katsura 2000: 202 for a like formulation. I should note that the use of "non-" as opposed to "not-" (or "-," or "¬" for that matter), though intended here to be as neutral as possible, has been the subject of some debate in the more logically oriented literature. See, for example, Jayatilleke 1967: 78–79, who makes a point of using "non-P" instead of "not-P" in overt opposition to Robinson 1967.
15. MK:18:8: *sarvaṃ tathyaṃ na vā tathyaṃ tathyaṃ cātathyaṃ eva ca / naivātathyaṃ naiva tathyam etad buddhānuśāsanam*. See also the discussion of this verse, and particularly of the word "*anuśāsana*" here translated as "teaching" but elsewhere interpreted as "graded teaching," in my discussion of the Modal Interpretation later (§2.2.2). Rahlwes additionally takes MK:18:6 as a positive *catuṣkoṭi*, but this is clearly mistaken, most pointedly because this verse involves no *prasaṅgic reductio* at all but rather relates three ways in which the teaching of *anātman* has been taught.
16. Regarding whom, see Tuck 1990: 56–64.
17. The "solution" proposed is that of D. T. Suzuki, presented by Robinson in the context of a discussion of "balance" between *śūnyatā* (emptiness) and *tathatā* (thusness). Robinson goes on immediately to state that

> Even though we were to admit that some nonsense is meaningful, attempts to blame "discursive understanding" for failure to answer the unanswerable would still be suspect prima facie. Questions should not be pronounced rationally insoluble until the full range of rational possibilities has been considered. It is doubtful whether "positive" and "negative" have anything to do with the meaning of "emptiness," except as signalling emotional acceptance or rejection. (Robinson 1957: 305)

That "the full range of *rational* possibilities" exhausts the full range of any and all *acceptable* possibilities is here clearly taken for granted.
18. The "two types of negation" referred to are *paryudāsa-pratiṣedha* and *prasajya-pratiṣedha*, discussed *vis-à-vis* the Qualitative Interpretation in §2.2.3.
19. MK:27:17–18: *divyo yady ekadeśaḥ syād ekadeśaś ca mānuṣaḥ / aśāśvataṃ śāśvataṃ ca bhavet tac ca na yujyate // aśāśvataṃ śāśvataṃ ca prasiddham ubhayaṃ yadi / siddhyen na śāśvataṃ kāmaṃ naivāśāśvatam ity api*.
20. See also Richard Jones, who states that MK:7:30, 8:7, 27:17, 27:25–27, and also possibly 15:5, 25:7, and 25:14 are all verses which "affirm the logical impossibility of the presence of opposite properties in one place" (Jones 1978: 493).
21. Kumārajīva's Chinese version of MK:27:17 reads: 若半天半人，則墮於二邊，常及於無常，是事則不然。
22. MK:27:25: *antavān ekadeśaś ced ekadeśas tv anantavān / syād antavān anantaś ca lokas tac ca na yujyate*. Ch. 若世半有邊，世間半無邊，是則亦有邊，亦無邊不然。
23. MK:27:27: *naitad apy upapadyate*. Qingmu's commentary follows the text closely throughout this passage.
24. In case it needs mentioning, it is not as if Nāgārjuna was incapable of utilizing mereological distinctions when these did prove useful to his argumentation. Westerhoff is well aware of this; indeed, his own translation of the VP speaks of Nāgārjuna's "refutation of the seventh [Nyāya] category, the constituents of an

argument (*avayava*, *yan lag*)" (Westerhoff 2018b: 142), where Nāgārjuna's argument revolves around the distinction between part and whole. See also Westerhoff 2018b: 164: "After a general mereological discussion applied to the parts of a syllogism in VP 33–39, Nāgārjuna now looks more specifically at the individual members of the syllogism."

25. For further clarification of this point, see n. 45 in §2.2.2.
26. The original Sanskrit of the *Akutobhayā*, which probably dates from the fourth century, has been lost. Huntington 1986 is a dissertation-length study and critical edition from the Tibetan.
27. See Tillemans 2009: 98 n. 6 and Westerhoff 2006: 391–392/2009: 89–90. Jayatilleke (1967: 82) rejects the interpretation of "the four alternatives as representing progressive degrees of truth" in preference for that in terms of parts adumbrated earlier. Westerhoff (2006: 391 n. 76/2009: 89 n. 81) mentions further possible expositions of "graded teaching" by Nāgārjuna in his *Ratnāvalī* and *Yuktiṣaṣṭikā* tangential to our concerns here.
28. For a thorough study of the history of doctrinal classification in China, see Mun 2005. The fact that nothing like the multifarious and individually complex systems of doctrinal classification produced in China existed previously in India is explained by Mun as stemming from the wholescale introduction into China of a large corpus of heterogeneous texts. He states:

    > When the body of Buddhist literature was imported into China over several centuries, Chinese scholars were naturally puzzled by numerous discrepancies and contradictions in the translated texts. These discrepancies and contradictions provide the logical beginnings of the *panjiao* (doctrinal classification) system in China. Since all the translated scriptures were considered the words of the Buddha, none of these teachings could be false. To account for diversity without rejecting some texts, Chinese scholars devised various *panjiao* systems. (Mun 2005: xvii)

29. See §2.2 for the original Sanskrit and English translation of MK:18:8. Kumārajīva's Chinese version (as quoted also in Li 1999b: 890) runs: 一切實非實, 亦實亦非實, 非實非非實, 是名諸佛法 (T 1564: 24a5).
30. See Li 1999b: 910–911:

    其實以四句來配‘三品人’簡言之，可作如下的安排：
    第一句“一切實”
    第二句“一切不實”
    對中品人說
    第三句“一切實不實”
    對下品人說
    第四句“一切非實非不實”
    對上品人說.

    I have laid out Li's statement in this manner in an attempt to render at least the tenor of the schematic diagram in which he depicts his formulations—a diagram I have been unable to reproduce. For related work by the same author, see Li 1999a, 1999c/2006a, and 1999d/2006b.

31. Ch. 上者觀諸法相非實非不實； 中者觀諸法相一切實一切不實； 下者智力淺故，觀諸法相少實少不實. For further discussion of this reading, see Robinson 1978: 56 and Wu 1992: 154ff, and for an identification of Qingmu's classification with that of Bhāvaviveka 清辨 as well an alternative fourfold schematization on a Tiantai 天台 basis, see Xingyun 1997: 368. For his part, Jakubczak too appears to subscribe to a version of this approach insofar as he asserts the *catuṣkoṭi* to be "a pedagogical and therapeutic instrument, i.e., it delineates the successive stages of understanding the fundamental Madhyamaka thesis of the emptiness (*śūnyatā*) of all entities" (*instrumentem pedagogicznym i terapeutycznym, tzn. wyznacza kolejne etapy zrozumienia fundamentalnej tezy madhyamaki o pustce (śūnyatā) wszelkich bytów*); these being represented as the "view of realism" (*pogląd realizmu*) of lemma (a), the "position of nihilism" (*stanowisko nihilizmu*) of lemma (b), the "view known as coincidentia oppositorum" (*pogląd znany jako coincidentia oppositorum*) of lemma (c), and the "way of describing existence typical of negative theology" (*sposobem opisu bytu typowym dla teologii negatywnej*) of lemma (d) (Jakubczak 2001: 65–66, echoed in 2010: 168–169).
32. Ch. 第一句是肯定語句：正. 第二句是否定語句：反. 第三句是綜合語句：合.
33. Ch. 第四句是超越於第三句：超越.
34. The "view of no view" is explicitly dealt with by Nāgārjuna in his *Vigrahavyāvartanī*, esp. verse 29 (for which see Westerhoff 2010: 63). It is implied, however, by numerous passages in both the MK and Nāgārjuna's other works, and discussed here in §2.4, "The Buddhist Tetralemma."
35. For this verse, see §2.4 here, and more generally Chapter 4. Siderits and Katsura make a related claim:

    > One might wonder whether the Mādhyamika is entitled to say that there is a hierarchy here [at 18:8]. To say that there is is to suggest that each position comes closer to accurately reflecting the nature of reality than its predecessor. And it is to suggest that the last position best represents how things ultimately are. If Mādhyamikas were to say this, they would seem to contradict their claim that nothing bears an intrinsic nature." (Siderits and Katsura 2013: 201–202)

36. Garfield already proposes this interpretation at Garfield 1995: 250.
37. This passage is also discussed by Tillemans (2009: 99 n. 13/2016: 83 n. 13).
38. For another scholar who, though in a different context, nevertheless likewise finds himself "forced to disambiguate" (312) Nāgārjuna's terms in order to make logical sense of him, see Hayes 1994.
39. MK:24:8: *dve satye samupāśritya buddhānāṃ dharmadeśanā / lokasaṃvṛtisatyaṃ ca satyaṃ paramārthataḥ*.
40. This is a doubtless more philosophically correct but certainly less eloquent version of what Duckworth previously referred to by the famous formulation "essentially the same but conceptually distinct" (Duckworth 2018: §1).
41. Admittedly, these comments refer to the negative *catuṣkoṭi*, whereas Garfield and Priest adopt the parameterization cited earlier to the positive *catuṣkoṭi* of MK:18:8. But although Garfield and Priest describe the positive and negative versions of the tetralemma as functioning in different manners, ultimately, they claim, these

"express the same insight" (Garfield and Priest 2009: 72), so there is no reason not to take Gorampa's critique here as on point. As for Westerhoff, although he explicitly cites a negative version of the *catuṣkoṭi* in the relevant discussion, there is no reason to think that his comments cannot be applied to the positive version too. On a related note, though Constance Kassor disagrees with elements of Tillemans's description of Gorampa's thought, she echoes his understanding here in stating that "in Gorampa's view, the tetralemma is a soteriological tool that aims to transform a practitioner's mind into a state that is free from conceptual proliferations. . . . When understood in this way, the tetralemma is nothing other than the complete negation of all possible forms of conceptualization" (Kassor 2013: 405). For Tillemans's clarification of his position on Gorampa, "as being an interesting case of someone who advocated no-parameterization and quietism—and *that's all*" (Tillemans 2016: 92, emphasis original) *vis-à-vis* Kassor's characterization of it, see Tillemans 2016: 91–92. For more on "What happened to the Third and Fourth Lemmas in the Tibetan Madhyamaka," see Tillemans 2016: 125–137. For book-length studies of the debate between Tsongkhapa and Gorampa, see Cabezón and Lobsang Dargyay 2007 and Thakchoe 2007.

42. See also MK:1:1 (cited in §2.2), which declares itself to apply universally to "any entity whatsoever / Anywhere" (*jātu vidyante bhāvaḥ kva cana ke cana*).
43. MK:22:9cd: *svabhāvataś ca yan nāsti kutas tat parabhāvataḥ*. And see also the similar line at MK:22:2cd.
44. See Tillemans 1999: 197 just cited and further discussion in §2.3.
45. Relatedly, Westerhoff rejects interpreting Nāgārjuna's contradictions through the application of non-classical logic due to the absence of "clear evidence" in, *inter alia*, "Nāgārjuna's own writings" (Westerhoff 2018a: 118) in support of such a logic. Yet he evidently sees no contradiction between this pronounced fealty to textual evidence and his proposal on the very next page to insert extra-textual parameters in support of his own interpretation. As C. W. Huntington commented here on a draft version of this chapter, "To selectively refer to one alternative and ignore the other when it suits your purposes is, incidentally, a genuine example of 'trickery' in the specific sense of 'sleight of hand'" (which, he went on to note, is not the way he used the term in his "The Nature of the Mādhyamika Trick": Huntington 2007). For my part, I take this occasion to clarify—in case any clarification were needed—that I do *not* charge Westerhoff, Garfield, Priest, Tillemans, and fellow parameterizers with *deliberately* misconstruing or distorting Nāgārjuna's texts to suit their own interpretive ends. On the contrary, I see no reason whatsoever to doubt their (internally variegated but overall collectively avowed) motivation to make sense of the texts in as reasonable a manner as they see possible. What I do point out, however, is that adding parameters as they do, though it be done for intellectually honorable intentions, *does* literally distort the texts, *is* motivated by logicalist assumptions alien (indeed, even at times inimical) to Nāgārjuna's thought, and *does* enable construals thereof not supported by the texts as they stand. None of this would even be a problem if the appointed task were that of philosophical construction; it is the pronounced commitment to textual hermeneutics that renders the procedure problematic.

46. Ruegg terms *prasajya* "non-presuppositional and non-implicative absolute negation," as opposed to the "presuppositional and implicative relative negation" of *paryudāsa* (Ruegg 1981: 37). He is characteristically thorough in citing the relevant literature at Ruegg 1977: 59 n. 10. Ames states that "Bhāvaviveka was, as far as is known, the first Mādhyamika to use the terms *prasajya-pratiṣedha* and *paryudāsa-pratiṣedha* to distinguish two kinds of negation (*pratiṣedha*)" (Ames 1986: 64), and he goes on to list several alternative translations of the terms. This does not mean, of course, that Bhāvaviveka was the first to use, as opposed to name, these two types of negations.
47. Among numerous others, Staal (1975: 38; 1976: 126), Lindtner (1982: 275), Ghose (1987: 24), and Garfield and Priest (2009: 79–81) all agree that "the negations in the *catuṣkoṭi* have to be interpreted as *prasajya pratiṣedha*" (Staal 1976: 126). Note that, contrary to the accepted definition of *paryudāsa* or "relational negation," Ruegg reads the classical commentators Bhāvaviveka and Candrakīrti as proposing that, though syntactically distinct from *prasajya* or "absolute negation," it logically functions as *prasajya* in the text, thereby effectively collapsing the distinction between the two types of negation (Ruegg 1977: 5).
48. Rahlwes discusses the same example on pp. 310–311 and 339–340 of Rahlwes 2022, which is the latest in the long line of attempts I am citing to draw on *prasajya* and *paryudāsa* negation to provide logically "formalized accounts of the *catuṣkoṭi*" (309). For further discussion of *prasajya* in the context of Nāgārjuna's use of it to ultimately renege on positionality altogether, see Mills 2018a: 52.
49. As already noted, Westerhoff too subscribes to such a distinction: in order to avoid contradiction, he states that "*we have to assume* that the two occurrences of 'not' . . . do not in fact refer to the same concept of negation" (Westerhoff 2006: 371/2009: 71, emphases added). See also Gunaratne 1980: 222–223, 230, and 1986: 219 for Venn diagrams not dissimilar to Katsura's.
50. The precise passage in Katsura's text I refer to is concerned with Vinaya, Abhidharma, and Yogācāra literature, but Katsura makes clear that his analysis applies to Nāgārjuna's tetralemma too, which is in any case the subject of his paper as a whole, entitled as it is "Nāgārjuna and the Tetralemma."
51. The passage in question is directly concerned with the *catuṣkoṭi* not as found in Nāgārjuna but as found in the Buddha's *Discourses*. The *catuṣkoṭi* form is itself equivalent in both, however, so there is no reason why Panikkar would argue any differently regarding Nāgārjuna. Indeed, much of the scholarly literature Panikkar cites is actually concerned with Nāgārjuna (see esp. Panikkar 1989: 200 nn. 12–16 and n. 24), so I take the application of his statements to the case of Nāgārjuna to be wholly unproblematic.
52. "(-/a)" is to be taken as referring to the first lemma of both the negative and positive tetralemmas, and so on *mutatis mutandis* for the others.
53. I thank Jay Garfield (personal communication) for calling my attention to this point.
54. See the distinction Katsura proposes between "~" as symbolizing *paryudāsa* and "–" as symbolizing *prasajya*, the application of this distinction to the positive *catuṣkoṭi*, and the conclusion that the third lemma thereof ("x is both A and non-A") thereby "does not violate the Law of Contradiction" (Katsura 2000: 204).

55. For Nāgārjuna's argumentation as to why the world can be neither finite nor infinite, see MK:27:21–24.
56. See MK:22:12, cited in §3.4.
57. He continues on the same page: "such is really the meaning of the third proposition, to wit, that a qualification of place, time, or truth must be added" (Wayman 1977: 17). For reference, MK:25:14 states: "Existent and non-existent / How could *nirvāṇa* be both? // These two cannot be in the same place / Just as light and dark." Skt. *bhaved abhāvo bhāvaś ca nirvāṇa ubhayaṃ katham / tayor abhāvo hy ekatra prakāśatamasor iva.* It is worth noting *en passant* that Nāgārjuna here foresees and explicitly rejects efforts to subvert the contradictoriness of the subject he is treating (in this case *nirvāṇa*) by means of the mereological interpretation.
58. Tillemans refers explicitly to Oetke's "modal interpretation of the tetralemma" (see Tillemans 1999: 204 n. 27).
59. Schayer's 1933 article is reprinted in Schayer 1988: 415–421 and has been translated into English by Balcerowicz (2001) and Tuske (2001); see also Mejor 2003: 11.
60. In passing, it is worthwhile noting that Tillemans's commitment to such "translations" demonstrates that the endeavor "to transcribe the *Kārikās* . . . into logical notation" (Robinson 1957: 307, cited in full in §1.2) propounded by Robinson in the mid twentieth century is still alive and well at the cusp of the twenty-first.
61. See also Westerhoff's reflexive question: "How are we supposed to make sense of passages such as these?" (Westerhoff 2018a: 118).
62. Westerhoff's attempts at "dissolving seeming contradictions" in Nāgārjuna on the basis of reducing them to the safely ignorable realm of the "merely apparent" are even more adamant, for in the space of just three pages he refers to them as "seeming," "apparent," or via cognate terms no fewer than eight times (see Westerhoff 2018a: 118–120).
63. See also his admission that, although Tsongkhapa's "interpretation offers advantages in terms of its logical clarity, but as an exegesis of Madhyamaka, his approach may seem somewhat inelegant, since it obliges us to add words almost everywhere in the Madhyamaka texts" (Tillemans 1999: 197).
64. In preceding pages, he has argued that "the four alternatives will be statements preceded by existential quantification" (Tillemans 1999: 199), and that "if we interpret the quantification in a referential manner—as *we must* do in this context—all four alternatives can be denied without the least logical deviance" (Tillemans 1999: 200, emphasis added). That "we must" so interpret Nāgārjuna's *catuṣkoṭi* is not argued for since it is apparently taken as axiomatically true that logical consistency is the aim.
65. On the basis of the passage just cited and others along similar lines cited earlier, I take Tillemans to be not merely considering but advocating such riddle-solving parameterization-cum-translation, but it is unclear to me how this tallies with his admission that such an approach "obliges us to add words almost everywhere in the Madhyamaka texts" and in fact "denature[s] the whole Nāgārjunian dialectic" (see earlier), or for that matter how it relates to his (subsequently published) view that Prajñāpāramitā and Nāgārjuna's early Madhyamaka should be distinguished from later Madhyamaka on the grounds that their (earlier) project should be taken "as a

form of quasi-skeptical suspension of belief in all positions. Taking these kinds of statements literally, without parameters, seems to me to be a way one could arrive at that skeptical form of quietism important to Nāgārjuna and the Buddhist author(s) of the Prajñāpāramitā sūtras" (Tillemans 2016: 89).

66. For representative examples of Siderits's method, see Siderits 2007 and 2015. For Siderits's stated approach regarding fusion, comparative, and confluence philosophy, see Siderits 2017.
67. My discussion here centers on Priest's explicit treatment of Nāgārjuna, but Ronald Green notes rightly that "From start to finish, Priest's book is a progressive argument meant to prove this interpretation" (Green 2020: 225) of the fifth corner as the ineffable.
68. I italicize "reinterpretation" to emphasize two points. First, and notwithstanding his protestations otherwise, Priest *is* engaged in textual hermeneutics (as he in any case must admit: "One cannot discuss texts without interpreting them; this is just Hermeneutics 100"—Priest 2018: xix). Second, Priest's is explicitly a *re*interpretation; that is, an effort to demonstrate that the *catuṣkoṭi* "makes sense" which acknowledges it is not actually *finding* that sense in the text but *making* it.
69. MK:0:2, regarding which see §4.2.
70. MK:24:1: *yadi śūnyam idaṃ sarvam udayo nāsti na vyayaḥ / caturṇām āryasatyānām abhāvas te prasajyate.*
71. See MK:24:4–5.
72. MK:24:20: *yady aśūnyam idaṃ sarvam udayo nāsti na vyayaḥ / caturṇām āryasatyānām abhāvas te prasajyate.*
73. MK:24:36: *sarvasaṃvyavahārāṃś ca laukikān.*
74. See MK:24:38.
75. VV:70 auto-commentary:

    > *yasya śūnyateyaṃ prabhavati tasya sarvārthā laukikalokottarāḥ prabhavanti / kiṃ kāraṇaṃ / yasya hi śūnyatā prabhavati tasya pratītyasamutpādaḥ prabhavati / yasya pratītyasamutpādaḥ prabhavati tasya catvāryāryasatyāni prabhavanti / yasya catvāryāryasatyāni prabhavanti tasya śrāmaṇyaphalāni prabhavanti sarvaviśeṣādhigamāḥ prabhavanti / yasya sarvaviśeṣādhigamāḥ prabhavanti tasya trīṇi ratnāni buddhadharmasaṃghāḥ prabhavanti*

    My translation here follows closely that in Westerhoff 2010: 41.

76. This is a translation from Candrakīrti's commentary (*Yuktiṣaṣṭikāvṛtti*) to the dedicatory verse of Nāgārjuna's *Yuktiṣaṣṭikā-kārikā*, as found in Loizzo 2007: 129–130. This latter work provides a critical edition and translation of the Tibetan text of Candrakīrti's commentary.
77. YṢ:0. See Lindtner 1982: 103/1997: 73; Loizzo 2007: 119; Tola and Dragonetti 1995a: 34.
78. YṢ:21–22. See Lindtner 1982: 109/1997: 79; Loizzo 2007: 121; Tola and Dragonetti 1995a: 37.
79. YṢ:60. See Lindtner 1982: 119/1997: 93; Loizzo 2007: 126; Tola and Dragonetti 1995a: 41. Regarding the "two supremes," Candrakīrti states that these are "the form body and the truth body" (Loizzo 2007: 208); that is, the *rūpakāya* and *dharmakāya*.

80. See Lindtner 1982: 45/1997: 101; Tola and Dragonetti 1995a: 74–75; Pandeya and Manju 1991: 142; Komito 1987: 84.
81. ŚS:24. See Lindtner 1982: 45/1997: 103; Tola and Dragonetti 1995a: 75; Pandeya and Manju 1991: 143; Komito 1987: 84.
82. ŚS:72–73. See Lindtner 1982: 67–69/1997: 119; Tola and Dragonetti 1995a: 81; Pandeya and Manju 1991: 148; Komito 1987: 95. For an argument to the effect that the "bad views" (*kudṛṣṭi*) Nāgārjuna denounces here are functionally equivalent to all views (*sarvadṛṣṭi*), see §4.2.
83. The most obvious textual loci from which to cite further evidence for the soterial mission of Nāgārjuna's thought are the overtly ethical texts: the *Ratnāvalī* and *Suhṛllekha*. Indeed, it would be difficult to know which verses from these *not* to select, and so rather than clutter my exposition with potentially near-endless citations, I have preferred to focus on the overtly metaphysical texts since demonstrating their soteriological orientation only strengthens my argument.
84. *Bodhicaryāvatāra* 10:1: *bodhicaryāvatāraṃ me yadvicintayataḥ śubham / tena sarve janāḥ santu bodhicaryāvibhūṣaṇāḥ*.
85. As the original Sanskrit texts of both the *Madhyamakālaṃkāra* and *Madhyamakālaṃkāravṛtti* are lost, I have relied on, and slightly modified, the translation in Blumenthal 2004: 59.
86. Citing Garfield and Priest 2002: 87.
87. See also Huntington 2003, which is a chapter-length study of Bhāvaviveka in the context of the Svātantrika-Prāsaṅgika debate. See also Yadav (1977: 452), for whom likewise Candrakīrti "considers as sick that form of life which seeks expression through metaphysical thinking. His is a request to think therapeutically." This is because Candrakīrti, following Nāgārjuna, following the Buddha, equates "metaphysical thinking with suffering" (Yadav 1977: 466).
88. I have had to rely on Ames's translation from the Tibetan since, first, the original Sanskrit text of Bhāvaviveka's *Prajñāpradīpa* is lost apart from a few scattered references in Candrakīrti's *Prasannapadā*, and, second, because (as with Nāgārjuna's YṢ: see earlier), in the words of Kajiyama (as translated in Ames 1986: 54), the Chinese translation (entitled 般若灯) completed by Prabhākaramitra 波頗 (574/5–633) in either 629 or 630–632 is "bad, unreliable and suppresses many sentences of the original text" (*Die Übersetzung ist aber schlecht, unzuverlässig und unterschlägt viele Sätze des Originaltexts*). In the light of such textual discrepancies, He and Van der Kuijp (2014: 336) postulate that "the Tibetan and Chinese translations of this work suggest that we must reckon with two different recensions." Unfortunately, a cursory survey of the Chinese translation (*Taishō* Vol. 30, 1566, 50c–135c) in comparison with Ames's English translation from the Tibetan bears out the great differences between these versions.
89. As evinced by my usage here and throughout this book, I have no gripe in subscribing to the Prāsaṅgika/Svātantrika distinction, but it should be noted that this is a Tibetan doxographical invention subsequent to the Indian debates themselves. Indeed,

> Early Mādhyamika explicitly claims to operate as a rejection, or deconstruction, of all attempts to create a value-free, objective view of truth or reality. From the very beginning this was the crux of the Mādhyamika critique, and in

> fact it was only much later, in reaction to the writings of Bhāvaviveka and his followers, that this total rejection of all fixed views and beliefs came to be specifically associated with the name Prāsaṅgika. (Huntington 1989: xii)

For an ample and nuanced discussion of the distinction as a whole, see Dreyfus and McClintock 2003, and also Ruegg 2010: 159–194, where Ruegg reviews the contributions in Dreyfus and McLintock 2003 on 179–189. For a nuanced study of just how the Prāsaṅgika and Svātantrika traditions were "invented by a few well-educated and creative individuals, standing amid the riptide of an Indian past quickly receding and a swell of translations sweeping into Central Tibet" (12), see Vose 2009, esp. chapter 2. A desire to maintain coherence of ambit, and thus not to follow tangents too far, has prevented me from engaging with the debate between Bhāvaviveka and Candrakīrti more at length. In any case, my aim here is to emphasize that, despite their distinctly divergent interpretations of Nāgārjuna's position, Candrakīrti and Bhāvaviveka—and the "schools" they represent—both acknowledged the same teleological schema, in the absence of which their philosophical positions and supporting arguments lose sense.

90. The passage juxtaposing edifying and systematic philosophy speaks of Candrakīrti, but context makes clear that Huntington is referring to "the vocabulary and attitudes critiqued by Nāgārjuna and Candrakīrti" (Huntington 1989: xi):

> Thus, although Candrakīrti has no fixed position to defend, it does not necessarily follow that his arguments are mere sophistry, for genuine meaning and significance is to be found in their *purpose*. The critical distinction here is between systematic philosophy, concerned with the presentation of a particular view or belief (*dṛṣṭi*), and edifying philosophy, engaged in strictly deconstructive activity (the Mādhyamika *prasaṅgavākya*). The central concepts of an edifying philosophy must ultimately be abandoned when they have served the purpose for which they were designed. Such concepts are not used to express a view but *to achieve an effect:* They are a means (*upāya*). (Huntington 1989: xii–xiii, emphases original)

Huntington reiterates the point at numerous places throughout his book, perhaps most forcefully when he writes "Mādhyamika philosophy cannot be properly understood when extracted from the matrix of its soteriological aims" (Huntington 1989: 13); and "the entire deconstructive project of the Mādhyamika needs to be read as a response to the question: How can all living beings find happiness, peace, and liberation from every form of fear and suffering?" (Huntington 1989: 201 n. 21).

91. For a succinct exemplification of the esteem in which Yinshun is held, I cite the opening words of his translator Shi Huifeng (a.k.a. Matthew Orsborn): "Not only was Venerable Master Yìnshùn (印順導師) one of the greatest figures in modern Chinese Buddhist history, he may also prove to be one of the greatest figures of Chinese Buddhist intellectual thought at any point" (Yinshun 2017: i). For a systematic introduction to Yinshun's life and work, see Bingenheimer 2004. For detailed study of Yinshun's innovative approach to Nāgārjuna and Madhyamaka more generally, see Travagnin 2009, partly summarized in Travagnin 2012 and revised with especial focus on the *Da Zhidu Lun* (大智度論 / **Mahāprajñāpāramitā śāstra* / **Mahāprajñāpāramitopadeśa*) in Travagnin 2022.

92. Yinshun 2017 is a fluent and copiously annotated English translation of Parts One and Two of this work. Here, however, I will be quoting exclusively from Part Four, which is directly concerned with Nāgārjuna. I thank Matthew Orsborn for allowing me to refer to a draft version of his as-yet unpublished translation of this while articulating my own translations.
93. Ch. 近代的學者, 從梵、藏本『中論』等去研究, 也有相當的成就, 但總是以世間學的立場來論究, 著重於論破的方法——邏輯、辨證法, 以為龍樹學如何如何. Foreseeably, Yinshun's criticisms of the preponderant consensus among his peers and markedly differing approach to Nāgārjuna led to "attacks he received from contemporary Chinese Buddhists . . . [and] lively and long-term debate within the contemporary Chinese Buddhist world" (Travagnin 2012: 253).
94. Ch. 種種四句, 無非依語言, 思想的相對性, 展轉 推論而成立.
95. For the original Sanskrit text and English translation of this verse, see §4.2. The Chinese version of Kumārajīva from which Yinshun and the other Chinese-language scholars of the MK generally quote (see Yinshun 1985: 229) gives the verse as: 如來過戲論 / 而人生戲論 / 戲論破慧眼 / 是皆不見佛.
96. For the original Sanskrit text and English translation of this verse, see §3.4. The Chinese version runs: 寂滅相中無 / 常無常等四 / 寂滅相中無 / 邊無邊等四. Note that Bocking (1995: 325) translates the verse from the Chinese rather differently as: "Within the characteristic of calm quiescence, / The four (views) of permanence, impermanence etc, do not exist. / Within the characteristic of calm quiescence, / The four (views) of limit, no limit, etc. do not exist."
97. Ch. 從分別善 巧, 辨析精嚴來說, 是大有功德的。但如忘失教意, 專在論議上判是非, 怕要失去龍樹的宗趣了!
98. Ch. 非常善巧的教說. The full sentence runs: "This teaching of the middle way can well establish all dharmas while avoiding all views. One could say that it is an exceptionally skillful form of teaching indeed." Ch. 中道說, 能善立一切法, 遠離一切見, 可說是非常善巧的教說. For reference, The Chinese version of MK:27:30, the final verse of the entire MK, runs: 瞿曇大聖主 / 憐愍說是法 / 悉斷一切見 / 我今稽首禮. For the original Sanskrit, English translation, and discussion, see §4.2.
99. For another work exemplifying his distinctive approach to Nāgārjuna and Madhyamaka, see Yinshun 2009; for more general theoretical works outlining what Yinshun considers to be *The Three Essentials for Studying Buddhism* (學佛三要), deems needful for *Studying Buddhism by Means of Buddhism* (以佛法研究佛法), and articulates as *My View on Religion* (我之宗教觀), see Yinshun 2003, 1998a, and 1998b respectively.
100. Unsurprisingly, given the logicalizing mission we have seen him adopt, Tillemans dismisses de La Vallée Poussin's understanding of the tetralemma as a "'therapeutic' use of language" as a "logically trivial interpretation" (Tillemans 1999: 190; see de La Vallée Poussin 1933).
101. See Huntington 2007: 127.
102. This point will find fuller elaboration in Chapter 4.

103. For more on a "dialectical" reading of the tetralemma, see the discussion of Wu Rujun in §2.2.2.
104. To take this a step further, note that "*nirvāṇa*" stems from the verbal root "*vā*" meaning "to blow" (as in air) coupled with the negative prefix "*nir*" (out, away) and the abstract noun suffix "*ṇa*." Strict philologists may rail, but I would like to think that "*vāṇa*" (blowing), as opposed to "*nirvāṇa*" (blowing out), is closely related (if not etymologically then, let us say, poetically) to "vanity." After all, is not to blow one's trumpet, as the saying goes, a vain affair? And is not to blow out to expire; that is, to extinguish the vain flame of self?
105. See the not dissimilar formulation in Huntington 1989: 136: "The entire conceptual edifice of the Mādhyamika must be allowed to collapse in on itself in order to fulfill its purpose." With regard to the tetralemma specifically, "Buddhist dialectic refutation moves beyond the dilemma and constantly makes use of the tetralemma. Furthermore, it uses the latter only to pass beyond it" (Faure 2004: 36).

Chapter 3

1. Mine is a relatively guarded formulation, but others have been more forthright, declaring, for example, that "it is hard to think of a position that endorses such a view [of Nāgārjunian emptiness] in Western philosophy" (Priest 2018: 56).
2. For a discussion of the variety of forms historically attested in the Western philosophical canon in the context of an initial attempt to augment these with Buddhist models, see Stepien 2020b: 11–13.
3. I adapt here the title of one of the *sūtras* Nāgārjuna studied, that generally known as the *Diamond Sūtra* (*Vajracchedikā Prajñāpāramitā Sūtra*).
4. For the Buddha's use of the tetralemma, see, for example, the *Brahmajāla Sutta* 2.27 in the *Dīgha Nikāya* (Walshe 1995: 81), and the *Cūḷamālunkya Sutta* 7 and *Aggivacchagotta Sutta* 9–12, both in the *Majjhima Nikāya* (Ñāṇamoli and Bodhi 1995: 536 and 591 respectively). For a discussion of the use of the *catuṣkoṭi* in the earliest Buddhist *sūtras*, see Westerhoff 2009: 74; for pre-Buddhist uses of the *catuṣkoṭi*, see Raju 1954: 694. In an evident effort to salvage some respectability for Nāgārjuna given his reiterated use of such a logically disreputable structure, Hayes conjectures that "The Buddha's use of this framework may have inclined Nāgārjuna to treat it with some respect, even if his own command of logic had advanced beyond the level of sophistication that the tetralemma represents" (Hayes 1994: 322).
5. Guanding T 1767, 008:

    非非。非不非。非亦非亦不非。非非非非不非。
    不非非。不非不非。不非亦非亦不非。不非非非非不非。
    亦非亦不非非。亦非亦不非不非。亦非亦不非亦非亦不非。亦非亦不非非非非不非。

非非非不非非。非非非不非不非。非非非不非亦非亦不非。非非非不非非非非不非。

I thank Tom Mazanec for reminding me of this passage.

6. See, for example, Raju: "The four-fold negation exhausts all the alternatives" (Raju 1954: 713); Murti: "Four and only four views are possible: two are primary and the other two secondary" (Murti 1955: 129), and "All possible modes of predication are classified under four heads: *bhāva* (existence, affirmation) and *abhāva* (non-existence, negation) are the primary modes which are conjointly affirmed (*ubhayam*) or disjunctively denied (*na bhāvaḥ, naivābhāvaḥ*) to make the third and the fourth class of predicates respectively" (Murti 1955: 228); Ruegg: "all conceptually imaginable positions are exhausted" (Ruegg 1977: 1), and "The 'tetralemma' is of course itself based in the last analysis on a binary set of two opposed terms, in conformity with the principles of contradiction and excluded middle; the full quaternary set is then meant to cover exhaustively all conceptually imaginable positions in which a putative entity might be postulated" (Ruegg 1981: 39–40 n. 97); Nagao: "*Catuṣkoṭi* consists of any four alternative propositions such as, for example, 'exists', 'does not exist', 'both exists and does not exist', and 'neither exists nor does not exist'. It is observed that the existence of all things is summed up and represented by these four propositions and that, dialectically speaking, there is no other possibility" (Nagao 1991: 179); Tachikawa: "The tetralemma is essentially the method whereby Nāgārjuna . . . sought to distribute in an exhaustive fashion the entire universe of discourse" (Tachikawa 1997: 149); Katsura: "The Tetralemma is a method to enumerate all the theoretically or logically possible propositions or views (*dṛṣṭi*) with regard to a pair of concepts" (Katsura 2000: 205); Westerhoff: "the tetralemma is usually employed in Mādhyamika argumentation to provide an enumeration of four exclusive and exhaustive logical alternatives, all of which are then shown to be deficient and thus rejected" (Westerhoff 2006: 391) (the exception being at MK:18:8 which, though presumably "exclusive and exhaustive," affirms rather than rejects the four alternatives); and Jones: "He [Nāgārjuna] uses the form of the four options simply to try to cover all positive and negative possibilities—i.e., he is saying there are no other options. . . . This approach obviously does not work unless it exhausts all logical possibilities" (Jones 2018: 49). Exhaustiveness likewise characterizes pre-Nāgārjunian uses of the *catuṣkoṭi*; thus, Williams states that the Buddha's use of it "is a rejection of all possibilities, whether affirmative or negative or any admixture of the two, or ordinary thought and logic" (J. Williams 2000: 41). Although I am in agreement with all the afore-cited statements insofar as they affirm the exhaustiveness of the *catuṣkoṭi*, my argument in §3.3 on "Tetralemma as Tetrāletheia" as to the inadequacy of binary analyses of the quaternary tetralemma should avert the reader to my disagreement with views that take the first two lemmata as primary (e.g., Murti 1955; Ruegg 1981) or (what I take to be equivalent) the tetralemma as regarding "a pair of concepts" (Katsura 2000). These and like interpretations take the tetralemma to be functioning within a bivalent logical schema, whereas I am proposing to take it as functioning within (or better, as exhausting) a four-valued propositional calculus.

7. Westerhoff (2006: 390 n. 72) mentions this identification by Wayman of the four lemmata as directed to four different opponents, and he also lists several other versions of the same argument.
8. Respectively, 24:7: *na tvaṃ vetsi*; 24:11: *mandamedhasam*; and 24:15: *aśvam evābhirūḍhaḥ sann aśvam evāsi vismṛtaḥ*.
9. MK:24:36: *sarvasaṃvyavahārāṃś ca laukikān pratibādhase.*
10. It has become customary (and, according to Garfield 2015: 62, preferable) to translate *svabhāva* as 'intrinsic nature' in contemporary English-language scholarship. Given the thrust of my argument as this emerges in what follows, I have preferred the etymologically closer renderings 'own-being' or 'selfbeing' (regarding which usage, see, e.g., Ruegg 1977; Taber 1998; Ye 2019; J. Williams 2000). As Ames states, *svabhāva* "literally means '[its] own (*sva*) existence or being or nature (*bhāva*)'" (Ames 1982: 161). This is echoed by Jakubczak, who translates *svabhāva* into Polish as *samobyt* and explains that it stems "from *sva*—'own' but also—'thanks to one's own self', 'of one's nature' plus *bhāva*—'being', 'existence'" (*od* sva—"*własny*," *ale też* —"*dzięki samemu sobie*," "*ze swej natury*" *oraz* bhāva—"*byt*," "istnienie") (Jakubczak 2002a: 261). For his part, Bugault translates *svabhāva* into French as *être en soi* but also provides for *nature intrinsèque* (Bugault 2002: 188). Katsura 2023 is the latest in a long line of papers (see Katsura 2023: 132–133) responding to Hayes 1994 and devoted to ascertaining the senses of *svabhāva*, *parabhāva*, *bhāva* and *abhāva* in MK:15.
11. MK:15:10: *astīti śāśvatagrāho nāstīty ucchedadarśanam / tasmād astitvanāstitve nāśrīyeta vicakṣaṇaḥ.*
12. I use 'dialectical' here with no Hegelian overtones to denote simply the critical investigation of truth.
13. See also Priest 2018: xx: "A dialetheia is a true contradiction—that is, something of the form $A \wedge \neg A$ which is true; and dialetheism is the view that there are such things."
14. For further details, see Priest 2006: xvii–xxi and 284–302.
15. Garfield has faced his own share of criticism from professional philosophers, though for more orientalist reasons. As he puts it, "I discovered when I—a Western, analytically-trained philosopher of mind—began to work on Buddhist philosophy that many in philosophy and cognitive science took this as evidence of some kind of insanity, or at least as an abandonment of philosophy, per se" (Garfield 1995: xiv). I can only assume that Garfield and Priest *together* have faced even more extreme antagonism.
16. In addition to the statements from Garfield and Priest 2009: 71 cited in §3.1, see also:

    > Classical Indian logic and rhetoric regards any proposition as defining a logical space involving four candidate positions, or corners (*koṭi*) in distinction to most Western logical traditions that consider only two—truth and falsity: the proposition may be true (and not false); false (and not true); both true and false; neither true nor false. (Garfield and Priest 2002: 99)

    These positions or corners appear to be four valuations of two truth values (i.e., 'true' and 'false'), though as we have seen in §2.3, Priest in fact speaks of "a four-valued semantic catuṣkoṭi, and a 5-valued ontological catuṣkoṭi" (Priest 2018: 73).

17. That Priest conceives of his notion of dialetheia as 'in contradiction' (!) with the Aristotelian tradition is clear from the final words of his book, where he declares its aim as "trying to overturn what has been the received wisdom on a topic so central to Western philosophy for over two thousand years" (Priest 2006: 302).
18. The alpha-privative refers to the fact that the word is a compound of 'a' + 'letheia', where the latter component comes from 'lethe', meaning 'oblivion' or 'concealment' (as in the name of the mythical river) to give 'un-concealment' or 'un-forgetting'.
19. For a discussion of Sanskritic views of truth as concealment in conversation with Heidegger, see Ganeri 2007: 1–2; for a careful discussion of "Heidegger on *Alḗtheia*, Buddhist Thinkers on *Satya*," see Kapstein 2001: 205–229; for a brief comparison between Mādhyamikas' understanding of own-being (*svabhāva*) and Heidegger's of being (*Sein*), see Arnold 2005: 191 and more amply Arnold 2019: 705–711; and for an application of dialetheic notions to Heidegger's thought, see Priest 2002: 237–248.
20. For more detailed discussion of the two truths by Nagao, see Nagao 1989: 13–22. For related discussions, see, e.g., Garfield 1995: 297–298 n. 109, the essays collected in Sprung 1973, and Newland and Tillemans 2011: 11–15, where the authors distinguish three senses of *saṃvṛti*: (1) as "concealing the actual way things are . . . 'true-for-the-ignorant', 'true-for-the-obscured', or 'true-for-the-benighted' "; (2) as "dependent arising (*pratītyasamutpāda*), more exactly as 'mutual dependence' (*parasparasaṃbhavana*)"; and (3) as "agreements governing the use of signs, that is, *saṃketa* . . . 'convention-governed symbols', 'agreed-upon usage' " (Newland and Tillemans 2011: 13). Collins (1982: 154–156) traces the notion of the two truths in Indian thought back to before the advent of Buddhism itself.
21. This is in part what motivates Sara McClintock's innovative and illuminating translations of *saṃvṛti* and *saṃvṛti-satya* as "camouflage" and "camouflagic truth" respectively (see McClintock 2023: 4 n. 8).
22. The clearest formulation is at MK:24:8–9. For the Sanskrit original and English translation of 24:8, see §2.2.2; for 24:9, see §5.1.
23. The clearest formulation of this is at MK:25:19–20. For the Sanskrit original, see §4.3.2, and for further discussion see also §5.1 and §5.2.3.
24. See also the similar formulation by Arnold: "The ultimate truth, in a sense, is that there *is* no 'ultimate truth'—a fact, however, that is proposed as ultimately true" (Arnold 2005: 120, emphasis original). An adequate presentation of the two truths, entailing as it would a presentation of Nāgārjuna's conceptions of emptiness (*śūnyatā*), dependent co-origination (*pratītya-samutpāda*), and their interrelatedness, is beyond my scope in the present chapter. For this subtle point about the emptiness of emptiness to be appreciated, however, I cite two of the more lucid summaries:

    > Now, since all things are empty, all things lack any ultimate nature; and this is a characterization from the ultimate perspective. Thus, ultimately, things are empty. But emptiness is, by definition, the lack of any essence or ultimate nature. Nature, or essence, is just what empty things are empty of. Hence, ultimately, things must lack emptiness. To be ultimately empty is, ultimately, to

> lack emptiness. In other words, emptiness is the nature of all things; for this reason, they have no nature, not even emptiness. (Garfield and Priest 2002: 101)

> To say that emptiness itself is empty, then, is only to say that emptiness is not an independent property antecedent to which there could *be* existents – which are not, however, thereby said not to exist, but precisely to exist in the only way that anything can (viz., reducibly, relatively, dependently). (Arnold 2005: 190, emphasis original)

This interpretation has recently been criticized, unconvincingly, by Ferraro 2013, to which Siderits and Garfield 2013 is a reply. It is worth noting that, if indeed "It is widely assumed among Indian philosophers that an entity cannot operate on itself" (Siderits 1988: 313), then this is yet another way in which Nāgārjunian emptiness subverts widely held assumptions. For that emptiness applies to emptiness cannot be doubted: this knife most certainly cuts itself (cf. Siderits 1988: 313). Finally, note that 'the emptiness of emptiness' (*śūnyatāśūnyatā*) is not strictly speaking a Nāgārjunian phrase, but is rather to be found in the *Madhyamakāvatāra* commentary by Candrakīrti no longer extant in Sanskrit (for a translation of the relevant verse, 6.186, see Huntington 1989: 180).

25. At the risk of being tripped up by overzealously punctilious critics, I suppose it behooves me to underline that my use of the 'pieces of the puzzle' metaphor is, precisely and a little playfully, metaphorical; it is not meant to entail any diminution of the matter at hand to a mere 'puzzle' or, for that matter, 'riddle'.
26. As noted by Williams, Nāgārjuna also ends his *Paramārthastava* (*Hymn to the Ultimate*) with "another of his gentle jokes" (Williams 2009: 178), in this case based on another of the standard epithets of the Buddha: *Sugata* or 'Well-gone'. In Tucci's unimprovable translation: "I have praised the Well-gone (Sugata) who is neither gone nor come, and who is devoid of any going. Through the merit so acquired may this world go along the path of the well-gone" (Tucci 1932: 325).
27. MK:22:11: *śūnyam iti na vaktavyam aśūnyam iti vā bhavet / ubhayaṃ nobhayaṃ ceti prajñaptyarthaṃ tu kathyate.*
28. MK:22:12: *śāśvatāśāśvatādy atra kutaḥ śānte catuṣṭayam / antānantādi cāpy atra kutaḥ śānte catuṣṭayam.* For reasons unclear to me, Siderits and Katsura (2013: 249) translate *śānte* as "who is free of intrinsic nature."
29. See MK:22:13ab: *ghanagrāho gṛhītas tu yenāstīti tathāgataḥ.*
30. See MK:22:13cd: *nāstīti sa vikalpayan nirvṛtasyāpi kalpayet.*
31. See MK:22:15: *prapañcayanti ye buddhaṃ prapañcātītam avyayam / te prapañcahatāḥ sarve na paśyanti tathāgatam.* See also Ruegg, who in regard to Nāgārjuna's statement in this verse that the *Tathāgata* is "beyond discursive development," notes Candrakīrti's explanation that this is so because "all discursive development is dependent on a substantial thing (*vastu*); but the *tathāgata* is no substantial thing (*avastuka*)" (Ruegg 1977: 13).
32. This statement paraphrases MK:22:14ab: *svabhāvataś ca śūnye 'smiṃś cintā naivopapadyate.*
33. MK:22:16: *tathāgato yatsvabhāvas tatsvabhāvam idaṃ jagat / tathāgato niḥsvabhāvo niḥsvabhāvam idaṃ jagat.* For further discussion of this verse, see §5.2.3.

34. MK:27:28: *antavac cāpy anantaṃ ca prasiddham ubhayaṃ yadi / siddhyen naivāntavat kāmaṃ naivānantavad ity api*. See also MK:27:18 for a parallel formulation regarding permanence and impermanence.
35. In Appendix 5 (on "The Story of the Bhikṣu Uttara") of chapter 42 (on "The Great Loving-Kindness and the Great Compassion of the Buddhas") of the *Mahā-prajñāpāramitā-śāstra* or *Mahā-prajñāpāramitā-upadeśa-śāstra* (大智度論, T 1509), a text whose traditional ascription to Nāgārjuna is now deemed highly doubtful, we find the story, recounted also in the Mūlasarvāstivāda Vinaya and the *Divyāvadāna*, of how the then Buddha Kaśyapa 迦葉 predicted that the monk (*bhikṣu*) Uttara 鬱多羅 would in future become Śākyamuni Buddha (see Chödrön 2001).
36. Nagao states that "for one whose point of departure is *śūnyatā*, even the claim that all is *śūnyatā* is absurd, for non-assertion or non-maintenance of a position is the real meaning of *śūnyatā*" (Nagao 1991: 42, also cited in Garfield 1995: 282 fn. 104). As should be clear from my comments earlier, I consider this characterization superior to straightforwardly positive ones insofar as it acknowledges the radically subversive nature of Nāgārjuna's rhetorical strategy, but nevertheless inadequate insofar as it avers the negative over the positive, and thereby falls victim to the other horn of hypostatization.
37. *Rhetoric* 1412 a 26 (Aristotle 1984: 2254, where, however, it is translated as something which "does not fit in with the ideas you already have.") I owe the reference to Ricoeur 2003: 29. Bagger discusses the etymological and philosophical uses of 'paradox' at Bagger 2007: 2–3.
38. For reference, "Paraconsistentists reject the universal validity of the rule of *ex falso quodlibet*, i.e., that every proposition follows from contradictions" (Mareș 2004: 265). This would result in sheer triviality.
39. See also:

> *Śūnyatā* is the removal of the constrictions which our concepts, with their practical or sentimental bias, have put on reality. It is the *freeing* of reality of the artificial and accidental restrictions, and *not the denial* of reality. *Śūnyatā* is negation of negations. (Murti 1955: 161, emphases original)

Robinson, for whom "it is possible to transcribe the *Kāṛikās* entirely, chapter by chapter, into logical notation" (Robinson 1957: 307), is clearly unable to conceive of a limit to logic beyond which one may pass.

40. See perhaps most pertinently MK:18:5, translated and further discussed in §4.2 and §5.2.2. As Ruegg states, "all the *koṭis* are to be negated with a view to breaking down the dichotomizing universe of conceptualization and discourse" (Ruegg 1977: 22).
41. See in this regard the eloquent statement by Williams: "an ontology is a conceptuality, and apophasis denies all conceptualities" (J. Williams 2000: 11).
42. MK:25:10cd: *na bhāvo nābhāvo nirvāṇam*.
43. That ontology is concerned with what is has been contested by certain modern philosophers who have criticized such an understanding as too simple; see, for example, the discussion in Hofweber 2020: §4.5. The word itself, however, is etymological testimony to such an understanding, comprised as it is of the Greek roots for "being, what is" and "the study of" (OED). An analytic philosopher of the caliber

of Quine, moreover, certainly sees no problem in the "simplicity" of "the ontological problem . . . [which] can be put in three Anglo-Saxon monosyllables: 'What is there?'" (Quine 1948: 21). As early as *Being and Time*, Heidegger already criticized the implicit, and hence inescapable, ontological commitment entailed in the very use of "ontology," a critique he amplified throughout his later work. While I underline here the etymology of "ontology," I see the standard understanding of "metaphysics," according to which "Metaphysics is about what there is and what it is like" (Jackson 1998: 4, cited in Tillemans 2016: 222), to not differ significantly for present purposes.

44. See in this regard Garfield:

> For a view is possible if, and only if, (1) there is some*thing* to view and (2) there is some way in which it is viewed. . . . But from the perspective in which we find emptiness, we don't find any entities or any characteristics, not even emptiness itself or the fact of its emptiness. Hence again, since we can't view emptiness even as empty, in view of its very emptiness, we can't have a view of emptiness. (Garfield 1995: 355–356, emphasis original)

While Siderits and Katsura are right to state, in their commentary to the aforementioned MK:22:13, that "The Tathāgata, having attained final nirvāṇa, is not available as an object to which conceptual distinctions might apply" (Siderits and Katsura 2013: 250), this does not bring out the reality-wide implications of the anontological reading I am proposing; that is, its applicability to conventional as well as ultimate reality. Kantor gets at this in his recognition that

> emptiness of inherent existence implies ontological indeterminacy. The specific term for this indeterminacy is the "middle way" (*zhongdao* 中道), which denies both the real existence and the complete nonexistence of things rooted in patterns of interdependence. Furthermore, no thing that pertains to the conventional realm has any invariant or definite identity (*juedingxiang* 決定相), which also means that those things are ontically indeterminate. (Kantor 2014: 346)

For further discussions of ontological (and ontic) indeterminacy in the thought of Nāgārjuna's Chinese Madhyamaka intellectual descendants, see Ho 2013, 2014, 2019 and Ziporyn 2019b.

45. See most perspicuously MK:26.
46. MK:18:7: *nivṛttam abhidhātavyaṃ nivṛttaś cittagocaraḥ / anutpannāniruddhā hi nirvāṇam iva dharmatā*. With regard to this verse, see also Ruegg, who explains that "outside the domain of discursive and conceptual thinking there is no propositional naming" (Ruegg 1977: 12), and Nagao, who states that "Ultimate meaning is ineffable not because it negates language, but because it is devoid of all mental activity" (Nagao 1989: 67). As I will go on to argue, the cessation of "the domain of thought" and the cessation of whatever is "expressed in language" are to be understood as intimately wedded (indeed, mutually entailing) in Nāgārjuna's thought because they both rest on the same base(lessness) of anontological emptiness in place of ontological being.
47. MK:25:24ab. For the original Sanskrit and further discussion, see §4.2.
48. MK:25:24cd. For the original Sanskrit and further discussion, see §4.2.

49. The Kantian and Hegelian overtones of Nagao's formulations need not detain us here.
50. As Siderits states in a different but overlapping context, "Madhyamaka actually agrees with Abhidharma that S ["Only that which possesses its nature intrinsically is ultimately real"] is the appropriate test of *dharma*-hood. They disagree only about whether anything actually has intrinsic nature and so counts as ultimately real" (Siderits 2019: 655).
51. For a translation of the Chan text (絕觀論, more fully 三藏法師菩提達摩絕觀論), see Morinaga 2012 (who translates the title as *The Ceasing of Notions*); for discussion, see McRae 2000 (*Treatise on the Transcendence of Cognition*), and Sharf 2014: 947–948 (*Treatise on Cutting Off Discernment*), who translates a line Nāgārjuna would surely have been proud of (無心即無物無物即天真。天真即大道) as "No mind is no thing, and no thing is reality itself. This reality is the great Way."
52. MK:24:36–37: *sarvasaṃvyavahārāṃś ca laukikān pratibādhase / yat pratītyasamutpādaśūnyatāṃ pratibādhase // na kartavyaṃ bhavet kiṃ cid anārabdhā bhavet kriyā / kārakaḥ syād akurvāṇaḥ śūnyatāṃ pratibādhataḥ*). Indeed, we will see in Chapter 5 that free action as a whole, and concomitantly truly ethical action as Nāgārjuna understands it, necessitates emptiness.
53. That a 'selfbeing being' is, for Nāgārjuna, a tautological designation, is apparent from the numerous places in his opus where he defines a being (according to the espoused tenets of his varied interlocutors) as precisely something that is possessed of selfbeing. See, for example, MK:15:4:

    Furthermore, without selfbeing or otherbeing
    How can there be a being?
    For a being is established
    If selfbeing or otherbeing is

    (*svabhāvaparabhāvābhyām ṛte bhāvaḥ kutaḥ punaḥ / svabhāve parabhāve ca sati bhāvo hi sidhyati*). 'Otherbeing' (*parabhāva*) is being dependent on the selfbeing (*svabhāva*) of an other. As Nāgārjuna has argued in the preceding verse, in refuting *svabhāva* he has effectively also refuted *parabhāva*, for this latter would necessarily depend on the *svabhāva* of an other. Given that no such *svabhāva* exists, no such *parabhāva* can exist either. The tautological nature of a phrase such as 'selfbeing being' (in my terminology) has not stopped commentators of all stripes from using phrases such as "hypostasized entity (*bhāva*) having self-existence (*svabhāva*)" (Ruegg 2000: 208), or "entity endowed with self-existence" (Ruegg 2000: 211). Surely, however, any 'hypostasized entity' is thereby imputed 'self-existence'. Otherwise, in what would the hypostasis consist? That said, it is difficult to avoid such circumlocutions altogether, especially as the definitional collapsing of *bhāva* into *svabhāva* does not, of course, do away with any and all conceptual distinctions between the two notions.
54. For the original Sanskrit and further discussion of this and related verses of the VV, see §4.2.
55. See in this light Arnold's characterization of Nāgārjuna's, as opposed to Ābhidhārmikas', understanding of *anātman*: "Nāgārjuna thus argues not against existence, per se, but against a particular *criterion* of existence—against, that is, the idea that to exist is finally to be some kind of *thing*" (Arnold 2019: 702).

56. *Niḥsvabhāva* is understood here as equivalent not to *svabhāvaśūnyatā* (selfbeing-emptiness, the real emptiness of purported selfbeings) but to *asvabhāva* (no-selfbeing).
57. As such, Huntington's statement that "when the Mādhyamika philosopher negates the reality of the world, he affirms neither a 'something' nor a 'nothing' in its place" (Huntington 1989: 58) is perfectly correct, though strictly speaking incomplete if applied to the *catuṣkoṭi*, for in its standard utterance this would affirm neither something, nothing, both something and nothing, nor neither something nor nothing.
58. See Ruegg 2000: 106, where *inter alia* he proposes 'propositional thesis' as a translation for *pratijñā*, 'assertion/asserted tenet' for *abhyupagama*, 'assertoric philosophical proposition/position' for *pakṣa*, 'doctrine of one's own' for *svamata*, and 'philosophical system' for *siddhānta*. Depending on context, I have rendered *pratijñā* as 'proposition' or as 'thesis'.
59. I see my point here as in agreement with McGuire's understanding "that for the Mādhyamika there is an ultimate truth, but it is non-propositional" (McGuire 2017: 392). I will return to McGuire's analysis, and specifically to his idea that "It is therefore incoherent, misleading and ultimately self-defeating to claim *śūnyatā* for one's own tradition" (397), in §5.4.
60. See in regard to all of this the statement by Huntington (1989: 106–107) cited in §3.5.
61. Indeed, this kind of criticism of Nāgārjuna's 'thesis of no thesis' is a commonplace throughout the critical literature; I can only hope that my understanding of it as elaborated throughout this book helps clear away at least some of the casuistry from ensuing debates. See also my point about "view" and "viewpoint" in §2.2.2.
62. See in this regard Kalupahana's comments as to MK:27:

> if that right view [i.e., Nāgārjuna's "middle position"] were to become another dogma, it would certainly contribute to conflict and suffering, thereby losing its pragmatic value. In other words, a right view is one for which there cannot be grasping, for if one were to grasp it it would turn out to be a closed view not an open one. (Kalupahana 1986: 80)

Kalupahana goes on to explain that what he means by 'open view' is one that "does not subscribe to an absolute discrimination as either/or. The very idea of openness imiplies [sic] non-grasping (*anupādāna*)" (Kalupahana 1986: 92). Furthermore, one who holds such a view "is free because he does not adhere to any dogmatic view that rules out other possibilities" (Kalupahana 1986: 92). Now, I am not sure what 'absolute discrimination' (as opposed to 'relative discrimination'?) means, and I am very unsure how Nāgārjuna's supposedly 'open view' is so due to its not 'ruling out other possibilities'. After all, the entire MK is designed to demonstrate the untenability of a wide (indeed, unbounded) range of views; Nāgārjuna does not eirenically accept all views; quite the opposite, he rejects all views precisely because any view is, to use Kalupahana's term, 'closed'. As for McCagney's characterization of Nāgārjuna's philosophy as one of 'openness', based in part upon her personal preference for "the positive term 'openness' [rather] than . . . the negative term 'emptiness' " (McCagney 1997: 35), this is not particularly instructive given that 'emptiness' is far from being 'negative' for Nāgārjuna.

63. See in this regard Ruegg, who characterizes "the apagogic process of reasoning and argument represented by the Mādhyamika's *prasaṅgāpādana*" as "a special form of maieutics" (Ruegg 2000: 137). See also Abé, who speaks of "emptiness as generative and regenerative processes" (Abé 2005: 309).
64. MK:24:38: *ajātam aniruddhaṃ ca kūṭasthaṃ ca bhaviṣyati / vicitrābhir avasthābhiḥ svabhāve rahitaṃ jagat.*
65. MK:15:5: *bhāvasya ced aprasiddhir abhāvo naiva sidhyati / bhāvasya hy anyathābhāvam abhāvaṃ bruvate janāḥ.* The phrase I have translated as "an othered being is not / A being" is *anyathābhāvam abhāvaṃ*. Wood (1994: 182) translates this as "the becoming-other of existence" while Jakubczak (2002b: 264/2010: 204) gives "non-being as a change of being" (*niebytem zmianę bytu*). Garfield (1995: 222) as well as Siderits and Katsura (2013: 158) provide more idiomatically acceptable versions: "An entity that has become different / Is a nonentity" and "the non-existent to be the alteration of the existent" respectively. Both these translations, however, lose the compound nature of the term *anyathābhāvam*; what Hegel would have called, in the context of very different philosophical mission, 'self-othering', where "the living Substance . . . is the mediation of its self-othering with itself . . . It is the process of its own becoming" (Hegel 1977: 10). That the self-realization of the Self in Hegel is radically different from the realization of self-emptiness in Nāgārjuna is brought out in the very same passage, where the German thinker declares Substance to be "in truth actual only in so far as it is the movement of positing itself."
66. Slightly modified for grammatical coherence. The phrase '*śūnyatā* of *dṛṣṭis*' is taken from the *śūnyatādṛṣṭi* spoken of at MK:13:8, where Nāgārjuna calls those who take *śūnyatā* to be a *dṛṣṭi* "incurables" (*asādhyān*).
67. For a detailed history of philosophers' attempts to interpret Buddhism as *The Cult of Nothingness*, see Droit 2003. For a recently published book-length refutation of the charge, see Jakubczak 2019, in which the author summarizes nihilistic interpretations of both Buddhism generally (31–34) and Madhyamaka specifically (34–41). The charge of nihilism is, of course, long-standing, and understandably so given the subtlety of *śūnyatā*. Huntington cites Candrakīrti's response, in his commentary to MK:24:7 (*Prasannapadā*, 491), thus:

    > Emptiness is taught for the complete cessation of conceptualization; therefore, the purpose of emptiness is the cessation of all conceptualization. You, however, in imagining that the meaning of emptiness is nonexistence, actually reinforce the net of conceptualization. On this account you do not understand the purpose of emptiness. (Huntington 1989: 205 n. 25, where the Sanskrit original is also to be found; my translation substantially modifies Huntington's)

    The topos of 'the cessation of all conceptualization' (*sarvaprapañcopaśamaḥ*) as 'the purpose of emptiness' (*śūnyatāyāṁ prayojanaṁ*) will be the focus of attention in Chapter 4.
68. For a discussion of Nāgārjunian emptiness as applied to self-contradiction in the Hegelian sense, see Stepien 2023a. I echo Tillemans in declaring that Nāgārjuna's "Madhaymaka for me is about quietism and *not* having philosophical positions, and

that includes a Hegel-like advocacy of true contradictions" (Tillemans 2016: 93 n. 11, emphasis original).

69. Note that Ye's nihilistic reading forms another link in the chain of supposed apologies on behalf of Nāgārjuna motivating much of the relevant scholarship (as we have seen already in Chapter 1). For in the final stages of his exposition (prior, that is, to analyzing its fit with Nāgārjuna's philosophy overall), Ye attempts to justify what he takes to be Nāgārjuna's nihilism by arguing that " 'nihilism' need not be treated as a derogatory term" (Ye 2019: 760).
70. See §3.6 for the Sanskrit text and translation of the entire verse. Other Madhyamaka passages countering a nihilist interpretation are provided by Westerhoff (2016a: 339–340), who, moreover, notes several reasons against the interpretation (337–340), surveys several ancient and modern proponents of the nihilistic interpretation, be they by non-Buddhists such as Uddyotakara, Kumārila, Śaṅkara, Rāmānuja, Madhva, and Mādhava (340–346), fellow Buddhists such as Asaṅga, Vasubandhu, and (controversially) Candrakīrti (346–352), or Buddhologists such as Louis de La Vallée Poussin, Eugène Burnouf, Hendrik Kern, Max Walleser, Arthur Keith, Joachim Wach, and Claus Oetke in addition to the more recent accounts by Thomas Wood, Paul Williams, and David Burton (352–357), before providing a cogent and nuanced alternative account (358–374).
71. Shulman here provides a footnote wherein he translates RĀ:59 as: "If, for somebody, following the refutation of existence, non-existence is essentially done away with, why, following the refutation of non-existence, is existence not done away with?" (*syād astidūṣaṇād asya nāstitākṣipyate 'rthataḥ / nāstitādūṣaṇād evaṃ kasmān nākṣipyate 'stitā*) (Shulman 2011: 317 fn. 45). For alternative translations, see Dunne and McClintock 1997: 18; Jampa Tegchok 2017: 86; Hopkins 1998: 101–102.
72. These are (1) "Nihilism as an Extreme View"; (2) "Nihilism as Annihilationism"; (3) "Nihilism as the Denial of Efficacy"; (4) "Nihilism as a Reified Non-Existence"; and (5) "Nihilism as Moral Nihilism" (Westerhoff 2016a: 362, 363–364, 364–365, 365, 366–369 respectively). Noteworthy is the fact that these classical Indian conceptions explicitly refuted by Nāgārjuna differ significantly from the five strands of nihilism identified by Karen Carr as operative in the Western context; these being what she calls *Epistemological nihilism* ("the denial of the possibility of knowledge"), *Alethiological nihilism* ("the denial of the reality of truth"), *Metaphysical or ontological nihilism* ("the denial of an (independently existing) world," *Ethical or moral nihilism* ("the denial of the reality of moral or ethical values"), and *Existential or axiological nihilism* ("the feeling of emptiness or pointlessness that follows from the judgment, 'Life has no meaning' ") (Carr 1992: 17–18, emphases original; I owe this reference to Jakubczak 2019: 29–30). A comprehensive study of 'comparative nihilism' awaits.
73. It should be clear from the foregoing that I find Spackman's "Conceptualist Interpretation of Nāgārjuna" (Spackman 2014), based as it is on parameterizing Nāgārjuna's statements about existent things "as statements not directly about existent things, but rather about the *concept* of existence, or about the *meaning* of terms like 'exists,' and about existents only indirectly" (Spackman 2014: 152, emphases original), on "simply reject[ing] the analysis of emptiness in terms of interdependent

existence" (Spackman 2014: 153) despite Nāgārjuna's clear and repeated textual espousals thereof, on reinterpreting those espousals on the basis that they "must be taken as truths at the conventional level" (Spackman 2014: 160), and thereupon concluding despite all the evidence to the contrary that "for Nāgārjuna, in the last analysis universal ontological interdependence is not a coherent concept" (Spackman 2014: 165), unconvincing. Far preferable in this context is Kantor's discussion of the Chinese translations by Kumārajīva of Nāgārjuna's MK (中論), VV (迴諍論), and the **Mahaprajñāpāramitopadeśa* (大智度論) traditionally ascribed to him, where Kantor observes that in Nāgārjuna's Madhyamaka

> All referents of our linguistic expression(s) imply conventional falsehood, as they are built upon interdependencies and correlative oppositions (*xiangdai* 相待) sustained by (their) emptiness. Like "up" and "down," Buddhist terms such as "suffering" and "liberation," *saṃsāra* and *nirvāṇa*, "ignorance" and "wisdom," "sentient being" and "Buddha," or "noble" (*sheng* 聖) and "common" (*fan* 凡) are merely correlative opposites, exclusively referring to each other via mutual negation, and thus mutually implying one another. (Kantor 2014: 344)

This leads Kantor to the understanding of Nāgārjunian emptiness as ontological indeterminacy I have mentioned in §3.5.

74. Ruegg (1977: 58 n. 4) provides useful summaries of the *loci classici* in which such 'unexplicated points' (*avyākṛtavastu*) appear, as well as of the classical and current literature explicating, as it were, their unexplicatedness. 'Silence' is, of course, a topic to which multitudinous discourses in diverse religious traditions have been devoted; for discussions of how silence relates to Nāgārjuna specifically, see, for example, Murti 1955: 36ff; Hayes 1994: §5; Nagao 1991: 35–49; and Sebastian 2016: §3.5. Collins 1982: 116–143 provides a highly illuminating account of the preceding context and philosophical import of silence. Regarding this last, see also Ruegg 1981: 35 fn. 92: "Silence as refraining from verbalization and as philosophically motivated aposiopesis is not mere absence of semiosis on the pragmatic level. And it can therefore be regarded as a semiotic sign in its own right, even though it abolishes the ordinary processes of the semantic level." Finally, Jakubczak differentiates between four senses of silence: (1) "The silence of (aware) ignorance . . . indicating ignorance of the answer" (*Milczenie (uświadomionej) niewiedzy . . . wskazujące na nieznajomość odpowiedzi*); (2) "The silence of the skeptic . . . an expression of the fundamental cognitive limitations of man" (*Milczenie sceptyka . . . wyrazem fundamentalnych ograniczeń poznawczych człowieka*); (3) "The silence of the mystic . . . an expression of the extra-empirical nature of transcendent being" (*Milczenie mistyka . . . wyrazem pozapojęciowej natury bytu transcendentnego*); and (4) "The silence of the Mādhyamika" (*milczenie madhjamika*). This last naturally receives the bulk of Jakubczak's attention, and it is characterized as being due "to the conviction that any, even correct (i.e., true) linguistic articulation can become an object of egoistic attachment" (*przeświadczenia, że każda, nawet trafna, tj. prawdziwa artykulacja językowa może stać się przedmiotem egoistycznego lgnięcia*) (Jakubczak 2017c: 86–87, reprinted in Jakubczak 2019: 388–389). We will soon see (in Chapter 4) just such an awareness of the trappings not

only of the linguistic articulation of views but of view-holding as such on the part of Nāgārjuna.

75. I cite here the lucid translation of the *Vimalakīrti-nirdeśa-sūtra* by Thurman (1976: 77). Note his comment, however, that "all silence is not to be exaggeratedly taken as the profoundest teaching, but only such a silence in the special context of profound thought on the ultimate" (132).
76. MK:18:7: *nivṛttam abhidhātavyaṃ nivṛttaś cittagocaraḥ / anutpannāniruddhā hi nirvāṇam iva dharmatā.*
77. See Garfield: "despite their ontic unity, the ultimate truth is epistemologically and soteriologically more significant than the conventional" (Garfield 1995: 297 n. 108). That ultimate (*paramārtha*) truth is *epistemologically* more significant is so because only by means of abandoning the concealment (*saṃvṛti*) of truth embodied in the conventional does one see revealed the ultimate as the conventional—and this realization itself constitutes the *soteriological* significance of ultimate truth.
78. In this connection, Turner's analysis of what he calls the "strategy of *opposing oppositions*" or of "*negating the propositional*," as opposed to merely making "*negative propositions*"; a discursive strategy, that is, according to which "the final, apophatic, negations *negate difference itself*, and so negate the negation between sameness and difference" (Turner 1995: 209, 35, 271, emphases original), could well be applied to Nāgārjuna.
79. See also in this context Ruegg's statement that "In sum, the *paramārtha* finds its only appropriate 'expression' in the silence of the saint (*ārya-tūṣṇīmbhāva*), propositions being applicable only to entities within the sphere of discursive development (*prapañca*) and dichotomizing conceptualization (*vikalpa*)" (Ruegg 1977: 12). In different contexts, Thurman and Collins both affirm the constitutive interdependence of silence and language. In discussing "the golden silence that issues effortlessly in the golden speech of Tsong Khapa and the Centrist [that is, Tibetan Madhyamaka] masters," Thurman states that "such speech does not 'break' such silence. It is balanced with it. It is the integration of silence and speech that is the central way" (Thurman 1984: 172–173). In speaking of speaking of *nirvāṇa* as leading to silence within "the Pali imaginaire," meanwhile, Collins states that "the ineffable is brought into being as an aspect of the effable," leading to "a silence-in-discourse that creates meaning as such" (Collins 2010: 185, 186).
80. Contrary to standard interpretations of Nāgārjuna's use of the term '*vyavahāra*' at MK:24:10 that render it as a simple alternative formulation for 'conventional truth' (i.e., *saṃvrti-satya*, 俗諦), Ogawa argues that "What Nāgārjuna means by the term in question is the verbalization of the truth or the truth as it is spoken of" (Ogawa 2019: 614). What I would specify in this context is that the term '*vyavahāra*' refers more specifically to the transactional-pragmatic level of truth/reality (see, e.g., Ruegg 2010: 406), whereas '*saṃvrti*' refers to the surface or conventional level (see also Nagao 1989: 39). Tibetan interpretations of '*paramārtha*' and '*saṃvrti*' are detailed by Thakchoe (2007: 46–78). Regarding the relationship between ultimate truth and (in) expressibility, see also Ruegg 2000: 109 fn. 5:

> The idea that ultimate reality—the *paramārtha* —as such is inexpressible (or ineffable, *anabhilāpya*, *nirabhilāpya*; cf. also *avyavahāra* and *acintya*) is to be distinguished in the history of Buddhist thought from the concept of the indeterminable or undecidable (*avācya*, *avaktavya* . . .). As something admitted in Buddhist thought, inexpressibility has also to be kept apart from the 'neither *x* nor not *x*' position represented by the fourth member of the 'tetralemma' (*catuṣkoṭi*), all of whose positions have in fact been repudiated by Buddhist thinkers.

I am arguing that Nāgārjuna did not only not consider *paramārtha-satya* inexpressible but used the *catuṣkoṭi* as an effective means by which to express it, and thereby to express the wholescale rejection of views.

81. MK:27:30. For the original Sanskrit, English translation, and further discussion, see §4.2.

Chapter 4

1. To my knowledge, Jay Garfield and Ethan Mills are unique among latter-day commentators in drawing attention to this. Garfield acknowledges that "There is a startling grammatical and poetic parallel between this closing verse and the dramatic dedicatory verses" (Garfield 1995: 354); yet, as will be demonstrated later, he is far from alone in not being willing to draw conclusions quite as radical as Nāgārjuna's text demands. For his part, Mills proposes two phases in Nāgārjuna's argumentation, where the latter undermines the former such that Nāgārjuna "ultimately takes no philosophical positions of his own," and while his "texts freely move between these phases . . . Still, a general tendency to move toward the second phase can be detected in the [MK] from the fact that the verses most amenable to phase two are found in the dedication (*mangalaṃ*), at the end of several chapters, and especially at the end of the text" (Mills 2018b: 97; see also Mills 2018a: 35–36 and my further discussion in fn. 89 later).

   Regarding my translation, technical Buddhist terms in Sanskrit are notoriously slippery; thus, for example, the *prapañca* in *prapañcopaśamaṃ*, which I have rendered 'conceptualization', has been translated variously as "conceptual construction" (Garfield 1995: 2), "conceptual diffusion" (Huntington 1989: 205 n. 25), "conceptual proliferation" (Yinshun 2017: 44 n. 12; Coseru 2017a: §3.3—who gives, however, "fabrication" as a "literal" translation), "conceptual prolixity" (Hayes 2013: 398), "conceptual elaboration" (Ames 2003: 45), "elaboration" (Dreyfus 2003: 322), "verbal elaboration" (Murti 1955: 348), "verbal proliferation" (Ogawa 2019: 615), "[verbal] proliferation" (Saito 2010: 1215), "proliferations" (Cabezón 2003: 301, 302), '*expansion*' (May 1959: 175 n. 562), "discursive development" (Ruegg 1977: 12; Tauscher 2003: 208), "discursive ideas" (Eckel 2003: 177) (cf. "*idées discursives*"—De Jong 1949: 29), "discursive thoughts" (Dreyfus and McClintock 2003a: 22; Saito 1984: 1), "discursive thinking" (Huntington 2003: 78), "linguistic fabrication" (Ho 2010: 162), "fiction" (Robinson 1978: 56), "obsessions" (Kalupahana 1986: 101), "hypostatization" (Siderits and Katsura 2013: 13; Siderits 2019), "manifoldness" (MacDonald 2015a: II, 17), and "the world of named things, the visible manifold" (Sprung 1979: 273). Thakchoe variously renders it and its Tibetan equivalent *spros pa* as "conceptual elaboration," "verbal elaboration," or "proliferation" (Thakchoe 2007: 107, 227, 88–89), and further notes that "this term is variously translated as 'self-reflexive thinking', 'reification', 'falsification', 'distortion', 'elaboration', or 'exaggeration' " (Thakchoe 2007: 212–213 n. 444), but he does not specify the relevant sources. Jakubczak devotes extended discussion to the term and translates it into Polish as *rozplenianie/-enie* (Jakubczak 2010: 162), which most closely approximates to English 'proliferation'. Schmithausen's long note on *prapañca* (1969: 137–142 n. 101) mainly pertains to Yogācāra materials, and is summarized by MacDonald as explaining "*prapañca* in its dual form of subjective mental acts and the objective products, or correlates thereof, viz., the world of manifold appearances" (MacDonald 2015a II: 42 n. 98). On this account, "*prapañca* as mental activity denotes a subjective act which is characterized by the fact that the subject does not remain calmly in the direct vision of reality but rather elevates above it or expands over it by reflecting and naming" (MacDonald 2015a II: 42 n. 98; cf. Schmithausen 1969: 140–141 n. 101). Meanwhile, based on his proposal "that the basic, recurrent element of sense [in the term *prapañca*] is the idea of making something longer, more spread out, or more elaborate, than what it originally is, and perhaps primarily by speaking of it, whether literally or figuratively, i.e., through conceptualization" (Salvini 2019: 675), Salvini opts for a combination of 'elaboration' and 'prolixity' (see Kantor and Salvini 2019: 606, and see also the term's "literal" translation as "diffusion," "expansion" in Buswell and Lopez 2014: 662). Salvini's sole-authored article not only enabled me to add the versions of De Jong 1949, Kalupahana 1986, and Saito 1984 to my list of translations here but also includes highly illuminating studies of the term's basic etymology and uses in non-Mahāyāna, Mahāyāna, and specifically Madhyamaka sources (the latter principally Candrakīrti) (Salvini 2019: 675 ff.). Furthermore, Siderits provides an informed and informative discussion of the term's use in early Buddhism and Abhidharma (Siderits 2019: 647–651). Finally, Saito 2019 provides a further list of modern translations, including into Japanese (2), and studies the usage of the term in the MK (2–3) as well as in MK commentaries (3–6). On this basis, Saito notes three possible meanings for the term within the MK; that is, as referring to "(1) the mental activity of 'conceptualization', to (2) the objects of mental activity, i.e., 'conceptualized objects' or 'conceptualized world', or to (3) the instruments of mental activity, i.e., 'concepts' or 'terms' " (Saito 2019: 6). He concludes that "taking into consideration all the usages of *prapañca* in Nāgārjuna's [MK] . . . as well as commentators' interpretations on some of the verses of [the MK] . . . it is most probable that, for Nāgārjuna, *prapañca* or the verb *prapañcayati* means a mental activity of conceptualization made in various sets of terms" (Saito 2019: 7). For reference, the typical Chinese translation is 戲論, which is most closely rendered into English by Inada as 'conceptual play' (Inada 1970: 180) or, in more extended senses, as "frivolous debate" (Buswell and Lopez 2014: 663), " 'frivolous discourse,' or, less literally, as 'word-play' or even 'blether' " (Tillemans 2023: 283, who also cites Lamotte's [1944: 41] translation from the Chinese into French "*vains bavardages*": "futile nonsense" [Chödrön 2001: 61a]). For a study explicitly devoted to this Chinese term as used in the MK, see Wan 1998b.

2. For this terminology, extended discussion of these differing methodological approaches, as well as discussion of the theoretical pitfalls of attempts to discern "the 'real meaning' of texts" (Tuck 1990: 14), see §1.3 on "Orientalizing Reasons." The terms used here are rooted in discussions found in Garfield and Priest 2002: 88 and Garfield 2015: 320.
3. As is to be expected, my list overlaps somewhat with that of Mills, who gives MK:5:8, 13:8, 25:24, and 27:30 as end-of-chapter verses renouncing views, and MK:18:5, 21:17, and 24:7 as likewise suggestive thereof (Mills 2018b: 97 fn. 15).
4. MK:0:1–2: *anirodham anutpādam anucchedam aśāśvatam / anekārtham anānārtham anāgamam anirgamam // yaḥ pratītyasamutpādaṃ prapañcopaśamaṃ śivam / deśayāmāsa saṃbuddhas taṃ vande vadatāṃ varam.* Note that, as per Macdonald, *śiva* in MK:0:2a may alternatively be taken as "a noun standing in apposition to *pratītyasamutpāda* which further describes *pratītyasamutpāda* taken in its ultimate sense. As a quasi-synonym of *nirvāṇa*, it refers to *nirvāṇa* in its aspect of safety and ultimate security" (Macdonald 2015b: 362). This reading would lead, in the terminology I have adopted, to a translation of the *śloka* as "Felicity; the cessation of conceptualization". Whether in nominal or adjectival form, however, and in line with MacDonald's own positively-connoted translation of *śiva* as "[ultimate] *wel*fare" (MacDonald 2015a II: 43 n. 100, emphasis added), my use of felicitous/felicity is *not* meant to

> suggest, in the face of explicit Madhyamaka statements that it is the stopping of consciousness (*vijñāna*) and thus the discontinuance of all conceptualizing and of all (invariably temporary) positive and negative affects associated with and based on conceptuality that makes way for the experience of *nirvāṇa*, that the attainment of *nirvāṇa* may be equated with or entails the experience of a positive affect. (MacDonald 2015a II: 43 n. 100)

It is noteworthy that Siderits and Katsura include an explanatory gloss in their translation of MK:0:2b, which is thus rendered: "[. . . for the purpose of *nirvāṇa* characterized by] the auspicious cessation of hypostatization." They further note that: "This verse serves not only as a dedication of the work to the Buddha but also as an announcement of purpose. . . . Nāgārjuna does not explicitly claim here that this work will help one achieve liberation from *saṃsāra* (it is Candrakīrti who says this is the purpose of the text), but what he does say suggests that this is the intention behind his work" (Siderits and Katsura 2013: 13). For a book-length study of what the Chinese commentarial tradition calls the 'eightfold negation' (八不) here, see Chen 1998. For an understanding of the eight negations as a device through which "every possible concept is proved to be *śūnya*" (68), see Sebastian 2016: §3.4.

5. MK:5:8: *astitvaṃ ye tu paśyanti nāstitvaṃ cālpabuddhayaḥ / bhāvānāṃ te na paśyanti draṣṭavyopaśamaṃ śivam.*
6. It will in fact recur at the very culmination of Nāgārjuna's treatment of *nirvāṇa*, at MK:25:24 (cited later).
7. MK:9:11: *darśanaśravaṇādīni vedanādīni cāpy atha / na vidyate ced yasya sa na vidyanta imāny api.*

8. MK:9:12: *prāk ca yo darśanādibhyaḥ sāṃprataṃ cordhvam eva ca / na vidyate 'sti nāstīti nivṛttās tatra kalpanāḥ*. While Ferraro (2018: 662) is of course right to observe that *na vidyate* "has the more literal meaning of 'is not found', 'is not seen' ", I have preferred the more idiomatic "do not apply" (cf. Siderits and Katsura 2013: 106).
9. The verse as a whole states:

   Dependent co-origination
   That we call emptiness
   This, a relative designation
   Is itself the middle way

   (*yaḥ pratītyasamutpādaḥ śūnyatāṃ tāṃ pracakṣmahe / sā prajñaptir upādāya pratipat saiva madhyamā*). Contra Garfield, Arnold, and others (see Introduction, n. 17), Oetke asserts that "this verse, notwithstanding its being frequently quoted in the literature, is of little avail for the interpretation of the work in which it occurs" (Oetke 2007: 24).
10. For a thorough study of the nuances of these and related terms, see Williams 1980. I have rendered *prapañca* as 'conceptualization' and *vikalpa* (following Ruegg 1977: 12) as 'dichotomizing conceptualization' to bring out both the "close connection between *vikalpa* in particular and *prapañca* in Madhyamaka texts," and the understanding that "basically the concern of *vikalpa* is with duality" (Williams 1980: 29, 27). This view is echoed by Jakubczak, for whom *vikalpa* is "a way of putting a thing in opposition to what that thing is not. Its function is hence to think in oppositions, dichotomies" (*sposobem ujmowania rzeczy w opozycji do tego, czym owa rzecz nie jest. Funkcja ta odpowiada zatem za myślenie opozycjami, dychotomiami*) (Jakubczak 2010: 158). It merits mentioning in this context that since Nāgārjuna's stated ambit, at least here, is whatever is *saṃskṛta*, the question of what exactly the category of conceptual-linguistic constructions he advises us to abandon in that they are inevitably deceptive/false includes (i.e., does this include non-conceptual mental content? Prelinguistic mental content? All mental content?) is textually undetermined. Nāgārjuna does not spell out such differentiations (as his intellectual heirs will in fact do), but contents himself with glossing the ambit of abandonment as "all conditioned phenomena" (MK:13:1c—see next verse cited). For the historical development of the Buddhist philosophical position regarding conceptualization, see Siderits et al. 2011, and most especially the contributions by Parimal Patil, Prabal Kumar Sen, Georges Dreyfus, and Jonardon Ganeri therein.
11. MK:13:1: *tan mṛṣā moṣadharma yad bhagavān ity abhāṣata / sarve ca moṣadharmāṇaḥ saṃskārās tena te mṛṣā*.
12. MK:13:8: *śūnyatā sarvadṛṣṭīnāṃ proktā niḥsaraṇaṃ jinaiḥ / yeṣāṃ tu śūnyatādṛṣṭis tān asādhyān babhāṣire*.
13. See also Garfield: "By a view, Nāgārjuna here means a theory on the same level of discourse at which reificationist-nihilist debates proceed . . . any understanding of emptiness as itself an essence" (Garfield 1995: 212, 215).
14. See in this light Siderits and Katsura's further comment to this verse that "to the extent that emptiness gets rid of all metaphysical views, including itself interpreted

as a metaphysical view, it might be called a meta-physic" (Siderits and Katsura 2013: 145–146).

15. MK:16:4ab: *saṃskārāṇāṃ na nirvāṇaṃ kathaṃ cid upapadyate.*
16. MK:16:5abc: *na badhyante na mucyanta udayavyayadharmiṇaḥ / saṃskārāḥ.*
17. MK:16:9–10: *nirvāsyāmy anupādāno nirvāṇaṃ me bhaviṣyati / iti yeṣāṃ grahas teṣām upādānamahāgrahaḥ // na nirvāṇasamāropo na saṃsārāpakarṣaṇam / yatra kas tatra saṃsāro nirvāṇaṃ kiṃ vikalpyate.*
18. MK:18:5: *karmakleśakṣayān mokṣaḥ karmakleśā vikalpataḥ / te prapañcāt prapañcas tu śūnyatāyāṃ nirudhyate.*
19. MK:18:9: *aparapratyayaṃ śāntaṃ prapañcair aprapañcitam / nirvikalpam anānārtham etat tattvasya lakṣaṇam.* Hideyo Ogawa states that the quiescent (*śānta*) nature of reality (*tattva*) Nāgārjuna speaks of in this verse "results from the avoidance of any conceptuality, so that *tattva* is what cannot be determined as this or that" (Ogawa 2019: 615). He goes on to draw on Candrakīrti to the effect that "by saying that *tattva* is beyond verbal proliferation Nāgārjuna means that it is ineffable (*vāgbhir avyāhṛtam*)" (Ogawa 2019: 616), and on the *Bodhicaryāvatārapañjikā* of the Mādhyamika Prajñākaramati (tenth–eleventh century) to the effect that "According to Prajñākaramati, ultimate reality is what is beyond verbal proliferation (*prapañcavinirmukta*); to be beyond verbal proliferation [i.e., beyond *prapañca*] is to be without any delimitation (*sarvopādhiśūnya*)" (Ogawa 2019: 617). In this context, Ogawa notes further that

    > In my view, what Nāgārjuna means by the term *śānta* [at MK:18:9] corresponds with this concept of being empty of delimiting factors. According to Prajñākaramati, what is called *upādhi* is a differentiator (*viśeṣa*), such as existence (*bhāva*) and non-existence (*abhāva*), being oneself and being others (*svaparabhāva*), which is simply an 'empirical' property (*sāṃvṛtadharma*); reality has no differentiators." (Ogawa 2019: 617 fn. 10)

    This resonates nicely with my characterization of reality as anontological in §3.5.
20. MK:22:11. For the original Sanskrit, see §3.4.
21. MK:22:10cd: *prajñapyate ca śūnyena kathaṃ śūnyas tathāgataḥ.*
22. MK:22:15: *prapañcayanti ye buddhaṃ prapañcātītam avyayam / te prapañcahatāḥ sarve na paśyanti tathāgatam.*
23. MK:25:21: *paraṃ nirodhād antādyāḥ śāśvatādyāś ca dṛṣṭayaḥ / nirvāṇam aparāntaṃ ca pūrvāntaṃ ca samāśritāḥ.*
24. For references to relevant scholarship, see fn. 74 in Chapter 3. Paul Fuller is clear that according to the early Buddhist textual sources,

    > To negate questions of the *avyākata* [Skt. *avyākṛta*] type, we do not find the 'correct' questions to be asked, or the correct answers to be given, but a completely different attitude is proposed. When right-view replaces wrong-view it is one order of seeing replacing an entirely different order of seeing, for at the stage of stream-attainment *all* views are abandoned. . . . The *avyākata* are not questions, as such, but expressions of craving. This is true of all views. It is by the cessation of this craving, expressed as the cessation of views, that the *avyākata* are overcome. (Fuller 20015, 124, emphasis original)

For his part, Collins analyzes these 'unanswered questions' as "the last and highest point on the continuum of views and attachment," at which "highest point (strictly speaking not on the continuum at all), there is the unconditioned freedom from view of the enlightened, desireless, and silent sage": "To hold a view here is to be under the sway of Māra—the god of death, whose realm is co-extensive with that of desire" (Collins 1982: 131, 117, 134). Collins goes on the provide a characteristically insightful analysis of the reasons for the prevalent misinterpretations of these points at pp. 135–138.

25. MK:25:22–23: *śūnyeṣu sarvadharmeṣu kim anantaṃ kim antavat / kim anantam antavac ca nānantaṃ nāntavac ca kim // kiṃ tad eva kim anyat kiṃ śāśvataṃ kim aśāśvatam / aśāśvataṃ śāśvataṃ ca kiṃ vā nobhayam apy atha.*
26. MK:25:24: *sarvopalambhopaśamaḥ prapañcopaśamaḥ śivaḥ / na kva cit kasyacit kaścid dharmo buddhena deśitaḥ.*
27. MK:26:12cd: *duḥkhaskandhaḥ kevalo 'yam evaṃ samyag nirudhyate.*
28. MK:27:29: *atha vā sarvabhāvānāṃ śūnyatvāc chāśvatādayaḥ / kva kasya katamāḥ kasmāt saṃbhaviṣyanti dṛṣṭayaḥ.* Following Siderits and Katsura (2013: 334), I have rendered *atha vā* as "So", but Oetke, following Lindtner, rightly points out that the expression could alternatively be rendered "In other words" (Oetke 2015: 226). The "rest" (*ādayaḥ*) recalls the similar term at MK:9:11 (regarding which see §4.2) and here refers to the other lemmata of the tetralemma, as per MK:27:28. As for the relationship between the doctrines of no-self and emptiness, I can only agree with Nagao, who states that, for the Mādhyamika, "*Śūnyatā* is actually a revival of the teaching of *anātman*, an expression of its true meaning" (Nagao 1991: 170).
29. MK:27:30: *sarvadṛṣṭiprahāṇāya yaḥ saddharmam adeśayat / anukampām upādāya taṃ namasyāmi gautamam.*
30. I elide here the distinction already noted by Ruegg (1977) and reiterated by Garfield (2002: 58; 2008: 524) between *dṛṣṭi* and *darśana*, according to which the latter denotes a non-conceptual mode of "direct awareness" (Garfield 2002: 58). While Garfield is right in stating that "Neither Nāgārjuna nor his mādhyamika followers ever deny the value or possibility of *śūnyatā- darśana*, (view of emptiness), though they are critical of the very idea of *śūnyatā- dṛṣṭi*" (Garfield 2002: 58), he too brackets the distinction in his discussion of the necessarily conceptual nature of view-holding.
31. VV:1: *sarveṣāṃ bhāvānāṃ sarvatra na vidyate svabhāvaś cet / tvadvacanam asvabhāvaṃ na nivartayituṃ svabhāvam alam.* VV:70: *prabhavati ca śūnyateyaṃ yasya prabhavanti tasya sarvārthāḥ / prabhavati na tasya kiṃcinna prabhavati śūnyatā yasya.* This final verse clearly echoes MK:24:14:

    All is acceptable for whom emptiness is acceptable
    Nothing is acceptable for whom emptiness is not acceptable

    (*sarvaṃ ca yujyate tasya śūnyatā yasya yujyate / sarvaṃ na yujyate tasya śūnyaṃ yasya na yujyate*). For my use of 'selfbeing', see my note in §3.2.

32. VV:21: *hetupratyayasāmagryāṃ ca pṛṭhak cāpi madvaco na yadi / nanu śūnyatvaṃ siddhaṃ bhāvānām asvabhāvatvāt.*

33. VV:29: *yadi kācana pratijñā syānme tata eṣa me bhaved doṣaḥ / nāsti ca mama pratijñā tasmān naivāsti me doṣaḥ.*
34. Westerhoff calls it "one of the most puzzling verses in the entire text" (Westerhoff 2010: 63).
35. Skt. *na mama kācid asti pratijñā.*
36. VV:9: *yadi ca na bhavet svabhāvo dharmāṇāṃ niḥsvabhāva ity evam / nāmāpi bhavennaivaṃ nāma hi nirvastukaṃ nāsti.* VV:59: *sarveṣāṃ bhāvānāṃ śūnyatvaṃ copapāditaṃ pūrvam / sa upālambhastasmādbhavatyayaṃ cāpratijñāyāḥ.* This is perhaps a good place to explain to the unacquainted reader that the VV is arranged such that the interlocutor's objections are listed in verses 1–20, followed by Nāgārjuna's rejoinders in the remainder of the text.
37. VV:63: *pratiṣedhayāmi nāhaṃ kiṃcit pratiṣedhyam asti na ca kiṃcit / tasmāt pratiṣedhayasīty adhilaya eṣa tvayā kriyate.*
38. VV:64cd: *atra jñāpayate vāgasaditi tanna pratinihanti.*
39. As Westerhoff comments, for Nāgārjuna "there is no *pratijñā* . . . [and] this reply does not imply Nāgārjuna getting caught on the other horn of the dilemma, that of the impossibility of making any substantial reply in a debate" (Westerhoff 20018b: 186). It is not immediately clear which sense of 'substantial' Westerhoff is thinking of here, but it is undeniably an unfortunate choice. For it is precisely the *emptiness* of substance which, for Nāgārjuna, enables replies— and for that matter all other phenomena— to function, to effect effects. What Nāgārjuna refutes here is better conveyed as the charge of being unable to make any *effective* reply in a debate. See in this regard Westerhoff's spot-on comment to VP:73:

    > [The Naiyāyika] assumes that Nāgārjuna's rejections will entail a denial of the functional efficacy of the items rejected. However, as Nāgārjuna points out at the beginning of VV, the emptiness of an entity (and thereby the rejection of its ultimate ontological status) in no way contradicts its ability to play a functional role at the conventional level. (Westerhoff 2018b: 281–282)

40. I have slightly altered the formatting of Westerhoff's translation for the sake of clarity out of context.
41. YṢ:1: *astināstivyatikrāntā buddhir yeṣāṃ nirāśrayā / gambhīras tair nirālambaḥ pratyayārtho vibhāvyate.* See also Lindtner 1982: 103/1997: 73; Loizzo 2007: 119; Tola and Dragonetti 1995a: 34–35; Li and Ye 2014: 4–5.
42. YṢ:23. See Lindtner 1982: 109/1997: 81; Loizzo 2007: 122; Tola and Dragonetti 1995a: 37; Li and Ye 2014: 50–51.
43. YṢ:41–47, for which the Sanskrit text is now extant for YṢ:44–47: *ye 'py upādāya bhāvānāṃ siddhim icchanti tattvataḥ / teṣām api kathaṃ na syur doṣās te śāśvatādayaḥ // upādāya tu ye bhāvān icchanty udakacandravat / nāpi tathyaṃ na cātathyaṃ hriyante te na dṛṣṭibhiḥ // rāgadveṣodbhavas tīvraḥ kaṣṭo dṛṣṭiparigrahaḥ / vivādās tatsamutthāś ca bhāvābhyupagame sati // sa hetuḥ sarvadṛṣṭīnāṃ kleśotpattir na taṃ vinā / tasmāt tasmin parijñāte dṛṣṭikleśaparikṣayaḥ.* See also Lindtner 1982: 113–115/1997: 87–89; Loizzo 2007: 124; Tola and Dragonetti 1995a: 39; Li and Ye 2014: 84–97. For YṢ:41–42 and 45, see also Huntington 2007: 109 fn. 11. In her study of a lost text attributed to Nāgārjuna with the title *Establishing the Transactional* (*Tha snyad*

grub pa / **Vyavahārasiddhi*), six verses of which are preserved (in Tibetan) within the Tibetan translations of the originally Sanskrit *Commentary on the Ornament of the Middle* (*Madhyamakālaṃkāravṛtti*) by Śāntarakṣita (c. 725–788) and the *Extensive Commentary on the Ornament of the Middle* (*Madhyamakālaṃkārapañjikā*) by Kamalaśīla (c. 740–795), Sara McClintock notes parallels between that Nāgārjunian text and YṢ:42, which latter she characterizes as "part of a much longer section in which Nāgārjuna articulates the disadvantages of views, theses, propositions, and standpoints, as well as the advantages of becoming free of these" (McClintock 2023: 18).

44. YṢ:50–51: *nirvivādā mahātmānaḥ pakṣas teṣāṃ na vidyate / yeṣāṃ na vidyate pakṣaḥ teṣāṃ pakṣaḥ paraḥ kutaḥ // kaṃcid evāśrayaṃ labdhvā śaṭhāḥ kleśabhujaṅgamāḥ / daśanti te na daśyante yeṣāṃ cittaṃ nirāśrayam*. See also Lindtner 1982: 115–117/1997: 89; Loizzo 2007: 125; Tola and Dragonetti 1995a: 40; Li and Ye 2014: 102–105; Huntington 2007: 109 fn. 11.
45. ŚS:73. See Lindtner 1982: 69/1997: 119; Tola and Dragonetti 1995a: 81; Pandeya and Manju 1991: 148; Komito 1987: 95. The Tibetan term Lindtner proposes as equivalent here to the Sanskrit *dṛṣṭi* is *lta ṅan* (*lta ngan*).
46. See ŚS:68, at Lindtner 1982: 65/1997: 117; Tola and Dragonetti 1995a: 80; Pandeya and Manju 1991: 147; Komito 1987: 94. The verse recalls MK:24:18, cited earlier.
47. See ŚS:2, at Lindtner 1982: 35/1997: 95; Tola and Dragonetti 1995a: 72; Pandeya and Manju 1991: 140; Komito 1987: 79. Lindtner (1982: 35) gives *abhidheyabhāva* as the Sanskrit for "all expressible things."
48. ŚS:62ab, at Lindtner 1982: 63/1997: 115; Tola and Dragonetti 1995a: 79; Pandeya and Manju 1991: 147; Komito 1987: 93. Note that Lindtner gives *viparyāsa* as the Sanskrit equivalent of the Tibetan *phyin ci log*, as he also does at ŚS:9 and ŚS:17 (Lindtner 1982: 63). *Viparyāsa* and *phyin ci log* both convey the sense of epistemic error or delusion. At ŚS:23, however, Lindtner (1982: 45) gives *viparyaya* (sic: *viparyāya*) for *phyin ci log*. This Sanskrit term, however, does not necessarily convey any negative import. Edgerton defines it simply as "contrariety, the being opposed (of signs, omens)" (Edgerton 2004: 491); that is, as referring to tetrachotomies (i.e., all oppositional views: quaternary rather than binary/dichotomous in the Indian context on the basis of the four, not two, positions possible in argument) in general. I thus call attention in passing to the incorrectness of Lindtner's proposed Sanskrit reconstruction at ŚS:23, which should be *viparyāsa* rather than *viparyāya*. Note also in this context that MK:23 as a whole is dedicated to the analysis of *viparyāsa*, which declines to give forms such as *viparyayaḥ* (nominative singular) at MK:23:13, 14, 16; *viparyayāḥ* (nominative plural) at MK:23:6, 17, 18, 19; and *viparyaya* (with *nirodhanāt* to form an ablative singular) at MK:23:23.
49. ŚS:72, at Lindtner 1982: 67/1997: 119; Tola and Dragonetti 1995a: 81; Pandeya and Manju 1991: 148; Komito 1987: 95.
50. This is true generally, but particularly so in cases of textual witnesses that appear to speak against what my citations in Chapter 1 showed as assumed by interpreters to be 'common sense'. Indeed, Huntington notes in relation precisely to "the Mādhyamika's rejection of all views" that "This element of Nāgārjuna's thought

has been responsible for the greatest controversy among both ancient and modern commentators" (Huntington 1989: xii).

51. The strategy here is straightforwardly analogous to that of parameterization for the sake of 'rescuing' Nāgārjuna from the evident philosophical absurdity of affirming mutually contradictory statements in the *catuṣkoṭi* I have detailed in Chapter 2.
52. To this charge, the best that Staal can do is admit on the same page: "But if Nāgārjuna got caught in paradoxes and contradictions, he is not worse off than most philosophers. What would make him an irrationalist is the desire to be illogical" (also cited in a different context in §1.2). This is a pretty weak defense, and one, moreover, that does not do much justice at all to Nāgārjuna's methodically systematic rejection of views as a means toward the realization of *śūnyatā* concomitant with the attainment of *nirvāṇa*.
53. Mills likewise identifies the dynamic at play but, given that his own interpretation relieves Nāgārjuna of contradictoriness, he places the burden of solution onto "Those who take Nāgārjuna to be presenting a truth-claim at the end of his procedure"; they—but not Nāgārjuna—"are faced with a dilemma: either Nāgārjuna is committed to a thesis that contains internal contradictions or he is committed to no thesis whatsoever. Neither of these is appealing if one wants Nāgārjuna to have a final truth-claim about emptiness" (Mills 2018a: 56).
54. Arnold himself is a prominent proponent of such parameterization. As he puts it, "Nāgārjuna's famous claim not to advance any philosophical "thesis" (*pratijñā*)—a claim ventured at VV 29—can be understood to express not a refusal to make any truth claims at all, but only a refusal of *the kinds of claims that are thought to require a certain kind of justification*" (Arnold 2010: 384, emphases added).
55. For further discussion of Tsongkhapa's logicalist take on Nāgārjuna—unsurprisingly used repeatedly to support analogous efforts among contemporary exegetes—in contradistinction to a rival Tibetan commentator such as Gorampa, see §2.2.2, and perhaps most relevantly my citation of Tillemans there to the effect that whoever adds parameters to Nāgārjuna's statements "has in effect denatured the whole Nāgārjunian dialectic" (Tillemans 2009: 93–94/2016: 77–78). Tillemans's overall point is that "much of the effort to read Tsongkhapa and other later Mādhyamika thinkers back onto Candrakīrti or Nāgārjuna is strained" (Tillemans 2016: 5).
56. Recall, for example, Westerhoff's offhand dismissal of the *catuṣkoṭi*'s irrefragably contradictory third lemma, "*as if it constituted a real possibility*" (Westerhoff 2009: 81), or for that matter Garfield's dictum that "Logic transcends metaphysics: It is a canon of reason, not a theory of reality, and a canon of reason ought to be equally valid no matter how the world is" (Garfield 2015: 249).
57. For another reading of Nāgārjuna that sees no problem in accepting him to be enacting a "performative contradiction," see Hans-Rudolf Kantor's understanding of 'emptiness' as a term that

> paradoxically denies what it simultaneously signifies, to bring about our genuine understanding of the true and ultimate meaning beyond linguistic expression(s). Such self-falsification via "performative contradiction" reveals what the term "emptiness" truly is: It is a "false name" [假名, also translated as

> 'provisional name'] which lays out the inseparability of truth and falsehood in our understanding. (Kantor 2014: 346)

58. As Tillemans notes in a different though not unrelated context, "It will probably be replied that the point is more about what the Mādhyamikas *should say* philosophically than what they did say" (Tillemans 2016: 11, emphases original). My point is that such a rejoinder would constitute an admission of abandoning textual hermeneutics for philosophical construction—which, again, is a perfectly valid, but methodologically distinct, procedure.
59. See my citation of Smith College 2010 at §2.2.2.
60. See Garfield 2002: 48 cited earlier, where he is conveying Ngog's position. As Garfield elaborates in the passage I cite from the same page here, "For Nāgārjuna generally, the dGe lugs to the contrary notwithstanding, says what he means. And, in the verses in question [i.e., rejections of view-holding in MK:27:30 and MK:13:8], nothing forces the kinds of implicit qualifiers that often *are* contextually forced" (Garfield 2002: 48, emphasis original).
61. The same applies to Ruegg; see, *inter alia*, the following:

> What Nāgārjuna is saying here, then, is surely not that he is not uttering a meaningful sentence (something that would be not merely paradoxical but quite absurd), but rather that he is not propounding a proposition claiming probative force concerning the (positive or even negative) own being (*svabhāva*) of any thing. Whatever other logical problems may arise in connexion with Nāgārjuna's procedure in this respect, there would appear to be no paradox here at all. (Ruegg 1977: 49–50)

> there appears to be no paradox in a philosopher's stating 'I have no thesis (postulating a self-existent *bhāva*)', for this sentence is not automatically equivalent to 'I have no philosophical thesis (of any kind)' (i.e., no *darśana*, *vāda*, etc.). And no logical inconsistency need then exist between Nāgārjuna's statement in VV 29 to the effect that he has no *pratijñā* and the actual procedure of this philosopher, and of other Mādhyamikas, who in effect set forth a philosophy (*darśana*, *vāda*, *siddhānta*). (Ruegg 2000: 132)

> Formally speaking, Nagarjuna's statement 'I have no *pratijñā*' [at VV:29] may look to us like a (semantic) paradox . . . [However,] it seems possible to understand it not as a first-order utterance in the object language but as a second-order metalinguistic one stipulating that none of the Mādhyamika's statements is to be taken as a thesis positing / presupposing / implying the existence of an entity having self-existence (*svabhāva*). (Ruegg 2000: 220)

Oetke takes extended issue with Ruegg's reading, criticizing the translation of the crucial phrase *nāsti ca mama pratijñā* in VV:29 as " 'I have no thesis' or even 'I do not state anything' " in favor of " '*Es gibt (aber) keine Behauptung von mir*' – '(But) there is no assertion of mine' " (Oetke 2003: 456, cf. Oetke 1989). Just as for Ruegg, however, "The distinction suggested by O[etke]. . . is anything but clear to me" (Ruegg 2000: 217; Oetke 2003: 456). Besides which, Oetke himself seems to abandon his own point in that he goes on in a later work to follow Bhattacharya's (1978) translation of the phrase as "I have, however, no proposition" (Oetke 2011: 311; cf. 317–319). To the extent that one can discriminate between them at all, this appears straightforwardly to resemble the sense Oetke earlier *rejects*.

Jakubczak (2006, reprinted in 2010: 195–202) refers to Ruegg explicitly in formulating his own view that "although Nāgārjuna repeatedly suggested that he does not hold his own views" (*Chociaż wielokrotnie sugerował, że nie posiada własnych poglądów*) (128), he nevertheless must do so the basis of the well-worn differentiation between theses postulating *svabhāva* (not held) and those (held) that are "simply a philosophical claim" (*po prostu twierdzenie filozoficzne*) (130). Although he does not discuss the distinction explicitly in these terms in his earlier work on "The Function of Positive Language in the Negative Philosophy of Madhyamaka" (*Funkcja pozytywnego języka w negatywnej filozofi madhjamaki*), presumably it lies in the background of Jakubczak's forthright assertion there that "In the treatises, Nāgārjuna's entire philosophical effort is directed . . . at demonstrating the internal contradictions inherent in philosophical views, in *all* philosophical views, and therefore at demonstrating the impossibility of maintaining *any* philosophical position" (*W traktatach cały filozoficzny wysiłek Nagardżuny nakierowany jest. . . na wykazanie wewnętrznych sprzeczności tkwiących w poglądach filozoficznych, we* wszelkich *poglądach filozoficznych, a zatem na wykazanie niemożliwości utrzymania* jakiegokolwiek *filozoficznego stanowiska*) (Jakubczak 1997: 106, emphases added).

62. It is thus ironic that, when it comes to discussing Nāgārjuna's "establish[ing] that everything is empty," Garfield and Priest themselves emphasize that "We must take the *everything* here very seriously, though" (Garfield and Priest 2002: 92, emphasis original).
63. Both cited in §4.2.
64. The relation of view-holding to clinging or attachment, and the consequent abjuration of all views on the part of the desireless Buddha, is well brought out with regard to the Theravāda tradition by Collins, who states that this

> aspect of the teaching, where dichotomy of right and wrong view is replaced by a continuum on which all views are seen against the psychological fact of attachment, shows us that when 'view' is seen as something bad, or detrimental to the monks' religious practice, in fact what is denoted is *any* view which is held 'with attachment'. It is because the Buddha and the enlightened sage are beyond attachment that they are beyond 'view' in this sense. (Collins 1982: 128, emphasis original)

This is a view I see as being echoed with regard to Nāgārjuna specifically by Jakubczak, who writes:

> Nāgārjuna's attitude is expressed by the statement: I do not hold views; that is, I do not cling. It is radically different from: I do not hold views, therefore I do not cling. Not holding views is derivative of not clinging, not the other way around. Nāgārjuna says: I do not cling, therefore I do not hold my own views. (*Postawę Nagardżuny wyraża stwierdzenie: nie mam poglądów, czyli nie lgnę. Jest ono radykalnie odmienne od: nie mam poglądów, dlatego nie lgnę. Nieposiadanie poglądów jest pochodne względem braku lgnięcia, a nie odwrotnie. Nagardżuna mówi: nie lgnę, dlatego nie posiadam własnych poglądów.*) (Jakubczak 2019: 342)

On the same page, Jakubczak goes on to state that "This attitude should therefore be clearly distinguished from that of the skeptic, who sees in the suspension of all views a way to achieve tranquility of mind" (*Postawę tę należy zatem wyraźnie odróżnić od postawy sceptyka, który w zawieszeniu wszelkich poglądów widzi sposób na osiągnięcie spokoju umysłu*). I return to this interpretation in §4.3.3. On the point under discussion here, however, see also McClintock's summary:

> Freeing oneself from addiction to views (*dṛṣṭi*) is, for the Buddhist practitioner, no less important than freeing oneself from the afflictions of lust, anger, jealousy, hatred, pride, and so on. This is because *all* addiction or clinging is a source of suffering, and this holds true for cognitive clinging just as much as it does for clinging in the more affective realms. Indeed, one might say that views—propositions, beliefs, or theories about the way things really are—have a special role in holding suffering firmly in place in our embodied lives, undergirding even seemingly mute or nonconceptual, yet nevertheless sticky, emotions. This is because views, which may permeate our perceptions unnoticed, are inherently distorting insofar as they superimpose ossifying, ultimately unreal identities (*svabhāva*) onto an unstable, ultimately indeterminate, ephemeral causal flux. (McClintock 2023: 2, emphasis original)

And finally, see also Siderits, for whom "*prapañca* [must] be understood as a subtle form of self-affirmation that results from the metaphysical realist conception of truth" (Siderits 2016b: 136). As he goes on to explain, "metaphysical realists are inclined to pound the table—to insist that there is such a thing as ultimate truth, that the truth is 'out there'. And in this insistence the Mādhyamika sees a subtle form of self-assertion—indeed so subtle as to perhaps defy detection and extirpation" (Siderits 2016b: 137).

65. From what I have said earlier regarding the mutually entailing nature of (binary or quaternary) opposites (see §3.7), it should be clear that all this goes as much for negative as for positive beliefs, for denials as for affirmations. See in this regard Ruegg: "Either term of the conceptual dichotomy (*vikalpa*) *atman/anātman* is an extreme deriving from discursive development (*prapañca*) and related to either eternalism or nihilism, the twin extreme positions that the Middle Way eschews by its very definition" (Ruegg 1977: 9).
66. See, for example: "For the question whether Nāgārjuna really advocates relinquishing all views [at e.g., MK:27:30 and MK:13:8] is in fact semantic: is it possible to understand the words Nāgārjuna utters to claim that he is not expressing propositions?" (Garfield 2002: 51–52); "The claim to assert no proposition [at VV:4 and 29] is a semantic claim that is bound up with the claim that language, like all other phenomena, is empty (Garfield 2002: 56); and "[Nāgārjuna] argues for the claim that he has no *pratijñā in the context of a debate about semantics* in *Vigrahavyāvartanī*" (Garfield 2008: 524, emphases original).
67. With reference to the ontic implications of emptiness and its assertion, Garfield goes on to say that Nāgārjuna's "is a recognition of the inability to make assertions from a nonperspectival perspective, together with the recognition that perspectives are ontologically determinative" (Garfield 2002: 66). This ties in nicely with his earlier assertion that "essentialism is virtually built into the grammar of our language" (Garfield

2002: 49). For a sustained and thoroughgoingly radical argument to the effect that "the law of non-contradiction (henceforth LNC) is incoherent in the absence of an essentialist ontology," with especial reference to the Chinese Tiantai Buddhist school founded by Zhiyi 智顗, see Ziporyn 2015: 253. Ziporyn elaborates that "'Real entity' and 'LNC' are two alternate descriptions of the same idea: a real entity is just defined as whatever accords with the LNC. The Buddhist rejection of any fixed and unambiguous boundaries for any single entity is also a rejection of the LNC" (Ziporyn 2015: 266).

68. See Garfield 2002: 269 n. 16:

> Moreover, a distinction must be drawn between knowing conventional truths and knowing ultimate truths. For it is central to any Buddhist understanding of the epistemological viewpoint that the nature of one's consciousness and cognition changes dramatically in enlightenment. Whereas in *saṃsāra* one knows objects conceptually, and they appear to one as inherently existent substantial entities, in nirvāna one knows things as they are, through direct, nonconceptual consciousness. Our account of what it is to relinquish all views, as well as our account of the status of emptiness, what one knows when one knows the ultimate, will have to respect this distinction.

The relationship between this statement and others avowing "The identity of the Two Truths" (Garfield and Priest 2002: 92)—such as "Ultimate reality is hence only conventionally real! The distinct realities are therefore identical" (Garfield and Priest 2002: 92) (an ontological claim) or "There are, therefore, no ultimate truths. . . . All truths, then, are merely conventional" (Garfield and Priest 2002: 96) (an epistemological claim)—is unclear.

69. This point is well made by Schmidt-Leukel (2016: 175–176), who despite this nevertheless appears to want to retain a hierarchical distinction between them in claiming that, for Nāgārjuna, "*nirvāṇa* is not reduced to the level of *saṃsāra*, but, on the contrary, *saṃsāra* is elevated to the level of *nirvāṇa*" (Schmidt-Leukel 2016: 174).

70. MK:25:24ab. This and preceding verses are cited in full in §4.2.

71. MK:25:19–20: *na saṃsārasya nirvāṇāt kiṃ cid asti viśeṣaṇaṃ / na nirvāṇasya saṃsārāt kiṃ cid asti viśeṣaṇaṃ // nirvāṇasya ca yā koṭiḥ koṭiḥ saṃsaraṇasya ca / na tayor antaraṃ kiṃ cit susūkṣmam api vidyate*. For further discussion of these verses, see §5.1 and §5.2.3. It will be noticed that I am proposing an equivalence between *saṃvṛti-satya* and *saṃsāra* on the one hand, and *paramārtha-satya* and *nirvāṇa* on the other. These sets of terms, I admit, are not strictly speaking coextensive, though (to the extent that one can speak of their referents) their referents are, I would argue, equivalent in the sense that the attainment of the relevant truth (e.g., *paramārtha-satya*) identifies the attainer as an inhabitant of the relevant realm (e.g., *nirvāṇa*).

72. Recall Williams 1980: 25 cited in §3.6, where he suggests that for a Mādhyamika entities do not "exist" but "inexist." Regarding the prefix "*vi-*," it is perhaps worth noting that it is also called into service at MK:24:9, where *vibhāga* is used to designate the act of distinguishing between the two truths (conventional/*saṃvṛti* and ultimate/*paramārtha*).

73. Eviatar Shulman makes this point as follows: "Rather than conceptuality being an attempt to define and understand reality, Nāgārjuna sees conceptuality as responsible for the creation of reality. Things are not objectively 'out there,' but are brought into being by ideation" (Shulman 2007 [2009]: 165). Of course, this positive account of the "creation of reality" must be leavened, in Nāgārjuna's system, with an acknowledgment that there is no 'reality', no 'being', no *bhāva/svabhāva*, created at all, which is why Shulman continues: "Moreover, once things are proven to be brought into being by the power of ideation, that ideation itself is realized to be unreal as-well, since it perceives objects which are not really there. Emptiness is said to be the play of unreal conceptualization perceiving unreal objects" (Shulman 2007 [2009]: 166). For further elaborations of the potential correspondences between Nāgārjuna's Madhyamaka and Yogācāra-style idealism, see Shulman 2015 and Gold 2015b. For Gold, "The fact that our words cannot reach beyond the horizon of the expressible is not an ambiguous Madhyamaka leaning within Yogācāra; it is the core Yogācāra contribution to the interpretation of the Mahāyāna doctrine of emptiness" (Gold 2015b: 240).
74. For support for my use of the English term "belief" in this context, I cite Charles Muller's "Inquiry into Views, Beliefs and Faith": "In Buddhism, the connotation of 'view', as a translation of the Sanskrit *dṛṣṭi* (from the root √*dṛṣ* 'to see') are often virtually the same as what we understand by the modern English word 'belief', especially when used in the negative sense of 'erroneous view' (*mithyā-dṛṣṭi*; *xiejian* 邪見)" (Muller 2018: 364). The very negative connotation of *dṛṣṭi* as *mithyā-dṛṣṭi*, of 見 as 邪見, in the Buddhist tradition at large, is itself eloquent evidence in support of reading Nāgārjuna's stated disavowal of all views as a disavowal of, precisely, *all* views. Muller goes on to characterize the broadly Buddhist view of views as one maintaining that "in their place as cognitive activities, they are not purely cognitive, as there is inevitably some kind of *desire* involved. Thus, no matter what, the expression of a view is seen to be an expression of some kind of craving" (Muller 2018: 372, emphasis original). To this I would add that not only is "the expression of a view . . . an expression of some kind of craving," but also that the *holding* of a view is, irrespective of its expressive status, a *holding* of some kind of craving. In any case, Jakubczak is surely right, if perhaps unduly tentative, in asserting that "in Buddhist thought, the concept of view is not formulated solely in an epistemological context, but also, and perhaps even primarily, in a psychologico-therapeutic, that is, soteriological, context" (*w myśli buddyjskiej pojęcie poglądu nie jest formułowane wyłącznie w kontekście epistemologicznym, lecz także, a może nawet przede wszystkim, w kontekście psychologiczno-terapeutycznym, czyli soteriologicznym*) (Jakubczak 2019: 356).
75. The debate as to what is typically referred to in the philosophical literature as the primacy of the "intentional" or the "linguistic" has been amply carried out by Chisholm, Sellars, and many others. As my stance on this point is tangential to my broader argument here regarding the mutually reinforcing nature of (self)being and belief, I prefer not to wade into these deep waters here, though I hope in passing that what I say about Nāgārjuna's (non)stance may be of value to professional philosophers generally familiar with the narrow ambit of Western philosophical thought alone. To the extent

that ultimates apply in history, the concept of "intentionality" in this sense dates back, ultimately, via Husserl to Brentano. As for the relationship between conceptually contentful belief and its linguistic expression, I follow D'Amato in that "I take it to be a relatively uncontroversial claim that the use of language requires conceptual thought, unlike the much more controversial claim that thought is determined by language (a strong version of the Sapir-Whorf hypothesis)" (D'Amato 2009: 52 n. 8). Finally, I see Patil's assertion that "generally . . . Buddhist philosophers do not accept the idea that propositional content and propositional attitude or even content and force are independent" (Patil 2011: 168 n. 40) as support for my contention that, for Nāgārjuna, to hold a view (irrespective of its content) is ineluctably to be involved in karmically determined and determinative activity.

76. Let us not forget that "By hypostatization is meant the process of reification or 'thingifying': taking what is actually just a useful form of speech to refer to some real entity" (Siderits and Katsura 2013: 15).

77. As Murti also states, "It is the contention of the Mādhyamikas that the final release is possible only through *Śūnyatā*—by the giving up of all views, standpoints and predicaments (Murti 1955: 269); "A view, because of its restriction, determination, carries with it duality, the root of *saṁsāra*" (Murti 1955: 270); and perhaps most forcefully:

> the Mādhyamika dialectic relentlessly exposes the falsity of every philosophical view. . . . It is a reversal of the natural process of looking at things through set ideas, the disabusing of the mind of *a priori* notions. . . . The essence of the Mādhyamika attitude, his philosophy (the *madhyamā pratipad*), consists in not allowing oneself to be entangled in views and theories, but just to observe the nature of things without standpoints (*bhūta-pratyavekṣā*). (Murti 1955: 209)

Candrakīrti's *Madhyamakāvatārakārikā* 6:119 is an eminent example of a classical Madhyamaka primary source making this point explicitly: "Attachment to one's view and likewise aversion to the view of another is itself evidence of reified thinking. When one sets aside attachment and aversion and conducts an analysis [of all views], he will soon find liberation" (Huntington 1989: 201 n. 26, Tibetan text also transliterated, insertion by Huntington). Regarding Candrakīrti, Huntington also states:

> When Candrakīrti goes so far as to say that Bhāvaviveka is not really a Mādhyamika at all, but rather a Logician (*Tārkika*) "taking the side of the Madhyamaka school out of a desire to parade the extent of his own dialectical skill" [citing Huntington 2003: 82], he is drawing attention not simply to the methodology of logical analysis but to the *motivation* of the Logician, who is driven not by selfless compassion but rather by a self-serving need for certainty rooted in rational conviction—a form of clinging no less seductive now than it was some two thousand years ago in ancient India. (Huntington 2007: 125–126, emphasis original)

Meanwhile, Jonathan Gold's study of Vasubandhu (fourth–fifth century), a distinctly non-Mādhyamika adherent of the Sautrāntika Abhidharma and Yogācāra schools at various times, has him too affirming that "the root, mistaken 'view'—the view of self (*satkāyadṛṣṭi*)—is implicit in all other views, all unenlightened perspectives. . . . So every 'view' participates in this false view of self" (Gold 2015a: 138); and "all doctrines, even Buddhist doctrines, are potentially dangerous for their capacity to reify self-construction . . . the key value in Mahāyāna [is] the freedom from views, the freedom from egotistical self-construction that comes of seeing things one way, our way" (Gold 2015a: 175).

Gold also proposes to read Dharmakīrti (sixth–seventh century), who was at the least Yogācāra-inclined, not through what amounts to the Geluk view initiated by Tsongkhapa, further propounded by Chaba Chökyi Senge (1109–1169), and (on Gold's analysis) informing Dan Arnold's (2012) interpretation of Dharmakīrti, but rather through the lens of an opponent of the Geluk reading such as Sakya Paṇḍita Kunga Gyeltsen (1182–1251), for whom "every conceptual cognition based on perception is not only subject to doubt, it is *mistaken*, because *every conceptual cognition is mistaken*" (Gold 2014a: 1052, emphases original).

Returning to Nāgārjuna, this is perhaps the aptest moment to cite the eloquent analysis of Janet Williams:

> In summary, the marks of Nāgārjunan apophasis are as follows: a rejection of dualism as based on the views of own-being, inconsistent with the Buddha's teaching of dependent co-arising; a consequent application of radical negation to both the affirmative and negative aspects of any binary; an undermining and dismantling of all views as tainted by dualistic-discriminative thinking; and establishment of 'no-view' or 'no-standpoint' as the ideal; the application of this apophatic recoil from views to ontology: the Absolute, the *Tathāgata*, neither exists nor does not exist; and, finally, an epistemological scheme which both affirms human discourse as true and denies it an absolute purchase on truth. (J. Williams 2000: 48)

78. To put this in terms used by Murti, ontological descriptions of reality are "negations of the real" in that the real "is essentially indeterminate (*nirvikalpa, niṣprapañca*)" (Murti 1955: 271).
79. YṢ:51, cited in §4.2.
80. Recall, for example, the discussion of 'common sense' in relation to Bugault and Oetke in §1.2, as well as the discussion of MK:9:11–12 in §4.2, where Nāgārjuna denies the existence—as well as the non-existence—of mental cognitions and all other perceptual acts, and actors . . . denials of which one could well ask "How could he deny *that*?"
81. See, e.g., MK:5:8, MK:13:8, MK:16:9, MK:22:15, MK:25:24, YṢ:1, YṢ:23, YṢ:41–47, all quoted earlier.
82. Gold's reading of Yogācāra is in turn reminiscent of Paul Fuller's understanding of early Buddhism:

> Although such assertions as the four truths may counter the views of other philosophical schools, I would argue that for them to be *sammā-diṭṭhi* [Skt. *samyag-dṛṣṭi*], for them to be right, they could not themselves be views at all. It is in this way that they are right-views. They may counter incorrect propositions, but they are not intended to be 'correct' propositions in the usual sense of the term. They are right, *sammā*, precisely because they cannot be an object of attachment. Though they are termed *diṭṭhi*, it is precisely because they do not share the unwholesome aspects of *micchā-diṭṭhi* [*mithyā-dṛṣṭi*,

> wrong-view] that they are termed *sammā-diṭṭhi*. The four truths may then correct and counter views, but as propositions, they are not intended to be held as *micchā-diṭṭhi* are held, but to reflect a detached form of cognition. It is right view, *sammā-diṭṭhi*, which implies this different order of seeing. (Fuller 2005: 2)

83. Arnold's reference is to Baker 1987: 173; he reiterates the reference at Arnold 2019: 698.
84. See also my reference to Collins 1982: 128 in §4.3.2, and see also more generally Collins's study of views and attachment in chapters 3 and 4 of that work, in which he cites numerous canonical passages supporting "the necessity of renouncing all views" (130).
85. Fuller's references are to Gómez 1976 and Hayes 1988: 52.
86. The passage from which these last words are taken is worth citing in full: "In other words, to say that one has right-view is to say that one has no-view. The consequence of achieving right-view is that one does not hold *any* views. The aim of the path is the transcendence of all views" (Fuller 2005: 2, emphasis original).
87. As Muller elaborates elsewhere, "In passage after passage in these [East Asian] texts it is stated quite clearly that ultimately, the only acceptable state of mind—Perfect Enlightenment—is one where all views are eradicated, and no further views are being constructed" (Muller 2013: 31). For a nuanced study of a "well documented historical confrontation between Chan and Madhyamaka" (Tillemans 2016: 4) on the question of (non-)conceptualization, see Tillemans 2016: 179–198.
88. For the Buddha as Tathāgata, the 'thus-come-gone', see §3.4 on "Tetrāletheia as Tathāgata."
89. A full treatment of the relation between conventional view-holding and its ultimate abandonment is beyond my concerns here, though I go on to explore the ethical implications of holding no view in Chapter 5. Suffice it for present purposes, in any case, to cite what I take to be an apt and accurate summary by Muller:

> the Buddhist approach [to changing one's views] operates from two distinct levels. The approach of the first level in Buddhism . . . [is one in which] Buddhist practitioners are led to adjust inaccurate and unworkable understandings of such matters as causation with a more accurate view of causation, or of reality. This is called the 'conventional' approach, in Sanskrit a *laukika*, or *saṃvṛti* standpoint. The second level takes a far more radical and transcendent position (in Sanskrit *lokōttara* or *paramārtha*), wherein the active effort towards the creation of a replacement view to which to adhere is seen as futile, since it is precisely the reification of the view that is problematic, and not necessarily the content. Thus, rather than advocating a change in one's view (e.g., from improperly understood causality to properly understood causality), the problematic nature of views in themselves is emphasized, and thus, a significant portion of Buddhist discourse—most prominently in schools such as Madhyamaka or Zen—but also to be found in a wide range of works of various Buddhist schools, directly advocate the practice of not lingering in any view. (Muller 2018: 10)

In highly analogous terms, Ethan Mills proposes that Nāgārjuna "has two general phases in his philosophical procedure, corresponding to his two main kinds of statements: those statements that support the philosophical position of emptiness and those statements that seem to deny that he has any position at all." While "The first phase is that of offering arguments for emptiness and against essence (*svabhāva*) . . . , The second phase is that of demonstrating that this idea of emptiness has the peculiar property of undermining not only all other philosophical views, but even itself, thus leaving a thorough Mādhaymika without any views, theses, or positions whatsoever" (Mills 2018b: 97; Mills 2018a: 35–36 expands on this idea).

This 'two level' or 'two phases' approach is discussed in a different key here in §5.3. It is in some ways reminiscent of the distinction proposed by Garfield between "the ordinary philosopher . . . [who] can be the subject of cognitive states such as beliefs whose direct object, via conception, is emptiness," and "the arhat, who directly perceives emptiness as it is unmediated either by apprehension of (other) conventional entities or by conception" (Garfield 2002: 52).

90. For the equivalence of enlightenment and emptiness, see e.g., Yinshun: "In general, the synonyms for *nirvāṇa* can all be called 'empty' [*śūnya*]" (Yinshun 2017: 233 n. 19, and more generally 225–235). For a discussion by the same author of *prajñā* / 般若 in connection with terms such as 知 (*vijñā*), 智 (*vijñāna*), 觀 (*vipaśyanā*), 見 (*dṛṣṭi*), see Yinshun 2010: 14.
91. See also Waldo, according to whom "In the end the knife of *prajña* [*prajñā*] cuts through itself—certainly a point Nāgārjuna wishes to underline" (Waldo 1978: 294). The metaphor of cutting through is indeed apt, for

> the empty (*niḥsvabhāva*) way of thinking or experiencing is not a theory advanced in opposition to theories based on substantialist *svabhāvic* thought. Rather, it cuts through all cognition, all theoretical standpoints that attempt to objectify reality and grasp its nature conceptually. (Emptiness serves to circumvent such thought, not to give it a correct object to ponder.) Nāgārjuna asks us to empty ourselves of such objectification, discrimination, and conceptualization—and then experience in terms of *prajñā*. (Ives 2015: 74, also cited in Sebastian 2016: 67)

92. See also in this regard Muller's insight:

> Regarding the state of viewlessness, a question sometimes arises as to whether the Buddhist *lokōttara* approach to Right View implies simply not lingering in views, or if it means having no views at all. The answer to this is that the two are the same. Viz., if the defining character of views is none other than reification, then not reifying any views is the same thing as not having any . . . Any view at all is by its nature a rigid reification, an empty shell or a rigid wall, that functions to obstruct the function of the naturally free-flowing Buddha mind, preventing it from adapting to the free-flowing, fluctuating world. (Muller 2018: 11)

93. Arnold continues:

> Specifically, what must finally be understood as possibly true is the claim that "all existents are empty, which is just to say that they are dependently originated"—a claim that clearly contradicts, for example, the claim (made by some theists) that at least one thing exists intrinsically or necessarily (and, therefore, is not "dependently originated"). And to say that the Mādhyamika

> claim contradicts a truth-claim proffered by some theists just is to say that the former claim, too, is proposed as *true*. (Arnold 2005, 137, emphasis original)

He reiterates his position at various points in his book, perhaps nowhere more clearly than when he writes:

> But this claim ("there is no such thing as the way things 'really' are") is itself a properly metaphysical claim. That is, the Mādhyamikas Nāgārjuna and Candrakīrti should be understood as making a universally obtaining truth claim to the effect that the way things really are *really* is such that we can never identify something "more real" underlying existents and our experience thereof. (Arnold 2005: 120, emphasis original)

Arnold likewise reiterates in a later work that, on his account, "Madhyamaka philosophers finally advance fundamentally metaphysical claims that are proposed as really true" (Arnold 2010: 372). In essence, Arnold's claim boils down to the idea that "To negate another's position quite obviously *is* to have a position of one's own" (Betty 1983: 129, emphasis original), mis-applied to Nāgārjuna's *prasaṅga*.

94. For an alternative iteration of the same point, see Mills 2018a: 39.
95. See also my extensive cataloguing of Nāgārjuna's statements as to the overarchingly soterial goal of his endeavor in §2.4, which I trust obviates the potential criticism that I am making such claims simply 'on faith', as it were. Rather, I have attempted, here as elsewhere, to substantiate my understanding of Nāgārjuna based on a strict reading of what he actually says (and no more).

Skeptical interpretations of Buddhism generally and Nāgārjuna specifically have almost as long a history as nihilist interpretations. For an overview of these (231–238), the various version of Greek-derived skepticism they rely on (238–270), and certain skeptical tendencies in early Buddhism (270–276), see Jakubczak 2019, the relevant chapter of which concludes (356–364) with an extended argument as to "Why Buddhism has nothing to do with skepticism" (*Dlaczego buddyzm nie ma nic wspólnego ze sceptycyzmem*). The specifics of the skeptical interpretation are tangential to my concerns here, so suffice it to say that on Jakubczak's reading the key distinction lies in the understanding that "The skeptical perspective is epistemological, the Buddhist perspective is psychologico-cognitive. For Pyrrho and Sextus, lack of views is the basis and condition of well-being; for the Buddha and Nāgārjuna, lack of views is an outcome, an expression of well-being" (*Perspektywa sceptyczna jest epistemologiczna, perspektywa buddyjska—psychologiczno-kognitywistyczna. Dla Pirrona i Sekstusa brak poglądów jest podstawą i warunkiem dobrostanu, dla Buddy i Nagardżuny brak poglądów jest wyrazem, ekspresją dobrostanu*) (Jakubczak 2019: 362, and cf. 329, where he states "for the skeptic, the absence of views is the beginning of the path that is to lead him to well-being, it is a way of pursuing well-being; for the Buddha, it is a point of arrival" [*dla sceptyka brak poglądów jest początkiem drogi, która ma go zaprowadzić do dobrostanu, jest sposobem dążenia do dobrostanu; dla Buddy jest to punkt dojścia*]). Meanwhile, for an interpretation of Nāgārjuna as not a skeptic but an anti-realist in that "he seeks to show the impossibility of a theory of the pramāṇas in order to close off one common route to metaphysical realism" (311), see Siderits 1988.

96. See in this context the distinction Huntington (1989: xii–xiii) proposes between "systematic" and "edifying" philosophy, and the "protreptic hermeneutics" of which Ganeri (2007: 116 fn. 28) speaks. See also Waldo 1978: 297: "Nāgārjuna does philosophy to produce a revolutionary change in his reader's approach to the world."
97. I am thus in full agreement with Huntington's understanding of the Mādhyamika's end as per his reading of Candrakīrti. The relevant passage is well worth citing in full:

> Candrakīrti has made it quite clear that the sole purpose of the doctrine of emptiness and the entire Mādhyamika critique lies in its function as a means through which all sentient beings can find release from fear and suffering. The great significance this "purpose" or "application" (*prayojana*) holds for him is both explicit, insofar as he has stated it in several places, and implicit, in that the overall structure of his treatise reflects the ethical and practical aspects of Mahāyāna Buddhism. This is not, however, simply a matter of apologetics, for independent of Candrakīrti's isolated remarks and the claims of the Mahāyāna tradition, a case can be made for the centrality of soteriological concerns strictly on the basis of an analysis of the Mādhyamika's approach to the problem of language and conceptual thought. It will become apparent as we proceed that the Mādhyamika is a philosophy which relates ideas to action in a particularly subtle fashion. This is not accomplished by arguing against one view as "wrong" and in favor of another as "right," but by demonstrating through any available means that the very fact of holding a view—*any* view—keeps one enmeshed in an endless cycle of clinging, antipathy, and delusion. If the Mādhyamika cannot be understood in this way—if we insist on interpreting these texts as a set of answers to epistemological or ontological questions—then we have missed the point. (Huntington 1989: 15, emphasis original)

98. For discussion of some relevant textual sources from the MK, VV, YṢ, and ŚS, see §2.4 on "The Buddhist Tetralemma"; Chapter 5 of the present book is conceived, moreover, as an exploration of the soterio-ethical purport underlying Nāgārjuna's philosophy as a whole.
99. MK:15:3: *kutaḥ svabhāvasyābhāve parabhāvo bhaviṣyati / svabhāvaḥ parabhāvasya parabhāvo hi kathyate*. See also the discussion of MK:15:4 in §3.6.
100. MK:24:19: *apratītya samutpanno dharmaḥ kaścin na vidyate / yasmāt tasmād aśūnyo hi dharmaḥ kaścin na vidyate*. In passing, I find Arnold's translation of *dharma* here (Arnold 2005: 259 n. 31) as 'existent' problematic, given that Nāgārjuna is arguing, precisely, *against* the existence of any existent. 'Thing' and 'phenomenon' are surely more neutral equivalents, the former more idiomatic, the latter perhaps more precise as a translation of this technical term.
101. That is, to use *prasajya* as opposed to *paryudāsa* negation.
102. The reference is to VV:5: If you deny existents after having apprehended them through perception / That perception by which existents were apprehended does not exist (Skt. *pratyakṣeṇa hi tāvad yady upalabhya vinivartayasi bhāvān / tan nāsti pratyakṣaṃ bhāvā yenopalabhyante*). My translation here is quite close to those in Bhattacharya 1978: 9 and Westerhoff 2010: 21 as I was unable to substantially improve upon them. For an alternative rendering, see Arnold 2005: 144–145. For an alternative elaboration of Madhyamaka responses to the *pramāṇavādin* charge

as formulated by the Nyāya and Yogācāra-Sautrāntika schools, see Siderits 1980 and 1981.

103. For translation and discussion, see Garfield 1996: 26–27/2002: 67.

104. See Candrakīrti's *Prasannapadā* 55.11–12, as translated by Arnold: "At this point, some object: Is this certainty [*niścaya*] that existents are not produced based on a reliable warrant [*pramāṇa*], or is it not based on a reliable warrant?" (Arnold 2005: 144, additions by Arnold). The Sanskrit is cited at 261 n. 7: *atra kecit paricodayanti: anutpannā bhāvā iti kim ayaṃ pramāṇajo niścaya uta-apramāṇajaḥ?*

105. This point recalls and elaborates in epistemological key on the discussion in §3.6 of a common meta-ontological framework but disparate ontological commitments between Nāgārjuna and his interlocutors. I am also reminded here of Ziporyn's point that "there is an implicit ontological essentialism embedded in the literal application of the copula" (Ziporyn 2015: 268).

106. See in this regard MK:16:9–10 cited in §4.2 on "Nāgārjuna's Abandoning Views".

107. I owe my adapted use of 'thetic' to J. Williams 2000.

108. In speaking of 'provisional theses,' I may be taken to be subscribing to the distinction Ruegg proposes between "a first-order utterance in the object language . . . [and] a second-order metalinguistic one" (Ruegg 2000: 220, cited in §4.3.1). I hope it should be clear from my further arguments, however, that I see Ruegg's parameterization of the latter as "stipulating that none of the Mādhyamika's statements is to be taken as a thesis *positing / presupposing / implying the existence of an entity having self-existence* (*svabhava*)" (Ruegg 2000: 220, emphasis added) as neither textually nor philosophically justified.

109. Recall MK:25:24ab, the final verse of the chapter on *nirvāṇa*:

The cessation of all cognizance
The felicitous cessation of hypostatization

For related discussion and the Sanskrit original, see §3.5.

110. See MK:7:34 (the concluding verse of his analysis of the conditioned / *saṃskṛta*), where Nāgārjuna uses the image of the dream as a simile for conventional reality:

Like an illusion, like a dream
Like a castle in the sky
So has arising, so has abiding
So has ceasing been explained

(*yathā māyā yathā svapno gandharvanagaraṃ yathā / tathotpādas tathā sthānaṃ tathā bhaṅga udāhṛtam*). Note that I have translated '*gandharvanagaraṃ yathā*' as 'a castle in the sky' since this conveys in a vernacular English expression the sense of Nāgārjuna's phrase. A literal translation would give 'a city of Gandharvas', these latter being a class of mythical sky-dwelling beings. Nāgārjuna uses the same image at MK:17:33 (the concluding verse of his chapter on action and fruit / *karmaphala*), and ŚS:66, where his enumeration of illusory imagery reaches heights unsurpassed elsewhere in his work:

Conditioned things are like a castle in the sky
Illusions, mirages, nets of hair
Foam, bubbles, fantasies
Dreams, wheeling firelight

For this last verse, see Lindtner 1982: 65/1997 117; Tola and Dragonetti 1995a: 80; Pandeya and Manju 1991: 147; Komito 1987: 94.

In relation to Nāgārjuna's use of such dream imagery, Garfield is careful to rebut Wood's nihilistic reading (see §3.6) with the following observation:

> The respect in which dependently arisen things are like a dream is this: They exist in one way (as empty) and appear to exist in another (as inherently existent). Just as dreams and mirages exist in one way (as illusions) and appear to exist in another (as objects of perception, or as water). But dreams and mirages are real dreams and mirages. So this verse should not be interpreted as asserting the complete nonexistence of all phenomena. (Garfield 1995: 177 n. 57)

111. For discussion, see Duerlinger 2013: 31. Garfield even cites Candrakīrti's use of the 'chariot' metaphor earlier in his paper. When glossing MK:18:8, Candrakīrti's *Prasannapadā* states, in Garfield's own translation, "A chariot is designated as a chariot in dependence on its parts, such as its wheels. That which is designated in dependence upon its parts is essentially unarisen, and that which is essentially unarisen is empty" (see Garfield 2008: 517). Garfield appears unaware of the consequent irony inherent in his later claim to be taking "the chariot path of rational inquiry."
112. YṢ:51, for the full text of which see §4.2.
113. Indeed, beyond chariots altogether, if we apply the model of 'relay chariots' espoused by Puṇṇa Mantāṇiputta in the *Rathavinīta Sutta*. For there we find an alternative use of the chariot metaphor, according to which the progressive purifications necessary for arrival at "final Nibbāna" are characterized by Puṇṇa as a succession of relay chariots, each of which is used to arrive at the next until, crucially, all are left behind. Otherwise, "he would have described what is still accompanied by clinging as final Nibbāna without clinging" (Ñāṇamoli and Bodhi 1995: 243). For a discussion of this *Discourse* with regard specifically to views and attachment, see Collins 1992: 121, to which I owe the reference.
114. MK:8:6: *phale 'sati na mokṣāya na svargāyopapadyate / mārgaḥ sarvakriyāṇāṃ ca nairarthakyaṃ prasajyate.* It is surely such textual precursors that Chan thinkers had in mind when taking liberation "to be totally unpredictable, unthinkable, beyond all expectation. It is perfectly 'aporetic' in the sense that there is no path (*poros*) that can lead to it" (Faure 2004: 120).
115. The interlocutor has been variously identified; see Garfield 2008: 511 fn. 7 for an enumeration of these; the thrust of Candrakīrti's response is not significantly altered by identifying his interlocutor as someone other than Bhāvaviveka.
116. Translation and Sanskrit text (from Vaidya's edition: Vaidya 1960) in Huntington 2007: 124 fn. 35: [Bhāvaviveka:] *kiṃ khalu āryāṇām upapattir nāsti?* [Candrakīrti:] *kenaitad uktam asti vā nāsti veti / paramārtho hyāryāṇāṃ tūṣṇiṃbhāvaḥ / tataḥ*

kutas tatra prapañcasaṃbhavo yadupapattir anupapattir vā syāt? Garfield (2008: 512 fn. 8), Arnold (2005: 146), and MacDonald (2015a: II, 211–212) provide alternative translations of this passage.

117. See MK:24, as noted earlier.
118. Yadav's formulation of metaphysics is *à propos* here, for on his account metaphysical thinking, being based in precisely the kind of propositional "logic of 'is' (*asti*) and 'not-is (*nāsti*)," is "a methodological fantasy" of ineluctably noxious consequence in that it amounts to "an argument for existence in bondage and self-love. . . . Metaphysics is a defense of the psychosis of identity" (Yadav 1977: 452, 466, 467, 469).
119. This is so, though, only given the appropriation of 'Philosophy' by academicians Aristotle would not have deigned to recognize under the title of 'Philosopher'. After all, as Aristotle puts it in the *Nicomachean Ethics*, "the end aimed at is not knowledge but action" (Aristotle 1984: 1730: 1095a5).
120. This is so despite Garfield's own acknowledgment of

> the essentially *soteriological* character of philosophical activity. For philosophy always begins in *aporia*, always aims at *noûs*, and always for the sake of *eudaimonia*. Or to put it another way, philosophy always begins in *avidya* [*avidyā*] and *saṃsāra*, always aims at *prajñā*, and always for the sake of *nirvana* [*nirvāṇa*]. (Garfield 2002: 260, emphases original)

121. Applying Tillemans's account of Kamalaśīla's criticism of Heshang (和尚) to Nāgārjuna, we may say that if he did "actually advocate no conceptual thought *across the board*, even in more ordinary contexts where decisions, intentions, and analyses *do* undoubtedly matter . . . [then] it is hard to see how he could function at all in most of the complex affairs of daily life and human society" (Tillemans 2016: 185, emphases original). As Tillemans observes, however, this does not seem to be what Heshang had—if I may put it this way—in mind:

> Heshang himself seems to have allowed that the nonconceptual state he was advocating was not one of complete absence of concepts—a type of perfectly blank mind or *tabula rasa*—but one in which notions, "whether they arise or not" . . . , are not thought about—are not *pursued by conceptual thought*. (Tillemans 2016: 186)

122. Regarding my reasons for not subscribing to this view, see my discussion of MK:18:8 in §2.2.2.

Chapter 5

1. MK:26:12cd. For the original Sanskrit and further discussion, see §4.2.
2. Also known as the *Rājaparikathāratnamālā* or *Precious Garland: An Epistle for a King* (Dunne and McClintock 1997: 2).
3. For alternative summaries, see Lindtner 1997: 292–295; Hopkins 1998: 22–83, which comprises analyses of the text in terms of "Advice for Living," "Advice for Liberation," and "Compassion and Wisdom in Public Policy"; and Jampa Tegchok 2017: ix–xi.

4. For an overview of the contents, see Padmakara 2013: 19–21, and Della Santina 2002: 6–7. Amber Carpenter characterizes the SL as "a sort of exhortation to live decently such as one might find indistinguishably in any moralist of any time, proceeding without anything distinctively Buddhist in its exhortations to, or conception of, virtue" (Carpenter 2016: 21 fn. 1).
5. For reliable translations and commentaries to the *Bodhicaryāvatāra*, see Crosby and Skilton 1995; Wallace and Wallace 1997. Williams translates the Sanskrit title more literally as "An Introduction (*avatāra*) to the Conduct (*caryā*) which leads to Enlightenment (*bodhi*)" (Williams 1995: xiv fn. 8).
6. This is the *kṣudravastuka* section of the *Dharmaskandha* or **Abhidharmadharmaskandhapādaśāstra*, a work "which, together with the *Saṅgītiparyāya*, belongs to the earliest stage of the Sarvāstivāda Abhidharma treatises" (Eltschinger 2015: 96)—though, as Eltschinger notes on the same page, the *kṣudravastuka* mentions seventy-eight rather than fifty-seven defilements. For a fuller study of the number of faults involved, see Hahn 1982b. For translations and commentaries of the relevant portion of Nāgārjuna's RĀ (i.e., RĀ:401–433), see Dunne and McClintock 1997: 73–78; Jampa Tegchok 2017: 329–343; Hopkins 1998: 149–154; Hahn 1982b: 164–171. This last work by Hahn also includes the Sanskrit text and provides a trilingual (Sanskrit-Tibetan-English) list of the faults themselves (181–183).
7. I reproduce here the versions in Hahn 1982b: 181–183.
8. For the relevant verses, see RĀ:434–439 on the six perfections and RĀ:440–460 on the ten stages or grounds. For an especially explicit attempt to stitch Śrāvakayāna and Mahāyāna models of attainment together in a coherent ethical system, see verse 440.
9. RĀ:438; my translation is calqued on those of Dunne and McClintock 1997: 78; Jampa Tegchok 2017: 346–347; and Hopkins 1998: 154–155.
10. See in this context Tillemans's statement that "Finally, quietism is not only a stance for philosophers who argue. It figures in meditation and practice too, as Mahāyānists generally agree that there comes a point on the Buddhist spiritual path where views (*dṛṣṭi*, *darśana*), and indeed all conceptual thinking (*vikalpa*, *kalpanā*), are to be left behind" (Tillemans 2016: 3). As Tillemans elaborates elsewhere,

    > For our purposes the particularity of the Madhyamaka is that it emphasizes philosophical analysis as a method leading to quietening of thought. It develops argumentation and analysis designed to undercut philosophical thinking by diagnosing where it goes wrong. Madhyamaka, or Nāgārjunian, quetism is thus the reasoned disengagement from all philosophical theses (*pakṣa*, *pratijñā*), positions (*abhyupagama*), and views (*dṛṣṭi*), and hence from all debates (*vivāda*) about them. (Tillemans 2017: 111).

    See also Waldo, for whom the MK is

    > a supremely transparent example of the limits of logic and language. The comprehending reader will come to see through it the absurdity of all metaphysical projects. In the context of the *bodhisattva* path this intellectual example is meant to resonate as an example of the folly of clinging to fixed patterns of thought, behavior, or emotion in any area of life. . . . Eventually the practitioner must leap free of all preconceptions into the realm of *śūnyatā*, which is beyond any question of being or not being. (Waldo 1975: 284)

11. As Carpenter asserts, "Nāgārjuna's distinctive ethical view . . . will turn out to be metaphysical not only because metaphysical positions have implications for ethics, but also because reflecting on metaphysics is a constitutive part of ethical practice" (Carpenter 2016: 27). See also the subtitle to her book on *Indian Buddhist Philosophy: Metaphysics as Ethics* (Carpenter 2014), or perhaps even more directly Owen Flanagan's assertion about Buddhism in general: "Outside of Plato in the West, I know of no other philosophical theory that draws such intimate connections among metaphysics, epistemology, and ethics" (Flanagan 2013: 206). Nevertheless, it is worth noting that my reference to Nāgārjuna's philosophy as 'globally coherent' refers, strictly speaking, to what Richard T. De George calls internal coherence; that is, the extent to which the elements of a philosophy "cohere with each other" (De George 1990: 39). In the case of Nāgārjuna, there in fact obtains a striking internal coherence, whereby untying one thread of his philosophy inevitably leads to fraying myriad others. As for *external* coherence, which on De George's model is to be understood as the extent to which the elements of a philosophy cohere with "general experience, knowledge, and beliefs" (De George 1990: 39), Nāgārjuna's philosophy is distinctly (and, as I have argued, consistently) *incoherent* in that it goes radically against the grain of the inveterate human tendency to reify the objects of experience and knowledge; indeed, against even the holding of such things as beliefs.
12. The coinage 'ceive' (along with correlates such as 'ception') is discussed in §5.3.
13. MK:24:9: *ye 'nayor na vijānanti vibhāgaṃ satyayor dvayoḥ / te tattvaṃ na vijānanti gambhīre buddhaśāsane.*
14. MK:25:19–20. For the Sanskrit original, see §4.3.2. As there, I am proposing here an equivalence between *saṃvṛti-satya* and *saṃsāra*, on the one hand, and *paramārtha-satya* and *nirvāṇa*, on the other. For further discussion, see also §5.2.3.
15. By 'ontological realization' I have in mind something like "to give real existence to something" and subsidiary senses such as "to make real or actual; to convert (something imagined, planned, etc.) into real existence or fact; to bring (a scheme, ambition, etc.) to fruition." By 'epistemological realization' I have in mind something like "to make real to the mind" and subsidiary senses such as "to present as real to the mind"; "to conceive of as being real"; "to become aware of or come to understand (a fact, situation, etc.)" (*Oxford English Dictionary*: realize, senses I and II).
16. This is in line with the distinction Tillemans proposes among the 'typical Prāsaṅgika Madhyamaka' of "post-third century writers like Candrakīrti" and Gorampa, the 'atypical Prāsaṅgikas' such as Tsongkhapa, and "Svātantrika-Mādhyamikas like Bhāviveka, Śāntarakṣita, and Kamalaśīla" (Tillemans 2016: 4 [and see 51–58], 5, 6).
17. As averred in §0.0, I owe the term 'soterial' "for cases where a notion is related to salvation (in Buddhist contexts: liberation) rather than to a theory or doctrine of salvation" to Kellner (2020: 39 fn. 2). Another way of making the point I am getting at here is to say that Nāgārjuna's abjuration of positionality includes the disavowal of even such theories or doctrines of salvation/liberation, and therefore moves beyond soteriology to soteries.
18. For discussion of the full passage wherein this term is found, see §2.2.2. For further elaboration of "Philosophical Quietism in Nāgārjuna and Early Madhyamaka," see

Tillemans 2017, and various points in Tillemans 2016, such as the reference to "the irenic positionless Nāgārjunian standpoint" (Tillemans 2016: 90).

19. For the classic statements, see Katz 1978, Proudfoot 1985, Forman 1990, and Stace 1961.
20. As Katz puts "the basic claim being advanced" in his paper, "mystical experience is contextual" (Katz 1978: 56–57).
21. Katz repeats this position *verbatim* thirty-five years later; see Katz 2013: 12. For the most thorough and sophisticated study of Buddhism and mystical experience, see Komarovski 2015a, which provides a fine survey of the scholarly literature insofar as relevant to the Buddhist case at pp. 26–43.
22. For an effective summary of the positions regarding Buddhist ethics in general adopted by relevant scholars, see Finnigan 2010: 267:

    > Keown (2001) and, later, Cooper and James (2005: 68) claim that Buddhist ethics is a type of virtue ethics. Siderits (2003[b], 2007) argues that it is unmistakably consequentialist, as do Williams (1998) and Goodman (2008). Velez [de Cea] (2004) and Clayton (2006) argue that Buddhist ethics is best understood as a combination of virtue ethics and utilitarianism whilst Harvey (2000: 49), though acknowledging the analogies, nonetheless maintains that a Buddhist ethical theory is significantly distinct.

    Like Tillemans, I am suspicious of these and other

    > such attempts to find a major Western ethical theory underlying Buddhism . . . [since] such unification is unlikely to be gained via a bottom-up approach where one reads extensively in the canon to find a clear recurring theory; rather, such unification is typically "discovered" or "found" via a top-down approach that imposes a view of what Buddhism *essentially is* on very often recalcitrant texts. (Tillemans 2016: 168, emphases original)

23. Recall in this regard my repudiation of Garfield's identification of "the relinquishing of all views" as "an *archē* beyond discourse" (Garfield 2002: 68) in §4.3.2.
24. 'Process' and 'promote' seem too 'pro' to be unproblematically adopted here so, while not wanting to needlessly clutter the main text, I propose that they should be understood to be, as it were, bracketed—'(pro)cess' and '(pro)mote'—so as to emphasize the Nāgārjunian insistence on hewing to the middle way between positive and negative positionality. As for 'cessation', this too can fruitfully be bracketed—as 'cess(ation)'—so as to emphasize the relationship (etymologically unattested) between process and cessation. For in a Nāgārjunian world, to exist in process is already to empt; that is, to exist in cessation, since what proceeds, in proceeding, ceases.
25. The coinage 'Buddhant' is here used to mean 'characteristic of a Buddha', specifically in this case as relating to a Buddha's perfect *prajñā* of reality. One could also call it 'arhatic' or 'arhatant' if one accepts Garfield's characterization of "the arhat, who directly perceives emptiness as it is unmediated either by apprehension of (other) conventional entities or by conception" (Garfield 2002: 52).
26. See also Harvey 2000: 17 (drawing on Keown 1992: 213–218) for still another translation and discussion. I will translate *cetanā* as 'intention', though (as we have seen to be common with such technical terms—see, for example, my discussion of *prapañca*

in Chapter 4, fn. 1), there is no shortage of alternative translations in use. For a representative list, see Meyers 2010: 140 fn. 9 (drawing on Karunaratna 1979: 86), and for detailed discussion of the meanings and translations of the term see Meyers 2010: 139 fn. 7 and 166–174.

27. MK:17:2–3: *cetanā cetayitvā ca karmoktaṃ paramarṣiṇā / tasyānekavidho bhedaḥ karmaṇaḥ parikīrtitaḥ // tatra yac cetanety uktaṃ karma tan mānasaṃ smṛtam / cetayitvā ca yat tūktaṃ tat tu kāyikavācikam*. Note that, technically, *anekavidhaḥ* in MK:17:2:c is a nominative singular, which perhaps explains why Kragh has rendered it "A manifold division" (Kragh 2006: 224). This would emphasize the overall unity of action, subdivided as it nevertheless is into distinct types. It merits noting that Kragh's commentary to Candrakīrti's *Prasannapadā Madhyamakavṛttiḥ* on these MK verses (Kragh 2006: 219–243) is an especially comprehensive and insightful study of the topic at hand as instantiated in the classical literature. Garfield is presumably translating MK:17:2b in speaking of "Nāgārjuna's statement that 'action is of two kinds: intention and the intentional'" (Garfield 2011: 179, where the Buddha's *mahāvākya* is also cited). For a slightly different rendering of Nāgārjuna's verse, see Garfield 1995: 232.

28. See also Williams: "for the Buddha *karman* is essentially volition (intention) which leads to actions of body, speech, or mind" (P. Williams 2000: 72).

29. This statement is, of course, not to be taken as denoting a relation of strict identity: action is not exactly the same as intention, though in the Buddhant (and more broadly Buddhist) conception intention is very much already action. See Meyers 2010: 139 fn. 7: "We tend to think of an intention as a cause of action, but *cetanā* is an action, *karma* in its own right."

30. Given its relevance to the point at hand, I cannot resist following Kragh (2006: 221 fn. 335) in citing here the explication provided in the early Chinese commentary to the MK attributed to Qingmu included in the text's canonical Chinese translation by Kumārajīva, the *Zhonglun* (中論). This reads:

> Intention is one of the dharmas of mental configurations. Amongst the mental configurations, it has the capacity to initiate that which is done, and this is why it is called karma. External actions of body and speech arise on the account of intention. Although there are things which are done through the other configurations of the mind, it is intention which is the basis of action, and this is why intention is said to be karma.

Ch. 思是心數法。諸心數法中能發起有所作故名業。因是思故起外身 口業。雖因餘心心數法有所作。但思為所作本。故說思為業 (T 1564:21). Like Kragh, I have provided here the translation by Bocking (1995: 258) on account of what I have found to be its unimprovable combination of fluency and accuracy, though I have replaced his rendering of 思 as 'conception' with 'intention' throughout.

Just as in English, so too the Sanskrit *cetanā* was rendered into Chinese by various terms, including 心 (standardly rendered as 'mind' or 'heart', and also used to translate several other Sanskrit terms, including some stemming from the same √*cit* root as *cetanā*, such as *citta*, as well as *abhiprāya*, *buddhi*, *garbha*, *manas*, and *jñāna* along with several cognates of this last, including *saṃjñā* and *vijñāna*), 志 (standardly rendered as 'intent', will', or 'aim', and also used to translate several other Sanskrit terms, including *citta* and *saṃkalpa*), 覺 (standardly rendered as 'consciousness' or 'enlightenment', and also used to translate several other Sanskrit terms, including *buddhi* and *vedanā*), as well as 思 (thought, reflection, longing, and also used to translate several other Sanskrit terms, including some stemming from the same √*cit* root as *cetanā*, such as *citta* and *cetayitvā*, as well as *abhiprāya*, *buddhi*, *smṛti* and *vikalpa*) and related compounds such as 思惟 ('thought') and 意思 ('purpose').

31. Garfield stresses the conceptual nature of intention repeatedly at Garfield 2016: 92–93; see e.g., 93 fn. 14: "*cetanā* is conceptual, and fundamental to ethical conduct." It is also worthwhile citing the observation made by Siderits: "That intentional action always involves conceptualisation is a basic premise in the study of motor cognition" (Siderits 2019: 647 fn. 4).
32. MK:18:5. For the original Sanskrit, see §4.2, and for further discussion see §3.5.
33. Nāgārjuna is naturally to be included among the Madhyamaka ethicists, but one thinks more readily of intellectual descendants such as Śāntideva.
34. McClintock's comments regarding Nāgārjuna's Madhyamaka heirs Śāntarakṣita and Kamalaśīla are *à propos* here:

> rational analysis . . . plays a critical role, because it allows one to rule out a whole range of incorrect views and replace them with views that while not able to directly encapsulate reality ["since the removal of ignorance does not take place at the level of language or concepts"], can nevertheless be ascertained as in accord with reality. On the basis of such views, one then undertakes the meditative cultivation that gradually eliminates the distortions of primordial ignorance (and hence, also, all "views"), such that one's thought and experience come to be in accord with reality. (McClintock 2010: 17)

Whether meditative cultivation is undertaken "on the basis of" certain philosophical views, or whether the relation works the other way around, or indeed whether "certain philosophical theories arose from meditative experiences and others did not, and . . . the origin of still others cannot be determined" (Franco 2009: 126), has been the subject of intense and ongoing debate. See, for example, Schmithausen (1973, 2014) and Franco (2009, 2018), both of whom are cited by Pecchia, whose own comments regarding Dharmakīrti's views (!) on the matter, moreover, are likewise well worth citing:

> It is thus not only worthy but also necessary to engage in mental cultivation for the follower of the Buddhist *dharma* who wants the results of philosophical analysis to be meaningful. What the yogin knows at the end of the path, when his cognitive abilities have been radically transformed, may or may not be different from what he knew during the path. The difference is that he now knows it with a different mind—a mind that does not obscure the objects of its cognition with its own concepts. Meditative practice is then a training for the mind to think out of its box and, in the long term, to become autonomous from thinking itself, from any kind of belief, even from the "right" ones. (Pecchia 2023: 679–680)

35. See Yadav's comment that, far from being rational, *nirvāṇa* "is cognitive nonsense; it is a 'scandal' to logic" (Yadav 1977: 463).
36. Of course, there is more going on in Dunne's claim that *nirvāṇa* is the preserve of "judicious, rational persons" than mere description, for it is clear that there is also at work

an implicit evaluative judgment. This clearly possesses prescriptive normative force, moreover, according to which one *should* be a judicious, rational person if one is to attain *nirvāṇa*, though whether that force is moral or merely prudential is unclear from the context. As we have seen in previous chapters, such privileging of rationality, and doing so moreover in treating topics explicitly characterized by the primary sources as beyond rationality's remit, is widely prevalent. Finally, while Dunne does not stipulate whether *nirvāṇa* is obtained by judicious, rational persons *alone*, I cannot help echoing Bernard Williams's quip as to "the tedium of immortality" (Williams 1993) to declare—tongue firmly in cheek—that a *nirvāṇa*-realm populated entirely by arch-rationalists seems anything but appealing: a kind of philosophers' conference panel, but deathly boring unendingly!

37. See Ram-Prasad 2001: 236 n. 53 for the relevant reference to Nāgārjuna. Dunne explicitly refers to Ram-Prasad's discussion in the context of his own treatment of liberation; see Dunne 2004: 229 fn. 10.
38. See Ram-Prasad's statement that, for what he calls the Yogācāra-Mādhyamika, "The ultimate simply is the insight that there is no duality" (Ram-Prasad 2001: 158). For his part, while Dunne acknowledges that "Dharmakīrti and his fellow Mahāyānists [presumably including Nāgārjuna] conceive buddhahood in such a way that while a buddha may still have perceptions, he no longer employs concepts . . . strictly speaking, a buddha does not employ reasoning (*yukti*)," nevertheless he prefers an "inverse" reading privileging reason after all (Dunne 2004: 250–251).
39. As so often, Garfield has already addressed the relevant point adroitly:

    > Buddhist ethics is about *path*. After all, Buddhism, . . . from the very beginning, is about solving a problem—that of the universality and pervasiveness of *dukkha*, and the route to solving the problem is the eightfold noble path. That path articulates the domain of ethics; hence ethics is a *means* to the achievement of liberation, not something to be fully achieved *upon* liberation. For that reason, we focus not upon perfection when addressing Buddhist ethics, but upon the means of self-cultivation. (Garfield 2016: 80, emphases original)

40. This phrase conveys an unstated but important assumption in Finnigan's argument. It is one, moreover, which effectively identifies her reading of Buddhist ethics here as broadly consequentialist-utilitarian, in the sense that it is the desired end-state of the action that justifies its performance. Noteworthy is the fact that this still leaves room open for a form of virtue ethics if the state in question (bliss, say) is taken to engender a virtue. In either case, it should be clear that the unspoken assumption I have identified here in Finnigan's account certainly eliminates a strict deontological interpretation, for the act is not undertaken on account of its conformity to any preestablished normative rules.
41. This phrase conveys another unspoken assumption. In the example given, if acting compassionately brings about bliss but also brings about, say, wisdom (let's stipulate that as a supporting state; i.e., one that reinforces the bliss) or resentment (let's stipulate that as a countervailing state; i.e., one that inhibits the bliss), then the account will be complicated precisely insofar as the relation among these states complicates the proposed founding relation between the initial act and the end-state. This has

non-negligible consequences for the account if it is to apply to lived experience, for it is clear that moral actions at least typically and perhaps invariably produce multiple phenomenologically attested feeling-states in the real world, and that, conversely, our feeling-states are constituted (among much else) by a multiplicity of moral (and non-moral) actions.

42. Perhaps the roles path stages play "in constituting or producing the teleological end" in Finnigan's 2011 account may be mapped onto what she later identifies as the 'instrumental' and 'constitutive' "ways of thinking about the nature of a path relative to a goal" (Finnigan 2017: 34, and see also Finnigan 2018: 168–169). It is unclear, however, how either an instrumental analysis in terms of "an *external effect*" or a constitutive one in terms of "an *internal objective*" (Finnigan 2017: 38, emphases original) would in fact map onto the symmetrically determinative function Finnigan requires in order for her analysis to stand up to scrutiny.
43. See also the fuller formulation later in the same paper:

    > Finnigan's recommendation . . . is in fact unavailable to a Buddhist of any stripe, and would constitute a wholesale abandonment of Buddhist metaphysics, philosophy of mind, and moral psychology. While Finnigan's account of awakened action might be an interesting *alternative* to Buddhism, it is not *Buddhist*. (Garfield 2011: 178, emphases original)

    Finnigan responds to these and other criticisms, including as voiced in Hansen 2011, in Finnigan 2011b.
44. See also Garfield's observation that "non-duality is non-dually cognized by a Buddha" (Garfield 2006: 69).
45. Recall Flanagan's acknowledgment (cited in §1.4) that "Even if there is a minority movement that fits the bill of naturalized Buddhism . . . it does not follow that it really deserves to call itself Buddhism" (Flanagan 2013: 4).
46. See also the discussion of this passage by Panikkar, who interprets it as "a reduction to the sublime" (Panikkar 2006: 28). The Woodward translation he provides of the first portion of the Buddha's *dénouement* is perhaps more eloquent than that by Bodhi here: "This question, Rādha, goes too far. You can grasp no limit to this question."
47. Thus, in Garfield's words, "Finnigan fails to see the radical distinction the Buddhist tradition draws between benighted and awakened action" (Garfield 2011: 179).
48. In fact, Finnigan appears to effectively admit as much in concluding with nothing more than two horns of a dilemma, each of which comes, as she sees it, with significant costs (Finnigan 2011a: 152).
49. See Collins, who states unequivocally that "The Buddhist doctrinal position can be stated simply. Nirvana is indeed the ultimate religious goal, a state of release from all suffering and impermanence, but no language or concepts can properly describe it. It is *atakkāvacara*, 'inaccessible to (discursive) thought'" (Collins 1998: 97). Naturally, this did not exhaust the range of Buddhist understandings—a point to which we come presently.
50. Or see also the related distinction between *nirvāṇa* as 'eu-topia' (Good-place) and 'ou-topia' (No-place) (Collins 1998: 89ff, esp. 112, and see also Collins 2010: 7).

51. For a corollary study of *nirvāṇa* in Pāli sources (though one that is primarily taxonomic as opposed to historical), see Collins 1998: 135–285.
52. See, therefore, in addition to Garfield's put-downs on pp. 175 and 178 cited earlier, his reproach regarding intentional (i.e., *cetānic*) action that "There is a problem here for Finnigan, and a fatal one, a problem that gets to the heart of what is wrong with her account: *no Buddhist philosopher has ever accepted the thesis that a buddha has cetanā*, and indeed the absence of *cetanā* in a buddha is central to every Buddhist account of awakened consciousness . . . [Finnigan's is thus] a heterodox position unavailable to any Buddhist, and for deep reasons" (Garfield 2011: 179, emphases original). Finnigan attempts to rebut this charge at Finnigan 2011b: 185–186 (and see 192 n. 5), but still without substantiating her claim with reference to any of the "historical and contemporary thinkers within the Buddhist tradition" she had initially adduced (Finnigan 2011a: 152).
53. See also Collins 1998: 117, which speaks of that "closure [which] is always implicit in a system, throughout its structure."
54. MK:22:16. For the original Sanskrit, see §3.4. See also the commentary to this verse by Siderits and Katsura, who observe that "For many Buddhists, the expression 'the Tathāgata' is not just the name of a historical person but stands as well for the supposedly transcendent reality of nirvāṇa" (Siderits and Katsura 2013: 251). There can be no doubting that in Nāgārjuna's case here this is the primary, if not sole, sense: a direct and unequivocal avocation of the ultimate identity between the ultimate reality of *nirvāṇa* and the conventional realm of *saṃsāra* as per MK:25:19 (on which, see earlier, and cf. the further comment to this effect at Siderits and Katsura 2013: 251). This appears to render Nāgārjuna thoroughly concordant with what Xing identifies as the 'mature' Mahāyāna view, wherein "Buddhas are not different from sentient beings in an ultimate sense since all possess the same *tathatā*, but from the perspective of conventional truth they are different, as Buddhas do not have *kleśas*" (Xing 2005: 181).
55. The reference is to Eckel, who states that "The Buddhist tradition often seems to play the role of the knotty exception in comparative studies of religion" (Eckel 2001: 125). If this can be said of Buddhism *vis-à-vis* other religions, then it is surely Madhyamaka which plays this role *vis-à-vis* its Buddhist brethren schools.
56. For the Sanskrit original and English translation of MK:25:19–20, see §4.3.2, and for further discussion see also §5.1.
57. MK:25:9–10: *ya ājavaṃjavībhāva upādāya pratītya vā / so 'pratītyānupādāya nirvāṇam upadiśyate // prahāṇaṃ cābravīc chāstā bhavasya vibhavasya ca / tasmān na bhāvo nābhāvo nirvāṇam iti yujyate.*
58. As Garfield comments on these verses, "the very same world is saṃsāra or nirvāṇa, dependent upon one's perspective" (Garfield 1995: 328).
59. MK:25:17: *paraṃ nirodhād bhagavān bhavatīty eva nājyate / na bhavaty ubhayaṃ ceti nobhayaṃ ceti nājyate.* The effective identification in this book of the Buddha, as the embodiment of *nirvāṇa*, with *nirvāṇa* itself, is eloquently attested by the anticipation of Nāgārjuna's 'non-qualifications' of the Buddha here and as follows in his analogous non-qualifications of *nirvāṇa* earlier in the same discussion. As examples, I mention MK:25:3 (cited in the next note), where he denies a number of existential qualifiers of

nirvāṇa; MK:25:4–10 (cf. verses 9–10 just cited), where he denies both existence and non-existence of *nirvāṇa*; MK:25:11–14, where he denies the third lemma ('both'); and MK:25:16, where he denies the fourth and final lemma ('neither'). See also Oetke (2015: 221):

> the thought conveyed by the two verses [MK:25:16–17] is that neither with respect to a Buddha after cessation nor with respect to a Buddha during lifetime would it be appropriate to characterize him either by 'he exists', or 'he does not exist', or 'he exists and does not exist' or 'he neither exists nor does not exist'. The reason is exactly the same as the one which justifies analogous dismissals with respect to Nirvāṇa.

60. See, for example, Nāgārjuna's incipit to the topic earlier in the same book, at MK:25:3:

    Not abandoned not attained
    Not annihilated not eternal
    Not ceased not arisen
    Thus is *nirvāṇa* said to be

    (*aprahīṇam asaṃprāptam anucchinnam aśāśvatam / aniruddham anutpannam etan nirvāṇam ucyate*). My translation here closely resembles that of Siderits and Katsura: 2013: 291.
61. MK:25:18: *tiṣṭhamāno 'pi bhagavān bhavatīty eva nājyate / na bhavaty ubhayaṃ ceti nobhayaṃ ceti nājyate.*
62. It may be worth noting in passing here that this shows Siderits and Katsura's gloss on Nāgārjuna's avowal at MK:25:10cd that "it is acceptable to say that *nirvāṇa* / Neither exists nor does not exist," according to which this "represents the position of an opponent, not Nāgārjuna" (Siderits and Katsura 2013: 297, and cf. 299–300), is incorrect, or at least unnecessary (cf. MacDonald 2015b: 374–375). For instead, I am proposing that Nāgārjuna is expressing here the kataphatic avowal (from the point of view of *saṃsāra*, as it were) of what he will go on to apophatically deny (from the point of view of *nirvāṇa*, as it were) in succeeding verses.
63. See also MK:24:19:

    Since no non-dependently co-originated thing
    At all is found
    Therefore no non-empty thing
    At all is found

    For related discussion and the Sanskrit original, see §4.3.
64. See MK:17:2–3 and the surrounding discussion earlier.
65. Williams's work is a study of Śāntideva's *Bodhicaryāvatāra*, but given the appositeness of (at least some of) his arguments to the positions I am ascribing to Nāgārjuna, I am using his rhetorical flourish to render in stark terms the issue at hand. I owe the reference to Garfield and Priest 2016: 4.
66. I will have more to say about *karuṇā* and its translation as 'compassion' shortly. I have here rendered the term as 'compassion' rather than 'care' (as I will do later) in order to make a point about passion and its absence.

67. See also Garfield, who characterizes *karuṇā* as, "on the Mahāyāna view, the direct result of a genuine appreciation of the essencelessness and interdependence of all sentient beings" (Garfield 2016: 89).
68. As should be evident from preceding discussions, the terms 'views' and 'actions' are to be taken not only as translations of *dṛṣṭi* and *karma* but as standing synecdochically for a broader compass of correlates, including, for example, *prapañca*, *pakṣa*, *pratijñā*, *vikalpa*, and *cetanā*.
69. More amply, I should perhaps speak of the relationship between Nāgārjuna's metaphysics of the emptiness *of things*, epistemology of the abandonment *of views*, and ethics of the pacification *of actions*. This latter I am calling eirenics.
70. While I arrive at my understanding of ception for different reasons, it is telling that, as Tillemans asserts of Nāgārjuna's intellectual heir,

    > On the Prāsaṅgika side, Candrakīrti . . . is definitely blurring the dichotomy between conceptual schemes and the perceptual given that is so important to his Svātantrika counterparts. When the distinction between conceptual thought and perception is deliberately fudged, that between the inventions of thought and the objects of perception is too—not surprisingly, Candrakīrti ends up having no use at all for foundationalist holdovers like appearances-cum-particulars. (Tillemans 2003: 100)

71. MK:3:1: *darśanaṃśravaṇaṃghrāṇaṃrasanaṃsparśanaṃmanaḥ/indriyāṇiṣaḍeteṣāṃ draṣṭavyādīni gocaraḥ*.
72. MK:3.8: *vyākhyātaṃ śravaṇaṃ ghrāṇaṃ rasanaṃ sparśanaṃ manaḥ / darśanenaiva jānīyāc chrotṛśrotavyakādi ca*.
73. Note, however, that Bodhi interprets the (textually unparameterized) 'all' to refer not to "the all-inclusive all (*sabbasabba*)" but to the narrower "all of the sense bases (*āyatanasabba*)" (Bodhi 2000: 1399 n. 6). The relevant passage is also cited in an alternative translation by Holder 2013: 231.
74. See, e.g., "form is nonself . . . Feeling is nonself . . . Perception is nonself . . . Volitional formations are nonself . . . Consciousness is nonself" (Bodhi 2000: 902 (III.22.II.I.59 (7)), or more amply

    > Any kind of form whatsoever . . . Any kind of feeling whatsoever . . . Any kind of perception whatsoever . . . Any kind of volitional formations whatsoever . . . Any kind of consciousness whatsoever, whether past, future, or present, internal or external, gross or subtle, inferior or superior, far or near—one sees all [form, sensation, perception, mental formation, and/or] consciousness as it really is with correct wisdom thus: 'This is not mine, this I am not, this is not my self'. (Bodhi 2000: 927 (III.22.II.III.82 (10))

75. Huntington goes on to note that "This ambiguity is graphically represented in the Buddhist doctrine of the six senses and their objects (*āyatanas*)" (Huntington 1989: 209 n. 101).
76. My example, pertaining as it does to the two truths, is, of course, not chosen at random given the subject under discussion, implicitly or explicitly, in much of this chapter.
77. That the distinction would come to dominate much subsequent discussion by Buddhist *Pramāṇavādins* such as Dignāga or Dharmakīrti as to the prime status of

pratyakṣa (perception) as a valid means of obtaining epistemological truth is another matter.

78. Note again that the relevant chapter of Ram-Prasad's work relates to what he calls the 'Yogācāra-Mādhyamika' school, in the course of which he discusses the likes of Vasubandhu and Sthiramati (c. sixth century), as well as Śāntarakṣita (725–788) and Kamalaśīla (740–795). Of course, the entire issue of sectarian identification is fraught, but the important point for present purposes is that the "double challenge" Ram-Prasad identifies most certainly applies to Nāgārjuna's account.
79. Epistemology is also central to Mark Siderits's formulation of the problem in terms of "The *Prapañca* Paradox." On his account, this relates to a

    > question that stems from the claim that the cessation of suffering is attained through stopping all *prapañca*. Suppose we take *prapañca* to mean conceptualisation, and we take the attainment of nirvāṇa to involve coming to see the truth about the world and ourselves. In that case it would have to be true that all conceptualisation falsifies. What, then, of the statement "All conceptualisation falsifies" (or *P* for short)? Since P, like any other statement, employs concepts, if it is true then it must be false. The upshot is that there could be no truth the grasping of which results in the cessation of suffering. (Siderits 2019: 645–646)

    Siderits goes on to propose a resolution of the paradox by means of radical contextualist semantics. While I find his account on the matter innovative and illuminating, in the following pages I will pursue an alternative approach.
80. Finnigan is here discussing what she identifies, following Dunne 1996, as Candrakīrti's broad conception of conceptuality, as opposed to the narrower conception they find in Dharmakīrti.
81. Dead, or a 'Robo-Buddha', "act[ing] directly on their perception without any intervening thought" (Siderits 2011a: 328). See also Jakubczak's reference to the Buddha's "divine madness" (*szaleństwie bożym*) (Jakubczak 2019: 326).
82. See also Sells 1994: 207, where he delineates the principles governing "The Aporia of Transcendence" and related apophaseis.
83. Many have tried, of course. For a rich excavation of early Prāsaṅgika and Svātantrika Madhyamaka attempts to ascribe to the Buddha both "pure realization of emptiness and constant compassionate activity" (133), see Vose 2009: 111–133. In the course of his exposition, Vose charts the views of exemplary Mādhyamikas such as Atiśa (Dīpaṅkaraśrījñāna) (c. 982–1054), who "is commonly credited with establishing Prāsaṅgika in Tibet" (23), and Jayānanda (twelfth century), who, "for the first time in the history of Indian Madhyamaka, writes of 'Svātantrika'" (36), in terms I take to be parallel to those I voice here. Thus, for example, both Atiśa and Jayānanda understand "consciousness to be inextricably imbued with subject-object duality" (112), which explains why "subject-object duality can play no part in 'knowing' the ultimate" (113), and this leads Atiśa to call "seeing emptiness" a "realizing through not realizing" (112) and Jayānanda to explain that "enlightenment is a process of 'not knowing'" (114).
84. See Dunne 1996: 525–526: "a buddha must speak, but the use of concepts and language would imply a spiritual ignorance (*avidyā*) that a buddha as transcendent must not have." Finnigan draws on Dunne's analysis explicitly to arrive at the like

conclusion that "a buddha would need to *employ* concepts in uttering speech acts," even though "conceptuality is bound to (or identical with) ignorance" (Finnigan 2010: 293 fn. 24, emphasis original, and 291). On the notion of Buddhic omniscience, see also McClintock, who echoes Dunne in addressing a "conception of omniscience as the proper goal of all rational and judicious persons," one effectively demonstrating "that the Buddhist path is a rational path, grounded in reason, which any rational person will be bound to follow if only he or she comes to see its rationality for him or herself," even though "the ultimate goal of the path cannot be achieved by rational analysis" (McClintock 2010: 13, 14, 17, and see Dunne 2004: 251 cited in §5.2.2). For a discussion of the ethical implications for Madhyamaka of Buddhic omniscience, see Tillemans 2016: 152–153.

85. See Griffiths: "It follows from these claims about construction-free awareness that Buddha's awareness cannot be implicated with speech" (Griffiths 1994: 159, and note that Griffiths translates *nirvikalpajñāna* as 'awareness without construction'). See also, however, the attempt (by Candrakīrti in the *Prasannapadā Madhyamakavṛttiḥ*) to square concept-laden speech with the circle of concept-free awareness in Griffiths 1994: 161–163. Predictably, and (in anticipation of the point soon to be made regarding God) analogously to like theistic efforts, the Buddhist tradition goes so far as to ascribe not just linguistic competence to the Buddha but downright omnilinguality, on which see again Griffiths: the "Buddha possesses complete and perfect skill in speaking every natural language" (Griffiths 1994: 116).

86. An especially salient reference to the diverse bodies of the Buddha is that detailed by Dunne (1996: 548–550), where it is argued that Candrakīrti's Buddha turns out to be one who "teaches in a magical, transcendent way" (549). For an astute historical overview of the 'three body' (*trikāya*) doctrine, see Williams 2009: 172–186, and for a far more substantial account see Xing 2005.

87. While my reading of Nāgārjunian apophasis on the Sellsian model was arrived at independently, I gratefully acknowledge the inputs and insights of Huntington, whose 'way of reading' Nāgārjuna (Huntington 1995) is, to my knowledge, the first attempt to read the two together. Regarding the issue of nameability here being discussed, Huntington writes:

> At the center of apophatic discourse is the effort to speak about a subject that can not be named. The suspension of the logic of non-contradiction necessary to accomplish this aim means, as Sells has shown, that apophasis has much more in common with poetry, narrative fiction, drama, and other forms of non-discursive writing than it does with traditional philosophical and theological texts. This is not to say that apophasis is devoid of deductive argument; however the appearance of argument and grounds in apophatic writing has generated a great deal of confusion among philosophers, theologians and critics who fail to appreciate that even the most rigorous logical form can be exploited for a variety of literary and rhetorical effects. (Huntington 1995: 283)

For further discussion of this passage and of Huntington's Sellsian reading of Nāgārjuna more generally, see Sebastian 2016: §6.1 and §6.2, where William Franke's brief treatment of Nāgārjuna (Franke 2015: 118) is also cited. In passing, I note with regret that Franke's anthologies (2007a and 2007b) of efforts "to probe the limits of language—and perhaps to exceed them" remain confined "within Western culture" (Franke 2007a: 1), "in the Occident" (Franke 2007b: 49), despite acknowledgment that a companion volume of relevant texts from "Eastern cultural traditions . . . would be an auspicious complement to the present effort" (Franke 2007a: 5).

88. Recall in this context the extra-textual additions and interpolations detailed, for example, in §2.2 and §4.3. As Sells asserts, "Apophatic texts have suffered in a particularly acute manner from the urge to paraphrase the meaning in non-apophatic language or to fill in the open referent—to say what the text really meant to say, but didn't" (Sells 1994: 4, also cited in Huntington 1995: 283).
89. See the references to Muller 2018: 10 and Mills 2018b: 97 and Mills 2018a in §4.3.
90. See Sells 1994: 2–3 for discussion of all these terms. See also Jakubczak 1997: 106, who with regard to Nāgārjuna's works proposes a perhaps over-simplified distinction between "the overall kataphatic form of expression of the hymns, as opposed to the apophatic form characteristic of the theoretical treatises" (*ogólną katafatyczną formę wypowiedzi hymnów, przeciwstawną apofatycznej formie charakteryzującej teoretyczne traktaty*).
91. See also Sells 1994: 178 and 3: "apophatic language is a language of double propositions in which no single proposition can stand by itself as meaningful" and "It is in the tension between the two propositions that the discourse becomes meaningful."
92. The foregoing paragraph has, of course, compressed a great deal of theoretical groundwork laid out gradually throughout Sells's work. For a summary of the principles involved, however, see Sells 1994: 207–209.
93. Jin Park 2017b and Janet Williams 2000 present readings for considering the Zen Buddhist context in analogous terms (the latter in great detail). As Park states, "With the simultaneous use of affirmation and negation, Zen Buddhism brings the nonduality thesis into daily reality" (Park 2017b: 80).
94. Recall that while admitting that "contradictions do not seem to be limited to tetralemma-style arguments," Westerhoff will go on to interpret these away as "merely apparent, but not as actual contradictions" (Westerhoff 2018a: 118, and see discussion in §2.1 and §2.2.2).
95. In this as in so much else, Nāgārjuna's discursive practice echoes and elaborates that of the Buddha, for whom, in the words of Williams, "The apophatic negation is not so much contained in the fourth clause of the tetralemma as in the overall structure of the discourse, which is a rejection of all possibilities, whether affirmative or negative or any admixture of the two, or ordinary thought and logic" (J. Williams 2000: 41).
96. All of the mystics Sells studies are theistic insofar as they are either Christian or Muslim, with the exception of Plotinus, whose status as a theist or pantheist is (still) the subject of scholarly debate. Contrariwise, Williams's study of "Apophasis in the Patristic Christian and Soto Zen Buddhist Traditions" argues that "Radical apophasis, through the deliberate disruption of linguistic norms and expectations, flushes the human need for icons of the ultimate out of the epistemological arena into a wider existential ground. All aspects of living become potential vehicles for the expression of the divine" (J. Williams 2000: 9–10). We will come to consider the epistemological and ethical implications of such discourse in due course, but for the moment

I emphasize the sheer radicality of Nāgārjuna's apophaticism as I have described it. This kind of

> apophasis leads to a negation of the concept of God or *nirvana* as something dualistically transcendent to the world, realizable only through a practice of death to the world; but it also avoids the trap of a one-sided negation which would reduce the ultimate to the immanent and identify spirituality with morality or aesthetics. The apophatic Ultimate is neither transcendent nor immanent; and is both. (J. Williams 2000: 227)

97. Sells states that "apophatic nonknowing is an essential feature of understanding, won with difficulty" (Sells 1994: 213).
98. The view on views found in the Pāli canon thus does not seem to be quite so distinct from that of Nāgārjuna as Tillemans makes out in claiming that

> Madhyamaka seems to interpret such a quietistic stance with a significantly different emphasis [from that in the Pāli canon]: quietism is not only the practical or prudential advice that one should stay out of useless or destructive debates but also a philosophical stance. There is a strong Madhyamaka argumentation that a philosophy of emptiness entails that one *cannot* have theses and views. (Tillemans 2016: 225, emphasis original)

99. See also Fuller 2005: 146: "This is *sammā-diṭṭhi*: a radically different order of seeing which transcends all views. I am arguing that the nature of right-view is such that it should not be regarded as a view."
100. Mills appears to arrive at a substantially similar conclusion via what he sees to be the two phases or "two types of activity" in Nāgārjuna's work: "arguments *for* emptiness" and "expressions of positionlessness" (Mills 2018a: 31, emphasis original). For on his account, "Rather than supporting a philosophical view about the nature of reality or knowledge, Nāgārjuna's arguments for emptiness are for the purpose of purging one of any view, thesis, or theory whatsoever, even views about emptiness itself" (Mills 2018a: 26). This in turn entails that "In phase one, one might be convinced that all beings really are empty; in phase two, one ceases to grasp at any one answer" (Mills 2018a: 38).
101. I have trans-transliterated Fuller's Pāli *dhamma* as the Sanskrit *dharma* here for rhetorical coherence.
102. As Kantor states of Chinese Madhyamaka, "the expression 'emptiness' reveals its true meaning only by denying what it signifies" (Kantor 2019b: 856).
103. Sebastian's formulations (2016) on this point are highly relevant:

> The sole aim of Nāgārjuna, it seems, is to free the human mind of the net of conceptualisation (*vikalpa-jāla*) and its corollary verbal proliferation (*prapañca*) (71) ... *Śūnyatā* shall be taken as an 'insight into propositionlessness' as all propositions, views and theories are discarded in the Mādhyamika. ... It means that no view is here adhered to (73). ... The sole import of Nāgārjuna's *śūnyatā* would be to the effect of the rejection of all views ... whereby a 'standpoint of no-standpoint' is arrived at (135). ... *Śūnyatā* is a metaphor for undoing all that is conceptually built upon as it points to the essencelessness of reality. (145)

See also McClintock 2023: 2–3, who states that,

> unlike many other abstractions, emptiness has the advantage of nudging us toward a place of greater relinquishment by offering up the intriguing prospect that, at the end of the day, there really is nothing to which we can profitably cling. In this way, the idea of emptiness, when properly deployed, can serve as a therapy to wean ourselves of views with their inevitable distortions.

104. Sells, as it happens, would go on to become one of Collins's colleagues in the University of Chicago Divinity School.
105. We are thus truly dealing here with a "kenosis of kenosis" (J. Williams 2000: 207), though with two caveats. First, whereas Williams understands 'kenosis' as "divine self-emptying" (205), here we must take the term to refer to what I would call '*nirvāṇic* self-emptying'. The second point is that, unlike any theistic conception of divinity as the "ground of being" (7), *nirvāṇa* in Nāgārjuna's Buddhist schema is itself already discursively 'self-emptying' in that it signals the very reality of self-emptiness. For an alternative discussion of *śūnyatā* and/as kenosis, see Keller 2005 and the discussion in Sebastian 2016: 146 (to which I owe the Keller reference).
106. As Williams states regarding the Buddha, and as I see readily applicable to Nāgārjuna, "both affirmative and negative views are to be transcended: the Middle Path is in a sense itself a radical negation" (J. Williams 2000: 41).
107. A corollary point is that Nāgārjuna's is not merely "the silence of skepticism about philosophy, a silence born of having moved beyond the desire for such knowledge" (Mills 2018a: 66) but something far more—indeed, infinitely—general. For whosoever inhabits such a state (a Buddha) no longer harbors views of *any* kind (not merely those "about philosophy") and has likewise passed beyond desire for *any* object (not merely for "knowledge").
108. Garfield is making the point of Nāgārjuna's Madhyamaka descendant Śāntideva (as of the Buddha) in the passage quoted, but the point very much applies to Nāgārjuna too.
109. Demonstrating in detail a text-historical lineage between the positions espoused in the texts cited by Fuller and the texts attributed to Nāgārjuna would be a worthy, not to mention difficult, scholarly task; one, however, beyond the scope of the present study. For an initial foray into identifying "two competing strands" in early Buddhism—an "analysis-insight strand" and a "quietist strand"—and arguing that Nāgārjuna "brilliantly combined both strands, pursuing analysis-insight as a means to quietism" (14), see Mills 2018a: 12–19.
110. In its modern iteration *ziran* is ordinarily rendered as 'nature', 'natural', or 'naturally' depending on context. It is therefore an especially apt term to signal the paradoxicality of the fact that, on a Nāgārjunian analysis, a world of entities full with self-nature (*svabhāva*) rules out the ceaseless flow of phenomenality: self-nature is unnatural, whereas to be natural is to be natureless, empty.
111. Apart from being bereft of attested text-historical bases (and, moreover, robbing the Buddha's insight of its universality and thus of a great deal of its existential weight), Kalupahana's proposal (see Kalupahana 1991: 326–327) to the effect that the elision of *idaṃ* in the Buddha's statement "*sarvaṃ idaṃ duḥkhaṃ*" initiated an important

"Brahmanical misreading" would imply an extraordinarily ungenerous interpretation of the entire Buddhist philosophical tradition, which thus apparently blindly accepted such a "problematic situation" without once considering it avoidable.

112. I write 'is' in inverted commas in another allusion to the fact that terms such as *anātman* and *śūnyatā*, denoting as they do precisely the absence of their substantial correlates, in so doing upend the ontological categories codified in our language.
113. See in this context Harvey's discussion of *saṃskāras* (which he translates as 'constructing activities') as karmically generative "actions of body, speech, or mind" committed out of ignorance, according to which "all actions are performed from the perspective of a particular way of perceiving and construing the world, an outlook and set of beliefs . . . In a person who has destroyed spiritual ignorance, though, actions no longer have the power to 'construct' any karmic results" (Harvey 2013b: 52). As for "the Peace which passeth understanding," this is T. S. Eliot's "equivalent" to "Shantih" in the final verse of *The Waste Land* (Eliot 1963: 86).
114. For further discussion of the terms used here, see Harvey 2000: 17–19, and see also Goodman and Thakchöe 2016: 12–17 on the philosophical issues involved in English translations of these and related terms.
115. Hence Harvey states that the enlightened one "is actually said to have 'passed beyond' *puñña* [*punya*] and *pāpa* (*Sn*. 636) and to have 'abandoned' them (*Sn*. 520)" (Harvey 2000: 43). See also Adam, who states that for "*Arahats* (including the Buddha): good conduct is beyond duality—neither bright [*sukka*] nor dark [*kaṇha*], neither karmically meritorious [*puñña*] nor detrimental [*apuñña*, *pāpa*], neither wholesome [*kusala*] nor unwholesome [*akusala*] . . . . Properly speaking such activity cannot be considered action in the normal sense" (Adam 2005: 76).
116. See *inter alia* my note to MK:25:17 in §5.2.3.
117. See MK:18:5 cited in §5.2.2.
118. Indeed, in introducing the term earlier I called the senses of 'peace' I am proposing 'twin' to emphasize that they are to be seen as two facets of a single face.
119. I borrow here Collins's evocative terms; see Collins 1998 and 2010 cited in §5.2.3.
120. In this usage I follow several contributors to Cowherds 2016a. For explicit discussion, see Goodman and Thakchöe 2016, for whom the translation of *karuṇā* as compassion

> is, at least in one respect, ill-fitting: the "passion" in "compassion" comes from the Greek *paschein*, "to suffer," and so is cognate with such English words as "passive," and expresses the venerable European conception of emotions as *passions* (things that befall us). *Karuṇā*, by contrast, has as its root *kṛ*, to do—the same root from which "*karma*" comes. (Goodman and Thakchöe 2016: 15–16, emphasis original)

Likewise Garfield, for whom translating *karuṇā* as 'compassion' is "a serious error. *Karuṇā* derives from the root *kṛ*, *to act*, and connotes a commitment to act for the benefit of others; compassion, on the other hand, derives from *passio*, *to feel*. To translate a term so clearly associated with action by one so clearly associated with passivity is seriously misleading" (Garfield 2016: 86 fn. 9, emphases original). For his part, Jakubczak (2004: 527) translates the term into Polish as *współczucie*, which literally breaks down into 'fellow/co-feeling' (*współ* + *czucie*), and is most typically rendered into English as 'sympathy' or 'compassion'.

121. The senses I have spelled out here may be seen to correspond to "two interpretations of Stoic detachment: detachment as freedom from emotionality . . . and detachment as resilience to the vicissitudes of the strongly felt, unstable attachments that threaten one's agency . . . (freedom from disturbance)" (McRae 2018: 73–74, following Wong 2006), where the former is termed *apatheia* and the latter *ataraxia*. For an account of Buddhist ethics which proposes that "the aim of ethics should be to promote one's own ataraxia and, with compassion, that of others" (100), see Priest 2017.
122. The bodhisattva's readiness for sacrifice on behalf of others is evinced perhaps most memorably in a tale according to which the embodiment of the bodhisattva Guanyin "gouged out both her eyes with a knife, then told the envoy to sever her two arms" in order to cure the land's afflicted king with the requisite medicine, confected as this had to be from "the arms and eyes of one without anger" (Yü 2001: 501).
123. The authoritative study of Avalokiteśvara/Guanyin is Yü 2001, which includes manifold discussions of the femininity of the figure in China, most sustainedly in the chapters on "Princess Miao-shan and the Feminization of Kuan-yin," "Feminine Forms of Kuan-yin in Late Imperial China," and "Venerable Mother: Kuan-yin and Sectarian Religion in Late Imperial China."
124. I am thus indebted to McRae's notion of a specifically Buddhist (as opposed to Stoic) form of detachment she calls 'equanimity' (McRae 2018: 83ff)—a close synonym of my 'peace'—and especially to her notion of an "ideal of loving through equanimity" (86). As she puts it, "detachment, on this view, enables one to feel—and cultivate—love and compassion [*karuṇā*: care] with less bias and more discernment" (87).
125. All of the sources I have referred to in fact discuss Nāgārjuna's more overtly ethically concerned Madhyamaka descendent Śāntideva. I can only hope that my attempt to demonstrate the soterio-ethical aim at the heart of even Nāgārjuna's most seemingly abstract notions impels greater scholarly attention to this hitherto understudied dimension of his own thought.
126. See Mills: "As I see it, Nāgārjuna's main goal is to lessen one's attachment to beliefs (even Buddhist beliefs), since grasping at and identifying with *my* views or *my* philosophical theories serves to reify my self in opposition to others" (Mills 2018b: 94, emphases original).
127. One example that evinces both profound ignorance of the tradition and an unfortunately all-too-evident motivation to present it derisorily is that of Felipe Fernández-Armesto, who states, in his purportedly "globe-wide" history of "the intellectual heritage of humankind" (Fernández-Armesto 2019: xiv), that "To achieve perfect Buddhist enlightenment, you have to suspend thought, forgo language, and obliterate all sense of reality . . . [This] represents radical withdrawal from perceived reality—a consequence of self-extinction, the inertia of nonbeing, beyond thought and language" (Fernández-Armesto 2019: 182–183). There are too many problems with Fernández-Armesto's account to go into here, so suffice it at least to note regarding the overall point that, for Nāgārjuna as much as for any Buddhist, enlightenment is the precise *opposite* of "obliterat[ing] all sense of reality" or "withdraw[ing]

from perceived reality." It is attained, moreover, not in "suspend[ing] thought," or "forgo[ing] language" but (as we have seen in our discussion earlier of the Buddha's omniscience and omnilinguality) in consummating them in aporetic transcendence of (the distinction between immanence and) transcendence, or, more prosaically, thinking, speaking, and more generally acting in a way that is not reducible to or explicable by conventional terms and rationales.

128. We cannot grammatically avoid speaking this way of *nirvāṇa*, but preceding discussions should have made clear that *nirvāṇa*, in the role it plays within Nāgārjuna's thought, cannot validly be characterized in any way.
129. See also the following statement for a fuller elaboration of this view:

> If we assume actions are adjudicable by some fixed moral standard, if we can pronounce any given act as moral or immoral only within the framework of a systematic theoretical dualism between good and evil, Nāgārjuna asserts, we actually rob it of its moral worth . . . empty ethics is the only kind of ethics we can embrace, for ethical absolutism, which in the Buddhist context Nāgārjuna knew entails unmitigated distinctions between right and wrong acts, leads merely to a disassociation of right and wrong that is so great that it effectively leaves us powerless to understand how one may change into the other, and thus powerless to bridge the gap that such moral absolutism ultimately creates between the interdependent world in which one lives and the freedom for which one strives. (Berger 2007: 53)

130. For further discussion of this *sutta* in a related context, see Collins 1982: 122, 130; and Fuller 2005: 153–155. As Jakubczak states in his study of related passages, "we are dealing here with an elaborate concept that embeds conflict in the very fact of thinking" (*mamy tutaj do czynienia z rozbudowaną koncepcją, która osadza spór w samym fakcie myślenia*) (Jakubczak 2019: 312). I will shortly point out just such a perspective informing Nāgārjuna.
131. Collins 1982: 140; see also pp. 127–131 for citation of several further textual sources regarding what Collins calls "the transcendence of views by the sage."
132. This explains why McGuire is able to speak of a characteristically "Madhyamaka Mode of Engagement" as "Frictionless Co-operation" (McGuire 2017: 394).
133. Pluralism rests on the idea that the various religions are equally valid mundane expressions of one supra-mundane reality. In the words of its most prominent exponent, it is the position that

> there is a transcendent and immanent Real, or Ultimate Reality, which is universally present to humanity and of which humans are aware, to the extent that they allow themselves to be aware, in the various ways made possible by their different conceptual systems and spiritual practices. (Hick 2012: 246)

To this may be contrasted the two other positions, which both take one religion to be superior to others. Exclusivism I define as the position that one religion (i.e., one's own) is uniquely (i.e., exclusively) right (where 'right' may mean 'metaphysically real', 'epistemologically true', 'soteriologically efficacious', or some other such designator depending on context). Inclusivism likewise takes one religion to be superior (in any of the senses just mentioned) but admits that other religions may be accounted valid means toward the realization of the one ultimately true religion's ends. Or, to put it in the words of Harold Netland, "exclusivism holds that true religious claims are found only among the teachings of one's own religion, whereas inclusivism maintains that it is possible that both one's own and other religions teach truth" (Netland 2012: 255). Note that my characterization here is stolen from a prior self—Stepien 2021a—where I treat related issues from an alternative angle (and specifically with a focus on Islamic mysticism). The literature on inter-religious relations is vast and ever-growing, so I refer the interested reader to that prior work for further references.

134. The sentence from which I have quoted is worth citing in full: "Practicing emptiness by relinquishing one's horizons for relevance means compassionately refusing to silence other things, refusing to pick and choose experiences according to self-centered likes and dislikes, and being able and willing to let go of what should work to realize artlessly what does work" (Hershock 2005: 139). Hershock's study is centrally concerned with Chan Buddhism, but his discussion of emptiness is obviously grounded, as it must be, in Nāgārjuna. Two points merit making in this context with regard to his notion of "improvisational virtuosity" as the acme of ethical practice. First, it appears to share important features with particularism, according to which "the possibility of moral thought and judgment does not depend on the provision of a suitable supply of moral principles" (Dancy 2004: 7). While it may be true that "Particularism can naturally be combined with some form of virtue ethics" (Goodman and Thakchöe 2016: 12, to whom I owe the reference to Dancy), it would certainly seem inimical to any form of deontology. Second, "improvisational virtuosity" may be interpreted as a form of "radical spontaneity," according to which the bodhisattva's conduct "is uncalculated, arising without premeditation or preconditions," allowing her to "Simply offer, moment by moment, what will open [her] situation to meaning the liberation of all beings" (Hershock 2005: 116). Christian Coseru's concerns from a different Buddhist context are also apposite here:

> if the bodhisattva can attain a type of freedom that is unimpeded by karmic hindrances, the efficacy of his or her actions (outside the web of interdependent causation) becomes deeply mysterious. . . . But in that case genuine compassion implies a kind of spontaneity that is not easily captured by notions of moral agency that depend only on the actual or foreseeable consequences of acts. (Coseru 2017b: 122)

As we have seen with the Buddha's own *karma*-less action, we are indeed dealing here with a phenomenon "deeply mysterious"; indeed, as I have argued at length and as Coseru suggests here, one irreducible to standard models of moral and ethical agency.

135. Interconnectedness is hardly unique to Madhyamaka; indeed, according to Tillemans, "the school in which interconnectedness occupies the strongest place is the Avataṃsaka/Huayan" (Tillemans 2016: 142). So whatever we might make of it would in any case not aid us in elucidating a specifically Madhyamaka ethics.
136. VV:70, cited at §4.2.
137. Recall ŚS:72, cited at §4.2.

Bibliography

Abé, Ryūichi. 2005. "Word." In *Critical Terms for the Study of Buddhism*, edited by Donald S. Lopez, Jr., 291–310. Chicago: University of Chicago Press.

Abu Sway, Mustafa. 2016. "On the Possibility of Rational Neutrality in Comparative Philosophy: A Response to Jonardon Ganeri." *Confluence: Journal of World Philosophies* 4 (Symposium: Is Reason a Neutral Tool in Comparative Philosophy?): 144–148.

Adam, M. T. 2005. "Groundwork for a Metaphysic of Buddhist Morals: A New Analysis of *puñña* and *kusala*, in Light of *sukka*." *Journal of Buddhist Ethics* 12: 61–85.

Alcoff, Linda Martin. 2017. "Philosophy and Philosophical Practice: Eurocentrism as an Epistemology of Ignorance." In *The Routledge Handbook of Epistemic Injustice*, edited by Ian James Kidd, José Medina, and Gaile Pohlhaus, Jr., 397–408. Abingdon, England: Routledge.

American Academy of Religion. 2021. "Annual Meeting." https://www.aarweb.org/AARMBR/Events-and-Networking-/Annual-Meeting.aspx.

Ames, William L. 1982. "The Notion of *Svabhāva* in the Thought of Candrakīrti." *Journal of Indian Philosophy* 10, no. 2 (June): 161–177.

Ames, William L. 1986. *Bhāvaviveka's Prajñāpradīpa: Six Chapters*. PhD diss., University of Washington.

Ames, William L. 1993. "Bhāvaviveka's *Prajñāpradīpa*: A Translation of Chapter One: 'Examination of Causal Conditions' (*Pratyaya*)." *Journal of Indian Philosophy* 21: 209–259.

Ames, William L. 2003. "Bhāvaviveka's Own View of His Differences with Buddhapālita." In *The Svātantrika-Prāsaṇgika Distinction: What Difference Does a Difference Make?* edited by Georges B. J. Dreyfus and Sara L. McClintock, 41–66. Boston: Wisdom.

Aristotle. 1984. *The Complete Works of Aristotle*. Edited by Jonathan Barnes. Princeton, NJ: Princeton University Press.

Arnold, Dan. 2005. *Buddhists, Brahmins and Belief: Epistemology in South Asian Philosophy of Religion*. New York: Columbia University Press.

Arnold, Dan. 2007. "Review of *Nāgārjuna in Context: Mahāyāna Buddhism and Early Indian Culture*, by Joseph Walser." *Journal of the American Academy of Religion* 75, no. 3: 684–688.

Arnold, Dan. 2010. "Nagarjuna's "Middle Way": A Non-Eliminative Understanding of Selflessness." *Revue internationale de philosophie* 253, no. 3: 367–395.

Arnold, Dan. 2012. *Brains, Buddhas, and Believing: The Problem of Intentionality in Classical Buddhist and Cognitive-Scientific Philosophy of Mind*. New York: Columbia University Press.

Arnold, Dan. 2014. "Response to Jonathan Gold's Review of Brains, Buddhas, and Believing." *Philosophy East and West* 64, no. 4 (October): 1057–1067.

Arnold, Dan. 2019. "The Sense Madhyamaka Makes as a Buddhist Position: Or, How a 'Performativist Account of the Language of Self' makes Sense of 'No-Self'." *Journal of Indian Philosophy* 47: 697–726.

Bagger, Matthew. 2007. *The Uses of Paradox: Religion, Self-Transformation, and the Absurd*. New York: Columbia University Press.

Baker, Lynne Rudder. 1987. *Saving Belief: A Critique of Physicalism*. Princeton, NJ: Princeton University Press.

Balcerowicz, Piotr, trans. 2001. "Studies on Indian Logic. Ancient Indian Anticipations of Sentential Logic." In *Materials of the International Seminar "Argument and Reason in Indian Logic," Kazimierz Dolny, June 20–24, 2001*, edited by Piotr Balcerowicz and Marek Mejor, 27–33. Warsaw: Instytut Orientalistyczny, Uniwersytet Warszawski.

Balcerowicz, Piotr. 2019. "Is There Anything Like Indian Logic? *Anumāna*, 'Inference' and Inference in the Critique of Jayarāśi Bhaṭṭa." *Journal of Indian Philosophy* 47: 917–946.

Balcerowicz, Piotr, and Marek Mejor, eds. 2001. *Materials of the International Seminar "Argument and Reason in Indian Logic," Kazimierz Dolny, 20–24 June, 2001*. Warsaw: Instytut Orientalistyczny, Uniwersytet Warszawski.

Berger, Douglas L. 2007. "Deconstruction, Aporia and Justice in Nāgārjuna's Empty Ethics." In *Deconstruction and the Ethical in Asian Thought*, edited by Youru Wang, 40–59. London: Routledge.

Berger, Douglas L. 2017a. "Cross-Cultural Philosophy and Hermeneutic Expansion." *Confluence: Journal of World Philosophies* 2, Summer (Symposium: Does Cross-Cultural Philosophy Stand in Need of a Hermeneutic Expansion?): 121–125.

Berger, Douglas L. 2017b. "Symposium Response." *Confluence: Journal of World Philosophies* 2, Summer (Symposium: Does Cross-Cultural Philosophy Stand in Need of a Hermeneutic Expansion?): 138–140.

Bernasconi, Robert. 2003. "Ethnicity, Culture, and Philosophy." In *The Blackwell Companion to Philosophy*, 2nd ed, edited by Nicholas Bunnin and E. P. Tsui-James, 567–581. Oxford: Blackwell.

Betty, L. Stafford. 1983. "Nāgārjuna's Masterpiece: Logical, Mystical, Both, or Neither?" *Philosophy East and West* 33 no. 2: 123–138.

Betty, L. Stafford. 1984. "Is Nāgārjuna a Philosopher? Response to Professor Loy." *Philosophy East and West* 34 no. 4 (October): 447–450.

Bhattacharya, Kamaleswar, trans. 1978. *The Dialectical Method of Nāgārjuna: Vigrahavyāvartanī*. Edited by E. H. Johnston and Arnold Kunst. Delhi: Motilal Banarsidass.

Bhattacharya, Kamaleswar, trans. 1986. *The Dialectical Method of Nāgārjuna: Vigrahavyāvartanī*. 2nd ed. Edited by E. H. Johnston and Arnold Kunst. Delhi: Motilal Banarsidass.

Bingenheimer, Marcus. 2004. *Der Mönchsgelehrte Yinshun) (*1906) und seine Bedeutung für den Chinesisch-Taiwanischen Buddhismus im 20. Jahrhundert*. Heidelberg, Germany: Edition forum.

Bocking, Brian. 1995. *Nāgārjuna in China: A Translation of the Middle Treatise*. Lewiston, NY: The Edwin Mellen Press.

Bodhi (Bhikku), trans. 2000. *Saṃyutta Nikāya: The Connected Discourses of the Buddha*. Boston: Wisdom.

Boghossian, Paul. 2016. "Is Comparative Philosophy Based Upon a Mistake? A Reply to Ganeri's 'Re:emergent Philosophy.'" *Confluence: Journal of World Philosophies* 4 (Symposium: Is Reason a Neutral Tool in Comparative Philosophy?): 149–153.

Bronkhorst, Johannes. 1993. "On the Method of Interpreting Philosophical Sanskrit Texts." *Asiatische Studien: Zeitschrift der Schweizerischen Asiengesellschaft / Études Asiatiques: Revue de la Société Suisse—Asie* 47, no. 3: 501–511.

Bruya, Brian, ed. 2015. *The Philosophical Challenge from China*. Cambridge, MA: MIT Press.

Bugault, Guy. 1983. "Logic and Dialectics in the *Madhyamakakārikās*." *Journal of Indian Philosophy* 11, no. 1: 7–76.

Bugault, Guy. 2000. "The Immunity of Śūnyatā: Is It Possible to Understand *Madhyamakakārikās*, 4, 8-9?" *Journal of Indian Philosophy* 28, no. 4 (August): 385–397.

Bugault, Guy, trans. 2002. *Nāgārjuna: Stances du milieu par excellence*. Mesnil-sur-l'Estrée, France: Gallimard.

Burley, Mikel. 2020. *A Radical Pluralist Philosophy of Religion: Cross-Cultural, Multireligious, Interdisciplinary*. London: Bloomsbury.

Burton, David. 1999. *Emptiness Appraised: A Critical Study of Nāgārjuna's Philosophy*. Richmond, VA: Curzon.

Burton, David. 2004. *Buddhism, Knowledge and Liberation: A Philosophical Study*. Aldershot, England: Ashgate.

Buswell Jr., Robert E., and Donald S. Lopez Jr. 2014. *The Princeton Dictionary of Buddhism*. Princeton, NJ: Princeton University Press.

Cabezón, José Ignacio. 1995. "Buddhist Studies as a Discipline and the Role of Theory." *Journal of the International Association of Buddhist Studies* 18, no. 2 (Winter): 231–268.

Cabezón, José Ignacio. 2003. "Two Views on the Svātantrika-Prāsaṇgika Distinction in Fourteenth-Century Tibet." In *The Svātantrika-Prāsaṇgika Distinction: What Difference Does a Difference Make?* edited by Georges B. J. Dreyfus and Sara L. McClintock, 289–315. Boston: Wisdom.

Cabezón, José Ignacio. 2007. "The Changing Field of Buddhist Studies in North America." *Journal of the International Association of Buddhist Studies* 30, no. 1–2: 283–298.

Cabezón, José Ignacio. 2009. "Language and the Ultimate: Do Mādhyamikas Make Philosophical Claims?" In *Buddhist Philosophy: Essential Readings*, edited by Jay L. Garfield and William Edelglass, 126–137. New York: Oxford University Press.

Cabezón, José Ignacio. 2021. "2020 AAR Presidential Address: The Study of Buddhism and the AAR." *Journal of the American Academy of Religion* 89, no. 3 (September): 793–818.

Cabezón, José Ignacio, and Geshe Lobsang Dargyay. 2007. *Freedom from Extremes: Gorampa's "Distinguishing the Views" and the Polemics of Emptiness*. Boston: Wisdom.

Cadge, Wendy, Peggy Levitt, and David Smilde. 2011. "De-Centering and Re-Centering: Rethinking Concepts and Methods in the Sociological Study of Religion." *Journal for the Scientific Study of Religion* 50, no. 3: 437–449.

Carpenter, Amber D. 2014. *Indian Buddhist Philosophy: Metaphysics as Ethics*. Abingdon, England: Routledge.

Carpenter, Amber 2016. "Aiming at Happiness, Aiming at Ultimate Truth—In Practice." In Cowherds, *Moonpaths: Ethics and Emptiness*, 21–42. New York: Oxford University Press.

Carr, Karen L. 1992. *The Banalization of Nihilism: Twentieth-Century Responses to Meaninglessness*. Albany: State University of New York Press.

Castro-Gómez, Santiago. 2005. *La Hybris del Punto Cero*. Bogota: Pontificia Universidad Javeriana.

Chakrabarty, Dipesh. 2000. *Provincializing Europe: Postcolonial Thought and Historical Difference*. Princeton, NJ: Princeton University Press.

Chen Xueren 陳學仁. 1998. 龍樹菩薩中論八不思想探究. 臺北：佛光.

Chi, Richard S. Y. 1969. *Buddhist Formal Logic*. London: Luzac and Co.

Chödrön, Gelongma Karma Migme. 2001. *Mahā-prajñāpāramitā-śāstra*. https://www.wisdomlib.org/buddhism/book/maha-prajnaparamita-sastra.

Clayton, Barbra R. 2006. *Moral Theory in Śāntideva's Śikṣāsamuccaya: Cultivating the Fruits of Virtue*. London: Routledge.

Clayton, John Powell. 2006. *Religions, Reasons and Gods: Essays in Cross-Cultural Philosophy of Religion*. Cambridge: Cambridge University Press.

Clouser, Roy A. 2005. *The Myth of Religious Neutrality: An Essay on the Hidden Role of Religious Belief in Theories*. Rev. ed. Notre Dame: University of Notre Dame Press.

Colas, Gérard. 2018. "Remarks on Nathan Sivin's Observations about Comparatism." *Journal of World Philosophies*, no. 3 (Winter): 75–97.

Cole, Alan. 2005. *Text as Father: Paternal Seductions in Early Mahayana Buddhist Literature*. Berkeley: University of California Press.

Collins, Steven. 1982. *Selfless Persons: Imagery and Thought in Theravāda Buddhism*. Cambridge: Cambridge University Press.

Collins, Steven. 1992. "Notes on Some Oral Aspects of Pāli Literature." *Indo-Iranian Journal* 35: 121–135.

Collins, Steven. 1998. *Nirvana and Other Buddhist Felicities: Utopias of the Pali Imaginaire*. Cambridge: Cambridge University Press.

Collins, Steven. 2010. *Nirvana: Concept, Imagery, Narrative*. Cambridge: Cambridge University Press.

Cooper, David E., and Simon P. James. 2005. *Buddhism, Virtue and Environment*. London: Routledge.

Coseru, Christian. 2014. "Logic, Mysticism, Both or Neither." *The Indian Philosophy Blog*, September 6, 2014. http://indianphilosophyblog.org/2014/09/06/logic-mysticism-both-or-neither/. Last accessed April 5, 2018.

Coseru, Christian. 2017a. "Mind in Indian Buddhist Philosophy." In *The Stanford Encyclopedia of Philosophy*, edited by Edward Zalta. https://plato.stanford.edu/entries/mind-indian-buddhism/. Last accessed March 15, 2021.

Coseru, Christian. 2017b. "Breaking Good: Moral Agency, Neuroethics, and the Spontaneity of Compassion." In *A Mirror Is for Reflection: Understanding Buddhist Ethics*, edited by Jake H. Davis, 109–128. New York: Oxford University Press.

Coward, Harold. 2000. *Scripture in the World Religions*. Oxford: Oneworld.

Cowherds. 2011. *Moonshadows: Conventional Truth in Buddhist Philosophy*. New York: Oxford University Press.

Cowherds. 2016a. *Moonpaths: Ethics and Emptiness*. New York: Oxford University Press.

Cowherds. 2016b. "Is *Moonshadows* Lunacy? The Cowherds Respond." *Philosophy East and West* 66, no. 2, April: 617–621.

Crosby, Kate, and Andrew Skilton, trans. 1995. *Śāntideva: The Bodhicaryāvatāra*. Oxford: Oxford University Press.

D'Amato, Mario. 2009. "Why the Buddha Never Uttered a Word." In *Pointing at the Moon: Buddhism, Logic, Analytic Philosophy*, edited by Mario D'Amato, Jay L. Garfield, and Tom T. Tillemans, 41–55. New York: Oxford University Press.

D'Amato, Mario, Jay L. Garfield, and Tom J. F. Tillemans, eds. 2009. *Pointing at the Moon: Buddhism, Logic, Analytic Philosophy*. New York: Oxford University Press.

Dānapāla 施護., trans. N.d. (T 1575) 六十頌如理論 (*Yuktiṣaṣṭikā-kārikā*). *Taishō* 30: 1575, 254b–256a.

Dancy, Jonathan. 2004. *Ethics Without Principles*. Oxford: Oxford University Press.

Davis, Bret W. 2019. "Beyond Philosophical Euromonopolism: Other Ways of—Not Otherwise Than—Philosophy." *Philosophy East and West* 69, no. 2 (April): 592–619.

De George, Richard T. 1990. "Ethics and Coherence." *Proceedings and Addresses of the American Philosophical Association* 64, no. 3 (November): 39–52.

De Jong, Jan Willem. 1949. *Cinq chapitres de la Prassanapadā* ("Buddhica: Documents at Travaux pour l'étude du Bouddhisme." Collection fondée par Jean Przyluski, publiée sous la direction de Marcelle Lalou, première série: Mémoires, tome IX). Paris: Paul Geuthner.

De La Vallée Poussin, Louis, ed. (1913) 1970. *Mūlamadhyamakakārikās. Mādhyamika-sūtras de Nāgārjuna avec la Prasannapadā Commentaire de Candrakīrti.* St. Pétersbourg: Académie Imperiale des Sciences.

De La Vallée Poussin, Louis. 1933. "Réflexions sur le Madhyamaka." *Mélanges chinois et bouddhiques* 2: 1–59.

Deegalle, Mahinda, ed. 2010. *Buddhist-Christian Studies*, 30. Honolulu: University of Hawai'i Press.

Deguchi, Yasuo, Jay Garfield, and Graham Priest. 2008. "The Way of the Dialetheist: Contradictions in Buddhism." *Philosophy East and* West 58, no. 3: 395–402.

Della Santina, Peter. 2002. *Causality and Emptiness: The Wisdom of Nagarjuna.* Singapore: Buddhist Research Society.

Dietz, S. 1983. "The Author of the Suhṛllekha." In *Contributions on Tibetan and Buddhist Religion and Philosophy: Proceedings of the 'Csoma De Kőrös Symposium' Held at Velm-Vienna, Austria, 13–19 September 1981 2. Wiener Studien zur Tibetologie und Buddhismuskunde 11*, edited by Ernst Steinkellner and Helmut Tauscher, 59–72. Wien: Arbeitskreis für Tibetische und Buddhistische Studien.

Donahue, Amy. 2016a. "For the Cowherds: Coloniality and Conventional Truth in Buddhist Philosophy." *Philosophy East and West* 66, no. 2 (April): 597–617.

Donahue, Amy. 2016b. "Reply to the Cowherds: Serious Philosophical Engagement with and for Whom?." *Philosophy East and West* 66, no. 2 (April): 621–626.

Drewes, David. 2015. "Oral Texts in Indian Mahāyāna." *Indo-Iranian Journal* 58, no. 2: 117–141.

Dreyfus, Georges B. J. 2003. "Would the True Prāsaṅgika Please Stand? The Case and View of 'Ju Mi pham." In *The Svātantrika-Prāsaṇgika Distinction: What Difference Does a Difference Make?* edited by Georges B. J. Dreyfus and Sara L. McClintock, 317–347. Boston: Wisdom.

Dreyfus, Georges B. J., and Sara L. McClintock. 2003a. "Introduction." In *The Svātantrika-Prāsaṇgika Distinction: What Difference Does a Difference Make?* edited by Georges B. J. Dreyfus and Sara L. McClintock, 1–37. Boston: Wisdom.

Dreyfus, Georges B. J., and Sara L. McClintock, eds. 2003. *The Svātantrika-Prāsaṇgika Distinction: What Difference Does a Difference Make?* Boston: Wisdom.

Dreyfus, Hubert L. 1993. "Heidegger on the Connection between Nihilism, Art, Technology, and Politics." In *The Cambridge Companion to Heidegger*, edited by Charles Guignon, 289–316. Cambridge: Cambridge University Press.

Droit, Roger-Pol. 2003. *The Cult of Nothingness: The Philosophers and the Buddha.* Translated by David Streight and Pamela Vohnson. Chapel Hill: University of North Carolina Press.

Duckworth, Douglas. 2018. "Gelukpa [dge lugs pa]." In *The Stanford Encyclopedia of Philosophy*, edited by Edward Zalta. http://plato.stanford.edu/entries/gelukpa/. Last accessed December 14, 2020.

Duckworth, Douglas. 2022. "Gelukpa [dge lugs pa]." In *The Stanford Encyclopedia of Philosophy*, edited by Edward Zalta. http://plato.stanford.edu/entries/gelukpa/. Last accessed November 23, 2022.

Duerlinger, James. 2013. *The Refutation of the Self in Indian Buddhism: Candrakīrti on the Selflessness of Persons*. Abingdon, England: Routledge.

Dunne, John D. 1996. "Thoughtless Buddha, Passionate Buddha." *Journal of the American Academy of Religion* 64, no. 3: 525–556.

Dunne, John D. 2004. *Foundations of Dharmakīrti's Philosophy*. Boston: Wisdom.

Dunne, John D., and Sara L. McClintock, trans. 1997. *The Precious Garland: An Epistle to a King*. Boston: Wisdom.

Dwivedi, R. C. 1985–1986. "Concept of the *Śāstra*." *Indologica Taurinensia*, no. 13: 43–60.

Eckel, Malcolm David, with John J. Thatamanil. 2001. "Cooking the Last Fruit of Nihilism: Buddhist Approaches to Ultimate Reality." In *Ultimate Realities: A Volume in the Comparative Religious Ideas Project*, edited by Robert Cummings Neville, 125–150. Albany: State University of New York Press.

Eckel, Malcolm David. 2003. "That Satisfaction of No Analysis: On Tsong kha pa's Approach to Svātantrika-Madhyamaka." In *The Svātantrika-Prāsaṇgika Distinction: What Difference Does a Difference Make?* edited by Georges B. J. Dreyfus and Sara L. McClintock, 173–203. Boston: Wisdom.

Eckel, Malcolm David. 2008. *Bhāviveka and His Buddhist Opponents*. Cambridge, MA: Harvard University Press.

Edgerton, Franklin. (1954) 2004. *Buddhist Hybrid Sanskrit Grammar and Dictionary. Volume II: Dictionary*. New Delhi: Munshiram Manoharlal.

Eliot, T. S. 1963. *Collected Poems 1909–1962*. London: Faber and Faber.

Eltschinger, Vincent. 2015. "Abhidharma." In *Brill's Encyclopedia of Buddhism, Volume One: Literature and Languages*, edited by.Jonathan Silk, 88–102. Leiden, the Netherlands: Brill.

Erb, Felix. 1990. *Die Śūnyatāsaptati des Nāgārjuna und die Śūnyatāsaptativṛtti* [*Verse 1–32*] (*unter Berücksichtigung der Kommentare Candrakīrtis, Parahitas und des Zweiten Dalai Lama*). PhD diss., University of Hamburg.

Erb, Felix. 1997. *Śūnyatāsaptativṛtti: Candrakīrtis Kommentar zu den „Siebzig Versen über die Leerheit" des Nāgārjuna* [*Kārikās 1–14*]. Stuttgart: Franz Steiner Verlag.

Faure, Bernard. 2004. *Double Exposure: Cutting Across Buddhist and Western Discourses*. Stanford, CA: Stanford University Press.

Fernández-Armesto, Felipe. 2019. *Out of Our Minds: What We Think and How We Came to Think It*. London: Oneworld.

Ferraro, Giuseppe. 2013. "A Criticism of M. Siderits and J. L. Garfield's 'Semantic Interpretation' of Nāgārjuna's Theory of Two Truths." *Journal of Indian Philosophy* 41, no. 2 (April): 195–219.

Ferraro, Giuseppe. 2018. "Some More Notes on Siderits and Katsura's Translation of Nāgārjuna's *Mūlamadhyamakakārikā*." *Asiatische Studien: Zeitschrift der Schweizerischen Asiengesellschaft / Études Asiatiques: Revue de la Société Suisse - Asie* 72, no. 2: 657–673.

Finnigan, Bronwyn. (2011) 2010. "Buddhist Metaethics." *Journal of the International Association of Buddhist Studies* 33, no. 1–2: 267–297.

Finnigan, Bronwyn. 2011a. "How Can a Buddha Come to Act? The Possibility of a Buddhist Account of Ethical Agency." *Philosophy East and West* 61, no. 1 (January): 134–160.

Finnigan, Bronwyn. 2011b. "The Possibility of Buddhist Ethical Agency Revisited—A Reply to Jay Garfield and Chad Hansen." *Philosophy East and West* 61, no. 1 (January): 183–194.

Finnigan, Bronwyn. 2017. "The Nature of a Buddhist Path." In *A Mirror Is for Reflection: Understanding Buddhist Ethics*, edited by Jake H. Davis, 33–52. New York: Oxford University Press.

Finnigan, Bronwyn. 2018. "Madhyamaka Ethics." In *The Oxford Handbook of Buddhist Ethics*, edited by Daniel Cozort and James Mark Shields, 162–182. Oxford: Oxford University Press.

Flanagan, Owen. 2013. *The Bodhisattva's Brain: Buddhism Naturalized*. Cambridge, MA: MIT Press.

Forman, Robert K. C., ed. 1990. *The Problem of Pure Consciousness: Mysticism and Philosophy*. New York: Oxford University Press.

Franco, Eli. 2009. "Meditation and Metaphysics: On their Mutual Relationship in South Asian Buddhism." In *Yogic Perception, Meditation and Altered States of Consciousness*, edited by Eli Franco, 93–132. Wien: Verlag der Österreichischen Akademie der Wissenschaften.

Franco, Eli. 2018. "On the Arising of Philosophical Theories from Spiritual Practice." In *Saddharmāmṛtam: Festschrift für Jens-Uwe Hartmann zum 65. Geburtstag* (Wiener Studien zur Tibetologie und Buddhismuskunde 93), edited by Oliver Von Criegern, Gudrun Melzer, and Johannes Schneider, 113–126. Wien: Arbeitskreis für Tibetische und Buddhistische Studien.

Franke, William, ed. 2007a. *On What Cannot Be Said: Apophatic Discourses in Philosophy, Religion, Literature, and the Arts (Vol. 1: Classic Formulations*. Notre Dame, IN: University of Notre Dame Press.

Franke, William, ed. 2007b. *On What Cannot Be Said: Apophatic Discourses in Philosophy, Religion, Literature, and the Arts (Vol. 2: Modern and Contemporary Transformations*. Notre Dame, IN: University of Notre Dame Press.

Franke, William. 2015. "Agamben's Logic of Exception and Its Apophatic Roots and Offshoots." *Concentric: Literary and Cultural Studies* 41, no. 2: 95–120.

Freiberger, Oliver. 2007. "The Discipline of Buddhist Studies: Notes on Religious Commitment as Boundary-Marker." *Journal of the International Association of Buddhist Studies* 30, no. 1–2: 299–318.

Fricker, Miranda. 2007. *Epistemic Injustice: Power and the Ethics of Knowing*. Oxford: Oxford University Press.

Fuller, Paul. 2005. *The Notion of Diṭṭhi in Theravāda Buddhism: The Point of View*. London: Routledge Curzon.

Ganeri, Jonardon, ed. 2001. *Indian Logic: A Reader*. Richmond, VA: Curzon.

Ganeri, Jonardon. 2007. *The Concealed Art of the Soul: Theories of Self and Practices of Truth in Indian Ethics and Epistemology*. Oxford: Oxford University Press.

Ganeri, Jonardon. 2012. *The Self: Naturalism, Consciousness, and the First-Person Stance*. Oxford: Oxford University Press.

Ganeri, Jonardon. 2016a. "A Manifesto for Re:emergent Philosophy." *Confluence: Journal of World Philosophies* 4 (Symposium: Is Reason a Neutral Tool in Comparative Philosophy?): 134–142.

Ganeri, Jonardon. 2016b. "Reflections on Re:emergent Philosophy." *Confluence: Journal of World Philosophies* 4 (Symposium: Is Reason a Neutral Tool in Comparative Philosophy?): 164–182.

Garfield, Jay L., trans. 1995. *The Fundamental Wisdom of the Middle Way: Nāgārjuna's Mūlamadhyamakakārikā*. Oxford: Oxford University Press.

Garfield, Jay L. 1996. "Emptiness and Positionlessness: Do the Mādhyamika Relinquish All Views?" *Journal of Indian Philosophy and Religion* 1: 1–34.

Garfield, Jay L. 2002. *Empty Words: Buddhist Philosophy and Cross-Cultural Interpretation*. New York: Oxford University Press.

Garfield, Jay L. 2008. "Turning a Madhyamaka Trick: Reply to Huntington." *Journal of Indian Philosophy* 36, no. 4 (August): 507–527.

Garfield, Jay L. 2011. "Hey, Buddha! Don't Think! Just Act!—A Response to Bronwyn Finnigan." *Philosophy East and West* 61, no. 1 (January): 174–183.

Garfield, Jay L. 2015. *Engaging Buddhism: Why It Matters to Philosophy*. New York: Oxford University Press.

Garfield, Jay L. 2016. "Buddhist Ethics in the Context of Conventional Truth: Path and Transformation." In Cowherds, *Moonpaths: Ethics and Emptiness*, 77–95. New York: Oxford University Press.

Garfield, Jay L., and William Edelglass, eds. 2009. *Buddhist Philosophy: Essential Readings*. New York: Oxford University Press.

Garfield, Jay L., and Graham Priest. 2002. "Nāgārjuna and the Limits of Thought." In Jay L. Garfield, *Empty Words: Buddhist Philosophy and Cross-Cultural Interpretation*, 86–105. New York: Oxford University Press. Originally published in *Philosophy East and West* 53, no. 1, January 2003: 1–21.

Garfield, Jay L., and Graham Priest. 2009. "Mountains Are Just Mountains." In *Pointing at the Moon: Buddhism, Logic, Analytic Philosophy*, edited by Mario D'Amato, Jay Garfield, and Tom Tillemans, 71–82. Oxford: Oxford University Press.

Garfield, Jay L., and Graham Priest. 2016. "Introduction: Why Ask about Madhyamaka and Ethics?" In Cowherds, *Moonpaths: Ethics and Emptiness*, 1–6. New York: Oxford University Press.

Garfield, Jay L., and Jan Westerhoff, eds. 2015. *Madhyamaka and Yogācāra: Allies or Rivals?* New York: Oxford University Press.

Gautama Prajñāruci 瞿曇般若流支, trans. (N.d.) (T 1631) 迴諍論 (*Vigrahavyāvartanī*. *Taishō* 32: 1631, 13b–23a.

Gadamer, Hans-Georg. 1994. *Truth and Method*. Translated by Joel Weinsheimer and Donald G. Marshall. New York: Continuum.

Gert, Bernard, and Joshua Gert. 2020. "The Definition of Morality." In *The Stanford Encyclopedia of Philosophy*, edited by Edward Zalta. https://plato.stanford.edu/archives/fall2020/entries/morality-definition/. Last accessed June 2, 2021.

Gethin, Rupert. 1998. *The Foundations of Buddhism*. Oxford: Oxford University Press.

Ghose, Ramendranath. 1987. *The Dialectics of Nāgārjuna*. Allahabad: Vohra Publishers.

Gokhale, Pradeep P. 1992. *Inference and Fallacies Discussed in Ancient Indian Logic*. Delhi: Sri Satguru.

Gold, Jonathan C. 2014a. "A Review of *Brains, Buddhas, and Believing: The Problem of Intentionality in Classical Buddhist and Cognitive-Scientific Philosophy of Mind* by Dan Arnold." *Philosophy East and West* 64, no. 4 (October): 1048–1057.

Gold, Jonathan C. 2014b. "Reply to Dan Arnold." *Philosophy East and West* 64, no. 4 (October): 1067–1068.

Gold, Jonathan. 2015a. *Paving the Great Way: Vasubandhu's Unifying Buddhist Philosophy*. New York: Columbia University Press.

Gold, Jonathan C. 2015b. "Without Karma and Nirvāṇa, Buddhism Is Nihilism: The Yogācāra Contribution to the Doctrine of Emptiness." In *Madhyamaka and Yogācāra: Allies or Rivals?* edited by Jay L. Garfield and Jan Westerhoff, 213–241. New York: Oxford University Press.

Gómez, Luis. 1976. "Proto-Mādhyamika in the Pāli Canon." *Philosophy East and West* 26, no. 2 (April): 137–165.

Gómez, Luis O. 1995. "Unspoken Paradigms: Meanderings through the Metaphors of a Field." *Journal of the International Association of Buddhist Studies* 18, no. 2 (Winter): 183–230.

Gómez, O. Luis. 2000. "Two Jars on Two Tables: Reflections on the 'Two Truths.'" In *Wisdom, Compassion, and the Search for Understanding: The Buddhist Studies Legacy of Gadjin M. Nagao*, edited by Jonathan A. Silk, 95–136. Honolulu: University of Hawai'i Press.

Gómez, Luis O. 2007. "Studying Buddhism as If It Were Not One More among the Religions." *Journal of the International Association of Buddhist Studies* 30, no. 1–2: 319–343.

Goodman, Charles. 2008. Consequentialism, Agent-Neutrality, and Mahāyāna Ethics." *Philosophy East and West* 58, no. 1: 17–35.

Goodman, Charles. 2016. "From Madhyamaka to Consequentialism: A Road Map." In Cowherds, *Moonpaths: Ethics and* Emptiness, 141–158. New York: Oxford University Press

Goodman, Charles. 2017a. "Śāntideva's Impartialist Ethics." In *The Oxford Handbook of Indian Philosophy*, edited by Jonardon Ganeri, 327–343. New York: Oxford University Press.

Goodman, Charles, and Sonam Thakchöe. 2016. "The Many Voices of Buddhist Ethics." In Cowherds, *Moonpaths: Ethics and Emptiness*, 7–20. New York: Oxford University Press.

Goshima, Kiyotaka. 2008. "Who Was Ch'ing-mu ('Blue-Eyes')?" *Annual Report of the International Research Institute for Advanced Buddhology at Soka University for the Academic Year 2007*, no. XI: 325–334.

Graham, A. C. 1992. *Unreason within Reason: Essays on the Outskirts of Rationality*. La Salle, IL: Open Court.

Green, Ronald. S. 2020. "Review of: Priest, Graham. 2018. *The Fifth Corner of Four: An Essay on Buddhist Metaphysics and the Catuṣkoṭi*. Oxford: Oxford University Press." *Journal of Buddhist Ethics* 27: 223–229.

Griffiths, Paul J. 1981. "Buddhist Hybrid English: Some Notes on Philology and Hermeneutics for Buddhologists." *Journal of the International Association of Buddhist Studies* 4, no. 2: 17–32.

Griffiths, Paul J. 1994. *On Being Buddha: The Classical Doctrine of Buddhahood*. Albany: State University of New York Press.

Guanding 灌頂. N.d. (T 1767) 大般涅槃經疏.

Gunaratne, R. D. 1980. "The Logical Form of Catuṣkoṭi: A New Solution." *Philosophy East and West* 30, no. 2 (April): 211–239.

Gunaratne, R. D. 1986. "Understanding Nāgārjuna's Catuṣkoṭi." *Philosophy East and West* 36, no. 3: 213–234.

*Guṇavarman 求那跋摩, trans. N.d. (T 1672) 龍樹菩薩為禪陀迦王說法要偈. *Taishō* 32: 1672.

Gyatso, Janet, ed. 1992a. *In the Mirror or Memory: Reflections on Mindfulness and Remembrance in Indian and Tibetan Buddhism*. Albany: State University of New York Press.

Gyatso, Janet. 1992b. "Introduction." In *In the Mirror or Memory: Reflections on Mindfulness and Remembrance in Indian and Tibetan Buddhism*, edited by Janet Gyatso, 1–19. Albany: State University of New York Press.

Hadot, Pierre. 1995. *Philosophy as a Way of Life: Spiritual Exercises from Socrates to Foucault*. Translated by Michael Chase. Oxford: Blackwell.

Hahn, Michael. 1982a. *Nāgārjuna's Ratnāvalī Vol. 1: The Basic Texts (Sanskrit, Tibetan, Chinese)*. Bonn: Indica et Tibetica Verlag.

Hahn, Michael. 1982b. "On a Numerical Problem in Nāgārjuna's Ratnāvalī." In *Indological and Buddhological Studies: Volume in Honour of Professor J. W. de Jong on His Sixtieth Birthday*, edited by L. A. Hercus, F. B. J. Kuiper, T. Rajapatirana, and E. R. Skrzypczak, 161–185. Canberra: Faculty of Asian Studies.

Hallisey, Charles. 2020. "Afterword: Reading Collins Today, and Tomorrow." In *Wisdom as a Way of Life: Theravāda Buddhism Reimagined*, edited by Steven Collins, 163–200. New York: Columbia University Press.

Hanh, Thich Nhat. 1993. *Interbeing: Fourteen Guidelines for Engaged Buddhism*. 2nd rev. ed. Berkeley, CA: Parallax Press.

Hansen, Chad. 2011. "Washing the Dust from My Mirror: The Deconstruction of Buddhism—A Response to Bronwyn Finnigan." *Philosophy East and West* 61, no. 1 (January): 160–174.

Harris, Stephen. 2011. "Does *Anātman* Rationally Entail Altruism? On *Bodhicaryāvatāra* 8:101–103." *Journal of Buddhist Ethics* 18: 91–123.

Harrison, Paul. 1987. "Who Gets to Ride in the Great Vehicle? Self-Image and Identity Among the Followers of the Early Mahāyāna." *Journal of the International Association of Buddhist Studies* 10, no. 1: 67–89.

Harrison, Paul. 1995. "Searching for the Origins of the Mahāyāna: What Are We Looking For?" *The Eastern Buddhist* 28, no. 1: 48–69.

Harrison, Paul. 2003. "Mediums and Messages: Reflections on the Production of Mahāyāna Sūtras." *The Eastern Buddhist* 35, no. 1/2: 115–151.

Harvey, Peter. 2000. *An Introduction to Buddhist Ethics: Foundations, Values and Issues*. Cambridge: Cambridge University Press.

Harvey, Peter. 2013a. "*Dukkha*, Non-Self, and the Teaching on the Four 'Noble Truths.'" In *A Companion to Buddhist Philosophy*, edited by Steven M. Emmanuel, 26–45. Chichester: Wiley Blackwell.

Harvey, Peter. 2013b. "The Conditioned Co-arising of Mental and Bodily Processes within Life and Between Lives." In *A Companion to Buddhist Philosophy*, edited by Steven M. Emmanuel, 46–68. Chichester, England: Wiley Blackwell.

Hayes, Richard. 1988. *Dignaga on the Interpretation of Signs*. Dordrecht, the Netherlands: Springer.

Hayes, Richard. 1994. "Nāgārjuna's Appeal." *Journal of Indian Philosophy* 22, no. 4: 299–378.

Hayes, Richard P. 2013. "Philosophy of Mind in Buddhism." In *A Companion to Buddhist Philosophy*, edited by Steven M. Emmanuel, 395–404. Chichester, England: Wiley Blackwell.

Hegel, G. W. F. 1977. *Hegel's Phenomenology of Spirit*. Translated by A. V. Miller. Oxford: Oxford University Press.

Heidegger, Martin. 1962. *Being and Time*. Translated by John Macquarrie and Edward Robinson. Oxford: Blackwell.

Heidegger, Martin. 1998. *Pathmarks*. Edited by William McNeill. Cambridge: Cambridge University Press.

Heim, Maria. 2018. *Voice of the Buddha: Buddhaghosa on the Immeasurable Words*. New York: Oxford University Press.

Heine, Steven, and Dale S. Wright, eds. 2000. *The Kōan: Texts and Contexts in Zen Buddhism*. New York: Oxford University Press.

Hershock, Peter D. 2005. *Chan Buddhism*. Honolulu: University of Hawai'i Press.

Hick, John. 2012. "Religious Pluralism." In *Routledge Companion to Philosophy of Religion*, edited by Chad Meister and Paul Copan, 240–249. Abingdon, England: Routledge.

Ho, Chien-hsing. 2010. "Nāgārjuna's Critique of Language." *Asian Philosophy: An International Journal of the Philosophical Traditions of the East* 20, no. 2: 159–174.

Ho, Chien-hsing. 2013. "Ontic Indeterminacy and Paradoxical Language: A Philosophical Analysis of Sengzhao's Linguistic Thought." *Dao* 12: 159–174.

Ho, Chien-hsing. 2014. "The Way of Nonacquisition: Jizang's Philosophy of Ontic Indeterminacy." In *A Distant Mirror: Articulating Indic Ideas in Sixth and Seventh Century Chinese Buddhism*, edited by Chen-kuo Lin and Michael Radich, 397–418. Hamburg, Germany: Hamburg University Press.

Ho, Chien-hsing. 2019. "Ontic Indeterminacy: Chinese Madhyamaka in the Contemporary Context." *Australasian Journal of Philosophy*. DOI: 10.1080/00048402.2019.1619791.

Hodgson, Marshall G. S. 1974. *The Venture of Islam 1: The Classical Age of Islam*. Chicago: University of Chicago Press.

Hofweber, Thomas. 2020. "Logic and Ontology." In *The Stanford Encyclopedia of Philosophy*, edited by Edward Zalta. https://plato.stanford.edu/archives/sum2020/entries/logic-ontology/. Last accessed December 14, 2020.

Holder, John J. 2013. "A Survey of Early Buddhist Epistemology." In *A Companion to Buddhist Philosophy*, edited by Steven M. Emmanuel, 223–240. Chichester, England: Wiley Blackwell.

Hopkins, Jeffrey. *Nāgārjuna's Precious Garland: Buddhist Advice for Living & Liberation*. Ithaca, NY: Snow Lion, 1998.

Hubbard, Jamie. 1995. "Upping the Ante: budstud@millennium.end.edu." *Journal of the International Association of Buddhist Studies* 18, no. 2 (Winter): 309–322.

Humphries, Jeff. 1999. *Reading Emptiness: Buddhism and Literature*. Albany: State University of New York Press.

Huntington, Jr., C. W. 1986. *The Akutobhayā and Early Indian Madhyamaka*. PhD diss., The University of Michigan.

Huntington, Jr., C. W., with Wangchen, Geshé Namgyal. 1989. *The Emptiness of Emptiness: An Introduction to Early Indian Mādhyamika*. Honolulu: University of Hawai'i Press.

Huntington, Jr., C. W. 1995. "A Way of Reading." *Journal of the International Association of Buddhist Studies* 18, no. 2 (Winter): 279–308.

Huntington, Jr., C. W. 2003. "Was Candrakīrti a Prāsaṇgika?" In *The Svātantrika-Prāsaṇgika Distinction: What Difference Does a Difference Make?* edited by George B. J. Dreyfus and Sara L. McClintock, 67–91. Boston: Wisdom.

Huntington, Jr., C. W. 2007. "The Nature of the Mādhyamika Trick." *Journal of Indian Philosophy* 35, no. 2 (April): 103–131.

Huntington, Jr., C. W. 2018. "Nāgārjuna's Fictional World." *Journal of Indian Philosophy* 46, no. 1 (March): 153–177.

Huntington, Jr., C. W. 2019. "Doing Buddhist Philosophy." In *APA Newsletter on Asian and Asian-American Philosophers and Philosophies* 19, no. 1, Fall (*Buddhist Philosophy Today: Theories and Forms*, guest edited special issue), edited by Rafal K. Stepien, 15–21. Newark, DE: The American Philosophical Association.

Huntington, Jr., C. W. 2020. "The Autobiographical No-Self." In *Buddhist Literature as Philosophy, Buddhist Philosophy as Literature*, edited by Rafal K. Stepien, 339–360. Albany: State University of New York Press.

Inada, Kenneth K. 1970. *Nāgārjuna: A Translation of his Mūlamadhyamakakārikā*. Tokyo: Hokuseido Press.

Ives, Christopher. 2015. "Emptiness: Soteriology and Ethics in Mahayana Buddhism." In *Philosophy of Religion: An Anthology*, 7th ed., edited by Michael Rea and Louis Pojman, 70–78. Stamford, CT: Cengage.

Jackson, Frank. 1998. *From Metaphysics to Ethics*. Oxford: Oxford University Press.

Jackson, Roger, and John Makransky, eds. *Buddhist Theology: Critical Reflections by Contemporary Scholars*. London: RoutledgeCurzon.

Jakubczak, Krzysztof. 1997. "Funkcja pozytywnego języka w negatywnej filozofi madhjamaki." In *Zrozumieć Wschód. Materiały z konferencji pt. 'Człowiek w zetknięciu kultur. Myśl Dalekiego Wschodu jako przedmiot poznania i źródło inspiracji. Uniwersytet Jagielloński, Kraków, 7 kwietnia 1997*, edited by Łukasz Trzciński and Krzysztof Jakubczak, 105–114. Kraków: Aureus.

Jakubczak, Krzysztof. 2001. "*Catuṣkoṭi*." In *Powszechna Encyklopedia Filozofii* II, edited by Maria Joanna Gondek, 65–66. Lublin: Polskie Towarzystwo Tomasza z Akwinu.

Jakubczak, Krzysztof. 2002a. "Nagardżuna. *Wigrahawjawartani*, czyli *Odwrocenie krytyki*." In *Filozofia Wschodu: Wybór Tekstów*, edited by Marta Kudelska, 251–262. Kraków: Wydawnictwo Uniwersytetu Jagiellońskiego.

Jakubczak, Krzysztof. 2002b. "Nagardżuna, *Mulamadhjamakakarika*, czyli *Podstawowe strofy Madhjamaki*. Rozdział XV: Badanie Samobytu (*svabhāva-parīkṣā*)." In *Filozofia Wschodu: Wybór Tekstów*, edited by Marta Kudelska, 263–265. Kraków: Wydawnictwo Uniwersytetu Jagiellońskiego.

Jakubczak, Krzysztof. 2004. "*Karuṇā*." In *Powszechna Encyklopedia Filozofii* V, edited by Elżbieta Grendecka, 527–529. Lublin: Polskie Towarzystwo Tomasza z Akwinu.

Jakubczak, Krzysztof. 2006. "O domniemanym sceptycyzmie madhjamaki." In *Indie w Warszawie: Tom upamiętniający 50-lecie powojennej historii indologii na Uniwersytecie Warszawskim. 2003/2004*, edited by D. Stasikand and A. Trynkowska, 127–134. Warszawa: Dom Wydawniczy Elipsa.

Jakubczak, Krzysztof. 2010. *Madhjamaka Nagardżuny: Filozofia czy terapia?* Kraków: Księgarnia Akademicka.

Jakubczak, Krzysztof, ed. 2017a. "Buddhism: Between Philosophy and Religion." Themed issue of: *Argument: Biannual Philosophical Journal* 7, no. 1.

Jakubczak, Krzysztof. 2017b. "*Introduction to the Issue*: Buddhism: Between Philosophy and Religion." In "Buddhism: Between Philosophy and Religion," edited by Krzysztof Jakubczak. Themed issue of: *Argument: Biannual Philosophical Journal* 7, no. 1: 5–8.

Jakubczak, Krzysztof. 2017c. "Widzenie pustki a doświadczenie mistyczne: przypadek madhjamaki." In "Buddhism: Between Philosophy and Religion," edited by Krzysztof Jakubczak. Themed issue of: *Argument: Biannual Philosophical Journal* 7, no. 1: 71–96.

Jakubczak, Krzysztof. 2019. *Poza bytem i niebytem: Filozofia buddyjska wobec zarzutu nihilizmu*. Kraków: Księgarnia Akademicka.

James, William. 1902. *The Varieties of Religious Experience: A Study in Human Nature, Being the Gifford Lectures on Natural Religion Delivered at Edinburgh in 1901–1902*. New York: Longmans, Green & Co.

Jampa Tegchok. (Khensur). 2017. *Practical Ethics and Profound Emptiness: A Commentary on Nāgārjuna's Precious Garland*. Translated by Steve Carlier (Bhikshu). Edited by Thubten Chodron (Bhikshuni). Somerville, MA: Wisdom.

Jayatilleke, K. N. 1967. "The Logic of Four Alternatives." *Philosophy East and West* 17, no. 1/4: 69–83.

Jizang 吉藏. N.d. (T 1824) *Zhongguanlun-shu* 中觀論疏. *Taishō* 42: 1824.

Jolley, Nicholas. 2000. "The Relation Between Theology and Philosophy." In *The Cambridge History of Seventeenth Century Philosophy*, Vol. 1, edited by Daniel Garber and Michael Ayers, 363–392. Cambridge: Cambridge University Press.

Jones, Richard Hubert. 1978. "The Nature and Function of Nāgārjuna's Arguments." *Philosophy East and West* 28, no. 4 (October): 485–502. Reprinted with minor alterations as chapter 4 of Jones 1993.

Jones, Richard Hubert. 1993. *Mysticism Examined: Philosophical Inquiries into Mysticism*. Albany: State University of New York Press.

Jones, Richard H. 2018. "Dialetheism, Paradox, and Nāgārjuna's Way of Thinking." *Comparative Philosophy* 9, no. 2: 41–68.

Kajiyama, Yūichi 梶山雄一. 1978. 佛教中觀哲學. Translated by Wu Rujun 吳汝鈞. 高雄：佛光.

Kalupahana, David J., trans. 1986. *Nāgārjuna: The Philosophy of the Middle Way* (*Mūlamadhyamakakārikā*. Albany: State University of New York.

Kalupahana, David J., trans. 1991. *Mūlamadhyamakakārikā of Nāgārjuna: The Philosophy of the Middle Way*. Delhi: Motilal Banarsidass.

Kant, Immanuel. (1755) 1900. "General History of Nature and Theory of the Heavens." In *Kant's Cosmogony*, translated by W. Hastie, 13–167. Glasgow: James Maclehose & Sons.

Kantor, Hans-Rudolf. 2014. "Philosophical Aspects of Sixth-Century Chinese Buddhist Debates on 'Mind and Consciousness.'" In *A Distant Mirror: Articulating Indic Ideas in Sixth and Seventh Century Chinese Buddhism*, edited by Chen-kuo Lin and Michael Radich, 337–395. Hamburg, Germany: Hamburg University Press.

Kantor, Hans-Rudolf. 2019a. "What/Who Determines the Value of Buddhist Philosophy in Modern Academia?." In *APA Newsletter on Asian and Asian-American Philosophers and Philosophies* 19, no. 1, Fall (*Buddhist Philosophy Today: Theories and Forms*, guest edited special issue), edited by Rafal K. Stepien, 8–11.

Kantor, Hans-Rudolf. 2019b. "Referential Relation and Beyond: Signifying Functions in Chinese Madhyamaka." *Journal of Indian Philosophy* 47: 851–915.

Kantor, Hans-Rudolf, and Mattia Salvini. 2019. "Words, Concepts, and the Middle Way: Language in the Traditions of Madhyamaka Thought." *Journal of Indian Philosophy* 47: 603–611.

Kapstein, Matthew T. 2001. *Reason's Traces: Identity and Interpretation in Indian and Tibetan Buddhist Thought*. Boston: Wisdom.

Kapstein, Matthew. 2017. "Interpreting Indian Philosophy: Three Parables." In *The Oxford Handbook of Indian Philosophy*, edited by Jonardon Ganeri, 15–31. New York: Oxford University Press.

Karunaratna, W. S. 1979. "*Cetanā*." In *Encyclopedia of Buddhism* IV, edited by G. P. Malalasekera, 86–97. Colombo: Department of Government Printing.

Kassor, Constance. 2013. "Is Gorampa's 'Freedom from Conceptual Proliferations' Dialetheist?" *Philosophy East and West* 63, no. 3, July: 399–410.

Katsura, Shōryū. 2000. "Nāgārjuna and the Tetralemma." In *Wisdom, Compassion, and the Search for Understanding: The Buddhist Studies Legacy of Gadjin M. Nagao*, edited by Jonathan A. Silk, 201–220. Honolulu: University of Hawai'i Press.

Katsura, Shōryū. 2023. "Nāgārjuna on *svabhāva*, *parabhāva*, *bhāva* and *abhāva*." In *To the Heart of Truth: Felicitation Volume for Eli Franco on the Occasion of His Seventieth Birthday, Part I* (Wiener Studien zur Tibetologie und Buddhismuskunde 104.1), edited by Hiroko Matsuoka, Shinya Moriyama, and Tyler Neill, 131–152. Wien: Arbeitskreis für Tibetische und Buddhistische Studien.

Katz, Steven T., ed. 1978. *Mysticism and Philosophical Analysis*. New York: Oxford University Press.

Katz, Steven T., ed. 2013. *Comparative Mysticism: An Anthology of Original Sources*. Oxford: Oxford University Press.

Keller, Catherine. 2005. "Scoop Up the Water and the Moon Is in Your Hands: On Feminist Theology and Dynamic Self-Emptying." In *The Emptying God: A Buddhist-Jewish-Christian Conversation*, edited by John B. Cobb, Jr., and Christopher Ives, 102–115. Eugene, OR: Wipf and Stock.

Kellner, Birgit. 2020. "Using Concepts to Eliminate Conceptualization: Kamaśīla on Non-Conceptual Gnosis (*Nirvikalpajñāna*)." *Journal of the International Association of Buddhist Studies* 43: 39–80.

Keown, Damien. 1992. *The Nature of Buddhist Ethics*. London: MacMillan.

Keown, Damien. 2001. *The Nature of Buddhist Ethics*. 2nd ed. London: Palgrave MacMillan.

Kidd, Ian James. 2017. "Epistemic Injustice and Religion." In *The Routledge Handbook of Epistemic Injustice*, edited by Ian James Kidd, José Medina, and Gaile Pohlhaus, Jr., 386–396. Abingdon, England: Routledge.

Kitagawa, Joseph. 1979. "Some Remarks on the Study of Sacred Texts." In *The Critical Study of Sacred Texts*, edited by Wendy Doniger O'Flaherty, 231–242. Berkeley: Religious Studies Series.

Komarovski, Yaroslav. 2015a. *Tibetan Buddhism and Mystical Experience*. New York: Oxford University Press.

Komito, David Ross. 1987. *Nāgārjuna's Seventy Stanzas: A Buddhist Psychology of Emptiness*. Ithaca, NY: Snow Lion Publications.

Kragh, Ulrich Timme. 2006. *Early Buddhist Theories of Action and Result*. Wien: Arbeitskreis für Tibetische und Buddhitische Studien.

Krstić, Tijana. 2015. "Islam and Muslims in Europe." In *The Oxford Handbook of Early Modern European History, 1350–1750: Volume 1: Peoples and Places*, edited by Hamish Scott, 670–693. Oxford: Oxford University Press.

Kuhn, Thomas S. 1970. *The Structure of Scientific Revolutions*. 2nd ed. Chicago: University of Chicago Press.

Kumar, Bimalendra. 1993. "The Critical Edition of *Yuktiṣaṣṭikā-kārikā* of Nāgārjuna." *The Tibet Journal* 18, no. 3: 3–16.

Kumārajīva 鳩摩羅什, trans. N.d. (T 1564) *Zhonglun* 中論. Commentary by Qingmu 青目. *Taishō* 30: 1564, 1b8–39c1.

Lakoff, George, and Mark Johnson. 1999. *Philosophy in the Flesh: The Embodied Mind and Its Challenge to Western Thought*. New York: Basic Books.

Lamotte, Étienne. 1944. *Le Traité de la Grande Vertu de Sagesse de Nāgārjuna (Mahāprajñāpāramitāśāstra), Tome I, Chapitres I–XV, Première Partie (Traduction annotée)*. Louvain: Bureaux du Muséon.

Larson, Gerald James, and Eliot Deutsch, eds. 1988. *Interpreting Across Boundaries: New Essays in Comparative Philosophy*. Princeton, NJ: Princeton University Press.

Levinas, Emmanuel. 2001. *Is It Righteous to Be? Interviews with Emmanuel Levinas*. Edited by Jill Robbins. Stanford, CA: Stanford University Press.

Lévy-Bruhl, Lucien. 1910. *Les fonctions mentales dans les sociétés inférieures*. Paris: Presses Universitaires de France.

Lévy-Bruhl, Lucien. 1926. *How Natives Think*. Translated by Lilian A. Clare. London: George Allen & Unwin.
Li Runsheng 利潤生. 1999a. 中論析義 (上冊. 香港: 佛教志蓮圖書館.
Li Runsheng 利潤生. 1999b. 中論析義 (下冊. 香港: 佛教志蓮圖書館.
Li Runsheng 利潤生. 1999c. 中論導讀 (上冊. 北市: 全佛文化.
Li Runsheng 利潤生. 1999d. 中論導讀 (下冊. 北市: 全佛文化.
Li Runsheng 利潤生. 2006a. 中伦导读 (上册. 北京: 中国书店.
Li Runsheng 利潤生. 2006b. 中伦导读 (下册. 北京: 中国书店.
Li Xuezhu 李学竹 and Ye Shaoyong 叶少勇. 2014. *Yuktiṣaṣṭikākārikā: Editions of the Sanskrit, Tibetan and Chinese Versions, with Commentary and a Modern Chinese Translation*. Shanghai: Zhongxi Book Company.
Li Zhifu 李志夫. 1986. 中印佛學之比較研究. 台北: 中華文化復興運動推行委員會.
Lin Tonqi, Henry Rosemont, Jr., and Roger T. Ames. 1995. "Chinese Philosophy: A Philosophical Essay on the 'State-of-the-Art.'" *Journal of Asian Studies* 54, no. 3 (August): 727–758.
Lincoln, Bruce. 2012. *Gods and Demons, Priests and Scholars: Critical Explorations in the History of Religions*. Chicago: University of Chicago Press.
Lindtner, Christian. 1982. *Nāgārjuniana—Studies in the Writings and Philosophy of Nāgārjuna*. Copenhagen: Akademisk Forlag.
Lindtner, Christian. 1997. *Master of Wisdom: Writings of the Buddhist Master Nāgārjuna*. Ratna Ling: Dharma Publishing.
Loewen, Nathan R. B., and Agnieszka Rostalska, eds. 2023. *Diversifying Philosophy of Religion: Critiques, Methods, and Case Studies*. London: Bloomsbury.
Loizzo, Joseph John (with AIBS Translation Team), trans. 2007. *Nāgārjuna's Reason Sixty with Chandrakīrti's Reason Sixty Commentary*. New York: The American Institute of Buddhist Studies at Columbia University, and Columbia University's Center for Buddhist Studies and Tibet House.
Lopez, Jr., Donald S. 1988. "Introduction." In *Buddhist Hermeneutics*, edited by Donald S. Lopez, Jr., 1–10. Honolulu: University of Hawai'i Press.
Lopez, Jr., Donald S. 1995. "Authority and Orality in the Mahāyāna." *Numen* 42, no. 1 (January): 21–47.
Lopez, Jr., Donald S. 2005. "Introduction." In *Critical Terms for the Study of Buddhism*, edited by Donald S. Lopez, Jr., 1–11. Chicago: University of Chicago Press.
Loy, David. 1984. "How Not to Criticize Nāgārjuna: A Response to L. Stafford Betty." *Philosophy East and West* 34, no. 4 (October): 437–445.
Lü Daji 吕大吉. 2016. 哲学与宗教学研究. Beijing: Beijing Book Co.
MacDonald, Anne. 2015a. *In Clear Words: The* Prasannapadā, *Chapter One* (Two Vols.). Wien: Verlag der Österreichischen Akademie der Wissenschaften.
MacDonald, Anne. 2015b. "The Quest for an English-Speaking Nāgārjuna." *Indo-Iranian Journal* 58, no. 4: 357–375.
MacFarlane, John. 2002. "Frege, Kant, and the Logic in Logicism." *The Philosophical Review* 111, no. 1 (January): 25–65.
Marcotte, Roxanne D. 2010. "The 'Religionated' Body: Fatwas and Body Parts." In *Medicine, Religion, and the Body*, edited by Elizabeth Burns Coleman and Kevin White, 27–49. Leiden, the Netherlands: Brill.
Mares, Edwin D. 2004. "Semantic Dialetheism." In *The Law of Non-Contradiction: New Philosophical Essays*, edited by Graham Priest, J. C. Beall, and Bradley Armour-Garb, 264–275. Oxford: Oxford University Press.

Masuzawa, Tomoko. 2005. *The Invention of World Religions, or How European Universalism Was Preserved in the Language of Pluralism*. Chicago: University of Chicago Press.

Matilal, Bimal Krishna. 1998. *The Character of Logic in India*. Edited by Jonardon Ganeri and Heeraman Tiwari. Albany: State University of New York Press.

Matilal, Bimal Krishna, and Robert D. Evans, eds. 1986. *Buddhist Logic and Epistemology: Studies in the Buddhist Analysis of Inference and Language*. Dordrecht, the Netherlands: D. Reidel.

Mattice, Sarah A. 2014. *Metaphor and Metaphilosophy: Philosophy as Combat, Play, and Aesthetic Experience*. Lanham, MD: Lexington Books.

May, Jacques. 1959. *Candrakīrti. Prasannapadā Madhyamakavṛtti. Douze chapitres traduits du sanscrit et du tibétain, accompagnés d'une introduction, de notes et d'une édition critique de la version tibétaine*. Paris: Adrien-Maisonneuve.

McCagney, Nancy. 1997. *Nāgārjuna and the Philosophy of Openness*. Lanham, MD: Rowman & Littlefield.

McClintock, Sara L. 2010. *Omniscience and the Rhetoric of Reason: Śāntarakṣita and Kamalaśīla on Rationality, Argumentation, and Religious Authority*. Boston: Wisdom.

McClintock, Sara. 2023. "Six Verses from Nāgārjuna's Lost Treatise *Establishing the Transactional*." *Journal of Indian Philosophy*. DOI: 10.1007/s10781-023-09536-6.

McGrath, Alister E. 2018. *The Territories of Human Reason: Science and Theology in an Age of Multiple Rationalities*. Oxford: Oxford University Press.

McGuire, Robert. 2017. "An All-New Timeless Truth: A Madhyamaka Analysis of Conflict and Compromise in Buddhist Modernism." *Contemporary Buddhism: An Interdisciplinary Journal* 18, no. 2: 385–401.

McLuhan, Marshall. 1964. *Understanding Media: The Extensions of Man*. New York: Mentor.

McMahan, David. 1998. "Orality, Writing, and Authority in South Asian Buddhism: Visionary Literature and the Struggle for Legitimacy in the Mahāyāna." *History of Religions* 37, no. 3 (February): 249–274.

McRae, Emily. 2018. "Detachment in Buddhist and Stoic Ethics: *Ataraxia* and *Apatheia* and Equanimity." In *Ethics without Self: Dharma without Atman: Western and Buddhist Philosophical Traditions in Dialogue*, edited by Gordon F. Davis, 73–89. Cham: Springer.

McRae, John R. 2000. "The Antecedents of Encounter Dialogue in Chinese Ch'an Buddhism." In *The Kōan: Texts and Contexts in Zen Buddhism*, edited by Steven Heine and Dale S. Wright, 46–74. New York: Oxford University Press.

Mejor, Marek. 2003. "Contributions of Polish Scholars to the Study of Indian Logic." *Journal of Indian Philosophy* 31, no. 1/3: 9–20.

Merquior, José. 1985. *Foucault*. Berkeley: University of California Press.

Meyers, Karin L. 2010. *Freedom and Self-Control: Free Will in South Asian Buddhism*. PhD diss., University of Chicago.

Mills, Ethan. 2018a. *Three Pillars of Skepticism in Classical India: Nāgārjuna, Jayarāśi, and Śrī Harṣa*. Lanham, MD: Lexington Books.

Mills, Ethan. 2018b. "Skepticism and Religious Practice in Sextus and Nāgārjuna." In *Ethics without Self: Dharma without Atman: Western and Buddhist Philosophical Traditions in Dialogue*, edited by Gordon F. Davis, 91–106. Cham, England: Springer.

Moeller, Hans-Georg. 2017. "Remarks on the Paradox and the Unmarked Space of Cross-Cultural Philosophy." *Confluence: Journal of World Philosophies* 2, Summer (Symposium: Does Cross-Cultural Philosophy Stand in Need of a Hermeneutic Expansion?): 126–129.

Morinaga, Soko. 2012. *The Ceasing of Notions: An Early Zen Text from the Dunhuang Caves*. Translated by the Venerable Myokyo-ni and Michelle Bromley. Boston: Wisdom.

Muller, A. Charles. 2013. "Zen Views on Views (*dṛṣṭi*): Are We Ever Rid of Them?" *The Japan Mission Journal* 67: 28–33.

Muller, A. Charles. 2018. "An Inquiry into Views, Beliefs and Faith: Lessons from Buddhism, Behavioural Psychology and Constructivist Epistemology." *Contemporary Buddhism* 19, no. 2: 362–381.

Mun, Chanju. 2005. *The History of Doctrinal Classification in Chinese Buddhism: A Study of the Panjiao System*. Lanham, MD: University Press of America.

Murray, Michael J., and Michael Rea. 2020. "Philosophy and Christian Theology." In *The Stanford Encyclopedia of Philosophy*, edited by Edward Zalta. https://plato.stanford.edu/archives/spr2020/entries/christiantheology-philosophy/. Last accessed December 31, 2020.

Murti, T. R. V. 1955. *The Central Philosophy of Buddhism: A Study of the Mādhyamika System*. London: George Allen and Unwin.

Nagao, Gadjin. 1989. *The Foundational Standpoint of Mādhyamika Philosophy*. Translated by John P. Keenan. Albany: State University of New York Press.

Nagao, Gadjin. 1991. *Mādhyamika and Yogācāra: A Study of Mahāyāna Philosophies*. Translated by Leslie S. Kawamura. Albany: State University of New York Press.

Ñāṇamoli (Bhikkhu) and Bodhi (Bhikkhu), trans. 1995. *Majjhima Nikāya: The Middle Length Discourses of the Buddha*. Boston: Wisdom.

Nance, Richard. 2007. "On What Do We Rely When We Rely on Reasoning?" *Journal of Indian Philosophy* 35, no. 2 (April): 149–167.

Nance, Richard. 2020. "Panegyric as Philosophy: Philosophical Dimensions of Indian Buddhist Hymns." In *Buddhist Literature as Philosophy, Buddhist Philosophy as Literature*, edited by Rafal K. Stepien, 85–111. Albany: State University of New York Press.

Narain, Harsh. 1964. "*Śūnyavāda*: A Reinterpretation." *Philosophy East and West* 13, no. 4 (January): 311–338.

Narain, Harsha. 1977. "The Nature of Madhyamika Thought." In *Madhyamika Dialectic and the Philosophy of Nagarjuna*, edited by Samdhong Rinpoche, 227–256. Sarnath: Central Institute of Higher Tibetan Studies.

Nattier, Jan. 2005. *A Few Good Men: The Bodhisattva Path According to the Inquiry of Ugra (Ugraparipṛcchā)*. Honolulu: University of Hawai'i Press.

Netland, Harold A. 2012. "Inclusivism and Exclusivism." In *Routledge Companion to Philosophy of Religion*, edited by Chad Meister and Paul Copan, 250–260. Abingdon, England: Routledge.

Newland, Guy, and Tom J. F. Tillemans. 2011. "An Introduction to Conventional Truth." In Cowherds, *Moonshadows: Conventional Truth in Buddhist Philosophy*, 3–22. New York: Oxford University Press.

Nongbri, Brent. 2013. *Before Religion: A History of a Modern Concept*. New Haven, CT: Yale University Press.

Nussbaum, Martha C. 1990. *Love's Knowledge: Essays on Philosophy and Literature*. New York: Oxford University Press.

Oetke, Claus. 1989. "Rationalismus und Mystik in der Philosophie Nāgārjunas." *Studien zur Indologie und Iranistik* 15: 1–39.

Oetke, Claus. 1990. "On Some Non-Formal Aspects of the Proofs of the Madhyamakakārikās." In *Earliest Buddhism and Madhyamaka*, edited by David Seyfort Ruegg and Lambert Schmithausen, 91–109. Leiden, the Netherlands: Brill.

Oetke, Claus. 1991. "Remarks on the Interpretation of Nāgārjuna's Philosophy." *Journal of Indian Philosophy* 19, no. 3: 315–323.

Oetke, Claus. 2003. "Some Remarks on Theses and Philosophical Positions in Early Madhyamaka." *Journal of Indian Philosophy* 31: 449–478.

Oetke, Claus. 2004. "On 'Nāgārjuna's Logic.'" In *Gedenkschrift J. W. de Jong*, edited by H. W. Bodewitz and Minoru Hara, 83–98. Tokyo: The International Institute for Buddhist Studies of the International College for Advanced Buddhist Studies.

Oetke, Claus. 2007. "On MMK 24.18." *Journal of Indian Philosophy* 35: 1–32.

Oetke, Claus. 2011. "Two Investigations on the *Mūlamadhyamakakārikās* and the *Vigrahavyāvartanī*." *Journal of Indian Philosophy* 39, no. 3 (June): 245–325.

Oetke, Claus. 2015. "Review of: Siderits, Mark, and Shōryū Katsura, trans. 2013. *Nāgārjuna's Middle Way: Mūlamadhyamakakārikā*. Boston: Wisdom." *Acta Orientalia* 76: 190–243.

Ogawa, Hideyo. 2019. "Two Truths Theory: What Is *vyavahāra*? Language as a Pointer to the Truth." *Journal of Indian Philosophy* 47: 613–633.

Padmakara Translation Group. 2013. *Nagarjuna's Letter to a Friend*. Kyabje Kangyur Rinpoche (comm.). Boston: Snow Lion.

Pandeya, Ram Chandra, and Manju. 1991. *Nāgārjuna's Philosophy of No-Identity*. Delhi: Eastern Book Linkers.

Panikkar, Raimundo. 1980. "Aporias in the Comparative Philosophy of Religion." *Man and World* 13, no. 3–4: 357–383.

Panikkar, Raimundo. 1988. "What Is Comparative Philosophy Comparing?" In *Interpreting Across Boundaries: New Essays in Comparative Philosophy*, edited by Gerald Larson James and Eliot Deutsch, 116–136. Princeton, NJ: Princeton University Press.

Panikkar, Raimundo. 1989. *The Silence of God: The Answer of the Buddha*. Translated by Robert R. Barr. Maryknoll, NY: Orbis Books.

Panikkar, Raimundo (Raimon). 2006. *Buddhism (Opera Omnia Vol. V)*. Maryknoll, NY: Orbis Books.

Paramārtha 真諦, trans. N.d. (T 1656) 寶行王正論 (*Ratnāvalī*). *Taishō* 32: 1656.

Park, Jin Y. 2017a. *Women and Buddhist Philosophy: Engaging Zen Master Kim Iryŏp*. Honolulu: University of Hawai'i Press.

Park, Jin Y. 2017b. "Zen Buddhism and the Space of Ethics." In *A Mirror Is for Reflection: Understanding Buddhist Ethics*, edited by Jake H. Davis, 73–91. New York: Oxford University Press.

Park, Peter K. J. 2013. *Africa, Asia, and the History of Philosophy: Racism in the Formation of the Philosophical Canon, 1780–1830*. Albany: State University of New York Press.

Pasternack, Lawrence, and Courtney Fugate. 2020. "Kant's Philosophy of Religion." In *The Stanford Encyclopedia of Philosophy*, edited by Edward N. Zalta. https://plato.stanford.edu/archives/spr2020/entries/kant-religion/. Last accessed December 23, 2020.

Patil, Parimal. 2011. "Constructing the Content of Awareness Events." In *Apoha: Buddhist Nominalism and Human Cognition*, edited by Mark Siderits, Tom Tillemans, and Arindam Chakrabarti, 149–169. New York: Columbia University Press.

Patton, Kimberley C., and Benjamin C. Ray, eds. 2020a. *A Magic Still Dwells: Comparative Religion in the Postmodern Age*. Berkeley: University of California Press.

Patton, Kimberley C., and Benjamin C. Ray, eds. 2020b. "Introduction." In *A Magic Still Dwells: Comparative Religion in the Postmodern Age*, edited by Kimberley C. Patton and Benjamin C. Ray, 1–19. Berkeley: University of California Press.

Pecchia, Cristina. 2023. "Meditation and Knowledge in Indian Buddhist Epistemology." In *To the Heart of Truth: Felicitation Volume for Eli Franco on the Occasion of His Seventieth Birthday, Part II* (Wiener Studien zur Tibetologie und Buddhismuskunde 104.2), edited by Hiroko Matsuoka, Shinya Moriyama, and Tyler Neill, 667–684. Wien: Arbeitskreis für Tibetische und Buddhistische Studien.

Perrett, Roy W. 2016. *An Introduction to Indian Philosophy*. Cambridge: Cambridge University Press.

Pettit, John. 1999. "Review of: Williams, Paul. 1998. *Altruism and Reality: Studies in the Philosophy of the Bodhicaryāvatāra*. Richmond: Curzon Press." *Journal of Buddhist Ethics* 6: 120–137.

Pind, Ole Holten. 2001. "Why the *Vaidalyaprakaraṇa* Cannot Be an Authentic Work of Nāgārjuna." *Wiener Zeitschrift für die Kunde Südasiens / Vienna Journal of South Asia Studies* 45: 149–172.

Plato. 2006. *Republic*. Translated by R. E. Allen. New Haven, CT: Yale University Press.

Pollock, Sheldon. 1985. "The Theory of Practice and the Practice of Theory in Indian Intellectual History." *Journal of the American Oriental Society* 105, no. 3: 499–519.

Prebish, Charles S. 1999. *Luminous Passage: The Practice and Study of Buddhism in America*. Berkeley: University of California Press.

Prebish, Charles S. 2007. "North American Buddhist Studies: A Current Survey of the Field." *Journal of the International Association of Buddhist Studies* 30, no. 1-2: 253–282.

Priest, Graham. 1995. *Beyond the Limits of Thought*. Cambridge: Cambridge University Press.

Priest, Graham. 2002. *Beyond the Limits of Thought*. 2nd ed. Oxford: Oxford University Press.

Priest, Graham. 2006. *In Contradiction: A Study of the Transconsistent*. Expanded ed. Oxford: Oxford University Press.

Priest, Graham. 2014. *One: Being an Investigation into the Unity of Reality and of its Parts, including the Singular Object which is Nothingness*. Oxford: Oxford University Press.

Priest, Graham. 2016. "Compassion and the Net of Indra." In Cowherds, *Moonpaths: Ethics and Emptiness*, 221–239. New York: Oxford University Press.

Priest, Graham. 2017. "Buddhist Ethics: A Perspective." In *A Mirror Is for Reflection: Understanding Buddhist Ethics*, edited by Jake H. Davis, 92–108. New York: Oxford University Press.

Priest, Graham. 2018. *The Fifth Corner of Four: An Essay on Buddhist Metaphysics and the Catuṣkoṭi*. Oxford: Oxford University Press.

Priest, Graham, J. C. Beall, and Bradley Armour-Garb, eds. 2004. *The Law of Non-Contradiction: New Philosophical Essays*. Oxford: Oxford University Press.

Proudfoot, Wayne. 1985. *Religious Experience*. Berkeley: University of California Press.

Quine, Willard Van Orman. 1948. "On What There Is." *The Review of Metaphysics* 2, no. 5 (September): 21–38.

Quine, Willard Van Orman. (1953) 1963. *From a Logical Point of View: 9 Logico-Philosophical Essays*. 2nd ed., rev. New York: Harper & Row.

Raghuramaraju, A. 2017. "Consolidation before Expansion: Revisiting Cross-Cultural Philosophy." *Confluence: Journal of World Philosophies* 2, Summer (Symposium: Does Cross-Cultural Philosophy Stand in Need of a Hermeneutic Expansion?): 130–134.

Rahlwes, Chris. 2022. "Nāgārjuna's Negation." *Journal of Indian Philosophy* 50, no. 2: 307–344.

Rajapakse, Regington. 1986. "Buddhism as Religion and Philosophy." *Religion* 16, no. 1: 51–55.

Raju, P. T. 1954. "The Principle of Four-Cornered Negation in Indian Philosophy." *The Review of Metaphysics* 7, no. 4, June: 694–713.

Ram-Prasad, Chakravarthi. 2001. *Knowledge and Liberation in Classical Indian Thought*. Basingstoke, England: Palgrave.

Rashdall, Hastings. 1920. "The Relation Between Philosophy and Theology." *Theology* 1, no. 4: 196–210.

Ray, Reginald A. 1997. "Nāgārjuna's Longevity." In *Sacred Biography in the Buddhist Traditions of South and Southeast Asia*, edited by Julianne Schober, 129–159. Honolulu: University of Hawai'i Press.

Ricoeur, Paul. 2003. *The Rule of Metaphor*. Translated by Robert Czerny. London: Routledge.

Robinson, Richard H. 1957. "Some Logical Aspects of Nāgārjuna's System." *Philosophy East and West* 6, no. 4: 291–308.

Robinson, Richard H. 1967. *Early Mādhyamika in India and China*. Madison: University of Wisconsin Press.

Robinson, Richard H. 1972. "Did Nāgārjuna Really Refute All Philosophical Views?" *Philosophy East and West* 22, no. 3 (July): 325–331.

Robinson, Richard H. 1978. *Early Mādhyamika in India and China*. New York: Samuel Weiser.

Rorty, Richard. 1982. *Consequences of Pragmatism*. Minneapolis: University of Minnesota Press.

Rorty, Richard. 1984. "The Historiography of Philosophy: Four Genres." In *Philosophy in History: Essays in the Historiography of Philosophy*, edited by Richard Rorty, J. B. Schneewind, and Quentin Skinner, 49–75. Cambridge: Cambridge University Press.

Roth, Paul A. 2017. "Translation and Understanding: What the Problems Are Not." *Confluence: Journal of World Philosophies* 2, Summer (Symposium: Does Cross-Cultural Philosophy Stand in Need of a Hermeneutic Expansion?): 135–137.

Ruegg, David Seyfort. 1967. *The Study of Indian and Tibetan Thought: Some Problems and Perspectives*. Leiden, the Netherlands: Brill.

Ruegg, David Seyfort. 1969. *La théorie du tathāgatagarbha et du gotra*. Paris: Publications de l'École Française d'Extrême-Orient (Vol. 70), Adrien-Masonneuve.

Ruegg, David Seyfort. 1977. "The Uses of the Four Positions of the *Catuṣkoṭi* and the Problem of the Description of Reality in Mahāyāna Buddhism." *Journal of Indian Philosophy* 5: 1–71. (Reprinted in Ruegg, David Seyfort. 2010. *The Buddhist Philosophy of the Middle: Essays on Indian and Tibetan Madhyamaka*. Boston: Wisdom.

Ruegg, David Seyfort. 1981. *The Literature of the Madhyamaka School of Philosophy in India*. Wiesbaden, Germany: Otto Harassowitz.

Ruegg, David Seyfort. 1992. "Some Reflections on Translating Buddhist Philosophical Texts from Sanskrit and Tibetan." *Asiatische Studien: Zeitschrift der Schweizerischen Asiengesellschaft / Études Asiatiques: Revue de la Société Suisse—Asie* 46, "Études Bouddhiques Offertes à Jacques May": 367–391.

Ruegg, David Seyfort. 1995. "Some Reflections on the Place of Philosophy in the Study of Buddhism." *Journal of the International Association of Buddhist Studies* 18, no. 2 (Winter): 145–181.

Ruegg, David Seyfort. 2000. *Three Studies in the History of Indian and Tibetan Madhyamaka Philosophy: Studies in Indian and Tibetan Madhyamaka Thought*, Part 1. Wien: Arbeitskreis für Tibetische und Buddhistische Studien Universität Wien.

Ruegg, David Seyfort. 2010. *The Buddhist Philosophy of the Middle: Essays on Indian and Tibetan Madhyamaka*. Boston: Wisdom.

Ruegg, David Seyfort, and Lambert Schmithausen, eds. 1990. *Earliest Buddhism and Madhyamaka*. Leiden, the Netherlands: Brill.

Ruseva, Gergana Rumenova. 2015. "On the Notions of Memory in Buddhism." *The Silk Road: Collection of Papers from the Third International Conference on Chinese Studies*. Organized by the Confucius Institute in Sofia, June 2015: 222–229.

Rutherford, Donald. 2019. "Descartes' Ethics." In *The Stanford Encyclopedia of Philosophy*, edited by Edward N. Zalta. https://plato.stanford.edu/archives/win2019/entries/descartes-ethics/. Last accessed June 2, 2021.

Ryba, Thomas. 1993. "Are Religious Theories Susceptible to Reduction?" In *Religion and Reductionism: Essays on Eliade, Segal, and the Challenge of the Social Sciences for the Study of Religion*, edited by Thomas A. Idinopulos and Edward A. Yonan, 15–42. Leiden, the Netherlands: Brill.

Saito, Akira. 1984. *A Study of the Buddhapālitamūlamadhyamakavṛtti*. PhD diss., Australian National University.

Saito, Akira. 2010. "Nāgārjuna's Influence on the Formation of the Early Yogācāra Thoughts: From the *Mūlamadhyamakārikā* to the *Bodhisattvabhūmi*." *Journal of Indian and Buddhist Studies* 58, no. 3 (March): 1212–1218.

Saito, Akira. 2019. "*Prapañca* in the *Mūlamadhyamakārikā*." *Bulletin of the International Institute for Buddhist Studies* 2: 1–9.

Salvini, Mattia. 2011. "The Nidānasamyukta and the Mūlamadhyamakakārikā: Understanding the Middle Way through Comparison and Exegesis." *Thai International Journal of Buddhist Studies* II: 57–95.

Salvini, Mattia. 2019. "Etymologies of What Can(not) Be Said: Candrakīrti on Conventions and Elaborations." *Journal of Indian Philosophy* 47: 661–695.

Samdhong Rinpoche, ed. 1977. *Madhyamika Dialectic and the Philosophy of Nagarjuna*. Sarnath, India: Central Institute of Higher Tibetan Studies.

*Saṃghavarman 僧伽跋摩, trans. N.d. (T 1673) 勸發諸王要偈. *Taishō*: 1673.

Sasaki, Ruth Fuller, trans., and Thomas Yūhō Kirchner, ed. 2009. *The Record of Linji*. Honolulu: University of Hawai'i Press.

Schayer, Stanisław. 1933. "Studien zur indischen Logik 2: Altindische Antizipationen der Aussagenlogik." *Bulletin International de l'Académie Polonaise des Sciences et des Lettres, Classe de Philologie*, fasc. 1–6 : 90–96.

Schayer, Stanisław. 1988. *O Filozowaniu Hindusów*. Edited by Marek Mejor. Warszawa: Polska Akademia Nauk, Komitet nauk Orientalistycznych, PWN.

Scherrer-Schaub, Cristina. 1991. *Yuktiṣaṣṭikāvṛtti: Commentaire à la soixantaine sur le raisonnement ou Du vrai enseignement de la causalité par le Maître indien Candrakīrti*. Bruxelles: Institut Belge des Hautes Études Chinoises.

Scherrer-Schaub, Cristina. 2007. "Immortality Extolled with Reason: Philosophy and Politics in Nāgārjuna." In *Pramāṇakīrtiḥ: Papers Dedicated to Ernst Steinkellner on the Occasion of His 70th Birthday*, edited by Birgit Kellner, Helmut Krasser, Hort Lasic, Michael Torsten Much, and Helmut Tauscher, 757–793. Wiener Studien zur Tibetologie und Buddhismuskunde 70.1 and 70.2. Wien: Arbeitskreis für Tibetische und Buddhistische Studien.

Schmidt-Leukel, Perry. 2016. "*Nirvāṇa* as 'Unconditioned' (*asaṃskṛta*) and 'Transcendent' (*lokottara*) Reality." *The Japan Mission Journal* 70, no. 3 (Autumn): 170–179.

Schmithausen, Lambert. 1969. *Der Nirvāṇa-Abschnitt in der Viniścayasaṃgrahāṇī der Yogācārabhūmiḥ*. Wien: Österreichische Akademie der Wissenschaften.

Schmithausen, Lambert. 1973. "Spirituelle Praxis und philosophische Theorie im Buddhismus." *Zeitschrift für Missionswissenschaft und Religionswissenschaft* 3, no. 73: 161–186.

Schmithausen, Lambert. 1997. "The Early Buddhist Tradition and Ecological Ethics." *Journal of Buddhist Ethics* 4: 1–74.

Schmithausen, Lambert. 2000. "Buddhism and the Ethics of Nature: Some Remarks." *The Eastern Buddhist* 32, no. 2: 26–78.

Schmithausen, Lambert. 2014. *The Genesis of Yogācāra-Vijñānavāda: Responses and Reflections*. Tokyo: The International Institute for Buddhist Studies.

Schopen, Gregory. 1997. *Bones, Stones, and Buddhist Monks: Collected Papers on the Archaeology, Epigraphy, and Texts of Monastic Buddhism in India*. Honolulu: University of Hawai'i Press.

Sebastian, C. D. 2016. *The Cloud of Nothingness: The Negative Way in Nāgārjuna and John of the Cross*. New York: Springer.

Sellars, Wilfrid. 1997. *Empiricism and the Philosophy of Mind*. Cambridge, MA: Harvard University Press.

Sells, Michael A. 1994. *Mystical Languages of Unsaying*. Chicago: University of Chicago Press.

Sharf, Robert H. 2014. "Mindfulness and Mindlessness in Early Chan." *Philosophy East and West* 64, no. 4 (October): 933–964.

Sharma, Arvind. 2005. *Religious Studies and Comparative Methodology: The Case for Reciprocal Illumination*. Albany: State University of New York Press.

Sharpe, Eric J. 1986. *Comparative Religion: A History*. 2nd ed. London: Duckworth.

Shen Jianying 沈剑英. 1985. 因明学研究. 上海: 中国大百科全书出版社.

Shulman, Eviatar. (2007) 2009. "Creative Ignorance: Nāgārjuna on the Ontological Significance of Consciousness." *Journal of the International Association of Buddhist Studies* 30, no. 1–2: 139–173.

Shulman, Eviatar. 2008. "Early Meanings of Dependent-Origination." *Journal of Indian Philosophy* 36: 297–317.

Shulman, Eviatar. 2011. "*Ratnāvalī*: A Precious Garland of Buddhist Philosophical Systems." *Indo-Iranian Journal* 54, no. 4: 301–329.

Shulman, Eviatar. 2015. "Nāgārjuna the Yogācārin? Vasubandhu the Mādhyamika? On the Middle-way between Realism and Antirealism." In *Madhyamaka and Yogācāra: Allies or Rivals?* edited by Jay L. Garfield and Jan Westerhoff, 184–212. New York: Oxford University Press.

Siderits, Mark. 1980. "The Madhyamaka Critique of Epistemology. I." *Journal of Indian Philosophy* 8, no. 4 (December): 307–335.

Siderits, Mark. 1981. "The Madhyamaka Critique of Epistemology. II." *Journal of Indian Philosophy* 9, no. 2 (June): 121–160.

Siderits, Mark. 1988. "Nāgārjuna as Anti-Realist." *Journal of Indian Philosophy* 16, no. 4: 311–325.

Siderits, Mark. 1989. "Thinking on Empty: Madhyamaka Anti-Realism and Canons of Rationality." In *Rationality in Question*, edited by Shlomo Biderman and Ben-Ami Scharfenstein, 231–249. Leiden, the Netherlands: Brill.

Siderits, Mark. 2000. "The Reality of Altruism: Reconstructing Śāntideva." *Philosophy East and West* 50, no. 3: 412–424.

Siderits, Mark. 2003a. "On the Soteriological Significance of Emptiness." *Contemporary Buddhism* 4, no. 1: 9–23.

Siderits, Mark. 2003b. *Empty Persons: Personal Identity and Buddhist Philosophy*. Farnham, England: Ashgate.

Siderits, Mark. 2007. *Buddhism as Philosophy: An Introduction*. London: Routledge.

Siderits, Mark. 2011a. "Buddhas as Zombies: A Buddhist Reduction of Subjectivity." In *Self, No Self? Perspectives from Analytical, Phenomenological, and Indian Traditions*, edited by Mark Siderits, Evan Thompson, and Dan Zahavi, 308–331. New York: Oxford University Press.

Siderits, Mark. 2011b. "Is Everything Connected to Everything Else? What the Gopīs Know." In Cowherds, *Moonshadows: Conventional Truth in Buddhist Philosophy*, 167–180. New York: Oxford University Press.

Siderits, Mark. 2015. *Empty Persons: Personal Identity and Buddhist Philosophy*. 2nd ed. Farnham, England: Ashgate.

Siderits, Mark. 2016a. "Response to Levine." *Journal of World Philosophies* 1 (Winter): 128–130.

Siderits, Mark. 2016b. "Does 'Buddhist Ethics' Exist?" In Cowherds, *Moonpaths: Ethics and Emptiness*, 119–139. New York: Oxford University Press.

Siderits, Mark. 2017. "Comparison or Confluence in Philosophy?" In *The Oxford Handbook of Indian Philosophy*, edited by Jonardon Ganeri, 75–89. Oxford: Oxford University Press.

Siderits, Mark. 2019. "The *Prapañca* Paradox." *Journal of Indian Philosophy* 47: 645–659.

Siderits, Mark, and Jay L. Garfield. 2013. "Defending the Semantic Interpretation: A Reply to Ferraro." *Journal of Indian Philosophy* 41, no. 6 (December): 655–664.

Siderits, Mark, and Shōryū Katsura, trans. 2013. *Nāgārjuna's Middle Way: Mūlamadhyamakakārikā*. Boston: Wisdom.

Siderits, Mark, Tom Tillemans, and Arindam Chakrabarti, eds. 2011. *Apoha: Buddhist Nominalism and Human Cognition*. New York: Columbia University Press.

Silk, Jonathan A., ed. 2000. *Wisdom, Compassion, and the Search for Understanding: The Buddhist Studies Legacy of Gadjin M. Nagao*. Honolulu: University of Hawai'i Press.

Silk, Jonathan A. 2002. "What, If Anything, Is Mahāyāna Buddhism? Problems of Definitions and Classifications." *Numen* 49, no. 4: 355–405.

Smith, Jonathan Z. 2004. *Relating Religion: Essays in the Study of Religion*. Chicago: University of Chicago Press.

Smith College. 2010. *Madhyamaka & Methodology: A Symposium on Buddhist Theory and Method*, April 23–25, 2010. https://www.youtube.com/playlist?list=PLPeMhGupBRES8oZM00LgFsSr3oRcPQiud (Videos) and http://docplayer.net/22172072-Madhyamaka-methodology-a-symposium-on-buddhist-theory-and-method-april-23-25-2010.html (Scholars). Last accessed March 12, 2021.

Soldatenko, Gabriel. 2015. "A Contribution toward the Decolonization of Philosophy: Asserting the Coloniality of Power in the Study of Non-Western Traditions." *Comparative and Continental Philosophy* 7, no. 2 (November): 138–156.

Spackman, John. 2014. "Between Nihilism and Anti-Essentialism: A Conceptualist Interpretation of Nāgārjuna." *Philosophy East and West* 61, no. 1: 151–173.

Sprung, Mervyn, ed. 1973. *The Problem of Two Truths in Buddhism and Vedānta*. Dordrecht, the Netherlands: D. Reidel.

Sprung, Mervyn. 1979. *Lucid Exposition of the Middle Way: The Essential Chapters from the* Prasannapadā *of Candrakīrti*. London: Routledge & Kegan Paul.

Staal, Frits. 1975. *Exploring Mysticism: A Methodological Essay*. Berkeley: University of California Press.

Staal, Frits. 1976. "Making Sense of the Buddhist Tetralemma." In *Philosophy East and West*, edited by H. D. Lewis, 122–131. Bombay: Blackie & Son.

Stace, Walter T. 1961. *Mysticism and Philosophy*. London: MacMillan.

Stcherbatsky, F. T. (1930) 1962. *Buddhist Logic* 2. New York: Dover.

Stepien, Rafal K. 2016. "Review Article of: Lin, Chen-kuo and Radich, Michael (eds.). 2014. *A Distant Mirror: Articulating Indic Ideas in Sixth and Seventh Century Chinese Buddhism*. Hamburg: Hamburg University Press." *Journal of the Oxford Centre for Buddhist Studies* 11: 237–264.

Stepien, Rafal K. 2018a. "Orienting Reason: A Religious Critique of Philosophizing Nāgārjuna." *Journal of the American Academy of Religion* 86, no. 4: 1072–1106.

Stepien, Rafal K. 2018b. "Do Good Philosophers Argue? A Buddhist Approach to Philosophy and Philosophy Prizes." *APA Newsletter on Asian and Asian-American Philosophers and Philosophies* 18, no. 1 (Fall): 13–15.

Stepien, Rafal K., ed. 2019a. *APA Newsletter on Asian and Asian-American Philosophers and Philosophies* 19, no. 1, Fall (*Buddhist Philosophy Today: Theories and Forms*, guest edited special issue. Newark, DE: The American Philosophical Association.

Stepien, Rafal K. 2019b. "Buddhist Philosophy? Arguments From Somewhere." In *APA Newsletter on Asian and Asian-American Philosophers and Philosophies* 19, no. 1, Fall (*Buddhist Philosophy Today: Theories and Forms*, guest edited special issue), edited by Rafal K. Stepien: 11–15.

Stepien, Rafal K., ed. 2020a. *Buddhist Literature as Philosophy, Buddhist Philosophy as Literature*. Albany: State University of New York Press.

Stepien, Rafal K. 2020b. "Introduction: Philosophy, Literature, Religion: Buddhism as Transdisciplinary Intervention." In *Buddhist Literature as Philosophy, Buddhist Philosophy as Literature*, edited by Rafal K. Stepien, 1–31. Albany: State University of New York Press.

Stepien, Rafal K. 2020c. "The Original Mind is the Literary Mind, the Original Body Carves Dragons." In *Buddhist Literature as Philosophy, Buddhist Philosophy as Literature*, edited by Rafal K. Stepien, 231–260. Albany: State University of New York Press.

Stepien, Rafal K. 2021a. "Interreligious Relations with No Self: A Mystical Path to Omnilogue?" *Journal of the Royal Asiatic Society*, Series 3, 31, no. 4: 721–741.

Stepien, Rafal K. 2021b. "Indian Buddhist and Continental Christianate Critiques of Ontology: An Exercise in Interreligious Philosophical Dialogue." *Interreligious Relations* 22 (January/February): 1–14.

Stepien, Rafal K. 2021c. "Substantialism, Essentialism, Emptiness: Buddhist Critiques of Ontology." *Journal of Indian Philosophy* 49, no. 5 (December): 871–893.

Stepien, Rafal K. 2022. "Contest, Game, Disgrace: On Philosophy and Buddhism." *Philosophy East and West*. 72, no. 4 (October): 1066–1088.

Stepien, Rafal K. 2023a. "Tetralemma and Trinity: An Essay in Buddhist and Christian Ontologies." *Comparative and Continental Philosophy* 14, no. 3: 236–254.

Stepien, Rafal K. 2023b. "Prolegomena to a Buddhist Philosophy of Religion." *International Journal for Philosophy of Religion* 94, no. 1: 63–89.

Stepien, Rafal K. 2023c. "Interdisciplinarity in Non-Disciplines: Archive and Academe in the Study of Religion." *Numen* 70, no. 5: 473–513.

Stewart, Georgina. 2016. "What's in a Name? In Support of *A Manifesto for Re:emergent Philosophy*." *Confluence: Journal of World Philosophies* 4 (Symposium: Is Reason a Neutral Tool in Comparative Philosophy?): 154–161.

Steup, Matthias, and Ram Neta. 2020. "Epistemology." In *The Stanford Encyclopedia of Philosophy*, edited by Edward N. Zalta. https://plato.stanford.edu/archives/fall2020/entries/epistemology/. Last accessed December 14, 2020.

Szaif, Jan. 1996. *Platons Begriff der Wahrheit*. Freiberg, Germany: Alber.

Szaif, Jan. 2007. "*Doxa* and *Epistêmê* as Modes of Acquaintance in *Republic V*." *Études Platoniciennes IV: Les puissances de l'âme selon Platon*, edited by Arnaud Macé, 253–272. Paris: Les Belles Lettres.

Taber, John. A. 1998. "On Nāgārjuna's So-Called Fallacies: A Comparative Approach." *Indo-Iranian Journal* 41, no. 3: 213–244.

Taber, John. 2013. "On Engaging Philosophically with Indian Philosophical Texts." *Asiatische Studien: Zeitschrift der Schweizerischen Asiengesellschaft / Études Asiatiques: Revue de la Société Suisse—Asie* 67, no. 1: 125–163.

Tachikawa, Musashi. 1997. *An Introduction to the Philosophy of Nāgārjuna*. Translated by Rolf W. Giebel. Delhi: Motilal Banarsidass.

Taishō shinshū daizōkyō 大正新脩大藏經. 1924–1932. Edited by Junjirō Takakusu and Watanabe Kaikyoku, et al. 100 vols. Tokyo: Taishō Issaikyō Kankōkai. Accessed at CBETA (Chinese Buddhist Electronic Text Association中華電子佛典協會, http://cbeta.org.

Tanaka, Koji, Yasuo Deguchi, Jay L. Garfield, and Graham Priest, eds. 2015. *The Moon Points Back*. New York: Oxford University Press.

Tauscher, Helmut. 2003. "Phya pa chos kyi seng ge as a Svātantrika." In *The Svātantrika-Prāsaṇgika Distinction: What Difference Does a Difference Make?* edited by Georges B. J. Dreyfus and Sara L. McClintock, 207–255. Boston: Wisdom.

Taylor, Charles. 2007. *A Secular Age*. Cambridge, MA: Harvard University Press.

Thakchoe, Sonam. 2007. *The Two Truths Debate: Tsongkhapa and Gorampa on the Middle Way*. Boston: Wisdom.

Thomson, Iain. 2000. "Ontotheology? Understanding Heidegger's *Destruktion* of Metaphysics." *International Journal of Philosophical Studies* 8, no. 3: 297–327.

Thurman, Robert. 1976. *The Holy Teaching of Vimalakīrti: A Mahāyāna Scripture*. University Park: The Pennsylvania State University Press.

Thurman, Robert A. F. 1984. *Tsong Khapa's Speech of Gold in the* Essence of True Eloquence: *Reason and Enlightenment in the Central Philosophy of Tibet*. Princeton, NJ: Princeton University Press.

Tiele, Cornelius Petrus. 1884. "Religions." In *Encyclopedia Britannica* (9th ed.) 20: 358–371. Edinburgh: Adam and Charles Black.

Tillemans, Tom. 1990. *Materials for the Study of Āryadeva, Dharmapāla and Candrakīrti*. Wien: Universität Wien.

Tillemans, Tom. 1995. "Remarks on Philology." *Journal of the International Association of Buddhist Studies* 18, no. 2 (Winter): 269–277.

Tillemans, Tom J. F. 1999. *Scripture, Logic, Language: Essays on Dharmakīrti and his Tibetan Successors*. Boston: Wisdom.

Tillemans, Tom. 2003. "Metaphysics for Mādhyamikas." In *The Svātantrika-Prāsaṇgika Distinction: What Difference Does a Difference Make?* edited by Georges B. J. Dreyfus and Sara L. McClintock, 93–123. Boston: Wisdom.

Tillemans, Tom. 2009. "How Do Mādhyamikas Think?: Notes on Jay Garfield, Graham Priest, and Paraconsistency." In *Pointing at the Moon: Buddhism, Logic, Analytic Philosophy*, edited by Mario D'Amato, Jay Garfield, and Tom Tillemans, 83–100. Oxford: Oxford University Press. Reprinted in Tillemans 2016.

Tillemans, Tom. 2016. *How Do Mādhyamikas Think?: And Other Essays on the Buddhist Philosophy of the Middle*. Somerville, MA: Wisdom.

Tillemans, Tom. 2017. "Philosophical Quietism in Nāgārjuna and Early Madhyamaka." In *The Oxford Handbook of Indian Philosophy*, edited by Jonardon Ganeri, 110–132. New York: Oxford University Press.

Tillemans, Tom J. F. 2018. "Metaphysics and Metametaphysics with Buddhism: The Lay of the Land." In *Buddhist Philosophy: A Comparative Approach*, edited by Steven M. Emmanuel, 87–107. Hoboken, NJ: Wiley-Blackwell.

Tillemans, Tom J. F. 2023. "Is Metaphysics Madness? A Sixth-Century Polemic Unpacked." In *To the Heart of Truth: Felicitation Volume for Eli Franco on the Occasion of His Seventieth Birthday, Part I* (Wiener Studien zur Tibetologie und Buddhismuskunde 104.1), edited by Hiroko Matsuoka, Shinya Moriyama, and Tyler Neill, 325–309. Wien: Arbeitskreis für Tibetische und Buddhistische Studien.

Tola, Fernando, and Carmen Dragonetti. 1995a. *On Voidness: A Study of Buddhist Nihilism*. Delhi: Motilal Banarsidass.

Tola, Fernando and Carmen Dragonetti. 1995b. *Nāgārjuna's Refutation of Logic (Nyāya): Vaidalyaprakaraṇa*. Delhi: Motilal Banarsidass.

Tola, Fernando and Carmen Dragonetti. 1998. "Against the Attribution of the *Vigrahavyāvartanī* to Nāgārjuna." *Wiener Zeitschrift für die Kunde Südasiens und Archiv für Indische Philosophie* 42: 151–166.

Travagnin, Stefania. 2009. *The Madhyamaka Dimension of Yinshun: A Re-statement of the School of Nāgārjuna in Twentieth-Century Chinese Buddhism*. PhD diss., SOAS, University of London.

Travagnin, Stefania. 2012. "What Is Behind Yinshun's Re-statement of the Nature of the *Mūlamadhyamakakārikā*? Debates on the Creation of a New Mahāyāna in Twentieth-century China." *Buddhist Studies Review* 29, no. 2: 251–272.

Travagnin, Stefania. 2022. *Yinshun and His Exposition of Madhyamaka: New Studies of the Da Zhidu Lun in Twentieth-Century China and Taiwan*. Sheffield, England: Equinox.

Tucci, Giuseppe. 1932. "Two Hymns of the Catuḥ-stava of Nāgārjuna." *Journal of the Royal Asiatic Society of Great Britain and Ireland* 2 (April): 309–325.

Tuck, Andrew P. 1990. *Comparative Philosophy and the Philosophy of Scholarship: On the Western Interpretation of Nāgārjuna*. New York: Oxford University Press.

Turner, Denys. 1995. *The Darkness of God: Negativity in Christian Mysticism*. Cambridge: Cambridge University Press.

Tuske, Joerg, trans. 2001. "Studies on Indian Logic. Ancient Indian Anticipations of Propositional Logic." In *Indian Logic: A Reader*, edited by Jonardon Ganeri, 96–101. Richmond, VA: Curzon.

Uryūzu, Ryūshin 瓜生津隆真. 1985. "ナーガールジュナ研究." 東京: 春秋社.

Vaidya, P. L., ed. 1960. *Madhyamakaśāstra of Nāgārjuna with the Commentary: Prasannapadā by Candrakīrti*. Darbhanga: Mithila Institute of Post-Graduate Studies and Research in Sanskrit Learning.

Velez de Cea, Abraham. 2004. "The Criteria of Goodness in the Pāli Nikāyas and the Nature of Buddhist Ethics." *Journal of Buddhist Ethics* 11: 122–142.

Vidyabhusana, Satis Chandra. 1971. *A History of Indian Logic*. Delhi: Motilal Banarsidass.

Vose, Kevin. 2009. *Resurrecting Candrakīrti: Disputes in the Tibetan Creation of Prāsaṅgika*. Somerville, MA: Wisdom.

Vose, Kevin. 2010. "Authority in Early Prāsaṅgika Madhyamaka." *Journal of Indian Philosophy* 38: 553–582.

Waldo, Ives. 1975. "Nāgārjuna and Analytic Philosophy." *Philosophy East and West* 25, no. 3 (July): 281–290.

Waldo, Ives. 1978. "Nāgārjuna and Analytic Philosophy, II." *Philosophy East and West* 28, no. 3 (July): 287–298.

Wallace, Vesna A., and B. Alan Wallace, trans. 1997. *A Guide to the Bodhisattva Way of Life by Śāntideva*. Ithaca, NY: Snow Lion.

Walser, Joseph. 2005. *Nāgārjuna in Context: Mahāyāna Buddhism and Early Indian Culture*. New York: Columbia University Press.

Walser, Joseph. 2018. *Genealogies of Mahāyāna Buddhism: Emptiness, Power and the Question of Origin*. London: Routledge.

Walshe, Maurice, trans. 1995. *Dīgha Nikāya: The Long Discourses of the Buddha*. Boston: Wisdom.

Wan Jinchuan 萬金川. 1998a. 中觀思想講錄. 嘉義：香光書鄉.

Wan Jinchuan 萬金川. 1998b. "由《中觀論頌 • "prapañca"》的解讀的三義." 萬金川. 詞義之爭與義理之辨. 台北：正觀: 25–91.

Wang Kexi 王克喜 and Zheng Liqun 郑立群. 2012. 佛教逻辑发展简史. 北京: 中央编译出版社.

Ward, Keith. 1971. "Kant's Teleological Ethics." *The Philosophical Quarterly* 21, no. 85 (October): 337–351.

Wayman, Alex. 1977. "Who Understand the Four Alternatives of the Buddhist Texts?" *Philosophy East and West* 27, no. 1 (January): 3–21.

Wayman, Alex. 1999. *A Millennium of Buddhist Logic*. Delhi: Motilal Banarsidass.

Westerhoff, Jan. 2006. "Nāgārjuna's *Catuṣkoṭi*." *Journal of Indian Philosophy* 34, no. 4: 367–395.

Westerhoff, Jan. 2009. *Nāgārjuna's Madhyamaka: A Philosophical Introduction*. Oxford: Oxford University Press.

Westerhoff, Jan. 2010. *Nāgārjuna's Vigrahavyāvartanī: The Dispeller of Disputes*. Oxford: Oxford University Press.

Westerhoff, Jan. 2015. *The New Madhyamaka*. https://podcasts.ox.ac.uk/series/new-madhyamaka. Last accessed April 5, 2018.

Westerhoff, Jan. 2016a. "On the Nihilist Interpretation of Madhayamaka." *Journal of Indian Philosophy* 44, no. 2 (April): 337–376.

Westerhoff, Jan. 2016b. "The Connection Between Ontology and Ethics in Madhyamaka Thought." In Cowherds, *Moonpaths: Ethics and Emptiness*, 203–220. New York: Oxford University Press.

Westerhoff, Jan. 2017a. *The Non-Existence of the Real World. Extended Synopsis*. Presented at the Theoretical Philosophy Work in Progress Seminar, University of Oxford, October 17.

Westerhoff, Jan. 2017b. "Nāgārjuna on Emptiness: A Comprehensive Critique of Foundationalism." In *The Oxford Handbook of Indian Philosophy*, edited by Jonardon Ganeri, 93–109. Oxford: Oxford University Press.

Westerhoff, Jan. 2017c. "Buddhism without Reincarnation? Examining the Prospects of a "Naturalized" Buddhism." In *A Mirror Is for Reflection: Understanding Buddhist Ethics*, edited by Jake H. Davis, 146–165. New York: Oxford University Press.

Westerhoff, Jan. 2018a. *The Golden Age of Buddhist Philosophy*. Oxford: Oxford University Press.

Westerhoff, Jan. 2018b. *Crushing the Categories (Vaidalyaprakaraṇa) by Nāgārjuna*. Somerville, MA: Wisdom Publications and New York: American Institute of Buddhist Studies, in association with the Columbia University Center for Buddhist Studies and Tibet House US.

Westerhoff, Jan. 2020. "Nāgārjuna." In *The Stanford Encyclopedia of Philosophy*, edited by Edward N. Zalta. https://plato.stanford.edu/entries/nagarjuna/. Last accessed January 15, 2021.

Whitehead, Alfred North. 1978. *Process and Reality: An Essay in Cosmology*. Corrected edition edited by David Ray Griffin and Donald W. Sherburne. New York: Free Press.

Williams, Bernard. 1993. "The Makropulos Case: Reflections on the Tedium of Immortality." In *The Metaphysics of Death*, edited by John Martin Fischer, 71–92. Stanford, CA: Stanford University Press.

Williams, Janet P. 2000. *Denying Divinity: Apophasis in the Patristic Christian and Soto Zen Buddhist Traditions*. Oxford: Oxford University Press.

Williams, Paul. 1980. "Some Aspects of Language and Construction in the Madhyamaka." *Journal of Indian Philosophy* 8, no. 1 (March): 1–45.

Williams, Paul. 1995. "General Introduction." In *Śāntideva: The Bodhicaryāvatāra*, translated by Kate Crosby and Andrew Skilton, vii–xxvi. Oxford: Oxford University Press.

Williams, Paul. 1998. *Altruism and Reality: Studies in the Philosophy of the Bodhicaryāvatāra*. Richmond, VA: Curzon Press.

Williams, Paul, ed. 2005. *Buddhism: Critical Concepts in Religious Studies. Volume III: The Origins and Nature of Mahāyāna Buddhism; Some Mahāyāna Religious Topics*. London: Routledge.

Williams, Paul. 2009. *Mahāyāna Buddhism: The Doctrinal Foundations*. 2nd ed. London: Routledge.

Williams, Paul, with Anthony Tribe. 2000. *Buddhist Thought: A Complete Introduction to the Indian Tradition*. London: Routledge.

Wong, David. 2006. "The Meaning of Detachment in Daoism, Buddhism, and Stoicism." *Dao: A Journal of Comparative Philosophy* 5, no. 2: 207–219.

Wood, Thomas E. 1994. *Nāgārjunian Disputations: A Philosophical Journey through an Indian Looking-Glass*. Honolulu: University of Hawai'i Press.

Wu Rujun 吳汝鈞. 1992. "印度中觀學的四句邏輯." 中華佛學學報第五期, 第五期. 臺北：中華佛學研究所發行.

Wu Rujun 吳汝鈞. 1997. 龍樹中論的哲學解讀. 臺北: 臺灣商務印書館.

Xing, Guang. 2005. *The Concept of the Buddha: Its Evolution from Early Buddhism to the Trikāya Theory*. London: Routledge.

Xingyun 星雲. 1997. 中論. 高雄：佛光.

Yadav, Bibhuti S. 1977. "Negation, Nirvāṇa and Nonsense." *Journal of the American Academy of Religion* 45, no. 4 (December): 451–471.

Yancy, George. 2007. "Introduction: No Philosophical Oracle Voices." In *Philosophy in Multiple Voices*, edited by George Yancy, 1–19. Lanham, MD: Rowman & Littlefield.

Ye, Shaoyong 叶少勇. 2011. 中论颂: 梵藏汉合校 · 导读 · 译注. 上海: 中西书局.

Ye, Shaoyong. 2019. "From Scepticism to Nihilism: A Nihilistic Interpretation of Nāgārjuna's Refutations." *Journal of Indian Philosophy* 47: 749–777.

Yijing 義淨, trans. (N.d.) (T 1674) 龍樹菩薩勸誡王頌. *Taishō* 32: 1674.

Yinshun 印順. 1998a. 以佛法研究佛法. 竹北: 正聞.

Yinshun 印順. 1998b. 我之宗教觀. 竹北: 正聞.

Yinshun 印順. (1952) 2000. 中觀論頌講記. 竹北: 正聞.

Yinshun 印順. (1971) 2003. 學佛三要. 竹北: 正聞.

Yinshun 印順. (1950) 2009. 中觀今論. 竹北: 正聞.

Yinshun 印順. (1985) 2010. 空之探究. 竹北: 正聞.

Yinshun 印順. 2017. *An Investigation into Emptiness: Parts One & Two* (空之探究). Translated by Huifeng (Shi). Towaco, NJ: Noble Path.

Yonezawa, Yoshiyasu. 2008. "*Vigrahavyāvartanī* Sanskrit Transliteration and Tibetan Translation." *Naritasan Bukkyo Kenkyujo kiyo* 31: 209–332.

Young, Stuart H. 2015. *Conceiving the Indian Buddhist Patriarchs in China*. Honolulu: University of Hawai'i Press.

Yü, Chün-fang. 2001. *Kuan-yin: The Chinese Transformation of Avalokiteśvara*. New York: Columbia University Press.

Zalta, Edward N. 2020. "Gottlob Frege." In *The Stanford Encyclopedia of Philosophy*, edited by Edward N. Zalta. https://plato.stanford.edu/archives/fall2020/entries/frege/. Last accessed December 31, 2020.

Ziporyn, Brook. 2015. "What Does the Law of Non-Contradiction Tell Us, If Anything? Paradox, Parameterization, and Truth in Tiantai Buddhism." In *The Philosophical Challenge from China*, edited by Brian Bruya, 253–278. Cambridge, MA: MIT Press.

Ziporyn, Brook. 2019a. "Philosophy, Quo Vadis? Buddhism and the Academic Study of Philosophy." In *APA Newsletter on Asian and Asian-American Philosophers and Philosophies* 19, no. 1, Fall (*Buddhist Philosophy Today: Theories and Forms*, guest edited special issue), edited by Rafal K. Stepien: 3–8.

Ziporyn, Brook. 2019b. "Seng Zhao's "Prajñā Is Without Knowledge": Collapsing the Two Truths from Critique to Affirmation." *Journal of Indian Philosophy* 47, no. 4 (September): 831–849.

Index

For the benefit of digital users, indexed terms that span two pages (e.g., 52–53) may, on occasion, appear on only one of those pages.

AAR. *See* American Academy of Religion
Abé, Ryūichi, 14, 310n.63
abelief, 9, 145–46, 147–48, 238–39, 241–42, 246–47, 253–54, 255–56. See also *dṛṣṭi*
Abhidharma, 42, 59–60, 129–30, 145–46, 159, 203–4, 295n.50, 308n.50, 314–16n.1, 328–29n.77, 337n.6
abhyupagama (tenet/position), 132, 309n.58, 337n.10
Abu Sway, Mustafa, 276–77n.26
action. See *karma*
Adam, M. T. 352n.115
aggregate. See *skandha*
agnosia, 237, 238–39, 241–42
Alcoff, Linda Martin, 76–77
aletheia, 133–34, 137, 304n.18. *See also* dialetheia; tetrāletheia
American Academy of Religion, 27–29, 266n.66, 266–67nn.67–68
Ames, William L. 121, 295n.46, 298n.88, 303n.10, 314–16n.1
anachorism, 70–71, 284n.59, 288n.76
anātman, 2–3, 144, 146, 148–49, 184, 244–45, 250, 253, 254–56, 291n.15, 308n.55, 319n.28, 325n.65, 352n.112
anontology, 6–7, 127, 139–41, 143–44, 146–51, 154–55, 184, 244, 307n.44, 307n.46
antagrahadṛṣṭi (extreme view), 22–23, 136, 139–40, 146, 153–54, 162, 190–91, 283n.56. See also *dṛṣṭi*
apathy, 248–49, 353n.121
apophasis, 42, 229–30, 237–43, 253–55, 306n.41, 313n.78, 328–29n.77, 345n.62, 347n.82, 348–49n.87, 349n.88, 349n.90–349–50nn.95–97
Aquinas, Thomas, 70, 265n.59, 281–82n.48
archē, 180–82, 241, 339n.23
Aristotle, 35, 49–50, 128–29, 133–34, 138, 273n.4, 306n.37, 336n.119
Arnold, Dan, 10, 59–60, 174–76, 185–95, 259n.17, 277n.27, 304n.19, 304–5n.24, 308n.55, 317n.9, 322n.54, 328–29n.77, 330n.83, 331–32n.93, 333n.100, 333–34n.102, 335–36n.116
arūpa-dhātu (formless world). See *rūpa*
Āryadeva, 38, 87, 119, 121–22
āssertion, 138, 147–48. *See also* utterance
athesism, 194–200. See also *dṛṣṭi*; *pakṣa*; *pratijñā*; thesism
atman, 144, 148–49, 183, 244–45, 325n.65
attachment, 1–2, 18, 21–22, 65–66, 105, 119, 120, 141, 156–57, 162–63, 169–70, 171, 172, 173, 179–84, 195, 197–98, 239–40, 242, 244–45, 246–47, 255–56, 258n.9, 282–83n.53, 297n.74, 318–19n.24, 324–25n.64, 328–29n.77, 329–30n.82, 333n.97, 335n.113, 337n.10, 350–51n.103, 353n.121, 353n.126. See also *dṛṣṭi*
Augustine, 24–25, 70, 265n.59
Avalokiteśvara, 249–50, 353n.122, 353n.123
Avataṃsaka. *See* Huayan
avyākṛtavastu (unexplicated points), 121–22, 154–55, 165, 225, 236, 312–13n.74. *See also* silence

Bagger, Matthew, 288n.75, 306n.37
Baker, Lynne Rudder, 186, 330n.83
Balcerowicz, Piotr, 270n.92, 281n.43, 296n.59

being. See *parabhāva*; *svabhāva*; *śūnyatā*
belief. See *dṛṣṭi*
Berger, Douglas L. 77, 250–52, 280n.40, 282n.50, 354n.129
Bernasconi, Robert, 77
Betty, L. Stafford, 262–63n.46, 288n.75, 288n.78, 331–32n.93
Bhattacharya, Kamaleswar, 45, 50–51, 288n.75, 323–24n.61, 333–34n.102
bhāva. See *svabhāva*
Bhāvaviveka, 39–40, 98–99, 104, 120–21, 198, 270n.92, 293n.31, 295n.46, 295n.47, 298n.87, 298–99n.89, 328–29n.77, 335n.115, 338n.16
Bhāviveka. *See* Bhāvaviveka
Bingenheimer, Marcus, 299n.91
Bocking, Brian, 271–72n.100, 290n.8, 300n.96, 340–41n.30
Bodhi (Bhikku), 1–3, 184, 225–26, 232–33, 252, 257n.1, 301n.4, 335n.113, 343n.46, 346n.73, 346n.74
Boghossian, Paul, 276–77n.26
Bronkhorst, Johannes, 281n.42
Buddha, 1–4, 7, 10, 12–13, 40–42, 65–66, 94, 98–99, 100, 101, 103, 110, 116, 117, 118, 121–22, 123, 125, 126–27, 129–31, 139–40, 141, 154–55, 156, 159, 164, 165, 166–67, 171, 183–84, 187, 189, 196, 197–98, 203–4, 207, 215–19, 221–31, 232–33, 234–35, 238–39, 241–42, 244–45, 246, 248–50, 251, 252, 254–55, 256, 257n.1, 257n.4, 258n.9, 260n.25, 260n.27, 267n.77, 270n.94, 270n.95, 272n.2, 274n.7, 283–84n.57, 292n.28, 295n.51, 298n.87, 301n.4, 302n.6, 305n.26, 306n.35, 311–12n.73, 316n.4, 324–25n.64, 328–29n.77, 331n.92, 332n.95, 339n.25, 340n.27, 340n.28, 342n.38, 343n.44, 343n.46, 344n.52, 344n.54, 344–45n.59, 347n.81, 347–48nn.83–86, 349n.95, 351n.106, 351n.108, 351–52n.111, 352n.115, 353–54n.127, 355n.134. *See also* Tathāgata
Buddhaghosa, 259n.15
Buddhapālita, 98–99, 120
Buddhate, 23–27, 29–30, 38–39, 263–64n.54, 264n.56, 269n.89
Bugault, Guy, 49–50, 52, 55, 58, 78–79, 129, 273n.4, 283n.56, 303n.10, 329n.80
Burley, Mikel, 267n.73
Burton, David, 20–21, 51–52, 63–64, 289n.2, 311n.70
Buswell Jr., Robert E. 270n.93, 314–16n.1

Cabezón, José Ignacio, 43, 135, 266–67n.68, 271n.99, 279–80n.39, 280n.40, 282n.49, 293–94n.41, 314–16n.1
Cadge, Wendy, 29, 30, 267n.69
Candrakīrti, 10, 38, 39–40, 45–46, 49–50, 66, 82, 98–100, 117, 120–21, 155, 178–79, 186, 188, 191–92, 194, 196–98, 234, 235–36, 261n.35, 288n.81, 295n.47, 297n.76, 297n.79, 298n.87, 298–99n.89, 299n.90, 304–5n.24, 305n.31, 310n.67, 311n.70, 314–16n.1, 316n.4, 318n.19, 322n.55, 328–29n.77, 331–32n.93, 333n.97, 334n.104, 335n.111, 335n.115, 335–36n.116, 338n.16, 340n.27, 346n.70, 347n.80, 348n.85, 348n.86
care. See *karuṇā*
Carpenter, Amber D. 337n.4, 338n.11
Carr, Karen L. 311n.72
Castro-Gómez, Santiago, 275n.9
catuṣkoṭi, 6–7, 17, 18, 21–22, 48–49, 50–51, 52–55, 60, 65–67, 69, 70–71, 79–81, 84, 87–93, 156, 165, 173, 175–76, 199–200, 202, 221, 225, 236–38, 240–41, 272n.1, 273n.4, 283n.56, 319n.28, 322n.51, 322n.56, 349n.94
  as anontological utterance, 137–41
  Buddhist, 115–25
  Buddhological, 111–15
  dilemma of, 126–30
  exhaustive, 130–33
  logical, 93–111
  mereological interpretation, 95–98
  modal interpretation, 98–106
  and no-teaching, 141–51
  qualitative interpretation, 107–11
  and silencing nothing, 151–55
  as Tathāgata, 135–37
  as tetrāletheia, 133–35

ceive. *See* ception
ception, 213, 215–16, 231–35, 250, 338n.12
cetanā (intention), 216–21, 230, 235–36, 242–43, 255–56–339–41nn.26–31, 344n.52, 346n.68
Chakrabarty, Dipesh, 30
Chan, 129–30, 143, 154–55, 186, 258n.9, 308n.51, 330n.87, 330–31n.89, 335n.114, 349n.93, 349–50n.96, 355n.134
Chengguang 澄觀, 129–30
Chen Xueren 陳學仁, 316n.4
Chi, Richard S. Y. 112–13
Chisholm, Roderick, 327–28n.75
Chödrön, Gelongma Karma Migme, 306n.35, 314–16n.1
Christianate, 22–30, 31–32, 36–37, 38–39, 70, 85–86, 263n.53, 264n.56
Christianity. *See* Christianate
Clayton, Barbra R. 339n.22
Clayton, John Powell, 269nn.90–91
clinging. *See* attachment
Clouser, Roy A. 267n.75
Colas, Gérard, 277n.30
Cole, Alan, 10, 11–12
Collins, Steven, 226–27, 240–41, 252, 259n.22, 260n.24, 304n.20, 312–13n.74, 313n.79, 318–19n.24, 324–25n.64, 330n.84, 335n.113, 343n.49, 343–44nn.50–51, 344n.53, 351n.104, 352n.119, 354n.130, 354n.131
comegoing, 150–51, 184, 197–98, 242–43, 256. *See also* Tathāgata
common sense, 49–51, 60–61, 78–79, 149–50, 184–85, 186–87, 198, 272–73n.3, 273–74n.5, 288n.79, 321–22n.50, 329n.80. *See also* logic; laws of thought
comparative philosophy. *See* cross-cultural philosophy
compassion. See *karuṇā*
conceptualization. See *prapañca*
confluence philosophy. *See* cross-cultural philosophy
consequentialism, 154, 211, 212–13, 223–24, 339n.22, 342n.40
contradiction. *See* paradox
conventional truth. See *saṃvṛti-satya*
Cooper, David E. 339n.22
correlative designation. See *prajñaptir upādāya*
Coseru, Christian, 84, 85–86, 314–16n.1, 355n.134
Coward, Harold, 14, 260n.25
Cowherds, 54, 61–62, 78–79, 279n.37, 352–53n.120
Crosby, Kate, 337n.5
cross-cultural philosophy, 4–6, 8, 18–19, 35, 39–40, 48–49, 54, 56–86, 261n.31, 264n.56, 276–77n.26, 280n.40, 282n.50–93–111, 114, 225, 285–88nn.68–74, 297n.66, 303n.15. *See also* Western philosophy

D'Amato, Mario, 54, 56, 327–28n.75
Dānapāla 施護, 45–46
Dancy, Jonathan, 355n.134
Dargyay, Geshe Lobsang, 293–94n.41
darśana, 36–37, 132, 196–97, 319n.30, 323–24n.61, 337n.10
Davis, Bret W. 77, 286n.71
Deegalle, Mahinda, 283–84n.57
De George, Richard T. 338n.11
Deguchi, Yasuo, 288n.75
De La Vallée Poussin, Louis, 45, 155, 300n.100, 311n.70
De Jong, Jan Willem, 314–16n.1
Della Santina, Peter, 46–47, 337n.4
deontology, 209, 212–13, 223–24, 342n.40, 355n.134
dependent co-arising. See *pratītya-samutpāda*
dependent co-origination. See *pratītya-samutpāda*
Descartes, René, 24, 49–50, 55–56, 70, 227–28, 265n.59, 281–82n.48
descriptive reduction, 32–33, 63, 70–72, 268n.79
Dharmakīrti, 35, 70, 186, 220, 225, 235–36, 281–82n.48, 328–29n.77, 341n.34, 342n.38, 346–47n.77, 347n.80
dialetheia, 6–7, 80–81, 84, 127, 133–34, 272–73n.3, 276n.17, 303n.13, 304n.17, 304n.19. *See also* aletheia; tetrāletheia

Dietz, S. 46–47
Dōgen 道元, 129–30
Donahue, Amy, 78–79, 279n.37, 286n.70
doxastic basicality, 52, 275n.11. *See also* epistemic basicality
Dragonetti, Carmen, 45–46, 117–156–57, 171, 297–98nn.77–82–320–21nn.41–49, 334–35n.110
Drewes, David, 13
Dreyfus, Georges B. J. 298–99n.89, 314–16n.1, 317n.10
Dreyfus, Hubert L. 26
Droit, Roger-Pol, 31, 267n.77, 310n.67
dṛṣṭi (view), 1, 2–3, 7–9, 16, 17–22, 42, 48–49, 55, 66–67, 91–92, 101, 102–4, 119, 121–22, 123–25, 127–28, 131–32, 141, 142, 144–51, 153–55, 156–73, 174–200, 201–3, 204–5, 209, 210–12, 216, 218, 219–20, 227–28, 229, 230–31, 233–34, 236, 237–43, 244, 246–47, 250–56, 257n.1, 260n.27, 261n.32, 262n.43, 262n.45, 263n.50, 288n.79, 293n.34, 298n.82, 299n.90, 302n.6, 307n.44, 309n.61, 309n.62, 310n.66, 312–13n.74, 313–14n.80, 316n.3, 317n.13, 317–18n.14, 318–19n.24, 319n.30, 320–21n.43, 321n.45, 321n.48, 321–22n.50, 322n.52, 323n.60, 323–24n.61, 324–25n.64, 325n.66, 326n.68, 327n.74, 327–28n.75, 328–29n.77, 329–30n.82, 330n.84, 330n.86, 330–31n.89, 331n.90, 331n.92, 332n.95, 333n.97, 334n.106, 335n.113, 337n.10, 339n.23, 341n.34, 346n.68, 346n.69, 350n.98, 350–51n.103, 351n.106, 351n.107, 353n.126, 354n.131. See also *antagrahadṛṣṭi*; *prapañca*; *vikalpa*
Duckworth, Douglas, 104–5, 293n.40
Duerlinger, James, 335n.111
duḥkha (suffering), 1–4, 7–9, 14, 20, 21, 65, 69, 89, 94–95, 115–17, 120, 131–32, 141, 145–46, 153–54, 161–63, 166, 183–84, 189–90, 197–98, 199–200, 201–2, 215–16, 218–19, 226, 229, 235–36, 242–43, 244–45, 246–47, 248–50, 255–56, 298n.87, 299n.90, 309n.62, 311–12n.73, 324–25n.64, 333n.97, 343n.49, 347n.79, 351–52n.111, 352–53n.120
Dunne, John D. 46, 220–21, 234, 284n.64, 311n.71
Dwivedi, R. C. 281n.47

Eckel, Malcolm David, 270n.92, 314–16n.1, 344n.55
Edgerton, Franklin, 321n.48
eirenics, 20, 202–3, 209–10, 212–14, 243, 244–48, 250, 255–56, 309n.62, 346n.69. *See also* peace
Eliade, Mircea, 268n.80
Eliot, T. S. 352n.113
Eltschinger, Vincent, 337n.6
emptiness. See *śūnyatā*
epistemic basicality, 52, 74–75, 275n.11. *See also* doxastic basicality
epistemic injustice, 74–75, 76–77. *See also* hermeneutical injustice
Erb, Felix, 46
essence. See *svabhāva*
Evans, Robert D. 281n.43
explanatory reduction, 32–33, 63, 71–72, 268n.79

Faure, Bernard, 24–25, 48, 61–62, 259n.16, 283n.55, 301n.105, 335n.114
Fazang 法藏, 129–30
Fernández-Armesto, Felipe, 353–54n.127
Ferraro, Giuseppe, 304–5n.24, 317n.8
Finnigan, Bronwyn, 221–27, 234, 339n.22–226, 342–43nn.40–43–343nn.47–48, 344n.52, 347n.80, 347–48n.84
five aggregates. See *skandha*; *rūpa*; *saṃjñā*; *saṃskāra*; *vijñāna*
Flanagan, Owen, 73–77, 78–79, 230, 284nn.60–63, 288n.74, 338n.11, 343n.45
Forman, Robert K. C. 211–12, 339n.19
Franco, Eli, 341n.34
Franke, William, 348–49n.87
Freiberger, Oliver, 271n.99, 279n.38
Fricker, Miranda, 76–77, 259n.15, 285n.68
Fugate, Courtney, 264n.57
Fuller, Paul, 3, 186, 239–40, 243, 318–19n.24, 329–30n.82, 330nn.85–86,

350n.99, 350n.101, 351n.109, 354n.130
fusion philosophy. *See* cross-cultural philosophy

Gadamer, Hans-Georg, 60–61, 280n.40
Ganeri, Jonardon, 77–78, 121–22, 251, 267n.76, 276–77n.26, 281n.43, 304n.19, 317n.10, 333n.96
Garfield, Jay L. 10, 16, 37, 52–53, 55–58, 60–63, 66–68, 69–70, 72, 78–79, 80–86, 87–88, 91–92, 101–6, 111, 114, 128–30, 133, 175–76, 177–79, 180–82, 184–85, 194, 195–98, 199, 259n.17, 261n.34, 262n.41, 268n.82, 276n.23, 276n.25, 276–77n.26, 277n.30, 278n.33, 278–79n.36, 281n.45, 281n.46, 281–82n.48, 282–83n.53, 284n.58, 285–86n.69, 288n.75, 288n.76, 288n.80, 288n.82, 288n.84, 293n.36, 293–94n.41, 294n.45, 295n.47, 295n.53, 298n.86, 303n.10, 303n.15, 303–4n.16, 304n.20, 304–5n.24, 306n.36, 307n.44, 310n.65, 313n.77, 314–16n.1, 316n.2, 317n.9, 317n.13, 319n.30, 322n.56, 323n.60, 324n.62–208–9, 213–14, 219, 224–25, 227–28, 230, 233–34, 242, 325–26nn.66–68, 330–31n.89, 334n.103, 334–35n.110, 335n.111, 335n.115, 336n.120, 339n.23, 339n.25, 340n.27, 341n.31, 342n.39–343nn.43–44, 343n.47, 344n.52, 344n.58, 345n.65, 351n.108, 352–53n.120
Gautama Prajñāruci 瞿曇般若流支, 45
Gert, Bernard, 209
Gert, Joshua, 209
Gethin, Rupert, 251
Ghose, Ramendranath, 295n.47
Gokhale, Pradeep P. 281n.43
Gold, Jonathan C. 185, 193, 327n.73, 328–29n.77, 329–30n.82
Gómez, Luis O. 186, 271n.99, 277n.28, 280–81n.41, 288n.83, 330n.85
Goodman, Charles, 210–11, 216, 250, 339n.22, 352n.114, 352–53n.120, 355n.134
Gorampa Sonam Senge (Go rams pa bSod nams Seng ge), 38, 104–5, 186, 293–94n.41, 322n.55, 338n.16
Goshima, Kiyotaka, 271–72n.100
Graham, A. C. 273–74n.5
Green, Ronald S. 115, 297n.67
Griffiths, Paul J. 35–36, 235–36, 264n.56, 268n.83, 348n.85
Guanding 灌頂, 130, 147–48, 301–2n.5
Guanyin. *See* Avalokiteśvara
Gunaratne, R. D. 50, 78–79, 94–95, 112–13, 124, 289n.7, 295n.49
*Guṇavarman 求那跋摩, 46–47
Gyatso, Janet, 259–60n.23

Hadot, Pierre, 13–14, 33
Hahn, Michael, 46, 337nn.6–7
Hallisey, Charles, 23–24
Hạnh, Thích Nhất, 63–64, 254–55
Hansen, Chad, 343n.43
Harris, Stephen, 250
Harrison, Paul, 59–60, 270–71n.96
Harvey, Peter, 2, 244–45, 246, 252, 257n.3, 339n.22, 339–40n.26–352nn.113–15
Hayes, Richard, 9, 50–51, 78–79, 186, 232–33, 258n.10, 274nn.6–8, 293n.38, 301n.4, 303n.10, 312–13n.74, 314–16n.1, 330n.85
Hegel, G. W. F. 24, 49–50, 100, 152–53, 303n.12, 308n.49, 310n.65, 310–11n.68
Heidegger, Martin, 24–25, 26–27, 35–36, 49–50, 134–35, 137–38, 149, 283n.55, 304n.19, 306–7n.43
Heim, Maria, 259n.15
hermeneutical injustice, 8, 76–77, 259n.15. *See also* epistemic injustice
Hershock, Peter D. 254–56, 355n.134
Hick, John, 354–55n.133
Ho, Chien-hsing, 307n.44, 314–16n.1
Hodgson, Marshall G. S, 23–24, 29–30, 265n.62, 267n.71, 269n.89
Hofweber, Thomas, 306–7n.43
Holder, John J. 346n.73
holding. *See* attachment
Hopkins, Jeffrey, 46, 311n.71, 336n.3, 337n.6
Huayan, 129–30, 355n.135

Hubbard, Jamie, 271n.99
Humphries, Jeff, 10
Huntington, Jr., C. W. 8–10, 11–12, 60–61, 82–83, 267n.77, 271n.99, 276n.25–91–92, 107, 120, 122, 138–39, 178–79, 195–97, 233–34, 254, 277–78nn.30–31, 287–88n.73, 288n.79, 289n.7, 292n.26, 294n.45, 298n.87, 298–99n.89, 299n.90, 300n.101, 301n.105, 304–5n.24, 309n.57, 309n.60, 310n.67, 314–16n.1, 320–21n.43, 321n.44, 321–22n.50, 328–29n.77, 333n.96, 333n.97, 335–36n.116, 346n.75, 348–49n.87, 349n.88
hypostatization. See *prapañca*

improvisational virtuosity, 355n.134
Inada, Kenneth K. 314–16n.1
ineffability, 84, 114, 211–12, 229, 288n.75, 297n.67, 307n.46, 313n.79, 313–14n.80, 318n.19
inexistence, 143–44, 326n.72
intention. See *cetanā*
intrinsic nature. See *svabhāva*
Islamicate, 23–27, 29–30, 265n.62
Ives, Christopher, 331n.91

Jackson, Frank, 306–7n.43
Jackson, Roger, 279n.38
Jakubczak, Krzysztof, 16, 179–80, 257n.5, 261n.33, 269n.88, 288n.75, 293n.31, 303n.10, 310n.65, 310n.67, 311n.72, 312–13n.74, 314–16n.1, 317n.10, 323–24n.61, 324–25n.64, 327n.74, 332n.95, 347n.81, 349n.90, 352–53n.120, 354n.130
James, Simon P. 339n.22
James, William, 288n.75
Jampa Tegchok (Khensur), 46, 311n.71, 336n.3, 337n.6
Jayatilleke, K. N. 50–51, 94–96, 98, 108, 111, 289n.2, 291n.14, 292n.27
Jizang 吉藏, 38, 63–64, 129–30, 261n.32, 290nn.8–9
Johnson, Mark, 14, 260n.27
Jolley, Nicholas, 265n.59
Jones, Richard Hubert, 52–53, 55, 112–13, 276n.17, 276n.21, 291n.20, 302n.6

Kajiyama, Yūichi 梶山雄一, 289n.3, 298n.88
kalpanā (conceptual construction), 134, 154–55, 183–84, 337n.10
Kalupahana, David J. 17, 261n.36, 309n.62, 314–16n.1, 351–52n.111
Kamalaśīla, 320–21n.43, 336n.121, 338n.16, 341n.34, 347n.78
Kant, Immanuel, 15–16, 21, 24, 31, 35, 49–50, 55–56, 209, 264n.57, 276n.22, 308n.49
Kantor, Hans-Rudolf, 263n.50, 267n.76, 307n.44, 311–12n.73, 314–16n.1, 322–23n.57, 350n.102
Kapstein, Matthew T. 280–81n.41, 281n.45, 286–87n.72, 304n.19
karma (action), 7–8, 20, 61, 126–27, 131, 163, 197, 201, 215–21, 235–36, 242–47, 253, 254–56, 327–28n.75, 334–35n.110–340–41nn.27–30, 346n.68, 352n.113, 352n.115, 352–53n.120, 355n.134
karuṇā (care), 7–8, 201, 203–4, 211, 230–31, 248–50, 254–56, 345n.66, 346n.67, 352–53n.120, 353n.124
Karunaratna, W. S. 339–40n.26
Kassor, Constance, 293–94n.41
Katsura, Shōryū, 12, 15–16, 45, 53, 67–68, 94–95, 97–98, 107–11, 159, 161, 163, 258n.10, 262n.43, 262n.44, 262–63n.46, 291n.14, 293n.35, 295n.49, 295n.50, 295n.54, 302n.6, 303n.10, 305n.28, 307n.44, 310n.65, 314–16n.1, 316n.4, 317n.8, 317–18n.14, 319n.28, 328n.76, 344n.54, 345n.60, 345n.62
Katz, Steven T. 211–12, 213, 288n.75, 339nn.19–21
Keller, Catherine, 351n.105
Kellner, Birgit, 257n.6, 338n.17
Keown, Damien, 339n.22, 339–40n.26
Kidd, Ian James, 74–75
Kitagawa, Joseph, 260n.25
Komarovski, Yaroslav, 339n.21

Komito, David Ross, 46, 118–173, 298nn.80–82–321nn.45–49, 334–35n.110
Kragh, Ulrich Timme, 217, 340n.27, 340–41n.30
Krstić, Tijana, 23–24
Kuhn, Thomas S. 75, 284n.64
Kumar, Bimalendra, 45–46
Kumārajīva 鳩摩羅什, 45, 95–96, 271–72n.100, 291n.21, 292n.29, 300n.95, 311–12n.73, 340–41n.30

Lakoff, George, 14, 260n.27
Lamotte, Étienne, 314–16n.1
laws of thought, 50, 78–79
Leibniz, Gottfried Wilhelm, 49–50, 55–56, 70, 265n.59, 281–82n.48
Levinas, Emmanuel, 264–65n.58
Levitt, Peggy, 29, 30, 267n.69
Lévy-Bruhl, Lucien, 273–74n.5
Lin Tonqi, 286n.70
Lincoln, Bruce, 27–28, 266n.66
Lindtner, Christian, 16–17, 40, 45–46, 117, 259n.17, 295n.47–150–51, 171, 172, 187, 297–98nn.77–82, 319n.28–203, 320–21nn.41–49, 334–35n.110, 336n.3
Linji Yixuan 臨濟義玄, 258n.9
Li Runsheng 利潤生, 99–100, 122–23, 292nn.29–30
Li Xuezhu 李学竹, 45–46, 171–320–21nn.41–44
Li Zhifu 李志夫, 281n.43
Loewen, Nathan R. B. 267n.73
logic, 6–7, 10, 16, 21, 39–40, 42, 49–56, 60–61, 63–66, 75, 79–83, 84–85, 86, 261n.33, 263n.49, 270n.92, 272–73n.3, 273–74nn.5–7, 275n.13–87–89, 90, 91–92, 93–116, 120–21, 123, 124–25, 127–29, 130–31, 132–34, 138–39, 142, 146–49, 156, 179–80, 191–92, 211, 221, 237–38, 244, 246–47, 276nn.17–18, 276n.20, 276n.22, 281n.43, 281n.44, 283n.55, 285n.67, 288n.75, 288n.81, 289n.3, 289n.5, 289n.6, 290n.10, 291n.20, 294n.45, 295n.48, 296n.60, 296n.63, 296n.64, 300n.100, 301n.4, 302n.6, 303–4n.16, 306n.39, 322n.56, 323–24n.61, 328–29n.77, 336n.118, 341n.35, 348–49n.87. *See also* common sense; laws of thought; paralogic
Loizzo, Joseph John, 45–46, 117–171, 297nn.76–79, 320–21nn.41–44
Lopez, Jr., Donald S. 13, 31, 259n.15, 270n.93, 270n.95, 314–16n.1
Loy, David, 288n.75, 288n.78
Lü Daji 吕大吉, 268n.80

MacDonald, Anne, 11–12, 46, 260–61n.29, 314–16n.1, 316n.4, 335–36n.116, 345n.62
MacFarlane, John, 55–56, 276n.22
Madhyamaka. *See* Svātantrika Madhyamaka; Prāsaṅgika Madhyamaka
Makransky, John, 279n.38
Manju, 16–17, 46, 118–173, 298nn.80–82, 321nn.45–49, 334–35n.110
Marcotte, Roxanne D. 267n.70
Mares, Edwin D. 306n.38
Masuzawa, Tomoko, 28–29, 30–31, 265n.64, 266n.67, 267n.74, 288n.78
Matilal, Bimal Krishna, 281n.43
Mattice, Sarah A. 77
May, Jacques, 314–16n.1
Mazanec, Tom, 302n.6
McCagney, Nancy, 309n.62
McClintock, Sara L. 46, 298–99n.89, 304n.21, 311n.71, 314–16n.1, 320–21n.43, 324–25n.64, 336n.2, 337n.6, 341n.34, 347–48n.84, 350–51n.103
McGrath, Alister E. 39–40, 272–73n.3
McGuire, Robert, 253–54, 309n.59, 354n.132
McLuhan, Marshall, 261n.30
McMahan, David, 12–13
McRae, Emily, 353n.121, 353n.124
McRae, John R. 308n.51
meandering, 149–51, 213–14, 256
meaning event, 237–39, 240–41
Mejor, Marek, 296n.59
Merquior, José, 259n.21
Meyers, Karin L. 216–17, 339–40n.26, 340n.29

Mills, Ethan, 19, 188–89, 237, 238–39, 240–42, 250–51, 254, 262n.45, 262–63n.46, 295n.48, 314–16n.1, 316n.3, 322n.53, 330–31n.89, 332n.94, 349n.89, 350n.100, 351n.107, 351n.109, 353n.126
mithyā-dṛṣṭi (wrong-view). See *dṛṣṭi*
Moeller, Hans-Georg, 279n.37, 282n.50
Morinaga, Soko, 308n.51
Muller, A. Charles, 179–80, 186, 237, 240–41, 257n.1, 327n.74, 330n.87, 330–31n.89, 331n.92, 349n.89
Mun, Chanju, 292n.28
Murray, Michael J. 25–26, 265n.59
Murti, T. R. V. 21, 61, 138–40, 151–52, 184, 263n.51, 290n.10, 302n.6, 306n.39, 312–13n.74, 314–16n.1, 328–29n.77, 329n.78
mysticism, 18–19, 52–53, 55–56, 67, 80–82, 84, 87–88, 211–12, 237–39, 241–42, 273–74n.5, 288n.75, 288n.78, 312–13n.74, 339nn.20–21, 349–50n.96, 354–55n.133

Nagao, Gadjin, 134, 141–42, 146–49, 302n.6, 304n.20, 306n.36, 307n.46, 308n.49, 312–13n.74, 313–14n.80, 319n.28
nāmarūpa (name-and-form). See *rūpa*
Ñāṇamoli (Bhikkhu), 184, 252, 257n.1, 301n.4, 335n.113
Nance, Richard, 11, 259n.19, 275n.12
Narain, Harsha, 139–40, 151–52, 153
Nattier, Jan, 270–71n.96
naturalism, 4–5, 73–77, 225, 284nn.60–63, 343n.45
negation. See *paryudāsa-pratiṣedha*; *prasajya-pratiṣedha*
Neta, Ram, 275n.11
Netland, Harold A. 354–55n.133
Newland, Guy, 304n.20
Nihilism, 31, 51–52, 132, 139–40, 151–54, 160, 190–91, 203, 276n.18, 293n.31, 310n.67, 311n.69, 311n.70, 311n.72, 317n.13, 325n.65, 332n.95, 334–35n.110
niḥsvabhāva. See *svabhāva*
nirvāṇa, 2, 3, 4, 7, 20, 65, 111, 117, 118–19, 120–21, 124–25, 127–28, 136–37, 139–40, 155, 156, 159, 161–62, 165, 173, 182, 184, 194–95, 197, 207, 209, 220–21, 224–30, 235–36, 237–38, 240–41, 243, 245–48, 250–51, 256, 275n.10, 289n.6, 296n.57, 301n.104, 307n.44, 311–12n.73, 313n.79, 316n.4, 316n.6, 322n.52, 326n.69, 326n.71, 331n.90, 334n.109, 336n.120, 338n.14, 341n.35, 341–42n.36, 343n.50, 344n.54, 344–45n.59, 345n.60, 345n.62, 347n.79, 351n.105, 354n.128
nirvikalpa. See *vikalpa*
no-self. See *anātman*
Nongbri, Brent, 31, 265n.63, 267n.75
nonpathic, 248–50, 254
Nussbaum, Martha C. 12, 15–16

Oetke, Claus, 50–51, 78–79, 112, 115–16, 262n.44, 262–63n.46, 273–74n.5, 282n.51, 289n.2, 296n.58, 311n.70, 317n.9, 319n.28, 323–24n.61, 329n.80, 344–45n.59
Ogawa, Hideyo, 313–14n.80, 314–16n.1, 318n.19
oppositionality. See *dṛṣṭi*
other-being. See *parabhāva*
own-being. See *svabhāva*

Padmakara Translation Group, 46–47, 337n.4
pakṣa (thesis), 7, 9, 132, 156, 182, 190–91, 196–97, 309n.58, 337n.10, 346n.68. See also *pratijñā*
Pandeya, Ram Chandra, 16–17, 46, 118–173, 298nn.80–82–321nn.45–49, 334–35n.110
Panikkar, Raimundo, 53–54, 80–82, 107–11, 225, 226, 288n.76, 295n.51, 343n.46
parabhāva, 105–6, 132, 190, 303n.10, 308n.53, 318n.19
paradox, 19, 31, 49–50, 51–54, 70, 84, 93, 94–96, 99, 101–3, 106, 107–15, 122–23, 124, 128–30, 133, 134–38, 141–42, 148–49, 152–53, 154–55, 163, 174–77, 183, 193–95, 202–3, 211–12, 224–25, 230, 235–36, 238–39, 273–74n.5,

276n.17, 288n.75, 288n.79, 289n.5, 292n.28, 293n.35, 294n.45, 295n.49, 295n.54, 296n.62, 302n.6, 303n.13, 304n.17, 306n.37, 306n.38, 310–11n.68, 322n.51, 322n.52, 322n.56, 322–23n.57, 323–24n.61, 325–26n.67, 347n.79, 348–49n.87, 349n.94, 351n.110
paralogic, 55–56, 127–28, 130, 131, 138–39, 155, 236, 244, 276n.17. *See also* logic
Paramārtha 真諦, 46
paramārtha-satya, 3, 51–52, 103–6, 111, 134–35, 136–37, 138, 147–48, 155, 182, 207, 275n.10, 304n.20, 304–5n.24, 313–14n.80, 326n.68, 326n.71, 326n.72, 346n.76
parameterization, 6–7, 66–67, 101–6, 111–14, 127, 133, 161–62, 174–79, 196–97, 220, 225, 236, 293–94n.41, 294n.45, 296–97n.65, 311–12n.73, 322n.51, 322n.54, 334n.108, 346n.73
Park, Jin Y. 288n.74, 349n.93
Park, Peter K. J. 31
paryudāsa-pratiṣedha, 97–98, 107, 109–10, 291n.18–295nn.46–49, 295n.54, 333n.101
Pasternack, Lawrence, 264n.57
Patil, Parimal, 317n.10, 327–28n.75
Patton, Kimberley C. 269n.86
peace, 119, 136, 163, 173, 204, 209–10, 244–48, 249–50, 254–56, 299n.90, 352n.113, 352n.118, 353n.124. *See also* eirenics
Pecchia, Cristina, 341n.34
Perrett, Roy W. 191–92, 284n.58
Pettit, John, 250
philosophical construction, 8, 44, 50–51, 56–58, 66–67, 72–73, 126–29, 279–80n.39, 280–81n.41, 281n.42, 282n.51, 323n.58. *See also* textual hermeneutics
philosophy. *See* Western philosophy
philosophy and literature, 9–16–259nn.16–21
Pind, Ole Holten, 46, 156–57
Piṅgala. *See* Qingmu
Plato, 24–25, 49–50, 69–70, 88–89, 132, 134, 274n.7, 283n.56, 338n.11
Pollock, Sheldon, 281n.46
positionality. See *dṛṣṭi*
practice. *See* eirenics
prajñā (wisdom), 21, 176–77, 187, 203–4, 241–42, 331n.90, 331n.91, 336n.120, 339n.25
Prajñāpāramitā, 21–22, 42, 129–30, 138, 139–40, 263n.52, 296–97n.65
prajñapti, 143, 164
prajñaptir upādāya (correlative designation), 14–15, 150, 160, 317n.9
pramāṇa (reliable warrant), 191–93, 284n.64, 332n.95, 333–34n.102, 346–47n.77
prapañca (conceptualization), 7, 10, 17, 20, 65–66, 105, 121, 123, 124–25, 127–28, 136, 138–39, 141, 142, 151, 154–55, 156, 159, 160, 162, 163–66, 174, 178–79, 182–83, 185, 187, 198, 210, 212–14, 216, 218–19, 227, 233–34, 235–36, 238–39, 242, 246, 293–94n.41, 305n.31, 306n.40, 310n.67, 313n.79, 314–16n.1, 316n.4, 317n.10, 318n.19, 324–25n.64, 325n.65, 327n.73, 329n.78, 330n.87, 331n.91, 339–40n.26, 346n.68, 347n.79, 350–51n.103. See also *dṛṣṭi*; *vikalpa*
prapañcopaśamaṃ (cessation of conceptualization). See *prapañca*
prasajya-pratiṣedha, 97–98, 107, 109–10, 291n.18–295nn.46–49, 295n.54, 333n.101
prāsaṅga, 18, 19, 64–65, 98–99, 123, 131–32, 139–41, 144–45, 149–51, 170, 180–81, 187, 191, 193–95, 201–3, 215–16, 220, 237–38, 256, 262n.37, 262–63n.46, 289n.3, 291n.15, 299n.90, 310n.63, 331–32n.93
Prāsaṅgika Madhyamaka, 75, 121, 122, 144, 195, 202, 209, 258n.10, 270n.94, 285n.67, 298n.87, 298–99n.89, 338n.16, 346n.70, 347n.83
pratijñā (proposition/thesis), 7, 9, 20–21, 68, 100, 132, 142, 146, 156, 167–70, 172, 175–79, 180–81, 182, 188, 191–92, 194–200, 262–63n.46, 281n.43, 309n.58, 309n.61, 320n.39, 322n.53, 322n.54, 323–24n.61, 325n.66, 334n.108, 337n.10, 346n.68

pratītya-samutpāda (dependent co-origination, dependent co-arising), 2–3, 10, 14–15, 50, 65–66, 116–19, 142, 143, 146, 159, 160, 166, 171, 173, 189–90, 215, 245, 246, 254–55, 260–61n.29, 275n.10, 297n.75, 304n.20, 304–5n.24, 316n.4, 317n.9, 328–29n.77
Prebish, Charles S. 271n.99, 279n.38
Priest, Graham, 52–53, 56–57, 61–62, 73–74, 78–79, 80–82, 84, 87–88, 101–6, 111, 114–15, 272–73n.3, 276n.25, 284n.60, 288n.74, 288n.75, 293–94n.41, 294n.45, 295n.47–128–30, 133–34, 297nn.67–68, 298n.86, 301n.1–177–79, 184–85, 254–55, 303–4nn.13–17, 304n.19, 304–5n.24, 316n.2, 324n.62, 326n.68, 345n.65, 353n.121
proposition. See *pratijñā*
Proudfoot, Wayne, 63, 70–72, 211–12, 268n.79, 288n.78, 339n.19

Qingmu 青目, 45, 66, 95–96, 99–100, 271–72n.100, 291n.23, 293n.31, 340–41n.30
Quine, Willard Van Orman, 75, 284–85n.65, 306–7n.43

racism, 31, 56, 78, 84, 258n.12, 272–73n.3
Raghuramaraju, A. 279n.37, 282n.50
Rahlwes, Chris, 291n.15, 295n.48
Rajapakse, Regington, 283–84n.57
Raju, P. T. 94–95, 112–13, 301n.4, 302n.6
Ram-Prasad, Chakravarthi, 215, 220–21, 234, 342n.37, 342n.38, 347n.78
Rashdall, Hastings, 265n.60
rationality. *See* common sense; laws of thought; logic
Ray, Benjamin C. 269n.86
Ray, Reginald A. 41, 271n.97
Rea, Michael, 25–26, 265n.59
reason. *See* common sense; laws of thought; logic
reductio ad absurdum. See *prāsaṅga*
religionate, 23–30, 34
religiosophy, 11–12, 24, 31–35, 42, 63, 64, 89, 92, 94–95, 115–16, 124–25, 201, 205–6, 209, 219–20, 231–33, 251–52
religious studies, 5, 22–24, 27–30, 31–35
Ricoeur, Paul, 306n.37
Robinson, Richard H. 50–51, 53, 63–64, 94–96, 111, 112–13, 138–39, 271–72n.100, 288n.79, 289n.2, 289n.3, 290n.8, 291n.14, 291n.17, 293n.31, 296n.60, 306n.39, 314–16n.1
Rorty, Richard, 276n.25
Rostalska, Agnieszka, 267n.73
Roth, Paul A. 282n.50
Ruegg, David Seyfort, 36–37, 50–51, 52–53, 79–81, 90–91, 98–99, 179, 198–99, 271n.99, 273–74n.5, 278n.34, 280–81n.41, 281n.43, 281n.44, 283n.56, 286–87n.72, 289n.1, 289n.7, 295n.46, 295n.47, 298–99n.89, 302n.6, 303n.10, 305n.31, 306n.40, 307n.46, 308n.53, 309n.58, 310n.63, 312–13n.74, 313n.79, 313–14n.80, 314–16n.1, 317n.10, 319n.30, 323–24n.61, 325n.65, 334n.108
rūpa (body/form), 2, 140, 260n.28, 297n.79. See also *skandha*
rūpa-dhātu (form-world). See *rūpa*
rūpakāya (form body). See *rūpa*
Ruseva, Gergana Rumenova, 259–60n.23
Rutherford, Donald, 227–28
Ryba, Thomas, 268n.80

Saito, Akira, 314–16n.1
Salvini, Mattia, 261n.36, 314–16n.1
*Saṃghavarman 僧伽跋摩, 46–47
saṃjñā (perception/cognition/notion), 2, 143, 161–62, 239, 340–41n.30. See also *skandha*
saṃsāra, 3, 14–15, 117, 136–37, 161–62, 182, 197, 207, 219, 226–30, 236, 244–46, 247–48, 250–51, 311–12n.73, 316n.4, 326n.68, 326n.69, 326n.71, 336n.120, 338n.14, 344n.54, 344n.58, 345n.62
saṃskāra (mental formation), 2, 161, 183, 215, 226, 241, 244–45, 317n.10, 334–35n.110, 352n.113. See also *skandha*
saṃvṛti-satya, 3, 51–52, 103–6, 111, 134–35, 136–37, 138, 147–48, 155, 182, 207, 275n.10, 304n.20, 304n.21, 304–5n.24, 313–14n.80, 326n.68, 326n.71, 326n.72, 346n.76

samyag-dṛṣṭi (right view). See *dṛṣṭi*
Sanlun 三論. *See* Jizang; Sengzhao
Śāntarakṣita, 120, 320–21n.43, 338n.16, 341n.34, 347n.78
Śāntideva, 35, 119, 203–4, 341n.33, 345n.65, 351n.108, 353n.125
sarvadṛṣṭiprahāṇāya (abandoning all views). See *dṛṣṭi*
Sasaki, Ruth Fuller, 258n.9
satya. See *paramārtha-satya*; *saṃvṛti-satya*
Schayer, Stanisław, 50–51, 112–13, 296n.59
Scherrer-Schaub, Cristina, 45–46, 203
Schmidt-Leukel, Perry, 326n.69
Schmithausen, Lambert, 260–61n.29, 314–16n.1, 341n.34
Schopen, Gregory, 270–71n.96
Sebastian, C. D. 312–13n.74, 316n.4, 331n.91, 348–49n.87, 350–51n.103, 351n.105
self. See *atman*
selfbeing. See *svabhāva*
Sellars, Wilfrid, 181–82, 327–28n.75
Sells, Michael A. 235–41, 347n.82, 348–49n.87, 349n.88, 349nn.90–92, 349–50n.96, 350n.97, 351n.104
Sengzhao 僧肇, 38, 129–30, 290n.9
Seon. *See* Chan
Sharf, Robert H. 308n.51
Sharma, Arvind, 28–29
Sharpe, Eric J. 28–29, 31
Shen Jianying 沈剑英, 281n.43
Shulman, Eviatar, 153, 203, 257n.5, 311n.71, 327n.73
siddhānta, 36–37, 132, 177, 309n.58, 323–24n.61
Siderits, Mark, 12, 15–16, 18, 45, 56, 67–69, 75, 114, 134–35, 159, 161, 163, 204–5, 250, 262n.43, 262n.44, 262–63n.46, 279n.37, 281n.44, 282n.52, 282–83n.53, 284–85n.65, 285n.66, 288n.74, 293n.35, 297n.66, 304–5n.24, 305n.28, 307n.44, 308n.50, 310n.65, 314–16n.1, 316n.4, 317n.8, 317n.10, 317–18n.14, 319n.28, 324–25n.64, 328n.76, 332n.95, 333–34n.102, 339n.22, 341n.31, 344n.54, 345n.60, 345n.62, 347n.79
silence, 5, 20, 30, 121–22, 141, 154–55, 165, 198, 215–16, 225, 236, 241–42, 247–48, 288n.75, 313n.75, 313n.79, 351n.107, 355n.134. See also *avyākṛtavastu*
Silk, Jonathan A. 270–71n.96
skandha, 2, 183, 215, 232–33, 239, 244–45, 340–41n.30, 352n.113
skepticism, 19, 188–89, 282–83n.53, 296–97n.65, 312–13n.74, 324–25n.64, 332n.95, 351n.107
Skilton, Andrew, 337n.5
Smilde, David, 29, 30, 267n.69
Smith, Jonathan Z. 27–28, 73–74, 265–66n.64, 266n.65, 266–67n.68
Smith College Madhyamaka & Methodology Symposium, 55–56, 91–92, 102–3, 195, 259n.17, 277–78n.31, 323n.59
Soldatenko, Gabriel, 275n.9
soteries. *See* soteriology
soteriology, 3, 5, 6–8, 13–14, 21–22, 33–34, 37, 54, 60, 65–66, 67–68, 69, 80, 89–93, 115–25, 127–28, 131, 132–33, 155, 156–57, 162–63, 166, 179–81, 184, 189–90, 194, 199–200, 204–5, 208–10, 213, 214–15, 218, 234, 240–41, 247, 250–51, 253, 257n.6, 276n.21, 281n.45, 282–83n.53, 286–87n.72, 288n.74, 298n.83, 299n.90, 313n.77, 327n.74, 332n.95, 333n.97, 333n.98, 336n.120, 338n.17, 353n.125, 354–55n.133
Spackman, John, 152, 311–12n.73
Sprung, Mervyn, 51–52, 275n.10, 289n.2, 304n.20, 314–16n.1
Staal, Frits, 51–52, 78–79, 98, 112–13, 124, 174, 289n.2, 295n.47, 322n.52
Stace, Walter T. 211–12, 339n.19
Stcherbatsky, F. T. 281n.43
Steup, Matthias, 275n.11
Stewart, Georgina, 276–77n.26
suffering. See *duḥkha*
śūnyatā, 7–8, 9, 14–15, 18, 20, 21, 42, 67–68, 75, 101, 110–11, 116–18, 124–25, 134–35, 136–37, 139–55, 257–58n.7, 258n.10, 263n.52, 270n.94, 271n.98, 273–74n.5, 275n.10, 285n.66,

śūnyatā (*cont.*)
291n.17, 293n.31, 301n.1, 304–5n.24, 306n.36, 306n.39, 307n.44, 307n.46, 308n.52, 309n.56, 309n.62, 310n.63-156, 160–61, 163, 164, 165, 166–69, 170, 173, 177–82, 183, 187, 188, 189–90, 196–200, 310–11nn.65–68, 311n.72, 311–12n.73, 316n.4, 317n.9, 317n.13, 317–18n.14, 319n.28, 319n.30, 319n.31, 320n.39, 322n.52, 322n.53, 322-23n.57, 324n.62, 325n.66, 325–26n.67, 326n.68, 327n.73, 328–29n.77-201–3, 204–5, 208–9, 210, 211, 212–16, 218–19, 221, 223–24, 227–28, 230–31, 233–34, 238–48, 250, 253–56, 330–31nn.89–91, 331–32n.93, 333n.97, 334–35n.110, 335n.111, 337n.10, 339n.25, 345n.63, 346n.69, 347n.83, 350n.98, 350n.100, 350n.102, 350–51n.103, 351n.105, 351n.110, 352n.112, 354n.129, 355n.134

svabhāva, 2–3, 105–6, 116–17, 120, 131–32, 134–35, 136–37, 139–40, 142–51, 152–54, 167–68, 169, 171, 174, 175–76, 179, 184, 190–91, 192–93, 194, 198–99, 227, 232–33, 239–40, 244–45, 250–51, 262n.43, 273–74n.5, 275n.10, 303n.10, 304n.19, 308n.53, 309n.56, 323–24n.61, 324–25n.64, 327n.73, 328–29n.77, 330–31n.89, 331n.91, 334n.108, 351n.110

Svātantrika Madhyamaka, 75, 98–99, 120, 121, 285n.67, 298n.87, 298–99n.89, 338n.16, 346n.70, 347n.83

Szaif, Jan, 283n.56

Taber, John. A. 271n.99, 303n.10

Tachikawa, Musashi, 112–13, 302n.6

Tanaka, Koji, 54

Tathāgata, 6–7, 110–11, 127, 135–38, 150, 164, 165, 184, 186, 187, 194, 197–98, 227, 242–43, 305n.26, 307n.44, 329n.78, 344n.54. *See also* comegoing; tathāgata-garbha

Tathāgata-garbha, 186

Tauscher, Helmut, 314–16n.1

Taylor, Charles, 272–73n.3

tenet. See *abhyupagama*

tetralemma. See *catuṣkoṭi*

tetrāletheia, 6–7, 18, 127–28, 133–37, 302n.6. *See also* aletheia; dialetheia

textual hermeneutics, 8, 34, 44, 50–51, 56–58, 63, 66–67, 72–114, 124, 126–29, 177, 277n.27, 279–80n.39, 280–81n.41, 281n.42, 282n.49, 282n.51, 294n.45, 297n.68, 323n.58. *See also* philosophical construction

Thakchöe, Sonam, 175–76, 293–94n.41, 313–14n.80, 314–16n.1, 352n.114, 352–53n.120, 355n.134

thesis. See *pratijñā*

thesism, 194–95. See also *athesism*; *dṛṣṭi*; *pakṣa*; *pratijñā*

Thomson, Iain, 26

Thurman, Robert A. F. 313n.75, 313n.79

Thus Comegone. *See* Tathāgata

Tiele, Cornelius Petrus, 73–74

Tillemans, Tom J. F. 37, 52–53, 79–80, 98–99, 104–5, 106, 111, 112–14, 258n.11, 262n.44, 271n.99, 275n.13, 282–83n.53, 283n.54, 289n.4, 292n.27, 293n.37, 293–94n.41, 294n.44, 294n.45, 296n.58, 296n.60-208–9, 210, 296–97nn.63–65, 300n.100, 304n.20, 306–7n.43, 310–11n.68, 314–16n.1, 322n.55, 323n.58, 330n.87, 336n.121, 337n.10, 338n.16, 338–39n.18, 339n.22, 346n.70, 347–48n.84, 350n.98, 355n.135

Tola, Fernando, 45–46, 117, 156–57, 171, 297–98nn.77–82, 320–21nn.41–49, 334–35n.110

Travagnin, Stefania, 261n.32, 290n.8, 299n.91, 300n.93

truth. *See paramārtha-satya*; *saṃvṛti-satya*

Tsongkhapa (Tsong kha pa bLo bzang Grags pa), 38, 63–64, 66, 104–6, 175–76, 281n.43, 281–82n.48, 293–94n.41, 296n.63, 322n.55, 328–29n.77, 338n.16

Tucci, Giuseppe, 221, 305n.26

Tuck, Andrew P. 58, 289n.7, 291n.16, 316n.2

Turner, Denys, 288n.75, 313n.78

Tuske, Joerg, 296n.59

two truths. See *paramārtha-satya*; *saṃvṛti-satya*

ultimate truth. See *paramārtha-satya*
Uryūzu, Ryūshin 瓜生津隆真, 45–46
utilitarianism, 342n.40
utterance, 6–7, 18, 93, 127–28, 130, 137–41, 147–48, 154–55, 229, 236–37, 240–41, 309n.57

vāda, 36–37, 132, 323–24n.61
Vaidya, P. L. 335–36n.116
Vasubandhu, 35, 186, 311n.70, 328–29n.77, 347n.78
vedanā (feeling). See *skandha*
Velez de Cea, Abraham, 339n.22
Vidyabhusana, Satis Chandra, 281n.43
view. See *dṛṣṭi*
vijñāna (discerning consciousness), 2, 183, 316n.4, 331n.90, 340–41n.30. See also *skandha*
vikalpa (dichotomizing conceptualization), 121, 124–25, 136, 138–39, 150–51, 152, 154–55, 161, 162–64, 179, 183–84, 187, 218, 235–36, 241–42, 313n.79, 317n.10, 325n.65, 329n.78, 337n.10, 340–41n.30, 346n.68, 348n.85, 350–51n.103
Vinaya, 271–72n.100, 295n.50, 306n.35
virtue ethics, 223–24, 339n.22, 342n.40, 355n.134
Vose, Kevin, 270n.94, 298–99n.89, 347n.83
vyavahāra-satya. See *saṃvṛti-satya*

Waldo, Ives, 75, 268n.84, 285n.67, 331n.91, 333n.96, 337n.10
Wallace, B. Alan, 337n.5
Wallace, Vesna A. 337n.5
Walser, Joseph, 37, 42, 46, 59–60, 270–71n.96, 271n.98
Walshe, Maurice, 301n.4
Wang Kexi 王克喜, 281n.43
Wan Jinchuan 萬金川, 100, 314–16n.1
Ward, Keith, 209
Waste Land, The, 352n.113
Wayman, Alex, 95–96, 111, 131, 281n.43, 296n.57, 303n.7
Westerhoff, Jan, 16, 18, 41, 45, 46, 53–55, 57–58, 72, 78–79, 84, 94–95, 96–99, 101–2, 103–6, 111, 112–13, 127–28, 154, 168–70, 175–78, 194, 203, 210, 237–38, 254–55, 257–58n.7, 258n.10, 262n.43, 263n.49, 263n.52, 275–76nn.15–17, 276n.20, 284n.62, 289n.5, 291–92n.24, 292n.27, 293n.34, 293–94n.41, 294n.45, 295n.49, 296n.61, 296n.62, 297n.75, 301n.4, 302n.6, 303n.7, 311n.70, 311n.72, 320n.34, 320n.39, 320n.40, 322n.56, 333–34n.102, 349n.94
Western philosophy, 4–6, 13–14, 15–16, 22–23, 24–27, 30, 31–35, 36–37, 258n.11, 260n.27–48–50, 69–86, 88, 107, 112–13, 126–27, 128–29, 133, 134, 181–82, 206, 209, 212–13, 243, 264–65nn.57–60, 267–68n.78, 268n.82, 272–73n.3, 278n.35, 278–79n.36, 281n.42, 281–82n.48, 284n.58, 284n.60, 301n.1, 301n.2, 303n.15, 304n.17, 306–7n.43, 310n.65, 327–28n.75, 336n.119. *See also* cross-cultural philosophy
Whitehead, Alfred North, 24–25
Williams, Bernard, 341–42n.36
Williams, Janet P. 240–41, 254–55, 306n.41, 328–29n.77, 334n.107, 349n.93, 349n.95, 349–50n.96, 351n.105, 351n.106
Williams, Paul, 2–3, 50–51, 120, 143, 164, 183, 216–17, 221, 230–31, 250, 270–71n.96, 302n.6, 303n.10, 305n.26, 311n.70, 317n.10, 326n.72, 337n.5, 339n.22, 340n.28, 345n.65, 348n.86
Wong, David, 353n.121
Wood, Thomas E. 151–53, 276n.18, 310n.65, 311n.70, 334–35n.110
Wu Rujun 吳汝鈞, 100, 111, 199–200, 293n.31, 301n.103

Xing, Guang, 226–27, 344n.54, 348n.86
Xingyun 星雲, 293n.31

Yadav, Bibhuti S. 121–22, 198, 260n.27, 298n.87, 336n.118, 341n.35
Yancy, George, 275n.9

Ye Shaoyong 叶少勇, 45–46, 152–53, 171, 303n.10–320–21nn.41–44
Yijing 義淨, 46–47
Yinshun 印順, 63–64, 122–24, 261n.32, 299n.91, 300n.93, 300n.95, 300n.99, 314–16n.1, 331n.90
Yogācāra, 186, 295n.50, 314–16n.1, 327n.73, 328–29n.77, 329–30n.82, 333–34n.102, 342n.38, 347n.78
Yonezawa, Yoshiyasu, 45
Young, Stuart H. 13, 40–41, 260n.25, 271n.97
Yü, Chün-fang, 353n.123

Zalta, Edward N. 276n.22
Zen. *See* Chan
Zheng Liqun 郑立群, 281n.43
Ziporyn, Brook, 267n.76, 307n.44, 325–26n.67, 334n.105